# SPINNAKER
# HANDLING

## Other titles of interest

*Sail, Race and Win, 2nd edition:* Eric Twiname, revised by Cathy Foster highlights the fact that a winning attitude is perhaps more important than having the best in design, hardware and technology.

*The Rules Book, 1993–1996 edition:* Eric Twiname, revised by Bryan Willis "presents an undeniably complex subject in a logical, easily followed format." SAIL Magazine

*How to Trim Sails:* Peter Schweer
A practical guide to getting the optimum from your sails. The most popular rig configurations found on today's yachts are described, and the correct standing-rigging tensions are given for a variety of sailing conditions.

*The Sea Never Changes – My Singlehanded Trimaran Race Around the World:* Olivier de Kersauson
A detailed account of one of the most difficult circumnavigations in the quest for speed under sail. With all of today's high-tech equipment, the challenge of the sea remains the same.

*The Boating Bible – An Essential Handbook for Every Sailor:* Jim Murrant
This handbook contains all the essential information sailors need in one easy-to-use volume. Thorough descriptions are given for all the topics covered.

*The Sailing Dictionary, 2nd edition:* Joachim Schult
This is a completely revised and updated edition of a highly respected and authoritative sailing dictionary. This comprehensive reference work has over 3500 entries and 1500 line drawings. "An essential purchase." Booklist

*Bent Aarre*

# SPINNAKER HANDLING

*Second Edition*

Translated by Christopher Croft
and Anne Firth

SHERIDAN HOUSE

Second edition 1993
Published by Sheridan House Inc.
145 Palisade Street
Dobbs Ferry, NY 10522

Copyright © English Language text Adlard Coles Nautical 1993

First published in Denmark by Clausen bøger, Aschehoug Dansk Forlag

**Library of Congress Cataloging-in-Publication Data**

Aarre, Bent.
    [Spilersejlads. English]
    Spinnaker handling / Bent Aarre : translated by Christopher Croft
and Anne Firth. — 2nd ed.
        p.      cm.
    Translation of: Spilersejlads.
    Includes index.
    ISBN 0–924486–51–1 : $14.95
    1. Sailing.    2. Seamanship.     I. Title.
GV811.5.A3713    1993
623.88′22—dc20                                          92–46223
                                                              CIP

Printed in Great Britain

ISBN 0–924486–51–1

# Contents

# Foreword

When a spinnaker sets, the sail area increases by 150 per cent – and it is then that things *really* happen!

The spinnaker offers fascinating sailing and provides a marvellous spectacle as the multicoloured sailcloth hauls the boat ahead to the peak of its performance. In an instant, an otherwise routine run becomes all speed and excitement.

Such a sail deserves a book of its own. How does the spinnaker work? How should it be handled? What must one look out for? This is what this book is about.

It goes without saying that it has been written with the racing sailor in mind, but I have tried to ensure that the recreational sailor too will find it both useful and interesting. The spinnaker has long been essential racing equipment but happily is now being used more and more for pleasure sailing also. Remember, though, that it can be dangerous to set the spinnaker alone, perhaps with only two adults and small children on board. The spinnaker calls for experience and precision if it is to be used correctly. Because the sail is not easy to handle, difficult situations can arise unless one is aware of the natural laws involved. It must be said that the spinnaker is capable of behaving more dramatically than one might at first expect!

As in the first edition of this book, sold out some years ago, I have included many illustrations, some now reworked, because one diagram can often convey far more than mere words. Henrik Hansen's action photographs bring many of the points to life.

Finally, I owe a debt of thanks to the author and journalist Jan Ebert for his unstinting help and advice.

*Bent Aarre*

# Then and now

Sailors have always sought ways of making their boats sail as fast as possible under whatever conditions they might meet. Every imaginable means of increasing sail area has been explored, but there are many natural limiting factors. There is no point in adding more and more sail if this just leads to loss of steering control, and the backwinding of existing sails that might themselves have been sufficient.

From the earliest times sailors have known how to increase the speed of small craft by setting a jib to windward with the help of a pole. In larger vessels, both merchantmen and warships, we know that use was made of so-called 'stunsails', which were set to windward outboard of these standing sails on the yard and held out using a stunsail boom – the forerunner of the modern spinnaker pole. On smaller single-masted vessels they used a so-called 'flying foresail', a large square sail set on the mainmast together with the fixed gaff mainsail.

These sails were the forerunners of what we now know as the spinnaker. Pleasure sailing began to develop in the 1850s, and it was in England, in a race in 1865 between two straight-stemmed cutters that a spinnaker was seen for the first time. The boat using the sail was called *Niobe* and, thanks to this sail, she won convincingly.

The origin of the English word 'spinnaker' is in some doubt. Some believe that it derives from 'to make her spin', meaning to give her a turn of speed, hence 'spinmaker' and later 'spinnaker'. Others believe that the word comes from the name of a cutter, the *Sphinx*, colloquially corrupted to 'Spinks', that used the sail in 1866. The sail became known as the 'spinker', then 'spiniker', and finally 'spinnaker' (according to Jeremy Howard-Williams, the sail expert).

The first spinnaker was asymmetric, rather like a baggy genoa, and was made of light cotton. It was sewn in panels at right angles to the foot of the sail and was boomed to windward on a long pole – the spinnaker boom – with the sheet set inside

Two English cutters shown racing in the 1870s. The spinnaker was first hauled close up, the enormous spinnaker pole was then lowered on a tackle, and the clew then hauled to its outer end on the guy.

With the spinnaker set, the other sails were of little use as they were almost completely backwinded by the spinnaker.

the forestay. In order to sail closer to the wind, the pole was dispensed with and the throat of the sail made fast to the stem or bowsprit. The sail was then called a 'balloon'.

This form of spinnaker remained in fashion, virtually unchanged, for nearly seventy-five years – right up until 1936, when yachts like the 6-metre (19½-foot) R-class carrying symmetrical spinnakers first made their appearance. These sails were constructed from two identically shaped halves, the markedly

3

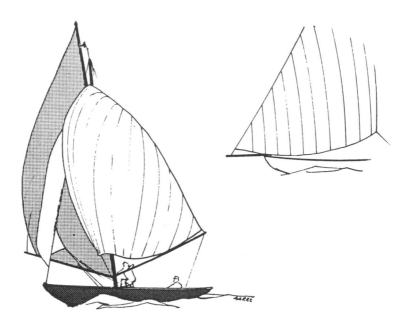

Small keelboat of 1912. At first there were no restrictions on the length of the spinnaker pole, and it was usual for it to be mounted on the mast – sharing the fitting for the main boom. When not in use it could be hoisted vertically. The inset shows the same type of spinnaker rigged as a balloon sail – very reminiscent of the present-day genoa.

curved sides also giving a deeper bosom. At the same time it was quite natural to sheet the spinnaker outside the forestay to reduce the chance of backwinding the mainsail and to allow the sail to set more freely. This was nothing less than a revolution, and sailmakers have competed ever since to produce the most effective spinnakers for all wind conditions.

By the end of the 1950s, having been used for a hundred years, cotton was replaced by nylon as the most popular material for making spinnakers. Nylon is lighter, stronger and more elastic than cotton and so, with certain limitations, is advantageous in a spinnaker. For this reason nylon is also preferred to the less elastic terylene or Mylar. These latter materials are, however, now used for most other sails.

Although limits to development are imposed under various

4

W-class racing, 1936. The first spinnakers, forerunners of those in use today, made their appearance in the mid-1930s.

rules, both international (eg the International Offshore Rules or IOR) and national (eg the Channel Handicap System in the UK), which govern spinnaker and boom measurements for the various classes, sailmakers are constantly experimenting with new and more efficient spinnaker designs – and the use of computers in this field has led to further advances. It is crucial that the run of the panels should follow the stresses in the sail as this will give strength and stability even to the lightest cloth.

At one time it was thought that Mylar would be the material of the future for spinnakers. In the event, though, it was found that the material was too unyielding to withstand the shock effect

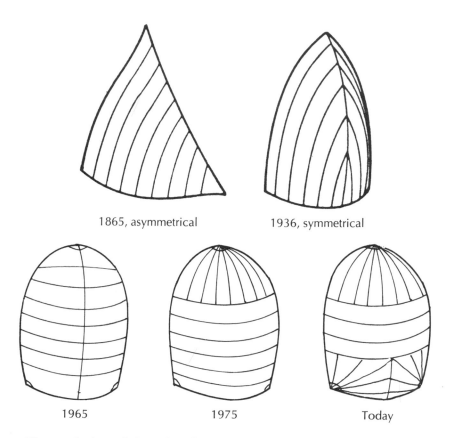

1865, asymmetrical       1936, symmetrical

1965       1975       Today

**The evolution of the spinnaker:** Sailmakers have always striven to devise the most stable and efficient designs. This has culminated in today's tri-radial sail. Its construction is complicated, reflecting the ultimate skills of the sailmaker. Towards the corners the seams follow the stresses, benefiting both efficiency and stability. The design is used in cruising as well as racing boats. The 1965 example was excellent when running before the wind, but was somewhat unstable in cross winds or in a light breeze, when a change to a flatter sail was necessary. The 1975 example, a top-radial design, was a first step towards greater stability and is still seen today. The modern tri-radial spinnaker comes close to being a true all-rounder, so that there is barely any need to carry more than one spinnaker — a considerable saving in cost.

of a sudden wind-slam, for example. Such a jolt could cause the sail to tear, and even the slightest misalignment in the seams of a spinnaker could have the same result. When sewn in nylon, however, the sail's 'give' enables these abnormal loads to be taken up.

Sailmakers continue to experiment with new materials in the hope of finding a cloth superior even to nylon. Racing provides the spur to these developments, but it is worth remembering that what is best for racing is not necessarily best for recreational use.

# *Preparations for hoisting*

The different methods of setting and lowering a spinnaker are largely determined by the size and type of boat – be it a dinghy, a light racing keelboat, an all-round cruiser, or ocean racer. However, all systems basically involve a spinnaker pole with topping lift and downhaul, a halyard made fast to the head of the sail, and a sheet on each clew.

## PACKING THE SPINNAKER

Let us consider the method on a 9–12 metre (28–35 foot) cruising/racing yacht. The sail should always be packed in the spinnaker bag, or turtle, so that it can be attached to the spinnaker halyard and hoisted quickly without tangling. This is best done in the cabin out of the wind.

Begin by finding one of the corners – any corner – and hold on to it. Keep following the leeches round until all three corners, that is to say the two clews and the top, are in your hand. If singlehanded, tie the three together with a light seizing and make it fast to a handrail or some similar point beneath the cabin top so that you can pack the sail into the bag.

To prevent the sail slipping out of the bag prematurely it is a good idea to run a seizing through the eyes in each corner and tie this to the top of the bag. If all the corners are identical in appearance, the top should be marked with a telltale to prevent confusion. In fact the top should be distinguishable from the other two clews since it ought to be fitted with a swivel to allow any twist in the sail to clear itself on hoisting.

## SHEET AND GUY

Although one talks of spinnaker sheets, the reality when sailing is that only the one on the lee side is a sheet. The other, to windward, is a guy that holds the spinnaker pole at a suitable angle to the wind. In the large sailing ships it was called a 'brace' because it was used to brace the yards, and hence the sails, at the

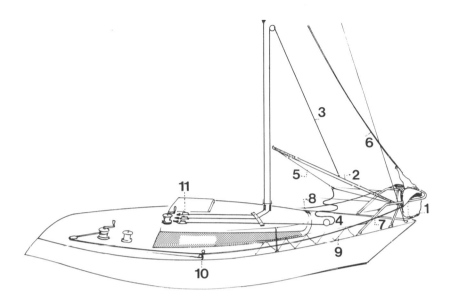

**Ready for hoisting**
**1** Spinnaker turtle containing sail. **2** Spinnaker pole. **3** Pole uphaul or topping lift. **4** Pole downhaul. **5** Bridle. **6** Spinnaker halyard. **7** Guy. **8** Sheet. **9** Hammock netting. **10** Barberhaul. **11** Jamming cleats.

Medium-sized boats should be fitted with a winch for the spinnaker sheet/guy on both sides and a separate winch for the genoa sheets. A winch for the spinnaker halyard is equally indispensable. Here the winch is mounted aft on the coachroof; this is normally best, but it could also be mounted on the side of the mast level with the boom. Since the downhaul also needs a winch, there should be jamming cleats just forward of the winch to enable it to be used for different hauls. The topping lift needs less effort, but even here a winch may be needed.

There should normally also be a winch sited on the coachroof for the mainsail, cunningham-haul, etc, but that is another story.

The hammock netting is secured to the guardrail; this is invaluable in preventing sails slipping overboard during sail changes.

An example of a barber-haul, often used to give a better lead when trimming the spinnaker leech. It was named after the Barber brothers, well-known Australian yachtsmen.

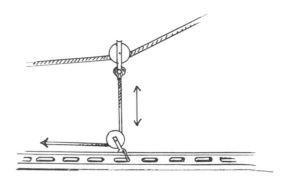

right angle to the wind. Although the term 'brace' may still be heard, the windward 'spinnaker sheet' is now almost universally known as the *guy*.

Whatever terms are used, though, the main thing is to distinguish between them because, with a spinnaker set, there is no room for error. 'Harden the sheet' and 'check the guy' are orders that are both clear and to the point. Follow this rule of clarity from the moment the spinnaker is hoisted and there will be no confusion as to which of the ropes acts as the guy for the spinnaker pole and which is the sheet.

When making ready to set the spinnaker, the sheet and guy are secured to the pulpit and from there the lines are led around outboard of the shrouds, lifelines, etc before finally passing through the spinnaker blocks at the stern. A barber-haul could well be included at some suitable point. This is used to move the sheeting point forward in situations where the block in the stern gives an unsatisfactory lead.

Braided polyester cordage of generous dimensions should be used for the sheets. Kevlar-reinforced sheets are not a good idea because they lack that slight give that could save the spinnaker from tearing in the event of a sudden wind-slam, for example. Snap shackles should be used to secure the sheets to the clews, but in smaller boats with just one spinnaker they can be secured using bowlines as for the foresail sheets.

The sheet blocks should be of generous dimensions to enable the sheets to run freely, and it is best if they incorporate a swivel to allow them to adjust to changes in the lead of the sheets.

The barber-hauls are more lightly loaded and smaller blocks

can be used. A strong, smooth eye may well be sufficient on smaller boats.

Winches should be conveniently sited by the cockpit or on the coachroof. The winches themselves should be of the best quality and not too small. Even if these are expensive, remember that it pays to have the best equipment for handling the spinnaker effectively. In a fresh wind, your safety may depend on it.

## THE SPINNAKER POLE

The spinnaker pole normally has its own stowage on the foredeck with one end attached to the after foot of the pulpit and the other end secured near the main shroud. It is best to use purpose-designed fittings for this.

Class rules normally limit the length of the spinnaker pole. The pole length should not exceed the J-measurement (the horizontal distance between the forward edge of the mast and the point where the forestay meets the deck, see page 89).

On some modern racing yachts the length of the main boom exceeds the J-measurement, thus making it possible to stow the spinnaker pole along the boom – avoiding the need to go forward to fetch it. When required, it is released from the boom and lifted on to the fitting on the mast. Both topping lift and downhaul can be left permanently attached when the pole is stowed in this way, again saving time.

Opinions vary widely as to how the spinnaker pole should be

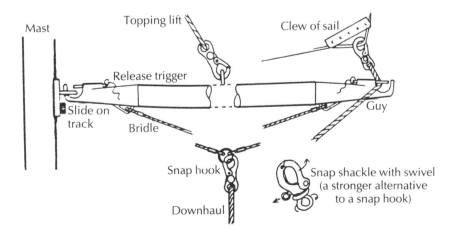

Mast     Topping lift     Clew of sail

Release trigger

Slide on track     Bridle     Guy

Snap hook     Snap shackle with swivel (a stronger alternative to a snap hook)

Downhaul

fitted out. Basically, the pole should be strongly constructed and fitted with a plunger-type snap hook at each end – both hooks facing the same way. The topping lift is attached to an eye mid-way along the pole and a bridle with an eye, to which a downhaul can be connected, is attached to the underside of the pole. In a fresh wind there can be very strong upward forces exerted on the pole when the spinnaker fills; the bridle helps to spread this load that might otherwise cause the pole to buckle. A quick-release line is attached to the catch of the snap hook so that the pole can be rapidly freed.

The other end of the pole is attached to an eye, possibly one of several, on the front of the mast. This eye should be integral with a slide capable of movement in a vertical track

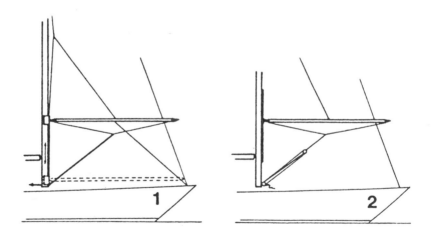

### Spinnaker pole uphaul/downhaul systems

1   While in position, the pole can be raised or lowered in its track using the asymmetrical bridle on the topping lift. The pole is thus always ready for use without the need for anyone on the foredeck. Such a system requires a mast clear of all projections, and all halyards, etc must be run internally. A strong elastic cord is run from the midpoint of the pole to the bow to ensure that the pole is always held hard by the clew of the spinnaker. This system is used in Dragons and some other classes, but is not suitable for cruisers.

2   The downhaul includes a purchase to make the crew's task easier. The line may be led to a cleat on the heel of the mast or aft to the cockpit.

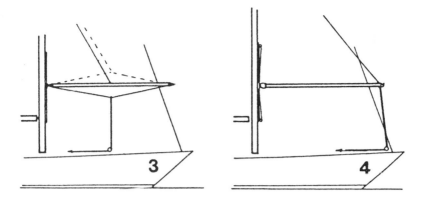

**3** This system is the one most commonly used and is suitable for all boats of up to about 10.6 metres (35 feet). A bridle is sometimes used on the topping lift.

**4** On large boats the uphaul and downhaul lines have to be led to the outer end of the pole to provide the greater leverage needed to work the spinnaker. This arrangement has the disadvantage that the pole cannot simply be end-for-ended when gybing, because each end requires its own downhaul. Lines are run in the mast to allow adjustment of the height of the pole in its track.

to allow the position of the pole to be trimmed. This slide is normally fitted with a spring-loaded plunger designed to engage in holes at intervals in the track. This arrangement is not entirely satisfactory, though, since the slide can be difficult to move when the spinnaker is pulling. A better solution is to equip the slide with up- and downhaul lines.

Thus in 'our' boat we have a spinnaker pole with the same fittings at either end and with attachments for the topping lift and downhaul. This is a great advantage when gybing, as we shall see later. Such an arrangement, though, is not adequate for larger boats, where too much hard work on the part of the crew would be needed. Instead, one end of the pole is shipped in a strong bell-shaped fitting on the mast while the topping lift and downhaul are attached to the outer end of the pole. Sometimes a boat will carry two spinnaker poles to make gybing easier (as described later) and it may be wise to carry a spare pole in the event of an accident.

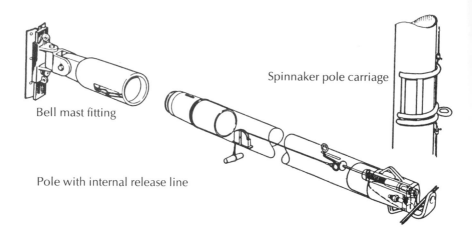

Bell mast fitting

Spinnaker pole carriage

Pole with internal release line

The pole is now released from its stowage on deck (or on the boom) and one end is attached to the slide in the mast track with the snap hook facing upwards. The slide should be positioned high in its track to ensure that the pole is more or less at the correct height when the spinnaker is set. With the outer end of the pole thus sloping down towards the stem, to windward of the forestay, the topping lift and downhaul are then attached to the pole using clips or snap hooks.

## THE TOPPING LIFT

The topping lift is led through a block or sheave well up on the front of the mast and from there down to a cleat at the foot of the mast, preferably with the facility for an additional lead aft to the cockpit to enable trimming to be carried out from there.

## THE DOWNHAUL

The downhaul is led through a block on the foredeck or on the heel of the mast. Again it is an advantage if the downhaul can be led aft to the cockpit. The line used should be of the same strength and quality as that used for the sheets.

## THE SPINNAKER BAG (OR TURTLE) ON DECK

The spinnaker, in its bag, is taken on to the foredeck shortly before hoisting and placed in the pulpit close to the forestay.

14

There should be a loop on the bottom of the bag and this should be secured with a seizing to the forestay deck fitting, fairlead or other suitable fixture. The ties holding the clews and top in place should now be freed, but care should be taken to prevent the sail slipping out of the bag to the extent that there is a risk of the wind catching it prematurely.

The guy (the windward sheet) should be *led through* the upward facing hook on the spinnaker pole and snapped to the windward clew of the sail. The leeward sheet is similarly snapped to the other clew. The last step is to snap the spinnaker halyard to the head of the sail and the spinnaker is then ready for setting.

## THE SPINNAKER HALYARD

The spinnaker halyard should be of the same strong, high-quality line as the sheets. It is rove through a robust swivel block on the front of the mast, just above the foresail block and clear of the forestay. The halyard may be led down outside the mast either to a cleat at the foot of the mast, or, via a block on deck, aft to the cockpit. Alternatively, the halyard can be led down inside the mast to ensure a clear lead and to minimise wind resistance. It is essential that the spinnaker halyard should run freely through any blocks or sheaves and it should be remembered that the more of these it passes through the greater the friction will be. When the halyard is not in use it is best to snap the hook to a convenient point in the pulpit forward of the forestay so that it is ready to clip to the spinnaker when required.

## A LAST LOOK ROUND

Before setting the spinnaker it is a good idea to make sure that everything is ready thus avoiding any unpleasant surprises. So check the following:

1   That the sail is packed carefully without twists.

2   That the sheets are led outside everything, ie the guard rails, shrouds and forestay.

3   That the spinnaker pole is secured to the mast fairly high up and the guy led through the upward facing hook on the end of the spinnaker pole. The hook must face upwards to allow the sheet to be freed when gybing. (The spinnaker will always exert an upward pull when filled.)

15

**4** That the downhaul is secured to the pole. It is important that the tension is kept on the downhaul because under no circumstances must the pole be allowed to lift above the horizontal, for control of the spinnaker would be lost. Make sure, therefore, that there is not too much slack. The line can conveniently be marked with tape for this purpose.

**5** That the topping lift is secured to the pole and hoisted sufficiently to allow the pole to rest against the forestay level with the top of the spinnaker bag.

**6** Finally, look up to make sure that the spinnaker halyard has not become entangled with the forestay or crosstrees.

# Setting the spinnaker

It is a tense moment for any sailor when the spinnaker is hoisted. Even in a moderate breeze things can get out of hand if anything goes wrong, and in a strong wind quite dangerous situations can arise. This is not said to alarm, but to help instil a healthy respect for the forces that are released when the sail area is suddenly increased by 150 per cent.

To keep things fully under control it is essential that the spinnaker is not allowed to fill before it is fully hoisted. To prevent this, the sail should be hoisted as quickly as possible, preferably in the lee of the headsail or genoa which should be left up to provide an effective wind shadow until the spinnaker is set.

A good strong winch is needed to ensure that the halyard is brought fully home. The guy should not be sheeted home until this has been done, otherwise the spinnaker will quite certainly fill before the crew is ready. The tail can, however, be pulled in quite safely while the hoisting is in progress. Once the spinnaker has been hoisted fully home, the pole position can be trimmed so that the pole itself is horizontal.

The helmsman plays an important part and is by no means a passive onlooker. He can give valuable help by bearing away to something like a dead run before the order to set the spinnaker is given. Not until the spinnaker is set, and the sheet and guy trimmed, should he return to his original course. When short-handed, the helmsman can help by taking the sheet or at least tailing it. On the other hand, working the winches to take in on the guy, and to give the final haul on the sheet, will require all the effort that the crew can muster

For safety reasons, beginners should always bear away to a dead run – regardless of wind conditions. An experienced crew, though, may justifiably hoist on a reach provided that the wind is not too strong. When something goes wrong it is most often for one of the following reasons:

Setting the spinnaker
on large and small
keelboats

**1**  The spinnaker gets a twist in it so that it sets in the shape of an hourglass. In this case first try to see which way the sail has been twisted and then pull in the direction that seems to offer the best chance of removing the twist. A swivel shackle at the head will help to eliminate the final twist. If this approach does not work, or if it actually makes things worse, then there is nothing for it but to douse the spinnaker and start all over again.

*Cause*: Carelessly packed spinnaker or sheet and guy attached to the wrong clews.

**2**  On hoisting, the spinnaker comes out of its bag in a ball and falls into the sea before the halyard can be hauled close up. Because the boat is moving through the water, the spinnaker

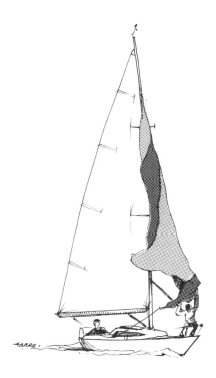

It is not easy to free the spinnaker when it has wound itself several times round the forestay and the helmsman is impatient . . .

will fill with water and before long it will be acting as a 'sea anchor' astern. Although this is embarrassing, it is seldom really dangerous. It quickly becomes clear that it is quite impossible to haul the spinnaker back on board since it is filled with several tons of seawater. The remedy is to take the wind out of the headsail by hauling it amidships, or even lowering it completely. Make sure the guy is attached firmly to the winch and free the sheet from the clew. It should then be possible to retrieve the spinnaker by hauling in on the guy. Under no circumstances let go of both clews, since this would allow the sail to float free attached only to the masthead with a resultant loss of all control. Another possibility is to cut the halyard, but if a kink, for example, should then stop the halyard running out through the block, the position may indeed be awkward.

*Cause*: Spinnaker packed wrongly or too tightly in its bag. (The effect of this is made worse if the sail is wet.) Or it may be that the bag is too small or has too narrow an opening.

**3** The spinnaker fills before it has been fully hoisted. The sail will flap about, and in a fresh breeze the boat can become out of control. It would be a slow and laborious job simply to continue to try to wind in on the winch, so the first thing to do is to spill the wind. To do this, ease the guy until the pole rests on the forestay and ease the sheet a little while the helmsman bears away to a dead run. Then ease further on the sheet so that the sail collapses, at which point it can then be hoisted close up.

*Cause*: The spinnaker may have been set when sailing too close to the wind, thus allowing the air flow to get round the genoa and fill the spinnaker. Or perhaps the guy was hauled in too early. If the spinnaker is set without a headsail up to shield it, there will always be the risk that it will fill too soon.

**4** The spinnaker has wound itself around the forestay. This should really only happen when the boat is rolling heavily and the spinnaker has just been set. In wet weather there may be an additional problem in that the sail tends to cling to the forestay, which in turn makes it likely that it will wind itself around even more, perhaps to the extent that the sail cannot be lowered. The resulting tangle can take a very long time to sort out – and may even prove impossible. In light airs, when there is also a heavy swell, this predicament can also arise when sailing with the spinnaker up, but with no foresail (arguably justifiable in these conditions purely from the point of view of speed alone).

*Cause*: The spinnaker has been set in a following swell or heavy sea without the foresail to protect the forestay. One way of preventing the problem is to use a 'ghoster', a very light sail shaped like a foresail but made from a fine mesh net. A ghoster is often carried by long-distance cruisers or racing yachts where spinnakers are set in a following wind, such as the trade winds, and where long rolling seas may cause the spinnaker to twist around an otherwise unprotected forestay.

The spinnaker has just been set and the crew are trimming the boat.

**1** The helmsman tends the mainsheet and carefully controls the steering. He keeps the sail well set by not sailing too close to the wind and by bearing away if the sail shows signs of collapsing. He can ease the guy singlehanded, but to haul in he may need assistance unless there is a winch with a jamming device to grip the sheet.

**2** The foredeck crewman has lowered the genoa to prevent it blanketing the spinnaker. This is necessary, especially in light winds.

**3** This crewman is fixing the kicking strap to the lee rail to flatten the mainsail for greater efficiency and to hold the sail steady in light airs and a swell that may cause the boat to yaw. This should not be done in a strong breeze since the kicking strap cannot be released quickly in the event of an unexpected gybe, especially if it is the metal stay type rather than a tackle.

**4** The fourth crew member trims the spinnaker sheet continuously, keeping an eye on the spinnaker itself by looking under the boom. He keeps the sheet loosened off as much as possible without the luff curling. He could also trim the sheet from just aft of the weather shrouds, from where he would also get a better view.

The backstay should be slackened off to allow the sail to set efficiently and to avoid undesirable backward bend in the mast.

▲ The wind has got hold of the spinnaker before it has been sheeted home. This is a typical result of sailing too close to the wind and thus being unable to take advantage of the lee afforded by the mainsail and foresail. Ease away the sheet to spill the wind and bear away to a dead run, then haul in on the guy. If this does not work, lower the sail and start again.

◄ The classic mistake: the 'hourglass'. The spinnaker was set, but alas it had been wrongly packed in its bag. All the crew members seem to be at a loss, but then it's not an easy problem to sort out. It is often necessary to lower the sail and start again.

On smaller keelboats, such as the Soling and Squib, the spinnaker can be hoisted directly from the cockpit, the leeward deck or a position by the hatchway. This arrangement is advantageous when racing because, by obviating the need for a crewman to go forward, it makes it easier to maintain an even weight distribution, something that is important when speed is of the essence. It also saves time since neither sheet/guy nor halyard need to be unclipped from the spinnaker which, when not in use, is simply lowered into the cabin with all three lines still attached, ready for hoisting again when needed.

Before hoisting the spinnaker, check that the guy is correctly led through the hook on the end of the pole and that the pole itself is correctly rigged to the mast. When the time comes to hoist the spinnaker, the slack on the guy should be taken up as quickly as possible so that the tack can be hauled out to the pole end before the halyard is hauled close up and the sheet trimmed to allow the spinnaker to fill.

As far as the pole is concerned, it may be mounted on the boom (as mentioned earlier), thus allowing it simply to be led forward into position on the mast. With all lines led aft to the cockpit this means that everything can be controlled from there – except of course the actual attaching of the pole to the mast. Even this can be 'automated' by attaching the pole to a carriage on the mast and using a special uphaul/downhaul arrangement to trim the height of the pole as required.

# Lowering the spinnaker

When lowering the spinnaker it is just as important that it should be done in the lee of the mainsail or genoa as it is when setting it, and the spinnaker should be allowed to blow out freely to leeward. In any conditions other than very light airs, a foresail should be hoisted to provide a windshield.

The sequence of events should be:

1 First, the helmsman should bear away.

2 The helmsman should also ease the guy until the pole is resting on the forestay.

3 The first crewman takes hold of the clew, having first sheeted home the sail.

4 If necessary, the crewman can also slacken off the topping lift and the downhaul sufficiently to allow the second crewman to reach the guy.

5 The halyard should be prepared for lowering. It is a matter of choice as to who does this. It may be the helmsman if the halyard has been led aft to the cockpit but, even better, it can be done by the third crewman if there is one. If shorthanded, the second crewman should be able to do the job once he has completed his other preparations.

6 The helmsman, or whoever is in charge of the halyard, gives the order to lower the spinnaker.

7 The guy should then be slackened off roundly by the helms-man and completely freed from the winch so that it runs out freely.

8 The halyard is gradually eased while, at the same time –

9 The first crewman gathers the spinnaker in, under the main boom and down into the cockpit. It is a good idea to pull it in while holding the foot of the sail, and to do this quickly. The second crewman should assist as soon as he can.

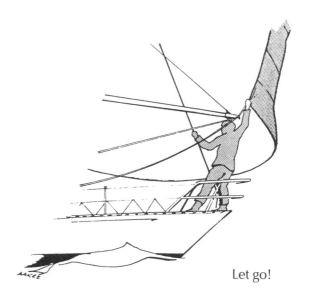

Let go!

**10** The pole should then be removed and stowed securely.

**11** On smaller boats, though, sheet, guy and halyard can remain attached as described earlier. On larger boats they should be unclipped and lashed together so that, by hauling on what was the guy (to windward in the cockpit), they can be dragged forward to the pulpit and secured ready for next time. One of the crew can than, at leisure, re-pack the spinnaker in its bag while out of the wind in the cabin.

As we shall see later, larger boats may be equipped with both sheet and guy on both sides for ease of gybing. In this case the guy should not be freed from the winch, as described in **7** on page 25. Instead, both guy and weather sheet should be unclipped from the tack. These two lines can be secured to a single snap shackle, one that can be snapped open even when under tension. One of the crew goes forward and, on the order to let go, opens the snap hook on the pole to allow the spinnaker to blow out freely in the lee of the other sails. It may be necessary to slacken the topping lift and lower the pole so that the crewman can reach the tack (as in the sketch above).

As the sail flies free, the tension in the guy is released. This may cause the pole to spring back, which is why one should never keep one's head to windward of the pole. People have lost teeth in this way, or even been knocked unconscious. Instead, keep your head below, or to leeward of the pole.

It is important that the spinnaker should be kept to leeward of the other sails while it is being gathered in. Especially in a strong wind, a firm hold should be kept on the leech to keep it close to the mainsail while the guy is left slack to allow the luff to blow out. (Although the leeches are identical it is usual to talk of the luff as the one attached to the pole, and the leech is the one attached to the sheet.)

The two most risky moments when lowering the spinnaker are:

1   If the halyard is slackened too quickly, catching the crewman unprepared, the sail can end up in the water. It will then act as an anchor and may be impossible to recover.

2   If the crewman fails to get a proper grip on the sail, it may slip out of his hands.

It is therefore a distinct advantage if there are two crew members working together: one sitting on the cabin top by the boom to receive the spinnaker behind the mainsail, and the other gathering in the loose sailcloth and passing it down into the cabin. Never try to bring the spinnaker aft of the mainsail or to lead it around the boom to windward. There is only one way: down on the lee side of the mainsail, under the boom, and down into the cabin. It is important to tidy up quickly, partly to be ready when the spinnaker is needed again, but also to be able to concentrate on the business of sailing on.

Spinnaker being gathered in correctly to leeward, hauled under the boom, and passed down into the cabin. If done quickly it should be possible to prevent most of the sail ending up in the water.

# Spinnaker sailing

With the spinnaker set, what might have been a routine run can become one with speed and excitement. But concentration must not be allowed to lapse; both helm and sail trim need continuous attention.

On a dead run the pressure of the wind fills the spinnaker, which takes up a hemispherical shape, and this pressure, combined with the suction generated behind the rear surface of the sail, drives the boat forward. Since the wind over the boat as a whole is travelling faster than the boat can sail, it creates an overpressure that spills over the sides of the sail – causing the leeches to spread apart. The shoulders, towards the top of the sail, need special attention. They lift the spinnaker and enlarge the sail area. The air flow over the shoulders also produces suction; this plays a large part in lifting the sail. As soon as the helmsman bears away a little, the spinnaker must be treated as a foresail. The air flow will then essentially be the same as it would be over a genoa. The air flow enters by the luff, flows over both surfaces of the sail, and spills off at the leech.

The faster air flow over the sail, as a consequence of bearing away, will drive the boat faster. This means that there is nothing to be gained by being on a dead run except in a fresh to strong wind when the boat is travelling at near its maximum speed anyway. The greatest advantage is obtained by sailing, say, 10–15° off the wind, especially when the winds are light. The extra speed obtained more than compensates for the slightly greater distance to be covered. This procedure is routine when racing on a leg that is directly downwind, so one in fact steers a zig-zag course with a gybe half-way to the mark.

The spinnaker has an advantage over the genoa in that it has greater sail area, but it lacks the genoa's taut luff and flat leech – features that aid the air flow over the sail. On the contrary, the spinnaker has no stability in the luff and its natural tendency is for the curve of the sail to move aft towards the leech, thus constricting the air flow with anything but favourable results.

The purpose of trimming the spinnaker is two fold: first, to ensure that the effect of the wind on the spinnaker is maximised, and secondly, to achieve forward rather than sideways thrust, since the latter will cause the boat to heel.

## THE SPINNAKER POLE

The most common mistake is to set the pole too low on the mast. It should be positioned well up the mast track to give the spinnaker the necessary lift to allow it to unfurl and present the greatest possible sail area to the wind. The difference is illustrated in cases **A** and **B** in the diagram on page 32.

Spinnaker air flow when running.

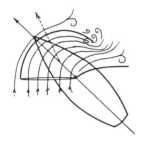

Air flow on a broad reach. The flow across the spinnaker causes thrust both forwards and athwartships, with the resultant thrust acting in the direction shown by the stippled arrow.

On a closer reach, even with the spinnaker well trimmed as shown, the sideways force is considerably greater, but even so the result is at least as favourable as in the example shown above. The keel prevents drift to leeward and the wind speed over the sail is greater now that the course is closer to the wind.

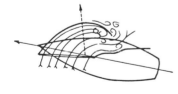

On a beam reach the air flow is spoiled because the curvature of the sail tends to move aft. This has an adverse effect. The sideways forces increase, the boat heels further, and this in turn causes increased sideways drift as a result of the angle of the keel. The mainsail has badly backwinded. In spite of all this there will still be some forward thrust, mainly because of the pressure reduction on the lee side of the spinnaker.

31

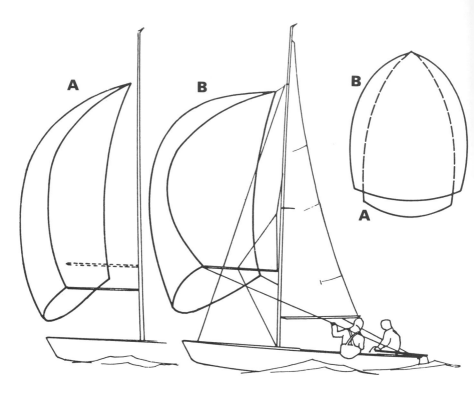

**A**  The pole is set too low, thus causing the leeches to become taut. This narrows the sail and presents a reduced sail area to the wind.

**B**  In this case the spinnaker is set correctly for moderate wind conditions. The sail lifts and presents the greatest possible area to the wind. The pole is horizontal and both tack and clew are at the same height above the water. If the clew dips, the sail will twist and efficiency will be lost. If clew and tack (attached to the pole) are at the same height, this is an indication that the pole is correctly set.

The exception to this is when sailing in light airs, when the first priority is to get the spinnaker to set at all. Keeping the pole low in this case allows even light airs to fill the sail. Then, once the spinnaker has filled, the pole can be raised to a position that gives optimum speed.

In principle, the pole should be horizontal to ensure that the sail presents its maximum area to the wind. There is no point

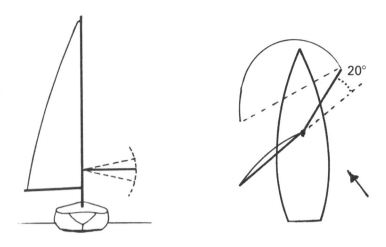

in effectively shortening the pole by allowing it to dip or lift. The wind should meet the sail at right angles (see diagram above); and for best results the pole should not be directly in line with the boom, but set about 20° further forward. The spinnaker sheet should be kept eased a little to avoid backwinding the mainsail. The luff needs constant watching because when the trim is right and the spinnaker pulling to maximum effect, the luff is just on the point of collapsing. The essential thing is to position the pole correctly and then trim the sheets to suit.

## TRIMMING

The correct trimming of the spinnaker is just as important as the positioning of the pole. Normally the sheet should be secured as far aft as possible to allow the spinnaker to lift high and wide, well ahead of the mast. This helps to avoid the wind being deflected into the lee of the mainsail. The sheet also needs to be slack to allow the spinnaker to assume the shape that gives

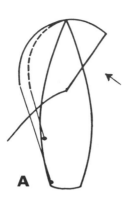

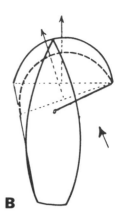

**A** The spinnaker should be sheeted as far aft as possible to give maximum distance between spinnaker and mainsail, and to allow the spinnaker to open as fully as possible.

**B** When in the position shown by the stippled line, the spinnaker is sheeted in too much, causing it to pull to leeward. With the wind as shown, the sheet should be eased to allow the sail to fill fully and draw ahead.

maximum forward thrust. In a fresh breeze with a lively sea, however, and when on a dead run, it is better to cleat the sheet further forward to prevent the boat from yawing – ie the 'pendulum' effect of the spinnaker swinging uncontrollably from side to side.

If the main boom obstructs the spinnaker sheet it will be necessary to adjust the sheet to avoid this. On a run, a barber-haul can be used to keep the sheet clear as it passes under the main boom. In more of a cross wind, with the main boom hardened in, the barber-haul can be eased off and the sheeting point moved aft once more. The barber-haul can be dispensed with altogether on a broad reach to prevent the leech from closing. On this course

A primitive but effective barber-haul in use. All on board are ▶ definitely enjoying themselves!

34

Spinnaker sailing at its best. Each boat is racing at maximum speed with spinnakers beautifully set.

▲ ▼ The spinnaker needs continual trimming. By standing up, the crewman has a good view and can keep the sheet trimmed to avoid collapsing the luff.

the sheet should be well free of the boom, although it might sometimes be necessary to free it by hand first. The important point is that the sheet should run free from the block aft to the clew of the spinnaker, even though it may just touch the leech of the mainsail.

It is usual to steer a steady compass course and this means trimming the sheet and guy accordingly. The wind, of course, is constantly changing direction, so it is the job of the crew to harden or slacken the sheet in response to this so that the spinnaker always draws to its maximum capacity. This means keeping the sheet as slack as the conditions allow. Only if the boat alters course, or if the wind changes for any length of time, should the guy be readjusted – and then this should only be to ensure that the pole is kept square to the wind. Remember, too, to keep an eye on the height of the pole relative to the clew. If the wind strength changes you may need to adjust topping lift and downhaul, or even – following a major change in wind direction – move the pole up or down in its track on the mast.

In very light airs the weight of the sheet itself can be a problem. With the guy sagging, its weight can pull the pole aft. For this reason, an experienced racing crew will carry a set of lightweight sheets (possibly strengthened with Kevlar to make them even lighter). If there is so little wind that it is doubtful whether the spinnaker will lift at all, one can even use very fine line as a sheet so that at least the weight of the sheet can't be blamed for any lack of performance.

It is worth bearing in mind that a damp spinnaker is less effective than a dry one. If the spinnaker has been in the sea it should be rinsed in fresh water; if you neglect to do this, the salt will remain in the cloth and attract any dampness in the air. In light airs, even the fall of dew can cause an evening race to be lost if the spinnaker has not been rinsed.

## CLOSE REACHING

The closest one can sail to the wind with a normal spinnaker is about 55–60° to the apparent wind, and even then opinions will differ as to whether it is worth while setting a spinnaker as close to the wind as that. If one carries a reaching spinnaker, a sail tailored especially for that purpose, then it is possible to steer even closer to the wind – say to within 40°. In fact, such a sail can be used with the true wind abeam in comparatively fresh

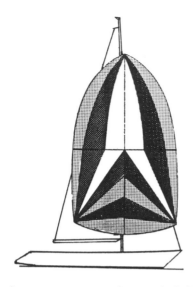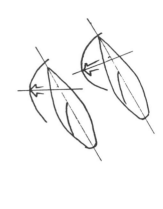

The star-cut spinnaker is slightly smaller and flatter than a normal spinnaker. It is therefore most suitable for close reaching, but can also be used with advantage when running in strong winds.

breezes, something rarely achievable with a standard spinnaker – although it does depend somewhat on the stability and manoeuvrability of the boat itself.

A normal spinnaker is not designed for this purpose and it would generally be better to set a genoa. Nor is there usually anything to be gained by letting the pole rest on the forestay to try to get the spinnaker to fill. The forward part of the sail may fill and draw, but the after part will act as a brake. At the same time the boat will heel, thus losing steerage way as well as speed. One would also need to sheet in the mainsail more than usual, to prevent the spinnaker backwinding the mainsail and rendering it virtually useless. The trick is to find the borderline for your boat between where it is, or is not, worth setting the spinnaker. One might expect it to be advantageous to lower the pole to stretch the luff, but in fact this would only cause the spinnaker to collapse. Even in this situation it pays to carry the pole as high as possible, because only then can the spinnaker spread and open its shoulders, thus flattening the sail. It is this flatter shape, albeit of limited width, that sailmakers aim to achieve when designing

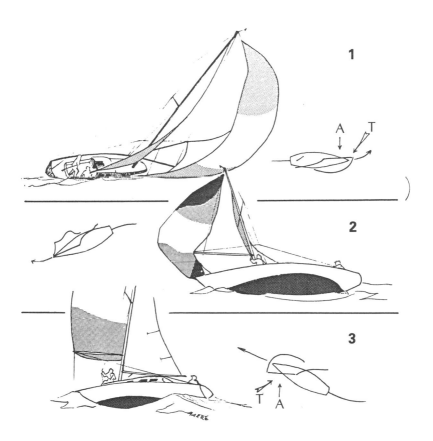

**1**   There is too much wind to make it worth while sailing so close to the wind. The boat is hard to control and will heel even further. The apparent wind (A) is at 55°, and only a star-cut spinnaker will set properly. (T) indicates the true wind.

**2**   The boat is broaching with the wind on the nose, thus causing the spinnaker to collapse. By immediately slackening both spinnaker and mainsheet the helmsman can regain control and bear away. Since the boat will be shuddering and the sail flapping, the situation may seem more dramatic than it really is. Do not slacken the guy or the spinnaker will fly out to windward, making it even more difficult to control. The main thing is to ease the force on the rudder by slackening main and spinnaker sheets – but only those.

**3**   One should bear away on to a tack to give an apparent wind of 75–80° to allow stable sailing conditions with a normal all-round spinnaker. If you need to tack closer to the wind than this, it will be worth while dropping the spinnaker and hoisting a genoa instead.

▲ **Close reaching**: Looking at these cruisers, you can see that one cannot sail too close to the wind with a spinnaker. The leech will close in and slow down the boat, so there is no point in trying to sail closer to the wind than these boats are doing here.

◀ The spinnaker is about to collapse. Since the pole is already resting on the forestay, there is no more easing that can be done here. If it really is necessary to maintain this course, the sheet must be hardened; it would be better to bear away a little to allow the sail to fill properly again.

a reaching spinnaker – more often than not a sail of the star-cut type (see page 40).

In most modern boats, especially boats with a broad flat stern, the rudder is subjected to heavy strain when the boat heels. The rudder may even be lifted so far out of the water that effective control is lost and the boat broaches. The increased force on the rudder, when the boat is heeled, will tend to take way off the boat. The balance of the boat is therefore of particular importance when the spinnaker is set. There are three key points to be considered:

1 The spinnaker sheet should be as slack as possible to help achieve an open, flat spinnaker (setting the pole high).

2 There should be a good deal of slack on the mainsheet and, in a fresh breeze, perhaps so much so that the forward part of the sail does not draw at all.

3 The crew should sit well out to windward to trim the boat as much as they can.

## FRESH WINDS

When sailing in winds of more than 25 knots, even an experienced crew will not be able to sail close-hauled with a spinnaker set. It is quite possible, though, to set the spinnaker with the wind abaft the beam or when on a dead run in such conditions, but it will still call for great care and a lot of hard work on the part of everyone on board.

At worst the boat may roll from side to side, thus causing a dangerous gybe, or the pole may dip into the water to windward with the result that the boat trips over itself. It is even possible that the vessel may grype up to windward so hard that the spinnaker slams violently, resulting in a broken mast. If the kicking strap is still fixed, all could be lost if the wind catches the mainsail on the opposite side, thus making it *impossible* to gybe. On the other hand, it is essential to have a strong kicking strap hauled taut in order to remove any twist in the mainsail that would itself play a major part in causing the boat to roll.

When sailing in such conditions it is essential to observe the following rules:

1 The helmsman must keep his eye aft to prepare for any approaching wind gusts (visible as dark stripes on the surface). Just before such a gust strikes, the helm should be put over to windward to prevent the boat gryping up uncontrollably.

2 The spinnaker should be centred with more or less equal sail area on each side of the boat. This means that the guy should be well eased so that the pole sets at about 45° forward of the beam. This gives the spinnaker more freedom to lift and

The boat is beginning to roll dangerously from side to side. The guy is hauled in so that the pole is set abeam. This makes the spinnaker pull the top of the mast to windward. The guy must be slackened immediately and the sheet hauled in to centre the spinnaker. Trimming would be easier if the barber-haul were hauled right home by the halyard. The kicking strap is correctly hauled taut to counter mainsail twisting.

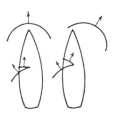

When the spinnaker is set too far to windward and there is a twist in the mainsail because the kicking strap is not hauled taut, there is no way of stopping the boat from rolling uncontrollably from side to side. The boat to port is better placed to avoid this. The short curve represents the top of the mainsail.

◀ Great sailing in stiff breeze. Although the boat is beginning to heel alarmingly, it looks as though the crew has everything under control.

The crew need to keep their ▶ wits about them here. The spinnaker is nicely centred, the kicking strap well hauled in, and the barber-hauls led well forward (perhaps a little too far forward), but the bow is tending to dip. The crew must speedily move aft to counteract this.

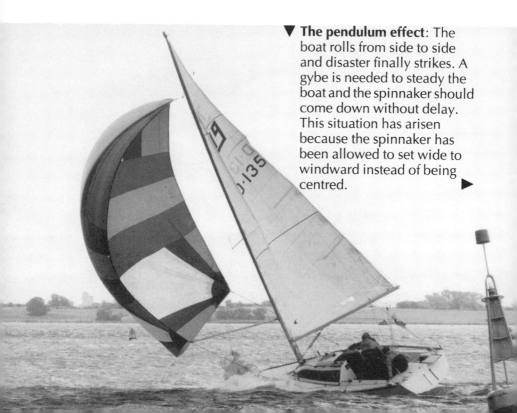

▼ **The pendulum effect**: The boat rolls from side to side and disaster finally strikes. A gybe is needed to steady the boat and the spinnaker should come down without delay. This situation has arisen because the spinnaker has been allowed to set wide to windward instead of being centred. ▶

**The pendulum effect**: Disaster! It can be seen that the spinnaker has not been hoisted fully home, something that would have contributed to the capsize. The boat in the foreground makes do with a jib, a sensible choice in such a strong wind.

so prevents it from dipping the bow. The spinnaker should draw well ahead as well as upwards; if it stands to windward of the centreline it will tend to make the boat roll or heel to windward, which in turn could lead to loss of control.

3　The spinnaker sheet must be led further forward by means of a barber-haul.

4　The kicking strap attached to the main boom should be hauled taut to avoid a twist in the mainsail.

5　When sailing in very strong winds it is a great advantage to have a specially designed storm spinnaker, although a star-cut sail can be used. If the weather deteriorates to near gale force, it will be too risky to keep a spinnaker set. It would be better in these conditions to set a jib or a genoa, but still using the spinnaker pole. This will leave the boat well balanced and easy to steer.

**Broaching**: This is what happens if one tries to sail too close to the wind when it is blowing hard. The boat will grype up uncontrollably and, with the rudder out of the water, steering is impossible. If both mainsheet and spinnaker sheet can be slackened during a pause between gusts, the boat will right itself and one can bear away on to a run.

## LOSS OF CONTROL

If everything goes wrong and, for example, the boat grypes up and the spinnaker drags the boat flat with water filling the cockpit, then there is a very real danger that the crew may be washed overboard. The water pouring in is capable of creating a vacuum that could simply suck out the crew with such force that it would be impossible for them to hold on. In heavy weather, therefore, it is essential that everyone wears lifelines – in addition to life jackets, of course. The cabin hatch cover, cabin doors and all other hatches must be kept shut.

## POSITIONING THE CREW

The best positions for the crew depend on the wind at the time. In light airs when running before the wind, it will pay to luff just enough to let the boat heel a little to allow the spinnaker to fill.

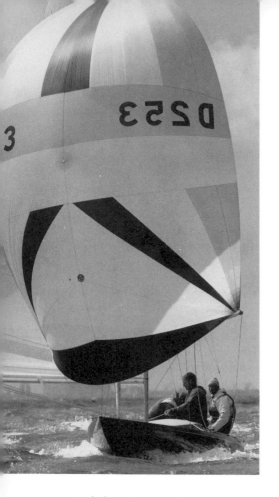

Stylish sailing – spinnakers under full control in a fresh breeze and in
light airs.

It also helps to let the stern lift to reduce the drag, and to this
end one crewman should sit to windward on the side deck while
another positions himself on the foredeck. The more wind there
is, the further aft the crew must be. If they are not in this position,
the enormous pull that the spinnaker exerts on the top of the mast
will cause the bow to dip deeper; this in turn will lead to loss of
speed and steering difficulties. As mentioned before, letting the
pole swing forward will help to compensate for this by giving the
spinnaker a better chance of lifting.

Here the guy has become detached from the pole and the boat is completely out of control. When a light boat with a broad stern heels this far over, its buoyancy takes the rudder almost out of the water. However, because it floats so high in the water, there is little risk of serious flooding.

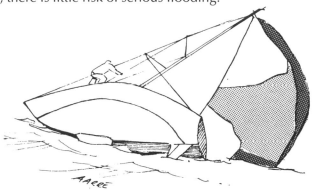

## GYBING

To gybe successfully requires experience and teamwork, especially in a fresh wind. The only way to overcome that anxious feeling is to practise, again and again, the drill for gybing. Gybing in light to moderate breezes should be done with the spinnaker drawing fully ahead throughout the gybe, whereas in a stronger wind the main thing is to concentrate on completing the gybe without losing control in the process.

Countless systems of gybing have been devised and tailored to the many different types and sizes of boats, but in every case the essential point is that the simpler the method the better the result is likely to be. One must remember, though, that the operation involves what almost amounts to a revolution on board, since lines that were slack now become taut and vice versa. It is not unknown for a skipper to assume that all will go smoothly if he shouts the orders loudly enough: Slacken away! Haul away! No, not that one! etc, etc. But slacken what? And how much? Gybing like that is doomed to failure.

It is important when gybing that crew members should always

**Gybing**: In a fresh breeze with a following sea, gybing should be carried out with the boat at full speed. It is then that the wind is exerting least pressure, and so the task is that much easier for the crew.

be anticipating the next move. For example, they will know that there will be a strong upward pull on the pole when the gybe is completed, and that the force of the wind will again lift the spinnaker when on the new tack. Should there be too much slack on the downhaul, the pole will lift too far and the spinnaker will be difficult to handle. If, on the other hand, telltales have been placed on the downhaul, topping lift, sheet and guy, it will then be possible to position and secure the various lines before the spinnaker lifts again. Sometimes a helmsman can forget to steer because he is *too* involved with what the crew is doing. His role of course is just as important as that of the crew and he must, for example, pay off and gybe at just the right moment. The boat tends to grype up when the main boom swings across in the gybe, and the helmsman must quickly bear up to windward to prevent this.

Some recommended procedures are described below:

**A   Gybing in light airs** (see diagram **A** opposite)

**1**   The foredeck crewman should stand forward of the mast facing aft. He or she should take hold of the sheet that is to become the guy after the gybe and wait ready for gybing.

**2**   The pole should be freed from the mast and attached to the sheet so that it is now fixed to both clews. The crewman should be positioned forward of the pole while holding on to it with both hands. The helmsman should aft the mainsail to free the wind and thus assist the spinnaker. He then bears away, gripping the mainsheet as close as possible to the sail, and 'wrenches' the boom across.

**3**   The crewman now frees the pole from the 'old guy' and, as the mainsail swings across, the pole is led out to the new side. The new inner end of the pole should be fixed to the mast while new sheet and guy are trimmed from the cockpit. Take care not to haul in on the guy before the pole is properly secured to the mast.

**B   Gybing in a fresh wind** (see diagram **B** opposite)

**1–2**   The helmsman should square off on to a dead run and the guy should be eased to allow the pole to point forward and upwards at an angle. Both barber-hauls should be hauled taut to stop the spinnaker flailing.

54

**Gybing a small or medium-sized keelboat**: The pole is identical at both ends, with topping lift and downhaul attached centrally.

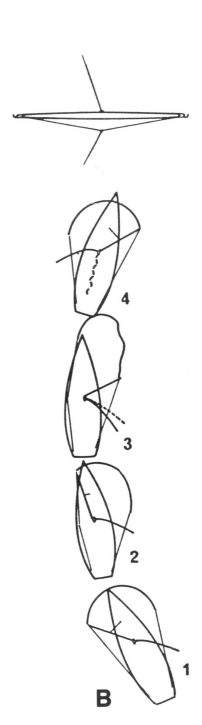

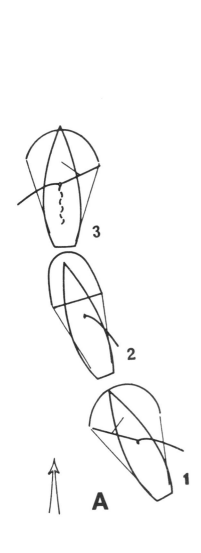

**Gybing**: Here the boats are gybing round a mark, but the leading boat is unlucky. The boats following have taken her wind, something the skipper should have foreseen and prevented by steering into wind the moment the mark was rounded.

**3** The pole is freed from the guy and the mast and is quickly cleated to the old sheet. It is not possible to pull in the sheet, and thus the pole must be guided to the sheet rather than vice versa.

For a brief moment the spinnaker will be flying free without a pole, but as the helmsman bears away still further the spinnaker will be in the lee of the mainsail and so will be easier to handle. The new sheet is braced by the barber-haul, which should be hauled in hard. There is now less pressure on the sail and the pole can once more be quickly secured to the mast fitting.

**4** Now the gybe can be completed in the usual way and the sheet, guy and barber-hauls trimmed. Remember to use a touch of opposite helm to prevent broaching when the boom swings over.

56

**C**

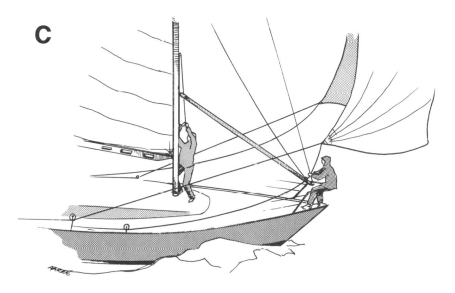

**Gybing with twin sheets and guy**: The boat is about to gybe on to the starboard tack. The crewman in the pulpit quickly clips the starboard guy on to the pole while the crewman by the mast is raising the pole to allow it to pass inside the forestay; after this he must raise it into position with the topping lift.

Remember to adjust the runners if the boat is equipped with these. Not all masts are strong enough to withstand these forces when supported by a stern stay alone, especially if a sudden wind slam makes the spinnaker snatch violently.

The gybe is most likely to be successful if the boat is sailing at maximum speed. The pull of the sail may be too great, for example, if gybing is attempted at the moment speed drops after planing or surfing. But of course the ideal time to gybe is during a period of calm between gusts.

**C   Gybing with twin sheet and guy** (see diagram **C** above)

On larger boats the strain of the sheet and guy is so great that it is no longer practicable to gybe by moving the pole from side to side; the weight of the pole alone is enough to make this difficult. Instead the pole is swung across while the inner end

**Gybing**: Rounding the mark in perfect style. All the spinnakers are drawing without any undue loss of speed.

remains fixed to the mast. This double-ended design of pole was illustrated in an earlier section.

Both sheet and guy are needed on either side since the pull of the spinnaker will make it virtually impossible to hook the pole to sheet or guy in anything more than a stiff breeze. The guys may even be of wire or Kevlar-reinforced line to resist stretching, while normal braided line with a little give is used for the sheets. Both sheet and guy are clipped to a common hook so that both can be freed from the spinnaker in a single operation.

The guy is led to a block on deck just aft of amidships and therefore does not need a barber-haul, whereas the sheet, which is led aft to its usual block will need one. There will need to be a separate winch for sheet and guy, ie four spinnaker winches in all. When gybing, no one has time to change over guy and sheet on the same winch.

When under way, the spinnaker is trimmed as usual: the guy to windward and the sheet to leeward. The windward sheet and leeward guy are left slack. A spinnaker gybe now needs at least four crewmen, if it is blowing at all. Two should be on the foredeck and two in the cockpit, in addition to the helmsman of course. Gybing should be carried out as follows:

1   There should be two crewmen on deck. One goes forward and settles himself in the pulpit with the leeward guy (hanging slack); the other must ease the topping lift sufficiently to allow the pole to swing across inside the forestay (see diagram on page 57). It may be worth while marking the topping lift to indicate how far it should be eased. If there is little room in which to manoeuvre the pole inside the forestay, especially likely if a foresail is set, then the mast fitting should be raised to give the pole room to swing across.

2   As the boat bears away on to a run, the guy should be eased to reduce the pressure on the pole. When the order to gybe comes from the cockpit, the pole should be released from the guy and swung across inside the forestay. The mainsail is gybed at the same time from the cockpit, preferably by someone not involved in controlling the spinnaker.

3   The crewman in the bow now clips the new guy to the pole – always a tricky job because it is essential to run the line correctly. If led wrongly, the guy may jam when tension arises. The best pole fittings have a release line and

ratchet for the snap hook that engages the moment the guy is attached.

4 When the mainsail gybe has been completed, the new guy can be hauled home by the crew in the cockpit and the pole then swings into position ready for the foredeck crewman to raise it with the topping lift.

5 The sheet is re-trimmed on the new leeward side where the guy is now hanging slack. Similarly, the old sheet is slack now that the new guy has taken over to windward.

**D**

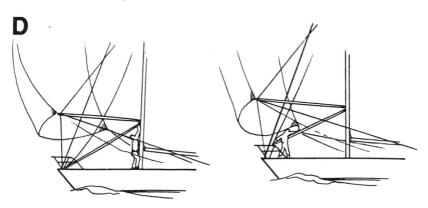

1 Rigging the new pole.

2 The free guy is led forward and clipped to the snap hook and the pole is swung into position.

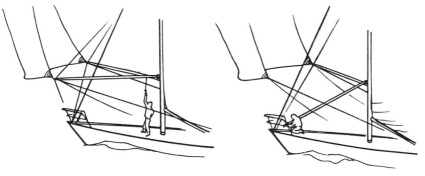

3 Briefly, both poles are in use while the mainsail is gybed. Sheet and guy are changed over on both sides.

4 The old pole is brought inboard.

With practice it should be possible to complete such a gybe quickly and safely. There is no danger of the spinnaker collapsing, because with careful trimming, the sail will draw nicely throughout the operation. This is because the pole is not attached to the sail during the gybe and therefore will not disturb its trim.

## D   Twin pole gybing (see diagram **D** on page 61)

On large offshore boats it is possible to use twin poles but, as described above, separate sheets and guys are needed in both clews. The method is the same except that, instead of pushing the pole across, the new one is rigged up (in its own mast fitting and with its own down haul and topping lift). This enables the new pole to be trimmed at leisure and the guy hardened in sufficiently to be ready for use as soon as the mainsail gybe has been completed.

It should be remembered that the racing rules forbid racing with more than one spinnaker pole. The extra pole may only be rigged for the gybe, and it must not be fixed until the old pole has been removed. If the boat is on a dead run in a lively wind, there is no way in which it is permissible to sail with both poles in place, using them alternately. It is not necessary, though, to remove the second pole completely; it can be left resting on the deck to show that it is not in use. (see photo opposite).

In smaller boats it is possible to gybe using two poles, without the need for separate sheets and guys on either side. Just make sure that the sheet is attached to the new pole before the pole is repositioned on the mast. In this case the guy becomes the sheet and vice versa, just as if the same pole were being changed from side to side. This method could be an advantage on cruising boats, but is hardly ever seen on smaller racing boats. The combined weight of the two poles together with the inconvenience involved would outweigh the advantages. It is really only in large ocean cruisers that two poles are used when racing, and then always with two sets of guys and sheets as already described.

**Gybing**: Gybing on to a starboard tack. The crewman is standing correctly facing aft. The pole is released from the guy and the mast, the sheet is then attached, and the pole replaced on the mast. The crewman in the cockpit (it could have been the helmsman) quickly pulls the pole across as soon as it has been replaced on the mast.

## TEAMWORK

One of the fascinating aspects of sailing with a spinnaker is the close relationship and teamwork it promotes between helmsman and crew. When cruising only under mainsail and jib (or genoa) there is little call for such close teamwork, except when going about. Once the sheets are trimmed on the new tack the crew will sit out to windward, and everything else is up to the helmsman.

While under way one or two crewmen will take care of the sheet, one standing to windward trimming it while the other operates the winch. A third crewman tends the mainsheet and a fourth (if there are that many) tends the guy and the halyards, while the helmsman takes charge of the navigation.

Offshore racer running before a force 6–7 wind. The slightly smaller star-cut spinnaker is well suited to such conditions, but it must be said that only experienced sailors will be able to cope in such circumstances.

The spinnaker is trimmed and centred to avoid rolling. The crew are sitting close together in the stern so that their weight helps to lift the bow. This also helps to shift the lateral plane and so counter any tendency to broaching. The mainsail is sheeted in for the same reason, and the kicking strap is hardened in.

In such weather there is the risk that the bow may bury itself in the back of a wave, thus submerging much of the foredeck. Should this happen there will not be time to drop the spinnaker immediately, so the guy should be eased until the pole rests on the forestay and the sheet also eased to reduce the wind pressure. At this stage it is about time to drop the spinnaker and set a jib instead.

Double-bell mast fitting with slide that can be adjusted up and down on the mast by means of a winch and internal wires. This is intended for large boats with two spinnaker poles. Such a system gives excellent results, even when a single pole is used.

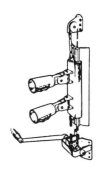

When there is a breath of wind the helmsman will bear away a little, the crewman on the sheet will slacken to the new course, the mainsheet will be eased and, if the change of course is permanent, someone will aft the guy a little. All this will be done without commotion, since a trained crew knows not only what to do but how to do it as a team. Probably none of them would be able to explain how they were able to do it all without one word being exchanged. Perhaps it was no more than the imperceptible heeling of the boat or the increase in wind that each would have felt on his face or neck. The crewman trimming the spinnaker knew that the helmsman would bear away, and he in turn knew that the sheet would be eased. The crewman tending the mainsail knew what the other two would do – even if he had not already sensed from the movement of the boat that it was sailing too close to the wind.

It takes a long time to build up such close teamwork and it is tempting to speculate that there might be an easier way. The reality is, however, that there is not, for nothing can take the place of experience and training. Fortunately, there are many ways in which this learning processs can be assisted and augmented – one means being the help of a book such as this.

**Above**: A Soling.
**Below**: A dinghy finely balanced.

# Special systems and gear

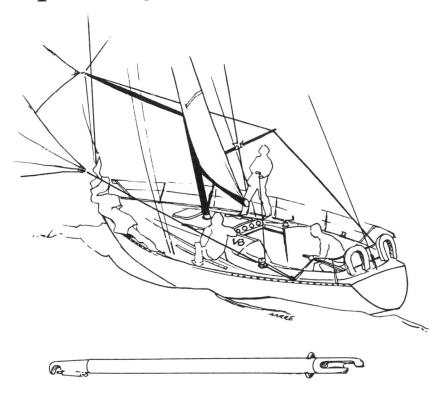

## THE JOCKEY POLE

To keep the guy clear of the shrouds and so avoid chafing, a special pole known as a jockey pole can be used. It is a short spar with a snap hook at one end and a sheave at the other end through which the cordage can ride, hence the name jockey pole (see diagram above). The spar increases the angle of the guy when the spinnaker pole is pointing ahead close to the forestay. When shipped horizontally, like a crosstree, it makes it easier to trim the spinnaker. As the mast fitting for the spinnaker pole is too high for the jockey pole, a special fitting is needed. When

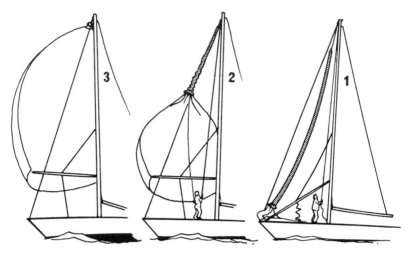

The spinnaker stocking.

clipped in place the jockey pole should be guided forward, thus allowing the guy to slip into position on the sheave. Note that it must always be shipped forward of the shroud and it can, if necessary, be secured to the shroud with a seizing. The diagram shows a crewman standing by the windward shroud while he trims the spinnaker – a good position that gives him a clear view of the spinnaker. If the wind is really pulling, there should be someone manning the leeward winch ready to help in hauling in on the sheet.

## THE SPINNAKER STOCKING

When sailing a cruiser shorthanded it can be a great help to have a spinnaker stocking or squeezer. This consists of a nylon bag the same length as the spinnaker. Its mouth is fitted with a plastic ring to squeeze the sail as it is pulled through, and there is a continuous line to enable the squeezer to be hauled up and down as shown in the diagram above.

The procedure starts by pulling the spinnaker into the stocking or squeezer, the end of which has a small hole to fit over the halyard swivel. Care must naturally be taken to avoid twisting the leeches, and the clews must be free at the bottom to enable the sheet and guy to be fitted. The stocking with the spinnaker

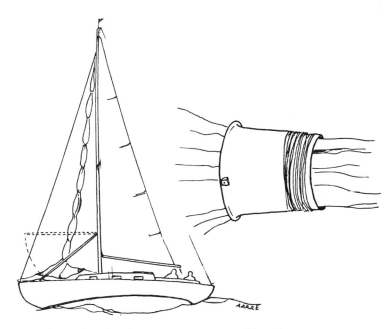

**Setting the spinnaker in stops** (any type of boat)
This is an old idea that has now been taken up again. Light thread was used in the past, but there was a risk that the thread might gather mid-way during hoisting and so cause the sail to set like an 'hour glass'. Things can be made much easier now by using elastic bands. By cutting the bottom off a plastic bucket and putting elastic bands round it as shown, it is a simple matter to pull the spinnaker through and to slip the elastic band into position at intervals of a metre or so along the sail.

The spinnaker can then easily be set without it blowing out prematurely. This method has obvious advantages when used, for example, prior to a race or before rounding a mark. When the moment comes, the guy and sheet are hardened in so that the lower elastic bands break and the wind does the rest.

inside can then be stowed in a sail bag until needed again. The rigging sequence is as follows (see diagram on page 68):

1   Rig sheet, guy and pole in the usual way. Then hoist the stocking, which is attached to the halyard swivel.

2   Haul on the continuous line to hoist the stocking sleeve to

Sailing with a spinnaker in a light keelboat or dinghy calls for youth and fitness . . . and you can only hope that you will not suffer later in life from problems with your back.

the top, thus allowing the spinnaker to unfurl. As soon as the lower part of the spinnaker catches the wind, the stocking will be eased up the rest of the way by the wind pressure. The sheet and guy should be roughly adjusted beforehand.

**3** The spinnaker is set with the stocking compressed into a concertina at the top.

To lower the spinnaker, ease away on both guy and sheet so that the pole can swing forward to the forestay. The sheet needs to be eased to reduce the pull on the spinnaker, and to allow the squeezer ring to be pulled down over the sail. It will be slow to start with, but as the wind is spilled the sail will slide into the stocking quite easily. Once the spinnaker is in, the whole thing should be lowered – although it can be left for a while if there are more pressing tasks to deal with.

In light airs there may be no need to slacken guy and sheet before pulling the stocking over the spinnaker, since the ring will slide down and collapse the sail quite easily. In a strong wind, on the other hand, the sheet will have to be slackened right off to allow the spinnaker to fly free and the squeezer ring should then be pulled down smartly.

Although it is most often used in cruisers, the spinnaker stocking can be very useful when racing shorthanded. The stocking can be hoisted and made ready to release the moment the boat reaches a windward mark. This manoeuvre usually requires a full crew – and a skilful one. It is also possible to leave the spinnaker up and to douse it only at the very last moment.

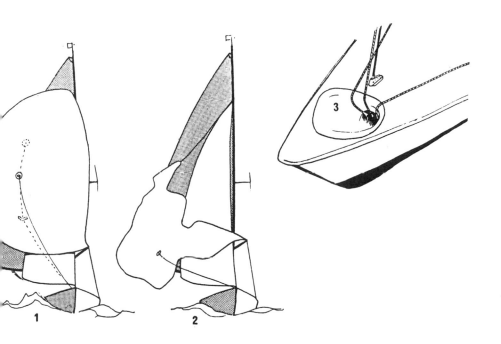

## Spinnaker chute on foredeck

Some racing dinghies and smaller keelboats have an elegant arrangement whereby the spinnaker is simply pulled from a chute on the foredeck. Not every class permits this arrangement, but where fitted it is much used.

The system is very simple to use and works like this. A line is attached to the middle of the spinnaker for extra strength, and this line is led down the chute and then aft to the cockpit through a long bag which holds the spinnaker below deck. To retrieve the spinnaker, all you have to do is haul on the line from the cockpit. Of course the sheet and guy need to be eased off, but there is no need to unclip them. Similarly, to set the spinnaker again, you simply rig the pole and haul on the halyard. The retrieving line can be attached higher on the sail and then led through a loop positioned lower down (shown by the dotted line). This allows the spinnaker to be partially folded when lowered, thus taking up less space in the bag below deck.

1

2

### Changing spinnakers

It can be an advantage when racing to be able to change spinnakers: for example, changing from a balloon-cut sail to a flatter one should the wind get up, or vice versa. If you have to lower one spinnaker before preparing and setting the new one, you pay the penalty in terms of speed for quite a long time.

By having an additional halyard and one, or even two, extra sets of sheets, the change can be carried out quickly and without losing too much time by setting the new spinnaker beneath the one already in place. It is done like this:

1   Lash bag containing the new spinnaker to the pulpit. Attach the halyard and sheet as usual, but with the windward clew lashed to

## SPINNAKER GEAR IN A DINGHY

Since a dinghy spinnaker is smaller and subjected to more modest forces, it can be handled more freely. Nevertheless, the skill necessary to handle a spinnaker in a light and lively dinghy should never be underestimated.

Without a spinnaker chute, the spinnaker must be retrieved into the cockpit and is best done to windward. The crewman is there already and he will be able to handle it on the spot, rather than having to gather it in under the boom to leeward.

**2a**                                **3**

the forestay and a seizing positioned as high up as possible. The helmsman should bear away on to a dead run.

2    Quickly hoist the new spinnaker. Ease the old spinnaker guy just enough to allow the pole to rest on the forestay and, if necessary, ease the topping lift to allow the pole to be reached. The crewman should free the guy to allow the old spinnaker to blow out to leeward. Remove the old guy and clip the new one to the pole. Undo the forestay seizing and trim the new spinnaker. It may be a good idea to use the old guy for this purpose and, in a strong wind, it is better to set the new spinnaker in stops.

3    Lower the old spinnaker.

While the helmsman steers downwind, the crewman removes the pole (on dinghies usually stowed alongside the boom), grasps the windward clew, lets go the sheet, and gathers in the spinnaker while the helmsman eases the halyard.

The spinnaker should be stowed in a bag hanging below deck; ideally there should be a bag on both sides so that it makes no difference which side the spinnaker is retrieved. Setting the spinnaker should be carried out to windward (except when reaching), and it may be necessary to gybe in order to get on to the right tack.

**Spinnaker chute**: These are Dragons. They are fitted with ▶
a spinnaker chute (or well) to facilitate setting and retrieval. When
lowering, the retrieving line – attached to the centre of the spinnaker
– is hauled in and the sail disappears down through the well in the
foredeck.

The best way to set the spinnaker is to gather the sail in
both arms and throw it into the air, while at the same time the
helmsman hauls smartly on the halyard so that the spinnaker is
up so quickly that there is no risk of it being ditched. Then aft
both sheet and guy and finally rig the pole. When reaching, it
is of course not possible to throw the spinnaker to windward;
rather, it should be hoisted to leeward as would be done in a
keelboat, ie with the pole mounted first. As before, the helmsman
works the halyard.

To achieve a really fast hoist (especially necessary when a
spinnaker is thrown up to windward), some dinghy sailors have

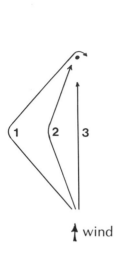

↑ wind

Asymmetric spinnaker on a 4.2 metre (14 foot) International dinghy. This type uses a bowsprit instead of a spinnaker pole. On very light racing dinghies, this is the system of the future – whatever the size of the boat. Since it is not possible to achieve a dead run with such a spinnaker, the boats is close reaching and gybing on to a new tack to reach the mark. Although the distance is greater, the speed achieved more than makes up for this.

Diagram: **1** The ultra-light boat will reach the mark first, even though by broad reaches. **2** In this way, all boats can take advantage of tacking with a normal spinnaker. **3** It never pays to run directly before the wind.

fitted their boats with a kind of double tackle inside the mast. One end of the halyard is secured at the top of the mast, and the halyard itself is led through a block and then out round a sheave let into the front of the mast. The block is secured to a second line led down into the boat and aft to the helmsman. When he hauls on this second line the effect is to double the motion of the halyard – although he has to exert twice the normal force.

Referring to the diagram opposite showing the arrangement of spinnaker gear in a dinghy, it can be seen that topping lift and

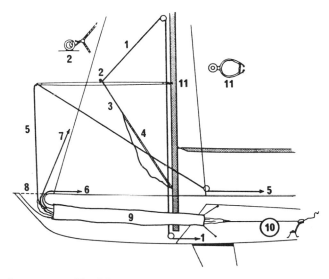

## Spinnaker gear – dinghies

**1** Topping lift. **2** Eye on pole and hook for topping lift.
**3** Downhaul. **4** Strong elastic shock cord attached to downhaul.
**5** Guy. **6** Sheet. **7** Halyard. **8** Chute mouth. **9** Canvas tube.
**10** Drum for stowing retrieving line. The line is run to a cam cleat
controlled by the helmsman. **11** Eye fitting on mast for attaching
the pole.

downhaul are combined in a single continuous line with a hook
in it. The elastic cord on the downhaul serves to take up the
slack and keep it close to the mast when not in use. If the pole
is stowed alongside the boom, the topping lift/downhaul can be
left permanently in place; if not, the hook should be detached.

A barber-haul is not necessary because a reaching hook is
fitted on the chainplate just forward of the shroud. This will
take the sheet and guy, but the sheet should be freed when
on a reach while the guy should remain clipped to the hook to
exert a downward pull that will greatly ease the pressure on the
downhaul – and perhaps take over altogether.

Halyard and sheet may be combined in a single continuous
line (though not if the special halyard tackle mentioned above
has been fitted). The tail of the halyard becomes the sheet when
the spinnaker is set and the sheet acts as the halyard when
lowering the spinnaker again. This arrangement means fewer
loose rope ends to get tangled in the cockpit.

# *Measurement rules set the limits*

Over 100 years ago there was a measurement rule that took no account of sail area, but instead concentrated on the hull weight (yacht tons); this rating was then used to work out individual handicaps. It is hardly surprising, then, that a cutter in the last century would use the greatest possible sail area, even though this made manoeuvring very difficult.

The development of new sail materials has not made sailing or racing any cheaper. You might expect that more stable and longer-lasting materials would extend the life of a sail and so lead to less frequent replacement. In fact, the opposite appears to be the case. Nylon and Kevlar are wonderful materials, but sails made of them cannot withstand as much as those made from the more old-fashioned Terylene (Dacron). Added to that, competition these days is so fierce that, if you want to make an impact, you must push the materials to their limits – thus making it extremely expensive to equip a boat for optimum performance.

Not that this is anything new. In the past, owners bemoaned the outlay for sails that lasted no time at all, even though they were fashioned from the finest materials then available – namely, Egyptian cotton. Consequently, it was not long before racing and class rules were introduced to limit sail equipment, and thus preclude more wealthy boat owners from having too great an advantage.

Although this has not been entirely achieved, progress has indeed been made, not least where spinnakers are concerned, and nearly all classes now limit the number of such sails that can be carried. Such limits have in turn influenced spinnaker development because it has been necessary to achieve design compromises to enable boats governed by these rules to be as well equipped as possible for spinnaker sailing in any weather.

While some classes are limited to just two spinnakers, under the International Offshore Rule (IOR) the position is quite clear – but also rather expensive as boats are permitted to carry between three and six spinnakers depending on the size of the boat in question. The actual numbers are as follows:

| Hull measurement (feet) | Number of foresails over 100% of J | Number of spinnakers |
|---|---|---|
| 16.0–22.9 | 3 | 3 |
| 23.0–32.9 | 3 | 4 |
| 33.0–39.9 | 4 | 5 |
| 40.0–44.9 | 5 | 6 |
| 50.0 and upwards | Any number | Any number |

With three spinnakers you can adequately cover, albeit expensively, most foreseeable requirements. For example, there could be one spinnaker for use in strong winds and for reaching, one all-rounder for use in moderate breezes and for running before a fresh wind, and one made of extra fine cloth (possibly nylon) to be used in light airs. A fourth might be added as a special storm spinnaker, or there might be two of different sizes for reaching. Higher up the classes there might be two light-air sails, one for very light airs (possibly made of fine gauze) and one for normal light airs.

The suit of sails must be right for the type of sailing envisaged and for the waters to be sailed. When racing over a short course some might prefer to carry several identical spinnakers, thus avoiding the need for packing simply by setting a new spinnaker each time one is needed.

The enormous expense of sailing under the IOR, using spinnakers many of which have only one use, has contributed to a decline in the number of boats competing. On the other hand, the sport has reached new peaks of performance at international level and it is no exaggeration to compare sailing under the IOR with 'Formula 1' motor racing.

This state of affairs has led to the drawing up of a somewhat less demanding system of measurement, the International Measurement System (IMS). Thus while the IOR governs certain specialist areas of ocean racing, such as the Admiral's Cup, the IMS helps to foster competition between more 'normal' ocean racers; these are still strongly built, but more modestly equipped without the use of the more costly and exotic materials.

Various rules have of course been developed for the classes for small boats. In some cases it may be possible to manage admirably with a single spinnaker – probably of maximum allowable size, but relatively flat and open and give a good performance when reaching. If you wish, though, to invest in a second spinnaker, the rules are so strict that only marginal differences may be permitted. The sailmaker would aim to make them both as large as allowed within the rules, but one would be made from a lightweight cloth and designed with deep curves to provide optimum drive in a moderate wind, while the other would be flatter and sewn with a heavier cloth for use in strong winds and when reaching.

If the main aim is to maximise the loading that the particular sail can stand, then the reacher will be a tri-radial,

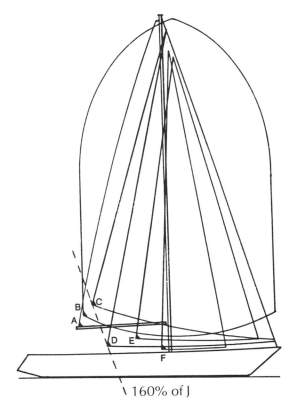

\ 160% of J

Example of sails that have been available for use with the spinnaker under the IOR. The broken line indicates the luff perpendicular (LP) measurement for the largest genoa, a dimension that must not be exceeded in the design of specialist sails.
**A**: Mainsail. **B**: Maximum spinnaker. **C**: Reacher. **D**: Maximum genoa. **E**: Spinnaker staysail (reduced genoa set further inboard to allow freer air flow over the spinnaker). **F**: Tallboy (narrow version of spinnaker staysail).

or tri-optimal, true-radial etc, depending on the terminology used by the sailmaker concerned. The lightweight or all-round spinnaker will not usually be exposed to such heavy loading, and some savings can therefore be made. You might make do with a radial top or radial clews combined with horizontal panels towards the centre. It is best to discuss such things with the

81

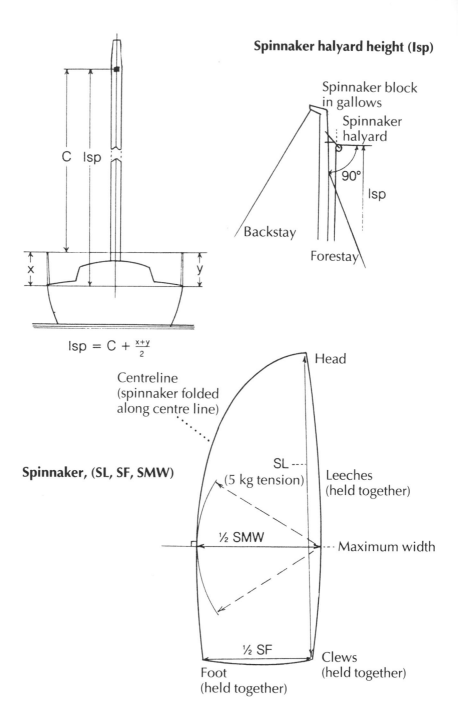

## Spinnaker halyard height (Isp)

Spinnaker block in gallows

Spinnaker halyard

90°

Isp

Backstay

Forestay

C Isp

x

y

$$Isp = C + \frac{x+y}{2}$$

**Spinnaker, (SL, SF, SMW)**

Centreline (spinnaker folded along centre line)

Head

SL (5 kg tension)

Leeches (held together)

½ SMW

Maximum width

½ SF

Foot (held together)

Clews (held together)

sailmaker when the time comes. In one-design and classboats the decisions are easier, since the class rules generally state the maximum size of the spinnaker – leaving only design and weight of cloth to be decided.

## MEASURING THE SPINNAKER

To measure the spinnaker it should be laid out and folded along the centreline so that the leeches coincide. The length of the leeches (SL) should be measured when applying a tension of 5 kg (11 lb) in the direction of the measurement. If this measurement differs from side to side, the longer one should be taken as the dimension SL. The foot of the sail is measured by taking the distance from clew to the lowest point of the sail (ie on the centreline) and doubling this to give the overall length of the foot (SF).

Measurement of the maximum width of the spinnaker (SMW) should also be done with the sail folded in this way. Measure from leech to centreline, at right angles to the centreline, at various points up and down the sail until the widest part is found. Double this measurement to give the overall maximum width of the spinnaker (SMW).

If two spinnakers are measured for the same boat, the measurements SL, SF and SMW must be given as the maximum

**Spinnaker pole length (SPL)**

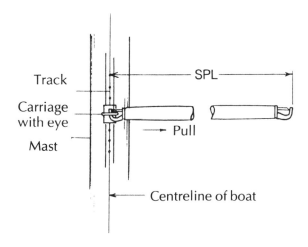

values obtained regardless of which spinnaker they apply to. Thus SL and SF could be taken from one spinnaker while SMW could be taken from the other.

## The spinnaker pole

The spinnaker pole length (SPL) is measured by placing it horizontally across the boat while still attached to the mast fitting, and then measuring from the centreline of the boat to the outermost part of the fitting at the pole end.

## The foresails

The foresail luff is measured from the tack to the head of the sail (T). The distance from the clew to the luff is measured at right angles to the luff (LP). This is best done by folding the sail along the line LP shown in the diagram, thus ensuring that the measurement is taken at right angles to the line of the luff. The measurement J is the horizontal distance from the front edge of the foot of the mast to the point at which the line of the forestay intersects the deck.

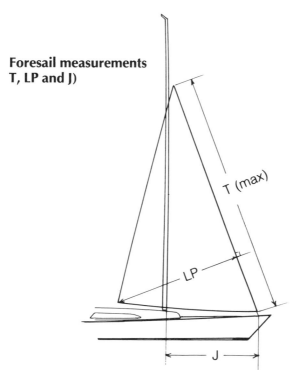

**Foresail measurements
T, LP and J)**

# Instruments

The impact of electronics now pervades the sailing scene, and some of what was once guesswork, allied to the feel and intuition that stems from experience, has now been converted into figures on a display.

A description of these electronic instruments and their uses could alone fill a book, so here we shall just consider those instruments that may be especially helpful during spinnaker sailing. First and foremost these are instruments that tell us:

- wind direction
- wind strength
- log reading
- compass course

Most instruments today can be obtained with either analogue (hands on a dial) or digital (numbers on a display) readout.

Shipmate instruments. These show compass course, relative wind angle, true wind angle, relative wind speed and boat speed in knots. These instruments incorporate both digital and analogue display.

Digital instruments can show values more precisely, but analogue instruments are far quicker to read. While a hand on a dial may not be quite so accurate, it can convey instantly to the trained eye the essential information, as with a glance at the old-fashioned clock. What is more, the hand on a dial gives an immediate indication of how that quantity is changing, something that a digital readout alone can never do.

It seems natural that the relative wind direction should be shown on a circular dial with a hand to show changes as they occur, whereas it takes time and practice to derive the same information from a display of numbers alone. Such instruments are invaluable when sailing at night or in a light breeze, enabling the helmsman to steer directly by the dial – even though he needs to check the compass from time to time to guard against any sudden shift in the wind that might push the boat off course.

When sailing with a spinnaker in daylight the direction of the wind will be crucial when deciding whether or not to continue,

Maxi-instruments mounted on the rear of the mast. Everyone on board can see them. *Photo: Courtesy of Brookes & Gatehouse Ltd.*

Some examples of analogue instruments. These show compass course, relative wind angle, relative wind angle with the scale expanded × 3 for use when close-hauled and running, relative wind speed, and boat speed in knots. The expanded scale instrument covers the sectors 0–60° and 120–180° – very useful for helping to achieve the best speed when close-hauled, but also excellent for helping to fine tune the spinnaker trim when running.

Examples of digital instruments.

The wind computer can display both relative and true wind angles, true wind speed, wind direction relative to north, and the boat's velocity made good.

say, on a reach with the spinnaker set, or whether it should be taken in. A good reacher may stand well enough without necessarily giving the best drive through the water, and the instrument will show whether it will pay to continue to the spinnaker or not. Again such instruments make it possible to see which combinations of wind speed and direction lead to the best results.

The log is important, measuring as it does the speed of the boat through the water. When reaching, for example, the straining of the spinnaker, the heeling of the boat and the foam whipped up by the rudder all conspire to give an impression of speed, whereas in reality they may indicate drama more than sheer speed. In fact, the log alone can tell you that speed is reduced when the boat is pressed too hard.

The log will also give a clear indication of what can be achieved by trimming the spinnaker. It might show, for example, that slackening the sheet a little more, even though this might make it slightly more difficult to keep the spinnaker properly set, would give an increase in speed of perhaps 0.3–0.5 knots, a gain well worth the trouble. When running, the log would show the increase in speed achieved by altering the angle of the pole with respect to the direction of the wind or by raising or lowering the pole itself. It is well to remember that such gains will show up only very gradually, especially in light breezes, because of the considerable inertia of the boat. The wind direction indicator would also help under these conditions by making it easier to maintain the desired course, thus avoiding an involuntary gybe – something to avoid at night. When lowering the spinnaker, experience will soon show where the indicator should point in order to ensure that the spinnaker is in the lee of the mainsail.

It would of course be wrong to sail by instruments alone. Such aids can never replace that indefinable feel for balance and trim that is part and parcel of the magic of sailing. Nevertheless, such instruments can provide real help to a degree that should not be underestimated.

# Foresails and spinnaker types

In the past there was a wide choice of special sails that could be carried together with a spinnaker. Such sails were much used on IOR boats where the rules required that the spinnaker should be of relatively modest dimensions. At the same time almost all boats were rigged to the top of the mast, which meant that there was a very large fore-triangle that could be filled with correspondingly large sails.

Today, though, fractional rigging predominates, ie the forestay is attached some way below the top of the mast. This effectively divides it in two: the free top and the part below the forestay. A ⅞ rig has, for example, ⅞ of the mast below the forestay and a free top of ⅛. This means that, as in the past, many boats have the greatest sail area in the mainsail so that the gains resulting from the use of special sails with a spinnaker are reduced. A larger mainsail also gives more wind shadow when on a run or a broad reach, thus making it more difficult to get a foresail to set properly unless boomed out to windward.

It is usual to leave the jib up when sailing with a spinnaker. A genoa, though, would normally be taken down. On classboats such as Solings, however, the need to go forward to recover the jib would cause too much disturbance in the boat. Also the lower, broad part of the jib can make use of the air that would otherwise pass unhindered under the spinnaker. Make sure, though, that the top of the jib is not obstructing the spinnaker, especially when reaching. The jib should be eased to allow the top to fall away so that it sets virtually parallel with the air stream.

A genoa is too wide, however, and will prevent the spinnaker from filling properly on a reach. On a run it will itself be obstructed by the mainsail and it will also greatly complicate gybing. Normally, therefore, the genoa is taken down when the spinnaker is set and is only hoisted again when the spinnaker is no longer needed. Sometimes, though, especially if the wind is light, it may be possible to make use of a genoa with a very flat reacher. But if the wind is too light the spinnaker will collapse, while if it freshens too much the use of both sails will be excessive. It is important to appreciate (and experience will soon convince you) that if the spinnaker collapses behind the genoa, it will be difficult to get it to fill again. This alone could lose you any advantage gained by using both sails together.

Especially when reaching, and with a flat spinnaker set, it pays to carry an ordinary jib to make best use of the air that spills under the spinnaker.

The low-set advocate collects the wind that would otherwise be lost under the spinnaker. Where rules allow it, it may be worth securing the sail a little way aft of the forestay to increase its distance from the spinnaker.

## THE ADVOCATE

One solution to the problems associated with the combined use of spinnaker and genoa is to have a special sail made. Such a sail is sometimes known as an advocate. This is a special genoa made with the same LP measurement as the boat's No 1 genoa, but with the luff extending only half-way up the forestay. The sail might be sewn from a lightweight Terylene, for example, possibly star-cut to match the stresses in the sail that are distributed radially from the clews.

The advocate would normally be set on the forestay once the genoa has been recovered. Special stay design may allow the advocate to be hoisted in the spare track once the genoa has been lowered, or it may be clipped on above the genoa – so obviating the need to unclip the latter from the stay.

Here we have a sail that makes effective use of the air that would otherwise have passed under the spinnaker, but without being so tall that there are problems in getting it to set properly. The advocate is most effective when on a broad reach, say with a true wind direction of 110° or so. With the wind further aft, the advocate would tend to be in the lee of the mainsail and would then lose it effectiveness.

Since it takes time to set and recover such a sail, there would be little to gain by using it on a triangular course (where only two of the tacks would be suitable in any case). The advocate is better suited to long-distance racing where, as the log will show, it can give an extra quarter or half a knot in the right wind conditions. That may not sound a lot, but it means the gain of a mile or so every few hours.

## THE REACHER (STAR-CUT)

When this type of spinnaker was introduced in the early 1970s it was considered revolutionary. It was now possible to carry a spinnaker as close as 45° to the wind – although it was not, and still is not, always worth while. The ability to sail so close to the wind was the result of the shape of this type of spinnaker and the way in which it was constructed (illustrated in the earlier section on reaching).

These aspects are of course connected since the shape was the result of sewing the panels to follow the sail loading – thus giving a more stable design. When cut in this way the spinnaker will not grow baggy from use in high winds or as age takes its toll. Nor will the curve of the sail begin to 'move' – something that often happened some fifteen to twenty years ago when nylon was less stable than it is now. When reaching, the curve in a less stable sail will naturally migrate towards the leech, the result of which is to backwind the mainsail. The spinnaker then acts more as an air brake rather than a source of forward drive.

When using a star-cut spinnaker it is especially important to carry the pole at the right height since, if the sail is at all distorted it loses its effectiveness and, if the wind is strong, it will be wrongly loaded. The point about reaching, of course, is that the wind is flowing transversely and the sail must therefore be smooth and open at the leech.

It is possible to check that the pole height is correct by slackening the sheet a little. If the luff begins to flap at the bottom, its shape is too hollow; this means that the pole is too high. If the pole is set too low the spinnaker will start to flap at the top because the shoulders are unable to open properly.

As already mentioned, the reacher is generally also useful when running in heavy weather. This is partly because the sail area is slightly less than that of the all-round spinnaker, but also because its construction is likely to be much stronger. One word of caution though. Care should be taken to ensure that the boat does not begin to roll and yaw, something that can happen when a flat spinnaker is used for running. The pole should be set well forward and the barber-haul on the sheet should be hauled in hard. The first makes for a more hollow and stable sail shape and the second ensures that the spinnaker has less play.

## ALL-ROUND SPINNAKER (RADIAL SPINNAKER)

The term radial refers to the layout of the panels that radiate from one or more of the clews. Initially the sail simply had a radial top, amounting to about one-third of the sail, while the remainder was sewn from horizontal panels. The aim was to stabilise the top so that the 'shoulders' would then help the sail set readily in a stable manner.

After a while radial clews were also introduced, leaving only a few horizontal panels in the middle. This tri-radial sail was similar to the star-cut design and the aim was the same, namely to provide a more stable shape. Sailmakers continue to experiment in developing this theme, and the area in the middle of the sale has become the focus of special interest. Individual sailmakers have their own ideas of how the central panels should be arranged and computer analysis plays its part in this aspect of design. Many fine spinnaker designs have emerged, even though fashion as well as technology is reflected in some of them.

The radial spinnaker is a typical all-round sail, but one that possesses special merit when it comes to reaching. This is partly because many sailors try to do without a specialist reacher and so look for a spinnaker that can do more or less anything. It is also attractive from the point of view that it is not always possible to

The original radial spinnaker, with radial panels at the top alone, is still seen on many boats. Newer designs have panels radiating from the clews as well, but still retain horizontal panels in the middle section.

change sails when wind conditions alter suddenly during a race, and a third point in its favour is that it pays to set the largest possible spinnaker in all light wind conditions.

The radial spinnaker is actually quite strong and can withstand considerable loads, provided of course that one does not choose to take advantage of the inherent strength of the design and opt for a very light sailcloth.

## THE GHOSTER (OR FLOATER)

The name of this sail says it all. It is an ideal sail in very light airs when the boat hardly moves through the water, or when there is barely any wind at all – no more than a ghost.

The rules may set a limit on size, but the general aim is to hoist as many square metres as possible. The other limit will

Relaxing after a hard spell.

be on shape. The sail must be fairly full to be efficient under these conditions but, if too full, it will be difficult to get the sail to stand in the lightest airs.

There have been many experiments made using superfine Mylar cloth weighing no more than a few grams per square metre, but results have been unsatisfactory. This is partly because such a spinnaker might tear, but also because it could burst in any sudden gust. Less obvious is the fact that using such a stable, unyielding cloth actually tends to reduce the stability of the sail itself. The reason seems to be that when the cloth has no elasticity it is unable to dampen the pressure variations exerted by the wind, and this in turn seems to hasten the onset of turbulence.

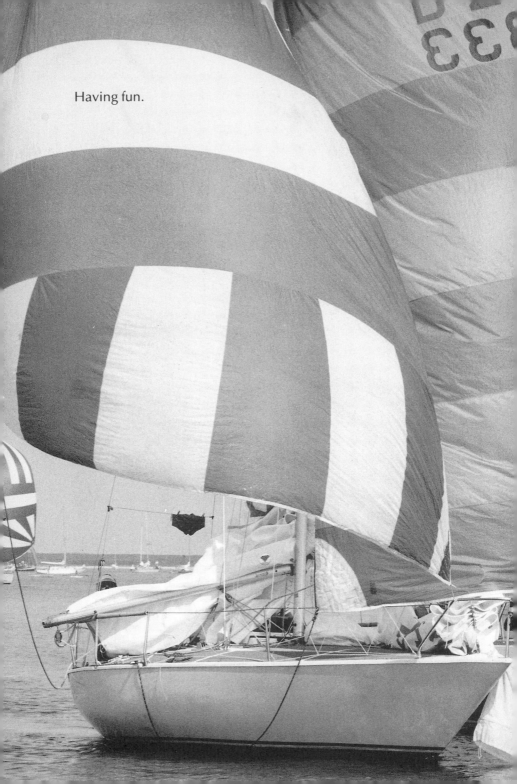

Having fun.

Sailing with a 'big boy' or 'blooper'.

## THE BIG BOY (OR BLOOPER)

For a time this sail was much used on IOR boats where it was permissible to carry a foresail flying free, ie not clipped to the forestay. But with the development of fractional rigs and larger headsails the big boy is used less frequently, although it can still be seen occasionally – especially on larger top-rigged IOR boats.

The idea was to make this sail the same size as the genoa, ie with the same LP and luff measurements, so that it would count as a foresail for measurement purposes. In shape it is far more baggy though, and the material is generally a fine nylon similar to that of the spinnaker. It can be set flying free alongside the spinnaker and the two together provide a greatly increased sail area.

The problem with the big boy is to get it to stand properly in the lee of the mainsail. To achieve this, one needs to slacken the halyard right off so that the sail can fly out to leeward to catch the free air stream there. To help the big boy to fly well out, the sheet can be led out to the end of the main boom as shown in the diagram opposite.

In very light winds it would pay to reef the mainsail because the area of canvas lost here would be more than compensated for by the freer air stream now enjoyed by the big boy. Reefing might also be necessary if the main boom is long (as in many modern designs), or in the case of fractional rigs because of the greater wind shadow.

Much extra work is involved in sailing with a big boy set, but on a long leg downwind the gain can be appreciable. When a gybe is necessary it is best to take the sail down and set it again on the new tack. It is possible to gybe with the big boy set, however. The trick is to let the whole sail fly out in front of the spinnaker and then sheet it in again on the other tack. This assumes that its halyard does not get tangled up with the spinnaker halyard. The big boy really needs its own halyard, because if it is set on the genoa halyard, which is lower on the mast, tangling will certainly occur.

## CRUISING SPINNAKER (ASYMMETRIC SPINNAKER)

The Americans call this a multi-purpose sail (MPS). It is really a headsail, but sewn in spinnaker cloth and shaped mid-way between a genoa and a spinnaker. Head, tack and clew are in their usual corners, as for a headsail, but the curves of the sail are full as in a spinnaker.

The sail is set in the normal way with the tack secured at the bow, but the luff is not hanked to the forestay. The sail can be used with advantage when the wind is on the beam, provided that the sail is not too baggy, and it is effective on a broad reach.

Asymmetric cruising spinnaker.

It is sheeted to the stern like a normal spinnaker and the shape of the sail itself can to some extent be regulated by easing or hardening the halyard or by adjusting the tack. Fitting a block in the bow allows this to be done conveniently from the cockpit.

On a run, the asymmetric spinnaker may well be blanketed by the mainsail so it pays to bear *the tack* (but not the clew) out to windward on a pole that should be set quite low down. The guy should be led through the pole in the usual way and then secured to the sail, so easing recovery. The sail can be lowered on to the foredeck or, if preferred, can be taken in under the boom (the tack being slackened using a line, as already mentioned).

The asymmetric spinnaker has neither the sail area nor the driving power of a pure spinnaker, but it is a great deal more effective than simply booming out a genoa. This sail is much used on large cruisers where the regular spinnaker may be too large for general cruising.

## DOUBLE GENOA

This is a sail designed especially for those who do not want to bother with a spinnaker when cruising, but who still seek some extra sail area to help when running or reaching. It is also handy for boats not designed to carry a spinnaker, such as Folkboats, etc.

In principle the sail consists of a genoa sewn from two layers of sailcloth, usually fine terylene or nylon similar to that used for spinnakers. With the wind on the beam the sail is carried like an ordinary genoa, but in a following wind the sail can be unfolded with one-half boomed out to windward while the other half remains set to leeward. This instant doubling of the sail area yields a handsome dividend, although not quite in the spinnaker class. Its dual role has also earned this sail the name of *uni-sail*. Its use presents few problems, but it is helpful to carry two sets of sheets – this making things easier when the two halves are opened out. Both sets can be fed through a single fairlead, provided the latter is large enough.

The pole can be carried without a topping lift or downhaul, as on Folkboats for example, but it would be more practical on larger boats to use a topping lift. This allows the pole to be fixed before the windward half of the sail is hauled into position using the sheet (which, strictly speaking, then becomes a guy when led through the pole).

The uni-sail enjoyed a great popularity for a time, but the increasing use of furled foresails has to some extent eclipsed it. But, as already mentioned, it remains a useful cruising sail for vessels such as Folkboats, where a genoa is not normally included in the sails for that class.

## THE SPINNAKER OF THE FUTURE

Sailmakers the world over continue to strive for further improvements in spinnaker design. Computer-aided design techniques – optimising sail shape to suit any given set of conditions – have become commonplace, and such progress has been made that it seems that only the most marginal gains remain to be attained. Nylon is still the material used for most spinnakers, but new

101

materials with even better properties may of course be developed one day.

One possible pointer towards the future is the spinnaker being developed by the Danish sailmaker Diamond Sails. This design allows the spinnaker to behave in some ways like a genoa in that, for example, the wind meets and passes over the luff at exactly the right angle, continues over the sail, and leaves the flat and open leech in such a way that turbulence is avoided. This spinnaker is flatter at the top and in the middle, but is more rounded in the leech than is now normal. Sailing with this spinnaker requires it to be trimmed differently. The pole, for example, needs to be carried lower down and further out to windward than would normally be the case.

The aim remains the same: to achieve a spinnaker that is completely stable, but that at the same time can be trimmed to the exact shape required to match changes in wind strength and direction.

# Cruising under spinnaker

When racing, both boat and crew are tested to their limits. Even though gear, if not life and limb as well, may occasionally be put more at risk than might be advisable, serious accidents seldom happen. The skipper will know his crew and their capabilities, and there will often be other boats to assist if needed.

On a family cruise things are very different. Quite often the skipper will have only himself to depend on and there may be no help at hand. The combined physical strength of the crew is likely to be lower than when racing, and the skipper may well think twice before deciding whether it is sensible to hoist a spinnaker when out to sea. On the other hand, there is one great advantage when cruising: there is all the time in the world!

Under these conditions, therefore, the spinnaker gear should be rigged quietly and with the utmost care and attention. Rushing around the deck and shouting confusing orders can only result in worry and uncertainty for everyone. Always wear a life jacket and always attach a lifeline when moving about on deck, not only for your own safety but because it will reassure and encourage the family in the cockpit when they see the skipper behaving responsibly and setting the right example.

Much in this book applies to family cruising – remember particularly to hoist or lower the spinnaker in the lee of the mainsail and foresail!

In light winds, say below 5–6 m/sec, sailing with a spinnaker should present no problem. Some prefer to start up the engine, but that bears no comparison with the thrill of feeling the spinnaker lift and drive the boat ahead. The speed is the same, but there the similarity ends. If the wind shows signs of freshening, then be sure to drop the spinnaker again. Even if your boat has an engine, the use of a spinnaker in the right circumstances will always be a satisfying experience.

In winds any stronger than 5–6 m/sec, it would be risky to set a spinnaker unless the crew has the necessary experience. In a fresh breeze, on a run, say, it would be better to boom out a jib or genoa to windward. Not only does the boat go faster, but the balance is improved which in turn makes steering easier.

In addition, one might set a further jib or genoa flying to leeward, either with a taut leech or flying free with the halyard eased well off. When a large genoa is boomed out, the spar may be too short to bear the clew far enough out to windward, in which case one can 'cheat' by securing the spar to the shroud – thus effectively extending its length. Alternatively, and depending on the strength of the wind, the best solution might be to use an asymmetric cruising spinnaker or a small, flat storm spinnaker.

The main thing is to enjoy the thrill of sailing without losing sight of safety. It has been wisely observed that 'only a fool does not fear the sea', to which I would only add that if you are not happy with the idea of sailing in the open seas, then don't. Respect for the sea, its power and its many moods, is after all part of the essence of sailing.

Colourful patchwork spinnaker on a cruiser. Advertising on a spinnaker is, incidentally, permitted to a limited extent by the International Yacht Racing Union.

# INDEX

# THE PLAINSMEN OF THE YELLOWSTONE

>>>>>>><<<<<<<

*A History of the Yellowstone Basin*

# The Plainsmen
# of the
# Yellowstone

*A History of the Yellowstone Basin*

*by*

*MARK H. BROWN*

UNIVERSITY OF NEBRASKA PRESS
Lincoln and London

*First Bison Book printing: March, 1969*

*Most recent printing indicated by the first digit below:*
6    7    8    9    10

Bison Book edition reprinted by arrangement with G. P. Putnam's Sons

*For Bill Felton, grand old pioneer,*
*who introduced me to some of Montana's real old-timers*
*and told me about many others.*

# CONTENTS

# ILLUSTRATIONS

*maps by palacios*

# THE PLAINSMEN OF THE YELLOWSTONE

>>>>>>>«<<<<<<

*A History of the Yellowstone Basin*

# 1

## *La Roche Jaune*

»»»»»»»«««««««« Famished Elk, a keen-eyed Chey-
enne scout, had ridden all night to overtake a detachment of cavalry
which had left Fort Keogh two days before. Now, a packet of dispatches
having been delivered, he had nothing to do but whip his leg-weary pony
along beside the column. It was the summer of 1878, and the troops
were searching for a small band of Indians reported to be along the
Yellowstone River somewhere below the post. The country through
which they were passing had been grazed recently by a great herd of buffalo: and the ground was covered with a labyrinth of interlacing trails.
Suddenly, this scout wheeled his horse to one side and then came back
to the soldiers at a shuffling tired gallop. He had *cut* the *sign* of the
hostiles.

Motioning to an officer, he followed the trail a short distance to a
campsite. After studying the droppings of the horses, size and number
of the lodges, and some small bits of litter, the Cheyenne identified the
Indians, estimated their number, established the date of the camp, and

predicted where they had come from and where they were going. "The record left by these Indians," a lieutenant wrote later, "was as complete as though it had been carefully written out."

On the frontier, *sign* included a wide variety of things—tracks, lost or discarded articles, an empty cartridge shell, drops of blood, litter at a campsite, movements of animals and birds, even the effects of raindrops, wind, or sunshine. To an experienced observer, these things often told stories with a vividness which words on a printed page cannot match.

Today, most of the *sign* that told of happenings on the northern part of the High Plains are gone. But not all of it. In the Yellowstone Basin, that vast stretch of rolling prairie, delicately colored badlands, and pine-covered mountains that covers an area as large as the state of North Dakota, *sign* can still be found.

Grass-grown scars of wagon trails wind up and down the ridges and across the flats. Rifle pits and rock shelters show how and where battles were fought. Depressions in the sod and scattered flat sandstones mark the location of buildings at old army posts and Indian agencies—buffalo grass still refuses to grow where one of the most fabulous fur trading posts once stood. In one abandoned graveyard rows of brown sandstones marked with only a number are silent evidence of the uncertainty of a soldier's life. At the foot of a gnarled juniper near the crest of a short rocky ridge a soldier left a handful of empty shells—mute evidence that a famous general did not tell the truth when he wrote about the fight. A pile of stones in the outline of a human form marks the spot where an unwise boy paid the supreme price for a bit of folly: a few miles away, back among the red scoria hills where the silence is broken only by the wind or the raucous cries of a crow or magpie, is a rude cairn of rocks and poles where lie the bones of his murderers. In a wide flat along a creek stand the buildings of an old ranch where loopholes face shallow trenches not far away—here white men fought each other.

These *sign* and others have not been swept away by the broom of time but often they do not tell a complete or well-connected story. Those who would know the history of this frontier must also seek the journals of explorers and Army officers, old books, the brittle, yellowed pages of contemporary newspapers, and the recollections of old-timers. Sometimes, unfortunately, even these are mute.

Today, no one knows with certainty who the first white man was who saw the Yellowstone—or when he saw it. Nor does anyone know how the name originated other than that some Frenchman called the river *la Roche Jaune*.

Perhaps some Crow Indian, while trading in the Mandan villages, described the *Elk* River to a Minitarí who rendered it *Mi tsi a da zi* to a French trader and he, in turn, translated it *Roche Jaune*. Perhaps it was named by a now-forgotten voyageur who, after wandering far in advance of his comrades, returned with stories about a beautiful valley filled with game—where the hills and mountains on either side had bold outcrops of grayish-yellow rock. All that is known with certainty is that from the time of the earliest traders on the Upper Missouri this river has been called *la Roche Jaune*—the river of the Yellow Rock.

The quaint spelling of the early traders and explorers corrupted these words into *Rejone*, *Rochejone*, *Rochejohn* and other similar phonetic renditions. David Thompson, noted explorer and geographer in the British fur trade of the Northwest, used the words "Yellow Stone" in notes he made at the Mandan villages in the winter of 1797-1798. A few years later Lewis and Clark referred to it in a similar manner in the progress report which they sent to President Jefferson when they left their winter quarters on the upper Missouri to push on to the Pacific. Although Roche Jaune continued in use during the early years of the fur trade, it was soon rendered Yellow Stone and this, eventually, became Yellowstone.

Truteau, an early trader from St. Louis, wrote the first description of the river in 1795:

A Canadian, named Menard, who for sixteen years has made his home with the Mandan, whither he came from the north, and who has been several times among the nation of the Crows in company with the Gros Ventres, their Allies, has assured me that this river is navigable with pirogues more than one hundred and fifty leagues above its mouth, without meeting any falls or rapids. . . . A fort built at the entrance of this river would be very profitable for the opening up of a large trade in peltries. . . .

A few decades later Fort Union, destined to play a fabulous role in the history of the region, was built at this crossroads of the Northwest.

Like the origin of its name, the source of the Yellowstone has a feature of uncertainty which furnished Jim Bridger with material for one of his famous stories. He sometimes told of seeing fish swim over the Continental Divide and this his friends laughed off as just another of Old Gabe's yarns. But it was true! Waters from the melting snow on Yount Peak, between the Tetons and the Absarokas, run down into a little valley where, as one of Jim's more literate companions noted in 1836, "it divides equally one half running West and the other East thus bidding adieu to each other one bound for the Pacific and the other for the Atlantic ocean. Here a trout of 12 inches in length may cross the mountains in safety." When the War Department had a mapping expedition in the Yellowstone country twenty-three years later, the leader was willing to admit—grudgingly however—that "Bridger's 'Two Ocean river' *may* be a verity."

About 120 miles north of Two Ocean Pass, the Yellowstone River, after flowing through one of the highest lakes in the world and a canyon famous for its beauty, turns abruptly at the Great Bend and takes a rather direct course toward its junction with the Missouri some 400 miles to the northeast.

Its basin is far-flung toward the south, reaching almost to the old Oregon Trail along the North Platte and the Sweetwater. Here are creeks, rivers and mountains with Indian names given to them no one knows when. The Powder River—named for the clouds of powdery fine sand which the wind often whipped up, the *Lazeka* or Tongue River, and two Rosebud creeks whose valleys once supported a profusion of wild rosebushes. The *Ets-pot-agie* and *Ets-pot-agie-cate*—Mountain Sheep River and Little Mountain Sheep River—were first translated the *Gros Cornu* and the *Petite Cornu*, and finally, the Big Horn and Little Big Horn Rivers. Likewise the name Wolf Tooth Mountains has been modified to Wolf Mountains. And there are many others.

In contrast to these, the creeks along the northern side are very short, never exceeding fifty miles in length. Old-timers in Montana split the basin into two parts with the channel of the Yellowstone as the dividing line. These they called the North Side and the South Side.

When the first white men came to explore, these prairies, mountains, and badlands were the home of the Crows. This fact was recognized by Thomas Fitzpatrick, Jim Bridger and Robert Campbell when, in 1851, they drafted some of the provisions of a treaty at Fort Laramie which set aside almost the entire Yellowstone Basin as a reservation for these people. However, the Crows were not the only tribe which roamed the valley of the Yellowstone.

This hunters' paradise was known far and wide. To it from the north came the Blackfeet, Assiniboines, and Gros Ventre of the Prairie. Flatheads, Shoshones, and Nez Percés slipped in through the mountain passes on the west. Cheyennes and Teton Sioux drifted in from the south and east. Even the Mandans, Minitarí, and Arickara came from their lodges along the Missouri. And as the Crows had large herds of fine horses, there were other attractions besides the abundance of game.

The Crows were well aware that they lived in a fine country. Their famous chief Arapooish, or Rotten Tail, described it explicitly to an early fur trader:

The Crow country is a good country. The Great Spirit has put it exactly in the right place; when you are in it you fare well; whenever you go out of it, whichever way you travel, you fare worse.

If you go to the south, you have to wander over great barren plains; the water is warm and bad, and you meet fever and ague.

To the north it is cold; the winters are long and bitter, with no grass; you cannot keep horses there, but must travel with dogs. What is a country without horses?

On the Columbia they are poor and dirty, paddle about in canoes, and eat fish. Their teeth are worn out; they are always taking fish-bones out of their mouths. Fish is poor food.

To the east they dwell in villages; they live well; but they drink the muddy water of the Missouri—that is bad. A Crow's dog would not drink such water. About the forks of the Missouri is a fine country; good water; good grass; plenty of buffalo. In the summer it is almost as good as the Crow country; but in the winter it is cold; the grass is gone; and there is no salt weed for the horses.

The Crow country is exactly in the right place. It has snowy mountains and sunny plains; all kinds of climates, and good things for every season. When the summer heat scorch the prairies, you can draw up under the mountains, where the air is sweet and cool, the grass fresh, and the bright streams come tumbling out of the snow-banks. There you can hunt the elk, the deer, and the antelope, when their skins are fit for dressing; there you will find plenty of white bears and mountain sheep.

In the autumn when your horses are fat and strong from the mountain pastures, you can go down into the plains and hunt the buffalo, or trap beaver on the streams. And when the winter comes on, you can take shelter in the woody bottoms along the rivers; there you will find buffalo meat for yourselves, and cottonwood bark for your horses; or you may winter in the Wind River Valley, where there is salt weed in abundance.

The Crow country is exactly in the right place. Everything good is to be found there. There is no country like the Crow country.

During the fur trading days this basin was more or less isolated. Fort Laramie and the famous trail along the Platte lay to the south. The posts along the Missouri lay well to the east and north. Traders did not find it easy to bring trade goods in or to take furs out of this area. Furthermore, raiding war parties made it a dangerous country in which to labor and after the work was over—as an old trader put it—"but little remains to compensate the trader for his time and trouble."

It is not strange that government officials regarded this as a suitable area in which to permit Indians to continue their nomadic way of life. Thus the Yellowstone country remained essentially an Indian country for almost three quarters of a century after Larocque and Clark explored it. Eventually, the Sioux used it as a prairie stronghold from which to launch parties of marauders and this finally brought down on their heads the wrath of the Government. When they were conquered and restrained, the basin filled with the herds of the rancher. Finally, as one pioneer put it, "Then came the Honyocker, with his cow in lead, his plow and his spotted sow" and the frontier was no more.

# 2

## The Horizon Beckoned

»»»»»»»»«««««««« When Louis XIV of France died in 1715, he was succeeded by a lad who was only five years old. His regent, the Duke of Orléans, was interested in North America and receptive to new ideas pertaining to this wilderness. One of the propositions which received much thought was that of linking the north shore of Lake Superior to Lake Winnepeg with a chain of forts, and then using the most westerly one as a base for exploration to the *Mer de l'Ouest*—the Sea of the West or, properly, the Pacific Ocean.

At first it was much easier to talk about this idea than to back it with adequate funds and capable leadership. So nothing of note developed until a disgruntled lieutenant, who had fought in the War of the Spanish Succession, returned to the Canadian woods and entered the fur trade. This man was Pierre Gaultier de Varennes de la Verendryé. The "de la Verendryé" part of his name, by which he was to become well known, was a designation which he had arbitrarily assumed.

La Verendryé soon became interested in stories told him by the Indians about the shore of a great lake where the water ebbed in and out and where there were many villages. Finally, his curiosity led him to offer to lead an expedition to search for this sea if the French government would provide him with 100 men and the necessary supplies. The Crown countered with the dubious promise of a fur trade monopoly if la Verendryé would finance and carry out the exploration which he proposed. This was a tempting prize if the gamble succeeded.

Although Pierre's funds were very limited, a number of his associates pooled their resources and gave him the needed support. With three sons, a nephew, and a party of Canadians, he set out from Montreal with high hopes. Seven years later, in the face of formidable odds, unrest and dissatisfaction among his men, his nephew and oldest son killed by the Sioux, he had managed to complete a chain of six stockades linking Rainy Lake to the Assiniboine River. But he had not been able to learn anything about the object of his quest.

At last some Assiniboine Indians told la Verendryé that there was a tribe living along the Missouri who knew the way to the Western Sea. Late in the fall of 1738, he led a small party westward to a village of this tribe, the "Mantannes," but his hopes came to naught when a thief stole the goods with which he hoped to barter for assistance. However, there was one concrete result. The hardships which the winter weather caused on the return trip convinced Pierre—he was then seventy-one—that he was too old to complete the task which he had set for himself. Fortunately, his sons shared his interest and enthusiasm.

After three years of fruitless search for guides, Pierre and his sons decided that they had collected enough bits of information to warrant making another effort. This time the party was to contain but four men —the Chevalier de la Verendryé, his brother François, and two men whose names were probably Edouard la Londette and Jean Baptiste Amoitte. Which one of Pierre's sons bore the title of Chevalier is not known. It was probably either Pierre Jr. or Louis Joseph.

On April 29, 1742, this little group left Fort la Reine on the Assiniboine River and arrived at the village of the "Mantannes" along the Missouri on the 19th of May. Here they hoped to meet the "Gens des Chevaux"—Horse Indians—whom they had been informed usually came to the village each spring to trade. After a futile wait until the latter part of July, the determined explorers hired two guides and set out to find these wandering traders.

The only record of the travels of this little group is the so-called "journal" of the Chevalier de la Verendryé; and this is really nothing but a summary report prepared for the governor of Canada. One point visited by this party can be positively identified—the hill near Ft. Pierre, South

Dakota, where they buried a lead plate. The village from which they started was described as being on a "westward flowing" river and the only bit of topography which fits this description is the Missouri in the vicinity of Sanish, North Dakota. Where the party went from the time they left the village on the "westward flowing" river until they buried the lead plate is a 200-year-old enigma.

Of the first part of this journey, the Chevalier wrote:

*We marched twenty days west-south-west, which to me did not seem the right direction; we found no one, but many wild beasts. I noticed in many places soils of different colors, as azure, a sort of vermillion, grass-green, shining black, a white as of chalk, and also the color of ochre. . . . We arrived the 11th of August, at the Mountain of the Gens des Chevaux. Our guides not wishing to pass over, we set about constructing a small hut for ourselves, there to wait the first savages we might discover. We built fires on all sides for signals, in order to attract someone to us, being resolved to join the first people that presented themselves.*

On the 10th of September one guide left them and four days later they "discovered a smoke to the south-south-west." On investigating this signal the Frenchmen found a village of *"Beaux Hommes"*—Handsome Men—whom they joined. The remaining guide now took leave and the little party was left on their own resources. During the remainder of the fall and winter the brothers wandered from one band or tribe to another, vainly seeking information about a route to the Western Sea.

The Horse Indians, whom they located on the 19th of October had been severely handled by the *"Gens des Serpent"*—Snake Indians—and the Chevalier persuaded them to unite with others and make war on their enemies. This resulted in bringing together a force of perhaps 2,000 men; and on the 1st of January this assemblage came in sight of mountains where their enemies might be expected. After traveling another week, the warriors left all their baggage in a camp and set out. The camp of the Snakes was located where it was predicted but, alas, it was deserted. Fearing that the enemy might be attacking their own people, the braves stampeded for the baggage camp.

The Chevalier and the two men had joined this war party, hoping to climb the mountains and view the country beyond. Not only were they disappointed in this but, during the two day retreat, they became separated from the Indians and rejoined the camp only after considerable difficulty. A severe blizzard struck immediately after their return and the little party now faced the prospect of wintering in an Indian camp.

After this abortive expedition, the large camp broke up. The explorers had now cast their lot with the *"Gens de l' Arc"*—Bow Indians— and this group traveled slowly "east-south-east." By March they had reached the permanent camp of the *"Gens de la Petite Cerise"*—Choke Cherry Indians—on the banks of the Missouri. While here they buried a lead plate on a hill just west of the site of the present town of Ft. Pierre, South Dakota. This was found on February 16, 1913. Stamped on one side was this inscription:

ANNO XXVI REGNI LUDOVICI XV PROREGE . . . . .
ILLUSTRISSIMO DOMINO DOMINO MARCHIONE . . .
DE BEAUHARNOIS M D CC XXXXI . . . . . . . . . . .
PETRUS GAULTIER DE LAVERENDRIE POSVIT . . . .

and scratched on the other side was

POSE PAR LE
ChevaLyeT de Lavr
to jo [to St.?] Louy la Londette
Amiotte
Le 30 de mars 1743

After burying this lead plate bearing the names of the King of France, the Governor of Canada, Pierre la Verendryé, and the members of this tiny party, the Frenchmen left the Choke Cherry Indians. Apparently traveling alone, they followed the Missouri River to their starting point, and then went back to Fort la Reine. They arrived home on July 2, 1743, "to the great joy of my father . . . and to our great satisfaction."

Where had these sons of la Verendryé been? The simplest and perhaps the best solution to this problem is to accept the meagre data in the journal at face value and plot it on a map. A "west-south-west" heading line drawn from the "westward flowing" portion of the Missouri near Sanish, North Dakota, will pass over or near the Sheep Mountains on the Yellowstone-Missouri divide (north and east of Miles City, Montana). These are about 170 air-line miles from the starting point and would have required that the party travel about eight and a half miles a day (for 20 days). This is very comparable to the twelve air-line miles a day which the party averaged between Fort la Reine and the "Mantannes" over a familiar route.

Apparently, the erratic wanderings during the fall were within the northern part of the Yellowstone Basin but they cannot be plotted. However, the Chevalier wrote that they traveled "east-south-east" from the "baggage" camp to the spot where the lead plate was buried. A reverse heading (WNW) plotted from the latter point will fall across the valley of the Little Big Horn. To have traveled from this point to the Missouri in 51 days would have required an average daily travel of seven or eight miles. Again, this figure compares favorably with data recorded in the *daily* journal of an explorer who, 60 years later, traveled with the Crows over similar terrain.

If these calculations are approximately correct, the first stopping place was the Sheep Mountains, and the Snake camp was in the Big Horn Mountains. One other bit of information strongly supports this hypothesis. The eight major bands or tribes which the brothers met—even though the names given cannot be positively identified with any in use today—were apparently congregated in the Yellowstone valley and the territory adjacent to it somewhere between the Powder and Big Horn rivers. These people were undoubtedly meat-eaters and their concentration can best be accounted for by an abundance of game. The immediate valley of the Yellowstone was the *finest hunting ground in the West.*

Although there is no positive proof that these intrepid sons of la Verendryé were the first white men to see the valley of *la Roche Jaune,* there are good reasons for believing that they were. Certainly they belonged to that breed of men to whom the country beyond the horizon was always a challenge.

Even though uncertainty shrouds the travels of the la Verendryés, there can be no doubt that these men existed. This much cannot be said for the next name associated with the exploration of the Yellowstone for the story of Charles Le Raye probably belongs to the folklore of the valley rather than to its history. But it is an interesting yarn.

According to Le Raye's "journal," he came from Canada in 1801 to trade on the Missouri. In the fall of this year he was captured by Indians on the Osage River in Missouri and taken, eventually, to the Ree villages in what is now South Dakota. During this journey he formed a friendship with a Frenchman named Pardo, and the following spring secured permission from his captor to accompany this man to the Mandan villages. That fall he went with a hunting party to the "River Jaun" and spent the winter at the mouth of the Big Horn. The next year, while in the custody of various Indians, he wandered to Canada, then to the head of the Minnesota River, and finally back to his captor who was camped along the Missouri near the mouth of the Vermillion River. Finally, on April 26, 1805, he stole a canoe and fled down the Missouri.

Such were the remarkable wanderings of Charles Le Raye. The geographical background of the story is quite accurate except for a few mistakes in the Yellowstone country which can hardly be overlooked; and the story is plausible except for certain bits which are at variance with known facts. In 1812 when this account was published, the Biddle edition of the Lewis and Clark journals had not been printed. Sergeant Gass' book had appeared five years before and, of course, stories of the Upper Missouri country had been told in the drawing rooms and saloons of St. Louis for many years. Perhaps the best explanation for Le Raye is that he was poured out of a whiskey jug.

David Thompson, the famous explorer and geographer of the British fur trade, never made an attempt to visit the Yellowstone country but, strangely enough, he made two contributions to its history. From data which he collected from Indians while at the Mandan villages in the winter of 1797-1798, he calculated that the source of the Yellowstone River was at 43° 39′ 45″ north latitude and 109° 43′ 17″ west longitude. The error was a mere twenty-one miles which, with a man of Thompson's stature, cannot be dismissed as just a lucky guess. Also he was the first to use the words "Yellow Stone" in his journals.

October 1804 found the tightly knit little party of Captains Merewether Lewis and William Clark building winter quarters near the Mandan villages—the traditional jumping-off place for exploring parties headed farther west. What happened here during the next few months was to have a very definite bearing on the exploration of the Yellowstone Basin, and these developments are almost as interesting as the activity which they fostered.

At the nearby Indian villages were several Frenchmen and a British trader named Hugh McCracken. The latter had come down from Fort Montagne á la Bosse, a post of the Northwest Company some 150 miles northeast on the Assiniboine River. When he returned shortly after the arrival of the Americans, Lewis and Clark sent with him a letter addressed to Charles Chaboillez, an official of the Northwest Company. In this letter they pointed out that the purpose of their exploration was for the "promotion of general science" and they requested, quite naturally, that,

If, sir . . . you have it in your power to furnish us with any hints in relation to the geography of the country, its productions, either mineral, animal, or vegetable, or any other information which you might conceive of utility to mankind, or which might be of service to us in the prosecution of our voyage, we should feel ourselves extremely obliged by your furnishing us with it.

British curiosity was immediately aroused. The Louisiana Purchase had been completed only a year before, and now an official party was surveying the area in which the British were trading. The officials at Fort la Bosse promptly sent a party to investigate. In charge of this little group was a trader named François Antoine Larocque—whose brother Joseph occupied a prominent position in both the Northwest and Hudson's Bay Companies. He was a capable man, well read, studious, and versed in both the English and French languages.

After a little friction in the beginning—probably over a misunderstanding—relations between the two groups settled down to an amicable basis. One of Larocque's associates noted in his journal that "the gentlemen of the American expedition . . . on all occasions seemed happy to see us, and always treated us with civility and kindness." The English liked Clark's frank and pleasant ways but Lewis' "inveterate disposition against the British stained, at least in our eyes, all his eloquence."

The British seem to have been genuinely helpful and, on one occasion, Clark noted in his journal that one trader, Hugh Henney of the Hudson's Bay Company, was a "Verry intelligint Man." However, there can be little doubt that this helpfulness stemmed from selfish interests for the British were deeply interested in the trade possibilities of this unexplored country. Nor is it surprising that the Northwest Company was anxious to have one of their traders accompany Lewis and Clark when they pushed on the following spring. However, the Americans did not wish any foreigners in their party and Larocque wrote in his journal, "I offered to accompany them on their voyage but for certain governmental reasons they declined my proposal."

When Larocque returned to Fort la Bosse on Februrary 12th with this unwelcome news, the company officials began to organize an exploring party of their own. They had all the information about the country west of the Mandan villages which the Americans had—and probably more. Clark makes no note of being provided with any information about the Yellowstone country but Larocque or one of his associates, or both, had talked with a "voyager" who had been to "La Roche Juene." The logical person to head such an expedition was, naturally, François Antoine Larocque.

Thus it came about that on June 2nd Larocque left Fort la Bosse

. . . *with two men; each of us had two horses, one of which was loaded with goods in order to facilitate relations with the savages which we might meet. . . . Our departure impressed everybody for it seemed more than likely that my men and I would not return.*

The plans for this exploration were very simple. Larocque was to join the Crows when they arrived at the Mandan villages for their annual trading visit, and wander with them during the summer. When he had gathered all the information possible, he was to leave the camp and return. Such a plan combined the maximum in safety and mobility for such a small party.

After reaching the Missouri, Larocque had to wait two weeks for the arrival of the "Rocky mountain savages." He put this time to good use in persuading the chiefs that he should be allowed to go with the Crows. When he met one argument, they proposed another and they finally wound up telling him of the harrowing experiences suffered by the Canadian, Menard, whom the Crows robbed after he had spent several months with them.

This reluctance of the Indians to see the traders go among the tribes farther west is easily understood. The Crows roamed the vast basin of the Yellowstone and each year came to the permanent villages of the Mandans and Gros Ventres to exchange horses for various goods—including articles secured from the traders. These goods then became part of the trading stock of the Crows when they visited the Flatheads who lived still farther west, and from whom they secured horses. Naturally, the Indians along the Missouri did not look with favor on traders going directly to those with whom they themselves traded.

Late in June the long-awaited visitors arrived. Four days later, the trading and visiting completed, a farewell council was held and the wandering traders broke camp. As they trailed away up the valley of the Knife, Larocque and his two men drove their pack horses before them among the ponies of the Crows.

In sharp contrast to the vague record of Chevalier de la Verendryé, Larocque's daily journal provides a concise and often vivid record of where he went and what he saw during the next four and a half months. In addition to being very careful to record all information of value to the fur trade, this trader set down much of interest about the topography, vegetation, wild animals, and daily life as this Crow village "flitted" from four to twenty-five miles a day.

From the mouth of the Knife River, this village moved along a rather direct route to the extreme southwestern corner of the present state of North Dakota. In the latter part of July, they topped the divide between the Little Missouri and the Powder Rivers near what are now called the Chalk Buttes. The first camp in the Yellowstone Basin was made along the Powder River, probably not far below the mouth of the Little Powder. These entries comprise the first recorded eye-witness descriptions of any part of the basin:

*Fryday 26th. We passed through a Range of hills whose tops and sides are covered with pine, and at the foot are many small creeks well wooded with Ash Maple, there are plenty of different kinds of mint* which emit a very odoriferant smell. We crossed three small Creeks running north and N.W. into the Powder River whose banks we had in sight from the top of those hills. The wind was N.W. & very strong, a hurricane blew at night. The course we have pursued on a very barren soil for 22 miles was West.

Saturday 27th. We arrived at noon at the Powder River after 6 hours ride by course W. by S. for about 20 miles. The Powder River is here about ¾ of an acre in breadth, its waters middling deep, but it appears to have risen lately as a quantity of leaves and wood was drifting on it. The points of the river are large with plenty of full grown trees, but no underwood so that on our arrival we percived herds of Elk Deers through the woods. There are Beaver dams all along the river. Three of these animals have been felled by our Indians.

When we arrived here the plains on the western side of the river were covered with Buffaloes and the bottoms full of Elk and Jumping deers & Bears which last are mostly yellow and very fierce. It is amazing how very barren the ground is between this and the lesser Missouri, nothing can hardly be seen but those Corne de Racquettes [prickly pear cactus]. Our horses are nearly starved. There is grass in the woods but none in the plains which by the by might with more propriety be called hills, for though there is very little wood it is impossible to find a level spot of one or two miles in extent except close to the River. The current in that river is very strong and the water so muddy as to be hardly drinkable. The Indians say it is always so, and that is the reason they call it Powder River, from the quantity of drifting fine sand set in motion by the coast wind which blinds people and dirtys the water. There are very large sand shoals along the river for several acres breadth and length, the bed of the river is likewise sand, and its Course North East.

The "Jumping deers" may have been white-tail deer or antelope although a few days later he referred to antelope as "Cabrio"; the "Elk Deers" were either black-tail deer or actually elk. One day he wounded a "large horned animal" which would indicate that there were also bighorn sheep in the area. The comment about the temper of the "yellow" bears is in complete accord with that set down by one of Montana's first pioneers:

In the valley of the Yellowstone, [grizzly bears] are very plenty and extremely ferocious, the white ones being the worst. I think that bears are more plenty and ferocious in the buffalo region than elsewhere.

Larocque seems to have been interested in everything from jumping deers to rattlesnakes, and from Indian customs to botany. However, no entry has caused historians more confusion than this one pertaining to geology. While camped along the Powder,

*I assended some very high hills on the side of which I found plenty of shells of the Cornu amonys Species . . . likewise a kind of shining stone lying bare at the surface of the ground . . . they are of different size and form, of Clear water color and reflect with such force as a looking glass of its size. It is certainly those stones which have given the name shining to that Mountain.*

The fossil shells were correctly identified as coiled cephalopods or ammonites. However, Larocque did not know that the "shining stones" —which are accurately described—were pieces of selenite, a crystalline form of gypsum, and neither have some historians who have commented about the entry. One wrote, "Larocque's statement is scarcely probable. . . ." As Pierre la Verendryé once made a reference to "shining mountains," this badland hill which sparkled in the sunlight has been confused with the Big Horn Mountains—to which Pierre did not refer and which the Chevalier did not describe at all!

After a few days rest along the Powder, the Crows continued southwestward up the valley of this river until they came in sight of the Big Horn Mountains. Moving leisurely up to the foot of the mountains, the camp turned northward to the headwaters of the Little Big Horn. Here the village idled along, cutting quirt handles of ash, teasing grizzly bears and then killing them for sport, and worrying over "woman" troubles. Of the latter, Larocque noted,

*. . . many women have deserted with their lovers to their fine tents that are across the mountain among them the wife of Spotted Crow who regulated the camp movements. . . . Horses have been Killed and women wounded since I am with them on the score of Jealousy. To day a Snake Indian shot his wife dead but it seems not without reason for it is said it was the third time he found her and the Gallant together.*

While in camp on the divide between the Little Big Horn and the Big Horn, scouts came into camp one morning with the news that rifle shots had been heard and that they had seen *running* buffalo. A band of warriors set out at once to investigate and a few hours later sent back word that thirty-five men had been seen on one of the branches of the "large Horn" River.

Immediately, everyone except a few old men and some women jumped on their horses and raced out of camp. Squaws carrying weapons and shields, like armor bearers of medieval times, followed closely behind their husbands. Finally, the movement acquired a certain amount of order and, after a stop to don their war clothes and listen to the camp crier make a final harangue, all dashed off in the direction of the enemy. Larocque, caught in the spirit of the moment, followed.

All of the strangers escaped except two scouts who were well in advance. These men

*were surrounded after a long race but Killed and scalped in a twinkling. When I arrived at the dead bodies they had taken but his scalp and the fingers of his right hand with which the outer was off. they borrowed my hanger [sheath knife] with which they cut off his left hand and returned it to me bloody as a mark of honour and desired me to . . . at him. Men women and children were thronging to see the dead bodies and taste the Blood. Everyone was desirous of stabbing the dead bodies to show what he would have done had he met them alive and insulted and frotted at them in the worst language they could give. In a short time the remains of a human body was hardly distinguishable. every young man had a piece of flesh tied to his gun or lance with which he rode off to the Camp singing and exultingly showing it to every young woman in his way. some women had a whole limb dangling from their saddles. The sight made me Shudder with horror at such Cruelties and I returned home in quiet different frame of mind from that in which I left it.*

However, warfare is a two-edged weapon and the trader soon experienced the other extreme. When scouts reported a large party nearby, the Indians saddled their ponies, packed a few valuable belongings and any small children on others, and then sat in their tepees with their weapons in their hands until the critical hour of daybreak had passed.

After visiting the mouth of the Big Horn Canyon, where Larocque made a side trip to view some of its wonders, the village moved down the Big Horn valley, along the northern slope of the Pryor Mountains, and then crossed over to "Shot Stone" (Pryor) Creek which they followed down to the Yellowstone. Here, on September 10th,

*. . . we arrived at two in the afternoon . . . we forded to a large Island in which we encamped. This is a fine large River in which there is a strong current, but the Indians say there are no falls. Fordable places are not easily found although I believe the water to be at its lowest. The bottoms are large and well wooded.*

Larocque had now completed most of the task assigned to him. He had scouted the country for fur, and had shown the Crows how to prepare beaver skins. The Crows had drawn a map for him showing the parts of the country where they could be found at different seasons of

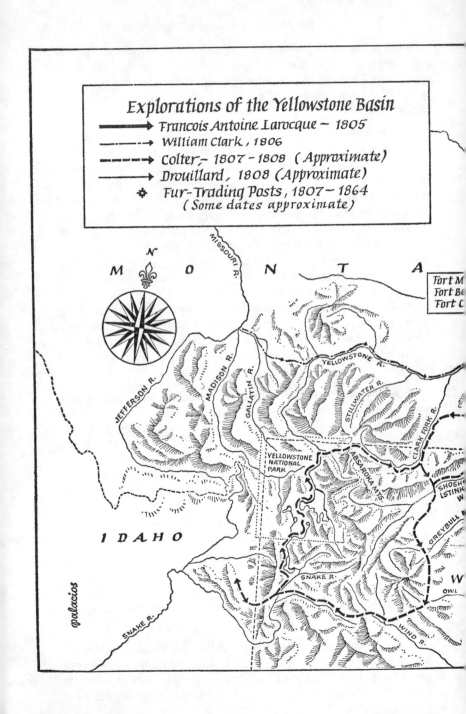

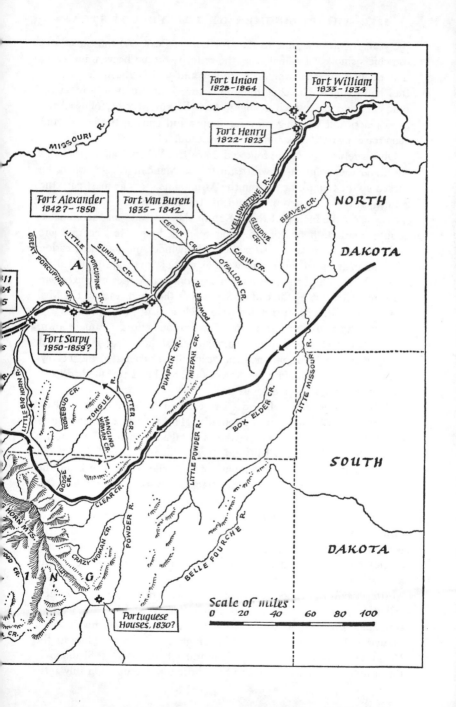

Fort Union
1828–1864

Fort William
1833–1834

Fort Henry
1822–1823

MISSOURI R.

NORTH

Fort Alexander
1842?–1850

Fort Van Buren
1835–1842

YELLOWSTONE R.

BEAVER CR.

DAKOTA

CEDAR CR.

GLENDIVE CR.

GREAT PORCUPINE CR.

LITTLE PORCUPINE CR.

SUNDAY CR.

A

CABIN CR.

O'FALLON CR.

11
24
5

Fort Sarpy
1850–1859?

PUMPKIN CR.

POWDER R.

MIZPAH CR.

LITTLE MISSOURI R.

LITTLE BIG HORN R.

ROSEBUD CR.

TONGUE R.

OTTER CR.

HANGING WOMAN CR.

LITTLE POWDER R.

BOX ELDER CR.

SOUTH

GOOSE CR.

CLEAR CR.

POWDER R.

DAKOTA

HORN MTS.

CRAZY WOMAN CR.

BELLE FOURCHE R.

I  N  G

Scale of miles
0    20    40    60    80    100

Portuguese
Houses, 1830?

the year. It was now time to start for Fort la Bosse. As the trader and
the chiefs smoked the final pipe, the latter swore by heaven and earth
that their young men would not follow and molest the little party as
they had Menard. Larocque took no chances—he put twenty miles behind him and kept watch at night. And the next day he followed the
good practice of stopping early for supper and grazing the horses, and
then traveling until dark and camping without a fire.

On his return, Larocque followed down the Yellowstone to the Missouri and then kept on downstream to the Mandan villages where he
picked up the trail to the post on the Assiniboine. For the most part, the
return journey was uneventful, and the travelers covered 13 to 37 miles
a day. Below the mouth of the Big Horn they got into an "abominable
country" with deep ravines and precipices. The horses' feet became sore
and they had to make shoes for them of rawhide, and on one occasion
three animals mired down and were extricated "with great difficulty."
Below the mouth of the Powder, smoke from prairie fires plagued them
for three days. But by the end of September they had reached the Missouri, and on the 17th of October were safely back at Fort la Bosse.

When the results of Clark's more pretentious effort became known,
the officials of the Northwest Company must have had a feeling of
smug satisfaction. Not only had their expedition penetrated the Yellowstone country a year before the American party, but Larocque had gathered information of far greater value.

On June 30, 1806, Lewis and Clark camped on a tributary of Clark
Fork in what is now western Montana. Here they made preparations
for the final bit of exploring. Lewis was to take ten men and go directly
to the Great Falls of the Missouri, then explore "Maria's" River, and
join Clark and his party at the mouth of the Yellowstone. Clark and the
remainder of the men were to back-track as far as the Three Forks of
the Missouri, recovering enroute the canoes and supplies which were
cached at the head of Jefferson River. At Three Forks the party was to
divide again. Sergeant Ordway and part of the men were to take the
boats down the Missouri: and the remainder were to accompany Clark
to the upper part of the Yellowstone valley and follow this river to the
rendezvous.

After seeing the canoes on their way, Clark turned up the Gallatin
valley for what is now called the Bozeman Pass. With him were Sergeant
Nathaniel Pryor, John Shields, George Shannon, William Bratton,
Francis Labiche, Richard Windsor, Hugh Hall, George Gibson, the
Negro servant York, interpreter Toussaint Charbonneau ("Shabono"),
the latter's squaw Sacajawea, and their little son "Pomp." On July 15th,

with the indispensable Sacajawea in the van pointing the way along "an old buffalow road," this party crossed the divide

. . . *at 2 PM.* . . . *struck the Rochejhone ½ a mile below the branch we came down & 1¼ M*ˢ, *below where it passes out of the Rocky Mountains. river 120 Yds wide, rapid and deep.*

There is no evidence that Clark was curious about the upper Yellowstone. He merely noted:

*The Roche passes out of a high rugid mountain covered with snow. the bottoms are narrow within the mountains but wider in the vally below.*

Yet a few days travel to the south lay one of the most curious regions in the vast area this party was ordered to explore. Half a century later scoffers still laughed at Jim Bridger's stories of the glass mountain, the river that flowed so fast that its bottom got hot, and the fish that swam over the Continental Divide. Kind providence seems to have delayed the *official* exploration of this area until time was ripe for its preservation as a national park.

As soon as Clark reached the Yellowstone he began to hunt for trees of sufficient size to make boats. At the end of the first day he wrote:

*I can see no timber Sufficient large for a canoe which will carry more than three men and such a one would be too small to answer my purpose.*

In the entry for the next day, he noted:

*The river and Creek bottoms abound in Cotton wood trees, tho' none of them sufficiently large enough for canoes. and the current of the Rochejhone is too rapid to depend on skin canoes no other alternative for me but to proceed on down the river until I can find a tree Sufficiently large &c. to make a canoe.*

On the fourth day of travel downstream, two of the men had accidents, one of which was serious. While attempting to mount his horse after shooting a deer, Gibson fell on a snag and drove it into the "Muskeler part of his thy." The next day this wound was exceedingly painful and Clark realized that a suitable tree must be found—and quickly. The men searched the bottomlands for several miles and finally found two trees which Clark thought could be used:

*I deturmined to have two canoes made out of the largest of those trees and lash them together which will cause them to be Study and*

*fully sufficient to take my small party & Self with what little baggage we have down the river. . . . those trees appeared tolerably sound and will make canoes of 28 feet in length and about 16 or 18 inches deep and from 16 to 24 inches wide.*

The next day brought unwelcome news—"Half of our horses were absent." When Clark attempted to put a guard on the remainder, they showed signs of having been spooked and ran away in the woods. This proved to be fortunate for the following day the men found fresh Indian *sign* near the camp indicating that the thieves had returned for those animals which they had missed. However, the horses got into a "small Prairie Serounded with thick timber in the bottom" and were not discovered.

As Clark had made no effort to guard the animals, their theft might have been expected. Signal fires had been noted to the south, and one of the men had seen an Indian on the opposite side of the river. Although the captain did not speculate on the identity of the thieves, the assumption has been made that they were Crows. There is a possibility—a very interesting possibility—that the smoke signals noted were the pre-arranged signals agreed upon by Larocque and the Crows when they parted. When a trading party did not come to their signal, the Crows investigated and, finding that these were not the men they had expected, then proceeded to make off with the horses.

The canoes completed, Clark detailed Sergeant Pryor, with Shannon and Windsor to assist, to take the remainder of the horses overland to the Mandan villages. Before separating completely, the canoe party was to wait at the mouth of the Big Horn and help the herders get their charges across to the south bank. Clark floated down to Clark Fork, which he mistook for the Big Horn, and helped cross the horses at this point. As Pryor was having troubles, Hall was added to the little detail.

The sergeant's troubles were unique! These were Indian horses, trained to run buffalo, and

*. . . in passing every gangue of buffalo the loos horses as soon as they saw the Buffalow would immediately pursue them and run around them. All those that [had] sufficient speed would head the buffalow and those of less speed would pursue as fast as they could.*

In order to make any progress, it was necessary that a man ride ahead and scare the buffalo out of the way. As he could not swim, Hall welcomed the detail. Alas, he did not know what was in store for him.

The party in the canoe traveled rapidly, Clark estimated that they covered 40 to 80 miles a day but, as he over-estimated the length of the river about 100 percent, they probably traveled about half that fast. "Pompy's Tower"—apparently named for Sacajawea's small son—enticed the party ashore, and they tarried long enough for Clark to estimate its dimensions and to carve his name and the date "July 25, 1806," near the top. On August 3rd, they reached the Missouri and, as the mosquitoes were particularly troublesome at the mouth of the Yellowstone, they left a note for Lewis and moved downstream to a more desirable campsite.

A few days later, on a "cool windey morning," two bull boats came down the river looking for all the world like overgrown, hairy tubs as they rode cork-like on the waves. In them, handling their stubby paddles with a rhythm that bespoke both haste and determination, were four men. To these paddlers—Pryor, Windsor, Shannon and Hall—Clark's canoes drawn up on the shore were a most welcome sight. But the news they brought was most unwelcome.

It was the same old story. Two days after separating from the party, the men had put the horses on good pasture late in the afternoon. The next morning every one was gone. The men wasted no time in a futile search but struck out for the Yellowstone. Here, near Pompy's Tower, they killed two buffalo and constructed a couple of unwieldy-looking craft such as they had seen at the Mandan villages. Contrary to expectations, they proved very sea-worthy. "Without takeing a drop of water," they had bobbed down the Wolf, Bear, and Buffalo Rapids where Clark had been fearful of splitting his canoes.

This exploration of the Yellowstone country was, obviously, very brief and superficial. Clark had made a general record of the country and had charted the channel of the river from the Great Bend to the Missouri. In justice to the captain, it must be said that this was all that he had planned as well as all he had time to accomplish.

Perhaps the most interesting feature of Clark's journal are his notes about the wild life which he observed. This is best summarized in his own quaint language. At the end of the second day in the valley he wrote:

Saw a large gangue of about 200 Elk and nearly as many Antilope also two white or Grey Bear in the plains. . . . Saw emence heards of Elk feeding on the opposit side of the river. I saw a great number of young gees in the river. one of the men brought me a fish of a species I am unacquainted; it was 8 inches long formed like a trout. it's mouth was placed like that of a Sturgeon  a red streak passed down each side from the gills to the tail.

When camped at Pompy's Tower they were annoyed by

emence herds of Buffalow about our [camp] as it is now running time with these animals the bulls keep such a grunting nois which is very loud and disagreeable sound that we are compelled to scear them away before we can sleep the men fire several shot at them and scear them away.

At a camp just above the mouth of Great Porcupine Creek, he noted:

The Buffalow and Elk is estonishingly noumerous on the banks of the river on each side, particularly the Elk which lay on almost every point in large gangs and are so jintle that we frequently pass within 20 or 30 paces of them without their being the least alarm$^d$. the buffalow are Generally at a greater distance from the river, and keep a continueing bellowing in every direction, much more beaver Sign than above the bighorn. I saw several of those animals on the bank to day. the antilopes are scerce as also the bighorns and the deer by no means so plenty as they were near the Rocky Mountains.

Below the mouth of the Powder, the buffalo were a source of considerable concern. On one occasion a "gang swam the river near our Camp which alarmed me for fear of their Crossing our Canoes and Splitting them to pieces." The next day they were obliged to land and wait for a herd to cross, the animals being "as thick as they could swim" in the river. As they neared the Missouri they encountered still another form of wild life—an experience they would gladly have foregone. "The Musquetors [were] excessively troublesom." Clark ends his Yellowstone journal with what must be considered a *musquetor* story. Noting a bighorn ram on a nearby hill, he

assended the hill with a view to kill the ram. The Musquetors was so noumerous that I could not keep them off my gun long enough to take sight and by that means Missed. [!]

As the party was proceeding slowly down the Missouri, they met two adventurous frontiersmen venturing into what had been an almost unknown wilderness but a year before. Joseph Dixon and Forest Hancock, two trappers from Illinois, were headed for a "trapping expedition up the River Rochejhone." These men followed Lewis and Clark back to the Mandan villages, questioning members of the party about what they had seen and, finally, asking John Colter to join them. Clark noted that they "offered to become sheerers with [him] and furnish traps &c"; and, as Colter had worked faithfully, the leaders released him and wished him "every suckess."

Unfortunately, there is but one description of this outstanding frontiersman. A trapping acquaintance recalled many, many years later:

> His veracity was never questioned among us and his character was that of a true American back-woodsman. He was about thirty-five years of age [in 1808?], five feet ten inches in height and wore an open, ingenious, and pleasing countenance of the Daniel Boone stamp. Nature had formed him, like Boone, for hardy endurance of fatigue, privations and perils.

He also noted that he had a "quick and ready thoughtfulness and presence of mind in a desperate situation, and the power of endurance, which characterizes the western pioneer."

There is no record of where the three men went to trap in the Yellowstone valley. A man who claimed to be the stepson of Hancock once told a Wyoming cowboy that the party wintered at the mouth of Clark Fork Canyon where the river breaks out of the Absaroka Mountains. Here they built a two-sided cabin against a recess in the canyon wall. This puncher also remembered that he had been told that Colter became bored during the winter and made an exploring trip by himself up into Sunlight Basin.

Be that as it may, Colter became dissatisfied with the partnership. Building a canoe, he took his share of the traps and fur and set out the next spring for far-off St. Louis. At the mouth of the Platte, not far below the present city of Omaha, he saw keelboats tied up along the bank, and the thin, blue smoke of campfires beckoned. The solitary traveler swung his canoe in to the shore and there to greet him were three friends of the trek to the Pacific—George Drouillard (Lewis and Clark's "Drewer"), Peter Wiser, and John Potts. They were bound for the Yellowstone with a fur trading expedition.

As the four swapped stories, Manuel Lisa, the *bourgeois* of this party, must have hovered near. This swarthy Spaniard was an ambitious, capable, and far-sighted trader, although he had some qualities which made him bitterly disliked as a leader. As Lisa was bound for the country from which this man had just come, the trader must have realized that it was imperative that he add Colter to his party. What inducements were offered have long been forgotten but, for the second time in as many years, Colter turned his back on the attractions of the settlements and headed for *la Roche Jaune*.

Records pertaining to this expedition are extremely scanty and fragmentary. A few notes in the record of a court, a brief comment written by a journalist the next year, and some notations which William Clark put on the maps he was preparing for publication—these are all.

Lisa built his post at the mouth of the Big Horn—of which Clark had written, "Good place for fort &c here the beaver country begins." Fort Manuel, sometimes called Fort Raymond, was not a pretentious affair, just a log cabin with a couple of rooms and a loft. As Lisa was aggressive, he promptly sent some of his men to hunt for customers. At least two men were dispatched to nearby villages to trade, one of them being Edward Rose. This trapper, the son of a white trader and a woman of mixed Cherokee and Negro blood, was regarded by some as a notorious outlaw. On this occasion he used Lisa's goods to ingratiate himself with members of this particular Crow village. This, naturally, brought down Lisa's wrath on his head and the two came to blows shortly before the trader left his post to return to St. Louis the following spring.

Notations on Clark's maps—apparently made from information furnished by the individuals concerned—indicate that Drouillard made two trips to contact Indians. On one he went into the upper part of the valley of Clark Fork, over to the Stinking Water (now the north fork of the Shoshone River), then through Pryor's Gap to Pryor Creek and, probably, back to Fort Manuel. The second took him up the valley of the Little Big Horn, eastward to a fork of the Tongue, then down Otter Creek and over the divide to Tullock Creek which he followed down to the mouth of the Big Horn. These travels would have taken him over much of the country between the Yellowstone and the Big Horn Mountains.

However, the trip which Colter made during this winter was one of the greatest feats of exploration during the days of the fur trade. The only written account is painfully brief:

[Lisa] *shortly after dispatched Coulter, the hunter before mentioned, to bring some of the Indian nations to trade. This man, with a pack of thirty pounds weight, his gun and some ammunition, went upwards of five hundred miles to the Crow nation; gave them information, and proceeded from them to several other tribes. . . . he returned to the establishment, entirely alone and without assistance, several hundred miles.*

The route traced on Clark's map was probably supplied by Colter himself. When this information is combined with a knowledge of the topography of the country involved, the following route seems probable.

Colter first went up Pryor Creek to the Pryor Mountains, from which vantage point he may have surveyed the country to the southward. Then he turned back to the campsite where he had wintered the year before. From here he went south, by way of Sunlight Basin, and traveled to the mouth of the Stinking Water. After visiting a Crow camp in this area he worked his way southward, probably by the way of the headwaters of Greybull River and the Owl Creek Mountains, into the upper part of the Wind River valley. As this was a favorite wintering spot, he may have found a village of Crows here and tarried for a time to prepare for the task before him.

After pushing out of the Wind River country by way of Togwotee Pass, he was out of the Yellowstone Basin and in the valley now called Jackson Hole with the formidable Teton Range towering in front of him. Resolutely facing the winter snow, Colter fought his way over Teton Pass and into the valley of the Teton River. In 1931, some twenty miles north of this pass, a rock was plowed up in a field. One side bears the date "1808," and the other, in rough letters, the name "John Colter."

From this point Colter probably doubled back into Jackson Hole and headed for Fort Manuel. Instead of returning the way he had come, he turned north along the base of the Tetons following, perhaps, an Indian trail which led to the Yellowstone Lake. Here he may have again engaged in some name scratching for in 1880, on a creek which bears his name but which was not named for him, a hunter found a large pine bearing an old blaze. In the center of this, under a large X were the letters "J C."

Clark's map indicates that Colter did not explore in the area which is now the Yellowstone National Park but passed down the Yellowstone River to Tower Falls. Probably he crossed the river here and took the only practical route eastward. This was an old Indian trail up Lamar River and Soda Butte Creek to the divide, and then down Clark Fork. For some reason which is not obvious, when Colter reached Sunlight Basin he doubled back over his outgoing route and went to the Stinking Water, then down this stream, over Pryor's Gap and down Pryor Creek to the Yellowstone.

This ended Colter's mid-winter journey. Most of it must have been accomplished alone, and the "pack of thirty pounds" doubtless included presents for the Indians as well as necessities. The essentials must have been few—the inevitable rifle, hatchet, knife, and flint and steel, together with a buffalo robe and, surely, a pair of snowshoes. In the winter's cold, with the snow deep in the high passes, and only wild animals for food—it was a marvelous achievement.

These trips made by Lisa's men constitute the last of the true exploring journeys in the valley of the Yellowstone. During the next twenty-five years, trappers were to pry into almost every niche and cranny. Actually, Larocque and Colter did most of the basic exploration in the Yellowstone country. However, Clark's contribution should not be overlooked. The maps which he complied were the best which were available for many years. There was one other expedition of note—the Yellowstone Expedition of 1819-1820. This deserves mention because of what *was not* accomplished.

After the War of 1812, there were deep-seated feelings of dissatisfaction about conditions in the Northwest. John Jacob Astor's project at the mouth of the Columbia River had collapsed: the Missouri Fur Company had encountered difficulties fostered by their counterpart on Canadian soil: and there were too-obvious evidences of British influence over those Indians who resided south of the border. To counteract these, the War Department—with the blessings of President Monroe—made plans for a show of force in the Northwest. These plans envisioned an exploring expedition of both scientific and military nature which, it was hoped, would lead to the establishment of military posts at strategic points. This development was to be followed later by the erection of minor posts, and the whole was to be connected by a road system.

Unfortunately, those in charge of the plans had grandiose ideas. Instead of planning to march the troops by land and carrying the supplies in tried and tested keelboats, it was deemed fitting that steamboats should be used to transport everyone and everything. The steamboats which were built failed to function satisfactorily and, as considerable money had been squandered on them, the wrath of Congress descended on the contractor's head—and on the entire expedition as well. One boat, the *Western Engineer*, did get as far as Council Bluffs on the Missouri.

Troops were sent up the Missouri in 1818, and these went into winter quarters near Council Bluffs where many died from scurvy. The scientific part of the expedition, under the direction of Major Stephen H. Long, gathered near the same place in the fall of the following year. By this time the funds which had been appropriated had been squandered on non-essentials and Congress was definitely hostile to the whole project. In 1820, as a poor apology for failure, an expedition was sent to the Rocky Mountains to explore the headwaters of the Platte, Arkansas, and Red Rivers. Thus the Yellowstone Expedition became Long's Expedition.

Perhaps it is not fair to condemn this fiasco too harshly. It did bring into focus the difficulties of the Western Frontier and, eventually, resulted in moving troops into the Northwest, and making official explorations. However, the vision of a military post at the mouth of the Yellowstone did not materialize for another quarter of a century.

# 3

## Absaroka

»»»»»»»«««««««« The word *Crow* is not a translation of the tribal name, Absaroka. An old Indian once told an Army officer that Absaroka was the name the Great Spirit gave them when he created them; and he noted that these Indians never called themselves Crows even though this was the name used by all their neighbors. In the Hiditsa language, *Absarokee* means "children of the large beaked bird"—*Absa* referring to a large crafty bird which no longer exists. And in the sign language, the sign for a Crow Indian is made by extending the arms forward at shoulder height and imitating the flapping of a bird's wings.

Legends indicate that the name may have originated with other Indians who had contact with the Crows. According to a Cheyenne story, when this tribe first met the Crows they had a pet "medicine" crow, and later they referred to them as the "Crow People." The Gros Ventre had a story that not long after the Crows split off from them, they had a fight with the Sioux. Some "Crows" were present but they just sat on the nearby hills and would not help their friends. Whereupon a "warrior called out to them and asked, 'Why they sat up there like a lot of crows?' and ever afterward they were called Crows."

Where the Crows lived before they came to the Yellowstone Basin is also shrouded with the haze of legend. One Crow account would indicate that they migrated from what is now eastern Nebraska and Kansas by way of the Platte valley. Another story, recorded by a trapper who was on the Yellowstone in the 1830's, states that about 1790 they came from the country north of the Missouri and east of the mouth of the Yellowstone. When Larocque traveled with them they apparently regarded most of the basin as their hunting grounds, a situation which continued to exist until about 1834. Fort Laramie was established this year, and the Teton Sioux soon began to edge into the southeastern part of the valley. Finding the country to their liking, they took over a sizeable portion.

During the days of the fur trade, these people still recalled very clearly just how they had divided from the Minatarí—sometimes referred to as Hidatsa, Gros Ventre, or Big Bellies. They told Edwin Denig, the *bourgeois* at Fort Union in the early 1850's, that at one time there were two factions, both of about equal strength and headed by ambitious leaders. While on a buffalo hunt, the wives of the two leaders quarreled about the manifolds or upper stomach of a cow. Words led to blows, and blows to knives, and in the scuffle one woman killed the other. The relatives on both sides then took part in the fight and soon there was a skirmish under way between the two groups. Several were killed and, in the end, the two factions separated. One stayed with the Mandans and the other migrated to the plains and mountains of the Yellowstone country and became the Crows.

However, these people did not allow this separation, which Denig placed about 1775, to interfere with their visiting. These visits became regular affairs and, as has been noted, developed into a kind of annual trading fair. About 1859 the Crows split again. One division continued to live near the mountains south of the Yellowstone and became known as the Mountain Crows. The other, which moved farther northward and roamed near the Missouri with the Gros Ventre of the Prairie, acquired the name of River Crows.

After Larocque returned, he prepared a study on the "Rocky Mountain Indians" for his superiors. This contains information about their tribal organization and an estimate of their numbers. According to this paper:

There are three principal tribes of them whose names in their own language are Apsarechas, Kee the restas and Ashcabcaber, and these tribes are again divided into many other smaller ones which at present consist but of very few people each, as they are the remainder of a numerous people who were reduced to their present number by the ravage of Small Pox, which raged among them for many years successively and as late as three years ago. They told me they counted 2000 Lodges or tents in their Camp when all together before the Small Pox infested them. At present their whole number consists of about 2400 people dwelling in 300 tents and are able to raise 600 warriors.

The small groups noted may have been maternal clans of which thirteen now exist.

The Crows were noted for being handsome people. The trader Denig, who could speak with authority, regarded the men as "decidedly prepossessing. . . . perhaps the handsomest body of Indians in North America. They are all tall, straight, well formed, with bold, fierce eyes, and as usual good teeth." Also, they were fair skinned in contrast to the other tribes and, naturally, fond of fine clothes and personal adornment. However, Denig, who had a sharp eye for a shapely female figure, was not favorably impressed by the women. To him

Of all the horrid looking objects in the shape of human beings these women are the most so. Bad features and worse shapes, filthy habits, dresses and persons smeared with grease and dirt, hair cut short and full of vermin, faces daubed over with their own blood in mourning for dead relations, and fingers cut off so that scarcely a whole hand is to be found among them, are the principal things which attract the attention of the observer. The young women are hard, coarse-featured, sneaky looking, with sharp, small noses, thick lips, red eyelids caused by venereal disease, and bare arms cloathed with a coat of black dirt so ground in as to form a portion of the skin. The old hags can be compared to nothing but witches or demons. . . .

Although the women were shorter in stature and less attractive than the men, this description is perhaps unduly severe. It is unfortunate that Larocque, who saw these people before they were contaminated by contact with the whites, did not leave his impressions. Certainly they were not as dirty as Denig indicates for he observed:

Both sexes are very Cleanly, washing and bathing every morning in the river, and in Winter in the snow. they keep their clothes always very clean, and as white as snow, with a kind of white earth. . . . A woman *never sets the Kettle on the fire in the morning without first washing her hands, and the men do not eat without the same precaution.*

Fortunately, Larocque did leave a description of how they dressed before the traders came among them. He noted that the men usually wore tight leggins rather than a breech clout, and that the tops of these were tucked under a belt or girdle. Their shirts were made of three antelope or deer skins, one forming the front, another the back, and the third the sleeves. These were attached to the top of the shoulder and left open under the armpit. Over this they wore a buffalo robe painted with pictures of their war exploits or decorated with beads and porcupine quills. Generally they wore a slip of skunk or wolf skin around the ankle with one end dragging behind, and some beads, hawk bells, and a couple of tufts of stained horsehair suspended from their head. A necklace of bear claws, or the entire paw ornamented with buttons, on the front of the shirt was also considered "very fashionable."

Women wore a pair of leggins which reached to the middle of the thigh and were tied with a garter below the knee. However, they were round like stockings and did not have fringes like those of the men. Their "shift or cottillion" reached the knee, or below, and was generally made of elk skin although some of the fine dresses were made of large antelope or bighorn sheep skins. Sleeves were attached in the same manner as with the men's shirts except that the opening under the armpit extended down each side far enough to permit them to suckle their children. Robes were also worn and, while these might be decorated with beads and quills, they were never painted. They did not wear ornaments in their hair but often painted their faces red. Children were dressed like their parents except that the boys went naked until they were eight or ten years old, "but the girls never."

Long hair was a fashion fad among the men.

*Those who have long hair gum them into 10 or 12 plat plastered over with white earth, except the end which is well combed. Those whose hair is not long enough lengthen them with horse hair which they gum into their own and divide in the same manner as the other.*

Larocque recalled seeing one man who had two *white* horsetails attached and "when he walked the hair dragged 2 feet behind him on the Ground."

They were good-natured, fun-loving people and were very sociable with each other. Old men collected in groups to smoke and visit, and even the children played in groups. Most of the plains Indians had a broad streak of humor in their makeup and the Crows were no exception. However, some of this humor was definitely "Indian" in character. One Crow woman recalled that when she was a girl, she and some of her friends once climbed a tree to get away from a bear and her cubs. Some young men who happened to observe the situation managed to tie one of the cubs to the tree, and then the girls could not get down until rescued by one of their parents. To the young men this was a good joke.

In comparison with their neighbors, the Crows were a kindly people. The crippled and decrepit were treated with consideration; and war parties usually spared the lives of any women and children whom they captured. In fact they were so kind to their captives that they usually made no effort to escape. However, they were a jealous and egotistical people—Larocque called "jealousy . . . their predominant passion." Murder was almost unheard of—a husband might shoot the horse of his wife's lover, or kill the woman, but he did no violence to the man involved. And the Crows were noted for the good order which they maintained in their villages.

Indians have been noted for being indulgent parents: the Crows were unusually indulgent. Fur traders detested the undisciplined children of the Absaroka. One clerk at Fort Union wrote that "Young Crows are as wild and unrestrained as wolves": and a trader once observed that "the greatest nuisance in Creation is Crow children, boys from the ages of 9 to 14 years." On occasion, crying babies were even allowed to disrupt the solemn proceedings of treaty commissions.

They are not so stupid as Indians are thought to be. They reason justly enough on such subjects as they have occasion to see and be acquainted with. . . . They know very well how to make unadvantageous bargains in their sales and purchases.

Although Larocque was perhaps the first white man to make the observation that the Crows were sharp traders, he was by no means the last. Denig wrote:

The trade with the Crows was never very profitable. They buy only the very finest and highest priced goods. . . .

Another prominent trader made a similar observation. Furthermore, they were wise enough to refuse to be debauched and swindled by the use of alcohol  the most profitable item in a trader's stock. They called whiskey "White man's fool water" and left it alone until the beginning of the reservation days in the late 1860's.

Many who came in contact with the Crows during the early days have noted that they were superb horsemen. Larocque wrote:

*Every one rides, men, women, & children. The female rides astride
as the men do . . . They are excellent riders being trained to it from
their infancy.*

In 1811, another trader noted just how young this training began:

*The children are perfect imps on horseback. Among them was one so
young that he could not yet speak. He was tied to a colt of two years old,
but managed the reins as if by instinct, and plied the whip with true
Indian prodigality.*

They took good care of their favorite war horses and buffalo runners
and were extremely reluctant to part with the best ones. Naturally, they
were good judges of horse flesh, and most men measured their wealth in
the size of their herds.

Chastity and stable marital relationships were definitely not Absaroka
virtues. Even today, membership in the various clans is traced through
the *mother* and not the father. Larocque made several references to
promiscuous relations and in one place noted that many men would
not go hunting without taking their favorite wife with them! Journals
covering the closing days of the fur trade indicate that what went on was
shocking even to hardened traders. In a typical entry, Denig described
this characteristic in blunt language:

*The bucks make it their whole business day and night to run after
the women, who, whether married or not, appear to be perfectly unaware that virtue and chastity has any existence even in the imagination.
Their conduct in these matters is carried on in broad daylight without
any regard to bystanders or lookers on . . . for they prefer to be seen
rather than to conceal any and all transactions between the sexes. . . .
a superfluous number of unmarried women are to be found, and those
who are married are neglected by their husbands who run after the rest.
The married women are not a whit better than the others. . . .*

It is not possible to entirely excuse Crow morals by noting that they
had these habits long before meeting the white people who took unto
themselves the prerogative of judging them. Even the Crows referred to
a virtuous woman who was expert at feminine tasks and physically attractive as a *good woman*. Also there were certain religious ceremonies
which could be performed only by a virtuous woman. Nor did all
women take kindly to some of the woman-stealing tactics of certain
societies. When one group tried to take the wife of His-Medicine-Is-
Bear, she called to her husband for help. He picked up his gun and

warned, "There is not one of you who are man enough to take her." Such action was practically unheard of and started a controversy. So not all of the Crows conformed to the pattern described by Denig.

All early observations are in agreement that the Absaroka were inveterate and skillful thieves. Men, women, and children were adept at pilfering and the only disgrace connected with it was to get caught at it. Perhaps the first record of Crow thieving is that set down by Larocque. When Le Borgne, the Big Belly chief, was attempting to dissuade him from going with these Indians, he related this incident:

A Canadian named Menard—who lived there about four years—was sent several years ago to trade in horses and beavers with the Rocky mountains [Indians], that they did everything to dissuade him but seeing his irrevocable determination they let him set out; that once arrived at the tents of the Rocky mountain savages, he had been well received and had procured nine horses, two women slaves, and a certain amount of beaver, after which he left the place well satisfied; that at length several young men followed him and stole seven horses from him during the night, that several nights after the two slaves deserted with the other horses, that some other young men rejoined him and took away all that he possessed, even his knife; that he returned weeping to the village of the Big Bellies, nearly dead, having only his cover [robe?] to make himself (with the aid of a flint rock) some shoes that he attached to his feet with cords. . . .

When bands of trappers began to wander through the Yellowstone country, the Absaroka had ample opportunities to practice this art. Any solitary trapper who was unfortunate enough to be discovered could expect to be robbed of everything he possessed. Parties were subjected to indignities of various kinds such as receiving old nags and worn robes in return for good horses and blankets, and having such supplies as tobacco, powder, and lead "begged" from them. It required a fine degree of judgment to know when to submit and when to threaten their tormentors with death and destruction. In 1831, a clerk of the Missouri Fur Company who had lived among the Crows summed up his rather extensive experience in a letter addressed to the Secretary of War:

They are thieves at home and abroad, and spare no chance to rob us, but never kill. This they frankly explain by telling us that if they killed, we would never come back, and they would lose the chance of stealing from us. They have no shame about stealing, and will talk over their past thefts with you with all possible frankness and indifference.

Some of this attention they justified in curious ways. In the winter of 1851-1852, two Metis from Fort Union were trapping along the Yellowstone River when their camp was jumped by a band of Blackfeet. One man was wounded but managed to hide while the other succeeded in making his way to a village of Crows. As soon as the Indians learned what had happened, a party went to the camp and appropriated all the equipment of the trappers. When the Metis claimed their property, the Crows explained that what they took was *fair* booty!

However, these encounters had an unpredictable quality. One trapper wrote in his journal that he and his three companions were robbed of everything except their arms, tobacco, powder, and lead—having threatened to fight to retain these. Shortly afterward, they met another band and the chief of this group requested that they accompany him to his camp where, he assured them, their property would be returned. The trapper told the Indian to go to Hell and resolutely turned his face toward Fort Laramie, the nearest trading post. Several weeks later he met his *partisan*, as the head of a trapper band was called, and learned that this man had met the same chief, received the same offer, and that the Indian actually did restore the stolen property!

Trader Robert Campbell had an experience which may point up a moral. On one occasion he lived in the lodge of the famous chief Arapooish, or Rotten Tail. Not wishing to trust *all* his property in the lodge, he secretly cached about 150 beaver skins. This cache was found and the skins taken—which was discovered by Arapooish. After making Campbell confirm what had happened, the chief announced that he would fast until all the skins were brought to his lodge. When they had been accounted for—and a few more—the offended chief told the trader to pack up and leave. Campbell philosophized later: "Trust their honor and you are safe; trust to their honesty, and they will steal the hair off your head."

Although the Crows had their faults, they had one great virtue—they were friendly toward the whites. On occasion, they have boasted that they never killed a white man. This *may* be true—but—even today there is a story told among the Crows that once when they were camped along the Big Horn a couple of white men came into camp one evening—and were not alive the next morning. Also, white men have recorded incidents which would cast doubt on this allegation. However, by and large they were friendly.

It is difficult to determine just *why* they were friendly. They were peaceable among themselves, and sometimes made peace agreements with their neighbors—the Blackfeet excepted. However, they were probably shrewd enough to realize that, pressed by the Blackfeet on the

north and the Sioux on the south and east, white friends were highly
desirable. In 1856, when Denig wrote his study of the tribe, he predicted grimly, "Situated as they are, the Crows cannot exist long as a
nation." There is a colorful story that when the beloved chief Arapooish
lay dying—he was on his way home from an abortive attempt to destroy the trading post on the Marias River which supplied arms to the
Blackfeet—he said, "Go back to my people with my dying words. Tell
them ever hereafter to keep peace with the whites." But to complete the
record, it must be noted that the alleged outlaw, Edward Rose, once
claimed that he advised these people that if they kept on friendly terms
with the Americans they had "nothing to fear from the Blackfeet
and can rule the mountains." Perhaps there is some measure of truth in
all these points.

The life which these people led was a self-sufficient and satisfying one
in many respects. Certainly it was a colorful one before the white man
transformed the Indian into an ugly caricature of himself. A camp was
never more fascinating than when it trailed out across the sagebrush-
covered prairies from one tree-lined watercourse to another, grey dust
rising from the horses' hooves and trailing tepee poles, a protective
screen of young men—"wolves"—thrown out far in advance, and the
chief and his principal men leading the assemblage. It was a sight to
make a man's blood tingle—even the caustic Denig who set down this
brilliant word picture:

When a camp is on the move in the summer, this tribe presents a gay
and lively appearance, more so perhaps than any other. On these occasions both men and women dress in their best clothes. Their numerous
horses are decked out with highly ornamented saddles and bridles of
their own making, scarlet collars and housing with feathers on their
horses' heads and tails. The warriors wear their richly garnished shirts,
fringed with human hair and ermine, leggins of the same, and headdresses of various kinds, strange, gay, and costly. Any and all kinds of
bright colored blankets, loaded with beads worked curiously and ele-
gantly across them, with scarlet leggins, form the principal portion of
the dresses of the young men or those whose feats at war have not yet
entitled them to the distinguished privilege of wearing hair. These bucks
are fancifully painted on the face, their hair arranged as has been described, with heavy and costly appendages of shells, beads, and wampum,
to the ears and around the neck. The women have scarlet or blue dresses,
others white cotillions made of dressed skins of the bighorn sheep, which
are covered across the breast and back with rows of elk teeth and sea
shells. These frocks are fringed along the edge and around the bottom.

The fringes are wrought with porcupine quills and feathers of many colors. . . . When traveling, the women carry to the horn of the saddle the warrior's medicine bag and shield. His sword, if he has one, is tied along the side and hangs down. The man takes charge of his gun and accoutrements in readiness for an attack however sudden. The baggage is all placed on the horses, at which they are very expert. Kettles, pots, pans, etc., each have their sack with cords attached. These are on the sides of the animal, and on top of the saddle is either one large child fit to guide the horse, or two or three small children so enveloped and so well tied as to be in no danger of falling. Often the heads of the children are seen popping up alongside of pup dogs or cub bears on the same horse. The lodge occupies one horse and the poles another. The meat and other provisions are put up in bales well secured. They are so expeditious in packing that after their horses are caught they are saddled, the tents struck, everything put on the horses and on the march in less than 20 minutes. The great number and good quality of their horses make a showy appearance. Both men and women are capital riders. The young men take this occasion to show off their persons and horsemanship to the women. A good deal in the way of courting is also done while traveling. The train is several miles in length, wives are separated from their husbands, daughters some distance from their mothers, which opportunities are not lost by these young and enterprising courtiers. They ride up alongside, make love, false promises, in short use any and all means to obtain their end.

Buffalo meat was their staff of life, and other parts of this animal provided a score or more of things necessary to their culture. They believed that buffalo meat was "hard meat" and would make good muscles. Later, when the herds were wiped out, some refused to eat beef. They called it "soft meat" and believed that it was not good for them. Trappers who lived among them witnessed various methods of killing in addition to the customary one of *running*. In the Wind River country, Crows were seen to drive small bands past men who shot them while on foot, on another occasion they drove up a narrow section of a canyon where hunters shot from the rocks above the animals. Sometimes a small herd was penned in a box canyon and killed as needed. On the open prairie, hunters might encircle a large area and drive everything to the center. When the catch began to mill aimlessly in the "surround," the kill began.

The only hunting which an Indian regarded as *sport* was baiting grizzly bears. This was done by several men surrounding a grizzly and wearing it down by making it charge first one and then another. In his traveling down the Little Big Horn, Larocque noted that the wild cherry trees were full of fruit and the bears, "extremely plentiful." Two or three were usually killed each day for their claws; and to kill a bear was regarded as something of an achievement.

War played an important part in the life of the men for it was here that a man acquired stature among his fellowmen. Offensive operations had some of the aspects of a sport for life was usually not risked unless the chance for gain—and a whole skin afterward—were good. Horse stealing was also a part of the business. However, when Crow met Blackfoot it was a grudge fight with no holds barred. Both old-timers and the Crows still recall the time when a Blackfoot horse stealing party made a raid through the Big Horn and Little Big Horn country during the early reservation days. Plenty Coups and a band of his warriors captured the thieves in the Bull Mountains up north of the Yellowstone, and impaled them on sharpened stumps of lodgepole pine. When asked what happened to the enemy, the chief replied, "They kicked themselves to death!"

Trading seems to have appealed to something in the Crow character for they were the Jew peddlers of the plains. In fact it is this trait which has led some to suspect that they were the "Horse Indians" for whom la Verendryé's sons waited in vain at the village of the "Mantannes." Certainly their annual trading fairs were well established years before Larocque joined them. This trader noted that they secured horses from the Flatheads and sold them at the Mandan villages for twice what they gave for them, and that the articles commonly traded were "battle guns, ammunition etc from the Mandans and Big Bellies in exchange for horses, Robes, Leggins & shirts, they likewise purchase corn, Pumkins & tobacco from the Big Bellys as they do not cultivate the ground." In addition to shuttling between the Flatheads and the Mandans, the Absaroka ranged far to the south. Larocque noted that they prized a certain kind of blue beads which came up by some means from the Spanish settlements of the southwest. In 1820, members of Major Long's expedition met a warrior and his squaw near the Spanish Peaks in southeastern Colorado who could speak the Crow language. And Denig knew that they "sometimes pushed their way as far as the Kiowas and Comanches and occasionally near the Spanish settlements of Taos and Santa Fe."

During the pre-reservation years, the Absaroka had two chiefs of particular note. One of these, Long Hair, was both a chief and a medicine man, and stories of his exploits were told for many years. When but a young man, he felt that he was destined for greatness, and said that the Great Spirit had promised him a sign which would be recognized by the people. After a couple of successful war parties his hair, which had been very short, began to grow and in "a brief season" almost reached his feet. Thereafter, he was known far and wide for his hair. One of the three trappers who left a record of its length wrote his impression while at Long Hair's camp in the early spring of 1837:

*This village is called "Long hair's band" after their chief whose hair is eleven feet and six inches long done up in an enormous queue about 18 inches long and six inches thick hanging down his back.*

About a century later, Plenty Coups showed a lock of this hair to General Hugh L. Scott and Scott Leavitt. At this time it measured "seventy-six hands" and the width of a finger—*over twenty-five feet.*

Trappers who lived in his camp recalled that he was also an admirable man whose word was law. He always did what he agreed to do and was so conscientious that nothing would tempt him to do anything which he thought would anger the Great Spirit.

Rotten Tail, or Arapooish as Washington Irving preferred to refer to him, was the greatest of the chiefs. He died in 1834, shortly after the Crow defeat at Fort McKenzie, and it was his death which made Long Hair the ranking leader. Almost twenty years after his death the Crows still referred to him as "the Chief," or "the Great Chief." He was about thirty years old when he became chief of the entire Crow nation: and Prince Maximillian, who saw him about a year before he was killed, described him as a "fine tall man, with a pleasing countenance." His people remembered him as a capable leader in camp and a fine tactician when on the warpath.

Denig, who wrote his biography in some detail, recorded the Indian accounts of his famous battles. Perhaps his greatest victory was in a fight with a village of Blackfeet in the valley of the Musselshell. Here he maneuvered his own camp in such a way as to indicate retreat; and when the village of the enemy was strung out on the move, he cut it to pieces. One hundred Blackfeet were killed, 230 women and children captured in addition to all the camp equipment, and 500 horses were rounded up. His death came in a suicide charge when he believed that his people might depose him for defeat in a battle which was not of his choosing.

A most unusual and colorful character was a minor chief named Woman Chief. She had been captured from the Gros Ventre of the Prairie when about ten years old, and became a Crow by adoption. A clerk at Fort Union saw her in October 1851:

In the afternoon the famous Absaroka amazon arrived. Mr. Denig called me to his office that I might have an opportunity to see her. She looked neither savage nor warlike. On the contrary, as I entered the room, she sat with her hands in her lap, folded, as when one prays. She is about 45 years old; appears modest in good manner and good natured rather than quick to quarrel. She gave Mr. Denig a genuine Blackfeet scalp which she had captured herself. How amazed was I when Mr. Denig afterwards presented the long black scalp to me! A scalp is an Indian curio of rare worth, for the reason that a brave so very seldom parts with those trophies.

Shortly after her capture, she showed a liking for the activities of the boys. Partly to humor her, and partly for his own convenience, her captor provided her with a bow and arrows and allowed her to guard his horses. In time she became a good marksman and a skillful hunter— but she did not attract the fancy of any of the young men. When her captor was killed, she promptly took charge of the lodge and the care of the other children.

The first of her warlike exploits was performed when a few lodges were trading at a post on the Yellowstone. Blackfeet jumped the camp and ran the people to the safety of the stockade wall. The war party then drew off, just beyond rifle range, and *signed* for someone to come out and talk with them. When no warrior accepted the dare, this woman jumped on a horse and rode out. A few Blackfeet advanced to meet her and when they failed to stop at her request she shot one and drove arrows into two others. Then to the discomfiture of the enemy, she galloped back to the fort unharmed. Not long afterward she led a successful horse-stealing foray and was well launched on her career as a warrior.

In time she assumed a place in the tribal council becoming the third-ranking person in a band of 160 lodges. Then, feeling that the duties of housekeeping were below a person of her standing, she took unto herself a *wife*—and finally three more wives! These, of course, dressed robes for trade thus increasing her wealth and standing. Finally, she assumed the responsibility of trying to arrange a peaceful meeting between her people, the Gros Ventre of the Prairie, and the Absaroka. When she and her companions met a small party of these people on the prairie, they sat down and smoked with them. While thus engaged they were murdered.

During the days of the fur trade, a number of white men joined the Crows. Some of these were renegades, most of them now nameless, who were held in poor repute by the traders and trappers who knew them. Others were men of ability—like Robert Meldrum—who were attracted to the life in an Indian camp.

Meldrum, or Round Iron as the Indians called him, was born in Kentucky in 1806, the son of Scotch-Irish immigrants. He probably came to the West with Captain Bonneville's trappers in 1832 and, after trapping for three years, went to live with the Crows. One trader recalled that he was a man of medium height, strongly built and weighing about 180 pounds, had dark sandy hair, keen grey eyes, and an attractive countenance. Although he possessed courage beyond question, he was neither quarrelsome nor overbearing. When he joined the Absaroka, he adopted Indian dress, let his hair grow, and took a squaw and established a lodge. As he had intelligence and courage, he rose to a position of some influence.

Although the details of Meldrum's life among the Indians have been forgotten, by the later 1840's he had become a trader for the American Fur Company. In 1848, he was in charge of Fort Alexander, a dangerous post opposite the mouth of the Rosebud. When this was abandoned in 1850, he helped build its successor, Fort Sarpy, and became its *bourgeois*. Some five or six years later a clerk at this post made a number of incriminating entries in his journal about Meldrum's liberality with the company's goods, as well as several notes about the amorous activities in which his boss was involved. These support Denig's view that even though a trader took an Indian woman—which practically all of them did—he should not try to enter Indian society on the level of the Indian.

When the American Fur Company abandoned the practice of maintaining a post on the Yellowstone, Meldrum was employed at Fort Union. Here he abandoned the habits of Indian life, dressed like a civilized man, and attracted considerable attention by the lack of slang and profanity in his speech. He died here in 1865, a few short years before this post, and the way of life it represented, passed out of existence.

Edward Rose and James Beckwourth were the two most colorful individuals who made the Absaroka their adopted people. Rose, who was the first to join the Crows, was a mixture of white, Cherokee, and Negro parentage. Beckwourth, or Jim Beckwith as he signed on the early fur trade rolls, was also dark complected being a mulatto or some mixture of white and Negro blood.

Rose, as has been noted, was one of Lisa's party which built the first trading post on the Yellowstone. Here he got into trouble with his *bourgeois* and went off in a huff to live with the Crows. His past history was something of a mystery. Rumor connected him with a notorious gang of pirates which operated on the lower part of the Mississippi and one contemporary referred to him as "a celebrated outlaw." However, everything known of him—after his squandering of Lisa's goods—is to his credit. Wilson Hunt, who had charge of John Jacob Astor's overland expedition to the mouth of the Columbia, engaged him as a guide in 1811. As this party was crossing the lower part of the Yellowstone Basin, Hunt became suspicious of Rose's friendly relations with the Crows and discharged him—probably without good reason. Rose went back to the Crows, and his name is noted from time to time in early journals.

He was killed in 1833. A war party surrounded Rose, doughty old Hugh Glass, and a Canadian named Menard when they were trapping along the Yellowstone. When the trappers took refuge in a spot from which they could not be easily dislodged, the Indians started a grass fire to burn them out. Faced with a hopeless situation—so the story goes—the men touched off a keg of gunpowder thus committing suicide.

Beckwourth enlisted as a trapper in General Ashley's party—that famous group which, individually and collectively, wrote their names indelibly in the history of the fur trade. He remained a trapper until Ashley withdrew from the business and then he cast his lot with the Crows. Old Caleb Greenwood, one of Jim's trapper companions who had an Absaroka squaw, whiled away an evening in a Crow camp telling a tall yarn about how Beckwourth had been born a Crow and how, through misfortune, he had been separated from his parents and raised by white people. Greenwood thought it was a good joke on his friend, but, as Jim was dark complected, the Crows believed it and accepted him as a long lost brother!

Beckwourth had a biographer who knew a good story when he heard one—and Jim had a first class reputation as a teller of tales. Between the two of them they turned out a book containing some fact and much fiction. Two of the most interesting incidents in his life were his participation, as an agent for the American Fur Company, in the Crow robbery of Thomas Fitzpatrick's party—an affair which reverberated to the halls of Congress (as will be noted later)—and a desperate Indian fight in which he claimed to have been, and probably was, the central figure.

Historian Francis Parkman heard the story at Fort Laramie in 1845, and estimated that it took place about six years before. However, a trapper named Zenas Leonard claimed to have witnessed the affray in November, 1834, when he was with a Crow camp about a half day's travel from No Wood Creek.

When going out on a buffalo hunt, a party of Crows saw a "considerable body" of people traveling on foot near some rough, craggy hills. Recognizing the strangers as Blackfeet, the hunters whipped up their horses and "treed" the war party among the rocks. Not being able to ride their enemies down, the Crows sent to camp for reinforcements: and the Blackfeet used the lull to build a sturdy fort of rocks, logs and brush on the brow of a hill. When the warriors had all arrived, the chiefs debated as to how to drive the enemy out of their stronghold. Meantime Leonard "repaired to an eminence about 200 yards from the fort among some cedar trees, where I had an excellent view of all their movements."

First the Crows charged the fort in line abreast. Then they rode past it in single file firing ineffectually as they hung on the opposite side of their ponies, and finally they made a series of futile charges on foot. However, they always failed to press home the charge and soon became demoralized by the losses which they suffered. When they were about to abandon the fight, "the negro . . . who had been in company with us" climbed on a rock and, in a scathing tongue-lashing, pointed the finger of scorn at their fighting qualities. Then he

. . . told them that if the red man was afraid to go amongst his enemy, he would show them that a black man was not, and he lept from the rock on which he had been standing, and, looking neither to the right nor to the left, made for the fort as fast as he could run. The Indians guessing his purpose, and inspired by his words and fearless example, followed close to his heels, and were in the fort dealing destruction to the right and left nearly as soon as the old man.

Here now was a scene of uncommon occurrence. A space of ground about the size of an acre, completely crowded with hostile Indians fighting for life, with guns, bows and arrows, knives and clubs, yelling and screaming until the hair seemed to lift the caps from our heads. As soon as most of the Crows got into the fort, the Blackfeet began to make their escape out of the opposite side, over the rocks about ten feet high. Here they found themselves no better off, as they were immediately surrounded and hemmed in on all sides by overwhelming numbers. . . . When the Blackfeet found there was no chance for escape, and knowing that there was no prospect for mercy at the hands of their perplexed and aggravated, but victorious enemy, they fought with more than human desperation. . . .

It was a no-quarter fight. The battle "was truly a scene of carnage, enough to sicken the stoutest heart—but nothing at all in comparison with what took place afterward." After retiring from the battlefield for a little rest, the Crows returned—the squaws to collect and wail over their dead, and the warriors to finish glutting their vengeance on the dead and wounded enemy. When the latter finished, the dead bodies could hardly be recognized as human forms. Leonard had seen almost more than he could stomach. And the following night, with its incessant wailings of the bereaved and the yelling of those who celebrated, "was entirely free from repose."

Beckwourth finally got into trouble, probably over a killing, and had to leave the Crows. In the late 1860's, he returned to scout for the troops stationed along the Bozeman Trail and died while visiting a Crow village.

The fur trade days, marred only by an occasional tense moment, were carefree, happy ones for the Absaroka and the rough white men who lived in some of their lodges. With a large hunting ground over which to wander, fine places to camp, an abundance of buffalo for meat and hides, and many horses—what more could such people want? Unfortunately, the last half of the century was to bring a sad change. Driven from part of their hunting grounds by the aggressive Sioux, confined to a reservation, the buffalo gone, perplexed by changes they could not understand—life was never to be the same.

# 4

## Brown Gold

»»»»»»»«««««««« About noon on September 23, 1806, with part of the men paddling and the remainder firing their rifles exuberantly "as a Salute to the Town," the canoes bearing Lewis and Clark's men swung in to the shore at St. Louis. Here they were "met by all the village and received a harty welcom from it's inhabitants &c." There is no record of what happened immediately afterward but there can be no doubt that the merchants and traders were not long in asking about the fur trade possibilities in the distant *up-river* country for fur was the life blood of this settlement.

For over a quarter of a century after the return of these explorers, it was not difficult to get the fur fever in St. Louis. *In* 1809 young Thomas James, later General James, caught the "spirit of trafficking adventure" and joined the second party Manuel Lisa took up to his post on the Yellowstone. *In* 1823 James Clyman, a land surveyor in from Illinois to draw his wages, went to visit General Ashley who had recently returned from the mouth of *la Roche Jaune*. A few days later he was recruiting men for Ashley from the "grog shops and other sinks of degredation." When this party of about 70 headed up-river, Clyman wrote, "A discription of our crew I cannot give but Fallstafs Batallion was genteel in comparison." And *in* 1833 Charles Larpenteur, a Frenchman by birth, signed on the rolls of a fur company "for 18 months, for the sum of $296 and such food as could be procured in the Indian country." Young Larpenteur did not return to St. Louis in eighteen months —or in eighteen years.

There was an interest in the Upper Missouri and Yellowstone country before 1806, and the information which Lewis and Clark brought back merely fanned an already smouldering fire into an open blaze. The aggressive Spaniard, Manuel Lisa, had been poised at St. Louis when the explorers returned. He and two others quickly formed a partnership and the following spring, as has been noted, a trading party under Lisa's personal direction headed up-river. Lisa believed in the military principle of "getting there fustest with the mostest."

Lisa planned to operate from a central post, gathering fur from both Indian trade and the work of his own trappers. This was a time-tried technique and it was to be used in the Yellowstone country until after the War of 1812 when General Ashley devised a better system of operation. As previously indicated, Lisa expended considerable effort during the first fall and winter he spent at the mouth of the Big Horn in gathering information so that he could properly organize subsequent activities.

It was early in July 1808 when Lisa left Fort Manuel—with the infuriated Rose struggling to load the post's swivel gun for a second shot at the keelboat carrying his erstwhile employer downstream. On his return to St. Louis, he had no difficulty in persuading ten influential men to join with him in forming the St. Louis Missouri Fur Company. Among his partners were William Clark, Pierre Chouteau, Sr., Auguste Chouteau, Jr., Pierre Menard and Andrew Henry—men who were to be prominent in the fur trade for years. And in the spring of 1809, an expedition of 150 men, with merchandise for several posts, got under way for the up-river country.

After Lisa left Fort Manuel—sometimes called Fort Lisa—in 1808, Colter made two noteworthy trips up the Yellowstone and over into the Three Forks country. On the first trip, he apparently hoped to meet the Blackfeet and induce them to come to the post to trade. Unfortunately, he met a party of Flatheads and Crows. While traveling leisurely with this hunting party, leading it toward the fort, a formidable party of Blackfeet jumped them in the valley of the Gallatin. Colter was severely wounded in one leg and, in self-defense, crawled into a thicket and helped drive off the attackers. This aroused the hostility of the Blackfeet and, ultimately, caused losses totalling thousands of dollars and cost many a trapper his life.

On the second trip Colter, with John Potts for a companion, returned to this country to trap. While paddling up a little creek near the Jefferson River, they were surprised by a band of Blackfeet. Colter bowed to the demands of the Indians and paddled to the shore where he was immediately disarmed and stripped. Potts, believing that his time had come, shot one warrior and was immediately riddled with arrows. After the Indians had vented their immediate rage by chopping up Potts' body and throwing the pieces in Colter's face, the leader turned the naked trapper loose on the prairie. His scalp was to be the prize for the warrior who was fleet enough to catch him.

Colter outdistanced all his pursuers but one. When this brave attempted to kill him with a spear, the shaft broke and the trapper stabbed his foe with the head. Continuing his flight toward the Madison River, Colter came out at the river bank where there was a pile of driftwood lodged against an island. Diving under this, he eluded the remainder of the infuriated warriors, and when night came he headed for the post on the Yellowstone.

Young Thomas James, who met him the following year, wrote that Colter rejoined his friends about a week later,

nearly exhausted by hunger, fatigue and excitement. His only clothing was the Indian's blanket, whom he had killed in the race, and his only weapon, the same Indian's spear which he brought to the fort as a trophy. His beard was long, his face and whole body were thin and emaciated by hunger, and his limbs and feet swollen and sore. The company at the fort did not recognize him in this dismal plight until he made himself known.

Thus when Menard and Henry brought the party of the Missouri Fur Company to Fort Manuel in the summer of 1809, the Blackfeet were hostile. Using this post as a base for their operations, the two leaders took a strong party into the Three Forks country the following spring. Here, between the Madison and Jefferson Rivers, they built a fort which the hostility of the Blackfeet forced them to abandon the following fall. Thus ended the efforts of the Missouri Fur Company to establish a post in this part of the Northwest which, coupled with reverses on the lower part of the Missouri, brought failure to the entire project.

As Henry and his men were abandoning the mountain country, the ambitious plan conceived by John Jacob Astor was getting under way.

This project envisioned a cycle of trade between a post at the mouth of the Columbia River, China, and the eastern part of the United States. The "overland" party, which was to establish the trading post—subsequently named Astoria—was under the direction of Wilson Price Hunt. This group came up the Missouri in the spring of 1811, and then turned westward across the southern part of the Yellowstone Basin. Hunt hired the alleged outlaw, Edward Rose, for a guide. It was while crossing the upper part of the valley of the Powder that Hunt became suspicious of Rose's contacts with the Absaroka, and this influenced him to discharge the adopted Crow.

The failure of Astor's post at the mouth of the Columbia, the difficulties in which the Missouri Fur Company became involved, and the abandonment of trapping activities in the valley of the Yellowstone had one thing in common—the War of 1812. This brought the American fur trade in the Northwest to a virtual standstill for about six years, and British-supported hostiles raided down the Mississippi as far as the northern part of the state of Missouri.

By 1818 the fur business had begun to revive; and the following year the Missouri Fur Company underwent another reorganization and the leadership passed from Lisa to Joshua Pilcher. By the fall of 1821, this company had another party back at the mouth of the Big Horn where they built a new post which they named Fort Benton. When $25,000 worth of fur was sent down a year later, the future looked bright. However, there was still a definite feeling among the Americans that their British competitors were hostile. Shortly the region was to be stirred by an incident which had international repercussions.

In the spring of 1822, two members of this company, Michael E. Immell and Robert J. Jones, left St. Louis with 180 men for the Yellowstone. These, together with those already at Fort Benton, brought the number of employees of the Missouri Fur Company in the mountains to about 300. Jones was a "gentleman of cleverness," and one of the owners of the company. Immell was considered a "trader of some distinction." He had been an officer in the Army but had resigned and gone up the Missouri with Lisa in 1809. One who knew him recalled:

He was an extraordinary man; he was brave, uncommonly large, and of great muscular strength. When timely apprised of his danger he was a host in himself.

After making a fall hunt in the vicinity of Fort Benton, Immell and Jones took a party of twenty-seven men to the Three Forks area. This time Immell found the beaver less plentiful than they had been when he was there in 1810, but the party managed to make a fair catch. As they were returning, they met a party of Blackfeet to whom they made some presents before parting "in the kindest manner." Immell suspected treachery; and twelve days later, when almost to a Crow camp near the mouth of Pryor's Creek, the force was ambushed. William Gordon, their clerk, who was fortunately ahead of the rest,

escaped by a run of about seven miles across a plain, pursued only by footmen, and returned at night to ascertain the extent of the mischief. I found the Indians encamped near the ground, and made off in the dark to provide for my own safety, and was received in a friendly way by a band of Crow Indians with which I fell in about dark the next night.

This survivor wrote a vivid, precise letter to Joshua Pilcher, then at Fort Recovery near the present site of Chamberlain, South Dakota:

Fort Vanderburgh

Mandan and Grosventre Villages      June 15, 1823

Dear Sir: It becomes my unpleasant duty to inform you of the defeat of our party by the Black Foot Indians, and the dire consequences of the same. After penetrating to the Three Forks of the Missouri, early in the Spring, although we found that country almost trapt out by the Indians, we had succeeded, by the greatest perserverence, in taking about [20] packs of beaver. On the 16th day of May, having reached the Upper Three Forks of Jefferson's River, and finding no beaver in that quarter, we commenced a retrograde march for the Yellow Stone. On the second day we fell in with a party of 38 Black Foot Indians. They came up boldly, and smoked, and remained with us during that night, making every profession of friendship; and in the morning, after making them presents of such articles as we could spare, they parted with us apparently well satisfied, having first invited us to come and establish at the mouth of the Maria River, as they said that they had been informed was our intention. They were in possession of every information in regard to two boats being at the mouth of the Yellow Stone, and their determination to ascend the Missouri to the Falls. This information must have been derived from the British traders, who have most probably instigated them to commit this outrage, and by them, no doubt, from some faithful correspondent in St. Louis. We did not suffer ourselves, however, to be lulled into false ideas of security by their friendly professions, but commenced a direct and precipitate retreat from the country, keeping strict guard every night, and using every vigilance at all times. This party of 38 had returned to their village, which was very close, and recruited to the number of between 3 and 400 men. These had intercepted us on the Yellow Stone, where they arrived two days before us. They lay in ambush for us on the side of a steep hill, the base of which was washed by the river, along which we had to pursue the intricate windings of a buffalo trace, among rock, trees, &c, by means of which they had secreted themselves. At this place the men were, of course, much scattered for a considerable distance, as two horses could not pass abreast. At this unfortunate moment, and under circumstances so disadvantageous, they rushed upon us with the whole force, pouring down from every quarter. Messrs. Immell and Jones both fell early in the engagement. A conflict, thus unequal, could not long be maintained. The result was the loss of five other men killed, four wounded, the entire loss of all our horses and equipage, traps, beaver, and everything. The balance of the party succeeded in escaping, by making a raft, and crossing the Yellow Stone. This took place on the 31st of May, just below the mountains, on the Yellow Stone. Not knowing to what extent the loss of the horses, traps, &c might affect any future plans I came with all possible expedition to this place, to acquaint you with the circumstance. I left Mr. Kemlee and the party near the mouth of Pryor's Fork, making skin canoes to bring down the Fall's hunt, amounting to about ——. Four of Mr. Henry's men have also been killed near the Falls. It appears, from information derived from the Black Feet themselves, that the British have two trading houses in their country on American territory, and, from some Snake Indians, we learned that they have several on the South Fork of the Columbia. Something decisive should be done.

> Believe me to be,
> Your sincere friend,
> s/ WILLIAM GORDON

Noting that "the flower of my business is gone. . . . I think we lose at least $15,000," Pilcher promptly reported the incident to Benjamin O'Fallon, U. S. Agent for Indian Affairs at Fort Atkinson, and the latter passed the information on to William Clark in St. Louis. Pilcher's letter, coupled with some serious trouble brewing at that moment with the Arickaras on the upper Missouri, made the Indian agent suspicious of British interference. He unburdened his mind in a letter to General Atkinson, and the press promptly put his views into print. In due time serious charges were laid on the desk of the British ambassador in Washington who passed them on to the Foreign Office in London and these officials, in turn, to the headquarters of the Hudson's Bay Company for explanation.

Unfortunately for the British, they were in an embarrassing position for the stolen beaver pelts, numbering about 1,000, had been traded at the Hudson's Bay Company's post at Edmonton. Furthermore, an entry in the journal kept at this post indicated that the traders were aware of the fact that they were trading for stolen property. In November of the following year, the London office of the Hudson's Bay Company, notified the Foreign Office that the stolen beaver were being unloaded at their wharf. They were prepared to deliver them to the American Minister—*"on being paid the cost of Salvage."* It is not known what settlement was finally effected; but the incident apparently had a salutary effect for, when Jedediah Smith's party was robbed in Oregon near Fort Vancouver four years later, Hudson's Bay Company officials took prompt steps to recover his property—"without any charge or demand whatsoever."

As the clouds of economic disaster were beginning to form for the Missouri Fur Company, another organization came to the Yellowstone country. One of the partners of this company was Alexander Henry, one of the original members of the Missouri Fur Company. The other was a distinguished gentleman who was to acquire for himself a fortune in the business of beaver pelts. He was William Henry Ashley, lieutenant governor of Missouri and a general in the state militia.

Ashley and Henry began their operations in the same manner as Manuel Lisa. They recruited a party of "enterprising young men" and went up-river, laboriously dragging their equipment, trade goods, and supplies in keelboats. On October 1, 1822, they pulled up on the point of land at the junction of the Yellowstone and the Missouri and began to build a rough stockade which they named Fort Henry. Major Henry, who was familiar with the country from his trip up twelve years before, "immediately commenced arrangements for business." Ashley remained long enough to see the party settled and then left for St. Louis in a "large Pirogue."

One of their "enterprising young men" was a greenhorn named Jedediah Strong Smith. In the next few years he was to establish himself at the top of the trapping fraternity and, because he worked with a Bible in one hand and a rifle in the other, earn for himself the sobriquet of *the knight in buckskin.*

The next spring a second party—the group Clyman referred to as being worse than "Fallstafs Battalion"—left St. Louis to join the men already in the field. This group was prevented from reaching their destination by the treacherous Arickaras who, in their palisaded village on the west bank of the Missouri, were in a strategic position to control traffic on the river.

Colonel Leavenworth and six companies of the 6th Infantry came up from Fort Atkinson to force a passage—assisted by Major Henry and the men who came down from Fort Henry, and Joshua Pilcher and his men plus some 350 Sioux. The colonel bungled the attack and then negotiated a meaningless "treaty" leaving the situation worse than it had been. All that Ashley and Henry could do was make the best of a bad situation.

Smith, already seasoned enough to be trusted with a party, was given part of the trappers. These he subsequently led westward across the southern part of the valley of the Powder, around the edges of the Big Horn Mountains and, after wintering with the Crows in the Wind River country, across the Continental Divide to the headwaters of Green River for a spring hunt. Henry and the remainder of the men returned to the mouth of the Yellowstone. Finding that the Blackfeet had been troublesome, he then abandoned the post and moved up to the mouth of the Big Horn where he built another.

This year of 1823 was a memorable one in the fur trade. The death of Immell and Jones had stirred up an international incident and left their company facing the spectre of financial ruin: Leavenworth had bungled the disciplining of the Arickaras: and Ashley and Henry had completed the organization of what was to become the most famous group of trappers ever assembled. Noteworthy as these incidents were, the year is best remembered for two rather unimportant—but extremely colorful—incidents which involved several of the *Ashley* men.

At the abandoned post at the mouth of the Yellowstone were two graves. In one was the body of Mike Fink who had acquired some stature as a frontier celebrity before his death. The other corpse was that of a man named Carpenter who would never have been remembered had he not become involved in the incident which cost him his life. Fink had been a keelboatman on the Ohio and Mississippi before he came up-river with Ashley and Henry. He was then 50 years old but still vigorous, and behind him was a record of brawling in all the river ports from Pittsburgh to New Orleans. And he was an exceptional rifle shot in a society where expert handling of a Kentucky rifle was commonplace.

Mike had two cronies, one the unfortunate Carpenter and the other a man named Talbot. The three had spent the winter of 1822-1823 with Jedediah Smith's party at the mouth of the Musselshell where they had quarreled and then patched up their disagreement. When the party came in to Fort Henry the following spring, Fink and Carpenter decided to test the firmness of their reconciliation with the customary ritual of shooting a cup of whiskey from each other's head. When they flipped "a copper," Mike won the toss for the first shot.

There are several versions of what happened. This one, if not the *true* account, is at least both logical and colorful—as is befitting an almost legendary incident:

Carpenter seemed to be fully aware of Mike's unforgiving temper and treacherous intent, for he declared that he was sure that Mike would kill him. But Carpenter scorned life too much to purchase it by a breach of his solemn compact in refusing to stand the test. Accordingly, he prepared to die. He bequeathed his gun, shot pouch, and powder horn, his belt, pistols and wages to Talbot, in case he should be killed. They went to the fatal plain, and whilst Mike loaded his rifle and picked the flint, Carpenter filled his tin cup with whiskey to the brim, and without changing his features, he placed it on his devoted head as a target for Mike to shoot at. Mike leveled his rifle at the head of Carpenter, at the distance of sixty yards. After drawing a bead, he took down his rifle from his face, and smilingly said, "Hold your noodle steady, Carpenter, and don't spill the whiskey, as I shall want some presently!" He again raised, cocked his piece, and in an instant Carpenter fell, and expired without a groan. Mike's ball had penetrated the forehead of Carpenter in the center, about an inch and a half above the eyes. He coolly set down his rifle, and applying the muzzle to his mouth blew the smoke out of the touch hole without saying a word—keeping his eye steadily on the fallen body of Carpenter. His first words were, "Carpenter! You have spilt the whiskey!" He was then told that he had killed Carpenter. "Its all an accident," said Mike, "for I took as fair a bead on the black spot on the cup as I ever took on a squirrel's eye. How did it happen!" He then cursed the gun, the powder, the bullet, and finally himself.

So it was passed off for an accident. Then, one day Mike boasted that he had killed Carpenter on purpose and was glad of it. Instantly, Talbot drew a pistol and shot him through the heart. Talbot went unpunished. Probably he went with Henry not long afterward to fight the Arickaras and, a few days after this fight, was drowned while attempting to swim the Teton River. Violence pursued Fink and Carpenter even after their burial. After the post was abandoned, some Blackfeet dug up the bodies to strip them of whatever clothes they were buried in but, finding them in a putrid state, did not molest them further.

The principal character in the second colorful happening of this year of 1823 was known to his associates as "*old* Hugh Glass." Like Mike Fink, this bullheaded trapper was not a young man. This adventure began somewhere in the valley of Grand River as Henry and his men were returning to the mouth of the Yellowstone after the fiasco with Colonel Leavenworth. One of his associates wrote:

. . . amongst this party was a Mr Hugh Glass who could not be re-
strand and kept under Subordination   he went off the line of march one
afternoon and met with a large grissly Bear which he shot at and
wounded   the bear as is usual attacted Glass   he attempted to climb a
tree but the bear caught him and hauled him to the ground tearing and
lacerating his body in a fearful rate

Several of his companions came up and killed the bear, but not before Glass was again badly bitten and clawed. Henry, not wanting to
abandon the man or to be delayed, persuaded two of his men to remain
and take care of the unfortunate man until he either died or recovered.
One of these *nurses* was a man named Fitzgerald and the other, a young
fellow recently turned nineteen who answered to the name of James
Bridger.

For five days the two waited, anxiously watching for hostile Indians
and—probably—hoping their patient would die. Finally, taking Glass'
rifle and personal belongings, the trappers took up the trail of their companions. At Fort Henry, the two reported that the old man was dead.
But old Hugh Glass was too tough to die. For ten days he nursed his
strength beside a nearby spring where he found a few berries, and then
he struck out for Fort Kiowa on the Missouri at the mouth of the White
River.

Somehow Glass—so weak he was barely able to walk, and without
even a knife or flint and steel—reached this trading post where he secured the indispensables. Then the old man headed up the Missouri
to exact stern retribution from the pair who had abandoned him.

According to one story which bears signs of having been told around a
campfire too many times, Glass finally stumbled into Henry's new post
at the mouth of the Big Horn just as the usual New Year's celebration
was getting started. Warmed by the holiday spirit and some whiskey, he
forgave Bridger—but not Fitzgerald. Late in the winter he set out for
Fort Atkinson, just above Council Bluffs on the Missouri. While en
route, the Arickaras killed his four companions and robbed Glass of
everything but "my knife and steel in my shot pouch," but he finally
arrived at the post where he found his quarry had enlisted in the Army.
The commanding officer made Fitzgerald return the stolen rifle and the
stubborn old trapper prudently relinquished his thoughts of revenge.
Thus ends the saga of "old Hugh Glass." Kind Fate gave him nine more
years to live before his luck finally ran out along the Yellowstone the
day he, Edward Rose, and a Canadian named Menard struck a spark
into a keg of gunpowder.

The winter of 1823-1824, and the following spring, marks the beginning of an important change in the development of the fur trade of the Yellowstone Basin. Jedediah Smith's party had a successful hunt but came to grief when they tried to take their furs down the Platte River, and the party which went out from Fort Benton to the headwaters of the Snake River brought back a good catch. The success of these two parties apparently caused Ashley to make a very important decision.

Up to this time the fur trade of the up-river country had been tied to the water routes and fixed headquarters like Forts Manuel (or Lisa), Henry, and Benton. Ashley now discarded the old practice of hauling goods upstream in keelboats and trading at a permanent post. Instead, he substituted a single trading session in the summer which became known as the *rendezvous*. Goods were brought in by a pack train to a predetermined point, usually in the valley of the Green River, and the trappers gathered at the same place. All the trading for the year was transacted in one short period at the end of which the pack train was loaded with the fur and started back to St. Louis, and the parties of trappers left for their favorite hunting grounds. This simple, effective procedure was an immediate success.

### THE ERA OF THE RENDEZVOUS

In 1825 General Ashley led his men on trapping and exploring expeditions which covered much of western Wyoming, northern Utah, and adjacent parts of Colorado and Idaho. After another successful season, one of his men suggested that the fur be taken from the rendezvous to the valley of the Big Horn, and then down this stream and on to St. Louis in boats. Thus it came about that when General Atkinson and the Yellowstone Expedition reached the mouth of the Yellowstone on August 17th, they were surprised to see Ashley coming down the river with twenty-four men and about 100 packs of beaver loaded in buffalo-skin boats. As Atkinson had plenty of room on his eight keelboats, he took the party and their cargo on board.

This Yellowstone Expedition of 1825, which reached and paused briefly at the mouth of the Yellowstone, was one instance where a matter of government policy was efficiently carried out. Congress had felt that something should be done to quiet the restlessness of the Indian tribes which had continued on down to the Immell and Jones affair and the Arickara fight after the War of 1812. To accomplish this end, it was decided to make a show of force and treat with the Indian tribes in the up-river country. General Atkinson and Benjamin O'Fallon, the Indian agent for this country, together with an escort of 476 soldiers, was sent up the Missouri with eight keelboats. As they had treated with the

Crows at the Mandan villages, the party did not attempt to go up the Yellowstone River.

Ashley's successful innovation brought, quite logically, a second change. The trappers, who had been somewhat restricted in their movements up to this time, now adopted the nomadic habits of the plains Indians and the area used for trapping grounds suddenly mushroomed —with Jedediah Smith and Captain Walker demonstrating that the only western limit was the Pacific Ocean. Thus the Yellowstone Basin became just one of the several parts of the whole mountain region which the trappers made their hunting grounds. The result was that for the next fifteen years the history of this important fur-producing area is no longer the story of certain companies operating within the area but of various parties traveling over the territory and leaving a maze of trails like rabbits playing around a brushpile after a fresh snow.

The trapping calendar called for an expedition in the fall before winter set in, and another in the spring after the ice went out of the streams. These were known as the fall and spring hunts. Winter was idled away in some snug refuge, and the summer was spent in a leisurely fashion going to the rendezvous, visiting friendly tribes, or— occasionally—exploring. The extent of this wandering, in the case of one trapper band in 1835, involved:

[*After leaving "Popoasia" Creek at the mouth of Wind River*] *Our course lead in a northern direction after reaching the Bighorn river, which we followed a few days and then crossed over to the Tongue river. . . . In this neighborhood, we spent the months of April, May, and part of June . . . . and were enabled to make a profitable hunt—having visited, in our toilsome occupation, the headwaters of the following rivers all of which are tributaries of the Missouri:—Tongue, Powder, Yellowstone, Little and Big Porcupine, Misscleskell, Priors, Smith's, Gallatin's, Otter, Rose-bud, Clark's, and Stinking rivers.*

This included the Yellowstone proper and nine of its tributaries.

Many of the trappers of this period were frontiersmen, or of frontier stock. Although many signed their name with an "X," some were educated and either kept journals or wrote interesting accounts of their adventures at a later date. Some joined on for adventure, some for health, and some to escape arrest. In addition to native Americans, there were French-Canadians, Spaniards, Frenchmen, Scotsmen, Irishmen, halfbreeds, Indians, Negroes, and at least one Portuguese. Typical of the curious antecedents of some were those of the traveling companion of a Jesuit priest who journeyed from the Great Bend of the Yellowstone to its mouth in 1840. Jean Baptiste de Velder was a Fleming from

Ghent and "an old grenadier of Napoleon, who had left his fatherland thirty years ago, and had passed the last fourteen in the mountains in the capacity of a beaver-hunter."

In appearance, these men sometimes resembled Indians more than white men. Part of their clothing they made themselves, and the remainder was either trade goods or of Indian manufacture. In 1838 a trapper's "equipments" usually consisted of one horse on which was placed one or two saddle blankets, a saddle and bridle, a sack containing six beaver traps, a blanket and an extra pair of moccasins, his powder horn and bullet pouch with a belt to which was attached a butcher knife, a small wooden container with bait for beaver, and a tobacco sack with pipe and flint and steel. Sometimes a hatchet was hung from the pommel of the saddle. His clothing consisted of a flannel or cotton shirt—or one of dressed skin if he was not that fortunate, a pair of leather breeches, a blanket or smoked buffalo robe, leggins, a coat made of a blanket or a buffalo skin with the hair on, a hat or fur cap, strips of blanket wrapped around his feet for stockings in the winter, and of course moccasins. His hair was usually worn long, falling loosely on his shoulders.

The favorite rifles were those made by Jake and Sam Hawken in St. Louis. A *Hawken* was a modified Kentucky rifle—the barrel being shorter, considerably heavier, and only stocked half way to the muzzle. The common caliber was .53 which took a half-ounce ball, as buffalo and Blackfeet sometimes took a lot of *killing*. Some of these were percussion lock and some were flintlock, the latter being preferred for buffalo running because the hunter never had to fumble around putting a cap on the nipple.

One striking characteristic of the trapping fraternity was their lack of thrift. One recalled that, "Scarcely one man in ten, of those employed in this country, even think of saving a single dollar of their earnings, but spend it as fast as they can see an object to spend it for. They care not what may come to pass tomorrow—but think only of enjoying the present moment." Some squandered the season's catch at the rendezvous and actually went back to work in debt for necessary supplies and equipment. As most of the men drank, they usually went on a big binge at the rendezvous—drinking, gambling, fighting, boasting, and dancing.

However, they were generally honorable in their business dealings. A trapper's word that he would pay a debt was all the security that was needed—a code which did not, however, interfere with all kinds of skulduggery at the high level of company management. Geology did not interest them and although they waded in streams which contained nuggets of gold, the only thing they sought was beaver. And while they were generous with their belongings, no *partisan* ever told anyone in a rival company where he intended to trap, and even trappers with a band did not disclose their favorite spots to their comrades.

As the men were of various nationalities, it is not strange that their speech was a curious mixture of idioms peculiar to the country and their profession. The artist George Catlin recorded one conversation he had with a free trapper at Fort Union:

"*Well* [said Catlin], *you must live a lonesome and hazardous sort of life; can you make anything by it?*"

"*Oh, oui, Monsr. putty coot, mais if it is not pour de dam rascalité Rickarree et de dam Pieds noirs, de Blackfoot Injin, I am make very much monair, mais (sacré), I am rob-rob-rob too much!*"

"*What, do the Blackfeet rob you of your furs?*"

"*Oui, Monsr. rob, suppose, five time! I am ben free trappare seven year, and am rob five time—I am something left not at all—he is take all; he is take all the horse—he is take my gun—he is take all my clothes —he is take the castors [beaver]—et I am come back with foot. So in de Fort, some cloths is cost putty much monair, et some whiskey is given sixteen dollars pour gall; so you see I am owe the Fur Comp 600 dollare, by Gar!*"

A band of trappers had some of the aspects of a military organization —but without strict discipline. The *partisan*, or leader, was sometimes one of the owners of the company and he was usually assisted by a clerk who kept simple accounts. The former directed the general movements of the company while the individual trappers supplied the detailed knowledge about good trapping spots once an area was reached. Large parties usually had one camp tender for each two trappers. These men cooked, took care of the pelts, and did other menial work.

Although the Yellowstone Basin was a favorite trapping ground, only the rendezvous of 1831 was held there. On this occasion the goods arrived late and the trappers gathered at a camp ground on the upper Powder which had been a wintering spot the previous year. This locality had an abundance of cottonwood thickets which attracted the buffalo and also provided an abundance of winter feed for the trappers' horses. Years later Joe Meek, who was barely old enough to be called a young man at the time, described this winter camp:

*Through the day, hunting parties were coming and going, men were cooking, drying meat, making moccasins, cleaning their arms, wrestling, playing games, and, in short, everything that an isolated community of* hardy men could resort to for occupation, was resorted to by these moun-taineers. Nor was there wanting, in the appearance of the camp, the variety, and that picturesque air imparted by the mingling of the native element; for what with their Indian allies, their native wives, and numer-ous children, the mountaineers' camp was a motley assemblage; and the trappers themselves, with their affection of Indian coxcombry, not the least picturesque individuals. . . .

And the night had its charm as well for,

Gathered about the shining fires, groups of men in fantastic costumes told tales of marvelous adventure, or sung some old-remembered song, or were absorbed in games of chance. Some of the better educated men, who had once known and loved books, recalled their favorite authors, and recited passages once treasured, now growing unfamiliar. . . . [Meek] learned to read by the light of the campfire. Becoming sensible . . . of the deficiencies of his early education, he found a teacher in a comrade, named Green, and soon acquired sufficient knowledge to enjoy an old copy of Shakspeare, which, with a Bible, was carried about with the property of the camp.

Another trapper recalled that he spent the winter of 1836-1837 near the mouth of Clark Fork with a party led by Jim Bridger. Here the men lived in "snug lodges of dressed Buffaloe skins." They passed the long winter evenings "entering into debates arguments or spinning long yarns until midnight . . . and I . . . derived no little benefit from . . . what we termed The Rocky Mountain College."

Ashley's success attracted others and by 1830 the competition, which had always been keen between the British and the Americans, now be-came intense. In 1828 the powerful American Fur Company established Fort Union opposite the mouth of the Yellowstone and began to send out parties. The following year, French-born Captain Benjamin Louis Eulalie de Bonneville, who had obtained a leave of absence from the Army, took a band of trappers into the mountains. All these were joined the next year by another group led by Nathaniel J. Wyeth, a New Eng-lander. Bonneville did not-make a success of the business and overstayed his furlough, but managed to pull the proper strings and get reinstated in the Army. He achieved fame of a sort as he established a trading post on the upper Powder—Antonio Matéo's "Portuguese houses"—which became a sort of landmark; and Washington Irving wrote a book about his adventures.

Wyeth was also a failure but he, too, is remembered. Thomas Fitz-patrick—one of the partners in the Rocky Mountain Fur Company after

Ashley sold out—contracted with him to bring $3,000 worth of goods to the rendezvous in 1834 and then reneged on the agreement (although he did pay the previously stipulated forfeit). The infuriated Wyeth took the goods over to the Snake River where he built and stocked Fort Hall —a permanent competitor in the territory.

The fur trade was a dog-eat-dog business during these years. Competition was carried so far that trappers were even encouraged to destroy the traps and sets of those employed by rival companies. However, there was one incident which stood out from among all the rest.

After the rendezvous on Green River in 1833, the parties of the Rocky Mountain Fur Company, Captain Bonneville, and Wyeth all crossed over into the valley of the Big Horn and headed northward. William Sublette and Robert Campbell were also along, being enroute to the mouth of the Yellowstone where they established an "opposition" post to Fort Union—with Charles Larpenteur driving two bulls and four cows, the first trail herd to enter the Yellowstone Basin. Bridger and Fitzpatrick divided the Rocky Mountain Fur Company men between them and got ready to slip away from the greenhorns and head for their favorite streams. Fitzpatrick—also known as White Head and Broken Hand— was headed for trouble.

White Head, with 50 or 60 men and several *dudes*—among them Sir William Drummond Stewart—turned eastward to the valley of the Tongue where he ran afoul of a camp of Crows. Kenneth McKenzie, the *bourgeois* of Fort Union, was doing his best to monopolize the Crow trade and to this end had established Fort Cass near the mouth of the Big Horn. This post was managed by Samuel Tullock, whom the Crows called the Crane because of his long neck. Tullock had two resident traders with the village Fitzpatrick met and one of these was none other than Jim Beckwourth. Jim and White Head were friends of a sort as they had both been members of Ashley's group of "enterprising young men."

Fitzpatrick took some presents and paid a courtesy call on the Crow chief. While he was gone some of the Crow warriors visited the trappers' camp and took the horses, numbering about one hundred, all arms and trade goods, and some beaver and traps. On their return, they met White Head whom they also robbed, taking even the capote from his back. There was nothing this *partisan* could do but to return to the Crow village and plead with his former comrade. Somehow, he managed to arrange for the return of some of the horses, traps, rifles, and a few rounds of ammunition for each man.

It was immediately obvious to Fitzpatrick that this piece of Crow deviltry was an attempt on the part of the American Fur Company to

embarrass the operations of its rival. He protested to the company officials, and also wrote a bitter letter to General Ashley, then a member of
Congress, in which he stated:

If there is not some alteration made in the system of business in this
country very soon it will become a nuisance and a disgrace to the United
States. With so many different companies roving from one tribe to another, each telling a different tale, and slandering each other to such a
degree as to disgust the Indians, they will all eventually become hostile
to the Americans.

In a letter to Tullock dated January 8, 1834, McKenzie wrote:

The 43 Beaver skins traded, marked, "R.M.F. Co.," I would in the
present instance give up if Mr. Fitzpatrick wishes to have them, on his
paying the price of the articles traded for them were worth on their
arrival in the Crow village, and the expence of bringing the beaver in
and securing it. My goods are brought in to the country to trade and
I would as willingly dispose of them to Mr. Fitzpatrick as to any one
else for beaver or beaver's worth, if I get my price. I make this proposal
as a favor, not as a matter of right, for I consider the Indians entitled
to trade any beaver in their possession to me or to any other trader.

The American Fur Company, having planned the robbery and secured the plunder, was now willing to return part of the loot if paid the
price of the goods exchanged, plus their profit in the transaction!

This feeling of triumph was to be short-lived. Wyeth had come by
Fort Union on his way to St. Louis, and McKenzie had charged him ex-
orbitant prices for a few necessities. When he passed Fort Leavenworth,
he stopped and reported that McKenzie had an illegal still in operation.
White Head's letter to Ashley was aired in Congress; and all of this,
piled on top of some high-handed dealings the previous year, was to
cause the officials of the American Fur Company some serious trouble.

In 1836 the remnant of the thrice-reorganized Rocky Mountain Fur
Company joined with the powerful American Fur Company. With this
union came, for all practical purposes, the end of the days of the roving
trapper bands; and the trading practices of the following years were
again tied to the use of permanent trading posts. Beaver hats had gone
out of style and by the mid-1830's trade in beaver skins was no longer
profitable. Coupled with this economic factor was the hard fact that the
exploitive type of trapping which had been followed had greatly reduced the beaver population. A third reason which dictated the merger
was that Ashley's successors in the Rocky Mountain Fur Company, while
able frontiersmen, had neither his business connections nor his financial

ability while the American Fur Company was powerful financially, ably administrated, and ruthlessly operated. Thus the history of the closing days of the fur trade in the Yellowstone Basin is the story of Fort Union and its satellite posts.

## THE UPPER MISSOURI OUTFIT

In the early days of the fur trade, the merchants in St. Louis tried hard to monopolize the trade of the Northwest. As a result, it was not until 1822 that the great American Fur Company established its Western Department in the western capital of the fur trade. Five years later it bought out the dominant company on the upper Mississippi and installed its officers in an organization named the Upper Missouri Outfit. To this new body was assigned all of the upper Missouri country above the Big Sioux River (in what is now the southeastern part of South Dakota). Among the personnel acquired in this merger was Kenneth McKenzie. This individual—a natural leader and a strict disciplinarian, a ruthless administrator, and an outstanding trader—was given the administration of the mountain field.

McKenzie's first step was to establish a headquarters at the strategic location formed by the junction of the Yellowstone and the Missouri. Construction was started on October 1, 1828 at a point about four miles above the actual mouth of the Yellowstone; and the post was first called Fort Floyd. The name was later changed to Fort Union. This was more than just a trading post. It was also a sort of central depot for a fort on the Missouri among the Blackfeet, and another—which was moved occasionally—on the Yellowstone to which the Crows came. And, as was befitting the importance of its central location and the rank of the personnel who administered its affairs, it was an imposing and elaborate establishment.

The fort was in the form of a quadrangle, 220 by 240 feet. The outside walls were made of squared pickets about seventeen feet high, and there were two-story, stone blockhouses on the southwest and northeast corners. Inside were the residence of the *bourgeois*, quarters for the employees, warehouses, workshops, a powder magazine, and stables for the livestock. In 1833, a visitor noted that there were "fifty or sixty horses, some mules, and an inconsiderable number of cattle, swine, goats, fowls, and domestic animals. The cattle are very fine, and the cows yield an abundance of milk." And milk was a great luxury in this wild land.

Fort Union dominated the trade in its immediate vicinity—"opposition" posts never lasted long—and the two satellite posts gathered in much of the trade of nearby Indians. In addition to these fixed facilities, traders were sent out from time to time to live and trade in the Indian camps. In this way, after the era of the rendezvous, the American Fur Company managed to dominate most of the trade in the Yellowstone valley.

On the surface, the profits in the fur business appeared to be enormous, and an inexperienced trader once estimated that $2,000 invested in eastern goods would return $15,000. One of the many interesting statements contained in the records of the Congressional investigation of 1831-1832 into the problems of the fur trade was made by the clerk of Immell and Jones. After admitting that the profits at the point of trade were 200 to 2,000 percent, William Gordon pointed out:

The real profits, however, fall far short of even the minimum stated owing to the very heavy expences which the trader has to incur in carrying on his business. . . . Not only does the trader have to supply himself the number of hands which ought to be necessary to carry on his business, but he has, in most instances, to have two or three times that number to serve as a protection to himself and property.

The business was a gamble in which the odds were often against the gambler.

In such a business, those trade goods were favored which provided the greatest margin of profit—and were most desired by the customer. Alcohol had both of these qualities, except where the Crows were concerned. Larpenteur, whom McKenzie hired after he had squeezed out Sublette and Campbell, summed up the situation in one sentence:

It must be remembered that liquor, at that early day, was the principal and most profitable article of trade, although it was strictly prohibited by law, and all the boats on the Missouri were thoroughly searched on passing Fort Leavenworth.

Even Jim Beckwourth moralized on one occasion and pointed out that a 40-gallon cask of alcohol, when diluted for the trade, would make 200 gallons in which there are "sixteen hundred pints, for each one of which the trader gets a buffalo robe worth five dollars!" And traders had devious ways of stretching these amounts even farther.

Although the government frowned on taking liquor into the Indian country, the Superintendent of Indian Affairs in St. Louis could grant permits for whiskey to be issued to boatmen on the Missouri if a bond was given that it would not be sold to Indians. Traders paid no attention to the intent of the regulation and even pack trains going overland to a rendezvous carried liquor—for their boatmen! And many ingenious schemes were used to smuggle alcohol by on the boats which had to pass inspection points on the Missouri. During the previously noted Congressional investigation, William Clark reported on this matter to the Secretary of War and recommended the "entire prohibition of the article in the Indian country, under any pretense, or for any purpose whatsoever." Congress also took a dim view of the situation and on July 9, 1832, passed a law which prohibited *taking* liquor into Indian country.

This law placed the traders at Fort Union in a desperate situation for, north of the border, their British competitors had no such restrictions, and the mobile trading outfits smuggled their supplies out by pack train. As the Upper Missouri Outfit brought all their supplies up on steamboats, it was impossible to avoid the inspectors. McKenzie's clever mind devised a solution to their dilemma—if they could not *import* alcohol, *they would make it at Fort Union*. Company officers in New York demurred, but the St. Louis officials overrode their objections and, on June 24, 1833, the steamboat *Assiniboin* delivered a still and a supply of corn to Fort Union. It was this still which McKenzie proudly showed to Wyeth a few weeks later.

The report which Wyeth turned in to the commandant at Fort Leavenworth set the wheels of the government in motion. In November the Superintendent of Indian Affairs in St. Louis wrote Pierre Chouteau, Jr. of the Western Division and asked for such explanation as he should "think proper to give." This official piously disclaimed any knowledge of what was going on, and then wrote a sharp letter to McKenzie for having placed the company "in an unpleasant situation." The trader, cut to the quick, made a lame excuse and then severed connections with the company. Such double-talk did not deceive the public, and it took all the political pressure that the company could muster to keep from losing their license to trade.

Several posts were built along the Yellowstone to serve the Crows. The first of these, Fort Cass or Tullock's Fort, was erected in 1832 by Samuel Tullock ("The Crane") near the mouth of the Big Horn. Wyeth, who saw it the next summer, noted that it was about three miles below the mouth of this river on the east bank of the Yellowstone. It was "about 130 feet square, made of sapling cottonwood pickets with two bastions at the extreme corners." Three years later it was replaced by Fort Van Buren located on the south side of the Yellowstone near the mouth of the Tongue. This post was burned in 1842 by Larpenteur, who then built Fort Alexander on Adams Prairie opposite the mouth of Armell's Creek (Armell being a garbling of Immell's name). It was used until about 1850 when Fort Sarpy was constructed on the south side of the Yellowstone about twenty-five miles below the mouth of the

Big Horn. This was the last of the posts among the Crows, and it was occupied for about nine years before it was abandoned.

Other than Wyeth's scanty notes about Fort Cass, Fort Sarpy is the only one of this series of which a description exists. Captain Raynolds, who saw it a few months before it was abandoned, noted:

We found the trading-house situated in the timber on what during high water would be an island, a channel, now dry, passing to the south of it. The "fort" is an enclosure about 100 feet square, of upright cotton-wood logs about 15 feet high, the outer wall also forming the exterior of a row of log-cabins which were occupied as dwelling houses, store-houses, shops and stables. The roofs of these structures are nearly flat, and formed of timber covered to a depth of about a foot with dirt, thus making an excellent parapet for the purposes of defense. The preparations for resistance to possible attacks being further perfected by loop-holes in the upper part of the outer row of logs. The entrance is through a heavy gate which is always carefully closed at night. No flanking arrangements whatever exist, and the "fort" is thus a decidedly primitive affair.

Although the captain stated positively that there were no blockhouses on the corners, a "bastion" in which a cannon was kept did exist in the outer wall, probably on one side of the main gate.

Life at any trading post had its moments of danger, but these posts on the Yellowstone were regarded as particularly dangerous assignments. This added element of danger grew out of the hostility which existed between the Crows and the Blackfeet. As the Blackfeet did not wish the Crows to have an opportunity to acquire weapons which would give them an advantage on the field of battle, they regarded the company employees at these posts as enemies because they provided the Absaroka with arms and ammunition. The Crows made the same objection to Fort McKenzie in the Blackfoot country. However, as the Blackfeet were more warlike than the Crows, they caused the whites more trouble in this respect: and, of course, the Sioux and Arickaras also raided.

Edwin Denig, who had a first-hand knowledge of the problems which filtered down to the *bourgeois* at Fort Union, wrote this about the Indian menace:

The banks of the Yellowstone, moreover, are infested by hordes of Blackfeet Indians and Sioux, both hostile to either Whites or natives. The well-timbered bottoms of the river and deep-cut coulees in the hills afford excellent lurking places for marauding parties ready to kill or rob whatever opportunity offers.

But all of these difficulties are of a trifling nature when compared to the situation of the traders around their own fort. Scarcely a week passes but attacks are made on those whose work obliges them to go beyond the gates of the stockade. The Sioux on one hand, and the Blackfeet on the other, constantly in search of the Crow Indians who are supposed to be near the fort, make this place the center of their operations. When the Crows are stationed in the vicinity all of the attacks fall upon them and well they retaliate. But when there are no Indians those who cut wood, guard horses, or go in quest of meat by hunting feel the murderous strokes of these ruthless warriors. Each and every year from 5 to 15 persons attached to the trading establishment have been killed, since commerce has been carried on with the Crows in their own district. . . . About six months in the year the fort was left to defend itself the best way it could with its small number of men. These were further reduced when the mackinaw boats left with the annual returns. At times those who remained could not with safety venture to the bank of the river to get water within a few steps of the gate. Whoever went forth to procure wood or meat placed their lives in extreme jeopardy. Every hunter there has been killed, and the fort often reduced to a famished condition when buffalo were in great numbers within sight. The few horses kept for hunting were always stolen, and those who guarded them shot down. . . .

After keeping up the war . . . for about 16 years neither the Crow Indians nor the traders could be brought to station themselves there for any length of time and the Yellowstone has been abandoned by both.

During the later days of Fort Sarpy when Robert Meldrum was in charge, a clerk named Chambers kept a daily journal. His entry for May 4, 1855, pictures vividly the perils of these days:

Made and press'd Beaver Bear Wolf Deer Elk Big Horn & Antelope Immediately after supper sun about one hour high Michael Stoup & a Pagan [sic-Piegan] Squaw were going down to the river the Squaw about twenty yards in advance when a party of Black Feet charged and kill'd the Squaw   three shots were fired at Michael without effect. At the same time I was lying down in my room   had a severe headache   I jumped & run but without my gun thinking it was Mr. Meldrom [sic— Meldrum] coming. Some of the men halloed Mr M's coming   As I got to the corner of the Fort three balls pass'd close by me   I run in the Fort   snatched up my gun & by the time I got out it was too late   the Woman was kill'd & scalped & the Hell Hounds off. A wet night.

However, there was a degree of uncertainty about the visits of the Blackfeet as entries made about three weeks later indicate.

Mon. 28— A party of Pagans arrived led by little dog   they say a large
party of Pagans & those inveterate dogs the Blood Indians
will be in tomorrow   Look for your top knots Boys

Tues. 29— About three hundred Pagans & Blood Indians arrived   we
closed the gates however a great many got in I suppose
about sixty

Wed. 30— things went along smoothly   traded some horses & robes
in opening the gates to let the Traders in Others would rush
in   Mr. Denig concluded to leave the small front gate open
the Little Dog's party treated us to a dance & Whilst our
attention was on the dance some few Blood Indians sliped
in to one of the house where an old Assiboin was sleeping
and cut his throat then dragged him out about forty yards
in front of the Bastion & commenced mutilating his body in
the most horrible manner. I was dispatched to take charge
of the Bastion   I had four men with me right under my
very eyes & at the muzzle of a Six pounder charged with
grape and Canister were crowded around the body of the
poor old man   they were not aware of the danger they were
in, the fuse was in my hand   one slight move from me & all
would have been over. . . . they left for home

However, it was a life of extremes—the entry for five days later read,
"A beautiful day done nothing."

When Denig was the *bourgeois* at Fort Union, he looked with disfavor on the habits which many employees acquired while stationed
among the Crows. One day, while explaining to a green clerk the principles of proper conduct for a trader, he pointed to Meldrum as a poor
example. The clerk recorded in his journal:

*Unless a white man were rich he became the sport of the savages when
he went about naked and wore long hair reaching to his shoulders, as was
the practice with some white men at Fort Alexander on the Yellowstone.
It was a mistake for a white man to adopt the life and customs of Indians, he loses their respect. Meldrum, bourgeois at the trading post
among the Crows, was an example. Though Meldrum is a soldier of
note, his scalps and his tropies from the hunt have not won him influence among the Absaroka; he is esteemed for his prodigal liberality,
on account of which he has fallen into debt instead of accumulating
money. He is said to be an efficient gunsmith but not an especially
shrewd business man.*

Various entries in Chamber's journal confirm Denig's opinion of Meldrum's prodigality; and they also present an unflattering picture of life at Fort Sarpy:

January 1855

Sun. 14— *A dull day as regards trade but lively in other respects. Gordon's camp treated us to a Scalp & Squaw dance, the roofs of the houses were covered with natives witnessing the performance. . . . On the whole it was a rather fine display & pleased Mr. Meldrom greatly. A cool Fifty came out of the pockets of P. [ierre] C. [houteau] sr. & Co, for that dance— rather costly affair.*

Mon. 22— *I find this morning that Murell [sic—Meldrum] not being satisfied with one whore house has converted the Store in to another this wont do. I must tell my Employers lock a Buck and a Bitch in the Store all night the goods all open, the Fort full of Indians the windows of the Stores hasped on the inside they can easily pass what goods they like out, this is the first offence of the kind I have known him guilty of but Mr. Lamarche says that the like is done often to his knowledge*

Tues. 23— *I find this morning that Murrell took to himself another wife last night A dirty lousy slut that was offer'd to me last fall. I enquired of her Mother what she recd for her she told me One Horse one Gun one chief's coat one N[orth] W[est] Blkt. one Indg B. Blkt two shirts one pr. leggins, six & half yards Bed ticking one hundred loads Ammunition twenty Bunches W[hite] Beads ten large Plugs Tobaco & some sugar Coffe Flour &c, Oh says the Old Crone I am rich now. I am chief for all this not one single copper is charged to his a/c. An honest man. The new Madam gave her coronation Feast it was well attended lots of Grubbers.*

Wed. 24— *The new Madam out in her finery A Scarlet dress with Six Hundred Elk Teeth. . . . Murrell's Mother in Law Wolf Skin as the Boys call her has put up a lodge in the Fort. P. C. & Co has another family to clothe & feed at their Expence Fort full of Indians filling their guts & receiving presents, a warm day*

This was not the end of Meldrum's squaw troubles. On the 9th of February, Chambers wrote:

*Mr. Meldrom left for the [Crow] camp he told me he was going for meat yes it is meat but it is squaw meat & Mag's meat at that since she has been gone he has acted more like a crazy man than one possess'd of sanity.*

Two days later the trader returned with the squaw but not long afterward as Denig was closing the big gate for the night "Princess Mag" left again. When asked if she was coming back, she replied, "No. I have had enough & got enough out of that old fool dog 'Sap-Kat a Hook. . . .' "

Such was life at Fort Sarpy in 1855—ambushes, squaw troubles, a *bourgeois* with a free hand, horses stolen by the Blackfeet and the Sioux, the stockade crammed with "squaws screaming Brats bawling" after a Blackfoot alarm, amorous couples quartered for the night in the store, couriers arriving from Fort Union stark naked after being robbed—but with the mail, and boats to be repaired for shipping the annual returns to Fort Union. Then there were other days when the clerk wrote, "A Beautifull day Very lonesome," or "Stormy day Snowed considerable done nothing."

Although no trace remains of the posts along the Yellowstone, the outlines of Fort Union are unmistakably marked in the prairie sod—a mute reminder of a way of life that has vanished. Fort Union was several things. Physically, the post was one of the largest and best constructed in the entire West. It was an important business establishment, and also the symbol of great influence and dictatorial power. To it came many important individuals connected with the fur trade and a host of characters of lesser importance whose lives were filled with colorful adventure. Because the post sat at the most important crossroads in the Northwest, it was the focal point for government surveying parties. And, as it was the only place in this vast wilderness where a visitor would be courteously entertained, comfortably housed, and well fed, the various *bourgeois* were host to a number of famous travelers. Some idea of the extent of the activities which took place here may be gathered from the fact that 600-800 buffalo were consumed each year, cartloads of meat being hauled in regularly and put on ice in the larder.

Kenneth McKenzie was not only the first *bourgeois* here, but also the most able. Born in Scotland and related to the great explorer, Alexander McKenzie, he entered the fur business as an employee of the British companies. He created an *empire* around Fort Union and ruled it like a feudal lord—until the affair of the still led to his downfall. Alexander Culbertson, who succeeded McKenzie, was born in Pennsylvania of Scotch-Irish parents. He began his career at Fort McKenzie, the post among the Blackfeet, where he married the daughter of a Blood chief.

As he was less arbitrary than his predecessor, he was more popular, and had a long and successful career as a trader.

One of the traders who followed Culbertson was Edwin T. Denig, a "small, hard-featured man," who came up the Missouri in 1833 and spent twenty-three years in the employ of the American Fur Company. Like many others he was fond of liquor although he did not regard himself "as the infernal drunkard represented"; and he had not one but two squaws. He once told a priest who reproached him for his plurality of wives that, as the older one was sickly, he felt he was entitled to an able-bodied wife but that it was not right to cast off the infirm one, as others would have done.

He was an able trader and a man of considerable ability in other fields as well. The journals of the great naturalist, John James Audubon, old records of the Smithsonian Institution, and the writings of Father Pierre-Jean De Smet, Henry R. Schoolcraft, F. V. Hayden and others bear witness to the fact that he was of assistance in gathering specimens for study, compiling native vocabularies, and collecting data about Indian customs. He kept up to date by reading newspapers and books sent up from St. Louis, and was an able conversationalist.

An unusual and intriguing figure during the early days of this post was Archibald Palmer, alias "James Archdale Hamilton," who was McKenzie's bookkeeper and chief lieutenant. He was an English nobleman who "from some cause or other" was obliged to leave home for a time. His associates remembered that he "always dressed in the latest London fashions," and took a bath and put on clean linen each day. "He wore ruffled shirt-fronts, and had a great gold chain around his neck, and was always polished, scented, and oiled to the highest degree." Visitors recalled that his mind was a storehouse of information about literature and art, and that he had a "free and easy acquaintance with the manners and men of his country." Although the employees regarded him as an eccentric character, he had a "sound old English head"—as evidenced by the fact that when some half-breeds got unruly and abusive, he told the clerk to put laudanum in their whiskey, which put them sound asleep in short order!

If there was any one item on the frontier which represented luxury, it was food—and the *first table* at Fort Union was famous in this respect. One clerk, who had just spent the winter living on jerked buffalo meat, tallow, and corn soaked in lye water to remove the hull, was amazed

on entering the eating hall, . . . [to find] a splendidly set table with a white tablecloth, and two waiters, one a negro. Mr. McKenzie was setting at the head of the table, extremely well dressed. [No one was al-

lowed to come to this table without a coat on.] The victuals consisted
of fine fat buffalo meat, with plenty of good fresh butter, cream, and
milk for those that chose; but . . . only two biscuits were allowed to
each one. . . .

Seventeen years later another newly arrived clerk was also overwhelmed—"There was chocolate, milk, butter, omlet, fresh meat, hot
bread—what a magnificent spread!" However, the fare for the common
laborers was predominantly buffalo meat.

Normally, there were two drinking sprees each year. One took place
after the annual steamboat had been loaded with the year's returns, and
had left for St. Louis. The other occurred at Christmas and might last
several days. Brawls were common and on one occasion the tailor and
carpenter had a fight in the store, during which a hunter was fatally
stabbed and thrown into the fireplace where he was discovered almost
dead. The two were tried and a jury sentenced them to be hanged. However, the judge did not think it safe to have this sentence executed so he
changed it to thirty-nine lashes.

Among the many interesting happenings was an incident which involved McKenzie and a free trapper named Augustin Bourbonnais.
Bourbonnais, with $500 worth of beaver, drifted into Fort Union to
spend the winter. Being young, very handsome, and possessed of a beautiful head of yellow hair, the trapper soon became popular with the opposite sex. One who fell under his charm was the "pretty young bed-
fellow" whom McKenzie had recently acquired. The trader "armed
himself with a good-sized cudgel," and, "hearing some noises he thought
he ought not to have heard," rushed into his quarters and ran the lover
out of the post. This affront to his dignity was too much for the Frenchman and he was next seen outside the fort with his rifle and pistol
threatening to kill McKenzie. As Bourbonnais persisted in watching the
gate for several days, the bourgeois counseled with his clerks and it was
decided to shoot the man. However, the mulatto detailed for the job
only wounded him in the shoulder: and the trapper, after being nursed
until the following spring, left and was never heard of afterward.

Thus the years passed at Fort Union, and with each passing year came
a slow but steady change in the nature of the trade. Beaver skins declined
in importance during the 1830's, and buffalo robes and other pelts
came to dominate the shipments that went down the Missouri each
spring. The heyday of the mountain trapper was over, and on September 15, 1851, a clerk at the post wrote in his journal that "since
beaver pelts have fallen in price, that far-famed class of trappers is
almost non-existant."

Business slowly dwindled and in 1864 Pierre Chouteau and Company, successors of the American Fur Company, sold out to Hubbell, Hawley and Company. The following year a representative of the company engaged Captain Grant Marsh to move the stock of goods to Fort Benton: and when the *Luella* backed away from the landing with the movable property on board, she closed the pages on the history of the fur trade days. In the summer of 1867, Colonel W. G. Rankin, commanding officer of the new Army post being constructed opposite the mouth of the Yellowstone, contracted for the old fort. Soldiers tore it down and incorporated the material into the new Fort Buford. Thus passed the last evidence of an empire based on fur. All that remains are the stories which dead men once set down.

## PESTILENCE

"Turn it as we may," moralized an Army doctor who knew the frontier, "three things, which have done the most to make the Indian what he is today, are not the state, the church, and the army—they are *alcohol*, *syphilis*, and *smallpox*." Syphilis was an insidious thing, alcohol has always demoralized, but smallpox killed at a catastrophic rate among the Indians of the Northwest.

Smallpox came up the Missouri in the spring of 1837 on the steamboat *St. Peter's*. When the boat stopped at Fort Clark, the Mandans insisted that their goods be put ashore; and they stole a blanket from a sick man. In a very short time this tribe had been reduced from a total of about 1,600 ("600 warriors") to a pitiful "13 young and 19 old men." Thus the epidemic of 1837-1838 began.

At Fort Union the situation was ghastly for a time. Many of the squaws at the post died, and Indians who came to trade contracted the disease. The traders, mindful of the danger of losing their best customers, tried to warn the visitors away but it was no use as "the Indians would say laughingly that they expected to die soon, and wanted to have a frolic until the end came."

What happened in the Yellowstone valley is shrouded with uncertainty. One trader reported that, "At the Crow post the disease was raging but there were no Indians near"; and it is thought that the Crows may have been in the Wind River country and escaped, at least for the time being. Curiously, although there are accounts of smallpox among the Crows, these outbreaks occurred at times other than the year of 1837.

The first report of this plague among the Absaroka was made by Larocque who quoted the Crows as saying that they had the disease about 1802. They also told him that they originally counted 2,000 lodges as compared to the 300 at the time of his journey with them. Denig, writing about 1856, describes an epidemic which occurred in 1833. According to this account, a party of warriors contracted the disease when they traded with a wagon train down on the Arkansas River, and these carried it back to the main camp.

As soon as possible after the arrival of the warriors the camp broke up into small bands each taking different directions. They scattered through the mountains in the hope of running away from the pestilence. All order was lost. No one pretended to lead or advise. The sick and the dead alike were left for the wolves and each family tried to save itself.

They certainly gained something by this course. At least the infection was not quite so fatal as among stationary tribes. For the rest of the fall and winter the disease continued its ravages but in the ensuing spring it had ceased. Runners were sent through their country from camp to camp and the reminant of the nation was once more assembled near the head of the Big Horn River. Terrible was the mourning on this occasion. More than a thousand fingers are said to have been cut off by relatives of the dead. Out of the 800 lodges counted the previous summer but 360 remained, even these but thinly peopled.

There is an Absaroka legend which may relate to this outbreak. According to this, a village was camped along the Yellowstone at the foot of what is now called Suicide Cliff (on the edge of the city of Billings). This is the story as Old Coyote related it to one of his grandsons:

There were two brothers. Two war parties went out from the camp at the same time. The two brothers went with one party. While the war parties were gone the people had an epidemic of smallpox. Most of the people died. The two brothers came back; their party had almost been wiped out and they were the sole survivors.

When the brothers came back they saw the dead on scaffolds. The brothers were courting two sisters. They saw many scaffolds on a hill and climbed up there. One brother said to the other, "Take a look at these dead people. What if they should turn out to be the girls we were courting?" They recognized the sisters on the scaffolds.

Their oldest brother was one of the chiefs. He was dead in the camp. There was no one to take care of the people any more. They dug into their parfleches. Took out their best clothes and put them on. One brother had a grey horse. This was his best horse. They got on this horse —rode double. Rode through the camp and sung songs just like when there was no sickness—some lodge songs, and lastly their brother's songs.

*After this ride they went up on the cliff and rode along the rim-rock singing their own songs. Then they blindfolded the horse and turned toward the edge of the cliff singing the Crazy Dog Lodge song. They were still singing when the horse went off the cliff.*

The second war party went over to the Missouri where they tried to steal horses from a Sioux camp. Unfortunately they were discovered and all killed except one man. After a series of adventures—a fast horse shot out from under him by the Sioux, *treed* on some large rocks by a *mad bull* (an old buffalo bull which has been run out of the herd), chased by a grizzly bear, and almost drowned while crossing the Yellowstone where he lost all his weapons—this warrior finally

crossed to the west side [of the Yellowstone] and came out near the camp. Here he noticed some scaffolds. Saw some personal belongings hanging on the scaffolds—recognized the dead by these things. Decided something was wrong because there were so many scaffolds. Came on to the camp. Noticed no smoke was coming from the tepees and went to one tepee that had smoke. One old woman who was about dead was in it —could not learn much. She told him that the survivors had left camp. He asked what he could do for her. She said, "My son, something terrible has happened to the people. Leave now and save yourself. I am beyond help now. Better leave before you get this terrible sickness."

He went through the camp and got good weapons. Dug into the bags and got the clothes he needed and went to the edge of the camp and got a horse. Went up the valley and picked up the trail of the survivors.

About two nights later he heard the voice of a young girl. Called to her, "My sister, my oldest sister where are you?" He found the young girl by a spring. Got off his horse and talked to her. Her eyesight was gone. Her sister had taken her to the spring and left her. He gave her some water. Girl started coughing—almost strangled—and then died. He felt bad when he came to camp—especially when he saw the young girl die. Became emotional and broke down and cried his heart out. He dragged the girl to a place where the wild animals could not get her. Then he followed the survivors again. Caught up with them by Grey Cliffs. Figured that the survivors were going toward the Great Bend of the Yellowstone.

About sundown he rode over a hill into camp. Saw a man going for horses—they recognized each other. This man rode up. He said, "Am I dreaming or is it your ghost? Your war party was gone a long time. We thought you were wiped out. Tell me about it." He told him, "The rest of the party was wiped out. I am the sole survivor. I have come home to nothing. Are any of my relatives alive?"

The other said, "A terrible thing has happened to us. This little camp is all that is left of our people. All your people are dead. We need a good man in camp. I am getting old. I have assumed leadership of what is left of our people. You are a good man. We need someone like you. See the tepee down on the end—the lowest one as the creek flows. There is a good woman there. She has lost everyone in her family. She is a good woman and some great power has spared her. She has all her things yet and a lot of horses. She has been taking care of the old ones and orphans although we have been pressed for food. She has rustled around and fed the poor ones. Before you do anything else, I command you to go to her camp. With her horses and your ability, we might survive. I know, as well as the remaining members of the people, you will be a great help to us. I will talk to her and she will understand."

He took the man to the woman's camp. They rode up. Called the woman out and the other man repeated what he had told the man. She agreed to all and said she would be at the disposal of her new-found husband. She will continue to help her people with her new husband. That is how they were married.

He was their leader from then on. He led them to where there would be plenty of food. Always looked out for the benefit of his people. It is said that all old people, even children had great respect for this man. From these people the story is passed on.

A legend, a story based on fact, a true account—*quien sabe?* It has been told among the Crows for several generations, and it describes the manner in which Denig has stated the remnants of the villages did survive.

# 5

## Early Travelers and Dudes

»»»»»»»«««««««« On the 16th of June, 1832, the steamboat *Yellow Stone* nosed up to the landing near the main gate of Fort Union. This was a momentous occasion for she was the first of her kind to stem the coffee-colored waters of the upper Missouri. Waiting for her on the bank were Kenneth McKenzie, his right-hand man "James Archdale Hamilton," and all the clerks, carpenters, hunters, and ordinary laborers—not to mention their dark-skinned women and half-breed offspring clustered in the background. On board was no less a personage than Monsieur Pierre Chouteau himself, head of the Western Department of the American Fur Company.

Among those who disembarked was a passenger who, strangely enough, was not concerned about the profits in beaver skins and buffalo robes. He was interested in Indians—Indians of all descriptions. In this respect he was an unusual man, and he expressed the purpose of his life in this stilted but sincere statement:

*In addition to the knowledge of human nature and of my art, which
I hope to acquire by this toilsome and expensive undertaking, I have
another in view, which, if it should not be of equal service to me, will
be of no less interest and value to posterity. I have, for many years past,
contemplated the noble races of red men, who are now spread over
these trackless forests and boundless prairies, melting away at the approach of civilization. . . . I have flown to their rescue—not of their
lives or of their race . . . , but to the rescue of their looks and their
modes . . . phoenix-like, they may rise from the "stain on a painter's
palette," and live again upon canvas, and stand forth for centuries yet to
come, the living monuments of a noble race. For this purpose, I have
designed to visit every tribe of Indians on the Continent. . . .*

This dedicated man was a sober-faced individual, thirty-six years old,
slightly above average height, and well proportioned with a tendency
toward slenderness. He had been a lawyer in Pennsylvania until he
taught himself to paint miniatures and changed from the legal profession to the field of art. Now, in the prime of life, he had aspirations to
become a collector, artist, anthropologist, historian, and author all combined in one. Letters to the *Commercial Advertiser* in New York also
stamp him as a reporter, and in future years he was to become a pro-
moter and a showman. His name was George Catlin.

McKenzie was a gracious host. He made the artist welcome at the first
table and the latter was duly appreciative of the food:

*. . . his table groans under the luxuries of the country; with buffalo
meat and tongues, with beaver's tails and marrow fat; but sans coffee,
sans bread and butter . . . and with good wine also; for a bottle of
Maderia and one of excellent Port are set in a pail of ice every day, and
exhausted at dinner.*

After the evening meal McKenzie, "Hamilton," and Catlin lingered at
the table cracking jokes, telling stories, and discussing art and literature
over their glasses of wine.

The studio space which the *bourgeois* assigned to Catlin was rather
curious but quite satisfactory. Catlin wrote that there were Crows,
Blackfeet, Chippeway, Assiniboines, and Crees camped nearby and,

*Amongst and in the midst of them am I, with my paint pots and canvas,
snugly enconced in one of the bastions of the Fort, which I occupy as
a painting room. My easel stands before me, and the cool breech of a
twelve-pounder makes me a comfortable seat, whilst her muzzle is looking out at one of the port-holes.*

Although he painted scenes in the nearby camps, most of the portraits were done in this "painting room." The chiefs took over the policing of the area and placed guards at the door who allowed only men of recognized standing to enter. Warriors of hostile tribes lounged around the walls of the room amicably recounting the details of their battles and exhibiting scalp locks as proof that they spoke the truth. Catlin, aware of the explosive nature of the situation, was amazed at the apparent absence of warlike attitudes. However, these feelings were not buried very deeply. As some Crees were leaving the post, giving *everyone* a hearty farewell, one brave lingered behind. Sticking his gun through a crack between two pickets in the wall, he shot a Blackfoot chief who was talking to McKenzie. From his vantage point in the bastion, the artist watched the ensuing skirmish on the nearby plain and, later, observed the medicine man perform his ceremonies over the mortally wounded leader.

Buffalo hunting fascinated Catlin, and he frequently went with the Indian hunters to watch them *run* these animals. Like all the visitors who followed him, he also went with the hunting parties from the fort. The favorite hunting ground at this time—and for years to come—was the broad valley of the Yellowstone just above its mouth where both Larocque and Clark had observed great numbers of buffalo. Catlin described one hunt, and this description is interesting, not because it was unusual, but because it is typical of those which other visitors described later. Like all such hunts, the men went "for meat" and not for sport.

On this particular occasion, a lookout on the bluffs across the Missouri signalled that there were "cattle a plenty" on the prairie along the Yellowstone. McKenzie picked a small party to accompany him to make the kill, and detailed several men to follow with one-horse carts to butcher and bring back the meat. The entire party was then put across the Missouri in a "scow" and the hunters galloped off leaving the wagons to follow. When the hunters had approached to within about a mile of the herd, they stopped to make the final preparations. First, they "tossed a feather" to determine the direction of the wind. Then each hunter quickly stripped both himself and his horse of every unnecessary article, tied a handkerchief about his head to keep the hair out of his eyes, and checked his gun. When all were ready, they mounted their impatient steeds and approached the herd in line-abreast until the buffalo took fright and ran. Then it was every man for himself.

Instead of selecting a fat cow, Catlin picked a big bull and managed to break its shoulder. As he pulled his horse up to sketch his animal, another wounded bull turned on a nearby hunter and lifted the horse with his head while "poor Chardon . . . made a frog's leap of some twenty feet or more over the bull's back, and almost under my horse's heels." Both horse and rider were severely shaken but not seriously hurt, and the artist soon proceeded with his sketches.

Presently the other hunters came back on their blowing horses to have a hearty laugh at the novice for picking an old bull whose meat was too tough to save. McKenzie had dropped five cows with five shots within a mile, and Catlin noted that this was something of a feat. It may have been, but years later Owen McKenzie, the *bourgeois'* half-breed son, held the record for being able to load and fire *fourteen* times during the distance of a mile while running buffalo, an accomplishment which called for superb horsemanship and precise handling of a rifle.

The men now rode slowly back to the ferry while some related stories of the hunting prowess of their employer. On their return to the fort, a couple of bottles of wine were set out to dampen a "half dozen parched throats," after which most of the men retired to their quarters. However, Catlin lingered a little longer

when . . . *the gate of the fort was thrown open, and the procession of carts and packhorses laden with buffalo meat made its entreé; gladening the hearts of a hundred women and children, and tickling the noses of many hungry dogs and puppies, who were stealing in and smelling at the tail of the procession. The door of the ice-house was thrown open, the meat discharged into it, and I being fatigued went to sleep.*

In addition to his painting, Catlin set down considerable information about the clothing, religion, customs, and dances of the various tribes. This material contains some errors, one of which borders on the amusing. Quoting "two gentlemen of the highest respectability," he blandly stated that the Crows "are one of the most honourable, honest, and highest minded races of people on earth," and that a "man of the strictest veracity" told him that "they never steal[!]" Someone must have cracked a joke and he failed to catch the point.

The artist probably left Fort Union late in July. McKenzie supplied him with a canoe of green timber and he pushed off with an old hunter and a free trapper. Leaving the paintings to be sent down with the next shipment of fur, he took with him only some packs of Indian articles, a few meagre supplies, and "my canvas and easel."

Twenty years afterward, Catlin was still remembered on the Upper Missouri. Frederick Kurz, a Swiss artist who was also a visitor at Fort Union, was highly critical of Catlin's drawings and writings. He noted:

[Catlin] is regarded here as a humbug. . . . I heard Mr. Kipp complain of Catlin. . . . With the exception of several instances where the author talks big, the book [North American Indians] contains a great deal that is true. The drawings, on the other hand, are for the most part in bad taste, and to a high degree inexact, especially the buffaloes. Indians never go on the hunt arrayed as if for war. That scene where the wolves surround the dying bull is silly make-believe; that one of the Indian vaulting on a single bull is another. . . . His buffalo herds consist of nothing but bulls—no cows and calves. . . . What astonishes one in Catlin's sketches . . . is that the faces are grotesque. . . .

On the 3rd of July, while Catlin was busy at Fort Union, the "Baron of Brausenburg" and two traveling companions landed in Boston. A year later, the "Baron" was at Fort Union, the second famous traveler to visit the post within a year. The German was, of course, not the Baron of Brausenburg but Alexander Philip Maximilian, Prince of Wied-Neuwied, the ruler of a small sovereignty along the Rhine. His traveling companions were Carl Bodmer, a Swiss artist who had studied in Paris, and Dreidoppel, the jäger or huntsman from his estate.

Although the prince had been a major general in the German army during the Napoleonic campaigns, he was a scientist at heart. He had spent two years in the jungles of South America and his *Reise nach Brasilien in den Jahren 1815 bis 1817* had established him as a scientist worthy of respect. He was now ready to turn his attention to the Indians and wild life on the plains of the Northwest.

In the spring of 1833, Maximilian met Captain William Drummond Stewart, an English *dude*, in St. Louis. Stewart had made plans to accompany a pack train to the annual trappers' rendezvous and urged the German to accompany them. However, General Clark recommended that he go up the Missouri on a steamboat of the American Fur Company. So the prince and his two men embarked with McKenzie on the *Yellow Stone* for the posts on the upper Missouri.

Maximilian's first visit at Fort Union lasted only two weeks—while the *Assiniboin* (on which they had traveled above Fort Pierre) was unloaded and the yearly shipment of furs loaded for the return trip, and while a consignment of trade goods was made up for the keelboat which was to continue on up to Fort McKenzie. However, the prince, with true German efficiency, packed much observation into this short period.

Two chapters in his monumental *Travels in the Interior of North America, in the Years 1832, 1833, and 1834* pertain to this period. These indicate clearly the extent of his interest, the preciseness of his observations, the breadth of his knowledge, and his ability to organize and record what he saw. Comments about the surrounding countryside show that little, if anything, of note escaped his eyes:

The neighbourhood around Fort Union is . . . a wide, extended prairie, intersected, in a northerly direction, by a chain of rather high, round, clay-slate, and sand-stone hills. . . . We observed on the highest points, and at certain intervals of this mountain chain, singular stone signals, set up by the Assiniboins, of blocks of granite, or other large stones, on top of which is placed a buffalo skull, which we were told the Indians place there to attract the herds of buffaloes, and thereby to insure a successful hunt. The strata of sand-stone occurring in the above mentioned hills are filled, at least in part, with the impressions of the leaves of phanerogamic plants, resembling the species still growing in the country. A whitish-grey and reddish-yellow sand-stone are found here. . . . The hills were partly bare, and very few flowers were in blossom; the whole country was covered with short, dry grass, among which were numerous round spots with tufts of Cactus ferox, which was only partly in flower. Another cactus, resembling mammillaris, with dark red flowers, yellow on the inner side, was likewise abundant. Of the first kind it seems that two exactly similar varieties, probably species, are found everywhere here; both have fine, large, bright yellow flowers . . . but in one species, the staminae are bright yellow, like the flower itself, and, in the other, of a brownish blood red, with yellow anthers. . . .

. . . Between the hills, there are, sometimes, in the ravines, little thickets of oak, ash, negundo maple, elm, bird-berry, and some others, in which many kinds of birds, particularly the starling, black-bird, &c., build their nests. The king bird and the red thrush are likewise found. Of mammalia, besides those in the river, namely, the beaver, the otter, and the muskrat, there are, about Fort Union, in the prairie, great numbers of the pretty little squirrel, the skin of which is marked with long stripes, and regular spots between them (Spermophilus Hoodii, Sab.), which have been presented by Richardson and Cuvier. . . . From its figure and agility, it is a true squirrel, and, therefore, rather different from the true marmot arctomys. . . . Besides these, there are several kinds of mice, particularly Mus leucopus. The flat hills of the goffer [sic—gopher] are likewise seen; this is a kind of large sand rat, living underground, of which I did not obtain a specimen.

And the fur trade and the personnel engaged in it were subjected to as searching observation and analysis as were the flowers of the cactus and the burrows of the ground squirrel.

While Maximilian collected notes, Bodmer sketched and painted and, while his work was not as voluminous as that of Catlin, it more than made up in quality what it lacked in quantity. Bodmer's painting, like the writing of his employer, was done with painstaking exactness although his work had a few minor faults. His Indian ponies tend to look like Arabian steeds, and some of his Indian figures appear to be too short and squat, a fault which is thought to have come from using Indian costumes on German models to complete some of his pictures after returning to Europe.

On the 6th of July the keelboat was at last loaded and the visitors began their journey on up the Missouri for Fort McKenzie. With the boat was Alexander Culbertson, then a young clerk, and later he wrote this description of the prince and his two men:

*The Prince was at the time nearly seventy [fifty-five] years of age, but well preserved, and able to endure considerable fatigue. He was a man of medium height, rather slender, sans teeth, passionately fond of his pipe, and speaking very broken English. His favorite dress was a white slouch hat, a black velvet coat, rather rusty from long service, and probably the greasiest pair of trousers that ever encased princely legs. . . . He was accompanied by an artist named Boadman [sic] and a servant whose name was . . . Tritripel [sic], both of whom seemed gifted to a high degree with the facility of putting their princely employer into a frequent passion. . . .*

By October the party was back at Fort Union, collecting additional notes and packing their collections to be sent down the Missouri on the steamboat the following spring. On the 30th of this month, with two young grizzly bears and a fox in cages and with several boxes of odds and ends, the visitors embarked in a mackinaw boat, with five boatmen, for the Mandan villages. Although Maximilian had a most successful trip, the bulky items which he had collected were loaded on the ill-fated *Assiniboin* the next spring, and she was destroyed by fire before she reached St. Louis. On his return to Germany, Maximilian wrote his *Reise in das innere Nord-America* and arranged the magnificent atlas which accompanied it—one of the most valuable items ever compiled about the Northwest.

While Maximilian was on the upper Missouri, the annual trappers' rendezvous was held in the valley of Green River. It will be recalled that when this gathering broke up, large parties crossed the Continental Divide into the Big Horn Valley and headed northward. Traveling with that part of the Rocky Mountain Fur Company which was under the leadership of Thomas Fitzpatrick, were three *dudes*. One of these was a

Mr. Brotherton, of whom nothing of interest is known. Another was Dr. Benjamin Harrison, son of General William Henry Harrison of Indian war fame. He was a man of "wild and adventurous disposition" who had been sent on the trip "with the view to breaking him from drinking whiskey"—obviously a very poor place.

The third tourist was Captain William George Drummond Stewart, the British officer whom Maximilian had met in St. Louis. He was a man of above average height, well proportioned, and with the bearing which might be expected of a man of aristocratic parentage who had served in the British Army. His nose was prominent, thin and beaked, his hair was black, and pictures indicate he wore a mustache. An Oregon-bound missionary observed that his nose had a "rum blossom" caused by too much New Orleans brandy and that "his general conversation and appearance was that of a man with strong prejudices and equally strong appetites, which he had frequently indulged, with only pecuniary restraint." However, the trappers did not object to his profanity and other habits, and they apparently accepted him as one of the fraternity.

He had been a soldier at the age of seventeen, was a lieutenant with the Fifteenth (the King's) Hussars at the Battle of Waterloo, and had been mustered out in 1821, a captain on half pay. Then, until he came to America at the age of thirty-seven, he had lived at Murthly Castle near Perthshire, Scotland. Apparently, he had tired of being the second son in a noble family and had come to America to hunt and amuse himself; however, it is not beyond the realm of possibility that he had connections with the British Secret Service.

Stewart and his companions were with Fitzpatrick when he ran afoul of the Crow camp on the Tongue. On this occasion the *partisan* left Stewart in charge of the camp when he went to visit the Absaroka chief. What happened is not known, but probably the Indians infiltrated the camp with professions of friendship. Then, shrewdly guessing that the captain was a greenhorn, they took over and stripped it bare.

Jim Beckwourth and his biographer set down a highly colored and rather improbable account of this whole episode which—apparently—was an attempt to clear the mulatto of master-minding the theft. Curiously, part of this story pertains to Stewart who—according to Jim—"insulted me in the grossest manner" and accused him "of complicity with the Indians, or, rather, of having instigated the fiendish plot." With obvious relish, the trader told how he humbled the Englishman:

*After the goods were secured and the horses brought up, it was discovered that Captain Stuart's horse, a fine iron-grey, was missing. It was* traced to the possession of High Bull, a very bad Indian. . . . Stuart valued his horse highly, as well he might, for he was a noble animal: he was, therefore, very anxious to obtain him. Fitzpatrick had acquainted Stuart that I was the only person in the nation that could procure the horse's restitution.

Accordingly, he visited me, and said, "Mr. Beckwourth" (he mistered me that time), "can you get my horse for me?"

I replied, "Captain Stuart, I am a poor man in the service of the American Fur Company. . . . The Indian who has your horse is my best customer; he has a great many relatives, and a host of friends, whose trade I shall surely lose if I attempt to take the horse from him."

However, Jim managed to restore the horse: and if Stewart had further strenuous adventures, they were never recorded.

Stewart made another trip to the rendezvous in 1837, taking with him Alfred Jacob Miller, a young artist whose work has only recently been properly appreciated. Later, the captain took him to Scotland where he painted several pictures for Murthly Castle. One of these was an enormous painting which depicted Stewart standing bravely at the head of Fitzpatrick's men, surrounded by Crow warriors who were doing their best to provoke a fight. After his elder brother died, Sir William became the seventh Baron of Grandtully and came into an estate. He returned to America and made another visit to the rendezvous in 1843. This one was long remembered by the trappers for his wagon train carried a fabulous selection of delicacies, and he had with him some seventy guests.

For seven years after Sir William Stewart and his companions left the Yellowstone country, there were no visitors of note. Then on August 29, 1840, a strange party topped the divide between the valley of the Gallatin and the Great Bend. In the lead rode a sturdy, thirty-nine-year-old man in the vestments of a Jesuit priest. Beside him was a trapper who had been a grenadier in the army of Napoleon, and scattered about them were ten Flathead warriors who were acting as an escort for this unusual pair. Both white men were natives of Belgium, and no doubt the soldier-trapper, Jean-Baptiste de Velder, would have died unknown to history had not the priest recruited him at the trappers' rendezvous a few weeks before. The man in the black cassock was Father Pierre-Jean De Smet, then on his first trip to the Northwest. During the next three decades he became known far and wide as "Black Robe" and no other soldier of the Cross was more beloved by all who knew him.

De Smet was a tactful, able man. He was also the congenial sort who could propound the gospel or tell a funny story. And he had abundant courage, but it was not of the gloomy martyrdom-seeking sort which has distinguished many of his profession. This was the sort of man who, with but a single white companion, rode into the savage frontier along the Yellowstone in the late summer of 1840. He was on his way to St. Louis to solicit funds for a mission among the Flatheads; and he was to record his experiences and observations on this and other journeys in voluminous letters which are equalled in human interest only by the meticulous observations of Prince Maximilian.

It was probably the Methodist, Jedediah Smith, who started the religious movement in the Northwest. In 1831 four Indians, either Flatheads or Nez Percé, came to St. Louis in search of Christian missionaries, and this resulted in Whitman and Spalding going to Oregon. In 1835, the Flathead chief, Insula, and his two sons journeyed to St. Louis to request "Black-robes"; and two years later a third deputation of five warriors were killed by the Sioux while enroute with a similar request. In 1839, two more Indians went down the Yellowstone and Missouri in a canoe with a group of trappers to make a similar request. When they stopped at St. Joseph Mission at Council Bluffs (just above the present city of Omaha), they met Father De Smet; and he wrote a letter for them to carry to Bishop Rosati in St. Louis. In the end, De Smet was given this assignment in the mountains. One Indian returned to the tribe with the news, and the other went with the priest the following year to the rendezvous where he met a delegation from the Flathead tribe. De Smet, de Velder, and the Indians then drifted northward and the latter were hunting buffalo in the Three Forks country when De Smet left the tribe to go to St. Louis to ask for assistance to establish a mission among these Indians.

After traveling down the Yellowstone for several days, this little party came to a Crow camp which received them cordially. One afternoon the priest was invited to twenty banquets—fortunately he had the foresight to take several "eaters" with him to empty his dishes and thus avoided offending his hosts. At the mouth of the Big Horn, this village was joined by another and more time was spent in feasting. Then the little party pushed on to Fort Alexander above the mouth of the Rosebud, which De Smet referred to as "The Fort of the Crows."

The traders received the travelers with "a great deal of benevolence and friendliness," and undoubtedly enjoyed this unexpected visit. But it must have been a strange sight for these rough men to watch the Flatheads. De Smet noted:

*At this place the Flatheads edified all hands by their piety. . . . we never failed to assemble in the morning and evening to say prayers in common, and to sing some canticles to the praise of God.*

At this point the priest sent the Indian escort back, and he and the old trapper faced the dangers before them—alone. In the nights which followed, the trapper snored "like a steam engine in full swing" while his companion rolled and turned and often spent hours without sleep. There were good reasons for the priest to be apprehensive. He observed later that although the howling of wolves and the roar of a grizzly bear were capable of

*freezing one with terror, this fear is nothing in comparison with that which the fresh tracks of men and horses can arouse in the soul of the traveler, or the columns of smoke that he sees rising around him.*

Below Fort Alexander the travelers were subjected to one alarm after another. On the morning of the second day out, De Smet awoke early to observe a large smoke only a quarter of a mile away. This sent them scurrying "at full gallop." At noon the next day they discovered a buffalo which had been killed but a couple of hours before; and in the morning of the following day they came to an abandoned campsite of a village of forty lodges—where the campfires were still smouldering. Small wonder that the veterans at Fort Union "could not get over their astonishment at the dangerous journey which we had concluded so fortunately." It was a relief to relax behind the sturdy walls of the post but,

*After having regenerated sundry half-breed children in the holy water of baptism, I left the fort on the 23rd of September.*

The next year De Smet returned with Father Nicholas Point and three lay brothers to found St. Mary's Mission in the Bitter Root valley. Father Point not only ministered to the Flatheads but at one time tried to reform the people at Fort Union. One clerk noted in his journal:

*Earlier there lived here for a time a Jesuit, Pére Point, who tried to inculcate strict morality. They let him preach without any opposition until he began to reproach Mr. Denig with a plurality of wives.*

Naturally, the *bourgeois* did not take kindly to such criticism.

The early fall of 1842 found De Smet again journeying down the valley of the Yellowstone enroute to St. Louis. He had left Father Point and the Flatheads camped along the Madison River, and an escort of ten warriors accompanied him as far as a large Crow camp in the upper part of the valley. This time the Crows recognized him when he was some distance away, and the village cryer announced his approach. Immediately the entire camp swarmed out of their lodges to welcome him. Although the Absaroka had been hospitable two years before, this time they entertained their guest like a respected friend. The principal men soon gathered in the lodge of the chief who acted as host, and the social pipe "went round that evening so frequently that it was scarcely ever extinguished."

This time the interest of the Crows centered on the priest's *medicine*, and particularly the aspect of prayer. De Smet had no difficulty in arranging for a service which was probably the first Christian worship held among these Indians. He erected three U.S. flags in the center of the camp and the village assembled before them. The priest and the ten Flatheads then knelt beneath the flags. The service was opened by intoning two canticles, then prayers were recited and explained, and the group sang two more canticles. At the end, the Apostles' Creed and the Ten Commandments were explained. Then the Crows asked De Smet to rid the camp of sickness and supply them with plenty. These things De Smet, of course, declined to attempt but he did promise them a "Black-gown" provided the chiefs would put an end to the thievish practices and oppose "vigorously" the corrupt morals of the tribe.

Again the escort was sent back, and De Smet continued on with "the Iroquois Ignatius, a Cree half-breed named Gabriel, and . . . two brave Americans, who, although Protestants, wished to serve as guides to a Catholic missionary." One of the Americans had spent eleven years in the service of the fur company and as they went along he continually pointed out places where battles had taken place—which made "our blood run cold." At one place it was not necessary for De Smet to use his imagination for on the ground lay the remains of ten Assiniboines which had been killed by some war party, their bones almost picked clean by the coyotes and birds. However, fifteen days after leaving the Crow village the little party reached Fort Union safely, having subsisted entirely on meat during this time.

This traveler made three other trips into the Yellowstone country. In 1846 he joined a mixed camp of Flatheads, Nez Percé, and Blackfeet shortly after they had beaten off a strong attack by the Crows. After this fight the mixed village went northward to Fort Benton on the Missouri, and the priest went down the Missouri to St. Louis from this point. The two other trips were made, not as a missionary, but to assist government officials in negotiating treaties with the Indians. These efforts, one in

1851 and the other in 1868, are a part of the story of increasing tensions which finally resulted in the Sioux War of 1876.

As De Smet was braving the dangers of the Yellowstone valley for a second time, John James Audubon was making plans for a trip to the western plains. The famous naturalist was at work on his second monumental work, *Quadrupeds of North America*, and this time he planned to do part of the collecting at the head of a small party. A noteworthy associate in this venture was a quiet, sedate, intelligent gentleman-farmer from Moorestown, New Jersey. Edward Harris and Audubon had met almost twenty years before when the latter was soliciting orders for his *Birds of America*, and they had one strong common interest—Harris was an amateur ornithologist.

There were three others in the party—John G. Bell, a taxidermist, Isaac Sprague, an artist, and Lewis M. Squires, a sort of general handy man. Perhaps Brag should also be listed: he was a pointer of which his master, Harris, was very fond. Brag was to make the trip safely only to die shortly after returning to the settlements.

Plans for the trip were worked out very carefully. Audubon, then fifty-eight years old but still vigorous and enthusiastic, had corresponded with Sir William Drummond Stewart—who headed a very elaborate expedition to the Green River rendezvous in 1843—and explored the possibilities of a trip overland to the Rocky Mountains. However, in the end, he declined Stewart's offer of a wagon and five mules in favor of a free passage to Fort Union on the *Omega* of the American Fur Company.

The *Omega* set the party ashore late in the afternoon of the 12th of June, 1843. Her time up the river had been 17 hours under seven weeks which was faster, by fifteen days, than any boat had hitherto made the trip. Several of the crew were glad to be rid of their visitors, among them Captain Joseph La Barge, later a famous steamboat captain on the Missouri. La Barge found the great naturalist very reserved, often overbearing, and with a tendency to belittle the efforts of others. Alexander Culbertson was in charge of the post at this time and in the journals kept by the members of the party are several familiar names. Boucharville—a famous French-Canadian hunter; Francis Chardon and Alexander Harvey—the infamous scoundrels; Denig; and Larpenteur are mentioned. The shadow of the first *bourgeois* still lingered on: Owen McKenzie, half-breed son of Kenneth McKenzie, was usually present when the party went buffalo hunting. And Etienne Provost, a famous trapper and explorer of the early fur trade days, assisted them in collecting specimens.

As much of the bird study hinged around physical details, members of the party were continually shooting specimens to weigh and measure, and examine for distinctive markings. Animals were also weighed and measured, no species from the smallest rabbit to the largest buffalo escaping their attention. Wolves which skulked nearby were shot from the walls of the fort or run down with horses, and hunters were employed to bring in animals such as bighorn which were hard to secure. A kit fox was discovered in the open and chased with a horse to establish some measure of its great speed. But the region did not abound with rattlesnakes—much to their disappointment.

Every member of the party kept busy at appointed tasks throughout their entire stay. Occasionally Harris dabbled in medicine, treating a white man or Indian, and was prone to mix assorted observations ranging from hay making to geology with his scientific notes. Neither of the principals were interested in Indians to any extent—Harris described an Assiniboine war dance as a "hideous uproar" and Audubon was even more caustic.

Early in August preparations were made to depart, and on the 16th the party pushed off down the Missouri in a forty-foot mackinaw boat. Those on board also included Provost, four boatmen, and Culbertson and his family. A tally showed that they had collected 153 birds and 48 quadrupeds, all of the latter being small animals however. When they docked at St. Louis on the 19th of October, the trip had cost a total of $1,994.86.

In 1847 an Irishman named John Palliser sailed from Liverpool to make the acquaintance of "our Trans-Atlantic brethren, and to extend my visit to the regions still inhabited by America's aboriginal people. . . ." By late August he was in Independence, Missouri where he met James Kipp, one of the bourgeois of the American Fur Company, who was about to start for the upper Missouri country with a pack train. Palliser went with Kipp and, on the 27th of October, arrived at the famous hostelry near the mouth of the Yellowstone.

During the winter he traveled up and down the Missouri from Fort Union, sometimes alone, sometimes with a small party. Once he made a long trip with only a dog and travois to carry the essentials. Fortunately, the worst misadventure he had was to be tossed by a wounded bull while hunting buffalo in the deep snow, the only damage being a shattered rifle stock.

The valley of the Yellowstone attracted him and late in the following April, with Boucharville, the famous hunter, and two camp tenders, he went up to the mouth of the Big Horn. Here they lived in luxury, at least as far as variety of meat on the table was concerned. The only labor performed, other than hunting, was some tailoring which necessity forced on Palliser. There were a few anxious moments when a party of Indians was discovered on the opposite bank of the Yellowstone, but the danger passed. Late in May, the Irishman and Boucharville embarked in a couple of bull boats and left the camp tenders to bring the horses down to the post, and then the two continued on down the Missouri to Fort Berthold where they did some more hunting.

Eventually, Palliser went down the Missouri on a steamboat of the fur company, and then returned to England. In 1853, several years after his return, he published a book, *The Solitary Hunter*, which told of his interesting experiences in a simple straight-forward manner. Apparently this book came to the attention of the British Colonial Office, for Palliser was selected to survey the southern boundary line of the British possessions between Lake Superior and the Cascade Range.

A combination of circumstances brought Rudolph Friederich Kurz to Fort Union on the evening of September 5, 1851. He was a young Swiss artist who had been inspired by his fellow countryman, Karl Bodmer, to select American Indians as a specialty. Unlike Bodmer, who was in the employ of Maximilian, Kurz was dependent upon his own resources. He landed at New Orleans in the fall of 1846, journeyed up the river to St. Louis, and in 1848 went up the Missouri as far as St. Joseph where he almost became a squaw man among the nearby Iowas. However, his attractive bride left him for her relatives and, in the spring of 1851 when the *St. Ange* came along bound for the up-river country, he persuaded Culbertson and Picotte—the agents on board—to take him along.

The agreement was that he was to be employed as a clerk if there was an opening and he desired to stay. Perhaps Culbertson would take him on up to the Blackfoot country. However, before going on up to the Blackfeet, Culbertson had to take a delegation of Assiniboines from Fort Union to the great Indian council which was to be held that summer at Fort Laramie. On board the *St. Ange* was Father De Smet, who was to go along on this trip, and also the wagons which were to be the first wheeled vehicles to traverse the plains between the mouth of the Yellowstone and the fort in the valley of the Platte.

Kurz was left with James Kipp at Fort Berthold, the post among the Mandans and the Arickaras, with strict instructions not to paint any portraits of the natives. Artists were taboo as the superstitious Indians had connected the *magic* of Catlin and Bodmer with the smallpox plague of 1837. However, the *St. Ange* brought cholera up the river, Kurz could not keep from drawing in his sketch book, and when the Indians began to die of this disease the artist had to go on up to Fort Union. Here Denig employed the thirty-three-year-old Swiss as a clerk.

Although he had an excellent opportunity to study Indians at this post there were some practical difficulties. His supply of oil for painting was limited to what was at the post. As this dwindled to a small supply, Kurz was disgusted when his employer decided it should be used to paint a dog sled. During the winter his watercolors froze when he attempted to use this media, and the following spring he ran out of paper. Although Denig was sympathetic and helpful, he irritated the artist by wanting a picture of a nude female figure painted for the reception room. This Kurz refused to do—"To paint a nude figure merely for the sake of appealing to his carnal passions and those of other men was beneath my dignity." The matter became a small bone of contention.

Although Kurz's sketch book contains many interesting drawings, it is ironic that perhaps the most valuable contribution this artist made was his diary with its intimate day-by-day picture life at this post during its last years. The entry for October 17th is typical of his concise and vivid observations:

Slept little last night. First, the Herantsa sang their war song. As I was getting to bed they began another chant in the interpreter's room and accompanied their singing with the drum. Of course, I could not fall asleep. After tossing from one side to the other for ever so long, I lost all patience, and, throwing my cloak around me, went to find out just what the hubub was about. The room, dimly lighted by the open fire and one candle, was crowded with performers and onlookers made up of redskins, white people, and half-breeds. According to Indian custom, eight Herantsa and seven Assiniboin sat opposite one another on the floor, encircled about by a pile of bows, quivers, knives, calico, etc., and were playing a game [of hand]. Two Assiniboin were making motions in every direction with their fists, or rather with their closed hands, swiftly passing, in the meantime, a bullet-ball from hand to the other, while the other members of their party sang "e, e, e, eh, e, e, e, ah" keeping time by beating a tatoo with sticks on washbasins and boiler tops. In an excited state of eager expectation, both singers and players swayed their bodies continually from the hips. . . . When [one player] felt sure that he knew he made a quick thrust with his left arm in the direction of the fist in which he supposed the ball to be, struck violently on his breast with his right hand, and, with a cry, designated the fist mentioned. . . . One of the Herantsa wished to make himself particularly conspicuous. He sat nearest the fireplace. He raked out all the ashes in front of him and concealed the bullet there, or rather he tried to make his opponents think he did. He moved his fists among the ashes in imitation of a buffalo bull working his way through mud and mire or rolling over in the dust; he grumbled and bellowed the while like an angry bull, threw ashes all over himself and around him, pawed and groaned like one possessed. His mimicry was unequalled. . . .

Trappers and hunters, lounging lazily in the sun inside the walls of the stockade, told him stories of adventure with hostile Indians—who often lurked within sight of the post. And the *bourgeois*, while sitting for his portrait and at leisure moments, not only added to Kurz's collection of stories but also told him much about Indian customs.

Little seems to have escaped the attention of the clerk. In one entry he discussed the results of the repugnance of a warrior for a pregnant squaw and closed with this observation:

Owing to this same repugnance on the part of their husbands, mothers suckle their children until the fourth or fifth year; it always impressed me as so droll to see boys with bows and arrows in their hands nursing like babies at their mother's breasts.

And in another entry he waxed caustic about the deliberations at Fort Laramie which resulted in the so-called "treaty" of 1851. Culbertson and the Assiniboine delegation returned from this meeting on the 31st of October and reported the happenings:

The news from Fort Laramie fails utterly to justify expectations. . . . The United States Agent, Colonel Mitchell, is said to have been befuddled most of the time from too much drink, to have made great promises to the Indians, to have appointed several braves to the rank of supreme chief without approval of the respective nations. . . . Mr. Culbertson has been named a colonel by his friend Mitchell. . . . Colonel of what? Here we have neither Regular army or militia.

As the winter passed, Denig sent many of his personnel to outlying camps to ease the burden on the commissary. Early in March Kurz was assigned to the "starvation troops" and spent some time at a horse camp. Here he lived in a tent with a man named Morgan, "a most civil, well-educated Scot," and his five dogs. He was glad to return to the post five weeks later. On the 17th of April, Culbertson arrived from the post on the upper Missouri; and on the following day Kurz, on board the boat as an oarsman, bid adieu to Fort Union. Late in the following September, the artist returned to his home in Berne, Switzerland, unexpected and seriously ill. Although he continued to follow art as a profession, he was never able to capitalize on his plans for a gallery of Indian paintings.

How a traveler could avoid dependence on the employees and facilities of the American Fur Company was a matter to which Palliser gave some thought after returning to England. Kurz, referring to him as "Mr. Palesieux," recorded the discussion of his ideas by the personnel at Fort Union. His idea was to outfit at the settlement with all the supplies and trading goods necessary, come out with his own pack train or steamboat, and then have a "blockhouse built and to hunt to his heart's content with huntsmen hired for that purpose." For obvious reasons, the traders did not look with favor on such an idea, and regarded it as impractical.

The man who planned and carried out this impractical idea in a grandiose manner was Sir George Gore of Sligo, Ireland. Sir George was an ardent sportsman and, with an annual income of $200,000, money was not a serious handicap in the indulgence of his whims. In the spring of 1854, he outfitted in St. Louis and, using Fort Laramie as a base, hunted in what is now Colorado. The following winter he stayed at Fort Laramie where he created something of a sensation among the mountain men. Also wintering here was a tall, lean frontiersman who had an incomparable knowledge of the Indians, game and terrain of the Northwest. Without any quibbling over wages, Gore promptly hired Jim Bridger to guide him into the Yellowstone Basin the following year.

As soon as spring came, Bridger led this fantastic party up Casper Creek and over to the headwaters of the Powder River. The procession was composed of four six-mule wagons, two three-yoke ox wagons, and twenty-one French carts, each painted red and drawn by two horses. With it were forty or more employees, one hundred and twelve horses—including some very fine ones, twelve yoke of oxen, three milk cows, and fourteen dogs. One wagon was required for Gore's arms—seventy-five rifles, twelve or fifteen shotguns, and a large number of pistols, all bearing the names of famous makers. Two vehicles were required to haul the fishing tackle, and a skilled fly maker was included in the retinue. And among the wagons was one which, by turning cranks attached to each of the four corners and lifting the top, could be converted into a comfortable "bedroom"!

Nor did this Irishman stand short on anything which would contribute to his comfort. He had a linen tent, about ten by eighteen feet, which had a striped lining. There was a brass bedstead that could be taken apart and packed in a small space, a portable iron table and washstand, and a "splendid" telescope mounted on a tripod. The kinds and amounts of food in his commissary were likewise extraordinary.

Several years later one of the employees described this sportsman to an Army lieutenant who was an amateur historian. The latter wrote:

Sir George was, in 1854, about forty-five years of age [sic—forty-three], of medium height but rather stout, bald head, short side-whiskers, a good walker but an indifferent horseman, a good shot from a rest but rather indifferent offhand. . . . He rarely, if ever, went [hunting] unattended, his party usually comprising seven men. He never loaded his own gun, but after firing passed it to an attendant, who gave him another already charged. . . . After breaking camp in the spring he rarely laid over a day until he went into winter quarters, moved leisurely, and camped early in the afternoon.

Later, Bridger told Captain—later General—Marcy that Gore usually invited him to dinner and, after the meal was over and they had a few glasses of wine, the Irishman would read to him. His favorite author was Shakespeare who was "a leetle too highfalutin" for the guide, but the adventures of Baron Munchausen did interest him. However,

". . . he be dogond ef he swallered everything that there Baren Mountchawson said, and he thout he was a dur'n liar." Yet, upon further reflection he acknowledged that some of his own experiences among the Blackfeet would be equally marvelous "ef writ down in a book."

During the spring the party hunted the headwaters of the Powder and then in the summer drifted slowly down the main valley of this stream to the Yellowstone River. Here they turned westward and proceeded to the Tongue where, eight miles above its mouth, the party "forted" and prepared to spend the winter. Unfortunately one of the men accidentally started a grass fire in the vicinity and the stock had to be moved to the mouth of the Tongue where Gore and a few of the party took care of them. Sir George had a small log cabin built for his own use and in this little shack, together with his favorite grey Kentucky thoroughbred, he spent the winter. The other horses were fed on cottonwood bark, but this animal received cornmeal.

The winter passed rather uneventfully—except that the Blackfeet discovered them and coveted their horses. A band of Piegans were successful in stealing twenty-one head: later, a party of Bloods attempted to get some horses from the corral but were discovered and one warrior was wounded. One man died and Gore very considerately dismantled a wagon box to get lumber for a casket—somewhat of a luxury where the usual shroud, if any, was a blanket or a buffalo robe.

Early in the spring, Gore went up the Tongue a short distance and crossed over to the valley of the Rosebud where a large village of Crows was found. Here he traded for some horses to replace those which had been stolen. Then Gore returned to the site of his winter encampment where he began to build two flatboats to carry part of his trophies and equipment down to Fort Union. While thus engaged "Major" Alfred J. Vaughan, the Indian agent for the upper Missouri, and Alexander Culbertson visited him while taking the Absaroka their annuity goods.

For some reason Vaughan took a dislike to Gore's presence. The following July, in an official report addressed to his superior in St. Louis, he commented caustically—and not wholly without cause:

The English Gentlemen whom you granted a pasport, to pass in and through the Ind country will return to your city in a month or so, having been in the Ind country from the time you granted him a pasport up to the present time  the pasport you find was granted him the 24th of May 1854  from my construction of the intercourse laws he has most palpably violated it.  he built from his own confession and that of many Employees which was forty-three in number a fort in the crow country some 100 feet square and inhabited the same nine months carrying on trade and intercourse with the Crow tribe of Ind  trading them all kinds of Ind Goods Powder & Ball he states, also his men that he killed 105 Bears and some 2000 Buffalo Elk & Deer 1600  he states was more than they had any use for having killed it purely for sport. The Inds have been loud in their complaints at men passing through their country killing and driving off their game.  what can I do against so large a number of men coming into a country like this so very remote from civilization, doing & acting as they please, nothing I assure you beyond apprising you of the facts on paper. . . .

As Gore's trading had been limited to securing some horses, much of this criticism was obviously a gross distortion of fact, and probably was inspired by the officials of the fur company. However, there is no doubt that Sir George killed wantonly. In St. Louis, after the trip was over, he told Captain Marcy that from the early summer of 1854 to the late spring of 1856,

. . . he had slaughtered the enormous aggregate of forty grizzly bears, twenty-five hundred buffaloes, beside numerous elk, deer, antelope and other small game.

Certainly this was wasteful, as were many things which happened on the frontier, but it is highly improbable that the Crows complained about it.

When the flatboats were completed, the trophies and part of the wagons were loaded and floated down to Fort Union. Gore went by land and hunted along the way. Here he arranged for his trophies and some of his equipment to go down the river on the fur company's steamboats; and he contracted with Culbertson for a mackinaw to carry the rest of his goods down the Missouri. During the dealing for this boat, or Gore's offering surplus wagons and supplies for sale, something happened which the Irishman interpreted as an attempt to take advantage of him. In cold fury, he gathered his extra wagons, harness, saddles, and supplies into a pile on the river bank and set fire to them. This pile he had guarded until the refuse was cold, when he had all the scrap iron picked up and thrown into the river. One of his men did purchase a cart, harness and some supplies. To these items Gore added so many articles that the man became alarmed lest the cost exceed his means. When he protested to the steward, Gore would accept only $12.00 for goods worth several hundred dollars.

And so, like all the others who had preceded him, Sir George Gore, his famous guide, and his secretaries, cooks, fly maker, gunsmiths, dog tenders, and servants embarked in a boat to float down the Missouri. After spending the next winter at Fort Berthold, Gore returned to the settlements. There never had been a dude that could equal Gore, and the Yellowstone Basin never saw another like him.

# 6

## Exploring the Known

>>>>>>>>><<<<<<<<<<< For half a century after Captain Clark's little party floated down the Yellowstone, the Government made no serious move to explore the Yellowstone Basin—unless the abortive "Yellowstone Expedition" can be classed as an attempt. During this period, trappers and fur traders searched every valley large enough to have a stream which could harbor a beaver, scouted the mountain passes, and became familiar with the broad stretches of prairie and badlands.

This exploration was a secretive sort of probing for no *partisan* or trapper willingly shared his knowledge with a rival. William Clark did gather from Colter, Drouillard, and others material to amplify and correct his maps, but by the middle of the century these were no longer adequate to meet the needs of the nation. So, in the 1850's, the Government set about *exploring* and mapping the area which had been familiar to large numbers of trappers for several decades.

In the spring of 1856, Lieutenant Gouverneur K. Warren, with W. H.

Hutton and J. H. Snowden as topographers, and Dr. F. V. Hayden as geologist, made a reconnaissance map of the Missouri River as far north as Fort Pierre. Here,

*instructions were now given me by General Harney to proceed with my party on the American Fur Company's boat to the mouth of the Yellowstone, and as far above as she should ascend, and return by means of a Mackinac boat. . . .*

His party augmented by an escort of seventeen men, Warren proceeded upstream as directed. After stopping at the mouth of the Yellowstone for two weeks while he procured some "land transportation" and watched Agent Vaughn distribute annuity goods to the Assiniboines, Warren's party

*. . . left the mouth of the Yellowstone, July 25, and, traveling leisurely up the left bank, reached a point one hundred miles from its mouth, beyond which it is impossible to advance with wagons along the valley of the Yellowstone without crossing to the opposite banks.*

Here Warren split his party and, taking some pack animals, proceeded through this badlands area to a point opposite the mouth of the Powder. This he regarded as being "a good and certain point with which any future reconnaissance should connect." He then returned to the place where he had left the remainder of his men and, using a skin boat, he floated down the river mapping the bends and islands while the bulk of the party returned over the same route which they had come.

This work provided the beginning for an accurate map of the upper Missouri, and the Yellowstone and its tributaries. Three years later the War Department launched a pretentious effort to continue the work which Warren had started. Captain W. F. Raynolds, with Lieutenant H. E. Maynadier as an assistant, was selected to head the survey; and the objectives were clearly stated in the orders:

*The objects of this exploration are to ascertain, as far as practicable, everything relating to the numbers, habits and disposition of the Indians inhabiting the country, its agricultural and mineralogical resources, its climate and the influences which govern it, the navigability of its streams, its topographical features, and the facilities and obstacles which the latter present to the construction of rail or common roads, either to meet the needs of military operations or those of emigration through, or settlement in, the country.*

*Particular attention should be given to determining the most direct and feasible routes:*

1. From the neighborhood of Fort Laramie to the Yellowstone, in the direction of Fort Union on the Missouri.

2. From the neighborhood of Fort Laramie northwesterly, along the base of the Big Horn mountains, towards Fort Benton and the Bitter Root valley.

3. From the Yellowstone to the South pass, and to ascertaining the practicability of a route from the sources of Wind river to those of the Missouri.

The route which the party was to follow was also worked out in some detail.

From the source of the Powder river the expedition should proceed down that stream to its mouth; thence along the Yellowstone to the mouth of the Tongue river, up which a detachment should be sent to its source. The remainder of the party should continue on the Yellowstone to the mouth of the Big Horn river, and ascend the latter stream to the point where it leaves the mountains. Here the two divisions of the party should be united. The approach of winter may require the expedition to pass the season in this neighborhood, or if time suffices, the expedition may ascend the Big Horn river to Wind river, where a favorable wintering place can be found.

The next season should be spent in examining the mountain region about the sources of the Yellowstone and Missouri, to ascertain the character of the routes leading south and west from the navigable parts of these rivers. On returning one party should descend the Missouri, using skin boats to Fort Benton, where a Mackinac boat should be in readiness. The other portion should decend the Yellowstone, in skin boats, to its mouth, where it should join the party with the Mackinac boat, and all proceed to the settlements.

To assist in this work, Raynolds was authorized to employ eight technical assistants; the sum of $60,000 was set aside from the appropriations to defray the expenses.

The commanding general of the Department of the West was directed to provide an escort of thirty "picked" infantrymen and an officer. Lieutenant Caleb Smith of the Second Infantry who commanded the escort the first year proved to be more trouble than he was worth. As Raynolds was a member of the Corps of Topographical Engineers, and not a *line* officer, Smith refused to take orders from him. After trying unsuccessfully to court-martial this subordinate, the captain welcomed a change the following year.

On the 4th of June, the party left St. Louis aboard the *Spread Eagle* and the *Chippewa*. Both boats were heavily loaded having on board not only the fur company's goods but also the annuity goods for the Sioux and the equipment of two Government parties. Two weeks later they arrived at Fort Pierre where Raynolds' group disembarked. After issuing the goods to the Sioux and organizing his party, which took another two weeks, Raynolds finally got under way. Skirting the northern end of the Black Hills, he crossed the divide between the headwaters of the Little Missouri and the Little Powder Rivers on the 21st of July.

Here a Sioux guide quietly disappeared—not neglecting to take with him the mule which had been provided for his use. In noting this loss, Raynolds commented, "My American guide, Bridger, is now on familiar ground and appears to be entirely at home in this country." Various entries in the captain's journal indicate clearly that Jim's intimate knowledge of the country did much to keep the party from becoming involved in difficult or impassable terrain; and his sage advice—to which Raynolds listened with proper respect—undoubtedly contributed to the success of the work.

As the party entered the Yellowstone Basin two humorous incidents occurred:

Three large [buffalo] bulls charged down upon us at one point in the march, to the great alarm of one of the escort, who dropped his gun, and, raising his hands, exclaimed, in all the accents of mortal terror, "Elephants! elephants! my God! I did not know there were elephants in this country." On another occasion as a band was passing close by the train, one of the teams started in full pursuit, and was with great difficulty checked. It was probably the first buffalo chase on record with a six-mule team.

Raynolds was unique in that he observed the Sabbath, and conducted a short service on this day. Although these services were not always well attended, the captain noted that the men looked forward to this day of rest and started the next week with renewed vigor. However, there did come a Sunday when necessity dictated that the party continue with their travel. On this occasion Raynolds

was amused on the march at the discussion between two of the party in regard to the day of the week. One insisted that it was Sunday, but the other replied: "I tell you it ain't. Dont you know the captain never moves on Sunday?"

As the party traveled down the Little Powder, and then the valley of the Powder, the captain was not favorably impressed with the rolling sagebrush-covered prairies. Good pasture was hard to find, quicksand was an additional hazard at stream crossings, the country was cut up by numerous gullies, and the water was poor. At the end of the first day in this country, Raynolds wrote: "The entire district is unfit for the home of the white man." When the party finally left the valley, this opinion had not changed greatly.

As the lower part of the valley of the Powder looked difficult for wagons, the party crossed over to Pumpkin Creek and went down it to its junction with the Tongue:

Bridger now advises that we travel up Tongue river some distance before crossing to the west, for the purpose of avoiding the bluffs on the Yellowstone. This is not in accordance with my pre-concieved plan, but I shall accept his advice out of deference to his remarkable knowledge of the country.

Traveling roughly parallel with the Yellowstone, but some ten to twenty miles to the south, the party crossed the Rosebud and went on to "Emmel's creek," named for the unfortunate Michael Immell. Here the ambitious Dr. Hayden—the geologist—and four others took French leave and went to examine the Wolf Mountains; and the irritated captain, whom they had not informed of their plans, used the incident to issue an order forbidding anyone to be absent overnight "without explicit permission."

Following down what is now called Armell's Creek, the party reached the valley of the Yellowstone. Raynolds' first impression was similar to those recorded by Larocque, Clark, De Smet, and others:

From the summit of the hill we obtained our first view of the Yellowstone valley itself, of which over 50 square miles was visible, literally black with buffalo, grazing in an enormous herd whose numbers defy computation, but must be estimated by hundreds of thousands.

Here the party camped for twelve days, preparing reports and maps, and writing letters, while they awaited the arrival of the fur company's keelboats which were bringing additional supplies. Robert Meldrum, the bourgeois at Fort Sarpy, came to visit, and from him Raynolds secured considerable information about the Crows and Indians in general, as well as possible routes. On the second day in camp, two Crows arrived—and not long afterward, a village. However, the novelty of these visitors soon wore thin and the captain noted:

The Indians were so troublesome about camp to-day that I posted a double guard at night for the purpose of freeing us from the annoyance of their visits.

When the party moved to the vicinity of Fort Sarpy, a few miles up-stream, the captain's perspective of the importance of this expedition received a rude jolt. Everything at the post was in confusion and the necessary supplies were mixed with the trade goods; and he was vexed to discover

the agent of the Fur Company had promptly commenced traffic with the savages, considerately allowing our matters to take care of themselves.

On the following day the Crows deflated his sense of values still further. While he was attempting to arrange for a council with these Indians, the horse of the head chief was missed and the "entire energies of the tribe were devoted to the recovery of the animal." Finally, early in the afternoon "the council convened for the discussion of such secondary questions as the relations of the Crows and the President."

On the 31st of August, their supplies replenished at last, the party continued up the Yellowstone valley to the Big Horn River and the nearby mouth of Tullock's Creek. Here the division took place which had been planned in the original orders for the mouth of the Tongue. Half of the group was turned over to Lieutenant Maynadier who promptly moved out up Tullock's Creek.

Bridger guided the remainder of the men up the Big Horn Valley to the Big Horn Mountains. Here the captain would have liked to explore the famous canyon, but he had to be content with examining its mouth and listening to the "glowing" descriptions provided by his guide. From this point they moved eastward and then southward along the eastern slope of the Big Horns following, in general, the route which seven years later was called the Bozeman trail. When they reached the North Fork of the Powder, a few miles west of the spot where Fort Reno was built in 1876, the party camped to wait for Lieutenant Maynadier.

This part of the journey was marked by bits of excitement. On one occasion a grizzly chased a man out of a plum thicket, knocked him down, and then retreated over a nearby hill with her three cubs. When on the headwaters of the Little Big Horn, Indians slipped into camp one night and stole a mule. Then they dogged the party for a week and, in spite of added precautions, pilfered small items from the camp and once wounded a man and killed a horse. Not long after this shooting, a Spaniard and fourteen Crows came into camp and from these information was secured which indicated that the nocturnal visitors were Absaroka from the village on the Yellowstone.

One day while the men idled in camp, Bridger and Raynolds rode down the Powder looking for Maynadier. They saw no sign of the party,

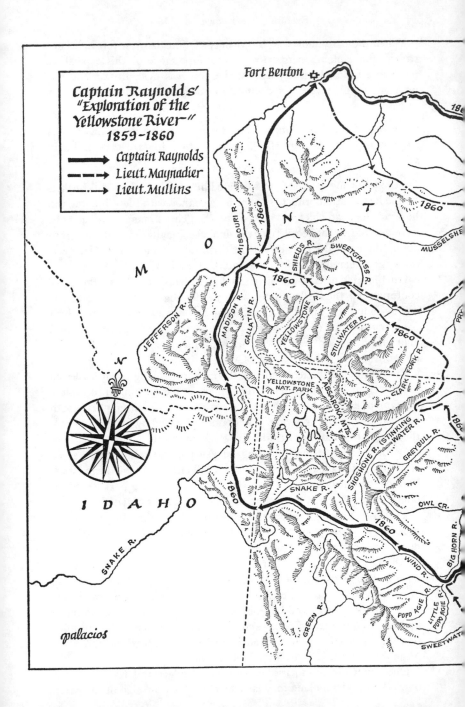

Captain Raynolds'
"Exploration of the
Yellowstone River"
1859–1860

→ Captain Raynolds
→ Lieut. Maynadier
→ Lieut. Mullins

Fort Benton

MONTANA

IDAHO

MISSOURI R.

JEFFERSON R.

MADISON R.

GALLATIN R.

SHIELDS R.

SWEETGRASS R.

YELLOWSTONE R.

STILLWATER R.

YELLOWSTONE NAT. PARK

ABSAROKA MTS.

CLARK FORK R.

MUSSELSHE

SNAKE R.

SHOSHONE R. (STINKING WATER R.)

GREYBULL R.

OWL CR.

WIND R.

BIG HORN R.

GREEN R.

POPO AGIE R.

LITTLE POPO AGIE R.

SWEETWAT

SNAKE R.

1860

palacios

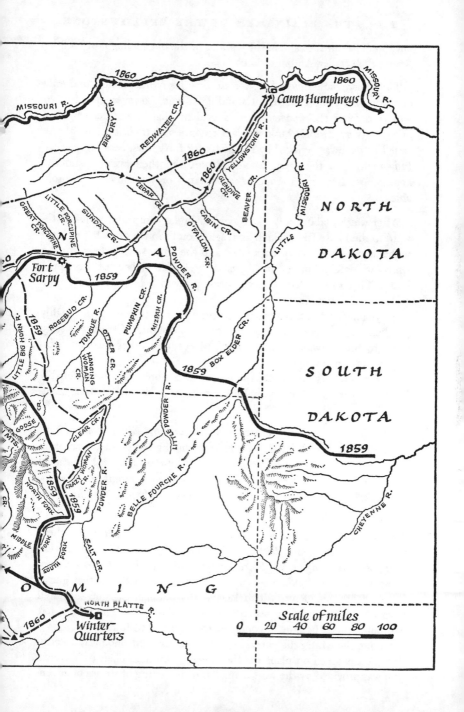

but Jim did show the captain the remains of the old trading post built by Bonneville's trader, Antonio Matéo:

The "Portuguese houses" . . . . are now badly dilapidated, and only one side of the pickets remains standing. These, however, are of hewn logs, and from their character it is evident that the structures were originally very strongly built. Bridger recounted a tradition that at one time this post was besieged by the Sioux for forty days, resisting successfully to the last the strength and ingenuity of their assaults, and the appearance of the ruins renders the story not only creditable but probable.

After waiting about a week, Raynolds broke camp and went southward to the Platte River which he reached on the 11th of October. Maynadier arrived a couple of days later, and the party settled down for the winter in some unfinished buildings at the Indian Agency of the Upper Platte. This was located on Deer Creek, midway between Fort Laramie and Independence Rock.

Maynadier's travels had taken him on a zig-zag course which roughly paralleled that pursued by Raynolds but at a distance of twenty to forty miles to the eastward. No troubles had occurred other than an occasional overturned wagon.

While in winter quarters, Captain Raynolds noted what was probably the first Protestant effort to establish a mission in the Yellowstone country:

Rev. Mr. Bryninger [Moritz Braeuninger] and three companions, [were] on their way to establish a mission among the Crows. They were German Lutherans, and had been sent out by the German Evangelical Synod of Iowa. God-fearing and devoted men, but ignorant of the world as well as of our language, and in consequence poorly fitted for the labors they had undertaken.

The captain gave them some financial assistance and persuaded them to winter at the agency. In the spring they left to found their mission near the mouth of the Big Horn Canyon, a spot which he had recommended. Late the following summer, Raynolds learned that they got as far as the Powder River where Reverend Bryninger became separated from his companions and was murdered by the Sioux. The others, left without a leader, became discouraged and returned to Iowa.

During the winter the party drafted maps, took astronomical observations, and worked on plans for the coming summer. Their only recreation was provided by the weekly mail and the telling of stories of adventure during the heyday of the fur trade. Raynolds thought "Some of these Munchausen tales . . . [were] altogether too good to be lost." Among those he recorded was this one:

I will close these specimen tales by one from Bridger, which partakes so decidedly of a scientific nature that it should not be omitted. He contends that near the headwaters of the Columbian river, in the fastness of the mountains, there is a spring gushing forth from the rocks near the top of the mountains. The water when it issues forth is cold as ice, but it runs down over the smooth rock so far and so fast that it is hot at the bottom.

No doubt listeners had laughed so often at his description of the Firehole River in what is now the Yellowstone National Park, that the scout enjoyed passing off a true story for a tall tale. To this frontiersman, friction between the rapidly flowing water and the stream bed was a logical explanation for the heated bottom of this river.

When Raynolds left his winter quarters on May 10, 1860, he had organized a pack train and planned to discard the carts and wagons when the going got rough. For the infantry escort, he substituted 30 men of the Second Dragoons under Lieutenant John Mullins; and this officer proved to be a much more valuable addition to the party than his predecessor. The party split at the start and then united at the junction of the Popo Agie and Wind Rivers which point is the beginning of the Big Horn. Here the final touches were put to the plans for the next five weeks. The captain wrote:

My own division will ascend the Wind river, and from its head cross to the Three Forks of the Missouri. Lieutenant Maynadier is to decend the Big Horn to the point at which we left it in September, and thence proceed westward along the base of the mountains, crossing the Yellowstone and reaching the Three Forks by Clark's route—the understanding being that we shall meet at the Three Forks on the last day of June.

Again the party was divided equally. Lieutenant Mullins accompanied Maynadier, and Paul Deval was their guide. Bridger went with Raynolds whose group included the energetic geologist, Dr. Hayden.

For a week Raynolds traveled up the valley of the Wind River. The captain had his heart set on crossing over to the headwaters of the Yellowstone, continuing down past Yellowstone Lake, and then moving over to the valley of the Gallatin, thus staying entirely on the Atlantic side of the Continental Divide while enroute to the Three Forks of the Missouri. During this week Bridger probably rode beside the leader with his tongue in his cheek for during the previous winter Jim had insisted that the proposed itinerary was impossible. Now they would see who was right.

On May 30th, Captain Raynolds wrote gracefully of his defeat:

Bridger said at the onset that this would be impossible, and that it would be necessary to pass over to the head-waters of the Columbia, and back again to the Yellowstone. I had not previously believed that crossing the main crest twice would be more easily accomplished than the transit over what was in effect only a spur, but the view from our present camp settled the question aversely to my opinion at once. Directly across our route lies a basaltic ridge, rising not less than 5,000 feet above us, its walls apparently vertical with no visible pass nor even cañon.

On the opposite side of this are the headwaters of the Yellowstone. Bridger remarked triumphantly and forcibly to me upon reaching this spot, "I told you you could not go through. A bird can't fly over that without taking a supply of grub along." I had no reply to offer, and mentally conceded the accuracy of the information of "the old man of the mountains."

Thus the headwaters of the Yellowstone, and what was to be called "The Wonderland" by early settlers, escaped official exploration for another decade.

Floundering through deep snow, Bridger led the party over the Wind River Range by way of Union Pass and down into Jackson Hole, and then over Teton Pass into Pierre's Hole. Here he skirted the western slope of the Tetons, headed north up Henry's Fork of the Snake, and crossed the easy divide which now bears Raynolds' name to the head of the Madison River. This stream they followed to the Three Forks, arriving one day before the date previously agreed upon.

While Raynolds was detouring to the west of the area he had hoped to enter, Maynadier was having no serious difficulty on the route planned for his party. Although neither of these officers made any mention of suggestions from Bridger, it is hardly a coincidence that the route traveled by the lieutenant should follow closely that of the road which Bridger laid out a few years later to connect the Oregon Trail and the settlements in the Montana gold fields.

While Maynadier and his guide had no difficulty in finding their way, the party came to grief at "Stinking creek," now designated the Shoshone River. This stream, rushing and roaring along in its gravelly channel, appeared to be only two or three feet deep, but when tested it was found "deep enough to swim a horse, and not fordable." Badlands prevented the party from hunting a suitable ford further upstream, and it was decided to attempt a crossing.

At first, two attempts were made to use a wagon box, which they calked and wrapped with canvas, for a ferry. This they tried to haul across but both times the rush of the water broke the improvised cable and the crazy craft went bobbing downstream, narrowly missing destruction. However, in this effort they discovered a reef of rock which stretched diagonally across the channel. The water was only about four feet deep over this except for thirty yards near the opposite shore where it was "nearly to the back of a medium-sized mule." By packing their goods high on the packsaddles of the largest mules, most of the supplies were crossed with only an occasional ducking.

Maynadier was reluctant to subject the instruments—a sextant and horizon, three chronometers, and three barometers—to the possibility of a ducking. These he lashed on top of the seats of the ambulance and, with four large mules hitched to the vehicle and three mounted men assisting the team and its driver, he attempted a crossing. When they reached the deep part near the opposite bank, the back wheels washed off the reef, locking the front ones under the side of the body. The instant the traces were slackened, everything was swept into the deep water just below the ledge of rock where the mules became entangled in the harness and were soon drowned, and the driver barely escaped with his life. The wreckage lodged on an island a couple of miles below but not before everything except the odometer was washed out and lost. That night the lieutenant wrote:

*We returned to camp wet, cold, hungry, and dispirited, and I passed the most wretched night it has ever been my lot to encounter. . . .*

The loss of the instruments was a serious one, but with the odometer for measuring distances the topographer could still plot the route. And so the party pushed on northward through Pryor Gap. Here they turned northwest across Clark Fork, Rocky Fork, and Stillwater River coming down to the Yellowstone River at a point below the present town of Big Timber. At the mouth of Boulder Creek, the party made a skin boat, crossed the river, and then parked their craft on a scaffold for future use. Now, instead of crossing to the Gallatin by the route used by Clark's party, Maynadier followed up Shield's River, crossed the Belt Mountains by Blackfoot Pass, and reached the rendezvous three days behind schedule to find Raynolds waiting—somewhat impatiently.

The two leaders spent the Fourth of July consolidating reports and making plans. Then, transferring Lieutenant Mullins to his party, Raynolds started down the valley of the Missouri for Fort Benton while Maynadier returned to the Yellowstone and prepared to descend this river. The skin boat was taken down and overhauled but its odor was "far from balmy," and the men named her, somewhat facetiously, the *Rose of Cashmere*. With a couple of men in the *Rose* and the remainder following along the bank with the pack train, the lieutenant started down the Yellowstone.

At Pompey's Pillar, the party stopped for two days to observe an eclipse, and to build a replacement for the foul-smelling *Rose*. When they stopped to renew acquaintances at Fort Sarpy, they found the post abandoned. These men reached the Missouri on the 31st of July and here, just above the mouth of the Yellowstone, Maynadier established a permanent camp which he named Camp Humphreys after the officer in charge of the Bureau of Explorations and Surveys. The employees at Fort Union extended the usual hospitality of the post, including a ball given in honor of the guests.

> . . . the ladies were daughters of the forest, . . . attired in the fashionable attire of the States, with hoops and crinoline, and [they] exhibited as much grace and amiability toward us, their guests, as could be found in any of the salons of any city in the land.

At Fort Benton, Raynolds dispatched Lieutenant Mullins with a party of twenty to map the divide between the Missouri and the Yellowstone. Bridger was assigned as a guide, and among the assistants was the indefatigable Dr. Hayden.

Mullin's party reached the watershed of the Yellowstone on the upper reaches of Big Porcupine Creek. Then Bridger led the group eastward along the Missouri-Yellowstone Divide until they came down into the valley of the Yellowstone east of the Mountain Sheep Bluffs. The journey was uneventful except for one day on the head of Big Dry Creek where Mullins encountered a large band of Crows. These Indians were in an ugly mood over the manner in which their annuities had been handled; but the lieutenant stood his ground and, with Bridger's assistance, managed to talk the chief out of a fight. On the 11th of August they joined their friends at Camp Humphreys. Raynolds had floated down the Missouri in a mackinaw boat without any mishaps and arrived four days before. The surplus animals were now sold and the party, dividing again, went down the Missouri to Omaha. Here the survey ended on the 4th of October, 1860.

Although the exploration of the Yellowstone was a *fait accompli* long before Raynolds' orders were prepared, this party accomplished much of value. The skeleton of a reliable map of a large section of the Northwest was prepared; and Raynolds, Maynadier, and Mullins collected in their journals a detailed picture of various features of this area. Travel with wagons between the mouth of the Yellowstone and the Platte had been pioneered eight years before when Culbertson and De Smet went to the treaty negotiations at Fort Laramie, and a few years later Gore had traversed the entire length of the valley of the Powder. However, Raynolds was the first to chart a road through part of this country, and Maynadier took the first vehicles down part of the valley of the Big Horn.

The captain was not favorably impressed by the agricultural possibilities of most of the country, although he admitted frankly that he did not think he was capable of properly evaluating all the factors in this respect. However, he did feel certain that there were precious metals in the Big Horn Mountains. The search for gold was discouraged at all times for,

if gold was discovered in any considerable quantity the party would have at once disregarded all the authority and entreaties of the officers in charge and have been converted into a band of gold miners. . . .

Maynadier felt confident that the Yellowstone was suitable for steamboat navigation, at least as far up as the mouth of the Big Horn. But Raynolds pointed out that the elevation of this stream at the Great Bend was 1,700 feet higher than the Missouri at Fort Benton, and noted:

Considering the difficulties encountered from the current of the Missouri, I cannot but think that the navigation of a stream whose waters possess such a greatly accumulated velocity is at least problematical.

However, he pointed out that,

the broad valley of the Yellowstone affords peculiar facilities for a railroad, and it is, moreover, the most direct route to the important region about the Three Forks, with all its agricultural and mineral wealth.

The captain also made other interesting observations. Among these were comments about the current government policy pertaining to the Sioux and the Crows; and, in regard to the buffalo, he predicted accurately that, "I think it is more than probable that another generation will witness almost the entire extinction of this noble animal."

It is doubtful if the completed report received the attention which it merited. The Civil War broke out shortly after Raynolds started to prepare it, and it was not until 1868 that it was finally published and distributed. The map was, of course, valuable; and, during the Sioux War of

1876, a second lieutenant with Crook's troops noted in his diary that he spent several evenings beside the campfire studying Raynolds' *Report on the Exploration of the Yellowstone River*.

This survey ended, for the most part, government exploration of the Yellowstone Basin. However, Raynolds noted that, "I regard the valley of the upper Yellowstone as the most interesting unexplored district in our widely expanded country." Kind fate was to keep the wonders of this area hidden from the general public for another decade. Then, quite fittingly, the man who headed the government exploration of this "*terra incognita*" was Dr. F. V. Hayden, who had rendered outstanding service to both Lieutenant Warren and Captain Raynolds.

# 7

## Coming Events Cast Their Shadows

>>>>>>>>>>«««««««« Shortly after noon on the 31st of July, 1851, the scow from Fort Union beached on the shore opposite the post and a strange party disembarked. In charge of this group was Alexander Culbertson, supervisor of all the American Fur Company's posts on the upper Missouri, and with him in a semi-official capacity was Father De Smet. The priest noted:

*We numbered thirty-two persons; the greater part were Assinboins, Minnetarees and Crows, who were repairing to the great Indian council to be held in the vicinity of Fort Laramie, and by the same route that we had chosen, which was scarcely less than 800 miles in length. Two four-wheeled wagons and two carts, for transporting our provisions and baggage, composed our whole convoy. The four vehicles were in all probability the first that ever crossed this unoccupied waste. There is not the slightest perceptable vestage of a beaten track between Fort Union and the Red Buttes, which are on the route to Oregon, and 161 miles west of Fort Laramie.*

This party traveled up the valley of the Yellowstone for a couple of days and then worked their way westward to the crest of the divide. Their first objective was Fort Alexander near the mouth of the Rosebud and, in order to avoid several impassable areas of badlands along the north side of the Yellowstone River, it was necessary to travel the Yellowstone-Missouri divide to a point near the fort and then work down to the river. This part of the journey was uneventful except that during the first several days great numbers of mosquitoes drove the travelers to the use of heavy gloves and coarse sacks which they pulled over their heads.

It took eleven days to reach the post on the Yellowstone where they waited a week for a barge which was bringing some of their effects. On the 17th of August, the barge ferried the party to the south bank of the Yellowstone, and then for four days they toiled up the valley of the Rosebud—drinking from stagnant, stinking pools and sometimes worried by "the impress of human feet in the sand, concealed encampments and half-quenched fires."

From the Rosebud, the little train laboriously crossed some rugged terrain to the Tongue where men and animals rejoiced at being able to enjoy water that was as "pure as crystal." As the party worked their way southward along the eastern base of the Big Horn Mountains they arrived "quite unexpectedly" at a little lake. This they named Lake De Smet in honor of the priest. As they passed into the valley of the Powder, the country became gullied and sterile to such an extent that the teamsters vowed they would never be caught driving a wagon there again. To make matters even worse they met three young Crows who recommended a route which the men were later to name "the route of a thousand miseries." Finally they came out on the Oregon Trail about 160 miles west of Fort Laramie and had to double back. When they arrived at the post on the 10th of September they found that the meeting place had been moved to the mouth of Horse Creek some thirty-five miles farther eastward.

The council which this party had journeyed so far to attend probably had its beginning five years before when Thomas Fitzpatrick was appointed Indian Agent for the Upper Platte and Arkansas Agency. *White Head*, one of the few trappers who was blessed with foresight and administrative ability, believed that conditions on the plains warranted a conference between the various Indian tribes and the Government, from which should come a general, all-inclusive treaty which would stabilize relations between the Indians and the whites. He spent considerable time promoting this idea and finally, in 1851, the General Appropriations Act did provide $100,000 to defray the expenses of a treaty-making conference. In August of this year, an imposing assemblage of plains Indians began to gather at Fort Laramie.

David D. Mitchell, Superintendent of Indian Affairs at St. Louis, headed the government delegation, which also contained the Adjutant-General of the Army, the editor of the *Missouri Republican*, Robert Campbell, and a lawyer named B. Gratz Brown. Campbell had been Sublette's partner in the first opposition post near Fort Union, and Mitchell had built Fort McKenzie, the American Fur Company's post among the Blackfeet. Two hundred and seventy soldiers were present to police the situation and keep enemy tribes from open hostilities. The Sioux, Cheyennes, and Arapahoes formed one friendly group, and in addition there were Shoshones, Crows, Arickaras, Minnetaries, and Assiniboines. One dragoon later estimated that there were 60,000 Indians present but De Smet put the figure at 1,000 lodges or 10,000 people.

The council lasted about a week. Perhaps the most knotty problem was that of tribal boundaries and this was finally turned over to three experts on both geography and Indians—Fitzpatrick, Bridger, and Campbell. The final draft of the treaty was signed on the 18th of September and two days later the anxiously awaited wagon train loaded with presents arrived. To the Indians, this was the most important part of the whole affair.

Several basic decisions were contained in the treaty: (1) The Indians recognized the right of the United States to lay out roads and establish military posts in Indian territory; (2) There were solemn obligations to maintain peace, and to reimburse the whites for any damages due to Indian depredations; (3) An annual indemnity of $50,000 was granted in return for damage done by white travelers to game, pasture, and timber; (4) The U.S. agreed to pay the $50,000 annually in goods useful to the Indians and to continue the payment for 50 years. Also, the normal territory of each tribe was outlined although it was recognized that hunting parties did not have to be limited by these boundaries.

Congress approved the treaty with the modification that the period of payment was reduced from 50 to 15 years—which change was agreed to by all the tribes except the Crows. In the end, this treaty was never officially promulgated by the President, the Indians forgot their good intentions toward the other tribes and the whites, and Fitzpatrick's bright dream brought no lasting benefits.

There is, however, one feature of this so-called treaty which is of particular importance in understanding some of the events which occurred during the next twenty-five years. That is the boundary of the area which it was agreed belonged to the Crows. This region extended from the Rattlesnake and Wind River Mountains in the south to the Musselshell River on the north, and from the upper reaches of the Yellowstone on the west to the channel of the Powder River on the east. *This included the entire Yellowstone Basin—with the exception of the eastern side of the valley of the Powder, and that part of the Yellowstone valley between the mouth of the Powder and the Missouri River.* After delivering the annuity goods to the Absaroka in 1859, Agent Alfred J. Vaughn wrote in an official report:

No country I have examined seems to me more adapted to the wild Indian than this. There is game in abundance for his subsistence, grass for animals, and wood enough for his fuel; and the red man asks nothing more. But from its very nature the hand of civilization will leave it undisturbed forever.

Vaughn's opinion may have appeared sound in 1859, but only a few years later the Crows signed a treaty at Fort Union which gave the government a right of way and unmolested travel up the valley of the Yellowstone. Between 1851 and 1866, the date of the above-noted treaty, two things happened which had a profound effect on what was to happen in the land of the Crows—the Sioux moved into part of this area, and the discovery of gold in the Northwest started several important movements.

When the elder la Verendryé was slowly extending his chain of posts westward from the Great Lakes region, the Teton Sioux were in the upper Mississippi valley and on the prairies immediately to the westward. By the time Lewis and Clark began their trek, they were established along the Missouri; and, later, Fort Laramie provided an excuse to roam still farther to the west and south. By 1851, these people were living in the area just to the east and southeast of the territory designated as Crow country.

These Dakotas—Oglalas, Sans Arcs, Miniconjous, Hunkpapas and Brules—were a proud, bold people known to their neighbors as the *enemies*. In the sign language of the plains, they were designated by the significant motion of drawing the edge of the hand, or index finger, across the throat meaning that they cut off the heads of their enemies—a fate which befell la Verendryé's oldest son and Father Aulneau in 1738 when on the western side of the Lake of the Woods.

Thus, in the century and a half before the great conference at the mouth of Horse Creek on the Platte, these Sioux tribes were moving west and southwest. Perhaps the chastisement suffered by the Santee Sioux for the Minnesota massacre in 1862 added a bit of incentive to move farther away from the whites. However, the Yellowstone Basin contained perhaps the strongest inducement of all for these interlopers to move into part of this area in the years immediately following 1851. The wife of an Army officer noted:

> At a formal council held at Fort Philip Kearney in July, 1866, between Colonel Carrington and certain Cheyenne chiefs, who were then in close relations with Red Cloud and other Ogillalla Sioux, but desirous of breaking loose from the tie, that they might receive protection from the whites, the following question was addressed to Black Horse:
>
> " Why do the Sioux and Cheyennes claim the land which belongs to the Crows?"
>
> Black Horse, The Wolf that Lies Down, Red Arm, and Dull Knife promptly answered:
>
> "The Sioux helped us. We stole the hunting grounds of the Crows because they were the best. The white man is all along the great waters, and we wanted more room. We fight the Crows, because they will not take half and give us peace with the other half."

In the decade following 1851, the Sioux appropriated for their own use a considerable part of the territory which it had been decided *belonged* to the Crows. And they arrogantly forced the whites to deal with *them* in matters pertaining to that part which they acquired by force.

While the Sioux were pushing the Crows into the northwestern corner of their own country, a development of far greater import was taking place in the mountains of western Montana. In 1852, indications of gold had been found, and eleven years later the fabulously rich deposits along Alder Gulch, a tributary of the Jefferson River, were discovered. A horde of people flocked in and settlements grew like mushrooms. These created a need for supplies of many kinds which had to be brought in either by way of the Missouri River or a road which connected with the Oregon Trail in what is now Idaho. Enterprising men began to raise grain and livestock in nearby valleys, particularly that of the Gallatin River, and they too developed needs. So there was an insistent clamor for a direct road to the east across the country of the Crows. And in their search for gold, prospectors traveled widely without regard for treaty stipulations. It is against this background that the events of the 1860's and 1870's must be placed: and in a society where the majority of the pioneers refused to take seriously the *rights* of Indians, there were ventures and dealings which were tainted with both selfishness and dishonesty.

As the first diggings discovered among the mountains were not highly profitable, prospectors began to search far and wide for richer deposits. One region which they eyed was the northwestern part of the Yellowstone Basin and, of course, the adjacent Big Horn Mountains. However, this was not an area which a few men could enter with impunity. In the spring of 1863, fifteen men organized a prospecting company to explore this territory. The captain was a seasoned frontiersman named James Stuart who, with his brother Granville, had made the journey to California in '49 when but a boy: and the two, together with a mutual friend, had set the first sluices in the Montana gold fields. Others were Samuel T. Hauser—later a prominent banker—Henry Edgar and Bill Fairweather, and George Ives who was hung before the year had passed for being an outlaw. Edgar and Fairweather were to have gone with Stuart but missed the rendezvous—fortunately—and, with five others of the group, had noteworthy adventures of their own.

On the 25th of April, Stuart's party had reached the Yellowstone just below the Great Bend. The party moved down along the north bank and one evening, when just below the mouth of the Stillwater, were startled to hear the reports of several guns and see some thirty Indians fording the river and calling out "How-dye-do" and "Up-sar-o-ka." By the time the Crows reached the camp, the men had their horses tied and were prepared for an emergency even though they were badly outnumbered.

Although it was obvious that there was going to be trouble, all that developed during the night was a series of scuffles between the prospectors and their light-fingered visitors over small pieces of property. By morning everyone had lost something and, when they started to pack up, the warriors

at once proceeded to forcibly trade horses, blankets, etc., and to appropriate everything they wanted. I saw that the time had come to do or die; therefore, I ordered every man to be ready to open fire upon them when I gave the signal. With one hand full of cartridges and my rifle in the other, I told the Indians to mount their horses and go to their camp. They weakened, got on their horses and left.

Twelve years later when Hauser edited Stuart's journal for publication he noted that this short comment did not do justice to the tense moment. Stuart, outwardly unperturbed and smoking his pipe, watched until the principal chief was separated from his warriors. Then, with a sharp order to his men, the captain covered the old warrior's heart. Each man covered a brave, and every Indian dropped his robe and leveled his gun also. With his eyes flashing, Stuart cussed the old chief out for his bad faith and then threatened to kill him if he did not call his men off at once. The chief stared at him defiantly for a few seconds "but finally a wave of his hand relieved our doubts, and his braves all lowered their weapons of death and suddenly sought their robes and ponies."

This sudden break in the tension was too much for young Hauser. He threw his hat in the air and shouted "with laughter."

*The second chief, who was a straight, tall, fine-looking young war-rior, and as brave as Julius Caesar, was perfectly pale with rage because the old chief hadn't signalled the fight, and the fact that I had laughed and exulted over it only increased his rage. Rushing up to me in a white heat, he placed his finger on my nose and then on his own, and quickly touched his gun and then mine, and pointed to one side. And while I didn't "see it," the other fellows did shouting with laughter . . . . the young brave had to retire without satisfaction which, I regret to say, he got afterwards. . . .*

On the 6th of May, the party crossed the Yellowstone to the mouth of the Big Horn where they surveyed a townsite and staked claims for adjoining lands. Five days later, while trailing up the western side of this stream, they had a mystifying experience:

*. . . . At seven o'clock, just as we were going to start from camp, tents down and horses packed, I looked across the river, and about a mile above us I saw three white men, with six horses, three packed and three riding. They were coming down the river [sic—traveling south, the same as Stuart's party], and I waited until they got opposite to us, distant about three quarters of a mile, and then hailed them. They would nei-ther answer nor stop, but kept the same course and at a little faster pace. . . .*

Stuart then sent two men to overtake the travelers while he and an-other crossed to the other side to meet them. After traveling five miles he met one of his men returning—without the strangers. They then picked up the trail and pushed their horses to their utmost for several miles; but finally decided "it would not pay to run ours down to see three fools. . . ." The identity of these furtive strangers remained unknown to Stuart for several months. However, this incident is properly part of another story, and at this point the strangers must be left in the broken country where they eluded the "captain" and his men.

The following day there were ominous *signs*. Far out on one side, bands of buffalo were continually being stampeded *toward* the party — indications that Indians were dogging their steps. That evening it threatened rain and the men took all the saddles, provisions, and bag-gage into the tents and piled them around the outside edges—a very fortunate thing. Stuart was worried for he was positive there were In-dians very close to the camp, and he elected to stand the first watch of the guard. About eleven o'clock the horses became nervous:

. . . we were both lying flat on the ground trying to see what made the horses so uneasy, and to this we owe our lives. Just then I heard Smith [the other guard] whisper that something was around his part of the horses, and a few seconds later the Crows fired a terrific volley into the camp. I was lying between two of my horses, and both were killed and very nearly fell on me. Four horses were killed, and five more wounded, while in the tents two men were mortally, two badly, and three more slightly wounded.

The tents were quickly jerked down, to prevent their being used again for a target, and those who were able to handle their guns crawled out and lay flat on the ground expecting another attack each instant. The man sleeping beside Hauser was wounded, and he had an anxious moment before he discovered that the bullet which had pierced the thick memorandum book in his left shirt pocket had merely lodged against one of his ribs. Throughout the remainder of the night, arrows whistled through the air "and so close were the Indians that we could hear the twang of their bowstrings." The next morning Hauser picked up forty-eight arrows within a radius of thirty or forty feet of where he had been lying.

Stuart wrote in his journal:

When at last day dawned, we could see a few Indians among the rocks and pines on a hill some five or six hundred yards away. . . . An examination of the wounded presented a dreadful sight. . . . We held a council of war; concluded that it was impossible to return through the Crow country, now that they were openly hostile; therefore, determined to strike for the emigrant road on Sweetwater river, throwing away all our outfits except enough provisions to do us to the road.

This fight and the evening of the following day brought two harrowing moments. One of those mortally wounded in the fight asked to be given a revolver and left behind.

We gave it to him, and a few minutes later were startled by the report of his pistol, and filled with horror when we saw that he had blown out his brains.

The next evening a man named Gerry carelessly pulled his rifle out from under a pile of blankets and was very seriously wounded by an accidental discharge. As his companions clustered around him, he asked Stuart for a candid opinion of his wound. Jim gave an evasive reply; and the man, with a revolver firmly clutched in his right hand, took leave of his friends and asked them to bury him in his army overcoat. All the men could do was to turn their backs and walk away.

Most of the men doubted if they would get out alive. Frequent smoke signals warned that the Indians hovered near but, by keeping vigilant watch and camping in the dark, the men arrived at the Oregon Trail—where a passing wagon train first mistook them for Indians. After finding a few *colors* along the Sweetwater, the men took the circuitous road back to Bannock where they arrived on the 22nd of June—"so dilapidated generally, that scarcely anyone knew us at first." It was going to be difficult to prospect in the Yellowstone Basin!

While Stuart's men were having their troubles, the little group of seven who were to have joined them had some adventures of their own. Two days after Stuart's first encounter with the Crows, these men were only a day's travel behind and pushing hard to catch up. Then, according to Henry Edgar's diary, "towards morning the horses became restless, and required a good deal of looking after," and when daylight came they discovered the "hills were alive with Indians." This was no band of thirty warriors but a village of 180 lodges.

These Absaroka took everything the men possessed but their arms, and would have taken these also had not the prospectors indicated that they would resist. After the Crow leaders had spent most of the next day deliberating, the men were told that if they continued on down the river they would be killed but if they went back they would be given horses.

A bunch of horses were driven up and given to us. I got a blind eyed black and another plug for my three; and rest of the boys in the same fix, except Bill Fairweather, he got his three back. We got our saddles, a hundred pounds of flour, some coffee, sugar, one plug of tobacco and two robes each for our clothes and blankets; glad to get so much.

They were directed to cross a nearby ford and go up the south side of the Yellowstone; but an old woman whom they met warned them that they would be killed if they followed these instructions.

When we came to the ford we camped and got something to eat and when it was dark saddled up and traveled all night; took to the hills in the morning; we were about forty or forty-five miles from our friends, the Indians.

Traveling at night and sleeping by day, dodging across the Yellowstone and back again to avoid a party of Indians which followed them, the men worked their way up the valley and over the Bozeman Pass to the valley of the Gallatin.

From this point they went directly west and, when they had the Madison River behind them, they stopped to prospect. Slowly they worked their way over the divide and into the valley of the Jefferson Fork of the Missouri. One day, while camped at the head of a small stream, four of the men left Edgar and Fairweather to watch camp while they prospected.

Bill went across a bar to see or look for a place to stake the horses. When he came back to camp he said, "There is a piece of rimrock sticking out of the bar over there. Get the tools and we will go prospect it."

Three *pans* later, they had $12.50 and the next day the party took out $150 "in good dust." This was the end of the rainbow which Stuart and his men had hoped to find—*this was the fabulous Alder Gulch.* Before winter came, miners took from this twelve-mile-long valley an estimated $10,000,000 in dust and nuggets.

While Stuart and his associates were looking far afield, others were content to search closer to the little settlements in the mountains. In the late fall of 1863 Thomas Curry, an Irishman who had recently come to the U.S., and two companions began to prospect in the valley of the Yellowstone south of the Great Bend. They found traces of gold at the mouth of Emigrant Gulch and were busily searching for profitable diggings when a band of Crows chanced to find them. The Absaroka helped themselves to all their food and supplies and then left them.

The men went back to Alder Gulch to winter and to accumulate another outfit, and in the spring returned for a second try. When Jim Bridger guided a wagon train through from the Oregon Trail, Curry learned of its presence and went down to the Great Bend to recruit additional miners. A few were receptive and, by mid-summer, thirty-six men were trying to develop the area he had located. However, the best anyone was able to pan out was about $2.00 a day and that was starvation wages. Late in August, a train captained by Cyrus Coffenbury arrived at the crossing of the Yellowstone and several men left it to explore the possibilities at these new diggings. However, the prospects at "Curry's Gulch" were not promising. Several turned back but David Weaver, Frank Garrett, and David Shorthill decided to follow the gulch back into the Absaroka Mountains and search for the source of the gold.

These men followed up the little stream some six miles. Here they came to a barren area where the stream flowed over solid bed-rock. Weaver recalled:

. . . Shorthill, picking up the shovel, stuck it down through the water, under a shelving rock, and brought up two shovelsful of the sand

and gravel, which were thrown into a "pan." It was the work of but a few seconds to "pan" this out. And there in the bottom of the pan lay unmistakably, the object of our long journey. There was perhaps a dollar's worth of gold in this first pan. I fancy I can hear yet the yell of delight which Shorthill gave, as well he might, for had we not traveled over two thousand miles and spent four long weary months at the heels of slow ox-teams, since we first "hitched up" on the prairies of Iowa?

Weaver remained at the find while the others went to bring their friends. On the 12th of September the miners organized the Shorthill District and adopted a set of by-laws. Years later, Deputy Recorder Weaver wrote:

Thereafter, the old or lower district was known as the Curry District, and the new discovery as the "Shorthill District," and the gulch, thus taken possession of by men of Bridger's and Coffenbury's emigrant trains, came to be referred to as the "Emigrant's Gulch."

When it became too cold for placer mining, the men went down to the mouth of the gulch where they built a cluster of little, dirt-roofed cabins which they named Yellowstone City. As there had not been time to bring in supplies, some of the men spent a long, hard winter. Flour sold for $28.00 a sack—in gold not greenbacks. Coffee brought $1.00-2.00 a pound, tea twice that amount, and smoking tobacco was worth its weight in gold—or $300 a pound with gold valued at $18 an ounce. One merchant arrived in the fall and the next year (1865) other traders came in and Yellowstone City became a "live mining town."

One settler was John J. Tomlinson who set up a water-powered saw mill nine miles down the valley at Mill Creek. His son, Philo, was the first white child born in the settlement. In addition to this sawyer, seven miners had their wives with them, and two of these families had children.

By the fall of 1865, the Crows had become ugly over this invasion of their territory; and many settlers, fearing for their safety, moved out. When Weaver left the following spring there were only about a dozen men left. When the report came in that Indians had ambushed a boat party shortly after they had left the Great Bend "for the states" and killed a man named Lawrence, the remainder packed an ox-cart and took the short-cut to Bozeman. Weaver returned in August at which time the diggings were almost abandoned. The mining days in Emigrant Gulch were practically over. It had never been a particularly rich find, and the total take was probably not over $28,-30,000.

James Stuart and his men were about fifty miles above the mouth of the Big Horn when, on May 11, 1863, they sighted the three mysterious travelers. These people had had one narrow escape from a large war party while coming down the Yellowstone, and were in no mood to meet strangers. John M. Bozeman and John M. Jacobs, accompanied by the latter's little half-breed daughter, were scouting out a short-cut from the Montana settlements to the Oregon Trail along the Platte— a private venture of a promotional nature. Bozeman, a young man, had come to the mountains about four years before from Georgia where, in an irresponsible sort of way, he had left a wife and three small children. As he had been rather unsuccessful in mining, he turned the energies of his restless nature and alert mind to promotional work. These activities resulted in marking out the short-lived Bozeman Trail, which was known by at least a dozen names, and the establishment of the town of Bozeman. His companion was a red-bearded ex-trapper who had spent twenty-one years in the mountains. After trapping had played out, he had traded cattle along the Oregon Trail and guided wagon trains.

Later, James Stuart's brother, Granville, learned of the adventures of this little party. Their fear of meeting unfriendly Indians was realized while traveling along the eastern slope of the Big Horn Mountains:

. . . two days later they came suddenly upon a band of seventy-five or eighty mounted Indians. Knowing they would be plundered of everything, if not murdered, and considering resistance hopeless, Jacobs managed to drop his rifle and bullet-pouch into the sage-brush before the Indians got to them. His anticipation was realized for they were at once stripped of almost everything, and many were for killing them on the spot; but finally, after a stormy discussion, they were given three miserable ponies in exchange for their horses and turned loose half-naked and without anything to eat. Moving slowly away, they waited until the Indians got out of sight, when they returned and found Jacob's gun and bullet-pouch; but unfortunately the latter only contained five balls at the time, and as they made all possible haste to get out of that dangerous neighborhood, they did not stop to kill and dry any meat, and before they knew it they had passed out of the buffalo range, and meeting with bad luck in killing small game . . . their five bullets were exhausted; and, after severe hardships, they finally got through to North Platte in a famishing condition.

Bozeman had little difficulty in interesting emigrants in this short route to the Montana gold fields and a wagon train began to gather about 100 miles north and west of Fort Laramie. Early in July, having assembled a sizeable train, Bozeman, Jacobs and a third guide named Rafeil started northward. For two weeks the train plodded along, traveling from six to twenty miles a day depending on the location of suitable water, and then one day, while halted for the usual mid-day rest—Samuel Word made this entry in his diary that evening:

July 20th (Monday)   Traveled six or seven miles this morning and encamped on the north prong of Lodge Pole Creek. We turned out our cattle and horses to graze and had eaten our dinner when the alarm of Indians was given. I was in the act of going to sleep at the time. I took out and discovered a body of Indians coming over the hills toward us. Word was given to bring in the stock and all were so busy looking after their guns and personal safety, that the order was not promptly responded to. The stock was however brought in and the guards put on. The Indians made friendly signs and we allowed them to come up. Their chiefs approached and asked for a parley with our "Captain," as they called him. The warriors, many of them prowled around our camp, stealing everything they could get their hands on, while others stayed around their chiefs. There were over 150 of them, belonging to the Cheyennes and Sioux, but few were Sioux. They came, they said to warn us not to proceed farther through their country, that they were combined to prevent a road being opened through there, that if we went on we would be destroyed, that they would be our enemies, that if we turned back they would not disturb us, etc, etc. One of them made an effort to kill our guide, but was prevented. They asked for something to eat, we gave them bread, meat and coffe, some would not eat, were sullen and mad. One made an effort to ride over the victuals, and I thought at one time we would have a fight, but they cooled down and left in squads after repeating their order that we must leave. Many of our men are timid and cowardly and immediately determined to go back. After the Indians left; while they were there, and today we have seen their signal fires and smokes on the high mountains from 30 to 50 miles to our left. Our guides tell us it is dangerous, and have ordered a retreat until we can get reinforcements. That is the conclusion this evening. We are disposed to leave it to the judgement of the guides as they have had experience with the Indians, their habits and the country. Some are in favor of going on anyway, others are not.

For a week the train eased southward, hoping that a large train of 75 wagons, reported to be behind them, would come up and provide reinforcements. Finally scouts came back with the information that this wagon train had decided to follow the old trail. Now there was nothing to do but retrace their steps and follow the Oregon Trail.

On the 31st of July, when this retrograde movement was well under way, Word noted:

*Ten of our boys started out this morning, going through to Bannock on horseback, packing their grub. Think it dangerous, doubt their getting through with their horses, if they do with their scalps.*

This group, guided by Bozeman, crossed the Big Horns and then turned northward down the valley of the Big Horn. Traveling mostly at night, they reached the Great Bend of the Yellowstone and crossed over to the Gallatin without meeting any Indians. However, their pack horse with the provisions tumbled into a deep gorge on the second day and they spent the next four days without food, a fast which was only partly broken when Bozeman managed to kill an eagle.

The following spring Bozeman was back again on the North Platte. This time both he and Jacobs were successful in bringing their trains through to the Montana settlements. Bridger also entered the business and took a train along the western side of the Big Horn Mountains, entering the Bozeman Trail after it had crossed the Big Horn River. Although there was a scarcity of grass along this route, Jim claimed his trail was better as it was 100 miles shorter and less exposed to attack by hostiles. These trains reached their destination early in July.

Other trains followed over the Bozeman Trail later in the season, the estimated total for the year being about 1000 wagons. One of these was a large train under the direction of "Captain" Townsend. One man with this train noted that they had "two French guides" and that

*the magnitude of our train, was 369 men, 36 women, & 56 children; 150 wagons, 636 Oxen, 79 horses, & 10 mules; valuation $130,000; there was also 194 cows. This train could shoot 1641 times without reloading.*

These people had four men killed and one severely wounded in an Indian attack on the headwaters of the Powder, but the hostiles did not make a determined stand. As travelers were favorably impressed by the new trails, the following year was to bring additional activity on these short-cuts to Virginia City.

While wagons were grinding out ruts to mark the new routes, the first major military expedition entered the Yellowstone Basin. This was sent out to chastize Indians thought to be in the eastern part of the area, and to establish a fort on the Yellowstone—a project which had been under consideration for over forty years. The force, under the command of General Alfred Sully, consisted of 4,000 cavalry, 800 mounted infantry, and two batteries of 12 pieces of artillery—with 300 government teams and 300 steers for beef.

Sully located Fort Rice on the western bank of the Missouri near the mouth of the Cannon Ball River. Then, leaving the infantrymen to complete the post, he took the remainder of the force and proceeded northward in search of the hostiles. Traveling with him was an emigrant train consisting of 160 teams and 250 people bound for the gold fields of Montana. On the 28th of July (1863), he scattered a Sioux village in the vicinity of the Kildeer Mountains and then headed for the Yellowstone. Although Indians dogged the column and sniped at those who strayed, the general's major problems involved food and water.

It was almost the middle of August when the expedition reached the divide between the Little Missouri and the Yellowstone. By this time the soldiers were reduced to a quarter of a ration per day—"two hardtacks, a little piece of 'sow belly' and a pint of coffee (when we could get the water)": and the heat during the middle of the day swelled the men's tongues until sometimes they could not talk. Finally, the troops reached the Yellowstone below the mouth of Glendive Creek and the men, forgetting discipline, rushed into the river alongside the horses to quench their thirst. Later in the afternoon two steamboats, the *Chippewa Falls* and the *Alone*, floated down and tied up nearby. On board were the much needed supplies.

Although the plans called for the establishment of a post on or near the site of old Fort Alexander, Sully did not think that such a desolate country needed a fort. Perhaps the fact that the third steamboat, which was loaded with the necessary building material, met with misfortune and sank below the mouth of the Yellowstone had something to do with this decision.

The steamboats now ferried the supplies to the west bank of the river while the wagons and teams forded the river. This operation took three days and cost the lives of several teamsters and a number of horses. Then the entire column went down to Fort Union where additional losses were incurred fording the Missouri. At this point the emigrants turned westward, and the troops began their return to Fort Rice.

It was the massacre of settlers living in southern Minnesota which set this first military expedition in motion. The second punitive effort which penetrated the Yellowstone Basin was motivated by troubles which took place just outside its southern border.

# 8

## A Futile Campaign

>>>>>>>>>>><<<<<<<<<< Those Indians who came to Fort Laramie when it was a trading post quickly learned that the great highway along the Platte River was a fertile field for plunder. Among these red freebooters none were more prominent than the Teton Sioux, Cheyennes and Arapahoes. The early 1860's saw an unusually large amount of Indian trouble because the Civil War had forced a reduction in the protection which the Army was able to afford. In fact there was such a dearth of troops that the North had to pad their scanty forces with "galvanized Yankees," as the Rebel soldiers who were paroled to fight Indians were called.

The year of 1864 was particularly trying. Raiding by the Cheyennes in western Kansas and eastern Colorado so infuriated the settlers that a mixed force of Colorado militia and regulars mauled White Antelope's camp on Sand Creek, a tributary of the Arkansas. Unfortunately, this camp was considered to be friendly—although it did harbor some bloody-handed culprits. The Sand Creek Massacre not only fostered greater hostility on the part of the Indians but such a howl of indignation went up from the mis-informed East that a Congressional investigation was held.

Conditions in the valley of the Platte were acute. Wagon trains moved with great difficulty; stagecoach travel without military escort was practically impossible; and large numbers of travelers collected at various locations, unable to proceed further with any degree of safety. Governor Evans of Colorado pointed out that the people of Denver and the vicinity faced a famine. Ben Holladay, kingpin of the Overland Stage Company, sent a long telegram to the Secretary of War in which he stated that his stages could move only with military escort and that small garrisons of troops were necessary for the existence of the stations. Such assistance, he argued, was neither adequate nor a solution to the problem. He wanted a seasoned Indian fighter like General Patrick Edward Connor placed in charge of the situation and given a sufficient force to put an end to the raids.

In response to this outcry, General Connor was moved from Camp Douglas in Utah, where he had been a thorn in the side of Brigham Young and his fellow Mormons, to the newly created District of the Plains with headquarters at Denver. Here the major problem was that of controlling the Sioux and their allies. These Indians, leaving their villages safe in the fastness between the Big Horn Mountains and the Missouri, were having a field day in the valley of the Platte. The danger from small bands which swooped down on stock, stragglers, and isolated habitations with the speed and sureness of a prairie hawk dropping on a mouse, was always present. And, in bands of several hundred to perhaps a couple thousand or more, well mounted on hardy ponies, they thumbed their noses at military escorts and garrisons. Theirs was the advantage of initiative, and the choice of time and place of battle.

There was no general agreement on *how* to solve the problem. The stage and telegraph companies wanted troops distributed all along the line while Connor favored a slashing winter campaign with a force of 1500-2000 well mounted troops. The latter was actually an impossibility as troops capable of such a campaign were not available.

Operations in 1865 were opened by Colonel Thomas Moonlight, the bumbling commander at Fort Laramie, who led a force of 500 cavalry into the Wind River country early in May. The Indians evaded him easily and moved over to the valley of the Powder where scouts reported there were 1500-2000 lodges of hostiles. Here the warriors were able to strangle traffic on the Oregon Trail, and block any movement up the Bozeman Trail. General Sully was directed to march westward from Fort Pierre with 1200 cavalry about the middle of May and establish a large post on the Powder 150-200 miles north of Fort Laramie. This was to be supplied from Fort Laramie; and Connor was directed to cooperate. However, these orders were countermanded and Connor went ahead with plans for a summer campaign which he was determined to lead in person.

Although Connor received plenty of *paper* cooperation, the sinews of war were hard to assemble. General G. M. Dodge, commanding officer of the Department of the Missouri under whose jurisdiction the newly-created District fell, telegraphed to General Pope that,

General Connor is laboring under great difficulty. Stores that should have been in Laramie six weeks ago are stuck in the mud, and the columns here started out half shod and half rationed. There is not one foot of road but what we have to guard our trains, and it uses up troops beyond all conception. Every regiment that has come here so far has been dismounted or the horses unserviceable.

The column which Connor was to command needed 200 wagons: his quartermaster, Captain Palmer, managed to gather 185 of which only 70 were government property. Many soldiers had enlisted for the duration of the Civil War and this was now over. Colonel Nelson Cole had trouble with the troops which he assembled in Omaha. The Sixteenth Kansas Cavalry actually mutinied at Fort Laramie—but Connor quickly corrected this situation at the point of a gun.

*Four* columns were put into the field. The eastern or right one, composed of about 1,100 men under Colonel Nelson Cole, started from Omaha. Its supplies were carried by a wagon train of 140 wagons drawn by six-mule teams. The mules were unbroken at the start and the drivers were "equally bad." The "center" column consisted of 700 men under Lieutenant Colonel Samuel Walker with rations for 40 days on pack mules. And in the "left" column were 475 men and the train of 185 wagons. The fourth or "west" column consisted of 200 men under Captain Albert Brown, and this one, after a short swing in the upper portion of the Big Horn valley, crossed the Big Horn Mountains and joined the "left" column on the headwaters of the Powder—thus leaving three columns for most of the campaign. Colonel J. H. Kidd and 250 men, who were to construct and garrison a supply depot where the Bozeman Trail crossed the Powder, also accompanied the "left" column.

This left column, which Connor commanded in person, was the best of the three in many respects. It had seven competent scouts including two of the very best—Mitch Buoyer, a half-breed Sioux who was married to a Crow woman, and cagey old Jim Bridger. And in the van were Frank North and about ninety-five Pawnees, a unique scouting and fighting organization that was a host within itself. Brown's force had 84 Omaha and Winnebago scouts.

Connor ordered Cole to proceed to the eastern side of the Black Hills and then turn north to Bear Butte where he might find Indians. He was then directed to skirt the northern end of the Hills "from thence you will strike across the country in a northwesterly direction to the north base of the Panther [sic—Wolf] Mountains where you will find a supply depot." Walker was directed to move northward from Fort Laramie, along the western side of the Black Hills to the headwaters of the Little Missouri, and then turn northwest and rendezvous with the others at the "Panther" Mountains. Both of these officers were further instructed:

You will not receive overtures of peace or submission from the Indians, but will attack and kill every male Indian over twelve years of age.

This stipulation became known in the East and was seized upon by those sentimentalists who were clamoring against the military policy of solving the Indian problem.

Cole left Omaha on the 1st of July, and Connor's column departed from Fort Laramie on the 31st: Walker got his men under way two days later. By the 14th of August, the "left" column was at the point where the Bozeman Trail crossed the Powder, and construction of Fort Connor was under way.

Two days later, North's Pawnees discovered the trail of twenty-four Sioux and, after trailing them about twelve miles, jumped the unsuspecting hostiles. Captain Palmer, Connor's quartermaster, went along:

Our war party outnumbered the enemy, and the Pawnees, thirsty for blood and desirous of getting even with their old enemy, the Sioux, rode like mad devils, . . . [and] rushed into the fight half naked, whooping and yelling, shooting, howling—such a fight I never saw before. Some twenty-four scalps were taken, twenty-four horses captured, and quite an amount of other plunder. . . . There was a squaw with the party; she was killed and scalped with the rest. On their return to camp they . . . rode with the bloody scalps tied to the ends of sticks, whooping and yelling like so many devils. In the evening they had a war dance. . . . No one who has never witnessed a genuine Indian war dance could form any conception as to its hideousness—the infernal "hoo yah" and din-din of the tom-tom. These howling devils kept up the dance, first much to our amusement, until long after midnight, when finally the General, becoming thoroughly disgusted, insisted on the officer of the day stopping the noise. After considerable talk Captain North, their commander, succeeded in quieting them, and the camp laid down to rest; but this war dance was kept up every night until the next fight, limited, however, to 10 o'clock P.M.

After a stop of eight days, the column moved northward along the eastern base of the Big Horn Mountains. Here the men reveled in an abundance of trout, game and good water. On one occasion the commissary was supplied in a novel fashion:

Several bands of buffalo had been feeding close to camp, and about 5 o'clock P.M., about twenty-five cavalrymen rode out and surrounded a band and drove them into a corral formed of our wagons, and there fifteen were slaughtered and turned over to the commissary department.

When the command topped the divide between the Powder and the Tongue, Captain Palmer and Bridger were riding with the Pawnees, well in advance of the general and his staff. As Palmer was admiring the great sweep of mountains and plains before him, the scout asked, "Do you see those ere columns of smoke over yonder?" pointing to a depression in the hills "fully fifty miles away." The captain could not—even with his glasses—but he thought it was politic to agree. Connor, who had now come up, could not see the smoke either and said so: and Jim rode on muttering something about "these damn paper collar soldiers." However, just to be certain, North and seven Pawnees were sent to reconnoitre.

The old scout had the last laugh. Just at sunset, two days later, two of the Pawnees caught up with the column as it was moving down the Tongue. There *was* an Indian camp in the locality which Bridger had indicated.

Leaving his wagon train, Connor took 250 men and 80 Indian scouts and moved out at once. Palmer was detailed to command the guard which was to protect the wagons; but, as he "had never been baptized with Indian blood . . . [or] taken a scalp," he begged to be replaced by another officer who was ill. Connor consented and some twelve hours later the quartermaster "was reminded" that he positively did not want "any dirty scalps." It was a difficult night, struggling through underbrush and over fallen trees in the darkness, and daylight found them some distance from the village and under the necessity of using every possible bit of cover.

About the middle of the forenoon Palmer, beginning to think there were no Indians near, managed to get ahead of Frank North. As he rode up a game trail out of a ravine, he was startled to suddenly see the camp before him. Quickly grasping his horse's nostrils, he slipped from the saddle and dragged his mount down the bank.

After issuing an order for his men to follow him and to hold their fire until he shot, Connor

rode his horse up the steep bank of the ravine and dashed out across the mesa as if there were no Indians just to the left; every man followed as closely as possible. At the first sight of the General, the ponies covering the table land in front of us set up a tremendous whinneying and galloped down toward the Indian village. More than a thousand dogs commenced barking, and more than seven hundred Indians made the hills ring with their fearful yelling. It appeared that the Indians were in the act of breaking camp. The most of their tepees were down and packed for the march. The ponies, more than three thousand, had been gathered in, and most of the warriors had secured their horses; probably half of the squaws and children were mounted, and some had taken up the line of march up the stream for a new camp. . . . The General watched the movements of his men until he saw the last man emerge into line. The whole line then fired a volley from their carbines into the village without halting their horses, and the bugles sounded the charge. Without the sound of the bugle there would have been no halt by the men in that column; not a man but realized that to charge into the Indian village without a moments hesitancy was our only salvation. . . . my horse carried me forward almost against my will, and in those few moments—less than it takes to tell the story—I was in the village in the midst of a hand to hand fight with warriors and their squaws, for many of the female portion of this band did as brave fighting as their savage lords. Unfortunately for the women and children, our men had no time to direct their aim; bullets from both sides and murderous arrows filled the air; squaws and children, as well as warriors, fell among the dead and wounded. The scene was indescribable. There was not much of the military in our movements; each man seemed an army by himself. Standing near the "sweat house," I emptied the contents of my revolver into the carcasses of three warriors. . . . The Indians made a brave stand trying to save their families, and succeeded in getting away with a large majority of their women and children, leaving behind them nearly all their plunder. They fled up a stream now called Wolf Creek, General Connor in close pursuit.

After chasing the Indians until their horses gave out—and it became too dangerous to press the pursuit farther—the soldiers returned to camp. Meanwhile, North and his Pawnees rounded up about 1,100 ponies. Then everyone worked for a couple of hours to burn the camp and its contents. While they were thus engaged, warriors returned to harass them and finally Connor had to use a howitzer to drive them off.

Early in the afternoon, the command began its return. North and the Pawnees led the way driving the captured ponies, while the remainder of the command fought the desperate hostiles who continued to charge the rear guard and dash at the captured ponies until nearly midnight. When the Indians finally drew off, everyone was almost exhausted and only forty men had any ammunition left. The command arrived at the wagon camp about 2:00 A.M. the next morning having been in the saddle or fighting for thirty hours.

This village, which was located on the south side of the Tongue opposite the present town of Ranchester, Wyoming, was that of a band of Arapahoes under Black Bear and Old David. Palmer estimated that the Indians numbered about 700, and that they destroyed 250 lodges. Connor reported that the camp contained "over five hundred souls" and that they "captured five hundred horses, mules and ponies, and took prisoners seven women and eleven children, and killed as near as I can estimate thirty-five warriors." The casualties were five soldiers killed or mortally wounded, one Omaha Indian killed, and two other soldiers wounded. A day or two later the captives were each given a pony and released to inform the chiefs that if they were interested in peace they should come into Fort Laramie in October for a conference with the general.

For a week following the fight, Connor moved down the Tongue. Scouts sent to the designated rendezvous returned with the information that there were no signs of the supporting columns. On the 6th of September, Connor, now worried about the remainder of his force, turned around and started back up the Tongue toward a good camping ground. Five days later, North and a detail of Pawnees came in with ominous news—along the Powder they had found five or six hundred cavalry horses and places where considerable equipment had been burned. Palmer, who was also in charge of commissary supplies, calculated that Cole was either out of food or on half rations.

Cole's command had moved along the route directed and, when on the Belle Fourche River north of the Black Hills, accidentally met Walker's troops. From this point the two columns, operating separately but staying close together, moved northwest striking the Powder about fifty miles above its mouth. It was now the 29th of August and Cole's rations were almost exhausted. A small scouting party was sent to the designated rendezvous, and this returned with the news that there was no sign of Connor and that part of the intervening territory was impassable for wagons. Rations were cut "to less than one half," and the men tightened their belts.

Up to this time neither party had seen any Indians, although trails had been noted leading down the valley of the Little Missouri. Now it was the Indians who found the soldiers and pressed matters. They attacked the herders while Cole was in camp and ran off part of the stock. These were recaptured with the loss of six soldiers. Then the colonel used his artillery to keep the hostiles at a safe distance, and they soon gave up the fight and retreated toward the Little Missouri carrying an estimated twenty-five dead. On the 2nd of September, both columns moved down the valley and that night were hit by an early fall storm. The following day they moved back to their first campsite on the Powder—Cole had now lost 225 horses and mules from "excessive heat, exhaustion, starvation, and extreme cold." After destroying the wagons and supplies which they could not move, both commanders headed up the Powder toward Fort Laramie.

To the troubles occasioned by starvation rations and difficult roads were now added harassing attacks by the Indians. On September 4th, they probed at Cole with a force of considerable size, an estimated 1,000 warriors taking part in one sally. Four days later, when near the mouth of the Little Powder, a courier arrived from Walker with a dispatch stating that he had been attacked by 3,000-4,000 warriors and was being driven back. Cole promptly went to his assistance and, after beating off the Indians, the two commands went into camp in an unprotected area. That night

a storm blew up, which grew worse as the night came on and finally became terrific in its fury. From rain it turned to hail, then rained again, then in succession snowed and sleeted, yet freezing all night long. My picket officers were forced to march their men in circles at the reserve posts to prevent freezing, as fires were not admissable. Nothing could be done to protect the stock from the peltings of this terrible storm, and numbers of them died during the night. When daylight dawned it had not abated in the least, and owing to the unsheltered position of my camp was especially severe on the men as well as the stock, so much so that I determined to move to some point where I could secure shelter in heavy timber to save the remnant of my rapidly falling animals.

I moved two miles and a half, marking my trail with dead and dying horses and mules. Arriving at a suitable place I camped, and by surrounding the stock with huge log fires and feeding them on cottonwood boughs and a little grass, decreased in a measure the rate of loss. . . . During the thirty-six hours the storm prevailed 414 of my animals perished. . . .

During the same period Walker lost 225 horses and 25 mules. The wagons which could not be moved were burned, together with the now-extra saddles and harness. Years later, cowboys idling with a round-up piled the tires from the wagon wheels into a great pile, which was picked up for scrap during World War I.

As soon as the storm ceased, the march was continued. Cole stated in his report:

*This move I was compelled to make under the cover of my artillery, owing to the fact that the Indians had, vulture-like, hovered around my exhausted and starving command, and as soon as preparations were made to move, knowing what the route must be, had made a detour around to a position on the bluffs in our rear, preparatory to dashing and harassing the rear of the column, which they did as soon as the command began its movements, but having no taste for the shells which were generously thrown amongst them, soon retired to their of late respectful distance beyond range.*

After a few more small skirmishes, the Indians—who had a strong dislike for artillery—gave up and were seen no more.

Connor became increasingly worried after North's report. Finally, Sergeant Thomas of the Seventh Iowa Cavalry and five Pawnees succeeded in finding the two columns. By this time the soldiers were down to less than quarter rations and were eating their horses and mules. When the men arrived at Fort Connor they looked more like tramps than soldiers.

While Connor's men had been hunting Indians, steps were taken to undo whatever good they might have accomplished. Those misguided individuals who were in favor of reducing the size of the army and of making a radical change in the policy of dealing with hostile Indians, had now gained sufficient political strength to permit them to dictate the course of action which should be followed. In fact, this movement had progressed to the point where the Powder River Expedition might not have even gotten started had General Dodge not employed stalling tactics at his level of command until the troops were beyond the reach of normal communications. Thus, while this force was in the field, plans were made to disband the troops and to hold a *palaver* at Fort Laramie the following spring—with the very Indians Connor's men were then fighting. However, before notifying the general that he had been relieved of his command, Dodge appealed to General U. S. Grant but the latter replied

*to the effect that the authorities in Washington were determined to stop all campaigns against the Indians. They had been made to believe* by the Interior department that all they had to do was withdraw the troops and the Indians would come in and make peace. . . .

These orders reached Connor while he was still in the field; and he immediately turned the troops over to Colonel Cole and set out for Fort Laramie. Here he relinquished his command and remained until his quartermaster had cleared his records. Then, smarting under the injustice done him, he left for Denver, enroute to his post in Utah. Captain Palmer noted that as soon as the soldiers returned to Fort Laramie, the Indians

again hastened to the road, passing General Connor's retiring column to the east of his line of march, and again commenced their devilish work of pillage, plunder and massacre.

While Connor was making his plans for this campaign, a road surveying expedition was working among the Niobrara River toward the valley of the Powder. Its ultimate destination was Virginia City in Alder Gulch. The impetus for this effort had come from the business men in Sioux City, Iowa, who could see no good reason why Omaha should enjoy all the pecuniary benefits of the travelers bound for the Montana gold fields. Congress had passed a bill providing $140,000 for the survey and improvement of several roads, and one of these was the pet project of the Sioux City merchants.

The expedition started, officially, at the mouth of the Niobrara on the 13th of June. "Colonel" James A. Sawyer was in charge, and the escort was comprised of 118 galvanized Yankees of the Fifth Volunteer Infantry and 25 soldiers from the First Dakota Volunteer Cavalry. The wagon train consisted of 15 wagons with three yoke of oxen, 18 double (or trail) wagons requiring six yoke, 5 emigrant wagons, and 26 mule wagons belonging to the escort. The chief guide was a squaw man, Ben Estes, who had been with Lieutenant Warren's surveying party in 1856, and he was assisted by a half-breed Sioux, Baptiste De Fond.

The survey experienced no trouble, other than an excessive amount of friction between Sawyer and the officer in command of the escort, until a point about twelve miles south of the present town of Gillette, Wyoming, was reached. Here Indians, thought to have been Cheyennes, killed one man and forced the train to corral for three days. Then, in a puzzling change of attitude, they allowed the train to proceed after leaving a wagonload of provisions. This change, the men deduced later, was due to the proximity of some of Connor's men. As the Indians harassed them from time to time, Sawyer sent out scouts to locate the whereabouts of the military expedition about which he had some vague information; and when they returned he took the wagon train south-westward to Fort Connor.

Here, Sawyer managed to exchange his obstinate escort for 40 men of the Sixth Michigan Cavalry commanded by Captain O. F. Cole; and then turned northward on the recently established Bozeman Trail. A few days later they met a small party bringing mail from Connor's column to Fort Connor, and these men appropriated half of the escort. On the headwaters of the Tongue a small band of warriors surprised Captain Cole and his lieutenant when they rode in advance of the rest to select a campsite. Cole was killed and the lieutenant escaped only by spurring his horse into immediate and precipitate retreat. As the captain was much liked by his men, they took his body with them hoping to return it to Fort Connor for burial.

The next forenoon the train rolled down to the crossing of the Tongue. Here there was a luxuriant growth of young trees and under-brush, and no precaution was taken to scout it. The wagons crossed without difficulty, but the train became strung out on the other side. While the loose cattle were drinking,

the air was suddenly filled with yells and shots. Out from the river, through the bushes rode the two herders, and also from among the bushes appeared a hundred or more devilish Indians, riding along on either side of our line, and pouring a continual volley of shot into our midst.

A corral was quickly formed and order was restored; but it was impossible to advance through the rolling country ahead. Finally, Sawyer ordered the wagons back to a flat near the river where a tight corral was formed just out of rifle range from the banks and brush along the stream. As two more men were killed, there were now three corpses in camp. The situation developed into a stalemate—the train could not move, and the Indians—apparently from the camp Connor had attacked—did not fancy a showdown with the soldiers and well-armed bull-whackers. Three volunteers slipped away to try to contact Connor and bring reinforcements and, as the men waited, the Arapahoes tried another tack. A few came in under a flag of truce and tried to convince the whites that they had mistaken them for a military outfit—and that they had no quarrel with ordinary travelers. Sawyer allowed these to retain their arms and to remain but when others tried to infiltrate the camp the next day the men became apprehensive and much excited.

The party now took matters into their own hands. Electing a leader from among themselves, they promptly put the savages out of the corral.

The new administration now proposed to destroy all but thirteen wagons and add the extra teamsters to the escort—thus making the chance of being able to fight their way through a little brighter. However, Sawyer stubbornly refused to destroy government property. So the train, having spent thirteen days in the fortified corral, started to retreat to Fort Connor.

This retreat was hardly under way when Captain Albert Brown and 100 men of the Second California Cavalry rode up. These were some of Connor's best troops and with them were Captain Nash and his Winnebago scouts. Brown restored Sawyer to command and escorted the train to the crossing of the Big Horn. On the 21st of September, having scouted the surrounding area for hostiles and discovered no signs, Brown allowed the train to proceed and he turned back.

The remainder of the journey was uneventful. They forded the Yellowstone just below where Livingston now stands and crossed the divide by way of the Bozeman Pass. On October 14th, the *Montana Post* of Virginia City noted that Sawyer had arrived two days before with 57 wagons and 350 head of cattle.

A month later, while in Salt Lake City, Sawyer wrote to the Iowa congressman who had pushed the bill for the road survey. He related all the advantages of the Niobrara route—grass, wood, and water—and its saving of 708 miles over the present route. Furthermore he stated that the road he had pioneered was good enough so that he did not have to uncouple his trail wagons at any time.

The following year Sawyer was sent out to complete the opening of this road. On the first of May, he left the mouth of the Niobrara River with a small force, numbering but seventy-two men including himself, and again went over the route he had laid out in 1865. However, the road was never used and the efforts of his men—like those of Connor's soldiers—went for naught.

# 9

## The Montana Road

>>>>>>>>>><<<<<<<<<< When the grass was well started in the spring of 1866, hundreds of Sioux and Cheyennes gathered about Fort Laramie to negotiate with the commissioners who believed that a pacifist attitude was all that was necessary to bring a cessation of the raiding along the Platte. These hostiles had taken the waving of the olive branch with some seriousness and were quite unprepared to see a large column of troops arrive from Fort Kearney on the 13th of June. The fact that the wagon train contained twenty-one women and children, together with the household goods of some of the officers, indicated all too clearly that this was no ordinary expedition.

The situation was one of dual perspective. Although the government was serious about this new *peace* policy, it had also decided that the Montana Road—alias the Bozeman Trail—was necessary for the settlements in the mountains. To make certain that the road was usable, military posts were deemed a necessity. As one hostile summed it up with brutal logic:

*Great Father sends us presents and wants new road, but white chief goes with soldiers to steal road before Indian say yes or no!*

It was no wonder that Red Cloud and other Sioux leaders left the council in disgust and anger.

The column which left Fort Laramie to fortify the Montana Road consisted of about 700 men under the command of Colonel Henry B. Carrington. Plans had been made to establish several posts, of which only three were ever built, and the force detailed to man them was to prove to be far too small to provide protection for the emigrant trains. The chief guide was Jim Bridger, then "somewhat bowed by age." With the troops was another guide named Williams; and Jack Stead, a runaway sailor boy from England who had a Cheyenne wife, was interpreter.

Before the summer was over another guide had been acquired—the erstwhile Crow *chief*, Jim Beckwourth. Carrington used him to make contacts with the Crows; and it was on one of these trips that he died in a Crow camp. There is a legend that he was poisoned by the Indians that they might keep his spirit with them always. Another acquisition after reaching the Big Horn Mountains was a group of about 50 miners. Their captain was a capable man named Bailey who worked at various tasks from making hay to carrying mail.

Carrington had expected to complete outfitting his column at Fort Laramie but there was little to be had. Carrington's wife wrote later that when he went to draw 100,000 rounds of ammunition there was available

*not a single thousand rounds for infantry arms . . . so it was assumed that we should have a happy journey, a happy peace, and a happy future . . . [However], Major Bridger told us that he had seen kegs of powder distributed to the Indians and carried away on their ponies; but . . . there was none for us.*

The command did draw twenty-six wagonloads of provisions, but soldiers had to be detailed to act as teamsters.

The troops left Fort Laramie on the 17th of June and eleven days later reached Fort Connor which was renamed Fort Reno. This was a "most unprepossessing" post with the quarters for officers and men, the guardhouse, and the magazine on the open plain. Only the warehouses and stables were enclosed by a rough stockade. Waiting here for instructions were three emigrant trains. Some of the officers' wives were quite surprised to find that the "lady travelers" did not believe that there were any bad Indians near the trail. This illusion was dispelled a

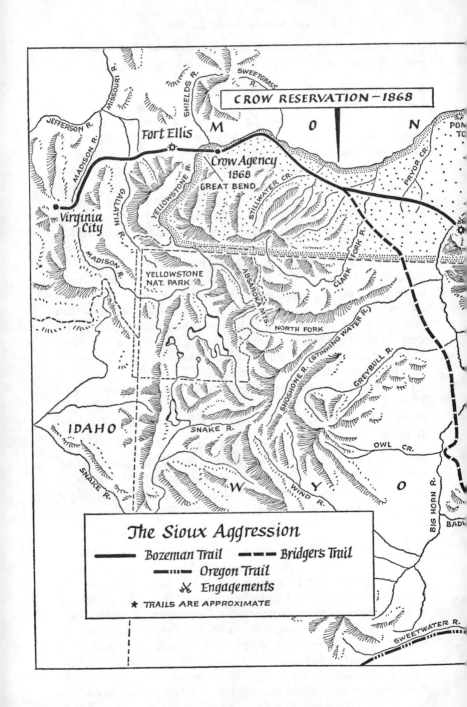

CROW RESERVATION—1868

The Sioux Aggression

—— Bozeman Trail   ----- Bridger's Trail
······ Oregon Trail
✕ Engagements
★ TRAILS ARE APPROXIMATE

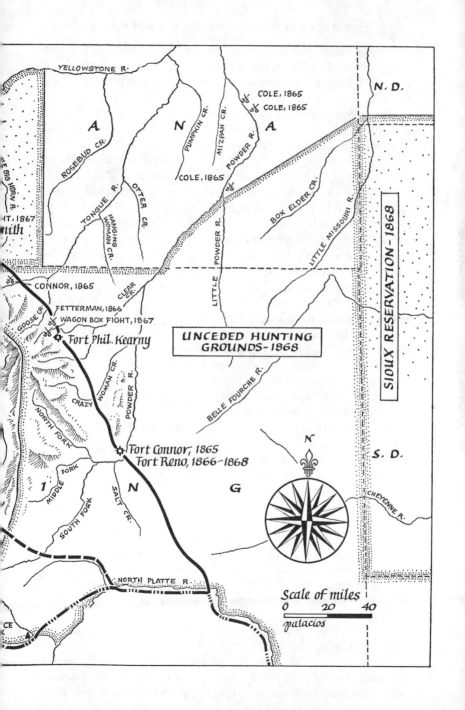

YELLOWSTONE R.

N. D.

COLE, 1865
COLE, 1865

A

N

A

E BIG HORN R.

ROSEBUD CR.

TONGUE R.

OTTER CR.

PUMPKIN CR.

MIZPAH CR.

POWDER R.

COLE, 1865

BOX ELDER CR.

LITTLE MISSOURI R.

T. 1867
uith

HANGING WOMAN CR.

LITTLE POWDER R.

CONNOR, 1865

CLEAR CR.

FETTERMAN, 1866
WAGON BOX FIGHT, 1867

GOOSE CR.

✣ Fort Phil. Kearny

**UNCEDED HUNTING
GROUNDS - 1868**

**SIOUX RESERVATION - 1868**

CRAZY WOMAN CR.

POWDER R.

BELLE FOURCHE R.

NORTH FORK

✣ Fort Connor, 1865
Fort Reno, 1866-1868

N

S. D.

1

MIDDLE FORK

SOUTH FORK

SALT CR.

N

G

CHEYENNE R.

NORTH PLATTE R.

Scale of miles
0    20    40
palacios

CE

day or two later when hostiles ran off the sutler's horses and mules. The detachment which was sent in pursuit did not recover the stock but they did capture a pony loaded with "favors recently procured at Laramie."

After delaying two weeks to get some necessary improvements under way, the colonel left two officers and a company of men to complete the work and garrison the post, and moved on. On the 11th of July, camp was made on the Big Piney Fork of Powder River at a place about four miles from the Big Horn Mountains. A few days later, after making a reconnaissance to the headwaters of the Tongue, Carrington decided to build a post on a bench near this creek. It is possible that the colonel did not make this decision. Ten years later an officer jotted down in his diary a bit of campfire gossip to the effect that the colonel's wife was a strong-willed woman. She decided that *she* liked the location and that the fort might as well be built at this spot as at any other.

While Carrington was absent on his reconnaissance, the Oglala Sioux sent word to the camp that if the colonel wanted peace he would have to return to Fort Reno—"they would not let the soldiers go over the road which had never been given to the whites, neither would they let them stay and build forts." Carrington arranged for a council on his return but the principal men who came in were from the Cheyennes. These finally expressed a desire for peace.

As it was necessary to complete the buildings as soon as possible so things could be made snug for the winter, both the soldiers and the civilians worked like beavers. Some idea of the difficulties involved are mirrored in the prices paid to contractors—$1. to 3.00 for each log delivered to the site of the fort, and hay was purchased at the rate of $126.00 per ton. On the last day of October the fort was near enough completed so that Carrington declared a "holiday" with a formal parade, flag raising, and speech by the commanding officer. Carrington's wife wrote this description:

> The fort proper is six hundred feet by eight hundred, situated upon a natural plateau, so that there is a gradual slope from front to rear. . . . A rectangle, two hundred by six hundred feet, is occupied by warehouses, cavalry stables, laundress quarters, and the non-commissioned staff.
>
> About the parade-ground . . . are officers' and men's quarters, offices, guardhouse, sutler's and band building.
>
> The stockade is made of heavy pine trunks, eleven feet long, hewn to a touching surface of four inches so as to join closely, being pointed and loop-holed, and firmly imbedded in the ground for three feet. Block-

houses are at two diagonal corners, and massive gates of plank with small wickets, all having substantial locks, are on three fronts, and on the fourth or southern front, back of the officers' quarters, is a small gate for sallies, or for officers use.

This post, named Fort Philip Kearney, was by far the most elaborate of the three as it was designed for a headquarters. Fort Reno was merely Fort Connor with some improvements and an encircling stockade added. The third post, Fort C. F. Smith, was built by Captain N. C. Kinney at the ford where the Bozeman Trail crossed the Big Horn. This was also a simple, stockaded post but it differed from the others in that two walls of the stockade were constructed of adobe bricks. A fourth, tentatively referred to as the "Upper Yellowstone" post, was to have been located beyond Fort C. F. Smith. However, it was never built.

As Fort Reno was at the extreme southern edge of the choice hunting grounds which the Sioux and their allies had appropriated from the Crows, it was not seriously harassed. And—except on one occasion— neither was Fort C. F. Smith which was near the region often occupied by the Crows. But Fort Phil Kearney was squarely within the hunting grounds claimed by the Sioux and they made their displeasure known in no uncertain fashion. Every work detail outside the stockade walls had to be carefully guarded: stock was run off whenever the vigilance of the herder relaxed: and the bodies of careless individuals who wandered off out of sight were almost invariably found later—if at all—naked, fancifully carved by knife and tomahawk, and bristling with arrows.

Eternal vigilance was the price of one's life, and sometimes even this was not enough. While the post was being completed, the civilian workers had their camp in a corral made of wagon boxes just outside the stockade. In the evening the men would gather near the fires within the circle to play cards and gamble; and on one occasion a man who had gone to bed was startled to hear three shots fired near the end of the wagon box in which he was reclining. Indians had crept through the picket line and killed two men and wounded a third who were seated near a campfire.

These civilians devised some ingenious gambling devices. One of these games of chance was

the race of a worm, or bug and very often . . . [lice]. They would chalk a small ring on a warmed tin plate and another outside this near the rim of the plate, when bets ranging from $10.00 to $100.00 would be made on the different worms, bugs or vermin that would get outside the outer ring first. The winner would sometimes clean up $500.00 on one race.

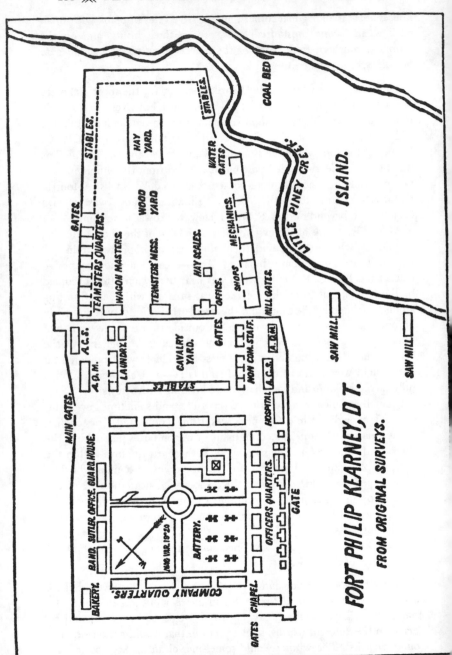

FORT PHILIP KEARNEY, D.T.

FROM ORIGINAL SURVEYS.

Although the President issued a statement early in December of this year to the effect that the Indians were peaceful, there rarely was a day during the first six months Fort Phil Kearney existed that Indians were not seen. To counter this claim, the colonel's wife compiled a list of the attacks which occurred during the summer and fall. The following occurred during the month of September:

*September 8th, at 6 o'clock* A.M.  *Twenty mules were driven from a citizen herd, during a severe storm, within a mile of Fort Phil Kearney; and two other demonstrations were made the same day. The colonel with one party, and Lieutenant Adair with another, were out until after 9 o'clock at night in pursuit.*

*September 10th.  Ten herders were attacked a mile south of the fort, losing thirty-three horses and seventy-eight mules. Pursuit was vigorous but unsuccessful.*

*September 13th.  At midnight a summons came from the hay contractors, Messrs. Crary and Carter, at Goose Creek, for help, as one man had been killed, hay had been heaped upon five mowing-machines and set on fire, and two hundred and nine cattle had been stolen by the Indians, who had driven a herd of buffalo into the valley, and thus taken the buffalo and cattle together out of reach.*

*Lieutenant Adair went at once with reinforcements, but found the Indians in too large force for continuance of the work.*

*The same day at 9 o'clock, Indians stampeded the public herd, wounding two of the herders. Captain Ten Eyck and Lieutenant Wands pursued until late at night. Private Donovan came in also with an arrow in his hip; but, just as he always was in an Indian fight, brave as a lion, and started out again as soon as it was withdrawn.*

*September 14th.  Private Gilchrist was killed.*

*September 16th.  Peter Johnson, riding a few rods in advance of his party, which was returning from a hay field near Lake Smedt [sic—De Smet], was suddenly cut off by Indians. Search was made that night by a party under Quartermaster Brown, but his remains were not recovered.*

*September 17th.  A large force demonstrated from the east, and took forty-eight head of cattle; but all were recovered on pursuit. [Ridgeway Glover, correspondent for Frank Leslie's Illustrated Weekly, was also found naked, scalped, and his back chopped by a tomahawk near the fort.]*

*September 20th.  Indians attacked a citizen outfit lying in the angle of the two Pineys; but were repulsed by aid from the fort, losing one red man killed and another wounded.*

*September 23rd.  Indians attacked and drove off twenty-four head of* cattle. They were pursued by Quartermaster Brown, in company with twenty-three soldiers and citizens, and after a sharp fight at close quarters, the cattle were recaptured, and a loss was inflicted upon the Indians of thirteen killed and many wounded [according to information secured later from the Crows].

September 23rd.   Lieutenant Matson, with an escort, bringing wagons from the hay field, was surrounded and corraled for some time by a superior force. He found upon the road the body of contractor Grull, who had been to Fort C. F. Smith with public stores, and was killed upon his return with two of his drivers. . . .

September 27th.   Private Patrick Smith was scalped at the Pinery, but crawled half a mile to the blockhouse, and survived twenty-four hours.

Two of the working party in the woods were also cut off from their comrades by nearly one hundred Indians, and were scalped before their eyes. A party of fifteen dashed at the nearest picket but did no harm.

Captain Bailey's mining party lost two of their best men.

By the 21st of December, the troops had participated in fifty-one skirmishes.

Late in August General Hazen made an inspection trip to the posts and picked up an escort of 26 men at Fort Phil Kearney. This, plus the requests for escorts by emigrants, made a heavy drain on the manpower available—even Chaplain White "only prayed *internally*, while putting his time physically into the best exercise of self defense." General Hazen assured Carrington that additional troops were on their way to bolster his scanty forces but all that arrived that fall was the fragment of one company—*sixteen "half armed" men.*

Horses used by the mounted infantry and cavalry dwindled in numbers until by the 10th of October only 40 were left at Carrington's post. By November, the men at Fort C. F. Smith were down to ten rounds of ammunition per man; at Fort Reno, to 30 rounds; and at Fort Phil Kearney, to 45 rounds. On that fateful morning of December 21st, Colonel Carrington had but 198 men. Yet in the early winter, in the face of this obvious shortage of men, up-to-date arms, and ammunition, two brave but foolhardy officers—Captains William J. Fetterman and Frederick H. Brown—wanted Carrington to allow them to lead a party of 60 mounted soldiers and 40 civilians against the Sioux villages in the valley of the Tongue!

The Indians hesitated to come to grips with the hated fort on the Piney. Carrington had some small howitzers and the hostiles had no stomach for the "gun that shoots twice"—a canister load contained 80 balls and could be something more than unpleasant. So the Sioux concentrated on maneuvers designed to decoy forces into ambush. On the 6th of December, one detail got into serious difficulty which cost the lives of a lieutenant and a sergeant while four others escaped death by the slightest of margins.

On the 21st of December, Mrs. Carrington recalled:

*The children ran in about 11 o'clock, shouting "Indians!" and the pickets on Pilot Hill could be distinctly seen giving the signal of "many Indians," on the line of the wood road; and the news was also furnished that the train was in corral only a short distance from the garrison.*

A detail of seventy-eight officers and men was organized to relieve the wood train; and as it was ready to move out, Captain Fetterman—a brevet lieutenant colonel—claimed the right to command the detachment by virtue of rank. Carrington gave his permission but, apparently, with a premonition of trouble for his orders were repeated three times. These were:

*Support the wood train, relieve it, and report to me. Do not engage or pursue Indians at its expence; under no circumstances pursue over Lodge Trail Ridge.*

Two experienced frontiersmen, James Wheatley and Isaac Fisher, joined the troops; Captain Frederick Brown slipped in without permission. The two reckless officers were now in command of a force sufficient—in their opinion—to whip the entire Sioux nation.

Fetterman moved out to a position on the near slope of the forbidden ridge where he could cut off the retreat of any Indians attacking the wood train. Some warriors were seen moving in front of the troops as they advanced and when the top of the ridge was reached, the force was extended in a skirmish line. Then, in utter disregard of orders, the force disappeared over the ridge. Soon scattered shots were heard, then continuous and heavy firing for perhaps fifteen minutes, and finally—silence.

In the meantime, Carrington sent a surgeon who soon returned saying that there were too many Indians for him to reach the troops. When the firing was heard, Captain Ten Eyck and seventy-six men—all the men for duty at the fort—together with two wagons with ammunition, were dispatched on the double; and orders were given to empty the guardhouse and hospital of every man capable of handling a gun.

When Ten Eyck reached the top of the ridge, the valley below seemed to be full of Indians, yelling and motioning for him to advance—but no sign of the troops was seen. When the Indians slowly drew back, the troops moved cautiously down the slope and

*where the Indians had been seen standing in a circle, [they] found the naked body of Brevet Lieutenant-Colonel Fetterman, Captain Brown, and about sixty-five soldiers of their command. At this point there were no indications of a severe struggle. All the bodies lay in a space not exceeding thirty-five feet in diameter. . . .*

Fetterman and Brown each had a bullet hole in the left temple and the wounds were so powder scorched that it appeared obvious they had used their revolvers to commit suicide when it was apparent all was lost.

*[At the post] there were . . . many anxious hearts, and waiting was perfectly terrible! . . . . It was after dark when Captain Ten Eyck returned, with forty-nine of the bodies, and made the terrible announcement that all were killed. . . . The body of Lieutenant Grummond had not been rescued, and there was some faint hope that stragglers might yet come in and break the absolute gloom of tragedy. . . .*

But none came. The next day Carrington and 80 men searched the battlefield and brought back the hacked and dismembered bodies of the missing. Seventy-five of the eighty-one had been killed by arrows, spears, and clubs.

Only the Indians knew how death came to Fetterman's command. Apparently, they decoyed the soldiers into a carefully prepared ambush where a force variously estimated from 1,500 to 2,000 overwhelmed them. Carrington found the bodies of Wheatley and Fisher, together with those of four or five seasoned soldiers, near some large rocks well in advance of the spot where the two captains fell. These two frontiersmen, with their sixteen-shot Henry rifles, apparently gave a good account of themselves. The report of the congressional investigation stated:

*Within a few hundred yards of this position ten Indian ponies lay dead, and there were sixty-five pools of dark clotted blood.*

The body of one civilian bristled with 105 arrows—mute evidence of the anger the warriors had vented on his body.

News traveled rapidly by *moccasin telegraph.* Within twenty-four hours after the fight, four Crow warriors came to Fort C. F. Smith and gave Captain N. C. Kinney, the commanding officer, information which did not reach him through his own channels for about six weeks. In a letter to the Governor of Montana, he wrote:

*The reported Indian loss in killed varies from 16 Sioux and 3 Cheyennes to 60 Sioux and 6 Cheyennes, and many wounded—from 90 to 300. These details of the Indian loss are learned from the Crow Indians, and I mention them, as their former reports of our loss tally with more authentic information since received.*

With forty percent of his force wiped out, Carrington was now in dire need of the troops which had been promised months before. The 236-mile trip to the telegraph station—across country believed to be full of hostiles, and with a blizzard brewing—was a task for none but the strong-hearted and hardy. The man who made it was John "Portugee" Phillips, a civilian who was not even a U.S. citizen. The sentry who saw the colonel let him out a gate recalled that he left the fort *alone.* Another soldier at Fort Reno was positive that he passed this post— *alone.* However, the telegraph operator at Horseshoe Station where the dispatch was filed remembered that Phillips arrived in company with two men. It was an epic journey—hiding in thickets in the daytime, traveling at night on a route parallel with the trail but not on it, and enduring temperatures of over twenty degrees below zero.

One story, well flavored with melodrama, relates that Phillips continued on down to Fort Laramie where he arrived Christmas night. Leaving Carrington's thoroughbred dying on the parade ground, he staggered into "Bedlam," the bachelor officers' quarters, where a ball was in progress. Muttering something about dispatches, he collapsed on the floor. Be that as it may, the exposure did affect his health and long after his death, Congress—belatedly—granted his widow $5,000 in recognition of his services and a settlement for stock run off by the Sioux as revenge for his part in the relief of the fort.

Life was doubly grim at Fort Phil Kearney—it was Christmas time and intensely cold. Wind drifted the snow against one side of the stockade until a man could walk over the top. Everyone lived in mortal terror of what could happen but the hostiles sat the blizzard out in their snug winter camps.

The reaction of the outside world was violently antagonistic. General Philip St. George Cooke—who was responsible for not reinforcing the posts along the trail—promptly relieved Carrington of his command. As soon as he was aware of what happened, General Sherman removed Cooke from his office. The press, *without any reliable information,* went all out with *true* versions and *eyewitness* accounts which were utterly fantastic. The report of the Congressional investigation noted:

> The difficulty, "in a nutshell," was that the commanding officer of the district was furnished no more troops or supplies for this state of war than had been provided and furnished him for a state of profound peace.

Carrington was cleared of negligence but the mischief was done. It took the colonel twenty-one years to get the government to print his official report of the disaster. To counteract the lurid lies of the press and the "official" silence of responsible individuals, Mrs. Carrington—with the approval of General Sherman—used her daily journal and wrote *Absa-ra-ka, Land of Massacre*, a narrative of her experiences and an exposé of official negligence, which presented the facts to the public.

General Cooke's order relieving Carrington added hardship to injustice. Lieutenant Colonel H. W. Wessels arrived shortly after New Year's day with two companies of infantry and three of cavalry to assume command. The colonel and his staff left two weeks later with a train of 40 wagons going down to Fort Reno for supplies. The women and children rode in wagons which the quartermaster had thoughtfully modified by closing both ends—with a door in front and a little sheet-iron stove. "That precaution alone," Mrs. Carrington wrote later, "secured us safe deliverance during the trip which ensued."

The snow was deep, and on the second night out the temperature dropped to over forty degrees below zero. Snow on the firewood melted and then the water froze around the edges of the campfires, bread had to be cut with an axe, and, during the night, blacksnake whips were used to keep the men from lying down in the snow and freezing to death. Inside the wagons, the children whimpered and the cold treated the little stoves "with outrageous contempt." When they reached Fort Reno the next day, two men had to have legs amputated—they died later.

Travel along the Montana Road in 1866, like life at the newly established posts, had its hazards. This daily journal—with descriptions of scenery and uneventful days deleted—is a candid picture of what Reverend William K. Thomas saw between Fort Reno and the mouth of "Bridger Creek" (west of the present town of Columbus, Montana). This Methodist minister left Belleville, Illinois, on the 15th of May, and reached Fort Reno on the 21st of July:

July 21. *Saturday night, Indians shot two oxen.*

July 22. *We left Powder River (Fort Reno) Sunday 3 o'clock in the* evening & made a dry camp about seven miles out, soon after camping four Indians were seen lurking around the herd, who raised quite an excitement among the boys. They were fired on and last seen making their way across the hills.

July 23.　Monday morning half past four we pulled out from camp, reached Crazy Woman's Fork at two o'clock and camped for the night, a dangerous place to camp on account of Indians. Two men were killed here two days ago by the Indians. We had expected an attack here but no Indians to be seen. A government train of a hundred wagons came up and camped with us; a fight took place between two of the government teamsters, one of them was dangerously stabbed.

July 24.　Tuesday morning we left camp at 5 o'clock, Government train goes ahead, two citizen's wagons and mine follow after it; Ox train of thirty wagons next, Kirkendall's mule train of forty wagons follows in the rear. Our drive was twenty miles to Clear Creek, a beautiful stream running from the mountains, clear as crystal, the advanced train reached here at 2 o'clock, the ox train stopped three miles back from here and was attacked by the Indians, there was not much damage done, one mule killed and one wounded. The worst fight was with six men sent back from the ox train to see what detained Kirkendall. When within a quarter of a mile of Kirkendall's train they were surrounded by twenty-five Indians, after fighting four or five hours they got to the train, killing two Indians, and carrying the wagon master Dillon mortally wounded, and left Kirkendall's team move up to ox train and corralled.

July 25.　Wednesday morning as the advance train moves out of camp the rear trains that did not get up last night are driving in, and will remain here until tomorrow. Wagon master Dillon that was wounded yesterday died last night. We got into New Fort Reno [sic—Fort Phil Kearney] at two o'clock today. . . . Col. Carrington commands here.

July 26.　Thursday the rearer trains came in; the teamster that was stabbed on Crazy Woman's Fork died yesterday and he and Dillon were buried this evening. Service by Chaplain White.

July 27.   Friday, we are still here recruiting our teams and looking for another train in.

July 28.   Saturday, a train of forty wagons came in to-day. Two or three families with it, they report two men killed and one wounded between Platte River and Reno by Indians.

July 31.   Tuesday, no hopes of leaving here for several days by order of headquarters. . . . I am meditating upon the adventure that I am about to take, counting the cost, summing up the danger, cold chills runs through my blood.

Aug. 1.   Very warm, laid in camp all day and read Bible.

Aug. 2.   Thursday at two o'clock the train of a hundred and twelve wagons moved from Fort Philip Kearney, the intention is to drive out five miles to Creek and camp, but accidently one of the wagon wheels in the train gave way which caused such delay that we did not reach the place desired. . . .

Aug. 3.   Friday morning about five o'clock we drove about a mile on our way to where there is plenty of water and breakfast with orders to wait until government train of forty wagons comes up & two companies of infantry. [This was Captain Kinney and the troops going to construct Fort C. F. Smith.] About a half mile drive from camp this morning on the hill side to the left of the road is a grave containing the bodies of five men who were killed a few days ago by Indians. As I passed by the grave I saw that the wolves had made an opening to the inmates and had torn the flesh from the bodies and left their ribs exposed. Such is the haste and depravity of man out here that he will hardly take time to pay his last respects to the dead—but leaves him for the wild beast of the field to cry and howl over and often feast upon.

Aug. 7.   Tuesday morning at five o'clock we leave camp North Tongue River. The road is very good today. . . . Just before we cross trout creek, to the left of the road is a lone grave, the inmate was deposited in July last, we could not make out his name, part of the headboard being gone, he left Chambersburg, Pennsylvania, May 8th, 1864, and was killed here by Indians. . . . wolves . . . had dug down until they left the inmate half uncovered and gnawed the flesh from his face. We could see that he had been scalped. . . . He had been deposited in a (I cannot say grave) a little narrow hole about two feet deep, with a few shovelfulls of dirt cast over him.

Aug. 11.   Saturday, we are now camping on the Big Horn River, the government trains that came through with us will stop here to establish a military post here. Quite a sad accident happened to us today. Three of the men belonging to the train while crossing the river in search of a ford, their horses unexpectedly pitched off into a deep hole. They were thrown from their horses in a struggle to get a shore, two of the men got out by taking their horses by the tail, when out they ran to the assistance of their comrade whom they saw swimming down the [?] and in need of assistance. But before they could reach him he sank and was not seen any more, until three or four hours after wards his lifeless body was taken from the stream.

Aug. 12.   Sunday morning we drove to Military Post (Ferry) about five miles. Laid by till Monday. . . .

Aug. 13.   Monday we commenced crossing the train, the mule and citizens' wagons were all landed safely by dark. In swimming the mules over three of them were drowned.

Aug. 14.   Tuesday morning one of the ox trains has just crossed and are now swimming their cattle over, a large train of three hundred and fifty wagons ten miles below on the river will be in tomorrow.

Aug. 15.   Wednesday morning at 6 o'clock we left Fort Smith on the Big Horn River, and drove about ten miles and camped at a little creek, plenty of grass and water and wood. We struck the divide. I upset my wagon today, no damage done. The ox train did not come up today.

Aug. 17.   Friday morning the train started out at about 6 o'clock over a rather sliding and hilly road, one of the freight wagons broke down about an hour after leaving camp. My

wagon and the two other citizen's wagons passed, went together two or three miles, they stopped behind thinking it
safer to wait for the train. I determined trusting in the Lord
to go ahead. We nooned on Beaver Creek about two miles
from where we left the train, drove about eight miles in
the afternoon, we saw plenty of antelope and buffalo.

The last entry was made on August 22nd when the little party—
"trusting in the Lord"—was not far from the Yellowstone River and
some twenty or thirty miles west of the present town of Columbus,
Montana.

On March 24, 1876, almost ten years later, the editor of the *Belleville Advocate* printed a letter which he had received a few days before:

EDITOR OF ADVOCATE

In 1866 I was crossing the Great American Plains over the Territory
of Montana, and so while traveling along, on the 8th day of September,
1866, on one of the tributaries of the Yellowstone River, I came across
four graves with headboards erected thereon bearing the following in-
scriptions:

Reverend W. K. Thomas, age 36 years of Belleville, Ill.
Chas. K. Thomas, age 8 years of Belleville, Ill.
James Schultz, age 35 years of Ottawa Co. C. W. (Canadian West)
C. K. Wright—
All killed and scalped by Indians on the 24th day of August, 1866.

These men were traveling with Hugh Kirkendall's wagon train, which
preceeded ours a week or ten days. I afterwards made the acquaintance
of Mr. Kirkendall in Helena, Montana, who told me that Thomas and
son wanted always to go on in advance of the train and so endanger
himself. I came across my notes of travel and found the above there, and
not knowing whether any person had ever written,—hence this.

very respectfully yours,
H. H. LOWMEIER
EDWARDSVILLE, ILLINOIS, March 16, 1876.

One train which came through late in 1866 was an unusual one under the direction of Nelson Story. This man was a seasoned freighter
before he came to Alder Gulch and located a good claim. However,
like a few others, he saw that the most profitable occupation was dealing in supplies needed by the miners. So, September of this year found
him on the trail to Virginia City with a wagon train loaded with

groceries and a herd of about 600 longhorns which he had purchased near Fort Worth for $10.00 a head.

No difficulty was experienced until they approached Fort Reno. Here, Indians ran off some of the cattle and wounded two men. Story's men recaptured the cattle and, leaving the wounded at the post, trailed on up to Fort Phil Kearney. Carrington stopped the herd three miles from the post as he wanted to save the meadows nearby for the "army stock," but he would not let them proceed. This was a ridiculous situation: the colonel was too busy constructing the post to provide an escort but he would not let the train camp near enough to derive any protection from the troops, or go on about their business. However, Story built a couple of corrals and settled down, as one of his men put it, "to twirl our thumbs."

After idling for two weeks, Story proposed to his men that they proceed without the colonel's permission. His plan was to move out at night, get far enough away so that the soldiers would not dare to come after them, and then keep on moving. All were in favor but one individual who was promptly "arrested" and not released until the train was well on its way.

Many years later, one of the members recalled:

There were 27 men in our party. There were 300 troops at the fort. But the Indians were more afraid of us than they were of the soldiers. We were armed with Remington breech-loaders and the troops had only old Springfield rifles. . . . The little brush we had with the Indians below Reno had taught them something of the effectiveness of our fire . . . and had got them scared. . . .

We . . . pulled out one night after the post was asleep. That first night's drive was so successful that we decided to keep up the plan of traveling nights and resting days. The result was that we were attacked only two or three times and each time was when we were resting during the day; we easily stood off the reds and had no trouble at all. Close to the fort there were more than three thousand Indians. As we moved toward the Big Horn country they became fewer.

When Fort C. F. Smith was reached, the men were able to relax their vigilance somewhat; and the remainder of the trip was made without trouble. The wagon train was taken to the settlements but the cattle were, probably, left in the valley of Shields River near the Great Bend. Story used this country as a holding range for stock which was later butchered for the meat markets. This marks the beginning of Story's ranching activities in the Yellowstone valley—activities which, a few years later, were to be a source of irritation to the early Crow agents.

Although James Stuart's ill-fated party of 1863 failed to discover gold in the Big Horn Basin, the idea persisted that this should be a profitable region. He led seventy-five men back into the area the following spring and went as far south as the Shoshone River but found nothing. During the latter part of July, 1866, Jeff Standifer led about one hundred men to the Rocky Fork of Clark Fork where the party split. Standifer and part of the men went on south into the Grey Bull, and Wind River areas, and finally to the valley of the Sweetwater. The others elected a man named Bailey as captain, and went to the upper part of the Big Horn Canyon to prospect. Here they found some bars with gold but water was a problem so they finally abandoned them and moved over to the vicinity of Fort Phil Kearney. Although one old-timer reported that Bailey was killed just before the party left these diggings, it is probable that this is the man who carried mail and guided at the post during the summer and the following winter. Most of his men—perhaps all who lived through that summer—went up to Fort C. F. Smith in the fall, and part of them came back to the Montana settlements with the last emigrant train that came up the Bozeman Trail.

Although several important events took place in the Yellowstone Basin between 1866 and 1870, it may be noted here that another prospecting expedition was organized at Cheyenne, Wyoming, four years after Standifer's party searched the Big Horn Basin. The object was "to prospect the Big Horn range and probably the Black Hills." Cheyenne newspapers gave the project considerable publicity and military authorities tried to stop it before it got started as the Black Hills had, at this time, been guaranteed to the Sioux. Finally, the leaders "solemnly promised" to stay out of forbidden areas.

By the time it started, the force had dwindled to about 120 men. According to one who probably accompanied the party:

The expedition crossed the Owl Creek range and prospected every stream from there to the Stinking Water. Here it divided and part went back, but the greater number came on to the Yellowstone. . . . The expedition dissolved on this river.

These men trundled along with them a bronze cannon which acquired the name of the Big Horn Gun. Before it ended up set solidly in concrete in front of the courthouse in Bozeman, Montana, Indian fighters and traders took it on two trips down the Yellowstone as far as the mouth of the Big Horn River.

In the spring of 1867, Tom Cover and William McAdow, proprietors of the "Gallatine Mills" in Bozeman, were interested in securing the flour contract for the posts on the Montana Road. Cover, not wishing to make the trip to the stations alone, persuaded John Bozeman to go with him. On the 17th of April, the two rode into Nelson Story's cattle camp near the Great Bend of the Yellowstone. Here they spent the night. The next noon, while in camp near the mouth of Mission Creek, several Indians approached them. A few days later, Cover wrote Acting Governor Thomas F. Meagher:

We perceived five Indians approaching us on foot and leading a pony. When within say two hundred and fifty yards I suggested to Mr. Bozeman that we should open fire, to which he made no reply. We stood with our rifles ready until the enemy approached to within one hundred yards, at which Bozeman remarked: "Those are Crows; I know one of them. We will let them come to us and learn where the Sioux and Blackfeet camps are, provided they know." The Indians walked toward us with their hands up, calling, "Ap-sar-ake" (Crow). They shook hands with Mr. B. and proffered the same politeness to me, which I declined by presenting my Henry rifle at them, and at the same moment B. remarked, "I am fooled; they are Blackfeet. We may, however, get off without trouble." I then went to our horses (leaving my gun with B.) and had saddled mine, when I saw the chief quickly draw the cover from his fusee, and I called to B. to shoot, the Indian fired, the ball taking effect in B's right breast, passing completely through him. B. charged on the Indians but did not fire, when another shot took effect in the left breast, and brought poor B. to the ground, a dead man. At that instant I received a bullet through the upper edge of my left shoulder. I ran to B., picked up my gun and spoke to him, asking if he was badly hurt. Poor fellow! his last words had been spoken some minutes before I reached the spot: he was "stone dead."

Cover managed to kill one Indian but the other four got off with the horses and the body of their comrade. Then, taking Bozeman's personal belongings, he started on foot for the cow camp where he arrived the next morning. The herders went down and buried the body, and the foreman remarked later that he could not understand how a man armed with the best repeating rifle available could have failed to kill *all* the renegade Blackfeet.

For over a year previous to this murder, Acting Governor Meagher had been pressing for the assignment of more troops to Montana. As he had been a brigadier general during the Civil War and had an excessive amount of ambition, both General Sherman, who was then in charge of the Division of the Missouri, and Secretary of War Stanton were suspicious of the man's judgment and his motives. When it became obvious that there were not enough troops available to allow a substantial increase in the number stationed in Montana, Meagher began to clamor for authorization to raise volunteer troops.

This request was based on a little fact and much fiction. The thing which did loom large in the minds of the settlers was the *idea* that there was a great deal of peril. Bozeman's murder was accepted by Meagher as proof of the alleged needs; and on April 24th he issued a call for 600 volunteers and, shortly afterward, requested authorities in Washington to increase the number to 800 men. Meagher's jockeying to create an Indian war continued through May and June but came to an end when he disappeared over the side of a steamboat at Fort Benton and was never seen again.

Governor Green Clay Smith, who assumed his duties about this time, inherited this mess. After trimming the ranks of the officers and number of men, the resulting force consisted of thirty-two line officers and four hundred and eighty-one soldiers. As his predecessor had promised the men all the loot they could capture from the Indians, everyone—including the press—tried to manufacture an Indian war. General Terry, who made an inspection trip early in August, reported that nothing had occurred to justify the state of alarm.

The volunteers actually went into the field, one camp being established at the mouth of the Musselshell, and another—Camp Thomas Francis Meagher—was on the Yellowstone at the mouth of Shields River. The latter force made one scout upstream as far as the present Yellowstone National Park and, on another occasion, chased a small party of Sioux downstream. According to one pioneer, "Beside these raids nothing was done during the summer but race horses, gamble, grumble, and quarrel among themselves." Any reason for the existence of this force came to an end on the 27th of August when Captain R. S. Lamotte began the construction of Fort Ellis just east of Bozeman.

Near the end of September, when Governor Smith sent "Colonel" Neil Howie down to Camp Meagher to muster the men out and convey to them the "heartfelt thanks & gratitude of the people of Montana," about 180 of them, under the leadership of a Captain Hughes, demanded that they be allowed to go prospecting along the Yellowstone. And they claimed that the necessary supplies should come from the now-disbanded organization. As Howie refused to sanction this steal, the men forcibly took over everything, including about two hundred horses and mules, and moved down the river. Howie, as brave a marshall as ever carried a gun in Montana, returned to Bozeman and tried to get some of the men from the camp on the Musselshell to help him crush this insubordination. Only twenty-six would go—and these only if promised any supplies which might be recaptured!—and Howie had to drop the matter.

Thus the Montana Volunteers came to an inglorious end. When the governor requested Congress to pay the $1,100,000 expenses incurred, this body refused, saying the amount was exorbitant. However, those who held the warrants flooded Washington with protests and, three years later, the Inspector General's Office sent Inspector Hardie out to go over the bills. He found matters thoroughly permeated with graft and when he finished, the claims which totalled $980,313.11 had shrunk to $515,343.00.

Although the Montana Volunteers could find nothing to do at Camp Meagher except to prospect, squabble, and irritate the Crows, the troops at the posts along the Bozeman Trail did not face any shortage of hostile Indians. The reputation which the trail had acquired the preceding year was bad enough to cause emigrants to use the other routes to the gold fields, so the only travel over the trail was government supply trains. During the preceding winter, supplies were short at Fort Phil Kearney, and troops at Fort Smith were reduced to desperate straits. In May two Sioux half-breeds, Mitch Buoyer and John Reshaw, brought the news to Bozeman that the horses belonging to the post on the Big Horn had been run off and that the men had to have provisions. Forty-two men volunteered and took a wagon train down without difficulty. In time heavily armed supply trains came through from the south and the tension eased.

In June, one train delivered a much appreciated shipment to Fort Phil Kearney—700 new Springfield rifles and 100,000 rounds of ammunition. Although the cavalry had seven-shot Spencer carbines (an effective rifle at close range), the infantry had been armed with muzzle-loading Springfields. At the end of the Civil War some of these were modified so that metallic cartridges could be used; and these "trap door" Springfields were comparable to the "rolling block" Remingtons which Story's men had used so effectively. It was this shipment of revamped rifles which gave new spirit to the infantry in the two desperate battles which lay a few weeks ahead.

In July the Sioux held a sun dance ceremony, and at its conclusion Red Cloud organized a strong force for the purpose of wiping out the two northern forts. According to a story which allegedly came from the Crows, this force was unable to agree which fort should be attacked first. So, the warriors divided into two groups according to their wishes. Then, as both groups were approximately the same size, it was decided to attack both posts at the same time. However, as Fort Phil Kearney was some ninety miles from Fort C. F. Smith, the attacks—for some reason—were not synchronized exactly.

During the latter part of July a small party was working in the hay-fields about two and a half miles from Fort C. F. Smith. Here they had built a flimsy corral about 100 feet square to hold their horses and mules. This consisted of a row of logs laid end to end on the ground above which had been built a sort of picket fence made of loosely woven willows. It offered no substantial protection, other than the logs on the ground, being merely a screen. Inside this *fence* was a picket line for the animals and the tents of the soldiers and civilians.

For several days the Crows had been visiting at the post and telling of the preparations for battle which were being made at a hostile camp not far away. Everyone regarded these friendly tips as just so much Indian talk; but, in the middle of the forenoon of the first day of August, a formidable force of Sioux drove the haying party into the corral and then proceeded to make a determined attack. At the beginning of the fight there were nineteen whites. Two soldiers foolishly insisted on standing up "to fight like men" and were shot down, and the bully of the group turned yellow and hid in a small hole. This left sixteen civilians and soldiers to carry the brunt of the fight, and one of these was killed later.

Lying flat on the ground, partly hidden by the willow pickets and firing over the top of the protecting logs, the whites fought stubbornly. They made the charges so costly that the Sioux warriors had no heart to press them home. Small blazes started in the corral by fire arrows were promptly extinguished; and attempts to burn the corral by starting grass fires nearby also failed. By late afternoon the Indians had had enough. According to one of the civilians, "Everything that was a foot or eighteen inches above the ground was simply shot to pieces by the Indians," and they killed all but two of the thirty-two horses and mules on the picket line.

While the fight was in progress, a captain whose men were escorting a wood train studied the situation through his glasses. When he reached the post, he was denied permission to go to the assistance of the besieged men. However, when the fighting stopped, the commanding officer allowed a party to investigate. This brought down on the head of the latter some caustic and—probably—well-merited criticism. As no official report of the fight is known to exist, it would appear that an attempt was made to hush up the matter.

The number of warriors engaged was estimated at 2,500 while the other "half" of the total force has been put as low as 1,500 and as high as 3,000. A *reasonable* figure is probably something less than the maximum stated. Estimates of the number killed are, no doubt, likewise inflated. After the fight, the Crows guided a party of whites to a rocky ledge a couple of miles from the battlefield where fifty bodies were found; and then offered to take them to another not far away where they said there were even more. However, the whites, believing that it was not prudent to venture farther, decided that the Absaroka were tell-.ing the truth when they stated that the Sioux losses were very high.

While "half" of the Sioux were engaged in the hayfield fight, the remainder of the warriors were moving against Fort Phil Kearney for a fight on the following day. Here, on August 2nd, they attacked a small party that was cutting wood about six miles from the fort at what was called "the pinery." What the overall plan of these operations was—*if any*—is not obvious. Perhaps they were decoy movements patterned after the strategy that was so successful with Fetterman. If so, the developments did not take the expected turn, and part of the success of the whites must be attributed to the rapidity of fire which the new breech loading Springfields made possible.

The small detachment which took the brunt of this attack was composed of twenty-five soldiers, two officers, and five civilians—thirty-two men. They, too, had a small corral for a camp and this one was formed of fourteen wagon boxes such as were used by government freighting trains. These were arranged in an oval near the edge of flat, open bench-land not far from Big Piney Creek.

Shortly after breakfast, the pickets were changed and the commanding officer, Captain Powell, went to the creek to take a bath. It was not long before the Sioux came streaming over the hills on the opposite side of the creek, and the sentries scurried back into the corral. For a few brief moments the men watched the Indians assemble. It was a thrilling and awesome sight, this great throng of various colored ponies, their riders decked out in warpaint, some with showy headdresses, giving vent to their feelings with yells and the singing of war songs. But this contemplation did not continue long for the men, keenly aware of the danger facing them, filled their hats and caps with cartridges, and took positions around the enclosure, some in the wagon boxes and others behind barrels of supplies or piles of ox-yokes. A few, remembering what had happened on that grim day the preceding December, took the shoelaces from their shoes and tied loops in either end so that they could pull the triggers with their feet should it be necessary to put the muzzles of their rifles under their chins and blow their own heads off.

Had the Indians pressed home one determined charge, all would have been over quickly. But that was not the way they fought. A large force would start a charge on foot apparently expecting to meet one volley and then come to grips with the defenders. This never happened —the first volley was followed by another, and then another. The crucial moment never came when the soldiers stopped to pour charges of powder and ram bullets down with their ramrods. The attack would falter, and then break. This happened again and again. Sometimes while these charges were under way, mounted warriors would circle and shoot fire arrows into the corral, but these never attempted a charge.

Thus the morning passed, the men in the wagon boxes shooting their hot rifles in desperate haste, and the Sioux circling and feinting for the opportunity which never came. Many of the soldiers became desperately thirsty under the blazing sun, and the stifling smoke from smouldering fires—started by the fire arrows—in the piles of manure added to the discomfort. As the number of dead began to mount, the hostiles began to realize that this was not another Fetterman fight; and in the early afternoon when a relief party from the fort approached— with the hated howitzer dropping shells among them—they had had enough. Packing their dead on ponies, the bewildered warriors began their retreat across the hills over which they had advanced so confidently but a few hours before.

In the corral, a lieutenant and two privates lay dead and another man was wounded in the shoulder. The remainder could hardly believe that they had survived, for the tops of the wagon boxes were badly splintered by bullets. The number of Indian dead was never positively determined. Captain Powell put their loss at 300 killed and wounded. Other estimates were higher. A few years later, after these Indians surrendered, one Indian is alleged to have put the number of dead at the fantastic figure of 1,137. Others refused to talk about the fight.

Although Red Cloud's forces had suffered severe losses, this chief did not relax the state of siege which he had clamped on the central part of the Bozeman Trail. The year of 1868 arrived with the Army occupying posts in an area through which all civilian travel had ceased over a year before: and part of the country which the "treaty" of 1851 stated belonged to the Absaroka was now overrun by their enemies.

# 10

## Mackinaws on the River Road

>>>>>>>>><<<<<<<<<< Although emigrants going *to* the Montana gold field regarded the Bozeman Trail as an important short-cut, travelers returning "to the States" sometimes chose to follow the river route. Above Fort Union, this *road* had two branches—one was the Missouri between Fort Benton and the mouth of the Yellowstone, and the other was the Yellowstone below the Great Bend. Anyone embarking at Fort Benton could book passage on a steamboat if he so desired, but those who floated down the Yellowstone used mackinaw boats.

These were flat-bottomed craft constructed of heavy planks.

The boats were sometimes made as large as fifty feet long and twelve feet beam. The plan was that of an acute ellipse, and the gunwale rose about two feet from the center of the boat toward both bow and stern. The keel showed a rake of about thirty inches from the bow or stern to the bottom. The hold had a depth of about five feet at the two ends of the boat, and about three and a half at the center.

Normally, the craft required four men at the oars and one at the rudder.

One of the first attempts to go down the river was made in the fall of 1864. About 120 men signed up to go on this trip, and late in September twenty-five men went over to the Great Bend where they planned to build twelve boats. However, when the remainder of the party arrived they found but two boats under construction and none completed. Part of the men pulled out in disgust but about seventy-five pitched in and helped with the work.

Early in October, the group pushed off in boats that were "little better than rafts." The river was low and the boats often stranded on sandbars. Provisions were inadequate and the hunters not overly successful, so the party was limited to half rations much of the time. To make matters worse, a severe snow storm hit and the river filled with mush ice. After battling these difficulties for a month, the boats froze in about twenty miles above Fort Union and the men had to abandon them and most of their baggage.

In spite of this questionable beginning, this route became popular the following year. A prospector who worked in Emigrant Gulch recalled:

*Another prominent settler was John J. Tomlinson, known as the "mill man." Tomlinson had brought across the "plains" machinery for the erection of a circular saw-mill. He selected a location for his saw-mill about nine miles down the valley from Emigrant Gulch on what has since been called "Mill Creek," deriving its name from this mill. He erected the mill on the bank of the Yellowstone, securing his water by making a ditch or "head-race" from a point on the north side of this creek some distance above its junction with the river. His purpose was to supply lumber for the construction of boats to carry men and goods down the Yellowstone River.*

Boats went down the river singly or in groups. One of the largest "fleets" on record numbered over 42 boats at the start and was owned by three firms. This one left the boat yard on September 27, 1865, and had among its passengers Hezekiah L. Hosmer, district judge and presiding justice of the Supreme Court of Montana, and his family. The sixteen-year-old son of this judge kept a very creditable journal which he himself published two years later, printing the pages on a small hand press and binding them between cardboard covers.

Of the 42 boats which started, 36 made the entire trip. On the 27th of September, young Hosmer noted:

Early this morning the boats were finished being thirty six in number and divided into four different fleets No. 1 Knox & Bradbury's fleet of 10 boats, these boats were sharp at the bow thirty two feet long, three feet high, eight feet wide in the center, and four feet wide at the stern.

The names of the boats in this fleet were as follows, No. 1. Jeannie Deans, No. 2. Montana, 3. (our boat) Antelope, 4. Lady Pike, 5. Helena City, 6. No name, 7. St. Louis, 8. Lady Jane, 9. Otter and 10. Autocrat.

The second fleet was Bivens' of nine boats, these were common flat boats, and were of different length   they had small cabins on the stern, they set sail on the 26th. and therefore I do not know the names of the boats.

The third, was the German Flats of nineteen boats these were common Flats or mud scows, the family boats had cabins but the others were plain scows used in the states for hauling mud.

The boats spoken of above were all built of pine lumber. Fleet no. 4. belonging to Van Cleave & Hanson, consisted of four boats. built of Cottonwood lumber, and sharp at each end like the original Mackinaw boat, but there were a few other boats which were built for the use of private families, one of these was the handsomest boat in the outfit which they called the "Gipsey Nell"   it was built similar to Knox's boats only on a smaller scale.

This journal contains a rather meagre account of some of the more routine matters. Of the organization, Hosmer wrote briefly at the end of the first day:

We cooked our supper of bacon and potatoes, and ate it, after they had all had their suppers, they formed a meeting and Charlie Davis an old Missouri steamboatman was elected pilot of the fleet, and Lieut. Robert Shilling a man who had seen considerable service in the late war, our military commander.

Scattered comments reveal that there were ten passengers in the *Antelope,* and that, while others cooked over a fire built on a pile of sand in the bottom of their boats, this group had a small stove: there was no hard and fast plan of travel—the groups did not stay close together, nor did they get widely separated: occasionally they grounded on sandbars, and one boat hit a rock and had to have her bottom patched. Most of the people slept on shore at night: on one occasion they were alarmed by the "peculiar whistle, long, trilling and frequent" of bull elk, and another time what was thought to be Indian *sign* caused the party to embark and spend the night in the middle of the stream.

When twelve miles above the Stillwater River, Hosmer noted that they met Sawyer's road surveying expedition. The passengers on the *Antelope* stopped to visit:

. . . the colonel was very kind and gave us some tomatoes, peaches and fresh milk, we stayed here two hours, during which time we got a narrative of their trip from Judge Smith.

Wolf Rapids provided a moment of thrills:

At about nine o'clock we passed the mouth of the Powder River. . . . At half past ten we heard a loud roaring ahead, not unlike that of a waterfall, we expected that the noise came from a rapid that we had dreaded from our very start, which Lewis & Clark called Wolf Rapid . . . , it was what we expected, soon after hearing the noise we came in sight of white surges in the distance, we sail on, the "Jeannie Deans" piloted by Davis entered the rapid first and trying to avoid the white surges, landed on a rock.

The "Montana," piloted by R. J. Paulison of Hackensack, N. J., followed Davis and got a rock at the bow, the current then took the boat around and it struck on a boulder at the stern, it was now aground both at the bow and stern, and in a helpless condition. Our boat came next piloted by Edward Hosmer, who made for the white waves, the rest followed us, and all passed through in safety, except No. 6 which received a slight injury at the head of the rapid, Davis' boat got on a rock close to another that stuck out of the water, and one man got out and pushed it off, Paulison as this boat passed threw a rope, which was caught, and they all got off safely.

Except for getting caught momentarily in a whirlpool near the mouth of Glendive Creek (?), the remainder of the journey was uneventful. Young Hosmer noted on one occasion that night "was always welcome"; and after it was over he wrote:

If it were not for the expectation of being fired into by savages every moment, the traveler would enjoy the trip hugely.

Not all the travelers who chose to boat down the Yellowstone "to America" had as uneventful trip as the Hosmer family. On April 11, 1866, a party of six miners together with a mixed group of twenty men (one being practically an invalid), two women and five small children pushed off from the Great Bend. The men in the latter were very poorly armed with only four guns and but a meagre amount of ammunition. On the morning of the fourth day, Sioux killed one of the miners and the remainder immediately abandoned their boat. The other party also disembarked, taking only such supplies as they could carry—and a leather valise containing several thousand dollars in gold.

The next morning a "violent" snow storm swept down the valley, and this, while it added greatly to the hardships, was a blessing in disguise for it provided effective protection from Indians who were seen shortly before the storm struck. These people divided into several groups and straggled back to the nearest settlement. However, a relief party did have to go out and assist the group containing the women and children. These were found at the mouth of Shields River, rather the worse for their experience. According to family tradition, Mrs. Piles, the wife of the invalid, made a second—and this time successful—attempt to bring her husband and three small children back to "the States." Perhaps, to a woman who crossed the plains five times in a wagon train and who had supported her family in Alder Gulch by operating a hotel in Virginia City, this was not a formidable experience.

In 1866 travel by this route became popular and several "companies" advertised that they would take passengers down the Yellowstone to any point above St. Louis for $25.00. This sum covered transportation from either Helena or Virginia City to the boat yards just above the Great Bend, and 100 pounds of freight per person. One fleet of sixteen boats left on the 27th of September which carried 250 miners from Alder Gulch and a half-million dollars in gold dust. They made the 2,700 miles to St. Joseph, Missouri, in 28 days and had but one serious mishap—the pilot boat sank at the mouth of Clark Fork with $3,500.

The following year, one little fleet had trouble with a village of Cheyennes and Arapahoes who were camped just below the mouth of the Big Horn. First, the savages professed friendship and requested the party to stop and trade, but when this request was ignored warriors followed along the shore and fired a volley at the boats. According to one pioneer:

*All of the bedding and boxes had been piled on the sides of the mackinaws and the volley did no damage to those down in the boats, but a man named Randall, who was standing up manning an oar, was shot in the breast and killed instantly. The boats were swept swiftly around a point and out of range of the Indians' rifles and the party were troubled no more by them on this trip.*

This party—sixty-seven men and two women—had another mishap near the mouth of the Powder. The boat containing the ladies was swamped and overturned (probably in Wolf Rapids). No one was drowned but all the baggage in the boat was lost.

Not many travelers used the Yellowstone route to "the States" after 1867. This fact would seem to be related to conditions on the Bozeman Trail where the Sioux had choked off travel. By 1868, the hostiles had bullied the government into making this state of affairs *official*; and, without even the moral support of troops anywhere in the area, no doubt the Missouri looked more inviting.

However, until the coming of the Northern Pacific Railroad in the mid-1880's, farmers and merchants in the Gallatin Valley continued to regard the Yellowstone as a highway over which produce could be transported to buyers. To these people any surveying party, construction crew, or Army post was a market worth trying to exploit—even when a major Indian war was under way! On May 23, 1876—only about a month before Custer and most of his men were wiped out—an officer with General Gibbon's troops made this entry in his journal:

*Colonel Chestnut [sic Chestnut], a Bozeman gentleman, arrived to-day in a mackinaw boat, bringing a cargo of vegetables, butter, eggs, tobacco and other goods. He had a crew of four men, and had made the run from Benson's Landing [not far from the present town of Livingston] without seeing any Sioux or meeting with any misadventure. The luxuries he brought found ready sale and gave great satisfaction. Not the least acceptable article was a keg of beer, reserved for the officers and resulting in a convivial reunion in the evening in the tent of Lieutenants Hamilton and Schofield. . . . The time passed jolilly, Colonel Chestnut was voted the best fellow going, and the occasion will long be remembered as one of the greenest of the green spots in the campaign.*

Others followed Chesnut but not all of them were voted "the best fellow going." Later in the summer another officer noted that there was a tendency for the men to call these merchants "commodore" on their arrival, and a few hours later—having priced their goods—to refer to them as "that old pirate."

When Forts Keogh and Custer were established at the close of Sitting Bull's War, the merchants in Bozeman continued to float goods— mostly vegetables, butter, etc.—down the Yellowstone. In 1877, flatboats were used to transport the women, children and infirm of the Nez Percé, captured in the Bear Paw Mountains, from Fort Keogh to the railroad at Bismarck, North Dakota. During the late 1870's and early 1880's boats were used occasionally for a quick passage down the valley by a single individual or small party: but when the railroad pushed its way along the Yellowstone the interest changed from transportation to irrigation.

# 11

## The Storm Clouds Gather

>>>>>>>>>>«««««««« In July 1867 a second council was held with the hostile Sioux at Fort Laramie. This time Red Cloud refused to negotiate as long as the forts along the Bozeman Trail were in existence. The Sioux believed that their efforts had forced Connor to retreat, and they knew they had dealt Carrington's forces one disastrous defeat as well as keeping the troops pinned down at the posts. Likewise, the white commissioners were not in favor of giving in to the Indians. In his report, General C. C. Augur pointed out that (1) the road was important to the public, (2) considerable money had been spent in fortifying the route, and (3) *abandonment of the road would have a bad effect on the attitude of the Indians*. Subsequent years were to reveal just how correct this third reason really was.

However, the government was involved in the military occupation of the South and the public was in no mood to consider expanding the Army to fight an Indian war. So, on March 30, 1868, Generals Sherman, Harney, Sanborn, Terry, and Sheridan, together with several other government officials and the indefatigable Father De Smet, left St. Louis to make a third attempt to treat with the Sioux. At the forks of the Platte, they negotiated successfully with Spotted Tail, the friendly chief of the Brules, and then moved on to Fort Laramie where they met a delegation from the hostile camps.

Although Red Cloud did not come in and sign the papers until the 6th of the following November, a treaty was drawn up and signed which contained—for the first time—an admission that the government had been defeated by the Indians with whom they were negotiating.

This agreement set aside for the exclusive use of the Sioux the area which is now represented by that part of South Dakota lying west of the Missouri River (plus a very small part of North Dakota—up to the 46th parallel). However, perhaps the most important part was the stipulations contained in Article XVI. These read:

> The United States hereby agrees and stipulates that the country north of the North Platte River and east of the summits of the Big Horn Mountains, shall be held and conceded Indian territory, and also stipulates and agrees that no white person or persons shall be permitted to settle upon or occupy any portion of the same; or without the consent of the Indians, first had and obtained, to pass through the same; and it is further agreed by the United States, that within ninety days after the conclusion of peace with all the bands of the Sioux nation, the military posts now established in the territory, in this article named, shall be abandoned, and that the road leading to them, and by them to the settlements of Montana, shall be closed.

On their part, the Indians promised to remain at peace, and to relinquish all claim to lands north of the Platte—except to hunt. They also agreed not to oppose railroad construction, except on the reserved lands, and not to molest white people or to steal stock belonging to them.

To understand the *true* causes of the Sioux War of 1876, it is necessary to be familiar with the stipulations of this treaty—particularly Article XVI—*and* the geographical location of places where battles with the Sioux took place during the next eight years. The extent of the hunting grounds guaranteed to the Sioux in Article XVI is somewhat vague, particularly the statement—"the country . . . east of the summits of the Big Horn Mountains." As the Big Horn Mountains do not extend north of the Wyoming-Montana state line, it would appear obvious that this was considered, for all practical purposes, to be the northern limit of these hunting grounds. This is confirmed by the fact that when the Sioux, Northern Cheyennes and Arapahoes signed an agreement (September 26, 1876) ceding all claim to the country described in this article, the line drawn for the northern boundary of this region began where the 46th parallel and the 104th meridian intersect and went southwest to the junction of the Little Powder and the Powder Rivers, and thence down the channel of the latter to the Wyoming-Montana boundary. What the arrogant Sioux did was to extend the area, over which they assumed control, northward to the Yellowstone and beyond!

This treaty could not be expected to change the roving, predatory nature of the Sioux—particularly after they had dictated the terms of the treaty—and time was to demonstrate conclusively that it created problems instead of solving them. Quite naturally, the settlers in Montana were furious over the vacillating policy of the Government.

Later, General Sherman made this sage observation:

*The motives of the Peace Commissioners were humane, but there was an error of judgment in making peace with the Indians last fall. They should have been punished and made to give up the plunder captured, which they now hold; and after properly submitting to the military and disgorging their plunder, they should have been turned over to the civil agents. This error has given more victims to savage ferocity. The present system of dealing with the Indians, I think, is an error. There are too many fingers in the pie, too many ends to be subserved, and too much money to be made; and it is to the interest of the nation and of humanity, to put an end to this inhuman farce. The Peace Commission, the Indian Department, the military and the Indian make a balky team. The public treasury is depleted and innocent people plundered in this quadrangular arrangement, in which the treasury, and the unarmed settlers are the greatest sufferers.*

The *wild* Sioux did not send representatives to Fort Laramie and this posed a problem of no small size for the commission as the treaty, to be effective, had to be approved by all the bands of the Teton Sioux. As nothing more could be done at Fort Laramie, part of the commission returned to Omaha and then went up the Missouri to Fort Rice, six miles above the mouth of the Cannonball River. Here the commission was stymied again for, although there were warriors present who belonged to the bands which it was necessary to contact, the principal men were many miles away. And none of the officials dared go hunting for them!

The solution lay in the sixty-seven-year-old priest. Father De Smet, although not an official member of the commission, volunteered to go and persuade the head men to come to Fort Rice. Accompanied by a

trader named Galpin, his Sioux wife, nine chiefs and eighty of their
warriors, he set out on the third of June. Two wagons carried "our little provisions" and the baggage of the savage escort. After traveling foi
a week, four scouts were sent out with a token gift of tobacco, and
these located the camp of the hostiles a few miles above the mouth of
the Powder River.

On the 19th of June, De Smet's party came in sight of the Powder
and saw a force of some four or five hundred warriors advancing to
meet them. The priest immediately had his "standard of peace hoisted,
with the holy name of Jesus on one side and on the other the image
of the holy Virgin Mary, surrounded with gilt stars" and the two groups
met with "shouts and songs." After traveling some ten or twelve miles,

we made our entry into camp in the midst of 4,000 to 5,000 Indians, big
and little, who received us with every sign of lively and sincere joy. Soon
afterward, I took possession of a large lodge, pitched in the center of the
camp, which had been prepared for me by order of the generalissimo of
the warriors, Sitting Bull, and which was guarded day and night by a
band of his most faithful warriors.

De Smet, being very tired at the end of this 250-mile journey, ate a little food and "took a little nap without delay."

The remainder of the afternoon and the evening was spent talking
with the principal men and the next day a formal council was held. For
this, an area of about a half acre was cleared in the center of the camp:

The whole place was surrounded by a series of tepees. . . . The banner of the holy Virgin occupied the center, and on one side a seat was
prepared for me of fine buffalo-robes. When all the Indians, 4,000 to
5,000 in number, had taken their places, I was solemnly introduced into
this salon champêtre, which was improvised for the occasion by the two
head chiefs, Four Horns and Black Moon.

Songs and dances by the warriors opened the council. Then came
the solemn lighting of the ceremonial pipe and its smoking by all the
individuals of importance. These preliminaries completed, De Smet
pointed out the dangers of continued warfare and enumerated the
kinds of assistance which could be provided at an agency. Four chiefs
then spoke, urging that a delegation be sent to hear what the commissioners had to say. After a singing which "roused the echoes of the
hills" and a dance that "made the ground tremble," the council closed
"tranquilly, in good order and harmony."

The next morning before sunrise, the party, accompanied by "eight
Hunkpapa deputies . . . and some thirty families of the hostile camp,"

started their return journey. On the 30th of June they were back at Fort Rice, much to the relief of the commissioners. The remainder of the treaty-making negotiations were simple; and after its conclusion Generals Harney, Sanborn and Terry addressed a letter of appreciation to De Smet for making it possible for them to complete their mission.

Except for Red Cloud's belated signing on November 6th, the treaty of 1868 was now completed. However, even before the work at Fort Ellis was finished, preparations were under way to evacuate the forts along the Bozeman Trail. Sometime before the 7th of August, the troops moved out of the hated fort on Piney Creek. The Indians, hovering on the nearby hilltops like buzzards watching the death struggles of some animal, were ready to swoop down as soon as the last man was gone and apply a torch. Before the soldiers were out of sight, a column of smoke told them that the fort had been fired.

While they were at Fort Laramie, the commissioners also negotiated a treaty with the Crows. One of the things which this treaty provided for was the establishment of an agency, and the employment of an agent and various other workmen as a blacksmith, carpenter, and engineer. Also, it provided for a school. Another item of interest was the boundaries of this reservation. This block of territory was bounded on the north and west by the channel of the Yellowstone River, on the south by the present Wyoming-Montana state line (45th degree of north latitude), and on the east by the 107th meridian (which passes close to the present city of Sheridan, Wyoming). In the next few years the Sioux were to be flagrant trespassers and the spot where they were to wipe out Custer and a considerable part of the Seventh Cavalry was well *within* the boundaries of the Crow Reservation.

# 12

## Rediscovering the Wonderland

>>>>>>>>>>«««««««« In the few short years which inter-
vened between the closing of the Bozeman Trail and the attacks on the
surveyors working on the route for the Northern Pacific Railroad, a
strange interlude took place at the extreme head of the Yellowstone
valley. This occurred in a more or less spontaneous manner, and the
final result marked the beginning of a unique national policy.

Like the Yellowstone Basin which Raynolds mapped in 1859-1860,
the region around the headwaters of the Yellowstone was not a *terra
incognita* at the time of its final discovery. Trappers had been over the
country some forty years before, marveled at what they saw, and regaled
their companions with descriptions of these "infernal regions." Perhaps
the first written account—a very brief one contained in a letter—was
published in a newspaper in 1827. Fifteen years later, on July 13, 1842,
the *Western Literary Messenger* published an anonymous account prepared by an ex-trapper named Warren Ferris. Garrulous Joe Meek, another ex-trapper, described the area to his biographer who recorded his

words in the manuscript for *The River of the West*, published in 1870.

Jim Bridger contributed his bit by needling the incredulous attitude of those whom he met. Perhaps, at first, he related only what he had seen. Then finding he was not believed, he proceeded to fabricate some tall yarns. A number of these have been preserved, such as the story about the hunter who tried to shoot an elk. Finally the hunter discovered that there was a glass mountain between him and the target. This had not only deflected his bullets but had made the animal appear near whereas it was twenty-five miles away. The *text* for this tale was taken, of course, from the cliff of obsidian—volcanic glass—which is now in the national park. Another story, sparked by the petrified wood which he had observed, pertained to the prairie where everything was petrified—shrubs, grass, birds, and animals. The fruit on the bushes were diamonds and rubies; and the birds were singing petrified songs. However, he carried this last idea a little further and told of riding across a canyon where the force of gravity was petrified!

Other things which were classed as fiction were actually facts. Among these was the observation of fish swimming over the Continental Divide at Two Ocean Pass, the stream where—in Bridger's opinion—the water flowed so swiftly that friction heated the streambed, and the place where fish could be caught and cooked without the fisherman moving. In 1879, after the reality of these phenomena had been proven, the editor of a leading western paper confessed that Bridger had told him about the wonders of the Yellowstone fully thirty years before. However, he discarded the article he had written about these things because he was told that "he could be laughed out of town if he printed any of old Jim Bridger's lies."

The public refused to believe that there were strange things near the lake on the upper Yellowstone, and now, in the late 1860's, history began to repeat itself. Prospectors began to comb the mountains just as the trappers had forty years before—and they too told stories about strange sights.

No doubt Old Jim helped in this revival of tales. Nathaniel P. Langford recalled:

*I first became acquainted with Bridger in 1866. He was then employed by a wagon road company, of which I was president, to conduct the emigration from the states to Montana by way of Fort Laramie, the Big Horn River and Emigrant Gulch.*

*He told me in Virginia City, Montana, at that time, of the existence of hot, spouting springs in the vicinity of the source of the Yellowstone and Madison rivers, and said that he had seen a column of water as large* as his body, spout as high as the flagpole in Virginia City, which was about sixty feet high. The more I pondered upon this statement the more I was impressed with the probability of its truth. If he had told me of the existence of falls one thousand feet high I should have considered his story an exaggeration of a phenomenon he had really beheld; but I did not think that his imagination was sufficiently fertile to originate the story of a spouting geyser, unless he had really seen one, and I was therefore inclined to give credit to his statement, and to believe that such a wonder really did exist.

Thus an interest in the "Wonderland" took root among the settlers in Montana. In 1867, and again in 1868, the citizens of Virginia City discussed making a trip to the area but nothing developed from this *talk*. However, in 1869, the matter progressed to the point where plans were made for a party of civilians, with an escort of soldiers, to explore this strange region. When the military escort failed to materialize, all but three of the men withdrew. David E. Folsom, Charles W. Cook, and William Peterson—subsequently known as the Folsom-Cook party —set out on the 6th of September to satisfy their curiosity.

Starting from Diamond City, a mining town near the Missouri below Three Forks, they crossed the Bozeman Pass and followed up the Yellowstone valley. Traveling leisurely and stopping to admire the sights along their route, they followed the river as far as Yellowstone Lake. Here they turned westward to the valley of the Madison River, which stream they followed back to their starting point. This trip took thirty-six days, and on their return they found their friends seriously considering a rescue party to go in search of them.

Apparently the men kept a detailed diary for later Folsom wrote an excellent article about what they had seen. However, just after their return, the men were reluctant to discuss what they had observed. Langford wrote later:

Bewildered and astounded at the marvels they beheld, they were, on their return, unwilling to risk their reputations for veracity by a full recital of them to a small company whom their friends had assembled to hear the account of their explorations.

In 1870 the first of two expeditions got under way which were to establish beyond all question the truthfulness of the stories about the strange sights in the country near the heads of the Yellowstone and Madison Rivers. This was no ordinary expedition which the citizens of the Montana settlements organized after almost four years of talking; and the military escort—even though it consisted of only one lieutenant, one corporal, and four privates—had the personal blessing of none other than General Philip Sheridan, then head of the Department of the Missouri.

Although this expedition became known as the "Washburn-Doane Expedition of 1870" the leading promoters were Nathaniel P. Langford and Samuel T. Hauser. The former was a prominent citizen and one of the founders of the famous vigilante committee that wiped out Henry Plummer's gang of outlaws, and the latter was a civil engineer and president of the First National Bank of Helena. Henry D. Washburn, a general in the Army during the Civil War and now Surveyor-General of Montana, was head of the expedition. Other members were Cornelius Hedges, a respected member of the Bar, Truman C. Everts, formerly U. S. Assessor for Montana, Walter Trumbull, son of Senator Trumbull of Illinois, Warren C. Gillette and Benjamin Stickney who were influential merchants, and Jacob Smith. If Smith was outstanding for anything it was to be for sleeping on guard duty and shirking in general. James Stuart was to have gone but was detained by jury duty. Lieutenant Gustavus C. Doane was a capable officer of pioneer stock who was interested in exploration.

The party left Fort Ellis on the 22nd of August and proceeded up the Yellowstone valley, following much the same route as the Folsom-Cook party until they reached Yellowstone Lake. Here they continued southward along the eastern shore, and then turned west around the head of the lake through a difficult country containing heavy pine forests, much down timber and brush, and occasional boggy areas. On the 9th of September, while in this area, Mr. Everts failed to appear when camp was made. At first no one was worried but several days passed without the missing man being found. Four days later, it "Stormed all night" and the men realized that they should not tarry long. After a week of futile hunting, one of the party and two soldiers remained behind to continue the search and the remainder crossed to the head of the Madison and continued their exploration.

On the 19th of September, they camped at the junction of the Firehole and Gibbon Rivers. It was here that an important idea began to take form. Langford set down this record of the incident:

Cornelius Hedges, of Helena, wrote the first articles ever published, urging the withdrawal of this region from private occupancy and dedicating it to the public, as a park. I distinctly recall the place and the occasion when he first broached the subject to the members of our party. It was in the first camp we made after leaving the Lower Geyser Basin. We were seated round the camp-fire, and one of our number suggested that a quarter section of land opposite the great falls of the Yellowstone would be a source of profit to its owner. Another member of the party thought the Upper Geyser Basin would furnish greater attraction for pleasure-seekers. Mr. Hedges then said that there ought to be no private ownership of any portion of that region, but that the whole of it ought to be set apart as a great national park. The suggestion met with a quick and favorable response from all the members of the party, and, to quote from a recent letter from Mr. Hedges to me, "the idea found favor with all, and from that time we never lost sight of it."

Although Hedges was the first to crystallize the idea of a "national park," the members of the Folsom-Cook party were also stirred by the thought that something should be done to preserve the area for the public; and the germ of the idea was probably planted before the group left Fort Ellis.

This party returned on the 27th of September and the small search group on the 2nd of October. Judge Lawrence of Helena offered a reward of $600 for the missing Everts, and two frontiersmen—Jack Baronet (perhaps Baronett or Baronette) and George Prichette—took up the search. These men found the man a few miles west of the mouth of the Lamar River.

Everts had experienced thirty-seven harrowing days. He became separated from his companions while passing through a large windfall; and the next day his horse took fright and ran away carrying "everything, except the clothing on my person, a couple of knives, and a small opera glass." Then he tried to catch the runaway and became lost. Eventually, he lost his knives but he did realize that the lens from his glasses could be used to start a fire—when the sun shone. Other than two little snow birds and a few handfuls of minnows, he subsisted entirely on the roots of thistles. When he was rescued his stock of roots was almost exhausted and his clothes were in tatters: and he was stumbling along carrying a burning stick (as a sure source of fire) and babbling to an imaginary companion. His rescue left one problem unsolved—his digestive system still retained the fibrous material from the roots which he had eaten. However, a frontiersman whom the party met two days later supplied a pint of oil he had rendered from the fat of a bear, and this provided a prompt and effective remedy.

Members of the party began to write articles soon after their return, and these were copied by eastern papers. Considerable publicity, flavored with human interest as a result of Everts' experiences, resulted. Lieutenant Doane's official report was exceptionally well done, and this was passed, through official channels, to the Secretary of War who forwarded it to Congress the following February.

As far as the general public was concerned, the Washburn-Doane Expedition *discovered* the Yellowstone "Wonderland." There remained for the Government the task of official confirmation. With the Montana newspapers putting their influence behind Hedges' idea that the area be set aside for a "national park"—a hitherto unheard-of thing—it was necessary that this be done promptly. The U. S. Geological Survey hastily reshuffled its plans for 1871 and put a party into the field under Dr. F. V. Hayden, who, eleven years before, had circled this area with Captain Raynolds. There were eighteen in this party including the outstanding pioneer photographer, William Henry Jackson, and the noted landscape artist, Thomas Moran. Jackson made some 400 superb photographs and these, coupled with Moran's fine paintings, did much to further the cause of the first national park.

General Sheridan, who was also interested in exploration, detailed his chief engineer, Captain J. W. Barlow, to head a second party. He was assisted by Captain D. P. Heap, Corps of Engineers (Barlow's counterpart at the Department of Dakota), two draughtsmen, and Mr. Hine, another photographer. A non-commissioned officer and five cavalrymen from Fort Ellis completed this party.

It was necessary for Hayden to do most of his outfitting at Fort D. A. Russell in southeastern Wyoming. The horses, mules, wagons, and supplies were then shipped over the Union Pacific Railroad to Ogden, Utah, and then taken overland, via Fort Hall and Virginia City, to Fort Ellis. The two parties left this post on the 16th of July and spent the next month and a half in exploring and mapping.

In general, their route followed up the Yellowstone to Gardnier River which they ascended to Mammoth Hot Springs, thence to the falls and Yellowstone Lake. Here they turned westward to the Upper Geyser Basin, south to Shoshone Lake, eastward around the head of Yellowstone Lake, and then northward by various routes to Mammoth Hot Springs, and out of the park area by way of the Yellowstone valley. This work added but little new knowledge, and its chief value was that it expanded the information gathered by the Washburn-Doane Expedition and provided a map of a portion of the area. Part of the data gathered by Captain Barlow was lost in the great Chicago fire although some of it was later duplicated from Captain Heap's notes. However, all of Hine's 200 plates were destroyed—everything except sixteen prints which were made the day before the conflagration started.

Beginning almost immediately after their return, Washburn's associates campaigned hard for their idea. The most active individual was Langford, whose initials permitted him to be nicknamed "National Park" Langford. He wrote articles which appeared in *Scribner's Magazine*, and lectured in Helena, New York, and Washington, D. C. Fortunately, these men had friends in Congress and on December 18, 1871, a bill was introduced to set aside this area as a "public park." This passed both houses of Congress and was signed by President Grant on March 1, 1872. Thus the Yellowstone National Park—the result of the vision of two public-spirited pioneers—became a reality. Quite appropriately, the first superintendent was "National Park" Langford.

# 13

## The Trail for the Iron Horse

»»»»»»»»«««««««« In 1853, the Government sent out three expeditions to survey possible routes for a railroad to the Pacific. One party was to work along the 35th parallel, another was to cross the central part of the country on the 38th parallel, and Isaac Stevens was directed to work out a route between the 47th and 49th parallels. Stevens' instructions also directed that he cross the Rocky Mountains near the source of the Missouri and Columbia Rivers, and follow the valleys of these two streams as closely as possible. Although this work indicated that it was feasible to build a railroad over this route, it remained for Captain Raynolds to draw attention to the fact that "the broad valley of the Yellowstone affords peculiar facilities for a railroad."

A group of energetic New Englanders became enthused with the idea of building a railroad over this northern route and continued to promote the idea all during the Civil War. On July 2, 1864, President Lincoln signed a chartering act for a line along the 45th parallel which would link Lake Superior and Puget Sound: and in 1869, Jay Cooke &

Co., the Philadelphia bankers who agreed to back the project, ordered a survey of the economic possibilities. This survey was made in two parts. W. Milnor Roberts, later chief construction engineer on the project, surveyed that portion of the route lying between the Missouri River and the Pacific Ocean. Roberts worked from west to east and, when he got as far as Bozeman, he decided not to venture further because of the hostile Sioux and Cheyennes.

While the Northern Pacific Railroad was building across the prairies east of the Missouri, survey parties worked out the route between the "Missouri Crossing" at Bismarck, North Dakota, and the Bozeman Pass. In the late summer of 1871, Major J. N. C. Whistler and a detachment of soldiers spent a little over a month escorting a reconnaissance party from Fort Rice to the mouth of Glendive Creek and back. At the same time, another party worked on the western end of this unsurveyed portion.

Captain Edward Ball and an escort from Fort Ellis shepherded a group of surveyors headed by a Mr. Muhlenburg who worked eastward from the Great Bend along the north side of the Yellowstone. Apparently there was some question as to whether the best route lay on the north or the south side of the channel. Of course, the south side belonged to the Crows but the editor of the *Avant Courier* of Bozeman took the view that if that was the best side the road should go there. With typical frontier disregard of treaty rights, he wrote: "We deprecate any policy towards the Indians which deprives the whites of any rights, or that retards the progress of civilization. . . ."

While Muhlenburg's party was working, Roberts returned to complete his general survey. He went down the valley with Major E. M. Baker, thirty soldiers, and "Major" F. D. Pease, the Crow agent. They experienced no difficulty other than to be caught in a snow, but the other party was too ambitious and stayed out longer than was prudent. On November 30th, the *Avant Courier* printed this account of the season's operations:

We received a call yesterday morning from Mr. G. D. Chenoweth, Assistant Engineer of the N.P.R.R. party on the Yellowstone, who arrived at this place Tuesday evening, having left Mr. Muhlenburg and the balance of the surveying party at the Crow Agency. Capt. Ball and the escort also returned to Fort Ellis Tuesday evening. Mr. Chenoweth reports terrible suffering among the whole party by cold. They had broken camp and were on the march when the severe snow storm of Friday came upon them in all its fury, the blinding snow coming in a hurricane, drifting to the depth of many feet in their line of march, and the party getting scattered, the greatest suffering prevailed. Twenty-three soldiers were frozen badly, and about forty all together were more or less frozen. They would tumble off their horses perfectly benumbed, and it required the greatest exertion of those not so badly affected to arouse them from the stupor that was fast coming upon them. One man connected with the surveying party, having become detached from the main body, was out all night, and had his feet so badly frozen that amputation will probably be necessary. The survey of Mr. Muhlenburg's party extended about one hundred and forty miles down the Yellowstone valley, and Mr. Chenoweth is highly pleased with the country, and is satisfied that the line surveyed on the north side of the river is the most practical route that could be adopted, which brings the road directly through the Bozeman Pass.

The party saw no hostile Indians on the trip, although fresh signs were visible every day. The Sioux are undoubtedly watching the movements of the surveyors every day. About one hundred and fifty lodges of Sioux were ascertained by the party as being camped on the Big Horn. The Crows were with the surveying party a portion of the time, making several sorties, capturing stock from the Sioux, which showed them to be in close proximity to the party. Some of the stock with the party perished from cold and hunger.

Although the hostiles did not molest these parties, precautions were taken the following year to enlarge the escorts. At Fort Rice on the Missouri, Colonel ("General") David S. Stanley assembled 33 officers and 553 enlisted men, three pieces of artillery, and 13 Indians and 5 half-breeds to act as scouts. Major E. M. Baker, commanding officer at Fort Ellis, started with eight companies of cavalry and infantry. This gave him a total of 20 officers and 349 enlisted men, together with 45 teamsters, employees, and civilians who were also armed. The surveyors' supplies were carried in three four-mule wagons, and 65 wagons and ambulances accompanied the escort.

As Major Baker's party passed the Crow Agency, he tried to get some of the Crows to go along but they told him "that they would like to go and fight the Sioux, but not to travel peacefully through their country." However, Mitch Buoyer, the half-breed Sioux with a Crow wife who had guided wagon trains over the Bozeman Trail, did engage as a guide. No difficulties were experienced in moving down the valley and finding the last stake which had been driven at the Place of Skulls, near the present town of Billings. The baggage train then proceeded about seven miles farther to a point just above and opposite the mouth of Pryor Creek. Here, in a rich meadow—surrounded on one side by the

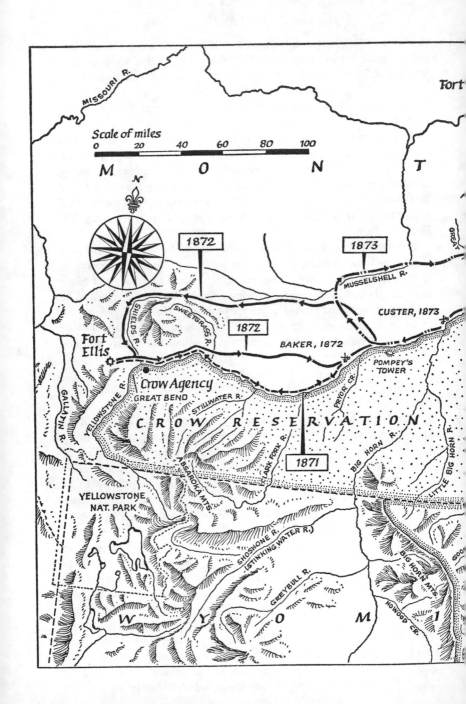

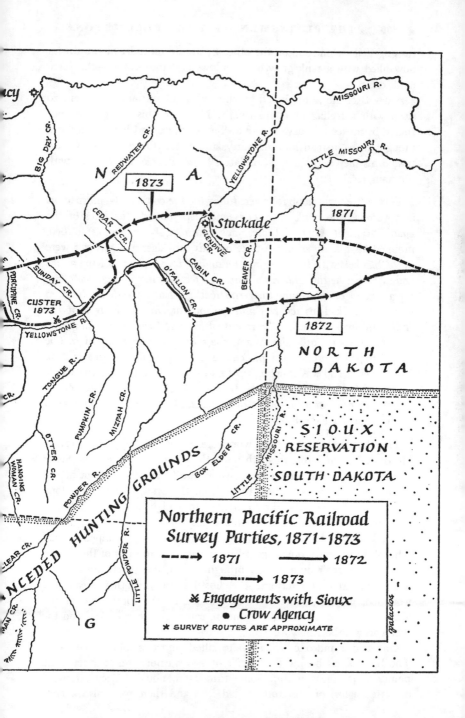

MISSOURI R.

BIG DRY CR.

N

REDWATER CR.

A

YELLOWSTONE R.

LITTLE MISSOURI R.

1873

CEDAR CR.

Stockade

GLENDIVE CR.

1871

PORCUPINE CR.

SUNDAY CR.

CABIN CR.

BEAVER CR.

O'FALLON CR.

CUSTER
1873

YELLOWSTONE R.

1872

NORTH
DAKOTA

TONGUE R.

PUMPKIN CR.

MIZPAH CR.

OTTER CR.

HANGING
WOMAN
CR.

POWDER R.

BOX ELDER CR.

LITTLE MISSOURI R.

SIOUX
RESERVATION

SOUTH DAKOTA

NCEDED HUNTING GROUNDS

CLEAR CR.

LITTLE POWDER R.

MAN CR.

G

Northern Pacific Railroad
Survey Parties, 1871–1873

- - - → 1871        ——→ 1872

——·→ 1873

✳ Engagements with Sioux
• Crow Agency
✶ SURVEY ROUTES ARE APPROXIMATE

palacios

rushing Yellowstone and on the other by an old meander of the stream now filled with a rank growth of willows and rose bushes—the force made camp.

A day later the camp, lulled by their pleasant surroundings, went to sleep with a feeling of contentment. However, this feeling was not shared by all for two days before a "Sioux" horse had been found and brought in by a small hunting party; and so the Officer of the Guard posted his men with care. Years later, J. W. Ponsford, a civilian with the train, recalled:

There were some camp followers following the command—prospectors and wolfers, who made their beds and slept outside the lines of the guards at night. One of these, Jack Gorman, before going to bed, propped his rifle up against a tree, but his cartridges and revolver were in the blankets with him. During the night (3 A.M.) he was lying awake and saw what he thought was a bunch of feathers moving and watching for a second or two found that the feathers had an Indian's head in them. He cocked his revolver and without moving his body shot the Indian through the head. The report of his pistol awoke the camp and the Indians commenced shooting at the soldiers but shot very high. The fact that Jack Gorman had placed his rifle up against a tree and an Indian saw it and was crawling up to steal it probably saved the whole command from being killed. The Indian that Gorman killed was crawling just in front of a big outfit of Indians. He had on just his breech cloth, mocassins and war bonnet.

This shot alerted the pickets who were soon firing "upon the moving forms dimly seen before them through the gloom." Although the Sioux managed to steal four mules and drive away all the cattle—about fifteen head—the soldiers soon drove them from the brush and timber along the slough. The warriors then retreated to a high bench about half a mile away and the soldiers took up the position which they had just vacated. Then, until about 7:00 in the morning, both sides sniped at each other and various warriors engaged in bravery runs in front of the troops. After one of their number was brought down, this practice was abandoned and shortly afterward the hostiles, carrying their dead and wounded, moved downstream and crossed to the south side of the Yellowstone. By 2:00 in the afternoon, camp had been broken and the surveyors were back at work.

One soldier and one civilian were killed, and two soldiers wounded. The Indians left behind the bodies of two warriors and fourteen dead ponies. One officer, writing some time later, noted, "They afterward admitted a loss of over forty killed . . . and there were also a large number wounded, probably nearly a hundred in all." The bulk of them were probably Hunkpapa under the leadership of Black Moon, and no doubt Sitting Bull was present. The *Avant Courier*, quoting a story prevalent at the time, stated that "these Sioux were on their way to the Gallatin valley to clean out the valley but having run across such a large band of horses and mules concluded to take them in first." And the editor, alert to the propaganda value of the account of the fight, complained loudly that "This valley is now left almost entirely unprotected. . . ."

Major Baker reported:

About 3 A.M. of the 14th [of August] the command was attacked by a band of Sioux and Cheyennes variously estimated at 400 to 1000. The companies were promptly formed by their company commanders and the Indians were easily repulsed.

This was the story in the proverbial nutshell—but it left considerable unsaid.

Although Lieutenant James Bradley, the amateur historian of the 7th Infantry, was not present, some of his fellow officers were. In his account of the fight, he stated:

When the attack was made on Baker's command . . . it found several gentlemen wide awake and absorbed in the mysteries of "poker," from which circumstance the fight is sometimes jocularly called the "Battle of Poker Flat." [After the alert, the troops formed promptly in front of their tents and] as soon as the infantry battalion was under arms Captain Rawn, its commander reported to Major Baker for orders and found him still in bed, stupefied with drink, skeptical as to the presence of an enemy, and inclined to treat the whole alarm as a groundless fright upon the part of the guard. It was difficult to get any order from him, but at last he directed Captain Rawn to hold his men in camp; and, disgusted and angry, that officer returned to his command and upon his own responsibility . . . [deployed his troops].

Later, when the Indians moved off, Baker told Rawn to get ready to follow them "but he soon forgot about it or changed his mind."

For a few days, the surveyors continued to work on their line but when they reached some broken country where the main body of troops could not follow closely Colonel Haydon, chief of the survey party, became worried. Although Baker assured Haydon he could provide adequate protection, the latter decided to abandon the work, and asked that he be escorted to the Musselshell in order that he might survey up that valley. Thus the survey stopped when at a point almost opposite

Pompey's Pillar. Apparently, Haydon later tried to make it appear that the escort was responsible for breaking off the work, for Bradley wrote somewhat acidly:

*Engineer Haydon, though wholly responsible for the failure to prosecute the survey to Powder River as had been originally designed, afterwards endeavored to shirk it upon the military.*

On the 26th of July, one day before Major Baker had marched from Fort Ellis, Colonel Stanley moved from Fort Rice. "General" Thomas L. Rosser, a former Confederate cavalry officer, was in charge of this survey party; and Basil Clement, a very competent ex-trapper who had been with Whistler the preceding summer, was his guide. After following Whistler's trail to a point 106 miles west of the Missouri, the engineers started to run a preliminary line "on a course as nearly as possible due west to the mouth of Powder River."

Not long after they crossed over the divide between the Little Missouri and the Yellowstone, Indians made a couple of demonstrations. On the 18th of August, Colonel Stanley and an escort took the engineers to the mouth of the Powder where they proceeded to build their initial "mound." While engaged a "foolish young man named Davis . . . strayed off to hunt agates." Soon the young engineer was seen returning at full speed with twenty-five or thirty Indians in hot pursuit. Stanley detailed the subsequent events in his final report:

*Our people outran the savages and after the exchange of a few shots, the Indians got off, and crossed to the west side of the Powder River, when their chief, the Gall (Uncpapa) came up to the bank of the river, laid down his arms, and called out that he wanted to talk to me. I laid down my pistol and moved forward to the opposite bank of the river, and proposed to meet him on the bare sand bar in the middle of the river. He declined doing this, and the talk that ensued amounted to very little. He wanted to know what we were doing, and when I told him, wanted to know what we were going to pay, and finally threatened to bring all the bands and give us a big fight.*

As Gall's men began to work into the timber behind him, Stanley broke off the parley and had barely moved back a short distance when the Indians fired on them. The soldiers replied and drove the Indians off, wounding one "pretty badly."

Rosser's men now began their line and ran it back up O'Fallon Creek and over the divide toward prairies lying to the eastward. Two skirmishes with the hostiles took place while the party was still within the

Yellowstone Basin; and the Indians dogged their steps much of the way back, finally killing two lieutenants and a mulatto who was Stanley's servant. Thus ended the second year of surveying in the Yellowstone valley.

The task facing the surveyors in 1873 was to close up the gap between the last stake driven by Haydon's men and the location point established by Rosser's party at the mouth of the Powder—a distance of about 175 miles. After reading the reports from the field parties, General Hancock stated, "It is now quite evident . . . it will require much larger bodies of troops than we now have disposable in this department. An accession of cavalry is especially required. . . ." This was accomplished by reassembling the 7th Cavalry, then at various stations in the South, and moving them up to Fort Rice.

Not only was this Regiment added, but the expedition which was organized during May and June of 1873 was roughly *three* times as large as the one Stanley had commanded the preceding year. And "General" Rosser had regarded it as much too unwieldy to perform the desired work.

The planning for this year was expansive in other ways—this time there were to be steamboats to move some of the supplies. To get the nautical activities under way, General Sheridan sent one of his aides, Major (Brevet Brigadier General) George A. "Sandy" Forsyth, to make a water reconnaissance of the Yellowstone. The boat selected was the *Key West*, commanded by Captain Grant Marsh who was alleged to have been capable of navigating on a heavy dew. Marsh left Fort Abraham Lincoln, near Bismarck, on the 3rd of May. Picking up a dependable scout named Luther S. Kelly—later widely known as "Yellowstone" Kelly—along the way, and loading on two companies of infantry at Fort Buford, the *Key West* entered the Yellowstone three days later.

During the next seven days, the boat was worked up to Wolf Rapids, just below the mouth of the Powder; and the captain estimated that he could get over this spot when the "spring rise" swelled the flow of the river. Then, having decided that there was a good spot for a supply depot near the mouth of Glendive Creek, the party returned to Fort Buford where the escort was discharged. Marsh then took the boat down the Missouri to Yankton from which point Forsyth sent his report to General Sheridan.

The escort which was assembled was indeed a large one. It consisted of all of the 7th Cavalry, except two troops, and 20 companies of infantry, together with a detachment of Arickaree scouts—a total of 80 officers and 1,451 men. The wagon train "amounted to 275 wagons and ambulances. The civilian employees numbered 373 men. The number of horses and mules to be foraged was 2,321."

Basil Clement was chief guide again, and among the others in this group was Charlie Reynolds. Reynolds' dislike of idle talk won for him the nickname of "Lonesome" or "Silent" Charlie Reynolds. Three years later he was chief scout for another expedition as colorful as this one—but one from which he did not return. And there were a few unusual individuals present. One was a Mr. Frost of St. Louis who was out for adventure, as were two English sportsmen, Messrs. Clifford and Molesworth, who had their own team and wagon. A fourth was Father Stephen. Lieutenant Colonel (General) Custer wrote his wife that while camped along the Yellowstone, just prior to starting the survey, they were amazed to see this priest and a single companion come driving up in a covered spring wagon drawn by a team of mules; having followed their trail "more than two hundred miles through hostile and dangerous country."

One lieutenant wrote to his mother that,

[General] Terry said in a little speech he made to us . . . that this was the most interesting of all the Indian campaigns. What with English lords, scientists, and outsiders of every military description you would imagine it a big picnic. . . .

The attitude that this expedition was a big lark persisted until the Yellowstone was reached.

A favorite sport was running game with greyhounds. The 22nd Infantry had a regimental pack—the star of which was a mongrel named Given; the Englishmen had a "set" of hounds; and Custer had a number of which he was proud. Poker playing was an obsession with many of the officers and "General" Custer had to take over his brother Tom's money to hold him in check. Too much liquor was consumed by some, among them Colonel Stanley. (Stanley's drinking and Custer's headstrongness were to lead to friction between the two before they returned.) And sometimes the band of the 7th Cavalry entertained the entire party with evening concerts.

Custer's hunting activities not only supplied his own mess with game most of the time, but also those of the other officers. The "general" also had his own cook with him, a Negress named Mary, who was a permanent fixture in his household. In the evenings, "Generals" Custer and Rosser would lie on a buffalo robe under the fly of a tent and talk over their cadet days at West Point and "listen to each other's accounts of battles in which we had both borne a part."

Not all was peace and harmony among the junior officers. Nepotism caused a schism in the 7th Cavalry and one lieutenant was prone to refer to Custer's brother Tom, his brother-in-law James Calhoun, and Captain Moylan as members of the "royal family." And no doubt he was a bit snobbish himself as he once commented that the infantry officers were "a very inferior class of society."

With Custer in the van hunting the *Key West*, part of the troops reached the Yellowstone near the mouth of Glendive Creek on the 13th of July. Captain Grant Marsh had arrived ten days before, and the command now went into camp to rest, replenish their stock of supplies, and build a shelter for the extra freight. Stanley located this stockade eight miles above the mouth of Glendive Creek, and when he moved on, one company of infantry and two troops of cavalry were left as a guard. About two weeks later, the expedition, which had been ferried to the north bank of the river, began their survey. A few days later, the *Josephine* arrived and followed on up to the mouth of the Powder where she unloaded additional supplies. In the fragmentary journal kept by the surgeon is this entry: "Thirteen barrels of whiskey destroyed today—thank God."

As the area of badlands above the mouth of the Powder made travel along the river impossible for the wagon train, Stanley often sent Custer and a small detail to locate a road. On the 4th of August, when above the mouth of the Tongue, Custer took about ninety men and three of the "royal family" and set out to locate one of these detours. About noon, he swung down to the Yellowstone several miles in advance of the main column. As the men were resting in a patch of cottonwoods, six mounted Sioux dashed boldly into the timber and attempted to stampede the horses. The troops saddled at once and moved out in pursuit, but Custer quickly became suspicious of these apparently overconfident warriors who loped along just ahead.

When he approached a heavy growth of timber he halted the detachment and then rode ahead, with a couple of orderlies, to reconnoiter.

*The six Indians in my front also halted, as if to tempt further pursuit. Finding . . . all efforts in this direction unavailing, their plans and intentions were quickly made evident, as no sooner was it seen that we intended to advance no further, than with their characteristic howls and yells over three hundred well-mounted warriors dashed in perfect line from the edge of the timber, and charged down upon Captain Moylan's squadron, at the same time endeavoring to intercept the small party with* me. As soon as the speed of the thoroughbred on which I was mounted brought me within hailing distance of Lieutenant Custer's troop, I directed that officer to throw forward a dismounted line of troopers, and endeavor to empty a few Indian saddles. This order was obeyed with great alacrity, and as the Sioux came dashing forward, expecting to ride down the squadron, a line of dismounted cavalrymen rose from the grass and delivered almost in the faces of the warriors a volley of carbine bullets which broke and scattered their ranks in all directions, and sent more than one Sioux reeling from his saddle.

Being outnumbered "almost five to one," Custer moved back to the timber where he had first been attacked and, with his rear protected by the river, began a defensive fight. At first the Indians charged up to "our line firing with great deliberation and accuracy"; and then, after suffering several losses without being able to force the soldiers to give ground, they attempted to burn Custer out. Fortunately, there was no wind and the grass was not tinder dry. Thus the fight dragged on until three o'clock in the afternoon. Mounting his troopers, Custer charged the now wavering Indians and "drove them 'pel-mell' for three miles."

Custer had one man and two horses wounded: the Indians left five ponies on the battlefield and carried off an estimated ten dead and wounded. Along the line of their hasty retreat, the warriors dropped quite a number of articles, among them some breech-loading rifles.

After the fight was over, the command found the bodies of Veterinary Surgeon John Honsinger, who was attached to the 7th Cavalry, and Mr. Baliran, a sutler, near what is now called Locke Bluff. These men had been repeatedly warned not to ride off by themselves and on this occasion, while attempting to go from the main command to Custer's detachment, they were ambushed by Rain-in-the-Face and two other warriors. When the column returned a month later they also found the remains of Private John Bell. No one could be certain whether he had been with the other two victims or whether he was hunting alone.

Shortly after this skirmish, the command picked up the trail of a village of about eighty lodges which Custer followed eagerly for four days. Finally, Stanley decided to let Custer take four squadrons of the 7th, together with Lieutenant Brush of the 17th Infantry and part of his force of guides and Indian scouts, and go in pursuit. Moving out at night when the moon was up enough to permit following the trail, Custer pushed along with all possible dispatch. Late in the afternoon of the next day, they came to the place where the Indians had crossed to the south bank of the Yellowstone. This point was about three miles below the mouth of the Big Horn, and the Sioux were now on the Crow Reservation.

At this point the Yellowstone was 600-700 yards wide and the water was—according to one lieutenant—"too swift and fierce for our heavy cavalry." After working all day, Custer was forced to give up the idea of crossing. However, just at sunset, a small party of Indians came down the river and discovered the troops but most of the men, dog-tired from their rapid march, lay down to sleep unaware that the hostiles knew where they were.

The next morning just at daylight, the slumbers of the troopers were rudely broken by a sharp volley and shouts and yells from the opposite bank of the river. The startled men were on their feet

*in an instant. As far up the river as we could see, clouds of dust announced the approach of our slippery foes, while rattling volleys from the opposite woods and the "zip," "zip" of balls about our ears told us that there were a few evil disposed persons close by.*

For half an hour the warriors sniped at Custer's men while three sharp-shooters returned the compliment. Among these was Private Tuttle, one of Custer's orderlies and a very fine marksman. After Tuttle had dropped three warriors he drew the concentrated fire of the Indians and was killed.

Soon the scouts and the Indians were exchanging what one officer facetiously termed "chaste complimentary remarks" and the latter were threatening to cross the river. Before long the scouts came tumbling down the bluffs to Custer screeching, "Heap Indian come." Five or six hundred warriors had crossed and soon these, "screaming and yelling," came charging in at the skirmish lines which Custer had hurriedly thrown out. The fight was short and sharp—the hostiles shooting the horses of Custer and another officer out from under them.

*In twenty minutes the squadrons were mounted and ordered to charge. Our evil-disposed friends tarried no longer, but fled incontinently before the pursuing squadrons. We chased them eight miles and over the river, only returning when the last Indian had gotten beyond our reach.*

Custer estimated that they had been engaged by 800 to 1,000 warriors, while others galloped back and forth on the bluffs along the opposite shore. Stanley arrived about seven o'clock, in time to order a few shells thrown at these distant Indians. These were "very well aimed, producing a wonderful scampering out of sight."

In his report, Custer stated:

The losses of the Indians in ponies were particularly heavy, while we know their losses in killed and wounded were beyond all proportion to that which they were enabled to inflict upon us, our losses being one officer badly wounded, four men killed, and three wounded; four horses killed and four wounded.

Careful investigation justifies the statement that including both day's battles, the Indian losses will number forty warriors, while their number of wounded on the opposite bank may increase this number.

The wounded officer was Lieutenant Charles Braden, whose thigh bone was shattered. An ingenious wagon master devised a sort of wheeled litter from the running gear of an ambulance and two poles about thirty feet long; and a detail of soldiers pushed and pulled this conveyance for approximately 300 miles until the man was finally placed in the cabin of the *Josephine* and taken down the river.

From various *sign* it was determined

the Indians were made up of different bands of Sioux, principally Uncpapas, the whole under the command of "S.B.," who participated in the second day's fight. . . .

Custer noted that,

the arms with which they fought us (several of which were captured in the fight) were of the latest improved patterns of breech-loading rifles, and their supply of metallic rifle cartridges seemed unlimited. . . . So amply have they been supplied . . . that neither bows nor arrows were employed against us.

In his report, Stanley recorded additional information which is of particular interest:

From citizens clothing, from coffee, sugar, and bacon dropped, from the shells of patent ammunition found on the field, from two Winchester rifles found upon the first field, it is certainly true that these Indians were the recipients of the bounty of the United States Government, and as they were mostly Uncpapa, they had at no long time since come from that center of iniquity in Indian affairs, Fort Peck.

The finger which Stanley pointed at the agency at Fort Peck was probably well merited, for the business of trading arms and ammunition to the hostiles was one of the scandals of the upper Missouri country.

From the standpoint of the survey for the Northern Pacific, these two fights are not particularly noteworthy. However, they are an important part of the background for the Sioux war of 1876 and, particularly, the

Battle of the Little Big Horn where these same Indians were part of the force which killed Custer and a large part of his regiment. It is possible that Custer's experiences in these two engagements were an important factor in determining his plan of battle on that fatal Sunday.

This battle, which occurred just below the mouth of the Big Horn on the 11th of August, all but ended the Sioux opposition. However, the Indians kept the column under surveillance and five days later an amusing incident happened. When the column was camped opposite Pompey's Pillar, some Indians hid behind this great rock. About eight o'clock in the morning "when the [north] river bank was covered with men, many in bathing, the Indians opened fire on them. The scampering of naked men up the hill was very comical." No one was killed and only one man was hurt.

After completing the survey, the expedition turned northward and followed Baker's trail to the Musselshell. Here Stanley prepared some reports:

> The night of the 19th I sent Reynolds and Norris, two daring scouts, to Fort Benton with dispatches. Mr. Frost, a young gentleman from Saint Louis, and two Englishmen, Messrs Clifford and Molesworth, who had accompanied the expedition for adventure, went through with the scouts.

Here Stanley turned eastward to the head of Great Porcupine Creek which he followed down to the Yellowstone where they picked up their old trail. However, on the "middle fork" of this creek he sent Custer and the cavalry, together with the engineers, by a direct route overland to the depot near Glendive Creek. Custer made an easy, rapid march, arriving at the stockade on the 6th of September. The infantry and the major part of the wagon train tramped wearily in three days later. Surplus supplies were loaded on the *Josephine*, which was waiting, and these together with the troops which were no longer needed were sent down the river. These details taken care of, Stanley began his return over the now-familiar road. Nine days later he was back at Fort Rice.

In the summary of his report, Colonel Stanley wrote:

> Ever since I have been in this department, the hostile Sioux have made their home upon the Rose Bud, Tongue River, or Powder River, and within a few days march of the several points I have recommended for a military post. [These were near the mouth of the Tongue, Great Porcupine, and Rosebud.] The Yellowstone is now the southern limit of the buffalo range in the Sioux country, and a strong post of infantry and cavalry mixed, with a good steam ferryboat (indispensable), will

overawe or destroy the hostile Sioux. *Until the Sioux are quelled nothing can be done to even test the capabilities of the country when it is settled. I have great hopes of the future of the Yellowstone and its tributaries.*

Congress did approve, in 1873, appropriations for the forts along the Yellowstone which the Army had favored for several years. However, another three years were to lapse before they were built.

As "General" Rosser's men were completing this survey line, events were taking place elsewhere which were to have a profound effect on the building of the Northern Pacific Railroad. During the summer, a financial panic swept the East and the great Philadelphia banking firm of Jay Cooke & Co. went down in the crash. Construction of the railroad, which had reached Bismarck on June 3rd of this year, came to an abrupt halt.

This was a severe blow to the hopes of the settlers in the valley of the Gallatin. The editor of the *Avant Courier* tried to keep these hopes alive but his stories had the tone of the proverbial small boy whistling in the dark. It was not until "General" Rosser built his famous bridge on the ice of the frozen Missouri during the winter of 1878-1879, that the Northern Pacific Railroad showed signs of pushing up the Yellowstone valley.

# 14

## Prospectors and Traders, 1874-1875

»»»»»»»«««««««« When it became obvious that there was no prospect of the Northern Pacific Railroad being built up the Yellowstone valley in the near future, the settlers in the Gallatin valley began to consider another means of alleviating their isolation. Beginning in January 1874, items began to appear in the *Avant Courier* to the effect that:

The Yellowstone Wagon Road and Prospecting Expedition, consisting of more than one hundred men, provisioned for six months and fully equipped to thoroughly prospect the country between Bozeman and the mouth of Tongue river on the Yellowstone and the adjacent country, will leave this place on or about the 10th of February, and its movements, discoveries, etc., will be watched with interest by every man in the Gallatin county, besides those in adjoining counties. Couriers will be sent back from the expedition at regular intervals, and a correspondent of this paper will accompany the expedition. . . .

This movement was sponsored and supported by the business and professional men of Bozeman, but those who were to make up the party were experienced prospectors and frontiersmen.

On the surface, this project appeared to be quite logical. The railhead was at Bismarck on the Missouri River. What the Gallatin valley needed was a road down the Yellowstone to the head of navigation, and then a steamboat link between these two points. The major problem was to establish a town along the Yellowstone which would correspond to Fort Benton on the Missouri. In one issue the editor of the *Avant Courier* discussed at considerable length the fact that, "It is the purpose of a portion of those who go with it to lay the foundations of a town. . . ." There were to be carpenters and blacksmiths in the party, and "enough men are going to make a good sized county."

The primary purpose of the founders was to do something which would benefit this frontier community. However, the rank and file who joined the party were interested in prospecting and this created a situation where the proverbial tail wagged the dog, instead of vice versa. This expedition did complete a rather remarkable prospecting trip— and it stirred up an exchange of correspondence between various government officials which is even more interesting than the adventures the men had with the Sioux.

Official circles had been stirred up the year before. In 1872, Paul McCormick, an ambitious individual, had been wagon master for the survey escort commanded by Major Baker. The next year he set about organizing an expedition to go into the Yellowstone country to prospect. This activity was reported, and on August 2, 1873, Lieutenant General Sheridan—then commanding the Department of the Missouri—dispatched a telegram which eventually reached Major N. B. Sweitzer, the Commanding Officer at Fort Ellis. This read, in part:

> You can notify the members of McCormick's party that they will not be permitted to invade the Crow Indian Reservation to hunt gold, but I do not consider we have any authority over the party outside the Reservation. The Judiciary of all the Territories, I believe, claim jurisdiction over all Territories within their limits not donated especially to Indians by act of Congress. . . .

Major Sweitzer, in his reports to higher headquarters, was inclined to view the Yellowstone Road and Prospecting Expedition as just another attempt to discover deposits of precious metals which were believed to exist in the Yellowstone valley—*largely on the Crow Reservation*. Military authorities did extract a promise from members of the expedition that they would stay out of forbidden territory, but this was given with tongue in cheek and no one paid any attention to it once they were well beyond the reach of the troops.

It was not long before there was a flurry of letters and telegrams passing between Governor B. F. Potts of Montana, Mr. C. Delano—the Secretary of Interior—Army officers from the Secretary of War down to the Commanding Officer at Fort Ellis, and the Crow Agent. Governor Potts, in particular, proved himself to be a letter-writing, telegram-sending busybody with his mind full of harebrained ideas.

From the very beginning, high ranking officers and government officials took a dim view of the whole affair. On March 13th, Secretary Delano wrote to Governor Potts:

*Referring to the so called "Exploring Expedition" which was the subject of Department telegrams of the 10th and 13 instants, I have to say that its departure from Bozeman is much to be regretted, and stringent measures would have been adopted to prevent it, had the facts been sooner known here. Although the promise made to the military authorities, that the expedition would not go upon Indian Reservations, may not be violated, there is nevertheless, grave apprehensions that the movement of such a formidable organization through the region of country more or less traversed by various bands of Indians, will provide collisions, that may culminate in a general Indian war.*

*You are earnestly requested to use every precaution to avert a disaster which would render abortive the efforts now being made with every prospect of success, not only for a continuance of the friendly relations now existing with reservation Indians, but for the purpose of invoking their assistance and influence in promoting a better feeling among the intractable Sioux.*

*The Department never entertained a doubt of the loyalty of the Crows, and I will thank you to inform them, that their friendship to the whites, is duly appreciated, and it is hoped that, no events will occur to render their proffered services necessary. If, however, circumstances should arise to require them, they may be made available.*

Governor Potts thought it was an excellent idea to get the Absaroka embroiled with the Sioux. His enthusiasm was not dampened in the least by Delano's disapproval, and he continued to bombard the Secretary with letters—even after the Expedition had returned from their foray. Finally, in a letter dated May 22nd—in which he acknowledged the receipt of letters dated *April 25 and May 2, 4, 6, 7, and 12*—Delano wrote not too accurately but nevertheless very emphatically:

In your letter of the 12th instant, this day received, you strongly urge that the Crow Indians be armed and furnished ammunition, and state that you believe it safe and judicious to do so.

Reliable information in the possession of this Department, is to the effect that the Crows have arms of superior quality and pattern, and more than there are adult members of the tribe to use them. And I think they are already supplied with as much ammunition as they should receive.

In your letter of the 7th instant, referring to the Bozeman expedition, you write that, "the Crow chiefs are anxious and beg the white men to return and every Crow warrior will go with them. The anxiety is intense among the Crows and they are now preparing for a campaign against the Sioux and will start in about ten days whether white men go or not. I think 300 white men and the Crow Nation could settle the Sioux question in one season."

The solution to the "Sioux question" cannot be reached by the method indicated. Its settlement would be, by such means, greatly retarded, and the Crow Indians instead of being encouraged, should be required to abandon their contemplated "campaign," which can only result in exciting the Sioux to greater hostility to the whites; endanger the success of the efforts now being made to bring the disaffected tribes upon Reservations and prevent the peaceful progress of the various wagon trains through the country from Judith Basin to Carroll; the road over which they pass being now reported by the War Department as exposed to raids by semi-hostile tribes.

I trust you will exert all your influence in aiding the Department to carry out the Indian policy which was inaugurated for the purpose of controlling the various tribes without force, unless as a last resort.

The information conveyed in your several communications, in relation to the "Bozeman Expedition" confirms the opinion I entertained of the enterprise and which was expressed in Department letter of the 13th, and in telegram of 10th and 13th March last, addressed to you.

I shall confidently rely upon your promised cooperation in preventing all future expeditions.

It is obvious from this correspondence that Potts welcomed the opportunity to stir up a war with the Sioux. This gives credence to an accusation made many years later:

Ostensibly the object of the expedition was to prospect for gold; but those possessed of inside information have been quoted as saying that its real object was to stir up the Sioux and Cheyennes in the Big Horn and Yellowstone valleys to commit hostilities, which would compel the

Government to take the tribes in hand and thereby open the Yellowstone and Big Horn for trade and provide a market for the agricultural surplus of the valleys. . . .

There were individuals in and around Bozeman who, conceivably, could have been interested in such a motive.

It is possible that there was more to the matter than this. There had been agitation to have the Crows removed from their reservation; and in 1873 these Indians had agreed to move provided they were given a reservation in the Judith Basin. The Government was agreeable to this proposal, but the settlement of Rocky Point—later Carroll—was becoming important as a point where steamboats could unload when the Missouri was low. And Carroll was connected with Helena by a freighting route which passed through the Judith Gap. As soon as this proposed move of the Crows became known, settlers immediately squatted all along this road and raised a big squawk about Government interference with their activities.

Troops stationed on the frontier were frequently called upon to protect settlers who were disobeying existing treaties or agreements: and it is to be expected that canny Army officers immediately began to probe this situation for its ulterior motives. General Sheridan who, as Commander of the District of the Missouri was responsible to the Secretary of War for what went on in the Yellowstone Basin, was not long in pointing his finger at those who were urging Governor Potts to promote an Indian war. In a letter dated April 15th—well before the above-noted deluge between the Governor and the Secretary of Interior, Sheridan outlined his views to General Sherman. It was his opinion that the fuss arose from a rival party which was interested in bringing freight to the settlements over what was known as the "Musselshell Route,"—which interests had also promoted the town of Carroll. As soon as these individuals found out about the Bozeman party, they raised the cry of "Indian troubles." Then when the Governor discovered that General Terry (at Fort Shaw) had provided some protection to the Carroll-Helena road, he had immediately claimed that the settlements were being left unprotected. Sheridan closed his letter with this blunt statement:

*I propose to let these parties fight their own battles, have refused either of them any assistance, and if the Interior Department will do the same, we will get rid of a subject which has no public interests in it.*

This is the background against which the activities of the Yellowstone Wagon Road and Prospecting Expedition must be placed. It is doubtful if the members of the party were aware of the fact that they were pawns in the schemes of others. They were interested in but one thing —"Whar is the gold in them thar hills?"

Interest in prospecting still ran high at this time. From time to time the Montana newspapers carried stories about deposits which had been found in the Yellowstone Basin—but which the finder had not been able to relocate. In the winter of 1873-1874 a glib liar named J. L. Vernon stayed in Bozeman. Here he tried to organize a party to help him exploit some rich gold deposits he said he had found on the south side of the Yellowstone between the Rosebud and the Powder. However, as he kept company with a couple of deserters and had a reputation for being dishonest, only ten men became interested in going with him.

The Yellowstone Wagon Road and Prospecting Expedition assembled at Quinn's ranch, sixteen miles out of Bozeman, on the 10th of February. Here, the party organized the following day and "Under the most favorable auspices and in fine spirits rolled out Thursday morning, amid the booming of artillery and the lusty huzzahs of the hardy pioneers."

Following the trails made by the escorts of the surveying parties, the expedition went down the north side of the Yellowstone to a point just above the mouth of Great Porcupine Creek. They picked up Vernon's party while enroute but this scamp was about as far down the Yellowstone as he dared to go and he soon left, taking two mules and a horse which were not his property. Here the train of the expedition crossed the Yellowstone on the ice, and then camped for several days while the men prospected the valley of Great Porcupine Creek.

Addison M. Quivey, a member of the governing council, later stated that the party at this point consisted of

147 men, with over two hundred horses and mules, twenty-eight yoke of oxen, and twenty-two wagons, with supplies of provisions for four months, and two pieces of artillery, with one hundred and fifty rounds of shell and canister. All the men were armed with the best breech-loading rifles, and were supplied with over forty thousand rounds of metallic cartridges for the same.

Most of the provisions, wagons, and teams had been provided by the people of Bozeman; and Governor Potts had been generous in furnishing arms and ammunition. One of the pieces of artillery was the Big Horn Gun which the expedition from Cheyenne had brought to Bozeman four years before.

The party was well organized having a captain, lieutenant, adjutant, signal officer, secretary, and a council of nine men which made many of the decisions. The captain, Benjamin Franklin Grounds, was well liked and very capable, and the members of the party were a hardy, level-headed lot. Many of the men had fought in the Civil War, and the remainder were capable frontiersmen.

Leaving their camp along the Yellowstone on the 26th of March, the expedition headed in a southeasterly direction on an old Indian trail. This brought them to the Rosebud at a point about twenty-five miles above its mouth. They then followed up this stream for approximately forty miles at which point they turned westward and, skirting the northern end of the Wolf Mountains, came down to the Big Horn about twenty miles northeast of old Fort C. F. Smith.

The first Indians were seen just after leaving their camp on the south side of the Yellowstone. From this time until they crossed the Big Horn a month later, the men had three stiff fights and one skirmish with hostile Indians. The total casualties were one man killed, another severely wounded, and a few with minor wounds. On one occasion the Indians killed twenty-one horses within the wagon corral but later the whites captured enough to even the score with a few left over. No estimate was made of the number of Indians killed although eight scalps were turned over to the Crows. At the scene of one fight, they left behind some food poisoned with strychnine; and on another occasion they buried an Indian in an obvious grave which was booby-trapped with a cannon shell and some scrap iron.

Perhaps the most determined attack was made as the train was traveling up Lodge Grass Creek, in the valley of the Little Big Horn. On this occasion hundreds of mounted Sioux burst from concealment and attempted to overwhelm the train. Previous to this, the attacks had taken place at camps where the whites were dug in with rifle pits for protection; but this time the whites had no such advantage.

The routine marching order was a strong defensive formation—the wagons in two parallel lines with the pack animals herded along between them, and a line of guards out on all four sides. On this occasion (as usual) there were eight men in both the advance and rear guards, with sixteen along each flank. The advance guard calmly stood their ground and soon cooled the ardor of the 200 who had started a confident charge on them: and in the meantime the rear guard, beset by twice as large a force, retired slowly to the corral which the drivers had quickly formed. When the circle was complete, all the men opened up and made things so hot for the Indians that they took cover in the timber along the creek, in ravines, and behind ridges.

Quivey who wrote very modestly about this fight, noted that the Indian fire was very ineffective as they would not expose themselves to take aim. However, about a hundred warriors got into a ravine some two hundred yards away and poured a galling fire on the animals in the corral. As it was necessary to dislodge this group, *six men* "stripped themselves of most of their clothing and prepared for the hot work." While their comrades laid down a covering barrage, these six charged and cleared the ravine. Lieutenant Bradley noted later that, "Sitting Bull declared afterward that he had never seen such men." After this amazing display of indifference to odds, the old soldier in charge of the two cannon shelled the timber and the fight was over.

In what was probably a candid evaluation, Quivey wrote:

*The Indians force could not have been less than one thousand, and many of them had needle guns of fifty caliber, center fire, as we picked up many battered bullets of that size, and found a good many metallic shells which they had used. They also had Spencer and Winchester and other breech-loaders, but probably the majority of them had muzzle loading rifles and many revolvers. Many of them had bows and arrows in addition to their firearms. Most of them were well mounted—much better than we were.*

Apparently the observations of this frontiersman were more precise than those reported by Custer the previous year.

When Lieutenant James Bradley wrote his account of this fight about two years later, he had not only listened to members of this expedition tell their versions but he had also picked up bits of supplementary information. He increased Quivey's estimate and identified the hostiles:

*The number of Indians who participated in the battle was variously estimated at 1000 to 1500. They afterwards admitted at Fort Peck that it was the combined force of three large camps under the leadership of the famous Sitting Bull. Their loss is unknown, but it is supposed to be not less than ten killed and many more wounded.*

He also made a sober comment concerning the commonly-held misconception about the fighting qualities of the Sioux. As Bradley was the first white man to see the naked and mutilated bodies of Custer and his men, his judgment was tempered with ghastly realism. He wrote:

*It almost justifies the conclusion to which it tempted Mr. Quivey "that the prowess of the Sioux has been vastly overestimated and that a small force of frontiersmen can whip the whole tribe at small cost." But it has since been found that it makes a vast difference whether the Sioux are engaged in an offensive or defensive fight. In the latter case*

. . . they prove themselves able to fight with something of the courage and resolution of civilized men.

After crossing the Big Horn the expedition picked up the Bozeman Trail and followed it back to Bozeman, arriving on the 11th of May. They had found no trace of gold in the lower Yellowstone country and only a few "colors" which indicated there might be deposits in the Big Horn Mountains. According to Quivey, no one knew any more about the navigability of the Yellowstone than "we did when we went away but it is very easy to make a good road as far as we went on the north side of the river, and doubtless in time it will be a great thoroughfare to the east."

The colors found in the lower part of the Big Horn valley served to keep alive the interest in the project. However, late in the following September, the secretary-treasurer of the organization wrote a lengthy statement for the *Avant Courier* in which he pointed out that it was for "our very best interest" not to plan further action. The reason for this sudden change in attitude was contained in a telegram which had been received at nearby Fort Ellis from the Headquarters of the Department of Dakota. This read:

St. Paul, Minnesota, Aug. 18, 1874

Commanding Officer, Fort Ellis:

It is reported that a mining party is about to leave or has left Bozeman for the Black Hills. If this be true, prevent its departure; or if it has already gone, overtake it, burn its wagons and outfit, disarm the men, arrest the leaders and confine them at your Post. If necessary use your whole force in execution of these orders, leaving only a small infantry guard at the Post. Acknowledge receipt and report the present situation and any action you may take.

s/ O. D. Greens, A.A.G.

A state of relative quiet existed along the Yellowstone in 1875—*except* for the marauding activities of the Sioux which, by this time, were accepted as a sort of unavoidable evil. No doubt the editor of the *Avant Courier* spoke for the settlers of the Gallatin valley when he wrote, in September of the preceding year:

It is a conceded fact that the tribe of Crow Indians are worth a regiment of troops to the Gallatin Valley. While they are on their reservation no raids are made by hostile Indians, and the settlers feel safe and secure, but during their absence the Sioux and Arapahoes come up the Yellowstone; cross through the different passes into the valley, drive off our stock and murder our citizens.

However, there was one significant bit of military activity which indicated that General Sheridan expected trouble in the Department of the Missouri. On the 19th of May, he ordered two members of his staff, Lieutenant Colonels James W. Forsyth and F. D. Grant, to make a reconnaissance of the Yellowstone River. In the orders, the general directed:

I want a careful examination made of the south bank of the Yellowstone and the mouths and immediate valleys of the rivers coming in from the Black Hills, and especially those of the Tongue River, Rosebud and Big Horn. . . .

It may be necessary, at some time in the immediate future, to occupy by a military force the country in and about the mouths of Tongue River and the Big Horn. You will, therefore, make a special examination of these points with this in view.

Mr. S. B. Coulson, the government contractor for moving freight on the upper Missouri, placed Captain Grant Marsh and the *Josephine* at Sheridan's disposal, and on the 26th of May the boat started up the Yellowstone. In addition to Forsyth and Grant, there were on board "several professors of the Smithsonian Institution, bent upon scientific research," "Lonesome Charlie" Reynolds, and an escort of seven officers, one hundred enlisted men, four mounted scouts and one Gatling gun.

The *Josephine* had no serious difficulty until she reached a point about twenty-seven miles above the mouth of the Big Horn. Here numerous rapids and islands made progress difficult and, after reaching a point about two miles above the present city of Billings, Forsyth decided it was not practical to try to go farther. The boat was turned around on the 7th of June and four days later she was back at the mouth of the Yellowstone. On their return to Bismarck, Forsyth and Grant dispatched a report to Sheridan in which they stated that they believed that the mouth of the Big Horn was the head of navigation, and they recommended the mouth of the Tongue as a suitable location for a military post.

While this reconnaissance was under way, the preparations for another venture were being completed on the bank of the river near the Great Bend. E. S. Topping, who joined the party later that summer, recorded the story of this project in one of the first histories dealing with the Yellowstone valley:

Maj. Pease, Zed Daniels and Paul McCormick conceived the idea that a trading post established near the mouth of the Big Horn would attract nearly all of the Crow trade, and that the rovers of the upper river, whose trapping grounds were nearly exhausted, would make this their headquarters. So they organized an expedition, and built three flat-boats. These they loaded with supplies, and on the seventeenth of June, 1875, with twenty-two men besides themselves, they commenced their voyage down the river.

During the following winter the *Avant Courier* carried advertisements for the YELLOWSTONE FUR COMPANY—*Fort F. D. Pease*—*P. W. McCormick and Newman Borchardt, agents.* One of these stated:

> We have on hand a well selected stock for Hunters, Trappers, and Miners. Will purchase all kinds of Furs, Peltries and raw skins at the highest market price. Parties contemplating coming to this country may rely upon finding everything needed for outfit-ting.

As Pease was the first Crow agent, and was married to an Absaroka woman, the proprietors certainly hoped to attract some Crow trade; and the post which they founded was used as a headquarters by a number of wolfers. However, there was more behind the project than this. The mouth of the Big Horn was well recognized as the head of navigation of the Yellowstone, and the idea of using this point as a transshipment point for freight was still very much alive. During the following winter "The Yellowstone Transportation Company" ran advertisements in the *Avant Courier* which stated that:

> The New and Light Draught Steamer YELLOWSTONE will leave St. Louis, Mo., April 15, 1876, for the head of navigation on the Yellowstone River and interme-diate points.

It is hardly conceivable that as ambitious a business man as Paul Mc-Cormick would not have been aware of the possibilities which might come from such a development. And, the members of the party were—according to a statement which Pease made thirty-six years later—*very much* interested in prospecting for gold. For obvious reasons, the foun-ders did not give the prospecting angle the publicity to which it was en-titled.

Thus, for various and sundry purposes, this little flotilla was pushed out into the swift current of the Yellowstone—probably from Benson's Landing. Only one of the boats made the trip without a mishap. One was swamped when its captain hit a pile of driftwood, and another hit a snag and upset just above the mouth of the Stillwater. Nothing was lost except three sacks of flour and some clothing, although the men did have to fish the Big Horn Gun and some rifles off the bottom of the river.

This party located their post on a large bottom opposite and just below the mouth of the Big Horn. The following March, a reporter—perhaps the editor—of the *Avant Courier* wrote this description:

Fort Pease is located on a high bottom, about ten feet above the present level of the river; is about 235 feet square; three sides of it is enclosed with log houses and the other with poles. It is evidently a good landing. There are 22 boats here at the present time.

After the buildings were up, McCormick returned to Bozeman for additional supplies—a task which occupied most of his time during the following fall. He started down the river with the last shipment in November. Then, fearing he might get frozen in, he went back to Bozeman for wagons and freighted the goods the remainder of the way, arriving in January. Pease left the party at the stockade and went on down the river in a small boat. According to a story which he told years later, he was arrested at Fort Buford for attempting to stir up trouble with the Indians. However, he escaped and continued on down the Missouri going, eventually, to Washington, D. C. Here he had no difficulty in "clearing" himself of the charges. However, the purpose of this trip is not clear.

The party saw hostile Indians soon after they started to build Fort Pease, and a sort of guerrilla warfare began which continued most of the summer and part of the fall. Eventually, six whites were killed and eight wounded; and Paul McCormick had a narrow escape from an ambush which turned his hair white. On one occasion a party of Crows crept up on a party of Sioux who were intent on ambushing a party of hunters. Then they came into the post where

a Crow played a trick on one of the boys . . . which was rather ghastly and yet was amusing. The Crow reached out a hand from under his blanket to be shaken, and when Muggins Taylor (who was the man greeted) took hold of it, it was left in his clasp. It was a hand which had been cut from a dead Sioux.

When winter came some of the men turned to "wolfing." Although much was said later about the great danger from the hostiles, these hunters scattered out in groups of two and three and spent the winter in little cabins and dugouts at some distance from the fort.

During the mid-winter, thirteen of the group which had collected at the post went back to Bozeman where they spread tales to the effect that the men were having fights with the Sioux "every two or three days," that the "Indians numbered several hundred," and that the post was in considerable danger. The *Avant Courier* helped promote this impression and, on one occasion, stated:

*Something should be done to save [the men] . . . from the merciless savages. Unless reinforcements are sent there we fear that the whole garrison will be masacreed.*

And the traders did nothing to contradict these statements, if, in fact, they did not foster them.

Someone asked the Commanding Officer at Fort Ellis to rescue these unfortunates, and on the 19th of February General Sheridan approved orders for Major J. S. Brisbin to go to their assistance. Three days later the major was on his way with 14 officers, 192 men, two pieces of artillery, and fifteen citizens from Bozeman. When near the mouth of the Stillwater, this detachment was joined by 54 Crows and twenty-three more civilians. The Crow agent even planned to go but was detained at the last moment. As the long-threatened Sioux war was now in its opening stages, the military authorities no longer had any objections to who fought the Sioux, or when, or where.

On March 6th, Brisbin dispatched a courier with the following telegram for General Terry, then in charge of the Department of Dakota:

> *Mouth of Big Horn, March sixth (6th), eighteen hundred seventy six (1876). Arrived at Fort Pease March fourth (4th) and relieved garrison. Fort was evacuated today at noon. Original garrison consisting of forty-six (46) men of whom six (6) were killed and eight (8) wounded. Thirteen (13) had left and gone to the settlements by night. I found in Fort eighteen (18) white men and a negro, and have brought them away. Saw no Indians but found five (5) war lodges here, of about sixty (60) Sioux who fled south. Think they were watching fort to pick up men who ventured out. We start for home tomorrow.*
> *s/Brisbin Commanding. (Major 2nd Cavalry)*

The Army, having set out to rescue a *beleagured* party, was stuck with the *story* that these people were actually in danger. In the official report written later, Brisbin retreated from his previous statement about the Indian threat and added an additional bit of interesting information. He wrote:

I brought away also the valuable property belonging to the men at Pease and took it to the mouth of the Stillwater where there is no danger of hostile Indians at present, and unloaded it. I saw no Indians, but small parties are about. My scouts report the Indians have removed their villages from the Big and Little Horn and are camped on the Rosebud.

Popular conception to the contrary, the true story of Fort Pease is *not* one of a continual and desperate fight with the Sioux. Although there had been fights with the Indians, when Brisbin arrived—according to Topping who was wolfing there at the time—"None of those at the stockade but the traders wished to leave, but all were forced to go." The most revealing record of what transpired on Brisbin's expedition was set down by "U Know," a reporter—probably the editor himself—of the *Avant Courier*. His "Notes on our trip to Fort Pease," which filled two columns on March 31st, is a mixture of candid reporting and sarcasm.

On March 4th, "U Know" wrote:

One mile brings us to opposite the mouth of the Big Horn River; one mile more, we descend to Fort Pease. The star spangled banner is visible in the distance, floating gaily in the breeze. Not a Sioux or sign of one was seen on the trip this far, but the boys did nobly, ran the gauntlet, charged gallantly and captured, without loss, those three barrels of cold poison, or whiskey. Thus our objective point is reached.

The following day he reported:

General Brisbin held a council with the occupants of the fort. They concluded, under the circumstances, to evacuate the place, though several of them did so reluctantly, believing they could hold their position until the boats would arrive in the spring. Several claimed that the whole subject of their situation had been misrepresented, and spoke in harsh terms of those who had evidently created the excitement. They stated that there had not been an Indian, or sign of one, seen since the 29th of January, and that they had no fear of any force of Indians taking ten men out of Fort Pease. They said they could get up and walk out, and to Bozeman, at any time, but they couldn't pack those three barrels of whiskey. The whole affair resembled what is called a farce or wild goose chase, a great fuss about nothing, or with comparatively little or no foundation.

Taking everything except the Big Horn Gun, a pet greyhound which escaped, and the flag which was "left waving in the air as an emblem of liberty," the fort was evacuated at noon on the 6th. U Know's final note read:

March 12—Command reach Stillwater. We reached the Agency after sixteen days on the round trip. Gen. Brisbin loaded up and brought back the goods of McCormick & Co., Dexter & Co., and the baggage of the other men who composed the Fort Pease garrison. You can rest assured there was not to [sic] much of that whiskey got back. Were you to take a glance of "dem red noses" once you would never think of disputing my word.

U Know put his finger on the real reason why this post had suddenly become so *dangerous. The profitable trade which had been expected did not materialize, and a full-scale war with the Sioux was in the offing.* On February 28th—before the relief column started—Paul McCormick and Benjamin Dexter signed a deposition to the effect that the Crows were molesting the wolfers, and that the Crow agent was at the bottom of the trouble. This affidavit was sent to the Secretary of Interior by Governor Potts. In due time, E. P. Smith, Commissioner of Indian Affairs, wrote Dexter E. Clapp, the Crow agent, and requested an explanation. Clapp was a sharp-sighted individual and his scathing answer amplifies U Know's observations.

In a lengthy letter dated April 15, 1876, Clapp replied that he did not believe the Crow thefts were a serious problem. As to the wolfers, he pointed out that the wolfers were trespassing,

killing wolves by poison on the Crow Reservation, a custom which causes great dissatisfaction among them. The Crows never allow a council to pass without complaining of this violation of their treaty.

With these questions disposed of, the agent proceeded to let fly at McCormick and Dexter:

As to the charge that I have incited the Crows to acts of violence towards the whites, or toward wolfers, it is utterly false and malicious. The parties making it know it to be so. Its falsity and absurdities is well known to every person connected with this Agency. I have in my possession affidavits, made before U. S. Commissioner Jones, by the Interpreter, by Good Heart and other chiefs, and by a member of the wolfing party that was robbed, to the effect that they never heard of the charge, until it was published in the Bozeman Times.

One object of the affidavit of McCormick and Dexter was to create a feeling that should assist in obtaining the aid of a military expedition to Fort Pease on the pretense of relieving men besieged there by the

Sioux, but really that McCormick and Dexter might get their private property at Fort Pease transported safely to Bozeman.

The expedition went under the command of Genl Brisbin, found no Sioux, and that none had been near there for a month, found the men unwilling to leave, and only forced them to leave by taking away all provisions, transported, perhaps a thousand dollars worth of property of McCormick and Dexter to Bozeman at an extra expense to the U S Government of from five to fifteen thousand dollars, and among other things, brought from Pease and deposited across the river from the Agency, and on the Reservation, two barrels of Whiskey.

Soon after the order revoking the extension of the Agency was received, and thereafter for two weeks, that whiskey made this agency almost a pandemoneum of drunkeness and brawling.

In a community where swindling the Government was looked upon by some as sharp, if not legitimate business, such a scheme was certainly not beyond the realm of possibility. Clapp obviously knew whereof he spoke; and the matter of the whiskey, which was left at a disreputable establishment just outside the edge of the Reservation, was enough to raise his anger to the boiling point.

# 15

## The Storm Breaks

»»»»»»»«««««««« *"The occupation by the settlers of the Black Hills country had nothing to do with the hostilities which have been in progress."* Thus wrote the commanding general of the Department of the Platte in his annual report, dated September 23, 1876. The author was Brigadier General George Crook, and at this time he had just returned to his headquarters in Omaha after leading two expeditions against the Sioux in the Yellowstone Basin. The Sioux War of 1876—Sitting Bull's War—was in full swing.

In making this statement, Crook was going squarely to the root of the trouble. In 1874, Lieutenant Colonel Custer had led a reconnaissance expedition through the Black Hills and his report of finding gold touched off a rush that filled the Hills with prospectors. As these mountains were on the reservation guaranteed to the Sioux by the Treaty of 1868, the Government found itself in an embarrassing position. Its efforts to eject the trespassers by force fizzled and the Sioux subsequently refused—at Fort Robinson on September 20, 1875—to part with this territory.

Contrary to the commonly-held opinion, *this brazen larceny was not the primary cause of the spectacular struggle with the Sioux*. The Indians did not make war on the whites because of it, nor did the government resort to force of arms to get that which they had been unable to secure by negotiation. This unsavory situation did, however, act as a screen to conceal the true cause: and to further becloud the picture, an estimated 1,500 warriors left the agencies during the spring and summer to join in the struggle. The real cause, in a "nutshell," was that some of the Sioux had committed so many flagrant acts of aggression that the Government had no alternative but to chastize them—thoroughly.

The foundations of this situation extend deep into the history of the western frontier. In 1727, the French, who were then beginning to probe the wilderness for a way to the *Mer de l' Ouest*, established a small settlement on the shores of Lake Pepin, an enlargement in the channel of the upper Mississippi. The hostility of the Sioux forced the abandonment of this foothold. Eleven years later the Sioux killed la Vérendrye's favorite son, a priest, and nineteen other men on an island in the Northwest Angle Inlet of the Lake of the Woods. As the settlers pushed these Indians farther westward, there was more friction. The early days around Fort Crawford, in northeastern Iowa and southeastern Minnesota were not exactly peaceful althought the trouble centered around other Indian tribes rather than with the whites.

The Teton Sioux were the first to move west of the Missouri; and the Santee, who remained in southern Minnesota, staged a bloody massacre of settlers there in 1862. It was the punitive expedition under General Sully, which pursued this tribe to the badlands of western North Dakota the following summer, that eventually reached the Yellowstone River in a bedraggled condition. The Teton Sioux proceeded to ally themselves with the Arapahoes, and a small fraction of the Cheyennes, and then take over the *Crow Country* to the east of the Big Horn Mountains. When they closed the Montana Road and forced the Government to treat with *them*, they were nothing but interlopers—a fact which rankled with discerning Army officers.

Thus by the early 1860's, the Hunkpapa, Oglala, Miniconjou, Sans Arc, and Brules had established themselves on the Dakota prairies and were roaming over the valleys of the Powder, Tongue, Rosebud and lower Big Horn. At times they even went into the country between the Yellowstone and Canadian border, and as far north and west as the Musselshell and the Gallatin. And they had a well established reputation of long standing as being marauders. A large part of the depredations which brought on Connor's futile campaign had been committed by them; and it was the attempt to put an end to most, if not all, of this trouble that the liberal concessions contained in the Treaty of 1868 were made.

Some of the Sioux made at least a pretense of living on the reservation set aside for them but there was a nucleus of renegades who scorned their cousins who lived around the agencies. Under such able leaders as Crazy Horse, Gall, Spotted Eagle, Broad Trail, Hump, Lame Deer, and others they roamed where they pleased and made war on anyone whom they thought they could attack successfully. The ring leader of this faction was the medicine man, Sitting Bull. While the treaty negotiations were under way in 1867, Charles Larpenteur saw this Hunkpapa at Fort Union. He told the trader:

"*I have killed, robbed, and injured too many white men to believe in a good peace. . . . I would rather have my skin pierced with bullet holes. I don't want to have anything to do with people who make one carry water on their shoulders and haul manure. . . . [Other Indians should] go into the buffalo country, eat plenty of meat, and when they wanted a horse, go to some fort and steal one. Look at me—see if I am poor, or my people either. . . . You are fools to make yourselves slaves to a piece of fat bacon, some hard-tack, and a little sugar and coffee.*"

As the Crows knew, in terms of topographic features, where the boundaries of their reservation were, it must be assumed that the Sioux —who were equally intelligent—had an adequate knowledge of the limits of their reservation, and the hunting grounds defined in Article XVI. In spite of the fact that these "unceded" lands constituted what is now the northeastern quarter of the state of Wyoming, this hard core of renegades did not see fit to stay within this area—they had a strong liking for the valley of the Yellowstone and what is now southeastern Montana. Thus when these Indians attacked the railroad surveying parties, their chiefs must have known they were a *long way* from the area where they belonged, and they must also have been aware of the fact that they were doing things which were *expressly* forbidden by the treaty then in force. Gall, in particular, was fully aware of these things as he had headed the delegation which De Smet took back from the mouth of the Powder, and he was the first to sign the treaty papers at Fort Rice.

Among the Indians who went in to the agencies there were a large number of unruly warriors. During the pleasant summer months, many of these joined the villages of the renegades and roamed with them. Those who remained behind found it hard to give up the old ways, and these organized forays of their own.

The troubles of the settlers in the area south of the Yellowstone Basin were the concern of the Department of the Platte; but, as these were similar to the difficulties along the Yellowstone River, what General Crook had to say in the opening part of the above noted report is particularly noteworthy. He stated:

At the date of my annual report for 1875, September 15th, the settlers along the line of the Pacific Railroad and in Wyoming, Nebraska and Colorado, were very much excited and exasperated by the repeated incursions made upon them by Indians coming from the north, and although many of the trails of stolen stock ran directly upon the Sioux reservation, the Agency Indians always asserted that the depredations were committed by certain hostile bands under Crazy Horse, Sitting Bull and other outlaw chiefs.

These bands roamed over a vast extent of country, making the Agencies their base of supplies, their recruiting and ordnance depots, and were so closely connected by intermarriage, interest and common cause with the Agency Indians that it was difficult to determine where the line of the peaceably disposed ceased and the hostile commenced.

In fact it was well known that the treaty of 1868 has been regarded by the Indians as an instrument binding upon us but not binding on them. On the part of the Government, notwithstanding the utter disregard by the Sioux of the terms of the treaty, stringent orders, enforced by military power, had been issued prohibiting settlers from trespassing upon the country known as the Black Hills.

The people of the country against whom the provisions of the treaty were so rigidly enforced naturally complained that if they were required to observe this treaty, some effort should be made to compel the Indians to observe it likewise.

As Articles III, IV, and V specifically prohibited depredations against the whites, Crook noted further:

It is notorious that, from the date of the treaty to the present, there has been no time that the settlers were free from the very offences laid down in the sentences quoted.

Indians have without interruption, attacked persons at home, murdered and scalped them, stolen their stock, in fact violated every leading feature of the treaty.

\* \* \*

In the winter months these renegade bands dwindle down to a comparatively small number, while in the summer they are recruited by restless spirits from the different reservations, attracted by the opportunity to plunder the frontiersman, so that by mid-summer, they become augmented from small bands of one hundred to thousands.

Sitting Bull's band has been regarded by the white people and Indians as renegades, and when it was decided by the Interior Department that they should no longer be permitted to roam at large, but be required to come in and settle down upon the reservation set apart for them, messengers were dispatched to them setting forth these facts; and that from and after a certain time unless they came in upon the reservations they would be regarded and treated as hostile.

The time having expired and the Indians failing to embrace the terms offered by the Government; by direction of the Lieutenant General Commanding, I commenced a campaign against these bands. . . .

Just as Crook was concerned about the raids into the valley of the Platte and adjacent territory, the Commanding Officer at Fort Ellis was concerned about the conditions in and along the northern part of the Yellowstone Basin. On March 7, 1875, Major Switzer addressed a letter to Crook's counterpart in the Department of Dakota at St. Paul, Minnesota. In this he stated:

These Indians controlled by Sitting Bull are the head and font of all the difficulties with the Indians belonging north of the Platte. . . . They are mostly Uncapapas, but bands of Broken Arrows, Blackfoot, Sioux and Yanctonians and usually about thirty lodges of Northern Cheyennes. . . .

Sitting Bull's bands are the ones who fought General Stanley, Col Baker, and the Citizens expedition last spring, that went down the Yellowstone and who raided in the Yellow Stone Valley and stole the Horses last Summer from the head of Gallatin Valley.

They are openly and defiantly hostile and occupying a section of country centrally situated to the different Indian Agencies excite these Indians more or less to hostilities to the whites and commit depredations about the different agencies to involve the Agency Indians in trouble.

These Indians keep the road from Montana to the east completely shut up and are of great injury to the development of Montana. . . .

These Indians hold complete control of the Yellow Stone and Powder River Country and fight any party of Citizens or Soldiers who go into it and are looked upon by a great many Indians at the agencies as being able to defy the power of the Government, the effect of which is *discontent and mutinous Condition among the agency Indians hard to control by the Government Officials and Chiefs disposed to be peaceful.*

The attacks made upon the surveying parties in 1872 and 1873, the prospecting expedition in 1874, and the men at Fort Pease in 1875 were only part of the troubles which occurred in the Yellowstone valley. The Sioux also committed depredations on the Crow Reservation and these incidents became the subject of correspondence between the Crow Agent and various officials, particularly the Commissioner of Indian Affairs in the Department of Interior.

Dexter E. Clapp served as the agent for the Crows during the period which preceded the War of 1876. He had been a general in the Union Army and was, apparently, a man of considerable ability. When he took over the agency late in 1874, it was located at the mouth of Mission Creek, some fifteen miles below the Great Bend. Late in the spring of the following year, he moved it to the mouth of *the* Rosebud Creek which is a small tributary of the Stillwater River. Although Clapp had good reasons for making this change, it intensified the problem of protection for the officer in command at Fort Ellis for the new location was 73 miles *farther* away. As Clapp's letters indicate, this became a bone of contention. Unfortunately, selfish interests of some of the citizens of Bozeman also became mixed in the affair and there was more involved in the ensuing wrangle than appeared on the surface.

In 1873 some Sioux were alleged to have stolen horses from within the enclosure at Fort Ellis. The next year they returned and ran off some 200 head that were within two miles of the post. Eight of these were later found among the ponies of the River Crows; and General Terry, then commanding the Department of Dakota, asked the Commissioner of Indian Affairs for an explanation. This task devolved upon the new agent.

Clapp explained that the horses had been found, and added that, "The same party that captured the horses at Bozeman remained around and harassed the agency for several days." Then he turned to another question:

*To the general principle on which General Terry founds his protest against the issue of breech-loading arms to Indians, I should certainly make no objection. If it were possible to confine them to the old gun, which answers all necessary purposes for hunting, it would be a most important desederatum; but the Sioux, who raid in this vicinity, are already supplied with breech-loading rifles. To attempt to deprive the Crows of the same advantage, or rather to take away from them the improved arms, which they already possess, would be unjust and disastrous.*

It did not take the Sioux long to locate the new agency which Clapp began to build in June 1875. About a month after construction was started, the Agent wrote:

CROW AGENCY, JULY 5TH, 1875

HONORABLE E. P. SMITH
Commissioner of Indian Affairs
SIR,

I am unfortunately obliged to report depredations and a murder committed at or near the New Crow Agency by Sioux Indians. On the morning of the 2nd inst, our timber train and camp was attacked near the mouth of the Stillwater by about thirty Sioux. This attack was easily repelled, although at great risk to some of the men.

The Indians captured one mule and drove off two oxen. Shortly after they killed Jose Pablo Tsoyio, whom I sent to the camp with several oxen, and captured the Agency horse which he was riding.

They concealed themselves in a small ravine, which he had to cross and allowed him to approach within fifty yards without discovering themselves. The poor man evidently made a brave fight for his life. I visited the place on the 4th and found that the Indians had for some unexplained cause departed in great panic, leaving behind them many articles of much value to themselves, and among them were found two small tents, that were made of Flour sacks, bearing the following brands "Anchor Mills XXX Flour, St. Louis, Inspected for Indian Department, F. S. Clarkston Inspector" Bag Manufactures, Bemis Bro. and Co. St. Louis Mo. The articles of Clothing and ornament are pronounced by Indian men to be distinctively of Sioux manufacture.

The party was in war paint and dress. On the morning of the 5th another party succeeded in running off from the Agency, a hired team of 22 mules and 2 horses, 4 Mules and 4 horses belonging to the Agency and 2 horses belonging to a workman, also about 40 head of Oxen and Beef Cattle. This party left a blanket behind bearing the Indian Department Brand.

About two weeks later the Crows were attacked at the mouth of the Big Horn by a body said to contain about 1500 lodges of Sioux, and after three days of fighting were driven from their reservation towards the Judith Basin.

On the night of the 4th three trappers came into our camp, and reported that they had been attacked near Ft. Smith by a body of 250 to 300 Sioux. They had Eleven horses which were either captured or killed. They succeeded in getting into the bushes and eluding the Indians. The party was in full war dress, and must have been on their way to this Agency.

I do not like to ask for a guard here, but feel that I should do so when the indications so strongly indicate determined war and pillage by the Sioux. We can defend ourselves while in Camp, but are liable to lose the remainder of our stock at any time; and I am obliged to send a large party to gather them up every morning.

The guard can be obtained only by an order from Washington as Genl Gibbon has refused to furnish any for the New Agency.

I earnestly ask, that, if a guard is to be furnished, the Order may be sent by Telegraph, as our special want is immediate.

Very Respectfully<br>your Obedient Servant<br>s/ Dexter E. Clapp<br>Agent

The attack on the trappers which Clapp mentioned involved a sharp fight. According to a frontiersman who knew the three men, this "is an almost incredible tale." Theodore Roosevelt, who managed to get the story from two of the men while he was ranching along the Little Missouri, also thought it was worth recording. What happened was that Tarzwell Woody—one of the most daring and capable frontiersmen on the upper Yellowstone, Charley Cockle, and a man named Hubble were jumped by a large party of Sioux one morning while tending traps. As all three were excellent marksmen, the Indians made no serious attempt to press the fight until the trappers had retreated to their camp where the whites made a barricade of saddles and, later, three dead horses. After charging the camp several times, both on foot and on horseback, and wasting considerable ammunition in reckless shooting, the Sioux finally decided that the price of these three scalps was too high. Woody, in telling the story to Roosevelt, said, "I only fired seven times all day. I reckoned on getting meat every time I pulled the trigger." When the war party drew off at night, the trappers slipped away with only their rifles and the clothes on their backs. They made their way to the agency where Clapp did not believe their story until the Sioux raided his camp shortly afterward.

The new agency was squarely on the route which had been used by hostiles in going toward the old agency and the passes leading to the Gallatin valley. A month after sending the first report of depredations, Clapp posted a second letter on the same subject:

Sir,

I have the following additional items of Sioux depredations to report. On the morning of July 21st The train of Nelson Story was attacked by a small number of Sioux in the Stillwater valley, about six miles from the Agency.

Captain Dusold, U. S. Detective, was fired at by two Indians from the bushes at a distance of but fourty yards, but strangely escaped unharmed. The men of the train pursued the Indians for some distance, and captured their saddles, clothing and trinkets, which they had stripped for the fight. They called to a half breed sioux scout who was with the train, that they were the advance of a large party, and "would give us plenty of fight."

This same morning a party came upon our herder who was with the Stock, one and one half miles from the Agency, drove him to the brush, took his horse and fourty three head of cattle. The next day with Captain Dusold, Mr Story and seventeen other men, I followed them up for twenty miles towards Clark's Fork. We recovered nine head of cattle most of them wounded; and found eight which they had killed.

On the morning of the 27th another party attacked two men who were herding our train cattle and killed one of them James Hilderbrand. His companion placed himself behind some rocks and kept the Indians off until help came from the Camp. The horse of Hildebrand was killed.

On August 1st seven Indians waylaid two men who had been sent from the old Agency to the Yellowstone Crossing one of them John Roues, a half breed, and Crow by adoption, and who is in my employ was shot in the breast, but will probably recover. Lieut Roe, who has just arrived from Fort Ellis, from the Judith Basin, reports that the Crow Chief Long Horse has been killed by the Sioux. A large amount of stock has been stolen by them at Carroll and at other places on the Carroll road. The most dangerous places in the country seems to be on the road from the Old Agency to Bozeman. This road is constantly watched by the Sioux and can be traveled safely only with a large party. Messages from the Crows indicate that they will soon come to the agency. They have lost by the Sioux about two hundred horses.

Very Respectfully yours—

s/Dexter E. Clapp

On the 10th of September, Clapp prepared his annual report. This was a lengthy document which detailed all the events of the past year, and among the items noted was an estimate that the Sioux had "hindered" the construction of the post to the amount of $4,500 to 6,000. He pointed out that the attacks of the Sioux had practically paralyzed the efforts being made to civilize the Crows; that the Crows observed that their enemies were mounted on fine horses, had the best of guns, and had clothing and supplies issued at the agencies; and that they complained "that the larger and most fertile portion of their reservation is permanently occupied by their enemies." Also, he emphasized that a bad impression was created when the whites could not protect themselves, much less the Crows, and

*I respectfully urge, that such action shall be taken as shall effectively quiet the hostile Indians in the Yellowstone country, and give to the whites peace, and to the Crows opportunity for the progress of civilization.*

The following spring, on March 4, 1876, this agent prepared for the Commissioner a detailed report of the happenings in the Yellowstone valley over the past eight months. This began:

*I have the honor to present the following report or memorandum of murders and depredations committed by Sioux Indians in the Yellowstone Valley since 1st of July last.*

*These sum up,*

| | |
|---|---|
| Men killed | 9 |
| "   wounded | 10 |
| Horses & mules stolen or killed | 86 |
| "   "   "   wounded | 3 |
| Oxen killed or driven off | 52 |
| Attacks made on whites | 17 |

*A large amount of property of various kinds stolen or destroyed*

*The Crows driven from the best of their reservation and several of them killed and many of their horses stolen.*

In the covering letter which accompanied this report, Agent Clapp again pointed out that the settlements of "eastern" Montana had been harassed regularly each summer, and that the Sioux who committed these depredations had lost articles bearing government marks:

*There is another very important consideration. The Crows have always been fast friends to the whites, and have largely assisted in protecting the eastern settlements of Montana. The Sioux are now occupying the eastern and best portion of their reservation, and by their constant warfare, paralizing all efforts to induce the Crows to undertake agriculture or other means of self support. I respectfully ask attention to the importance of establishing a Military post, or at least a summer camp on the Yellowstone, near the mouth of the Big Horn. . . . As it is now, not only are men murdered and property destroyed each year, and the* permanent good intended to the friendly Crows prevented, but large tracts of the best Agricultural and pasture lands of Montana made inhabitable.

It was the complaints stemming from this ever increasing list of depredations—from the Platte to the Missouri and from the prairies of North Dakota to the valley of the Gallatin—that finally forced Secretary Delano to lay aside the olive branch and ask the Army to do by force of arms that which his peace policy had failed to accomplish. The old letter books of the Crow agency indicate clearly why there could be but one way to solve the problem of the renegade Sioux. Some of the Army officers had recognized this fact ever since 1865 when General Connor had been ordered to withdraw his troops from the Powder River country. It had never been a question of IF but rather a question of WHEN.

Although old reports provide a picture of the causes for this war, there are no data which allow a precise appraisal of the kinds and amounts of arms which the hostiles possessed. Some estimates, like Quivey's, are probably quite reliable. Others, made by soldiers who campaigned against them, should be viewed with some degree of skepticism for there is the matter of *face* involved. Not every warrior had a Winchester, Henry, or Spencer as Custer's report of the fights on August 4th and 11th, 1873, would lead one to believe; but they did have a considerable number of these up-to-date arms and, in some fights, an abundant supply of cartridges for them.

As to the source of these weapons there is, again, only fragmentary information. However, sketchy as this is, it is both conclusive and damning. On September 25, 1876, Thomas Mitchell, the Indian agent at Fort Peck on the Missouri, wrote to the Commissioner of Indian Affairs that a warrior who had been in the Battle of the Little Big Horn—the so-called Custer massacre—had asked him if Sitting Bull and his followers could come in for the approaching winter. Mitchell reported:

In reply to the question, "Where did you get your ammunition" he answered, The soldiers brought it to us (meaning that it had been taken from the bodies of the dead soldiers,) and the traders from the Burning Grounds furnish us with some.
He states that the Burning Grounds embrace a country extending from south of the Black Hills to the Platte River.

No doubt Mitchell could have added some interesting comments had he seen fit for it was not necessary to go clear to the Platte to find unscrupulous traders who were willing to bootleg modern arms and ammunition to hostile Indians. In June 1873, the Secretary of Interior had asked Durfee and Peck, the traders at this agency, to explain why the steamboat *De Smet* had delivered arms and ammunition to them in boxes marked "Hardware." To this query they had piously replied that only enough had been shipped to supply their own employees—no doubt a new version of the whiskey stories of the fur trading days! It is no wonder that Colonel Stanley pointed his finger at Mitchell's post and called it a "center of iniquity."

There are many letters bearing the dates 1873 and 1874 which tell about illicit trade in arms, ammunition, and whiskey on the upper Missouri. Much of this centered about Fort Benton and it was kept up until on March 31, 1875, the Secretary of Interior notified the two largest merchants in this town—and in all of Montana for that matter—that their licenses to trade on Indian reservations had been revoked.

This bootlegging of arms and ammunition was no secret. In a letter to the Commanding General of the Department of Dakota, dated February 14, 1874, Major Switzer at Fort Ellis made this cynical comment:

*There appears to be no limit to the amount of ammunition and arms these Indians can get, except the means to purchase with.*

And on August 1, 1876—when the campaign against the Sioux was at its height—Governor Potts wrote to General Sherman, then General of the Army, that

*Messrs I. G. Baker & Co. and Messrs T. C. Power & Co., government traders at Fort Benton [noted above], are now selling more arms and ammunition than at any time in the history of trade at that Post and much of it will find its way to Sitting Bull.*

However, in the years just before the war began, a few of the shortcomings of the past were being corrected. A Congressional investigation had aired some of the *dirty linen* of the Indian Bureau with faint signs of progress. The agent at the Red Cloud Agency (just south of the Black Hills) had been removed for incompetence and speculation; but his replacement left much to be desired. One contractor living in nearby Cheyenne had been tagged for fraud in Indian contracts and, at the other corner of the Yellowstone Basin, Captain Ed Ball, the official inspector at the Crow Agency, Agent Dexter E. Clapp, and Nelson Story, a contractor in Bozeman, were engaged in a mudslinging match over alleged fraudulent dealings in provisions for the Absaroka. In Washington, Reverend E. P. Smith, Commissioner of Indian Affairs, had been accused of doing much which brought the

peace policy into disrepute, and also of being corrupt. One Army officer noted his passing with this blunt comment:

> . . . *after vainly trying to stem the tide without refuting the evidence*
> *Smith retired from office and sank into deserved obscurity.*

These things which happened between the summer of 1868 and
January 1, 1876, made war with the renegade Sioux and their allies inevitable. There can be no doubt but that Crook was correct when he
wrote that the rape of the Black Hills, which began late in 1874, "had
nothing to do with the hostilities which have been in progress." It was a
curious situation. On one hand, as Crook put it, the raiding Sioux were
"scourges to the people, whose misfortune it has been to be within
reach of the endurance of their ponies." And on the other hand, greedy
white traders eagerly traded bright, new repeating rifles to them for
their buffalo robes.

# 16

## Crook and Terry Take Over

### THE WINTER CAMPAIGN

>>>>>>>>><<<<<<<<<< On the 17th of February, 1876, several Army officers and a tall, lean plainsman climbed aboard a train in Omaha. Their destination was Cheyenne, Wyoming. Previous to this time telegraph operators' keys had clicked, and orders had been sent to the commanding officers of several posts in the general vicinity of this raw frontier town. As the train pulled from the depot, quartermaster officers were searching for specified materiel, and troop commanders were busy putting their outfits in readiness. At Fort Fetterman, atop a bleak hilltop just south of the Platte at the point where the Bozeman Trail branched off to the north, a wagon train, a herd of mules, and a great pile of grain was being assembled. Part of the force which was to exact the retribution which Sitting Bull and his renegades had been assiduously cultivating for some twenty years was at last taking form.

The touch which put this machinery in motion was a recommendation made by an inspector in the Indian Bureau. He had suggested that a regiment of cavalry make a quick winter campaign and strike a heavy blow against a band of Sioux, estimated at about 500, which were believed to be northeast of the Big Horn Mountains in the valley of the Tongue or the Powder. The blow envisioned was one such as Custer struck Black Kettle's camp in the valley of the Washita about seven and a half years before. General Sheridan, who was now in command of the Division of the Missouri, had directed this operation. His touch was apparent on this occasion in that the grim-faced scout who followed the officers aboard the train was Ben Clark, one of the most able frontiersmen the general had known on the southern plains.

Two divisions of Sheridan's command were involved. One was the Department of the Platte which was under General George Crook. This officer, who had proved to be a capable Indian fighter while in command of the Department of Arizona, had replaced General Ord in the headquarters in Omaha. The other was the Department of Dakota with headquarters in St. Paul. Here the general in charge was Alfred H. Terry, a capable man but without experience in plains warfare.

The troops with which Sheridan hoped to crush the Sioux were located in three general areas—the posts in southeastern Wyoming, Forts Shaw and Ellis in western Montana, and the forts along the Missouri near Bismarck. His plan, if such a rough idea can be considered a plan, was for these troops to converge on the prairie stronghold in three columns and crush the slippery renegades between them.

In this plan there was no provision for anything but the roughest sort of coordination of effort; and, worst of all, was—apparently—based on the fallacy that each column would be practically self-sufficient. Within a few weeks this plan was badly snarled. Before the summer was over the two department commanders were trying to work out a plan of action in the field while separated by a stretch of territory across which only the most nervy of messengers would attempt to venture. This was not a picture of efficiency, irrespective of how colorful some of the campaigning had been. The Indians were to exploit this situation to the utmost, defeating the troops in detail and ending the summer in something resembling a draw.

Unlike Connor's expedition, about which only a modest amount of information is available, the activities of these troops were recorded in detail. With General Terry's troops was Lieutenant James Bradley, the avid historian and journal-keeper of the 7th Infantry. Matthew Carroll, one of the partners of E. G. Maclay & Company, was wagon boss of the Diamond R outfit which freighted for the Montana troops, and he kept a most interesting diary. One of General Crook's aides was Lieutenant John G. Bourke, another amateur historian and the keeper of a voluminous journal. Four newspaper correspondents accompanied

Crook during the summer, one of whom left a particularly good record of what he observed. And, of course, almost every Tom, Dick, and Harry who was in any way connected with the 1876 campaign recorded their reminiscences in later years—without, however, the on-the-spot accuracy which is highly desirable.

The focal point for the beginning of the field operations in the Department of the Platte was Fort Fetterman. This was a small post at the southern terminus of what Bourke invariably called the "Montana Road." As the facilities here were limited, the arrival of some of the troops was timed as close to the date set for departure as was possible. The column which was assembled consisted of ten companies of cavalry and two companies of infantry. Supplies were transported by 86 six-mule wagons and 400 pack mules, one of the principal items of freight being grain, or forage as the soldiers called it. Crook accompanied the column but delegated the immediate command to Colonel Joseph J. Reynolds, commanding officer of the 3rd Cavalry then stationed at Fort D. A. Russell just outside of Cheyenne.

The pack train on which Crook was depending for rapid movement when near the Indians was a development of which he was proud. Tom Moore, the civilian in charge of this outfit, had served with Crook in Arizona and, like Ben Clark, had been brought in for this assignment. The mules were carefully selected and each animal carried a load of 250-325 pounds in addition to a pack saddle. Each five animals required a packer. Bourke noted that they were "robust, hard-working, and good natured fellows, great eaters and generally good story tellers"; and after messing with them for a time he found they were also "very observant, proverbially hospitable . . . and only a few were heavy drinkers." This particular train was divided into five equal segments each of which had its own bell mare. This animal was ridden by the cook of each unit—in Bourke's opinion—"an important personage in every sphere of life, but notably an officer of dignity and trust in a pack train."

Crook's aide was not favorably impressed by the scouts who were led by Colonel Thaddeus Stanton, an old "fire eater" who had charge of the Paymaster's section in the Omaha headquarters. Although he later modified his opinions somewhat, they impressed him as being

*as sweet a bunch of cut throats as ever scuttled a ship. Half-breeds, Squaw-men, bounty jumpers, thieves and desperadoes from the various Indian agencies composed the outfit. . . . Some of these, a minority it is true, but a respectable minority, were men of high type of character, of great previous experience and likely to be of inestimable use in any sudden emergency.*

Ben Clark, the chief scout, had been brought up from the southern plains because Sheridan had a great deal of confidence in his ability. Others were men who were prominent in this area as Louis Richaud, "Big Bat" and "Little Bat" (Baptiste Pourrier and Baptiste Garnier, respectively), Louis Changrau, Speed Stagner, and last, but not least, Frank Grouard.

Grouard was an odd character with—probably—a questionable past. His father, said to have been of French descent, was a Mormon missionary to a group of islands near Tahiti in the South Pacific. While here he married a native girl and Frank was born to this union. Eventually, the Grouard family returned to the United States where it broke up. Little Frank was "adopted" by friends of the Grouards' and when about sixteen he ran away to Montana. In Frank's sometimes-unreliable biography, the statement is made that he was captured by the Sioux and spent several years with them, first with Sitting Bull and then with Crazy Horse. No doubt he lived with the Sioux—Frank was very dark complected and some old warriors believed as long as they lived that he *was* an Indian. But he probably was not a captive for "Clubfoot" George Boyd addressed a long letter to the Bismarck *Tribune* (November 8, 1876) exposing him as a thief and general no-account who had lived with the renegade Sioux. Boyd was a well known scout in eastern Montana and claimed first hand knowledge of some of the things about which he wrote. Be that as it may, he apparently served Crook faithfully and well. Bourke wrote that he

*was one of the most remarkable woodsmen I have ever met . . . no question could be asked him that he could not answer at once and correctly. His bravery and fidelity were never questioned; he never flinched under fire, and never growled at privation.*

The column which was assembled was not a particularly military appearing outfit. Protection from the cold was the first consideration—especially for the cavalrymen—and many of the men wore fur caps, buffalo or bear skin overcoats, and "overboots" made of buffalo skin which extended well above the knees. Undoubtedly the most unmilitary appearing man was the commanding general. His attire consisted of

*boots, of Government pattern, number 7; trousers, of brown corduroy, badly burned at the ends; shirt, of brown heavy woolen; blouse, of old army style; hat, a brown Kossuth of felt, ventilated at the top. An old army overcoat, lined with red flannel, and provided with a high collar made of the skin of a wolf shot by the general himself, completed his costume, excepting a leather belt with forty or fifty copper cartridges, held to the shoulders by two leather straps. His horse and saddle were alike good, and with his rifle were well cared for.*

On the first day of March, the men faced the broad open stretches of prairie on the north side of the Platte. There was fresh snow under foot, and a cold, biting wind stung their faces; but spirits were high as there had been a report that Sitting Bull and some of the hostiles were camped along the Powder about 100 miles away. At the first camp, the Sioux ran off the cattle they planned to use for beef, and thereafter for a week Indian sign of some kind was observed each day. By the 6th of March the column had passed the ruins of Fort Reno and were camped at the point where the Montana Road crossed Crazy Woman Fork of Powder River. Here Crook cut his forces to fighting trim. He ordered his officers to shake down the baggage and see that each man—officers and enlisted men alike—had

*one buffalo robe, or two blankets and no more. The clothing on their backs was all that should be carried. No tentage to be allowed, but every man might take a piece of shelter tent and every two officers, one tent fly.*

Each line officer was to mess with his troops and the staff officers were to eat with the packers of the mule train. Each man was to carry 100 rounds of ammunition, and an equal amount was to go with the pack train, along with rations for fifteen days.

On the following day, the wagon train and the infantry were sent back to old Fort Reno; and just after nightfall, by the light of a "very fine three-quarters moon," the column formed and moved out "toward the North Star." Many of the men were struck by the beauty of the scene as the "column of cavalry wound up the steep hillsides like an enormous snake . . . . backed . . . by the majestic landscape of moonlight on the Big Horn Mountains."

But scenery was no substitute for sleep and when the column stopped at a bleak campground on the Clear Fork of the Powder, the men wrapped themselves up in their overcoats and furs and were soon asleep on the frozen ground. Their repose was of short duration for about eight o'clock they were awakened "by a bitter pelting storm of snow which blew in our teeth whichever way we turned, and almost extinguished the petty fires near which our cooks were trying to arrange breakfast." For the next week, as the column followed down the valley of the Tongue, cold and snow provided major hardships. Temperatures of twenty degrees below zero were common, and for two days it was forty below. Bacon had to be chopped with an axe and table utensils had to be warmed in the ashes of the campfire before touching them to the lips.

Even with this discomfort, Lieutenant Bourke was able to find bits of humor for his journal. On one occasion he compared the troops, with moustaches and beards coated with icicles and their "raiment of furs and hides," to a column of Santa Clauses. On another date he recorded the soliloquy of an Irish recruit which he overheard at a campfire:

"Och, thin boi Jaysus, sure for didn't Oi inlist in the Feet! Bee once cowl, they hev nothing to do but march with the wagons and mar-r-rch back home agin. Shure the cavalry dus be mar-r-r-rching all the time! They takes uz across the mountains all noight, in a sthar-rum of sch-now, widout a boite of gr-r-grub, bee God, and thin Giniral Crook will say, "now bois make yersilves as comfartibble as yiz can— Throw yirsilves down on yer picket pins for a math-thrass and cover yirsilves wid yer lar-rhiat roapes."

As the column moved slowly down the Tongue, a few trails were found which headed eastward toward the valley of the Powder, but there were no fresh *sign* in front of the troops or to the left. Sometime after crossing the Wyoming-Montana line—the "Engineer Officer" having no exact idea of where they were—Crook turned eastward to the valley of Otter Creek where the scouts saw two Indians who immediately fled.

The general decided to pursue them at once. Six companies were detailed from the column, given rations for one day, and then turned over to Colonel Reynolds with instructions to follow the trail and rendezvous with the remainder of the troops somewhere on the Powder. Lieutenant Bourke, who, as a staff officer, had no line assignment, secured permission to go with Captain Teddy Egan's company. The forces separated late in the afternoon, and Grouard led the detachment eastward across broken country with the "accuracy of a bird," at the same time "following like a hound the tracks of the two young Indians."

When the first faint light of morning came, the men were almost to the valley of the Powder. Here Reynolds halted the troops while Grouard went ahead to scout. As the men tried to beat a little warmth back into their hands and feet, Frank

galloped back among us in great glee and announced to General Reynolds that right down in the valley beneath us . . . lay a village of more

*than a hundred lodges, with great herds of ponies grazing on the . . .
river bottoms.*

After a hasty staff meeting, Reynolds detailed one battalion (two companies) to charge the village and drive the Indians out, another under
Captain Moore was to dismount and pour down a covering fire from
the bluffs just back of the camp, and the third was to follow the first,
capture the pony herd, and burn the village.

The lodges were located on a "V" shaped piece of bottomland which
was bordered on the west by steep bluffs and on the east, by the channel
of the Powder—the two meeting at the apex of the angle. A grove of
cottonwoods with a thick undergrowth of wild plum bushes provided
further protection—the only avenue of approach being from the
south. In a hasty race with the coming daylight, the two battalions
pushed down a couple of miles through some rough breaks, and moved
into position for the attack just as the boys were driving bunches of
ponies to water.

As Bourke rode with Egan's company down into the last ravine just
in front of the village,

*an Indian boy, herding his ponies, was standing within ten feet of me.
I covered him with my revolver & could have killed him; Egan said, "let
him alone, John." The youngster displayed great stoicism, maintaining
silence until we had passed him and then shouting the war-whoop to
alarm the village.*

Egan's command scrambled up out of the ravine and charged at a trot
—"our animals being too tired and cold to do more."

The Indians swarmed out of their lodges like hornets out of a nest
and the warriors, taking shelter in the brush in front of the camp, opened
a lively fire that wounded three men and killed six horses. Although
Egan's men took the first line of timber, they were forced to fight dismounted to hold their position. The support which was expected from
Moore's men on the bluffs did not materialize for half an hour; and
when it did come it was located too far to the left and rear to be effective,
some of the bullets falling among their own comrades. Finally, Major
Mills and his men came up on foot and, passing between Egan's men
and the bluffs, drove the Indians out of the camp and into the breaks.
In the meantime Captain Noyes, assisted by the scouts, rounded up
over 700 horses and mules, "many with American brands."

With a skirmish line holding the warriors at a distance, the balance of
the men now went to work to destroy the camp which consisted of about
105 lodges. Bourke discovered that he had two toes frozen and, being

unable to walk, sat down and observed the scene around him. He noted that there were a considerable number of tepee covers made of canvas "obtained at the agencies," and that all of the lodges were "surprisingly rich in everything a savage would consider comfortable and much that would be agreeable in a white man's house." In addition to robes, fine clothing, and rawhide trunks,

in each lodge, knives and forks, spoons, tincups, platters, mess-pans, fry-ing-pans, pots and kettles of all kinds, axes, hatchets, hunting knives, water-kegs, blankets, pillows and every imaginable kind of truck was seen in profusion.

Of the weight of dried and fresh buffalo meat and venison, no ade-quate idea can be given; in 3 or 4 lodges I estimated that there were not less than 1000 pounds. Ammunition in abundance; pig lead, metallic cartridges, and percussion caps enough for a regiment. One hundred and fifty saddles were burnt in the flames of the tipis, which each ex-ploded with a puff! as its little magazine of powder ignited.

As this officer watched the work of destruction, he was amazed to note that Reynolds had ordered everything destroyed

in a command suffering from hunger, tons of 1st class meat and provi-sions were destroyed and many things of positive value to the men were wantonly burned up.

Nor was this the worst which happened:

We abandoned, to our shame be it said, the corpses of our gallant dead, 3 or 4 in number and one poor wretch, shot in arm and thigh, fell alive into the hands of the enemy and was scalped before the eyes of the command.

From this point on, Bourke has written two accounts with conflicting views. In his classic *On the Border with Crook*, published in 1891, he stated:

General Reynolds concluded suddenly to withdraw from the village, and the movement was carried out so precipitately that we practically abandoned the victory to the savages.

With the village destroyed, the horse herd captured, and the doughty warriors in a position from which it would have been costly to have at-tempted to dislodge them, it would appear that the action was as suc-cessful as could be expected. And this was the way the men felt about it at the time.

Reynolds' detachment now marched southward up the valley of the

Powder and went into camp just south of the present Wyoming-Montana line. At Camp Inhospitality—"a name well deserved and well bestowed"—the men took stock of their situation. There were "no rations, not even for our poor wounded men," and no blankets or robes for protection while sleeping. Reynolds' lack of foresight was painfully apparent to all. But, even on an almost empty stomach, Bourke had no acute feelings of dissatisfaction with the results of the day's work for he wrote in his journal:

Our men are, of course, very tired [having "marched between 68 and 75 miles since yesterday morning, besides fighting (5) hours to-day"]: guard duty is done by "running tours" of the whole company, but we feel almost satisfied with our day's work which has been praiseworthy and brilliant enough when we take into regard the disadvantages we had to contend against to gain any success at all.

Many awoke the next morning with "frosted noses, feet & fingers"; and Bourke and correspondent Robert Strahorn—who had fought like a veteran trooper—spent the night on a saddle blanket with a stiff untanned buffalo skin for a cover. The lieutenant wrote ruefully the next morning—"We might just as well have employed a board for a blanket."

The identity of the Indians is shrouded with uncertainty. Bourke wrote at the time:

The head chief . . . was "Crazy Horse" who had with him, "Little Big Man." The Indians represented were Ogallallah Sioux, Minneconjou Sioux and Northern Cheyennes [with a few others].

As Grouard had lived with Crazy Horse not long before, he should have known. However, the lieutenant noted that the "forty new canvas lodges clustered together at the extremity by which we had entered belonged to some Cheyennes": and the Cheyennes still maintain that this was Two Moon's village. If half of the camp was Northern Cheyennes, this might well be.

The fate of the captured horses is equally confusing. The next morning a small "squad" of hostiles ran off "our herd of ponies." (As Reynolds refused to attempt their recapture, "the officers vented their ill-feeling in splenetic criticism and openly charged Reynolds with incapacity.") However, the Indians ran afoul of Crook's men shortly afterward and *all* or *part* of them were recaptured, the number depending on whether Crook's or Bourke's account is accepted. A considerable number were killed for food and to prevent recapture and, although Crook stated that, "The next day all the ponies remaining in our hands were killed," Bourke wrote in his journal after their return to Fort Fetterman that the *captured ponies* were distributed to deserving scouts and soldiers! *Quien sabe?*

The troops were reunited about midday. Bourke noted that although the general

*was much pleased to learn of our having encountered the Sioux and taken their village he seemed annoyed and chagrined upon being told that we had left our own dead upon the ground and that our ponies had been recaptured through our own carelessness, but he said nothing. . . .*

On the following day, the column reached the supply train at old Fort Reno. The weather had now began to moderate and the horses and mules became badly fagged traveling over muddy trails. Four days later, plodding wearily through the mud, the column reached Fort Fetterman. In reply to Crook's report, General Sheridan promptly wired instructions to

*make what dispositions he found needfull to recuperate the command's horses and then resume campaign against hostile Indians.*

As the Indians themselves had escaped almost unscathed, the expedition did not accomplish its objective. When the second column was being assembled, Spotted Tail, the most friendly of the Sioux chiefs, commented sarcastically to one of Crook's staff, "If you don't do better than you did the last time, you had better put on squaws' clothes and stay at home."

What Crook thought of the action on the Powder now became painfully evident for he preferred charges against Colonel Reynolds and Captains Noyes and Moore for misbehavior before the enemy. These court-martial cases were tried the following winter. Noyes, who imprudently allowed his men to unsaddle after rounding up the ponies— while there was still fighting in the village—was sentenced to be reprimanded for an "error in judgment." This Crook did with a gracious comment which took part of the sting from the action. Moore was convicted of neglect of duty (cowardice in battle) and Reynolds, of "misbehaviour in the presence of the enemy." When these cases were reviewed by President Grant, the convictions were allowed to stand but the sentences imposed by the board were suspended.

Crook's action stirred up a small furor. Reynolds tried to get the general to withdraw his action, and then asked correspondent Strahorn not to mention the matter in his dispatches—a request which enraged the press. One fact would indicate that these steps were justified—before the next expedition got under way there were a considerable number of desertions. It was not unusual for soldiers to "go over the hill" on the frontier, but this time they made no secret of the fact that they would not serve under men who abandoned their dead and wounded to the enemy.

### GIBBON AND TERRY MARCH

On the 17th of March, at the very time that Crook's men were destroying the hostile camp in the valley of the Powder, General Gibbon's men marched from Fort Shaw on Sun River. Plodding through mud and snow, they reached Fort Ellis eleven days later. After stopping a day to draw supplies, they moved on to the mouth of Shield's River where they went into camp to wait for Major Brisbin and his men who had just returned from "relieving" Fort Pease. It was here that the news of Crook's fight reached the Montana Column.

At this point General Gibbon assembled six companies of the 7th Infantry, four companies of the 2nd Cavalry, and three pieces of artillery—a force of 27 officers and 426 men. Their supplies were loaded in a train of 36 wagons. This total was augmented shortly afterward by additional supplies and a company of the 7th Infantry which had come down to the Crow Agency from Camp Baker in the Musselshell country. And, after some palaver, the general succeeded in enlisting twenty-three Crow warriors as scouts. To assist in handling the Absaroka, two squaw men, Thomas Leforge and a man named Bravo, were also enlisted. Lieutenant James Bradley requested and was given the assignment of commanding this group.

Among the irregulars was the Sioux half-breed and Crow squaw man, Mitch Buoyer, who had been engaged as a guide. Two of the white civilians were a man named Bostwick who had been employed by the *dude*, Sir George Gore, and Muggins Taylor, one of the wolfers at Fort Pease. It was Taylor whom General Terry later sent up the Yellowstone with the dispatches containing the news of Custer's defeat. One of the Crows was the seventeen-year-old warrior named Curly who became involved in the mass of legend as an alleged *survivor* of Custer's detachment in the Battle of the Little Big Horn.

It was the 12th of March when the Montana column, now complete with guides and Indian scouts, marched from the vicinity of the mouth of the Stillwater. Winter still lingered as eleven inches of snow had fallen while Gibbon and his staff were at the Crow Agency. With the Crow scouts fanned out ahead feeling for the enemy over a ten or twelve mile front, the command moved deliberately down the Yellowstone. On the morning of the 21st, when in camp on the north bank of the river just above the abandoned Fort Pease, Bradley made this entry in his journal:

*Will Logan (son of Capt. Logan) accompanied by a soldier arrived this morning from the supply camp bearing mail and dispatches. It appears that General Crook has not yet retaken the field and will not before the middle of May, and that General Custer will not start from Fort Abraham Lincoln until about the same time. We were to have acted in conjunction with these forces, but we are now, when well advanced in the Sioux country, left unsupported. General Crook's victory was not so decisive as we have regarded it, while the fighting seems to have demonstrated that there are heavier forces of warriors to encounter than had been counted upon. General Terry fears that the Indians may combine and get the better of us; and that we are therefore to cease our advance for the present and remain in this vicinity until further orders, in a state of inactivity unless sure of striking a successful blow.*

Thus Sheridan's *plans* for a late winter campaign came to an abrupt end.

On the following day, Bradley wrote,

*Four cavalrymen left for Fort Ellis at 1 o'clock A.M., carrying mail. It is dangerous service, as these small parties are exceedingly liable to be cut off by the Sioux.*

These dispatch carriers—sometimes soldiers, sometimes civilians, and, on a few occasions, Indians—were the unsung heroes of this campaign. Some weeks later Bradley recorded a measure of this danger when he noted that General Terry offered a civilian $200 to carry a message to General Gibbon when the intervening distance was not over 75 miles.

These daring souls provided the important link between General Sheridan and his troops. Messages from Chicago were sent to Omaha and then over telegraph lines paralleling the Union Pacific Railroad to Corrine, Utah, at which point they were relayed to Helena, Montana. Here messengers took over and carried them south to Fort Ellis, over the Bozeman Pass, and down the Yellowstone to the troops. During the summer, such couriers shuttled back and forth between Crook's camp on the headwaters of the Tongue and Fort Fetterman on the Platte. On two occasions, messages were carried between the Yellowstone River and Crook's camp on Goose Creek—a distance of well over 100 miles when thousands of Sioux and Cheyennes were known to be in the intervening area.

Gibbon now moved down to the still-intact Fort Pease and went into camp. Captain Ball and two companies of cavalry scouted the Big Horn valley as far as the site of Fort C. F. Smith, turned east across the valley of the Little Big Horn, and returned by way of Tullock Creek. The Crows then scouted the Yellowstone valley as far as the mouth of the Rosebud. Neither party found any sign of the Sioux; but one morning not long afterward Bostwick's horse and mule were gone and when the Crows rushed to the little island where they had put their ponies, they found "every head was gone—thirty-two in all, gobbled up by the Sioux." To the cleverest thieves on the plains, this was most humiliating and, "The Crows had a good cry over their loss, standing together in a row and shedding copious tears. . . ." This coup, which was probably pulled off by the Cheyennes, was a daring piece of work for Two Moon later told Tom Leforge that he had wrapped his blanket about him and boldly wandered through Gibbon's camp.

Curious as to whether this theft had been made by Indians from the Fort Peck area to the northeast, or hostiles from south of the Yellowstone, Gibbon began to move again. With the cavalry following along the north bank and some of the infantry in mackinaw boats which had been salvaged at Fort Pease, he went downstream to a point some fifteen or twenty miles below the mouth of Great Porcupine Creek. Here Bradley requested permission to do a little "village hunting" himself and Gibbon reluctantly consented.

With twenty volunteers from the infantry, five Crows—who did not volunteer—and the squaw man, Bravo, Bradley left the camp at dusk. Four o'clock the next morning found them concealed in a ravine at the northern end of the Wolf Mountains between the Rosebud and the Tongue. From a nearby hilltop, the lieutenant and the Crows studied the country between them and the not far distant Tongue. "The smoke was raising in different columns and uniting in a cloud which hung low over the valley": and buffalo, obviously disturbed by hunters, "in bands of ten to a hundred passed . . . until I estimated that not less than five thousand had gone by."

Bradley wanted to go closer and count the tepees in the camp but the Crows "violently opposed" the idea. Finally, he accepted the Indian estimate of at least two or three hundred lodges and that night returned to camp. In this he was most prudent:

*It afterward turned out that this camp contained about four hundred lodges, or from eight hundred to a thousand warriors, but for all that there were not wanting men among those bold rascals of mine that would have had me attack it with our twenty-seven. But they all lived to be thankful that we didn't. A sight of the Custer field, six weeks later,* with its two hundred and six naked and bloody corpses, the victims in part of this very village, satisfied them that we had done well not to poke a stick into the hive.

The command had broken camp and was ready to move when this scouting party returned. After an hour's deliberation, Gibbon decided to leave the camp where it had been, cross the major part of the force, and attack the village which had been discovered. Unfortunately—perhaps fortunately—everything seemed to go wrong. After losing four horses on one attempted crossing, the general abandoned the idea—much to the disgust of the Crows who were inclined to regard this failure "as a device to conceal our cowardice." As this decision was made a party of some seventy-five Sioux rode boldly up on the south side of the river making it obvious that a surprise attack was out of the question.

Gibbon now decided to confine his activities to keeping the hostiles on the south side of the Yellowstone. The next day he sent two companies to scout to the mouth of the Tongue, and two days later mail arrived which contained the information

that General Terry had taken the field in person, and that we may look for the arrival of Custer at the head of the entire 7th Cavalry in about a month. In the meantime we are ordered to remain in this vicinity and hold the Indians, if possible, on the south bank.

As a couple of excited Crows came in from the Wolf Mountains and reported a strong force of warriors was moving toward the Yellowstone, Gibbon moved to support his scouting party, and the command went into camp opposite the mouth of the Rosebud.

The troops remained in this camp for the next two weeks during which time a few minor incidents occurred. Two soldiers and a teamster went hunting without permission and were picked off by the Sioux. Another scout made by Bradley revealed that the village he had previously discovered was now on the Rosebud only about eighteen miles from the soldiers. Obviously, the Sioux were not in the least awed or worried about Gibbon's force. It was while at this camp that the previously noted "Colonel" Chesnut arrived with a mackinaw boat filled with luxury provisions and supplies and he was followed five days later by a second boat. Apparently these daring merchants were not greatly worried about the hostile Sioux. And just after darkness fell on the 27th of May, a civilian and two infantrymen, Bell and Stewart, started down the Yellowstone in a rowboat with dispatches for General Terry.

On the 4th of June, a Diamond R train of ten wagons, under the direction of Matt Carroll, rolled in with 50 tons of supplies. With them was Bravo and replacement mounts for the Crow scouts which this squaw man had secured from the village at the Agency. On the following day, Gibbon again began to move down the Yellowstone, following the road worked out by Colonel Stanley's escort party in 1873. Captain Clifford, with his infantry in two mackinaw boats, misunderstood his orders and, instead of floating only as far as the next camp ground, went all the way to the mouth of the Powder where he met General Terry on board the steamboat *Far West*.

Terry now dispatched Bell and Stewart—who had made a successful journey in the rowboat, together with a Crow who was with Captain Clifford, with a message for their commanding officer. These men reached the Montana Column at 2:00 A.M. the morning of the 9th: and a few hours later Gibbon met his Department Commander along the Yellowstone some twenty-five miles below the mouth of the Tongue. After this meeting of the two generals, Bradley made a summary of the situation:

> The arrival of the 7th Cavalry at Glendive Creek disproved the reported gathering of the hostiles in that quarter, and the whole force is now to push up the river after the village we had first discovered on the Tongue River and afterward in the Rosebud. The 7th Cavalry under Custer will scour the country south of the Yellowstone, while we return up the north bank to prevent the Indians from escaping to this side. As it is feared they may attempt to do so, four companies of the 2nd Cavalry were placed under orders to move back at once. . . . The infantry will soon follow, and we will then go into camp near the mouth of the Rosebud to await further orders. Meantime the steamer [Far West] returns to Glendive Creek, to bring up the stores left there to the Powder.

The Dakota Column, the third prong of the enveloping movement envisioned by Sheridan, had been plagued with difficulties. Inclement weather and deep snow had held central Dakota in its grip and it was not until the fore part of May that the preparations were finally completed. Lieutenant Colonel—brevet Major General—George Armstrong Custer was to have led this force but during the winter he had become embroiled in a scandal involving the post traders at the army posts.

This stinking mess pointed straight at General Belknap, a personal friend of President Grant's who was then Secretary of War, and Grant's own brother, Orvil. The Congressional investigation was headed by Congressman Clymer, and Custer—flamboyant and outspoken as usual —was his star witness. Although the commanding officer of the 7th

Cavalry had but little evidence to offer which would stand in court, he was a source of considerable irritation to the President. When Custer left Washington to return to the field, he failed to observe the absolute letter of two rather insignificant military regulations governing officers on temporary duty in the capitol.

Grant now lashed out against his subordinate in a manner ill-befitting the chief executive. When Custer reached Sheridan's office in Chicago he found that the President had wired the Division commander that he was not to be allowed to take the field in the pending campaign. To a fighting man, this was a blow below the belt. Fortunately, Custer was able to show that Grant himself had been partly to blame for his disregard of official protocol, and he made what defense he could. Then he placed a humble request, through channels, that, if he could not command the column, he at least be allowed to go to the field at the head of the regiment of which he was the commanding officer. General Sheridan (as commanding officer of the Division of the Missouri) and General Terry (as commanding officer of the Department of Dakota) added favorable endorsements. President Grant, perhaps fearing additional public criticism for this petty act, yielded and granted the request. Thus—it would appear—the stage was set for the spectacular tragedy which was to cost the lives of 265 men.

When the Dakota Column left Fort Abraham Lincoln on the morning of May 17th, General Terry accompanied the troops as the commanding officer while Lieutenant Colonel Custer—smarting under what he felt was unjust humiliation—rode at the head of the 7th Cavalry. Terry, although liked and respected by his staff, *was not* the seasoned Indian fighter which his subordinate was.

This column totalled about 1,200 men all told. The 7th Cavalry was the hard core of this body, and with it were three companies of infantry and a platoon with three Gatling guns. A train of about 150 wagons carried over 250 tons of supplies, and an additional 200 tons were loaded on the *Far West*. In addition, a herd of beef cattle provided fresh meat during the early part of the movement.

There were about forty Indian scouts—mostly Arickaras under Bobtailed Bull. Of these, Custer's favorite, Bloody Knife, was the best known. Among the civilian scouts were Robert and William Jackson, half-breed Blackfeet, and two interpreters. One of the latter was the negro named Isaiah "Teat" Dorman. "Lonesome Charley" Reynolds, who had been with the railroad surveying expeditions and the Black Hills Expedition of 1874, was chief of the scouts. And along more or less as guests were two schoolboys, Boston Custer and Armstrong "Autie" Reed. These were "General" Custer's youngest brother and nephew; and they were carried on the rolls as a forage master and a herder. Except for Captain Marsh's foresight, there might have been two other visitors along. While the *Far West* was being readied, Mrs. Custer and the wife of Lieutenant Algernon Smith visited the captain one day and tried to wangle passage to the Yellowstone country. The canny captain had chosen a boat which did not have adequate space for such tourists!

Although presentiments of disaster are not infrequent when soldiers separate from their families, Mrs. Custer has left a poignant picture of what she saw as she rode beside her husband on this occasion. At the Indian quarters, old men, squaws, and children *moaned* a traditional song in a minor key and the scouts, beating their drums, echoed this "weird and melancholy" tune. In front of Laundress Row, the small children marched with a mimic column of their own while their mothers, with streaming eyes, held babies for a last look at their fathers. And when the band bravely struck up "The Girl I Left Behind Me," the wives of the officers who had steeled themselves to "wave a courageous farewell" gave up the fight and retreated behind the doors of their quarters. A mist enveloped everything that morning and when the sun broke through a mirage appeared which took up about half of the line of marching cavalry and for "a little distance it marched, equally plain to the sight on earth and in the sky."

Terry and his staff went overland with the troops, and the *Far West* and the column established contact with each other near the mouth of Glendive Creek. Marsh then moved on up to the mouth of the Powder at which point Custer led the column down to the Yellowstone River.

On the afternoon of June 10th, Major Reno and six troops of the Seventh, together with a Gatling gun and its crew and about seventy pack mules, left on a scout. Mitch Buoyer, on loan from Gibbon, was the guide. Reno's orders called for him to go up to the forks of the Powder, cross over to the Mizpah, and follow it and the Tongue down to the Yellowstone where he was to rejoin the column.

Reno did not follow these orders. He went as far as the forks of the Powder, and from this point Buoyer led him across the valley of the Tongue to the Rosebud which he struck just below the site of the village Bradley had located. After trailing this village up stream for a day and a half, the Major turned around and proceeded to the mouth of the Rosebud. Then he sent a courier to notify Terry of his whereabouts. Terry, considerably irked by this violation of orders, moved on up and went into camp with the detachment. Then, using the *Far West* as his headquarters, he, Gibbon, and Custer set down to evaluate the scanty intelligence about the enemy. In the meantime—

## THE BIG HORN AND YELLOWSTONE EXPEDITION

When he disbanded the column at Fort Fetterman late in March, Crook sent the troops to their various stations to recuperate while he and his staff returned to their headquarters in Omaha. Here they marked time until the winter snows melted, the mud dried, and the grass began to grow again. On the 9th of May the general and his assistants boarded the train for Cheyenne and what was designated as the Big Horn and Yellowstone Expedition began to take form soon afterward.

While this second column was being assembled at Fort Fetterman, Crook journeyed to Fort Robinson to survey conditions at the Red Cloud and Spotted Tail Agencies. Here he found that, with one or two possible exceptions, the chiefs were not in favor of allowing their young men to scout against their friends and relatives. Also, it soon became obvious that the employees of the Indian Department were using their influence to block all cooperation on the part of the Indians. The extent of this opposition became highly obvious as the General and his party were returning to Fort Laramie. Smoke signals were noted coming from the vicinity of the Indian camps shortly after his departure and Crook learned later that a war party—apparently awed by the unexpected size of his escort—had killed a solitary mail carrier whom they had met on the road.

Shortly after noon on the 29th of May, Crook's force crossed the Platte and headed north—the infantry in the lead, the wagon train in the center, with a somber mile-long "black line of mounted men" bringing up the rear. The military portion totalled 47 officers and 1,002 men. There were fifteen troops of cavalry under the command of Colonel William B. Royall, and five companies of "Walk-a-heaps" under Major Alex Chambers. The supplies were carried in a wagon train of 103 six-mule wagons, and Tom Moore was on hand again with a pack train of over 1,000 mules. Ten newspapers—from San Francisco to New York—were represented by five correspondents. Among these were Robert Strahorn, who had already proved that he was a stouthearted campaigner, and John Finerty, an Irishman representing the Chicago *Times*, who was to prove that he, too, could fight as well as write. And this time there were three scouts Louis Richaud, Baptiste Pourrier (Big Bat), and the man who stood ace-high in Crook's estimation, Frank Grouard.

Although the weapons of the men were in first class condition, the column was not outstanding in its military appearance. Crook dressed in a rough hunting rig—"worn shooting jacket, slouch felt hat, and soldier's boots, with ragged beard braided and tied with tape." The only

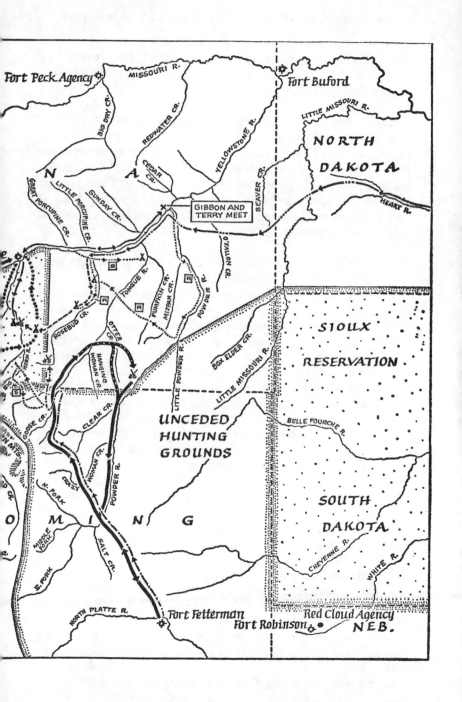

other protection which he had from the inclement weather which came with the late summer was a "private soldier's light-blue overcoat." By the time early fall came, the members of his staff presented an equally distinguished appearance:

Bourke, the senior aide and adjutant general of the expedition, is picturesquely gotten up in an old shooting-coat, an indescribable pair of trousers, and a straw hat minus ribbon or binding, a brim ragged as the edge of a saw, and a crown without a thatch. . . . Schuyler, the junior, is a trifle more "swell" in point of dress. His hat has not quite so many holes; his hunting shirt of brown canvas has stood the wear and tear of the campaign somewhat better, and the lower man is garbed in a material unsightly but indestructible.

And in the Fifth Cavalry, which joined the force two months later, "you could not have told officer from private."

The march north to the headwaters of the Tongue was uneventful except for the fickle weather. Two days after the column started the temperature, which had been pleasingly warm, dropped to zero and the next day it snowed and sleeted. Everyone wrapped in their overcoats, and Finerty observed that "the brigade looked much better, because more uniform, than usual." At the Crazy Woman Fork of the Powder, sixty-five miners—enroute to the Yellowstone from the Black Hills— joined the soldiers. Later, these men proved themselves to be cool, efficient, irregular troopers. It was during this stage of the journey that Crook expected his Indian scouts to join him. As their whereabouts were still unknown when he reached Fort Reno, the three scouts were sent to locate the Crows and join the column later.

On the 7th of June, camp was made at the junction of Prairie Dog Creek and the Tongue, and a few days later moved back up the latter to Goose Creek. Here, where the town of Sheridan now stands, the troops settled down to wait for the arrival of their Indian allies, each man spending his leisure according to his tastes. Crook and two other officers hunted for butterflies and unusual birds, the miners went prospecting, a lieutenant and one of the packers turned to sketching, while the others raced horses, fished, and played various games. "Newspapers were read to pieces and such books as had found their way with the command were passed from hand to hand and read eagerly." Couriers came and went bringing, among other things, the intelligence that most of the young men had left the Sioux agencies and had—presumably—joined the hostiles.

After a week of waiting, Grouard and Richaud, accompanied by a "gigantic Crow chief," rode into camp with the news that 175 warriors were not far behind. Late that afternoon Finerty saw

a grove of spears and a crowd of ponies upon the northern heights, and there broke upon the air a fierce, savage whoop. The Crows had come in sight of our camp. . . . We went down to the creek to meet them, and a picturesque tribe they were. Their horses—nearly every man had an extra pony—were little beauties, and neighed shrilly at their American brethren. . . .

Old Crow, Medicine Crow, and Good Heart, the principal chiefs, were presented to Crook at once and, almost before the soldiers realized what had happened, a cluster of little war lodges had taken form in the middle of the camp.

Grouard and his two companions had found the Crow camp near the site of old Fort C. F. Smith. As the Absaroka had been in touch with the scouts with Gibbon's men, Grouard and the Crow chiefs were able to inform Crook of the location of Montana Column and also the whereabouts of the Sioux camp. Now that Crook had the necessary scouts and information concerning the whereabouts of the enemy, he called a staff meeting just after retreat and outlined his plans. Bourke jotted down his "terse instructions":

We were to cut loose from our wagons, each officer and soldier carrying four days' rations of hard bread, coffee, and bacon in saddlepockets, and one hundred rounds of ammunition in belts or pouches; one blanket to each person. The wagons were to be parked and left behind in a defensible position on the Tongue or Goose, and under the protection of the men unable for any reason to join in the forward movement; all the infantrymen who could ride and who so desired were to be mounted on mules from the pack-trains with saddles from the wagons or from the cavalry companies which could spare them. If successful in attacking a village, the supplies of dried meat and other food were to be saved, and we should then, in place of returning to our train, push on to make a combination with either Terry or Gibbon, as the case might be.

The next day was to be spent in making ready, and the advance would begin the following morning.

While the general was outlining his plans, those who were crowded around the Crows

saw several warriors raise their heads and say "Ugh, ugh! Sho-sho-ne." They pointed southward, and, coming down the bluffs in that direction,

we saw a line of horsemen, brilliantly attired, riding at whirlwind speed
. . . . the newcomers crossed the creek, and, in column of twos, like a
company of regular cavalry, rode in among us. They carried two beautiful American flags, and each warrior bore a pennon . . . [and] were
splendidly armed with government rifles and revolvers. Nearly all wore
magnificent war bonnets and scarlet mantles. . . . The meeting between
them and the Crows was boisterous and exciting. Demoniacal yells rang
through the camp, and then this wild cavalry galloped down to headquarters. . . .

Here, Bourke noted:

Scarcely had this brief conference ended when a long line of glittering
lances and brightly polished weapons of fire announced the anxiously
expected advent of our other allies, the Shoshones or Snakes, who, to the
number of eighty-six, galloped rapidly up to headquarters and came left
front into line in splendid style. No trained warriors of civilized armies
ever executed the movement more prettily. Exclamations of wonder and
praise greeted the barbaric array. . . . General Crook moved out to re-
view their line of battle, resplendent in all the fantastic adornment of
feathers, beads, brass buttons, bells, scarlet cloth, and flashing lances
. . . . and when the order came for them to move off by the right
[they] moved with the precision of clock-work and the pride of veterans.

This fine appearance was the result of the work of their leader, Tom
Cosgrove, formerly a captain in the 32nd Texas Cavalry. This Confederate cavalryman was chief of scouts at the Shoshone Agency, and he
was assisted by two other Texans and a French-Canadian half-breed.

The Indians continued to be the center of attraction during the remainder of the evening and—to the dismay of some—throughout the
night as well. First came a "grand council" around a "huge fire of crackling boughs." In the center of the assembly was General Crook—"looking half bored, half happy"—and the members of his staff, together with
the three scouts who acted as interpreters, and the Indian chiefs. On
one side were two rows of officers and on the other, the Indian scouts.
And behind them, partly illuminated by the dancing flames were throngs
of soldiers.

This meeting ended a little after ten o'clock as it was supposed that
the Indians were weary after their all-day ride.

The erroneousness of this assumption was disclosed very speedily. A
long series of monotonous howls, shrieks, groans, and nasal yells, emphasized by a perfectly ear-piercing succession of thumps upon drums
improvised from "parafleche" attracted nearly all the soldiers and many

of the officers not on duty to the allied camp. Peeping into the various lodges was very much like peeping through the key-hole of Hell.

Crouched around little fires not affording as much light as an ordinary tallow candle, the swarthy figures of the naked and half-naked Indians were visible, moving and chanting in unison with some leader. No words were distinguishable; the ceremony partook of the nature of an abominable incantation. . . . One of the Indians, mounted on a pony and stripped almost naked, passed along from lodge to lodge, stopping in front of each and calling upon the Great Spirit . . . to send them plenty of scalps, a big Sioux village, and lots of ponies. The inmates would respond with, if possible, increased vehemence. . . .

With this "wild requiem" ringing in his ears, a soldier in the hospital breathed his last; and the remnants of the beef herd, frightened by the pandemonium, stampeded for the hills.

The next morning the Indians, showing no signs of weariness from their all-night ceremonies, assembled in a huge semi-circle of "barbaric splendor" around the tents and wagons of the quartermaster. Here they received, with true aboriginal solemnity, rations, ammunition, and—where needed—arms. Then they turned to sharpening knives and lances, making coup sticks, drying meat, and other preparations peculiar to their manner of campaigning. However, the activity which attracted the most wide-spread attention took place on a well-grassed flat along the creek where Major Chambers set about mounting 176 of his infantrymen on mules from the pack train. After a bit of instruction the circus began. Grouard recalled later, "I never saw so much fun in all my life. The valley for a mile in every direction was filled with bucking mules, frightened infantrymen, broken saddles and applauding spectators."

Tom Moore organized a small detachment of twenty packers among whom, in the typical cosmopolitan manner of the Western frontier, were two Englishmen who had served with the British during the wars in India. The sixty-five miners also made ready—perhaps hoping to go through to the Yellowstone.

The force marched at five o'clock on the 16th of June—803 cavalrymen, 176 mounted infantry, 262 Indian scouts, 20 packers and 65 miners: their objective was the Sioux village which was supposed to be in the valley of the Rosebud. To some it was a thrilling sight. The Indians rode along the flanks of the column in careless order, "war bonnets nodding, and lances brilliant with steel and feathers." Wild roses and other prairie flowers which the horses trampled underfoot gave off a delicate perfume, and "buffalo spotted the landscape in every direction." However, the buffalo were too great a temptation for the Indians to resist and, leaving everything they did not need with the camp tenders (squaws and small boys), they dashed off "like mounted maniacs." Although Crook disliked having the animals disturbed, the choice parts from thirty of the beasts made a welcome addition to the scanty fare when camp was made that night on the headwaters of the Rosebud. It was late at night when the scouts returned from searching the country ahead. They had found a campfire in a small gulch from which a band of Sioux hunters had fled so precipitately that they left behind an India-rubber blanket.

The next morning before there was any hint of dawn on the horizon, the men, having brewed some coffee over little fires, moved northward down the South Fork of the Rosebud. By eight o'clock the head of the column had reached the little valley immediately west of the Big Bend of the Rosebud, at which point this stream turns from an easterly direction toward the north. Here Crook allowed the men to rest while he awaited the return of some Indian scouts who were probing the broken country lying to the north. A half hour later the reports of rifles were heard which experienced ears interpreted as the sounds of a skirmish. Hardly had this conclusion been reached when a score or more of the scouts appeared over the hills to the north and rode at full speed toward the soldiers. Crook immediately deployed the infantry as skirmishers at the foot of the slopes and

hardly had this precaution been taken, when the flying Crow and Snake scouts, . . . came into camp shouting at the top of their voices, "Heap Sioux! Heap Sioux!" gesticulating wildly in the direction of the bluffs which they had abandoned in such haste. All looked in that direction, and there, sure enough, were the Sioux in goodly numbers, and in loose, but formidable array. The singing of the bullets above our heads speedily convinced us that they had called on business.

This battlefield cannot be easily described. Its topography is a mixture of long slopes, low ridges, a few deeply cut drainageways, occasional steep rocky hills with here and there a scattering pine tree, and, at the eastern end, a broken area. Predominantly, it is an open country well suited to the slashing maneuvers which were the favorite tactics of Plains Indians. Three miles north of the Big Bend, the valley of the Rosebud narrows abruptly to a width of 150 to 200 yards. This so-called canyon is walled in by steep, rocky slopes with some cover of pines on either side. However, it can hardly be called a formidable "defile" as some descriptions indicate.

The initial attack caught the troops somewhat unprepared as the rear of the column was still closing up. Grouard was probably correct when he stated that the Indian allies swarmed out and engaged the hostiles on the slope just north of the valley for "all of twenty minutes" before the soldiers began to advance. The strategy of the Sioux seems to have been to draw the troops out of position and then attempt to destroy them in detail. Finerty noted, after one advance:

*The Sioux, having rallied on the second line of heights, became bold and impudent again. They rode up and down rapidly, sometimes wheeling in circles, slapping an indelicate portion of their persons at us, and beckoning us to come on.*

One of Crook's aides wrote later:

*The warriors dashed here, there, everywhere; up and down in ceaseless activity; their gaudy decorations, waving plumes and glittering arms, forming a panoramic view of barbaric splendor, once seen, never to be forgotten.*

*Our efforts were directed toward closing in with the enemy by a series of charges, and theirs to avoid close contact until, by the nature of the ground, our forces began to get scattered, and then their tactics changed from the defensive to the offensive. Each separate detachment was made the objective of terrific onslaughts, the warriors charging up to them, careening on their horses, and firing from behind them, while exposing as little of their own persons as possible. All the time they were whooping and yelling. . . . And woe to the officer or soldier who, at such a moment, lost his presence of mind.*

Thus, during the first two or three hours of the fight, the troops became scattered over a front of some three miles in length while swarms of warriors on swift ponies eddied about them. The soldiers on the eastern part of the battlefield, supported by the deadly sniping of the packers and miners and under Crook's direct supervision, were not involved in any serious trouble. About mid-day the general, becoming tired of the indecisive action, ordered a detachment to go down the valley and attack the camp which he believed to be a few miles further north. Shortly after these men left, a second force was dispatched to support them.

The first echelon, guided by Grouard, had just reached the mouth of the "canyon" when they heard heavy firing in the vicinity of Crook's position. Two messengers caught up with them here with orders to return at once—and the men, having seen the narrow valley before them, were more than happy to do so. Royall's troops, who had been involved in some heavy fighting on the western part of the battlefield, had finally worked their way back to Crook's position—in what the general later called a tardy compliance with his orders. Crook now found he had plenty of trouble on his hands without hunting for a village: and the two detachments which were ordered back worked their way up a ravine and emerged in the rear of the Indians who were engaging Crook. This unexpected turn apparently disconcerted the hostiles and they retreated to the north and west leaving Crook's men in possession of the battlefield. Why the Sioux broke off the fight is not clear. One Cheyenne stated later that they were tired and hungry, having ridden all night and fought all day. As they had fought when and where they saw fit, this explanation is probably correct.

Crook's men went into camp in the valley where they had first been attacked. They were tired, almost out of ammunition, but in reasonably good spirits. A few weeks later they were to realize how fortunate they were to have fought the great Sioux *general*, Crazy Horse, and a large force of Sioux and Cheyennes to a draw. But Crook always felt that the heavily-beset Royall had cost him a "victory" by not rejoining him promptly. Royall believed that he had done the best he could, and ill feeling existed between the officers for years.

What the battle lacked in decisiveness it more than made up in color as many noteworthy incidents occurred. While Captain Guy V. Henry and his men were engaged in a furious hand-to-hand struggle, this officer was knocked from his horse and temporarily blinded by a bullet which broke both cheek bones. As men and horses eddied back and forth, the gallant captain almost fell into the hands of the enemy. However, a Shoshone scout, noting several Sioux warriors about to count coup, charged in and stood them off until a rescue could be effected.

During the early part of the fight, at the eastern end of the battlefield, the Sioux drew Major Mills' men into some rough breaks and then turned on them. Major Randall and Lieutenant Bourke "rallied and led back to action" the Crow and Shoshone scouts and the ensuing skirmish became a melee. Then more Sioux arrived and the scouts were forced to withdraw. Left behind unnoted was Sergeant John Van Moll, "a brave and gigantic soldier" who had gone into the fight on foot.

A dozen Sioux dashed at him. Major Randall and Lieutenant Bourke . . . [now] turned their horses to rush to the rescue. They called on the Indians to follow them. One small, misshapen Crow warrior, mounted on a fleet pony, outstripped all the others. He dashed boldly in among the Sioux, against whom Van Moll was dauntlessly defending himself, seized the big sergeant by the shoulder and motioned him to jump up *behind. The Sioux were too astonished to realize what had been done until they saw the long-legged sergeant, mounted behind the little Crow, known as "Humpy," dash toward our lines like the wind.*

Stories of similar incidents are still recounted among the Northern Cheyennes. During the final stages of the battle, six Cheyennes were caught in a cross-fire in a little valley immediately to the west of the caprock on "Crook's Hill," and one of them, a warrior named Limpy, had his horse shot out from under him. This warrior was deformed to the extent that one leg was shorter than the other, and it was impossible for him to jump. Young Two Moon—an uncle of the chief Two Moon—had to make two passes before he could effect a rescue. On the last one, Limpy climbed on top of a large sandstone rock and when the pony "almost stopped" he slipped up behind his rescuer. The other incident occurred in a wide ravine at the eastern end of the battlefield and probably took place in the melée from which Van Moll was rescued. When the chief Comes-In-Sight was unhorsed, his sister, Buffalo Calf Road Woman, drove her pony into the middle of the fight and paused long enough for him to jump up behind her. Because of this event, the Cheyennes have always referred to the battle as the place "where the sister saved her brother."

Such was the Battle of the Rosebud where Crook and his 1,325 men matched wits and valor with the dashing Sioux tactician, Crazy Horse, and an estimated 1,500 Sioux and Cheyenne warriors. Crook's report listed nine men killed (and one Shoshone scout), twenty-one wounded, and thirteen Indians left dead on the field. Crazy Horse is said to have admitted later that he lost thirty-six killed and sixty-three wounded—and one hundred and fifty ponies. However, it would appear that the official casualty list is either incomplete or inaccurate for Bourke put the total casualties at 57 when he described the fight in his journal.

When the Crows and Shoshones returned to their villages for a celebration immediately after the battle, they took most of their wounded with them. Among the Absaroka, one warrior exhibited unusual fortitude. During the fight, Grouard saw a Crow lying on the ground who had been shot in the thigh and the bone "terribly shattered." The curious thing about this man was that he was watching the fighting very intently and now and then would "yell like a madman." Probably this warrior was Bull Snake who had been wounded while making a series of *bravery runs* in front of the enemy. Fox-Just-Coming-Over-Hill—later renamed Old Coyote—told his grandsons years afterward that this was the toughest individual he ever knew. When he was moved to the Crow village, this leg was bound to a splint and fastened to his pony's neck—thus holding it parallel to the ground. In crossing the Big Horns the injured member sometimes got tangled in the underbrush and twisted so as to grind the ends of the broken bone together. When this happened Bull Snake would remark—cheerfully, "There goes another piece of bone into fine meal." Fox-Just-Coming-Over-Hill was acutely aware of the trials of the injured for he too was seriously wounded.

By the 19th, the command was back at the camp along Goose Creek. Two days later a wagon train, carrying the wounded on beds of freshly-cut grass and guarded by infantry, rolled out for Fort Fetterman. With them went Calamity Jane who had been discovered posing as a driver among the teamsters. The column now marked time while Crook discussed the problems of the campaign with General Sheridan. As it took three days—when everything went well—for a message to go from the field to the headquarters in Chicago, it took time to develop plans.

While this slow process was going on, the men turned to whatever amusement they could find. Fishing was popular both as a sport and as a source of food to break the monotonous camp fare. Catches of 100 trout in a day were not uncommon, and Bourke estimated that over a period of four or five weeks the 1,550 men in camp consumed *at least* 15,000 trout! Crook and some of the officers hunted and explored in the Big Horn Mountains during the intervals while messages were passing to and from Chicago. Many of the men were careless because the illusion existed that they had taught the Indians to leave them alone, an attitude that was strengthened by the fact that there were no Indian alarms for over two weeks after the battle. Crook himself was lax in this respect and finally his adjutant noted that the general "has set an example of recklessness that cannot be too strongly condemned."

The thing which suddenly aroused Bourke's feelings of apprehension about his chief was the experiences of a scouting party. On the 6th of July Crook sent Grouard and Big Bat, supported by Lieutenant F. W. Sibley and 25 picked troopers from the 2nd Cavalry to make a reconnaissance and locate the enemy. Finerty, bored by the inactivity, was allowed to go along but his enthusiasm received a dash of cold water just before the party started. Several officers joked him but "Grim Captain Wells only said to his orderly—'Bring Mr. Finerty a hundred rounds of Troop E ammunition.' This command was more eloquent than an oration."

The party moved out northward along the route of the old Bozeman Trail and when near the Little Big Horn River Grouard discovered a large war party approaching. The party retreated and hid among some bluffs, but the Indians discovered their trail and they were in trouble. Grouard led the troops back into the mountains along an old hunting trail. Then, thinking that they had not been followed, they stopped to make coffee and give their well-blown mounts a needed rest. The next thing they knew the Indians had them pinned down in a little patch of timber at the foot of a mountain. Finerty wrote later, "I had often wondered how a man felt when he thought he saw the inevitable, sudden doom upon him. I know it now. . . ."

After a short skirmish, during which they probably killed a chief, the two scouts advised Sibley to abandon their horses and made a stealthy retreat on foot. The lieutenant reluctantly—but wisely—agreed, and the two capable scouts led the men back into rough terrain where the Indians could not go on horseback. Then they headed for the camp where they arrived at 6:30 on the morning of the 9th. Lieutenant Bourke noted in his journal:

> When the party reached camp . . . they were all completely prostrated, having marched over mountains for two nights and one day without food or sleep.

Whatever illusions remained about the temper of the Sioux were rudely shattered the next day when scouts Louis Richaud and Ben Arnold arrived at daybreak with important dispatches from Sheridan. They also brought the news that most of the young bucks had left the Red Cloud Agency and that the 5th Cavalry had forced these Indians to abandon two wagon-loads of arms, ammunition, and other supplies apparently destined for the hostiles. The heart-chilling information was in the dispatch pouches—Sheridan had telegraphed the gist of Terry's sad report that disaster had struck the 7th Cavalry. After receiving Crook's report on the Rosebud fight, Sheridan had wired, "Hit them and hit them hard." Now the Department commander offered to augment Crook's force with the entire 5th Cavalry and urged that the Indians be hit the "hardest blow possible." The full realization of the magnitude of the problem which the Army had on its hands was slowly beginning to dawn on everyone from the commander of the Division of the Missouri down to the lowest private in the ranks. If anything was needed to emphasize this situation, an Indian attack on the camp that night furnished the final touch.

Two days after Richaud and Arnold arrived with the dispatches, Bourke and the other members of Crook's staff watched with admiration and anticipation as

3 men, dressed in army blue, faded and travel worn, trotted up to General Crook & announced themselves as bearers of advices from General Terry!

The men were Corporal Stewart and privates Bell and Evans—Stewart and Bell being the two intrepid souls who had braved the Sioux to take a rowboat down the Yellowstone to hunt for the Dakota Column a month before. Each carried a copy of a letter from General Terry. The Commanding General of the Department of Dakota had at last—on the 12th of July—established contact with his counterpart in the Department of the Platte.

Terry wrote:

> "Hdqrs. Dept. of Dakota, In the field,
> Camp on North side of Yellowstone River,
> near mouth of Big Horn, July 9<sup>th</sup>, 1876

Genl George Crook
Comdr Department of the Platte (in the field)
General,

On the 25<sup>th</sup> ult. General Custer, crossing over from the valley of the Rosebud to the Little Big Horn found on the last named stream an enormous Indian village. He had with him his whole Regiment and a strong detachment of scouts. At the time of the discovery of the Indians he had but eight (8) companies close at hand, but with these he attacked in two detachments, one under himself of five companies, the other, under Major Reno, of three (3) companies. The attacks of these two detachments were made at points nearly, if not quite three miles apart. I regret to say that Custer and every officer and man under his immediate command were killed. Reno was driven back to the bluffs where he was joined by the remainder of the Regiment. He was surrounded by the enemy and obliged to entrench himself, but succeeded in maintaining himself in this position without heavy loss until the appearance of General Gibbon's column induced the Indians on the evening of the 26<sup>th</sup> to withdraw. Two hundred and sixty-eight [sic 265] officers, men, and civilians were killed and there were fifty-two (52) wounded. This affair occurred about twenty (20) miles above the junction of the Little Big Horn and the Big Horn. While Custer's column was in motion, Gibbon's column of about one hundred and fifty (150) cavalry, one hundred and sixty (160) Infantry and three (3) Gatling guns, was advancing to join Custer and cooperate with him in the attack upon the Indians. He was ferried across the Yellowstone at a point just below the mouth of the Big Horn, on the 24<sup>th</sup> ultimo. On the 25<sup>th</sup>, it had advanced through country of extreme difficulty, the Infantry twenty-two (22), the

Cavalry thirty-six (36) miles. Custer had been informed that Gibbon's column would reach the mouth of the Little Big Horn, on the evening of the 26$^{th}$ ult. Reno's position was reached on the morning of the 27$^{th}$ ult. It is estimated that not less than twenty-five hundred warriors were in the fight. Besides the lodges in the village, a vast number of temporary shelters were found, showing that many Indians were present there, besides those who properly belonged to the village. A reconnaissance southward was made on the 28$^{th}$ ultimo and a very large trail was found leading down the stream, a distinct trail from the one (a heavy one) which Custer had followed from the Rosebud.

Captain Ball of the 2nd Cavalry, who made this reconnaissance, was of the opinion after leaving the valley the Indians divided into two bands, one making toward the mountains and the other towards the South and East. It was a difficult task to get our wounded away, as the character of the country had not permitted ambulances to accompany the troops and mule litters had to be made. They have now been sent by boat to Fort A. Lincoln. In view of the shattered condition of the 7th Cavalry and the damage done to our small pack train, I have thought it best to bring the troops down to this depot [Fort Pease] to refit. I have sent for horses and mules for the dismounted men of the 7th Cavalry and for two (2) more companies of Infantry. I have tried to communicate with you but my scout each time has been driven back by Indians or rather reports that he was driven back. This morning, I received from General Sheridan a copy of your dispatch to him, giving an account of your fight of the 17$^{th}$ ultimo, and as it gives me information of your position at that time, I hope that the bearers of this may be able to find your trail and reach you.

The great and to me wholly unexpected strength which the Indians have developed seems to me to make it important and indeed necessary that we should unite or at least act in close cooperation. In my ignorance of your present position and of the position of the Indians, I am unable to propose a plan for this, but if you will devise one and communicate it to me, I will follow it. The boat which took down our wounded, will, I hope, return with a supply of horses and mules, with material for the repair of my saddles, &c and with some reinforcement.

I expect her back about the 18$^{th}$ inst. and soon after that I hope to be able to move. I hope that it is unnecessary for me to say that should our forces unite, even in my own Department, I shall assume nothing by reason of my seniority, but shall be prepared to cooperate with you in the most cordial and hearty manner, leaving you entirely free to pursue your own course. I am most anxious to assist you in any way that promises to bring the campaign to a favorable and speedy conclusion.

As my base of supplies is movable (being a steamboat) I can start out from any point on the Yellowstone which may afford the readiest means of joining you and I think I shall be able to take with me from 15 to 20 days rations on pack saddles, though no forage. If, however, I should move up the Rosebud, I could take a wagon train with me.

The following officers were killed on the 25th ultimo, General Custer, Colonel Custer, Captain Keogh, Captain Yates, Lieutenants Hodgson, McIntosh, Cook (Adjutant), A. E. Smith, Calhoun, Porter, Sturgis, and Riley. Lieutenants Crittenden, 20th Infantry (attached to the Cavalry). Assistant Surgeon Lord, A. A. Surgeon Dr Wolf. Lieutenant Harrington missing. Also Mr Boston Custer and Mr Reed, brother and nephew respectively of the General.

I am General

Very truly yours,

s/ALFRED H. TERRY

Brigadier General

When Bourke copied this letter into his journal, he followed it with this comment:

*The story is now assured. Custer had with imprudent rashness pushed ahead into the thickest of the enemy, seeking glory not to be eclipsed or even shared by his superiors and comrades. His fate was most horrible, above all when we regard the involvement of others' lives in the same deadly conflict. The brave couriers . . . had not much to add to the official narrative. . . .*

The remark, no doubt made facetiously, that there has been more ink used in writing about the Battle of the Little Big Horn than there was blood spilled on the battlefield could almost be taken for the literal truth. This has created an unfortunate situation for this battle, and the dramatic death of the 265 soldiers and scouts which occurred in it, made a large contribution to the *folklore* of the Western Frontier but *it contributed hardly a whit to settling the question of these renegades.* It was Crook's three campaigns, coupled with the work of Colonel Miles and the Fifth Infantry, that brought this struggle to a successful conclusion—while Custer's tragic blunder has achieved a renown far above its *historical* merit.

Plans which led to the fatal movement of the 7th Cavalry were formulated by General Terry, Colonel Gibbon and Lieutenant Colonel Custer on the 21st of June. When Terry's adjutant issued orders to Custer, Gibbon's troops were already a day's march on their way, and the 7th Cavalry was ready to move within an hour or two. Terry's orders, which are the starting place for arguments about Custer's motives, read:

Camp at the Mouth of
Rosebud River,
June 22, 1876

LT. COL. CUSTER, 7th Cavalry:
COLONEL:

The Brigadier General commanding directs that as soon as your regiment can be made ready for the march, you proceed up the Rosebud in pursuit of the Indians whose trail was discovered by Major Reno a few days ago. It is, of course, impossible to give you any definite instructions in regard to this movement, and were it not impossible to do so, the Department commander places too much confidence in your zeal, energy and ability to wish to impose upon you precise orders which might hamper your action when nearly in contact with the enemy.

He will, however, indicate to you his own views of what your action should be, and he desires that you should conform to them unless you shall see sufficient reason for departing from them. He thinks that you should proceed up the Rosebud until you ascertain definitely the direction in which the trail above spoken of leads. Should it be found, as it appears to be almost certain that it will be found, to turn toward the Little Big Horn he thinks you should still proceed southward, perhaps as far as the headwaters of the Tongue, and then turn toward the Little Big Horn, feeling constantly however, to your left so as to preclude the possibility of the escape of the Indians to the south or southeast by passing around your left flank.

The column of Col. Gibbon is now in motion for the mouth of the Big Horn. As soon at it reaches that point it will cross the Yellowstone and move up at least as far as the forks of the Big and Little Big Horn. Of course its future movements must be controlled by circumstances as they may arise; but it is hoped that the Indians, if upon the Little Big Horn, may be so nearly enclosed by the two columns that their escape will be impossible.

The Department commander desires that on your way up the Rosebud you should thoroughly examine the upper parts of Tullocks Creek, and that you should endeavor to send a scout through to Col. Gibbon's column with information of the result of your examination. The lower part of this creek will be examined by a detachment of Col. Gibbon's command.

The supply steamer will be pushed up the Big Horn as far as the forks of the river are found to be navigable for that space, and the Department commander desires you to report to him there not later than the expiration of the time for which your troops are rationed, unless in the meantime you receive further orders.

Respectfully,
s/ E. W. SMITH
Capt. 18th Infantry,
Acting Asst. Adjt. Genl.

The focal point in these orders lies in a single statement: "[The Department commander] desires that you should conform to [his views] *unless you shall see sufficient reason for departing from them*." Did Custer depart from them for "sufficient reason" or for the reasons which his fellow officers ascribed to him? No one knows.

The hoped-for result of such a maneuver—considering the high degree of mobility of these Indians—was but little better than wishful thinking: and, considering the opinion held of Custer, the hopes of Gibbon's men to take part in any fight were even more slender. This was well recognized for Bradley, who marched with these troops, wrote:

It is understood that if Custer arrives first he is at liberty to attack at once if he deems prudent. We have little hope of being in at the death as Custer will undoubtedly exert himself to the utmost to get there first and win all the laurels for himself and his regiment.

The lieutenant also noted enviously that, not only did Custer have the Ree scouts, but that he had been directed to detail six of his Crows to the Seventh; and:

Our guide, Mitch Buoyer, accompanies him also. This leaves us wholly without a guide, while Custer has one of the very best that the country affords. Surely he is being afforded every facility to make a successful pursuit.

At mid-day on the 22nd of June, the Seventh began its march up the valley of the Rosebud: and on the evening of the 24th the regiment camped near the site of the present village of Busby. Here scouts came in with the information that the trail of the big camp had turned west toward the valley of the Little Big Horn. Custer had the camp alerted —many had already gone to bed—and shortly before midnight the column was in motion again. By two o'clock in the morning, they were near the crest of the divide between these two streams. When daylight came, Custer studied the valley from a vantage point but—probably —was not able to make out the camp which was some fifteen miles away. However, a detail which had gone back to try to find some things lost by the pack train, came in and reported that they had seen an Indian taking hardtack from a box which had been dropped.

Apparently believing that he had been discovered by his quarry—which, ironically, was not the case—Custer made plans to attack a village about which he had practically no intelligence. Captain Benteen and one battalion (125 men) was directed to scout toward the left (southwest) and "to pitch into anything he might find." Major Reno was given another battalion (115 men) and ordered to proceed down the valley of the creek—now Reno Creek—which lay immediately ahead, and Custer followed with the two remaining battalions which totaled 225 soldiers. The pack train of about 175 mules, six or seven packers, and an escort of 70 troopers was left to follow the trail of the main body. After marching down this creek for about two hours, unmistakable evidence of Indians was noted in the valley of the Little Big Horn. Custer now sent his adjutant to Reno with verbal orders to pursue the Indians—whom Custer believed were fleeing—with all reasonable speed, attack them, and "you will be supported by the whole outfit."

The hostiles were camped in the valley which, at this point, was a beautiful, flat, grassy plain over a mile in width and lying entirely on the west side of the river. Cottonwoods, with some willows and underbrush, edged the winding stream. On the eastern side, Reno Creek joined the northward-flowing Little Big Horn a mile or two to the south of the southern end of the great camp. Between this creek and the central part of the camp, a high, rugged bluff rose steeply from the bank of the stream: and across its northern end was Medicine Tail Coulee beyond which, parallel with the river, stretched a sagebrush-covered ridge which was over a mile in length.

Reno followed the creek which now bears his name to the river and crossed as quickly as the thirsty horses would permit. Then the battalion galloped northward towards the clouds of dust which could be seen rising above the tops of some cottonwoods which screened the camp from view. After advancing about two miles—and shortly after the first shots were fired—the men saw an angry swarm of warriors riding to meet them. Instead of charging, Reno dismounted his men and formed a line of skirmishers. Surging around the left end, the Sioux quickly flanked the line; and the major swung his troops back into the nearby timber along the river. The warriors infiltrated the cover behind the soldiers and Reno, now badly frightened or thoroughly flustered—or both, ordered a retreat. As he sat on his horse ready to start, with Bloody Knife—Custer's favorite Ree scout—beside him, a bullet struck the latter in the head and spattered bloody brains on the officer.

There was a mad scramble and, with Reno at their head, the troopers galloped back toward the point where they had crossed. Pouring on a telling fire with everything from bows and arrows to repeating rifles, Sioux and Cheyenne warriors raced beside the right side of the disorderly battalion and forced what Reno was later to call a "charge" toward the river. For the Indians it was just like running buffalo only more exciting. Fortunately, the men hit the stream at a point where they could ford without too much difficulty. They splashed across, swarmed up the almost-precipitous sides of the bluff, and then stopped on the top to collect their wits and allow their shaking horses to blow. Left behind in the woods—to rejoin their comrades hours later—were seventeen men, and thirty-two more were killed or wounded in this rout. Among the dead was "Lonesome Charlie" Reynolds, killed in the timber as he warned another of his danger.

Benteen and his men now came up, having found nothing to "pitch into." The captain—who was a steady veteran when the chips were down—immediately sent a courier to hurry the pack train along, and set about bringing order out of chaos. While these things were being done—about 4:30 in the afternoon—heavy firing was heard in the distance to the northward. One of Benteen's company commanders took it upon himself to move out to a high hill a mile or so farther north, and later the rest of the force joined him. From this point the men saw a large number of Indians moving aimlessly about on the long ridge to the north of Medicine Tail Coulee. Before long the warriors began to leave the area where they had been milling about and advanced determinedly upon the soldiers.

Reno and Benteen now pulled back to the place where they had united their forces, which was a better spot to make a stand, and improvised scanty defenses. For the remainder of the day, and the most of the next, the men—exposed to the blazing sun, without water, and with but little opportunity to eat—fought a desperate fight to survive. The fifteen men who, under the cover of four good marksmen, slipped down a ravine to the river and brought back water for the wounded were later awarded Congressional Medals of Honor. By mid-afternoon of the second day, the sniping almost ceased. Near evening the troopers watched the great camp move westward over the rolling hills in a haze of grey dust that was tinted by the rays of the evening sun. It was estimated that this closely-packed column was at least three miles long and a half, perhaps three quarters, of a mile wide.

Evening brought welcome changes. Horses and mules were watered —for the first time in over a day: the campground was moved slightly to get away from the stench of dead animals: the dead were buried in a common grave: and cooks prepared the first meal since supper two days before. But there was nothing to do except wait, and wonder when Custer would come and rescue them from their predicament.

In the meantime, Gibbon's men were coming up the eastern side of the valley of the Big Horn. Early in the morning of the day following the Battle of the Little Big Horn, Bradley was scouting well in advance of the column when his Crows found the trail of four ponies. *Sign* indicated that the riders were fleeing in haste and "we found much to our great surprise that they belonged to some of the Crows whom I had furnished to General Custer." Three Indians were sighted on the west side of the river and these were persuaded to come back and converse across the stream while

*I kept the remainder of the detachment on the bluffs. Presently our Indians turned back and, as they came, shouted out at the top of their voices a doleful series of cries and wails that the interpreter, Bravo, explained was a song of mourning for the dead . . . . when they came up, shedding copious tears and appearing pictures of misery, it was evident that the occasion was of no common sort. Little Face in particular wept with a bitterness of anguish such as I have rarely seen. For a while he could not speak, but at last composed himself and told his story in a choking voice, broken with frequent sobs. As he proceeded, the Crows one by one broke off from the group of listeners and going aside a little distance sat down alone, weeping and chanting that dreadful mourning song, and rocking their bodies to and fro. . . .*

"It was a terrible, terrible story. . . ." The Crows had watched from a distance while the Sioux sallied forth from the village in overwhelming numbers and destroyed all but a small portion of the command. This they had surrounded in the hills and when the scouts left they believed that it was impossible for this group to hold out much longer.

*I therefore rode back until I met the command, which was halted just before I came up, and narrated to the General the ghastly details as I had received them from Little Face. He was surrounded by his staff and accompanied by General Gibbon . . . and for a moment there were blank faces and silent tongues and no doubt heavy hearts in that group. . . . But presently the voice of doubt and scorning was raised, the story was sneered at. . . . General Terry took no part in these criticisms, but sat on his horse silent and thoughtful, biting his lower lip and looking to me as though he by no means shared the wholesale skepticism of the flippant members of his staff.*

After making his report, Bradley allowed the demoralized Crows to stay with the column, and not long afterward all of them left abruptly and headed for their camp. The column continued on up the Big Horn to the mouth of the Little Big Horn and then followed this stream to a point some eight or nine miles below Reno's position. Here scouts reported a strong force of hostiles not far away, and Terry ordered camp made in a strong position. The next morning the column advanced to the campsite where blood-stained clothing was found. When Bradley, who with his mounted infantry had been scouring the hills on the eastern side of the river, came in and quietly reported that he had just counted 197 bodies on the slopes of a long ridge everyone knew that the story told by the Crows was true.

Reno's men had noted the dust of the approaching column. When reasonably certain that this was caused by soldiers, the major sent two Rees and two officers to make contact. Bradley was soon in the camp of the remnant of the Seventh, and Terry and his staff followed shortly afterward. Lieutenant Godfrey of Company K wrote in his diary that Bradley inquired for him and when they met the first question he asked was where was General Custer. Bradley replied that

he did not know but supposed him killed, as he had counted 197 bodies he did not think any of them escaped. I was dumbfounded. . . .

There remained the disagreeable task of burying the dead which had laid exposed to the hot sun for three days. As practically all of the bodies had been stripped and many were badly mutilated, identification was practically impossible except for the officers. Burial was equally difficult as there were only a few implements with which to dig. Using hunting knives, tin cups, and similar instruments, the men scraped a little dirt over the corpses where they lay and left them—to the wolves and coyotes.

The fifty-two wounded were laboriously transported to the *Far West* which Marsh had skillfully brought up to the mouth of the Little Big Horn. Then the captain dropped down to the Yellowstone where he ferried the command across to Fort Pease. This task completed, the *Far West* headed downstream on a record run of 710 miles in 54 hours to take the wounded—and the news—to Fort Abraham Lincoln. Speedy as the trip was, *moccasin telegraph* had brought rumors of the disaster before Marsh's arrival.

Thus ended the disaster on the Little Big Horn. The dead totaled 265 although some of the bodies were never found. How many warriors the Indians lost was never known. For that matter, no one has ever estimated with certainty how many warriors were in the fight. Some estimates are as low as 1,500 and others as high as 4,000. Neither is it known with certainty whether the Indians had one leader who directed the fight or whether each band had its own leader, for the Indians, like the whites, had their petty jealousies. Certainly Crazy Horse, Gall, Hump, Spotted Eagle, and Lame White Man played prominent parts. And although some have claimed that Sitting Bull was present while the battle was fought, there are persistent reports that when the battle started he left in haste, with his wives, and was later overtaken at the Two Leggins Crossing of the Big Horn some eighteen miles away.

Only the Indians knew positively what happened to Custer's detachment. For years most of them were afraid to relate what they knew—some never would talk—and the stories which have been gathered contain certain striking disagreements. Custer had followed Reno's men to the mouth of Reno Creek and then turned off to the right and continued northward among the hills on the east side of the river. There is, however, one indisputable fact. Custer had "the royal family" —so long the cause of bitter friction within the regiment—with him at the end. The bodies of the three brothers—George, Tom, and Boston, Lieutenant James Calhoun (Mrs. Custer's brother-in-law), and the colonel's nephew, Armstrong "Autie" Reed, were all found on that fatal ridge.

Typical of some of the myths which have sprung up is that about the ammunition carried by the soldiers. There are stories that the cartridge cases were defective and that the extractors cut through the rims making it necessary to dig these out of the chamber with hunting knives or hammer them out with a ramrod after the piece was fired. Among the hundreds of shells recovered by the National Park Service by means of metal detectors, there are four—only FOUR—which bear evidence of being dug or driven out of the chamber. None of these were found in positions believed to have been occupied by soldiers during the battle.

Immediately after the Battle of the Little Big Horn, Sheridan moved to reinforce both Terry and Crook. The major part of the Fifth Infantry, then at Fort Leavenworth, Kansas, was sent post haste to join Terry. Traveling by train to Yankton, South Dakota, and by steamboat the remainder of the way, Colonel Nelson A. Miles and this regiment reached Terry's camp on the 2nd of August. Early in June, the Fifth Cavalry had been concentrated near the southern end of the Black Hills to stamp out the traffic between the agency Indians and the hostiles. To command this force, Sheridan had detailed Colonel Wesley Merritt from his own staff. On the 12th of July these troops were ordered to join Crook's column but this was not accomplished until the 3rd of August.

The diary of Lieutenant Bourke who, as Crook's adjutant was a very knowledgeable individual, indicates that the month of July could hardly be called one of inactivity—even though the troops whiled their time away by trout fishing. Mail carriers came and went between Fort Fetterman and the camp on Goose Creek, and the dispatches in their pouches were evidence of far-flung developments which focused on the campaign which had been temporarily halted. Crook desired some Utes for scouts. The agent thwarted this request—until indicted for fraud. Then Sheridan gained control of the agencies and the enlistment was accomplished. On the 20th, information arrived that Congress had—at long last—passed a bill to provide for the construction of two posts on the Yellowstone: eight days later Sheridan wired, "I will build both posts . . . if the stage of water will permit and will supply them well so that the force operating in the fall and winter can draw from them." And there was considerable correspondence concerning the Battle of the Rosebud about which Crook and his staff were—if anything—unduly sensitive, insisting that this *draw* had been a "victory." Finally, Sheridan gave the action his approval and wrote that General Sherman (then General of the Army) had said, "You need not mind the newspapers." Another interesting development was that Colonel Ranald Mackenzie and six companies of the 4th Cavalry had been ordered from Fort Sill in Indian Territory to fill the gap left by Merritt's withdrawal from Fort Robinson.

The most interesting correspondence was that which passed between Crook and Terrry. Both were Department commanders and the dividing line between their areas of responsibility was the line between the Wyoming and Montana Territories. Crook had not hesitated to take his troops across this line on two occasions, and Terry's orders to Custer envisioned crossing into Wyoming. *But cooperative action with each other was quite another matter.* Terry had offered to "assume nothing by reason of my seniority" but Crook—the junior officer of the two—was not free to accept this offer. It was a military principle that the senior officer present assumed command: Terry, a well-liked, scholarly officer, was not an experienced Indian fighter while Crook was one of the best and the latter had a well seasoned body of troops. This situation was to delay future operations and also to cause considerable irritation. When Bourke wrote his *On The Border With Crook* he saw fit not to mention this matter, but this second-just-turned-first lieutenant wrote what he pleased in his journal.

Three days after the arrival of Terry's daring couriers (a week later four Crows arrived with copies of the same letter), Crook dispatched an answer. He wrote, in part:

*I had determined to attack the Indians immediately after the arrival of my supply train [which took the wounded from the Battle of the Rosebud to Fort Fetterman], but about that time I learned that the hostiles had received reinforcements and I also learned at the same time that I could get the eight companies of the 5th Cavalry, so I concluded to defer the movement until the arrival of those companies which have now been ordered here. I expect to be joined by them about the last of the present month. . . .*

\* \* \*

*I am rationed up to the end of September and will share with you and your command everything I have as long as it lasts. Should the two commands come together, whether the Indians be in this or your department, if you think the interest of the service will be advanced by the combination, I will most cheerfully serve under you. When the 5th arrives, I expect to have about (1600) sixteen hundred fighting men, besides some friendly Indians and it is my intention to move without further delay.*

This letter was entrusted to a man named Kelly, "a half-witted sort of fellow, possessed of an under-stratum of cunning and common sense." With only a small bundle of supplies, the man started out on foot and, by traveling at night and sleeping in the daytime, managed to get through. Finley, who talked with him several weeks later, noted:

*No one expected him to succeed . . . ; yet he did. . . . He had determined, if he fell by accident into the hands of the Sioux, to play off as a madman, because the savages rarely ever injure a maniac. . . . Kelly, in my opinion, was near enough to the crazy line to play the role to the entire satisfaction of the Indians.*

It was not long after the Battle of the Little Big Horn before Crook's men had no reason to feel slighted by a lack of attention by the Sioux. For two weeks in the middle of July, hostiles hovered about the camp almost constantly, harassing the pickets, attempting to steal horses, and trying to burn the camp out. Smoke from fires filled the air for days, and these scorched earth tactics added to Crook's worries. On the 23rd of July, Crook wrote Sheridan that he was "immeasurably embarrassed" by the delay of Merritt's troops. The Shoshones—213 warriors led by their venerable chief Washakie and the ex-Confederate

Cosgrove—had arrived two weeks before and now were becoming dissatisfied and restless. Grass was drying and the whole country from the Rosebud to the Powder was full of fires: a properly located fire could drive them out of the country. And he feared that he was being watched constantly which would eliminate any element of surprise which might accrue from joining Terry. "I am at a loss what to do."

The Utes, thirty-five in number, arrived unexpectedly on July 30th —adding momentarily to the consternation of the camp which was, at the moment, fighting a fire in the Shoshone camp. On the 3rd of August, the hearts of all were gladdened by the arrival of Merritt and the 5th Cavalry, a feeling which was further intensified by greetings between old friends as many of the men had campaigned together under Crook in Arizona.

Now that his command was complete, Crook wasted no time in stripping it down to the barest of essentials. Every man, from himself down to the lowest private, packers and civilians included,

was to have the clothes on his back and no more; one overcoat, one blanket (to be carried by the cavalry over the saddle blanket), and one India-rubber poncho or one-half of a shelter tent. . . . We had rations for fifteen days—half of bacon, sugar, coffee, and salt, and full of hard bread; none of vinegar, soap, pepper, etc. There were two hundred and fifty rounds of ammunition to the man; one hundred to be carried on the person, and the rest on the pack mules, of which there were just three hundred and ninety-nine. The pack train was in five divisions, each led by a bell-mare; no tents allowed, excepting one for the use of the surgeons attending to critical cases. "Travois" poles were hauled along to drag the wounded in case it should become necessary.

. . . . General Crook did not allow us either knife, fork, spoon, or plate. Each member carried strapped to the pommel of his saddle a tin cup, from which . . . he might quaff the decoction called coffee. Our kitchen utensils comprised one frying-pan, one carving-knife, one carving-fork, one large coffee pot, one large tin platter, one large and two small tin ladles or spoons, and necessary bags for carrying sugar, coffee, bacon, and hard bread. I forgot to say that we had also one sheet-iron mess pan.

All the surplus was turned over to the quartermaster with the wagon train, and at daylight on the 5th of August the column was moving again.

Colonel Merritt assumed overall command of the cavalry. Colonel

T. H. Stanton, the old "fire-eater" from the office in Omaha who had been with Crook in March, was given command of some irregulars who dubbed themselves the Montana Volunteers. These were commonly known throughout the command as the "Montana Thieves" because they would steal the clothes off the backs of the staff officers who traveled with them if given the opportunity. One curious character among them was an Indian named Ute John who had lived among the Mormons. He would talk to no one about the campaign except Crook—"Hullo Clook," he would say, "hou you gettin on? Heh? Where you tink dem Clazy Hoss'n Sittin Bull is now, Cluke?"

William F. "Buffalo Bill" Cody, who had been chief scout for the Fifth Cavalry in and around Fort Robinson, was also along. Bourke characterized him as a "gentlemanly man of pleasing address and quiet bearing . . . . a good shot, a fine rider, and a fair scout. In the last mentioned capacity he plays a very insignificant part in association with our Indians . . . because they know almost every foot of this vast country."

The command moved down the Tongue for a couple of days and then, failing to find any fresh Indian sign, crossed over to the Rosebud, striking this stream a short distance below the battlefield of June 17th. Here the scouts soon found a great campsite which was ten or twelve days old. This was about four miles long and a mile wide, and the tepees had been arranged in seven circles. The pony herd, which Grouard estimated at 10,000 to 20,000 head, had cropped the valley almost as bare as a desert. Following this trail, the command moved down the valley—the Shoshone scouts amusing themselves by throwing corpses from their burial places in the trees to hunt for trinkets and weapons, and teasing rattlesnakes into a coil and then lancing them, "Exclaiming at the same time: 'Got tamme you! Got tamme you!' which was all the English they had been able to master."

In the morning of the third day's travel down this valley there was a hubbub among the Indians, and at the same time dust rose in the distance from ponies which were also being ridden in circles—the universal Indian warning sign. Then the officers near the front saw

compact squadrons . . . moving diagonally out across the broad plain, taking equal intervals, then coming squarely toward us at a rapid trot. . . . Each company, as it comes forward, opens out like the fan of a practiced coquette, and a sheaf of skirmishers.is launched to the front. . . . Behind them are the solid regiments of Miles and Gibbon, the long trains of wagons and supplies. It is General Terry and his whole array. . . .

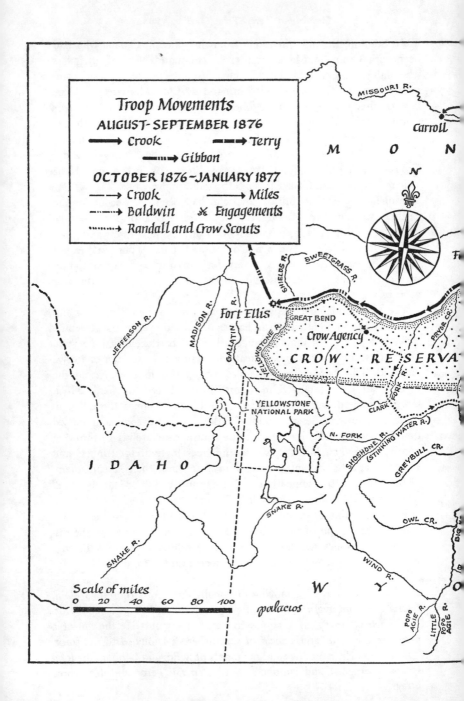

Troop Movements

AUGUST–SEPTEMBER 1876
→ Crook ⇢ Terry
⇢ Gibbon

OCTOBER 1876–JANUARY 1877
⇢ Crook → Miles
⇢ Baldwin ✕ Engagements
⇢ Randall and Crow Scouts

MISSOURI R.

Carroll

M O N T

MADISON R.

JEFFERSON R.

GALLATIN R.

YELLOWSTONE R.

Fort Ellis

SHIELDS R.

SWEETGRASS R.

GREAT BEND

Crow Agency

C R O W   R E S E R V A

PRYOR CR.

CLARK FORK R.

YELLOWSTONE
NATIONAL PARK

N. FORK

SHOSHONE R.

STINKING WATER R.

GREYBULL CR.

I D A H O

SNAKE R.

SNAKE R.

OWL CR.

WIND R.

POPO AGIE R.

LITTLE POPO AGIE R.

BIG

W Y O

Scale of miles

0   20   40   60   80   100

palacios

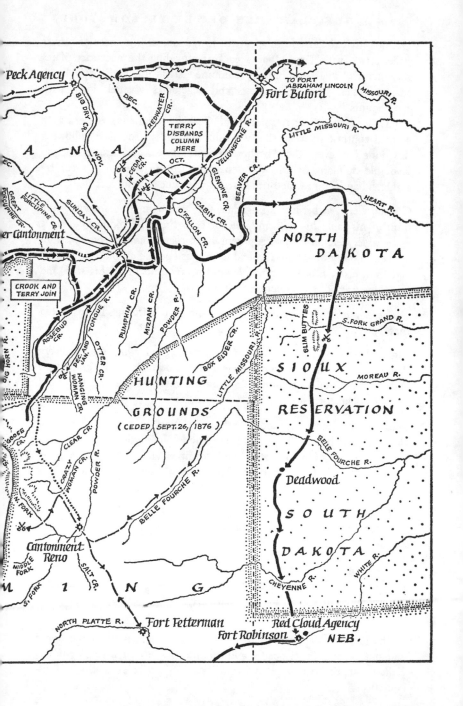

Peck Agency

TO FORT
ABRAHAM LINCOLN

Fort Buford

MISSOURI R.

BIG DRY CR.

DEC.

NOV.

REDWATER CR.

LITTLE MISSOURI R.

TERRY
DISBANDS
COLUMN
HERE

A N A

DEC.

LITTLE
PORCUPINE CR.

GREAT
PORCUPINE CR.

SUNDAY CR.

K. CEDAR CR.

OCT.

YELLOWSTONE R.

GLENDIVE CR.

BEAVER CR.

HEART R.

er Cantonment

CABIN CR.

O'FALLON CR.

NORTH

DAKOTA

CROOK AND
TERRY JOIN

PEC. IND TONGUE R.

ROSEBUD CR.

OTTER CR.

HANGING
WOMAN CR.

PUMPKIN CR.

MIZPAH CR.

POWDER R.

S. FORK GRAND R.

GLIM BUTTES

BIG HORN R.

BOX ELDER CR.

LITTLE MISSOURI R.

S I O U X

MOREAU R.

HUNTING

GROUNDS

( CEDED  SEPT. 26, 1876 )

RES ERVATION

GOOSE CR.

CLEAR CR.

CRAZY WOMAN CR.

POWDER R.

BELLE FOURCHE R.

BELLE FOURCHE R.

Deadwood

N. FORK

Cantonment
Reno

MIDDLE
FORK

SALT CR.

S O U T H

DAKOTA

WHITE R.

M I N G

St FORK

NORTH PLATTE R.

Fort Fetterman

CHEYENNE R.

Fort Robinson

Red Cloud Agency

NEB.

Crook invited Terry to lunch—which was served on a piece of canvas under a tree, with Tom Moore's packers providing the necessary plates and utensils. That evening the combined staffs ate at Terry's headquarters where they "had meats and vegetables washed down with good liquors."

To the weatherbeaten soldiers of Crook's command, there was a marked contrast between the two columns; and in the days following this junction even the Shoshone scouts noted and expressed unfavorable opinions on this difference. At this first evening meal together, a lieutenant in the Fifth Cavalry was struck by the fact that,

General Terry, as became a brigadier, was attired in the handsome uniform of his rank; his staff and line officers, though looking eminently serviceable, were all in neat regimentals, so that shoulder straps were to be seen in every direction. General Crook, as became an old campaigner and frontiersman, was in a rough hunting rig, and in all his staff and line there was not a complete suit of uniform.

There were other differences besides those of uniforms. It was noted that Terry

had with him a complete wagon train, tents and equippage of every description. We had a few days bacon and hard-tack, coffee and sugar, and a whole arsenal of ammunition on our mules, but not a tent, and only one blanket apiece.

One officer, "almost exploding at a revelation so preposterous," exclaimed to another, "Look at Reno's tent—he's got a Brussels carpet!" A couple of weeks later, while camped along the Yellowstone, Bourke noted that a steamboat which arrived from one of the supply depots had

quite a number of rocking chairs and such useless truck going to show the accumulation of impedimenta that had been permitted to a dangerous extent.

The most serious difference was in morale. Crook's tattered men had an *esprit de corps* that was largely lacking in Terry's column. Finerty noted that they "looked tired, dirty, and disgusted." To Bourke's more experienced eyes:

The massacre of Custer had fallen as a wet blanket upon the hopes and ambitions of his associates and the time passed in refitting upon the Yellowstone had been a period of idleness productive of apathy and discontent.

Later he noted that there was actually "some indifference" among the officers as to the outcome of the summer's work.

Plans were quickly made to continue the campaign. The next morning Miles and the 5th Infantry was ordered to take the wagon train—including all the sick and disabled, and extra horses and supplies—back to the Yellowstone, and to patrol the river in a steamboat. Crook and Terry combined and set out on the trail which the former had been following when the meeting took place. Another difference now became obvious: Terry's pack train

*was the saddest burlesque in that direction which it has ever been my lot to witness. . . . [This was] a string of mules, of all sizes, each led by one soldier and beaten and driven along by another—attendants often rivalling animals in dumbness. . . . On the first day's march after meeting Crook, Terry's pack train dropped, lost, or damaged more stores than Crook's command had spoiled from the same causes from the time the campaign commenced.*

The Shoshones had no difficulty in understanding the implications of this sorry exhibition and before many days passed were saying that Crook's men could do more without the "Yellowstone soldiers" than with them.

The trail of the hostiles now led eastward and when it crossed the Powder near the mouth of Mizpah Creek, Terry left it and led the troops down to the Yellowstone. Crook was in need of rations, clothing, and shoes for the infantry. These supplies were not available, and it soon became obvious that they might not be forthcoming even after the steamboats had stripped all the supply dumps along the river. After one day's delay, Washakie urged Crook to take the meager supplies which were available and push on, leaving Terry and his cumbersome pack train to follow if he so desired. But Crook was the junior officer, and Terry wished to hold the commands together. Two days later, seeing that the military men were completely bogged down, the old chief shook hands with Crook and started home with his now thoroughly-dissatisfied warriors.

While the steamboats went hunting for the necessary supplies, the troops settled down to what proved to be a week of idleness and hardship. There was but little to eat and several rains, two of which were extremely severe, drenched Crook's unprotected men. Both Bourke and Finerty wrote detailed descriptions of nights spent with a "solid sheet of rain falling" and "vivid flashes of lightning followed by tremendous peals of thunder." The latter summed his experiences up in one expressive sentence—"I had slept in the rain several times on this trip, but the experience of that night was the nearest approach to hell on earth that I have known."

The delay and the hardships frayed tempers. Terry and Crook got along amiably but Bourke noted that "human nature crops out among subalterns at a fearful rate." Of Reno and Brisbin, he wrote with cutting sarcasm:

Reno saved, more by good luck than good management, the remnant of the 7th Cavalry at the Custer Massacre. He saw enough at that fight to scare him for the rest of his life. He will never make a bold movement for ten years to come.

And:

Brisbin is one of the political dead-beats who have crowded into the Army since the war . . . . under his guidance his Battalion will never be surprised by Indians, because "Jim" will smell them for twenty miles and avoid danger. He has never heard a shot fired in a fair fight.

Although the Ree scouts combed the surrounding territory, they did not discover any significant movement to the north. However, the rumor persisted that Sitting Bull and Crazy Horse were likely to cross the Yellowstone. The Rees did find that the large trail which the troops had been following continued on eastward. Crook suspected that these Indians were on their way to the agencies to refit after which they would probably harass the settlements in the Black Hills and the area along the Platte. As it was his responsibility to protect this region, he now had a reason to split his men out of the unwieldy force which circumstances had placed him, if not against his will, at least against his better judgment.

On the morning of the 24th of August, Crook's column, miserable and bedraggled from a drenching the night before, headed back up the Powder to pick up the trail they had abandoned seven days before. Five Ree scouts accompanied them—a welcome addition—and in their commissary were rations for fifteen days. At evening on the second day out, Terry and Buffalo Bill rode into camp and the two generals had a final conference. When it was over, Terry decided to patrol the Yellowstone while Crook continued on, and each would notify the other of any important developments.

The trail continued eastward to the Yellowstone-Little Missouri divide and then began to fray out as small bodies split off. Crook, now near the headwaters of the Heart River and down to three day's rations, faced three alternatives—he could return to the Yellowstone, he could continue on eastward to Fort Abraham Lincoln, or he could follow the Indians southward. Sending the Rees to the fort on the Missouri with dispatches for Sheridan, the general ordered the men on half rations and headed southward, hoping that he could reach the settlements in the Black Hills.

For the next seven days the soldiers pushed steadily southward across desolate, open prairie—pelted almost daily by cold rains, every step a battle with the gumbo mud, almost nothing to eat except the nauseating, leathery meat of played-out horses and what they could scavenge from the country, and no wood for 80 or 90 miles. There were few marches in the history of the West which could equal it for hardship and none which could surpass it.

The only bright spot in this trek was when Mills and a small detachment, which had been ordered to push on ahead, captured American Horse's village just east of Slim Buttes. Mills—with more pluck than good judgment—attacked the camp and then sent a courier to Crook with an urgent request for assistance. All of the Sioux, except the chief and twenty-seven of his people, escaped but the combined forces easily held off Crazy Horse and his warriors who rode up from a village a few miles away. The lodges yielded relics from the Custer fight and considerable plunder which was useful to hungry and impoverished troops. Best of all, some of the captives provided valuable intelligence concerning the probable whereabouts of the other bands of hostiles during the remainder of the fall and winter.

Crook now re-dispatched the advance party—this time on captured Indian ponies—and the column toiled on after them. On the 13th of September, the seventh day of the horsemeat march and three weeks after separating from Terry, supplies which Sheridan had ordered sent up from Fort Robinson reached the men. While his troops camped on the Belle Fourche River to recuperate, Crook and his staff pushed on to Deadwood, then to Fort Robinson, and finally on to Fort Laramie for a conference with General Sheridan. The latter had already begun to plan a fall campaign.

After Terry's final conference with Crook, the 7th Cavalry scouted the vicinity of Glendive Creek, and then crossed the Yellowstone and went as far north as the Yellowstone-Missouri Divide. Finding nothing, the general broke up his column on the 3rd of September. The Montana and Dakota troops were ordered to return to their former posts; and Miles and the 5th Infantry and six companies of the 22nd Infantry were left on the Yellowstone to establish a post at the mouth of the Tongue. Actually, construction of the Tongue River Cantonment was started on the 28th of August by Lieutenant Colonel N. J. C.

Whistler who had come up the river with the two companies of the Fifth which Miles had left behind him at Fort Leavenworth.

This post, the forerunner of Fort Keogh, was built in a grove of big cottonwoods between a bend in the Tongue and the bank of the Yellowstone where the winter winds would be broken by the rugged bluffs just to the north across the river. It consisted of

shelters made of logs placed on end in a trench and "capped" with a "plate" or log, on which rested a roof of poles and earth; not uncomfortable, as far as warmth was concerned, in the winter, but terribly damp and leaky in the heavy rains of the spring.

The following year an officer's wife lived in one of them while the quarters at Fort Keogh were being built. She recalled that the mud chinking had a way of falling out after rains and referred to them as "vermin-infested, ramshackle huts" and "dark dismal dens."

### MILES AND HIS WALK-A-HEAPS

Colonel Miles, an ambitious and energetic officer, had no intention of allowing his troops to settle comfortably in camp and permitting the Indians to move unchallenged in the country about them. He had campaigned in the winter on the plains of Indian Territory, and he was convinced he could operate during the winter months even if Terry did think otherwise. To this end he made plans and gathered a force of capable scouts.

Chief of this group was Luther S. Kelly—better known as Yellowstone Kelly. He had a good education, liked to read, and never drank or caroused. Eventually, the soldiers nicknamed him "Kelly the Silent" and "Kelly the Sphinx." Others who have almost been forgotten were Joe Culbertson, half-breed son of fur trader Alexander Culbertson; George Boyd who was clubfooted in both feet; "Liver-eating" Johnson who, in an Indian-trapper fight, had pretended to eat a piece of the liver of a Sioux warrior; Billy Jackson, the half-breed Blackfoot who was left in the timber when Reno started his hasty retreat; Vic Smith, an outstanding marksman with a rifle; and Johnny "Big Leggins" Bruguier whose name Miles and others have invariably misspelled. Bruguier, a half-breed Sioux, was the son of a fur trader who ran a post where Sioux City now stands. He had fled to Sitting Bull's camp to escape arrest on a murder charge. Miles met him during a parley with the Sioux medicine man and hired him several weeks later. Tom Leforge, the squaw man who assisted Lieutenant Bradley, enlisted a group of Crow scouts but this group dissolved abruptly in the early fall.

While the men were working on the cantonment, Leforge and his Indians made a large circle toward the south and east, and Miles scouted out a road to Fort Buford opposite the mouth of the Yellowstone. The trail which Miles' party laid out followed, generally, the route to Hay Creek (opposite Glendive) which was laid out in 1873 by Colonel Stanley, and from this point it followed down the valley of the Yellowstone.

Some supplies were brought up to the post from Camp Glendive, one of Terry's supply dumps. The Sioux discovered this activity and early in October drove a train of 94 wagons and the escort of four companies of infantry back to the depot. After replacing forty-one of the drivers who refused to venture out again, the train made a second start. This time, with five companies of infantry extended in line of skirmishers on the flanks, the hostiles gave way although they had increased in numbers to an estimated seven or eight hundred warriors. On the second day an insolent note—perhaps written by Johnny Bruguier—was found on the road. This read:

Yellowstone
*I want to know what you are doing traveling on this road. You scare all the Buffalo away. I want to hunt in this place. I want you to turn back from here. If you don't I will fight you again. I want you to leave what you have got there and turn back from here.*

*I am your friend,*
SITTING BULL
*I mean all the rations you have got and some powder. I wish you would write as soon as you can.*

After preparing an answer to this absurd demand, Colonel Otis continued on his way. Finally three minor chiefs came in and the commander gave them some hard bread and a couple of sides of bacon and informed them that if they wanted to surrender they would have to go to the cantonment.

In the meantime, these difficulties were reported at the post. Miles immediately assembled a force of 394 riflemen and one piece of artillery and, crossing to the north side of the Yellowstone, struck out to try to intercept the hostiles. With only brief stops to prepare meagre meals, the command "marched all day through burning dust and sand" and then "marched all night long." After scaring the Indians away from the vicinity of the wagon train, Miles finally caught up with the main camp on Cedar Creek. Sitting Bull "held a long pow-wow" with Miles under a white flag: the colonel demanded that they surrender but the chief stalled for time. Finally, Miles agreed to draw back to his last camp if the Indians would come and confer with him after they had held a council.

In the morning it was obvious the Indians had only tried to maneuver a delay, and Miles struck out after them. When Sitting Bull rode up again, the colonel gave him no satisfaction. Trumpeter Brown wrote this account of what happened:

*Sitting Bull then rode off in disgust to his warriors who occupied the bluffs in our front; one of the Indians was seen setting the prairie on fire in our front, the Genl ordered one of the scouts to go and stop him; the scout rode out and as he reached the point of the bluff he yelled at the Indian but fired at the same time. The Indian rolled over in the burning grass, we did not stop but kept straight ahead for the redskins on the bluffs. The opera had commenced, bullets whistled lively over our heads without doing much material damage; the big gun broke loose on them which scattered them in all directions; had it not been for the cannon they might have done much greater damage; it was only our best marksmen could be able to make them bite the dust, but occasionally they were seen to thrown up their hands and tumble from their ponies; all that day we fought them through fire and smoke which nearly suffocated us. . . .*

The troops followed the village for several days and finally drove the Indians across the Yellowstone. When the soldiers came down to the opposite bank, the Sioux waved a white flag again and this time agreed to go to the agencies and surrender, Miles taking "five of their chiefs as hostage." How many surrendered is not clear. Official reports say that there were 400 lodges involving 2,000 men, women, and children: the trumpeter wrote in his journal that "11 hundred of this band surrendered." Be that as it may, only about forty lodges *actually* gave up and went in.

Sitting Bull and an estimated 400 of his people split off before this parley and headed for Fort Peck on the Missouri where he believed, perhaps with some grounds, that he would not be molested. Here he was joined a little later by Gall and some other chiefs with about ninety lodges, thus increasing his band to an estimated 600 warriors.

When Miles returned to the Cantonment, he did not tarry long. On the 6th of November, he marched northward up Sunday Creek with "434 rifles," seven scouts, and a wagon train with rations and supplies for 30 days. This column scouted as far north as Fort Peck. Leaving a small detachment at this agency, Miles went west as far as the mouth of the Musselshell, and then sent a small party on to Carroll to check on the traders at this place. Lieutenant Baldwin, a seasoned veteran with two Congressional Medals of Honor, was given three companies and thirteen wagons and sent back to Fort Peck.

Here Baldwin learned that Sitting Bull was camped a few miles away. However, when he reconnoitered the location, he found the Indians on the defensive and decided that his force was not large enough to force the issue. When on his way back to the cantonment, on the headwaters of Redwater Creek, the lieutenant came rather suddenly upon a "large Indian village." He charged without delay and the Indians fled precipitously, leaving 119 lodges and all their property, and about 60 ponies. The trumpeter, who had the information second hand, wrote that Baldwin "ran into a small band of Sioux" which tallies with one Indian account that most of the men were away hunting. The loss of these lodges and supplies in mid-December was a severe blow to Sitting Bull's followers—and perhaps helped them make up their minds to seek the sanctuary north of the Canadian border. Baldwin's men reached the post on the 22nd of December to find that the rest of the column had already returned. The men were worn, and the mules and horses badly used up—but Miles allowed them only six days of rest before they were again in the field.

It was after this expedition that Trumpeter Brown witnessed a regrettable incident:

> While the command was out Lieut Hargous arrived from the Crow Agency with a party of Crow Indians to be kept at the post as scouts, they were camped on Tongue River on the east side of our quarters. . . .
>
> The next day after our arrival in the Post a party of Sioux rode into camp under a flag of truce, they passed the Crow village, and as they got past the Crows ran out and opened fire on them. the Sioux did not return the fire but took a direct line for our camp, the Crows followed and continued firing; the Sioux on seeing them closing in on them turned and began to fire also. The Officers and troops ran out but it was of no use, before anything could be done the Crows had killed and scalped and mutilated the bodies of five, the Sioux thinking the soldiers were also going to fire on them, also took flight, the remaining, the Crows followed.
>
> The Officers undertook to arrest the Crows but they left their lodges and hid among the hills. They were afraid they would be hung for firing on a flag of truce. The Sioux killed two of the Crows squaws when they were coming to this post and they only avenged their deaths.

What band these Sioux came from was never known, and any chances for a possible surrender were irretrievably lost by the Crows' action. This *faux pas* also cost Miles practically all his Indian scouts for most

of the Crows left immediately afterward for their camp. Only squaw-
man Leforge, two Crows, and a very brave Bannock warrior were left.

### THE POWDER RIVER EXPEDITION

While Miles was campaigning between the Yellowstone and the Missouri, Crook was busy in his Department. The management of the Indian agencies had been turned over to the Department of the Army
during the preceding summer and Sheridan lost no time in assuming
these new responsibilities. Crook, who had been unable to plug the
gaps in his rear during the summer, now prepared to deal sternly with
the stubborn chiefs at the Red Cloud Agency.

The Oglalas had moved twenty-five miles away from the agency
headquarters and, on the morning of October 24, cavalrymen rounded
up about 500 of these Indians, together with 700 ponies, and seized
50 rifles. The camps were then herded back to the agency where Red
Cloud, Red Leaf, and other warriors were put in the "calaboose." On
the next day the Indians were assembled and the general "gave them
the first plain talking to they had ever received." Red Cloud was
notified that he was no longer considered a chief, and the friendly
Spotted Tail was presented with an ornate certificate of his appoint-
ment to the position of head chief. This done, Crook wired Sheridan
that, "I feel that this is the first gleam of daylight we have had in this
business."

With his rear under control at last, Crook proceeded to Fort Laramie
where he put the final touches to the organization of the third column
—the "Powder River Expedition"—which was scheduled to leave Fort
Fetterman shortly. As the troops with the Big Horn and Yellowstone
Expedition were badly used up, replacements were necessary. This
time the column was built around Colonel Ranald S. Mackenzie and
six companies of the 4th Cavalry which had been brought up from Indian Territory, where this brilliant but sometimes irascible officer had
quelled the Kiowas and Comanches. Added to this regiment were four
companies from the 3rd and 5th Cavalry, making a total of 28 officers
and 790 men. Colonel R. I. Dodge was in command of 33 officers and
646 men who made up the infantry and artillery companies. Tom
Moore and 65 packers were on hand with 400 of their long-eared
charges; and the supplies were loaded in a train of 168 wagons.

In addition to ordering Mackenzie to join the column, Sheridan
sent Frank North, then post guide and interpreter at Sidney Barracks,
to enlist a company of 100 Pawnee scouts—North and his Pawnees
having acquired something of a reputation in the business of fighting

Indians. With no agents to balk him this time, Crook enlisted some 150 Sioux, Arapahoes, and Cheyennes whom he mounted on ponies confiscated at the Red Cloud Agency. Three days after the column started, over 100 Shoshones and Bannocks under old Washakie's sons and led by Cosgrove and Eckles, joined. These 360 warriors represented an explosive mixture with tribal hatreds of long standing but fortunately no match ever touched the powder keg. The nearest thing to a squabble occurred when Lieutenant William Philo Clark, an ambitious officer of the 2nd Cavalry who was without a command, tried to organize all the scouts into a group under his control. North would have none of Clark's little *empire* as his orders from Sheridan stated clearly, "You are to be captain of the company. . . ." There were four interpreters, one of them being Bill Rowland, a Cheyenne squaw-man who spent the remainder of his life among the Cheyennes in Montana; and Frank Grouard and "Big Bat" also went with the column.

This was the force which picked its way through the floating ice on the Platte on the 14th of November and moved northward from Fort Fetterman on the "old familiar road to Reno . . . [which] stretched out in a long snaky line . . . over the low bluffs." On the fourth day out, the men reached Cantonment Reno which had been set up as a supply depot—along with Deadwood and the Tongue River Cantonment—for expeditions in the field during the winter. Here the command stopped and camped: and at evening Crook dispatched a small party of Arapahoes and Sioux to scout along the base of the Big Horn Mountains.

The Indian scouts returned on the third day. On Clear Creek, 50 miles to the north, they had captured a young Cheyenne who had talked freely about the whereabouts of the various villages before he realized that he was in unfriendly hands. That night Crook dispatched a courier to Fort Fetterman with a telegram for Sheridan:

Scouts returned today and reported that Cheyennes have crossed over to the other side of the Big Horn Mountains and that Crazy Horse and his band are encamped on the Rosebud near where we had the fight with him last summer. We start out after his band tomorrow morning.

As the messenger left on his ninety-mile ride, snow was falling and the landscape was blanketed with white. Bourke wrote in his journal, "This was exactly what we wanted to enable such a large command to creep up upon the enemy undetected."

Moving northward along the Bozeman Trail some twenty miles to Crazy Woman Creek, Crook prepared to leave his wagons and use his pack train. However, before the column got under way again a friendly Cheyenne came into camp under a white flag. He brought the information that the little camp to which their captive belonged had become alarmed and fled to warn Crazy Horse of the presence of the troops. Confronted with this unpleasant news, Crook sent a small party of scouts up Crazy Woman Creek to hunt for the Cheyenne village. That afternoon the remainder of the Indian scouts, all of the cavalry except one company, and the pack train started to follow the trail of the scouts.

Early the next day, the scouts returned saying that they had found the main camp of the Cheyennes. They had no idea how many lodges there were but insisted that there were "heap ponies." Mackenzie moved the command to the cover of a projecting spur of the mountains—now called "the Horn"—and waited. At nightfall, with the North Star for a compass and the aid of a few Indian guides, the troops began their march. For a while the light from the moon lit up the country through which they passed, and when it set "only the feeble but grateful glimmer of the stars illuminated the trail, winding in among the recesses of the mountains." As they neared the camp, a maze of little ravines and cut banks in the *trough* along which they were advancing made progress "slow, painfully slow": and Mackenzie's natural impatience was aggravated by the guides who kept coming back every few minutes to urge the column on.

Throughout the night Lieutenant Bourke had ridden near Mackenzie. As the troops approached the village in the twilight between darkness and the dim light of dawn—chilly from the cold of the preceding hours, the aide sensed both the tenseness of a man just before battle and the weight of responsibility resting on the shoulders of the commanding officer. Behind lay three inconclusive engagements and a heart-breaking march. Now, on this wintry morning of November 25th, in a little valley of the Red Fork of the Powder, opportunity beckoned again. Bourke wrote:

We soon heard in a vague but awe-inspiring sort of indistinctness the thump! thump! thump! of war drums, and the jingling of their rattles sounding the measure of a war dance. Only a distance of a mile intervened, but the light had broken in the East. The hostile drums ceased beating, a sign the Cheyenne village had finished its dance and retired to rest. Now or never!

Sharp Nose, the Arapahoe chief, came running up to General Mackenzie and asked if the whites were ready. The response was in the affirmative; then it seemed as if I could hear a sigh of relief from suspense go up from that dense throng of soldiery, as the command "gallop" was "given," and with the thundering roar of a waterfall, the column dashed through the embrochure of the canon into a cylindrical space where the village was situated [and] burst like a tornado upon the unsuspecting village. . . .

The menacing rumble produced by the hooves of a thousand galloping horses beating on the frozen ground and the sudden, shrill whinneying of their own ponies soon startled the Cheyennes from their warm beds. A few sharp yells of alarm and the entire camp was boiling with motion. Boys ran to save the pony herds, squaws grabbed up their babies and herded their young children toward the far end of the village while the warriors, with such arms as they had picked up as they left their couches, began a rear-guard action.

In the van, riding with the Pawnees on the right of the line, Frank North and his brother Luther suddenly saw a Cheyenne youth near the willows along the little stream. Firing with lightening speed, their rifles made but a single report, and, following close behind, Bourke's horse

balked at a prostrate object—it was the dead body of an almost naked Cheyenne youth, shot as he was running out to save their herds. Around his neck was wound his "lariat," ready to be used to catch the first pony he expected to come to.

Thus fell the first of the three sons that Dull Knife, the head chief, was to lose in this battle.

From his position near the center of the line, Lieutenant Clark witnessed a bold, precisely executed rescue of a Sioux chief:

Three Bears . . . rode a horse which became crazed by excitement and unmanageable, and being wonderfully fleet, dashed with him, ahead of all others, into the very center of the hostile camp, where bullets were flying thick and fast, and where the hostiles were making a sharp resistance to protect their families. Feather-on-the-head, another scout, seeing the trouble his friend was in, urged his own fast pony forward with vigorous strokes of the whip, at the same time throwing himself from side to side on his pony to avoid the shots of his enemies. Thus he followed Three Bears through the bushes and across the stream, down among the tepees, and into the very center of the village, where Three Bear's horse had fallen dead, shot through the neck. His rider scarcely touched the ground when Feather-on-the-head, sweeping past, took him behind himself and bore him safely away. . . .

This first dash cleared all of the village except the western end which the enemy stubbornly defended, and the scouts now rounded up a large part of the pony herds. During the brief lull which ensued, the soldiers appraised the situation which faced them:

*The village nestled closely to the thread of the stream, which at this point flowed nearly east and west, its banks thickly fringed with willow and cottonwood. Through these, the smoke curled upward from the tipis, arranged in an elliptical form, covering a space whose transverse axis was not short of a mile.*

The valley was a sort of cul-de-sac a mile and a half or two miles long. Its upper end terminated in two, very narrow canyons and the lower end was closed in a like manner by a narrow gorge. A towering wall of red sandstone, near which the stream flowed, sealed off the southern side of the valley—it was at the eastern end of this barrier that Mackenzie's men began their charge. Paralleling the stream on the north was an open area, a half mile or more in width, which was a mixture of gentle slopes, rocky knolls, and nasty gullies cut in the blood-red soil. And to the north of this a steep, rocky mountain slope, seamed with small ravines, blocked further movement in that direction. It was among these knolls and ravines in the northwestern part of the valley that the Cheyennes, unable to retreat farther, fought so determinedly that Mackenzie made no attempt to dislodge them.

Using the western end of the village as a starting place, the Cheyennes tried to get into position to recapture their ponies but the Shoshones succeeded in scaling the red wall and from this vantage point put an end to all offensive movements. The battle now settled down to a long range sniping duel. One of the early casualties was Lieutenant John A. McKinney. Mackenzie ordered his company to break up a group of Indians who were gathering to the north of the central part of the camp. In the charge, the soldiers came suddenly upon a *hidden* gully and, as the lieutenant wheeled his troopers away, Indians who had been hidden there rose up and blasted him from his horse.

In the afternoon, North and his Pawnees braved the bullets of the snipers and occupied the village. With great glee the Pawnees and some of the Shoshones pounced upon the abandoned war drums and "for hours kept up an uninterrupted charaviri, deriding the misfortunes of their enemy and exalting their own prowess." Fires were now started and dense columns of smoke rolled up as the stores of dried buffalo meat caught fire, and supplies of ammunition, fixed and loose, exploded with "loud reverberations" as the flames spread from tepee to tepee. Fine robes and clothing, together with unusual objects, were appropriated by the scouts. "Nor was the number of guns taken inconsiderable. We captured many, some of extra fine makes and finish."

The soldiers searched particularly for articles taken from Custer's men. Bourke compiled a long list of the findings—horses branded US, pocketbooks with money, sergeants' rosters, clothing—including a buckskin jacket believed to have belonged to Tom Custer, letters— some stamped and ready to mail, watches, photographs, and much gear used by the cavalrymen. He also noted: "The scalps of two young girls, neither over twelve years old, one an American, the other a Sho- shonie; Buckskin bag containing the right hands of twelve Shoshonie babies." Big Bat found High Wolf's medicine necklace—a beaded band with pendants consisting of eight Indian fingers—which he gave to Bourke, an object which eventually landed in a case in the U. S. Na- tional Museum.

During a lull in the sniping, Bill Rowland worked up close enough to talk to the hostiles. From Dull Knife he learned that—although he was ready to surrender—his people would not give up. The chief, con- firming the merit of Crook's policy of fighting Indians with Indians cried out bitterly to the Sioux and Cheyenne scouts, "Go home. You have no business here. We can whip the white soldiers alone, but we cannot fight you too."

The next morning, scouts located the hostiles in a rocky canyon several miles away. For them it had been a grim night in the winter cold—without shelter or even adequate clothing, nothing to eat but their ponies, and with the bitterness of defeat. Eleven babies had frozen to death in their mothers' arms, and three more died the next night. While the scouts were locating the Cheyennes, soldiers went over the campground and completed their work of destruction. Everything that would burn was burned, axes were thrown in the fire to draw the tem- per, kettles were mashed and broken, and even tin cups were chopped in two. Leaving the little valley strewn with wreckage, the troops left at noon to return to the balance of the column. The engagement which was to break the resistance of the Sioux had been fought and won.

Mackenzie's report, dispatched to Crook the morning after the bat- tle, contained this candid appraisal:

*The village, consisting of (173) one hundred seventy three lodges and their contents was destroyed, almost (500) five hundred ponies were taken and (25) twenty five Indians were killed where their bodies fell into our hands, but from reports which I have reason to doubt, I believe a much larger number were killed.*

*Our loss was: Killed, one officer and (5) five men; Wounded, (25) twenty five soldiers and one Shoshonie Indian Scout. (15) Fifteen Cavalry horses were killed and (4) horses belonging to Indian scouts.*

One of the wounded died while enroute to Crook's camp, and the surgeon pronounced the Indian scout, whose name was Amzi, beyond all hope. Amzi had been shot through the intestines early in the day. He came in to the field headquarters about dark and was placed in the hospital tent where the surgeon directed the officer in charge, Lieutenant Homer W. Wheeler, to give him a little stimulant. Wheeler gave the Indian some brandy and, of course, did not forget himself. After a while the Indian called, "Oh, *John*. Heap sick. Whiskey." The lieutenant complied again, and the performance was repeated several times during the night. The next morning, the Shoshone was gone and was not seen again until the second day when—unable to sit on his pony any longer—he rode up to Wheeler's hospital train. He was put on a travois and dragged, eventually, to Cantonment Reno where he made a miraculous recovery. However, he did not bear a charmed life for he was shot a year or so later while on a horse stealing expedition.

The column now turned back to Cantonment Reno where the Shoshones left for their camps—greatly worried by the buckskin bag and its twelve little hands. After being delayed a few days by severe storms, Crook moved eastward to the headwaters of the Belle Fourche and then turned down this stream to the vicinity of the Black Hills. It was bitter cold, traveling was difficult, and sufficient forage could not reach the column to keep the animals in condition. On the 20th of December, a dispatch from Sheridan reached Crook with the information that his transportation bill was $60,000 per month whereas his allowance was $28,000. "Those few words," his adjutant noted, "mean that this campaign must terminate speedily." There was nothing to do but retrace their steps to Cantonment Reno, and thence back to Fort Fetterman, which post they reached nine days later.

When the expedition was being made up, Major Randall was sent north to enlist a detachment of Crows. As the expedition was withdrawing, Bourke met the major and 76 Absaroka at the cantonment and got their story. Randall had enlisted the Indians in the Judith Basin from which place they had gone to Fort Ellis and crossed over to the Great Bend. Then they followed down the Yellowstone to Clark Fork where they turned south and went to the headwaters of the Stinking Water (now the Shoshone). This stream they followed to the Big Horn River and then continued east over the mountains to the headwaters of the Tongue, and thence south on the Bozeman Trail to the cantonment. This thirty-one day trip "had been severe beyond all example. For (9) days they had to subsist on raw buffalo entrails. Crossing the Big Horn Mountains, they encountered five (5) feet depth of snow on the level."

They had found the trail of Dull Knife's Cheyennes at the mouth of Prairie Dog Creek, and followed it nine or ten miles toward the Rosebud. From *sign* the Absaroka estimated the pony herd at not over 500, and they brought in nineteen of the best of those which they found abandoned. At a campsite which they examined, they counted a hundred campfires: there were no lodges—only little couches of grass and willows on which to sleep.

The Cheyennes found Crazy Horse camped in the valley of the Tongue near the mouth of Otter Creek. Just how hospitable the Oglalas were to their starving comrades is not clear. Years later some of the Cheyennes maintained that the Sioux did their best to supply their wants. However, Bourke, who saw these people surrender the following spring, noted that they "were in a miserable plight and told a sad story of want and destitution." More eloquent than their words, was the desire of many to enlist and go fight their former allies.

While Crook was keeping a lookout on the southern edge of the Yellowstone Basin near the Black Hills—and Bourke was worrying, needlessly, that the Sioux had probably scattered "like a flock of frightened partridges"—Crazy Horse's village was in the sheltered valley of the Tongue near the present Montana-Wyoming line. The troops at the Tongue River Cantonment became aware of this fact one night late in December when warriors dashed into the beef herd, ran off about twenty-five head, and headed up the valley of the Tongue. Miles quickly organized a force of 436 men and set out in pursuit.

The troops left the cantonment on the 29th of December, the day Crook's column returned to Fort Fetterman. Plagued by numerous stream crossings—one hundred before they returned—and weather which alternated between thawing and freezing, the force made its way laboriously up the Tongue. Early in the morning of the sixth day out, a small party of hostiles struck suddenly and killed a soldier. Large Indian trails were seen in the vicinity of Otter Creek, and near the mouth of Hanging Woman the command passed a large campsite which had been used recently.

Early in the morning of January 7th, the scouts brought in eight women and children whom they had captured in the valley of the Tongue a couple of miles in advance of the column. According to the Cheyennes, these people had been visiting a village near the head of the Belle Fourche River and were returning to one of the campsites already passed by the troops. Big Horse, a man who was with the party, was doing a bit of reconnoitering and escaped. Fleeing up the valley, he found Crazy Horse's village and gave the alarm. A party of over 100 warriors rode down the valley at once to attempt a rescue. When but a short distance from the troops, they met the scouts whom Miles had sent back to hunt for the camp. These they pinned down in some brush and had in a tight spot until the soldiers came up and rescued them. Miles now went into camp and the Indians retired.

This campsite was on a flat bottomland along the river a few miles south of the mouth of Hanging Woman. Immediately north of the camp was a cutbank *bluff* topped by a small conical *hill*, and from this point the valley widened out to the width of a mile or more—bordered with the badlands hills and sparsely timbered breaks typical of this valley. Miles prepared to move out early the next morning but the Sioux and Cheyennes came down in force from their camp a few miles above. The colonel posted his troops on the cutbank just above his wagon train and moved his two pieces of artillery to this commanding elevation: and, as soon as the Indians discovered the cannon, they spread out and occupied the bluffs and hills which edged the valley.

Miles dignified the sniping which followed by calling it the Battle of Wolf Mountain, and he and others wrote highly colored and somewhat inaccurate accounts of what happened. The most interesting incident took place on a high, flat-topped hill which commanded the eastern edge of the valley. In his memoirs, the general stated:

. . . the key of the position was a high bluff to the left of the line of troops. . . . The Indians who held it were led by Big Crow a "medicine man" who had worked himself up to such a frenzy that he had made the Indians believe that his medicine was so strong that the white men could not harm him. He rushed out in front of the warriors, attired in the most gorgeous Indian battle costume . . . , jumped up and down, ran in a circle and whooped and yelled. . . . In the midst of his daring acts of bravado, Big Crow fell . . . and his loss, together with the success of the charge that had been made and the important ground gained, seemed to cause a panic among the Indians, and they immediately fled in utter rout up the valley. . . .

From such material *folklore* is created.

It was true that this butte was a key position. However, there were two parts to the top and it did not require any particular amount of daring to take the small detached ridge which the soldiers occupied. Big Crow and seven companions were on the larger portion of this hill. According to one Cheyenne, these Indians were in a depression and

Big Crow, who was not a medicine man but a noted warrior, decided to make a series of bravery runs—four being the required number. Moving *chick-chack*—in a zigzag manner—this Cheyenne circled the unprotected edge of the hill which faced the little ridge held by the soldiers some 200 yards away. After the second run, his friends asked him not to expose himself so recklessly, and on the third run he was knocked down by a bullet which inflicted a mortal wound. Two of his comrades, running in the same manner, now dashed out with a buffalo robe, placed the stricken warrior on it, and—on the second trip—dragged him to shelter. Such was the action in which Big Crow was killed. As for the reason why the fight was broken off, trumpeter Brown wrote in his diary:

The firing ceased at 12 o'clock M: for it began to snow [so hard] that it was impossible for either of the parties to continue the combat. We went back to the camp for the night.

So much for the veracity of one successful Indian fighter.

Miles lost one man killed and seven or eight seriously wounded, one of whom died later. Lieutenant Baldwin noted in his diary that the Indian loss "must have been considerable"; trumpeter Brown wrote, "The loss of the Indians was estimated at 15 killed and 25 wounded." However, the action had served its purpose as far as the Indians were concerned—Crazy Horse had stalled the movement of Miles' column until his camp had been able to move. When the soldiers moved up the valley the next morning they found their quarry was gone.

For the next eight days trumpeter Brown's diary notes briefly the hardships of an infantryman: "One foot of snow on the ground on the level. . . ."—"Weather cold, many frozen hands and feet"—"Thermometer at 40° below zero. One of the wounded men . . . died. . . ." —"Marched to our fifth camp and dug up the body of Belty and carried him home with us. A very heavy storm blew up just as we got into camp." On the 18th of January he wrote:

Moved out for the Cantonment, which was about eight miles from us on the Yellowstone: the men highly elated at the prospects of glowing fires in nice snug and warm quarters, shelters from the bleak mountain winds, well cooked meals and a good wash. The advance struck out at daylight, but owing to the worn condition of the teams we were delayed. It was two o'clock before we reached the post. . . . The main difficulties on this march will be perceived by the foregoing. In the deep snow, and after a thaw, the rotten condition of the ice on the river allowing our teams to break through. Melting of snow in the mens shoes causing wet feet was the cause of many frozen feet, when the march was delayed and the water froze in the shoes.

### THE END OF THE STRUGGLE

The persistent pressure exerted by armed columns moving through the choice hunting grounds and into the secluded valleys used for winter campgrounds had at last given the victories of the preceding June a hollow ring. Fear and discontent followed the destruction of Dull Knife's village, and Miles' vigorous campaigning had further emphasized to the hostiles that the days were gone when they could thumb their noses at the soldiers with impunity. Defeat had come and the only thing which remained to be done was to surrender.

Both Crook and Miles now set about to capitalize on the effects of their winter work. Already there was a steady trickle of starved and discontented hostiles coming to the Red Cloud Agency and these totalled 386 by the end of March, 1877. The handful of women and children captured just before the *Battle* of Wolf Mountain contained the wives of some prominent Indians. Miles treated them kindly and induced two of the women, one of whom was Sweet Woman, to accompany the Sioux half-breed, Johnny "Big Leggins" Bruguier, to the hostile camp where they were to try to get a delegation to come in and discuss a surrender.

This little party left the Cantonment on the 1st of February and a small escort went with them as far as the battlefield on the upper Tongue. From this point the three emissaries and their pack mule followed the trail of the Indians westward, finally finding the village on a small tributary of the Little Big Horn not far from the present town of Lodge Grass. According to the Cheyenne account, the party slipped quietly into the village and Bruguier quickly took refuge in the sanctuary of the Sacred Hat Lodge. Here he remained until Sweet Woman had an opportunity to explain their mission. The sugar, coffee, bacon, tobacco, and other presents packed on the mule, together with the story of kind treatment told by the women, created a favorable impression and the nervy Bruguier succeeded in convincing a number of the Cheyennes that they would be treated fairly if they surrendered to Miles.

On the 19th of February, Big Leggins was back at the Cantonment with nineteen chiefs and prominent warriors. Among these were Two Moon, Little Chief, Hump—a Sioux, and the famous medicine man, White Bull or Ice. Miles had no difficulty in persuading these to surrender and, leaving nine of their number as hostages, they returned to their camp. On the 22nd of April, some three hundred hostiles, mostly Cheyennes with a few Sioux, came in and gave up their horses and arms.

Working independently of Miles, Crook arranged with Spotted Tail to lead a delegation to the hostile Sioux. This amiable chief left the agency near Fort Robinson on the 13th of February with a party of 200 warriors. With them went two squaw men, "Old Joe" Mericate (or Merricato) and F. C. Boucher, who were capable of writing messages. Although "Old Spot" had been overly optimistic about the amount of time necessary to accomplish the desired end, he returned with part of the Cheyennes near the end of the first week in April. The remainder, being unable to travel as rapidly due to the condition of their ponies, arrived two weeks later.

Crook now threatened to take troops to the field and the Oglalas became concerned about their relatives. Red Cloud, no doubt anxious to curry favor with the general, requested permission to go out and hurry Crazy Horse's village. Crook gave his consent but refused to give the chief any "official" status. Crazy Horse and his people finally arrived on the 6th of May. Lieutenant William Philo Clark, a keen student of Indian ways and a good sign talker, was delegated to accept the surrender. Bourke, who went along to watch the proceedings, left this description of the noted warrior:

*"Crazy Horse" behaved with stolidity, like a man who saw he had to give in to fate, but would do so as doggedly as possible. I went over to see him, going in company with Frank Grouard who had been "Crazy Horse's" captive for (3) three or (4) four years. Frank is the only one "Crazy Horse" seems at all glad to see; to the rest he is sullen and gloomy.*

*His face is quiet, rather morose, dogged, tenacious, and resolute. His expression is rather melancholic. When we approached, a couple of squaws were busy making coffee and preparing supper. "Crazy Horse" remained seated on the ground, but when Frank called his name, "I a ashimco nit co," he looked up and gave me a hearty grasp of the hand. He looks quite young, not over (30) thirty years old, is lithe and sinewy and has a wound in his face. (scar) The other Indians give him a high reputation for courage and generosity; say he never allows one of his warriors to hide ahead of him when advancing toward the enemy. . . . He is always taciturn and rarely jokes or smiles.*

Although the Sioux war dragged on until the summer of 1881—due to the fact that Sitting Bull and a large number of his people retreated north of the Canadian line—Crazy Horse's surrender marked the close of the major part of the trouble with the Sioux. General Sheridan, in his annual report for 1876-1877, tabulated the number of hostiles who had surrendered up to that time:

On the 25th of . . . [February] 229 lodges of Minneconjous and Sans Arcs came in and surrendered to the troops at Cheyenne Agency, Dak. . . . . From the 1st of March to the 21st of the same month over 2,200 Indians, in detachments of 30 to 900, came in and surrendered at Camps Sheridan and Robinson, in the Department of the Platte, and on the 22nd of April, 303 Cheyennes came in and surrendered to Colonel Miles at the cantonment on the Tongue River in the Department of Dakota, and more are reported on the way to give themselves up. Finally on the 6th of May, Crazy Horse with 889 of his people and 2,000 ponies, came into Camp Robinson and surrendered to General Crook in person.

Cheyennes were enlisted as scouts at both Fort Robinson and the Tongue River Cantonment. In February, before the Cheyennes had actually surrendered, Miles enlisted the medicine man White Bull—one of the nine hostages—and put a uniform on him before his companions had left the post to return for their people. Bourke recalled an interview with Turkey Legs who had come in to Fort Robinson with the first contingent of Dull Knife's people. This chief, who was partly paralyzed, was immensely proud of his warriors.

"These" he said, waving his trembling hands around the semi-circle of grim-faced warriors who stood by him, "these are the Cheyennes. You who have fought us (pointing to General Crook and General Mackenzie) know what we are. We claim for our people that they are the best fighters on the plains."

Turkey Legs was proud with just reason for the Northern Cheyennes not only made excellent scouts but they had other admirable qualities as well. Finerty, who returned to Montana two years later to accompany Miles on an expedition against Sitting Bull, became well acquainted with some of them. He noted:

The Cheyennes are proud as Lucifer, and rarely beg. They fight like lions, and are, taken altogether, Indians of the dime novel type. Some of them are amazingly intelligent, and . . . are of gentlemanly deportment.

As Bourke watched the Sioux and Cheyennes surrender at Fort Robinson and nearby Camp Sheridan, he apparently had a feeling of satisfaction at seeing the war terminated successfully. However, as he recalled what had happened in previous years, he was deeply concerned about the future. On one occasion he wrote:

*If our government will only observe a half of its promises, the Indians will comply faithfully with their agreements, I am certain; the great danger of the future is not from the red man's want of faith, so much as from the indifference of our Government to the plainest requirements of honor.*

Bourke's foresight was all too accurate. The moving of Dull Knife's people to Indian Territory set the stage for the epic struggle of these people to return to that part of the Yellowstone Basin which they regarded as home. And broken promises with the Sioux were the fundamental cause for the tragedy which was called the Ghost Dance War. Indian agents looked upon their positions as opportunities to feather their own nests—and those of their relatives—and their conniving was hated by the Indians. Spotted Tail recognized this basic evil and, at a council with Crook on April 14, 1877, made this penetrating observation:

*Now, we have a new Great Father. I want you to tell him when he sends a new agent to send one with plenty of money to take good care of my people.*

# 17

## Policing the Yellowstone

>>>>>>>>>«««««««« Although the surrender of the bulk of the hostiles at the various agencies, and Sitting Bull's retreat to Canada, brought a measure of peace and security, life on the plains of Montana continued to have its dangers. These troubles did not end until Sitting Bull's surrender in 1881, and then they were followed by threats, some real and some imagined, from the Indians on the reservations. Thus in the spring of 1877, the soldiers at the new posts in the Yellowstone valley assumed police duties which were to last for about a decade and a half.

When the Cheyennes and Oglalas went in to surrender, a band of Minneconjou Sioux decided to go buffalo hunting in the Rosebud country. Lame Deer—or perhaps more properly, Lame Antelope—was the principal chief, and with him were a few lodges of Cheyennes under White Hawk. Very soon these became the object of Miles' attention, and he set out with four troops of cavalry and six companies of infantry to capture them.

Before daybreak on the 7th of May, this force was hidden in a small valley near the mouth of Lame Deer Creek—then called Muddy Creek by the Indians. With Miles were Hump, a Sioux chief, and two Cheyennes, White Bull and Brave Wolf. The two Cheyennes and Johnny Bruguier had discovered the Indian camp along Muddy Creek a mile or more south of the present town of Lame Deer, and the attack was launched at daylight. Part of the cavalry swept past the village and rounded up the horse herd and the remainder took the camp, while the Indians fled hurriedly to the pine covered hills and bluffs just to the west.

Hump and White Bull recognized Lame Deer and called out for him to surrender saying that he would not be harmed. Miles then rode up and held out his hand saying, "how-how-kola"—kola being the Sioux word for friend. The chief, apparently suspicious of a trap, laid his rifle down—cocking it and covering the breech with his foot as he did so. Then he grasped Miles' extended hand. Behind Lame Deer was his nephew, Big Ankle, who was in an ugly mood. This young man walked back and forth, muttering that he was a soldier—that no one should cross the place where he stood—that his grandmother had been killed —and that he loved her.

White Bull, sensing trouble in the making, warned the colonel by "pointing with his mouth" to the cocked weapon. Then he rode up to the belligerent warrior and attempted to take his rifle from him. In the ensuing scuffle, the piece was discharged. Immediately, Lame Deer jerked his hand free, snatched up his rifle, and took a snap shot at Miles which killed an orderly who was just behind the colonel. In the short, deadly skirmish which followed, Lame Deer and three of his warriors were killed and any hope for surrender vanished. Four soldiers were killed and seven were wounded. The Indian loss was placed at seventeen dead. Four hundred and fifty horses were captured and fifty-one lodges "richly stored with robes, horse-equipments, and every other species of Indian property" were burned.

An amusing thing happened among the Cheyennes. Early that morning White Hawk came to visit Tall White Man. As the latter came out of his lodge, he saw the troopers advancing and, calling out that the soldiers were coming, he ran for the hills and "kept on running." Three warriors came along and helped his three wives to escape. After the fight was over these men told Tall White Man, "We are going to keep your wives. You were supposed to protect them. You ran away." So Beater Woman (or Taste Strong) became the wife of White Moon, Morning Holler went to the lodge of Sun Bear, and Crawling took Little Woman. Years later, the husband got Beater Woman back, but the other two remained with their new husbands until they died.

A few weeks after this fight, Miles' forces were augmented by eleven troops of the 7th Cavalry and six companies of infantry. With four companies of the 5th Infantry mounted on captured ponies, the colonel was now ready to chase any hostiles who came near. Lame Deer's people went eastward to the upper part of the Little Missouri country and about the middle of June a force under Major Lazelle was ordered to pursue them. Two weeks later another body of troops was dispatched to assist Lazelle. Although these soldiers were not able to bring the Sioux to bay, they ran them back into the valley of the Powder and harassed them to such an extent that late in the summer they went in to the agencies and surrendered. While these troopers were chasing the Minneconjoux, a large force of scouts patrolled the north side of the Yellowstone but Sitting Bull's Sioux made no attempt to return to the valley in force. Another task which was performed was to bury the dead on the Custer Battlefield. Troop I of the 7th Cavalry under Captain Henry J. Nowlan was detailed for this duty. The bodies of seven officers were exhumed for burial elsewhere: and there was some difficulty in identifying Custer's remains. Leforge, who sat on the ground "not more than ten feet distant," noted that "they gathered up nothing substantial except one thigh bone and the skull attached to some part of the skeleton trunk."

Between the 24th of August and the 15th of September, the upper part of the Yellowstone valley was the stage for the part of the most tragic of all the Indian wars. White settlers in western Idaho, by flagrant and protracted aggression, goaded some of the Nez Percé into hostile action. These were honest, peaceable Indians, unskilled in the ways of war, yet under Chief Joseph and his three able lieutenants they made a noteworthy march. Leaving the reservation near Lewistown, they went up the middle fork of the Clearwater, across the rugged Bitterroot Mountains, then southward and eastward across the Yellowstone National Park, and from thence northward to the Bear Paw Mountains just south of the Canadian line. Here they were surprised and forced to surrender. This movement of approximately 2,000 miles—encumbered by their families, baggage, and all their horses—is regarded as one of the greatest retreats in history.

When these Indians entered the Yellowstone Park, they had already twice-whipped General Howard's troops in pitched battles and had stolen his pack mules in a night raid. In the Battle of the Big Hole, after Colonel Gibbon's men had driven them out of their camp in a surprise dawn attack, they re-took their camp and then pinned the troops down in a patch of timber on the mountainside where the soldiers had to fight desperately to keep from being wiped out. It was a strange war. Soldiers recalled later that Joseph had the uncanny ability of being able to use terrain to his advantage and his warriors fought more like white soldiers than Indians. Many of them were excellent marksmen. And the most unusual feature of the struggle was that, for the most part, they did not molest civilians.

During their first day in the Park, they came upon nine tourists—the "Raidersburg party"—among whom was a married woman and her twelve-year-old sister. Joseph's scouts rode into their camp one morning and were not unfriendly until Mr. Cowan, the husband of the woman, "premptorily" ordered them out of camp. This irritated them and they took the whites back to the main party. About noon Joseph directed that they be given some wornout plugs and turned loose. Then, instead of riding quietly away, two men ducked into the brush and the Indians—now suspicious—opened fire.

Cowan, wounded in one thigh, slid off his horse beside a fallen pine, and his wife and her sister immediately dismounted beside him. One warrior grasped Mrs. Cowan to pull her away:

*Looking back over my shoulder, I saw an Indian with an immense navy pistol trying to get a shot at my husband's head. Wrenching my arm from his grasp, I leaned over my husband, only to be roughly drawn aside. Another Indian stepped up, a pistol shot rang out, my husband's head fell back, and a red stream trickled down his face from beneath his hat. The warm sunshine, the smell of blood, the horror of it all, a faint remembrance of seeing rocks thrown at his head, my sister's screams, and all was blank.*

While this was taking place, Mrs. Cowan's brother was captured. Then the Indians, with their three captives, resumed the march. The next day, after crossing the Yellowstone between the lake and the upper falls, the Nez Percé held a council and decided to release a deserter, whom they had just captured, and the two female captives. However, Mrs. Cowan refused to trust the deserter and insisted that they release her brother in his stead. To this they agreed. A warrior took them back across the river and started them downstream toward Bozeman with the admonition to ride "All Night, All Day, No Sleep." In the afternoon of the second day they met a detail of soldiers who were hunting for signs of the Nez Percé and, eventually, the three reached Bozeman safely.

General Sherman and a party were touring the Park but they escaped meeting the hostiles. Less fortunate was a party of nine tourists and a negro cook who were camped not far from where the Indians crossed the Yellowstone. Warriors killed one and wounded another in an attack on the camp. Later, a small band of unruly braves on a foray killed one of the survivors at a hotel near Mammoth Hot Springs where they had imagined themselves safe.

Fortunately the revolver with which Cowan was shot was either improperly loaded or the powder was damp for the bullet merely flattened itself against his skull. He regained consciousness and was seen by another Indian who shot him in the hip and left him for dead a second time. Again, he regained his senses and this time was found by General Howard's scouts who were trailing the Nez Percé. They left him beside a campfire which spread and burned him severely. At last the troops arrived, carried him to the Yellowstone, and then sent him down the valley to an overjoyed wife.

When Joseph swung eastward and headed for the Yellowstone Park, General Howard—whose troops were doggedly following the trail— surmised that the Nez Percé were heading for the plains east of the Absaroka Mountains. Realizing that he could not bring them to bay, he sent a telegram from Virginia City to the War Department asking that troops be sent to make an interception. At this time the re-formed 7th Cavalry under Colonel Sturgis was in a camp a few miles above the Tongue River Cantonment, and Sheridan ordered part of this regiment into the field.

Sturgis took six troops, about 360 men, and moved into a position where he could watch the headwaters of both Clark Fork and Stinkingwater (Shoshone) Rivers. As Joseph headed eastward from the Yellowstone River, he followed an old hunting trail to the northeastern corner of the Park. At this point his scouts spotted Sturgis and the astute chief proceeded to make a fool of the colonel. A small decoy party— making a big dust by dragging pieces of brush at the ends of their lariats—headed toward the Stinkingwater: and Sturgis rose to the bait like a hungry trout striking at a fat grasshopper. The main body now doubled sharply on their trail and reached Clark Fork by way of a very rocky, narrow canyon that had "such precipitous walls on either side that it was like going through a gigantic rough railroad tunnel." Now the Nez Percé had no one between them and the Canadian border.

"Captain" S. G. Fisher, an intelligent frontiersman who was chief of Howard's Bannock scouts, wrote an account of this maneuver in his diary:

*After leaving the summit the enemy followed the trail toward the Stinkingwater about two miles, and then attempted to elude pursuit by concealing their trail. To do this, the hostiles "milled," drove their ponies around in every direction, when, instead of going out of the basin* in the direction they had been traveling and across an open plain, they turned short of [sic] it to the north, passing along the steep side of the mountain through the timber for several miles.

Sturgis caught up with Howard a day later, very much irritated at having been drawn out of position. Now there was nothing to do but try to run the Indians down. Taking fifty men and a couple of howitzers from Howard's command, Sturgis made a forced march of some fifty or sixty miles the next day. By noon of the following day, September 13th, his men had crossed the Yellowstone a short distance above the mouth of Clark Fork, and were in contact with the rear guard of the Nez Percé. The hostiles were about to work their way up Canyon Creek to the prairie which stretched northward toward the Musselshell River.

In this locality, the northern side of the immediate valley of the Yellowstone is bordered by rough, rocky breaks; and the line of separation between these breaks and the prairie just beyond is a ledge of cap rock —the *roche jaune* of the Yellowstone valley. The upper reaches of Canyon Creek make a break in this rock barrier through which it is possible to gain access to the prairie, and the Indians were headed toward this gap when the 7th Cavalry caught up with them. Canyon Creek itself is a dry wash some fifteen or sixteen miles in length. Throughout the first third of its extent, it fingers into the rough breaks, then it passes through a little valley bordered by rolling hills, and finally crosses a gently sloping terrace or "bench" some five miles in width which parallels the north bank of the Yellowstone.

As the troops came up, a few warriors had just attacked a stage station at the mouth of the creek and fired some hay stacks, the smoke of which could be seen in the distance by the troops. Fisher's diary contains this description of the action which followed:

The soldiers drove . . . [the *Nez Percé*] slowly across the flat, or rather what was a gradual descent cut by small ravines and dry "washes." The Indians fought entirely on horse-back, firing mostly from their animals at long range, doing but little harm. From this point, we got a good view of the camp and their herd, which was scattered along the other side of the creek for a mile or more. Canon Creek is a narrow "wash," with banks from ten to twenty feet high. . . . I saw but one cavalry charge made, consisting I think of only one company which dashed across the creek. The charge was not followed up, the soldiers falling back across the creek again. During this time the enemy's herd passed slowly across our front in the direction of the canon, evidently being driven by the squaws and children, the warriors keeping between us and the horses and holding us in check. As soon as their herd had entered the canon the Indians got in among the rocks and cottonwood timber that skirted the creek, dismounting and concealing their horses in the ravines and washes close by. Here the hardest fighting was done. . . .

At this point the fight developed into a sniping duel and evening came before the soldiers advanced very far. The next day the soldiers got close enough to see the Indians "by the aid of field glasses" but that was all.

The official report makes Sturgis' handling of the situation look quite rosy, and contains this statement:

The losses of the Indians in this engagement and in the pursuit on the following day, was twenty-one killed; the loss of the troops was three enlisted men killed and Captain T. H. French, 7th Cavalry, and eleven enlisted men wounded; the number of ponies lost by the Indians was altogether about nine hundred.

Early on September 14th, Sturgis resumed the pursuit, preceded by a large party of Crow scouts, who killed five more of the rear guard of the Nez Percés and captured four hundred of the entire number of ponies taken by Sturgis' command.

In a letter written many years later, Fisher made this comment about the casualties:

General Sturgis reported twenty dead warriors found on the field and trail: but he was surely mistaken. I saw only two dead on the trail and the Crows claimed that they killed one of them. I do not think a single dead Indian was found on the battlefield. . . . Several of my Indians hunted the ground over the next day and could find no dead Nez Percés to scalp. I don't say there were none killed, but if any had been their friends packed them off or cached them somewhere.

This was a polite way of saying that the official report contained more *fiction* than fact. In later years an old Nez Percé warrior remembered only two or three men being wounded on the 13th, and three killed the next day by the Crows: and he recalled the loss of but thirty or forty horses—probably worn out animals which dropped behind. The soldiers never got close enough to capture any Nez Percé ponies.

Thus Joseph's people passed over the horizon and out of the Yellowstone Basin. Sturgis turned back and joined Howard on the banks of the Yellowstone. Mackinaw boats, carrying supplies from the Gallatin valley to the new army posts, came along and the wounded were put on board and sent down to the post at the mouth of the Tongue, now called Fort Keogh. Howard also sent a message to Miles giving him the approximate direction and speed the Indians were traveling and asked him to try to stop them. The colonel received the information on the evening of the 17th and the next day was on his way with six troops of cavalry, five companies of mounted infantry, and thirty Cheyenne and Sioux scouts—about 600 men.

Miles caught up with the unsuspecting Nez Percé who had stopped near the northern edge of the Bear Paw Mountains for a much needed rest—believing that they were safely in Canada. His scouts rounded up the pony herd without any difficulty, but when the soldiers attempted to take the camp, Miles received a rude jolt. The first charge cost him *two officers and twenty-two men killed and almost double that number wounded.* Miles and his men could not stomach losses of that magnitude so they encircled the camp and sat down to wait. Five days later, on the 5th of October, Joseph surrendered 87 men, 184 women, and 147 children. Seventeen of his people had been killed and forty wounded.

Howard and a small escort arrived shortly before the surrender. According to the general's adjutant, Miles showed Howard the dispatch pertaining to the surrender—which the old *general* had graciously allowed the *colonel* to take. This apparently gave the troops from the Department of the Columbia, who had trailed the Indians throughout the entire retreat, proper credit. However, another was substituted for it which gave to Miles and his men *all* the credit for the capture. As Miles had been one of Howard's aides during the Civil War, this was a particularly ungracious act, and when the general saw the newspaper reports he was cut to the quick.

After the surrender, Miles gave each of his Indian scouts five ponies as a reward for their "gallant services," and they left at once for the post. Their arrival brought some consternation for, although they could indicate that Mrs. Miles' husband was unharmed, they could not assure the wives of the other officers that their men folks were safe. Johnny Bruguier's arrival with the dispatches three days later put an end to this uncertainty. Fortunately for the women, both of the officers killed were bachelors.

Miles held the Nez Percé in a camp near the post, expecting to return them to their reservation. Unfortunately, the same selfish forces which drove the Indians to war now objected loudly and strenuously to their return. Government officials bowed to their wishes, even though it violated the terms of the surrender agreement, and sent the captives to Indian Territory. Here about one third sickened and died.

Miles, be it said to his credit, fought to have the surrender terms honored and eight years later, when in command of the Department of the Columbia, succeeded in getting Joseph and the remainder of his people returned to the Northwest.

A special act of Congress, dated July 22, 1876, authorized the construction of two posts in the Yellowstone valley. The one at the mouth of the Tongue began its official existence on the 11th of the following September. Lieutenant Colonel George P. Buell and parts of the 11th Infantry established the other on May 10, 1877 when they occupied the high bench immediately above the junction of the Little Big Horn and the Big Horn Rivers. The third fort within the Yellowstone Basin began as Cantonment Reno. It was established on October 12, 1876 pursuant to Special Orders No. 131 issued by the Department of the Platte on September 22nd of the same year. It was three miles above the old Fort Reno of the Bozeman Trail days; and on July 17, 1877 was moved north to a location three miles west of the present town of Buffalo, Wyoming. On August 30th, the name was changed from Cantonment Reno to Fort McKinney, in honor of the officer killed at Dull Knife's village.

When steamboat navigation opened with the "June rise" in the spring of 1877, boats churned up to the Tongue River Cantonment and unloaded equipment, lumber, various supplies, and a large construction crew. With these men was Captain Heintzelman, quartermaster of the Department of Dakota, who was to supervise the construction of the two posts in Montana Territory. Although steamboats were sometimes able to go up to the mouth of the Little Big Horn, it was not feasible to deliver freight farther than the mouth of the Big Horn. Therefore, a supply dump for the Big Horn Post was established near this point on the bank of the Yellowstone. From Terry's Landing, as this place was called, an estimated 6,000,000 pounds of lumber and supplies were freighted the remaining thirty-three miles during the summer and fall of 1877. Sawmills were set up to supply the rough framing lumber, the one for the Big Horn Post being located on the Little Big Horn not far from the Custer Battlefield. The first one for Fort Keogh was located along the Tongue just above the Cantonment. This one burned and the second was established about fifteen miles up the Tongue at a place known as Pine Hills. Thus the rough lumber was obtained near each location, but all the shingles, finishing lumber, doors and windows, etc. had to be brought in by steamboat.

These posts were officially named on the 8th of November, 1877: the Tongue River Cantonment became Fort Keogh and the Big Horn Post, Fort Custer. Fort Keogh, named after Captain Myles Walter Keogh who died with Custer, was destined to become the more important of the two; and plans were made for it to be the headquarters of a "District of the Yellowstone." Its buildings were of better design and, perhaps, better construction. During the early years, almost twice as many troops were stationed here: however, when the Crow Agency was moved to its present location and the reservation for the Northern Cheyennes was established nearby, the complement of troops at each post was about equal. Keogh was also destined to outlast Custer, the latter being abandoned on April 17, 1898 while troops were stationed at the former for another ten years.

Both posts were of the same general design with officers' quarters and barracks facing a central parade ground and other buildings located nearby. At Fort Custer about 80 buildings were planned but all of these were never completed while plats for Fort Keogh indicates that about 60 buildings were contemplated at the latter post.

A windstorm in the late summer of 1879 was partly responsible for providing a place for the library of the Fifth Infantry at Fort Keogh, as well as other facilities for recreation. The son of a captain of this regiment recalled:

*One of the barracks blew down and was reconstructed in two buildings. One had a dance room and stage on the second floor. The ground floor was used for a chapel, Sunday School and court-martial room. The other building had a reading room and library on the ground floor. Major Girard, Post Surgeon and Doctor, established a place in a room at one end of the building where the soldiers could buy a sandwich and a cup of coffee.*

He also recalled that the living space for the families of officers was not extensive:

*The officers' quarters were all double buildings, and the allowance of quarters for a captain was two rooms and a kitchen. . . . a little ingenuity got an additional room on the ground floor. Of course the upper story was only an attic, but with the high mansard roof and dormer windows, four completely furnished rooms were easily obtained and a Captain got seven rooms and a kitchen.*

In the winter, winds blowing under the houses would cause rugs to billow up from the floors until a banking of horse manure put an end to the movement of air. Water was stored in barrels in the rear of the houses and these were filled by the "water wagon." In severe cold weather these would freeze solid and then would have to be taken into the kitchen and placed by the stove to thaw out. The water wagon was

replaced in the spring of 1880 when an ingenious individual overhauled the steam engine used at the sawmill which had burned, and
put it to work near the river pumping water for the post.

Married enlisted men lived in log houses which they built themselves
with the assistance of their friends. As the women usually did washings,
this part of a post was appropriately named "Suds Row."

Before the coming of the Northern Pacific Railroad (which reached
Fort Keogh in the early winter of 1881) steamboats, bull trains, and
stages provided the connecting links with the outside world. The first
steamboats came up to Fort Keogh (and adjacent Milestown) on the
"June rise" when the normal flow in the Yellowstone was augmented
by the melting snow in the mountains, and continued to ply the river
as long as there was sufficient water in the channel. Wagon trains
powered by mules or "bulls" freighted in supplies although they could
not compete with the freight rates of the steamboats in season. And
enterprising merchants in the Gallatin valley floated produce down the
Yellowstone in mackinaw boats.

Several trails connected Forts Keogh and Custer with distant points.
One road ran up the north side of the Yellowstone to Fort Ellis and
Bozeman. Another ran south from Fort Custer up the valley of the
Little Big Horn, crossing the divide to Tongue River at Pass Creek, and
then continued southward along the Bozeman Trail. Mail from the
"States" usually came in from Bismarck: this road followed the trail of
the railroad surveying parties from Fort Abraham Lincoln to the mouth
of the Powder and then continued along the south side of the Yellowstone to the Tongue. Another road connected Milestown and Deadwood. There were two ways to go to Fort Buford. One was to go north
from Fort Keogh and follow the route laid out by Culbertson and De
Smet in 1851; however the most popular way was to follow the Fort
Keogh-Bismarck road to a point just above the mouth of O'Fallon
Creek, ferry to the left bank of the Yellowstone, and then continue on
down the valley.

Fort Buford at the mouth of the Yellowstone was important as a re-
lay point for both freight and passengers as steamboats could often
reach this point even though the Yellowstone was too low to continue
farther. The son of Captain Ovenshine, an officer in the Fifth Infantry,
recalled:

*In the fall of 1878 he returned to Montana with his wife, two girls and
two boys. We took the "Josephine" at Bismarck and went up the Missouri to Fort Buford, crossed the Missouri and went into camp with the
escort that had brought Mrs. Miles and her baby from Keogh to Buford.*

That night there was a prairie fire and my mother and children fled to the river bank while the soldiers started a backfire. Fortunately the wind shifted and blew the fire away.

Some of the recruits sent to Fort Keogh were not so fortunate, as items in the early issues of the *Yellowstone Journal* indicate that they were marched overland from the end of the Northern Pacific Railroad at Bismarck some 300 miles away.

The year of 1878 was relatively quiet as Sitting Bull's warriors stayed above or near the Canadian border. With no campaigning to do, some soldiers were employed in building telegraph lines along the Yellowstone. In August, Colonel Miles, believing that there was no danger from Indians, left his post to reconnoitre the upper Yellowstone valley and to visit the National Park. He took with him ten officers, an escort of 100 veteran soldiers, twelve guests among whom were five ladies and three children, and "a strong wagon train, a well-equipped pack train, and all the appliances, camp equipage and field equipment necessary."

When camped at the mouth of Mission Creek, near the Great Bend of the Yellowstone, a courier from Fort Ellis rode into camp with the news that a party of hostile Bannocks were crossing the Park, apparently following the same route used by the Nez Percé the year before. These Indians had a reservation near Fort Hall, Idaho, and there had been friction between them and the whites for several months. At last they had gone on the warpath, allegedly because settlers had allowed hogs to feed on the bulbs of the camas plants on Camas Prairie. Probably the fundamental cause was the failure of the Government to provide sufficient food but, be that as it may, some of the hostiles were now headed toward the upper Yellowstone driving along a considerable number of stolen horses.

Sending the non-combatants and the baggage train to Fort Ellis, the colonel divided the remaining seventy-five soldiers into two parties. Forty men were sent to watch the pass at the head of Boulder Creek while he took the remaining thirty-five and went back to a Crow camp on Clark Fork. Here he enlisted seventy-five Absaroka—"It then appeared more like an Indian expedition than a march of white soldiers." This motley force reached the point where Clark Fork issues from the mountains ahead of the unsuspecting Bannocks. An attack was made on their camp just at dawn—with one humorous mishap. When the moment arrived for the bugler to give the signal for the attack this key individual tripped over some sagebrush and fell heavily upon his trumpet, bending it so that it was useless.

The fight was short but before it was over there was scarcely a Crow and not a single Bannock horse in sight. A few Crows did return after getting their loot safely away and helped persuade some of the hostiles who had hidden in the brush to surrender. Eleven Bannocks were killed and thirty-one were captured, and the Absaroka acquired some 200 horses and mules. Miles lost three killed—Captain Andrew S. Bennett of the 5th Infantry, an interpreter, and a Crow scout. Lieutenant Colonel Buell and his men from Fort Custer arrived too late for the fight. Miles handed the captives over to Buell, together with the body of the captain which was eventually returned to Wisconsin, and turned to assembling his party for their tour of the Park.

Miles wrote in his memoirs, "the winter of 1878-1879 was uneventful. . . ." It was—along the Yellowstone. But it was anything but quiet in the western part of Kansas and Nebraska.

In August 1877, not long after the mass surrenders at Fort Robinson, the Northern Cheyennes were moved—against the will of many—to the reservation of the Southern Cheyennes in Indian Territory. The climate here did not agree with many of them, some died, and a year later about one third of these people, under the leadership of Dull Knife, Little Wolf, and Wild Hog, determined to return to the northern plains or die in the attempt. On the 9th of September, 1878, an estimated 89 men, 112 women, and 134 children, slipped out from under the noses of the soldiers who were watching them and began a march which ranks among the epics of the West. Outrunning the cavalry in their rear and eluding other forces which tried to intercept them, these Cheyennes left a trail of terror behind them in Kansas and western Nebraska.

When they reached Nebraska about half of them, including Dull Knife and Wild Hog, were captured and taken to Fort Robinson but the remainder under Little Wolf slipped into the Sand Hills where a snow storm hid their trail. Dull Knife's band, after being ill-treated to the limit of their endurance, broke out of their prison and forced the soldiers to kill some sixty of their number. Dull Knife and his family became separated early in this attempted flight and, after three harrowing weeks in the mid-winter cold, came in to the cabin of interpreter Bill Rowland. A few months later he was allowed to join his people in Montana.

Little Wolf's band stayed hidden all winter. In the spring they swung along the eastern edge of the Black Hills and entered southeastern Montana. On the 25th of March, Lieutenant W. P. Clark—whom they knew at Fort Robinson as "White Hat"—and some Cheyenne scouts captured them at Charcoal Butte near Box Elder Creek without firing a shot. Of the original group of 336 who started this brave journey, 33 men, 43 women, and 38 children finally reached their friends at Fort Keogh. Miles treated this group kindly and immediately requested Little Wolf and his men to enlist in his band of scouts. After a slight delay, all the warriors joined. The following summer John Finerty, the fighting correspondent who was with Crook in 1876, accompanied Miles when he chased Sitting Bull back across the Canadian border. Finerty saw considerable of the Cheyennes on this campaign and he left a flattering picture of their manly qualities.

Little Wolf came to grief the following winter near Fort Keogh. Some twenty years before a man named Famished Elk (or Poor Elk) had made improper advances toward his wife and bad feelings had resulted. While under the influence of liquor, Little Wolf found his daughter gambling with this man for candy in a trader's store. The old feeling of resentment flared and the enraged chief shot and killed Famished Elk. Sobered almost instantly by the realization of what he had done, the chief said he would go to the top of a nearby hill and anyone who wanted him could find him there—murder of a tribesman was an unpardonable sin among the Cheyennes.

The relatives of the victim were entitled to destroy the property of the chief but, because of the circumstances involved, other Cheyennes exerted pressure on them to desist. Bill Rowland—the Cheyenne squaw man who had been an interpreter at the Sioux agencies—then persuaded the self-deposed chief to seek the protection of Fort Keogh. In time, matters quieted down. However, Little Wolf, though still a chief, remained an exile from his people until he died—a pathetic figure who impressed all who knew him with his quiet dignity and manly qualities. And the Cheyennes never forgot that he had been an able leader and a mountain of courage when he led them across the plains from Indian Territory to Montana.

Another tragic incident had its beginning not long before Little Wolf surrendered to Clark. Black Coyote, an unruly warrior in his band, killed two men in a camp quarrel and was banished. His wife, the famous Buffalo Calf Road Woman who had rescued her brother, Comes-In-Sight, in the Battle of the Rosebud, and a few relatives elected to follow the outcast into exile. Including the children, this little party totalled eight. On the 5th of April, when in the vicinity of Mizpah Creek, this band of renegades discovered a sergeant and a private working on the Fort Keogh-Deadwood telegraph line. They severely wounded the sergeant, killed the private, and stole their horses. Five days later, they were captured by a small detail under the command of Sergeant Glover, an ambitious non-commissioned officer of the 2nd Cavalry. As the case was adjudged to be a civil one, the three warriors involved were lodged in the Custer County jail at Miles City, and their case was heard in the first territorial court ever held in the territory east of Bozeman.

On this occasion, a one-room "cabin built of hewn logs" which stood on *Milestown's* Main Street served as a courthouse: and the session lasted ten days, May 27-June 5, 1879. Present as a reporter for *The New York Times* was Thompson R. McElrath who, two months later, launched Miles City's famous newspaper, the *Yellowstone Journal*. In a long letter to *The New York Times* dated June 8th, he noted that the case of the three Cheyennes possessed "a special historical interest":

. . . Competent council undertook the defendants case, but had the evidence against them been only a tithe as strong, they would undoubtedly have been convicted. . . . The theory that the only good indian is a dead one is in full force among the civilians through our frontier, though the army, appreciating their bravery and recognizing their powerlessness, take a more merciful view of their red-skinned opponents.

The unfortunate trio sat through the trial with impassive features, and with little apparent interest in the proceedings, though I noticed that Hole in the Breast occasionally put his hands to his head as though he realized the gravity and hopelessness of his position. The testimony of each witness was repeated by an interpreter, and permission was given to the prisoners to put any questions they desired, a priviledge that was uniformly declined. They were all convicted, and on the fourth instant sentence was passed on all four.

The jail facilities are limited at this place, and short thrift was given them, the seventh of July being appointed for their execution. Two of the condemned Cheyennes, however, rejected even this period of life, and were found dead in their cell on the following morning. They had sought death in a cool and deliberate manner, so unparalleled as to provoke the admiration of even their white foes. Although handcuffed, and chained by the ankles to a bull-ring in the floor, they had succeeded in hanging themselves by a belt-strap to an iron bar in the aperture of the cell door. The same strap was used by both, one waiting until the other was dead, and then lifting down the corpse, deliberately removing the strap and adjusting it for his own hanging.

One of those who threw away the last few days of his life was Black Coyote. The third choked himself later by using the cord from one of his moccasins.

Marauding bands made the spring of 1879 a busy one for the soldiers in the Yellowstone Valley. General Sheridan listed the various incidents in his annual report. The summary for March is typical of the three months:

March 1st, Several head of stock were stolen by Indians from McDonald and Dillon's ranch near Powder River, Montana. March 4th, twenty-three head of stock were also stolen from Countryman's ranch, near the mouth of the Stillwater. March 28th, Indians attacked two white men near the mouth of the Big Horn River, killed one, H. D. Jackson, and wounded the other, named James Stearns; a man named Dave Henderson was killed the same day, near Buffalo Station, on the Yellowstone. Horses were run off from Pease Bottom, near the mouth of Buffalo Creek, and sixty-seven ponies were stolen from the Crows at their agency. The Indians committing these depredations were ascertained to be Sioux from the north, with a few Nez Percés; Captains Mix and Gregg with their troops of 2nd Cavalry were dispatched in pursuit, but after a very hard chase were unable to overtake the marauders.

After having detailed the depredations, Sheridan outlined the steps taken to correct the situation:

Many depredations having recently been committed by Indians in the vicinity of the Missouri and the Yellowstone Rivers, it was ascertained that large numbers of hostiles, half-breeds and foreign Indians, from British Columbia, including the Indians under Sitting Bull, were roaming upon United States territory, south of the boundary line. From a number of reliable persons who had seen the main hostile camp, this was estimated at not less than five thousand Indians, of whom two thousand were warriors, with twelve thousand horses. Half-breed Indians had also been trading with the hostiles and furnishing them with ammunition, so in July Colonel Miles was sent from Fort Keogh, Montana, with a strong force to break up their camp, separate the doubtful Indians from those avowedly hostile, and force the foreign Indians to return north of the boundary.

Colonel Miles' force consisted of seven companies of 5th Infantry, seven troops of 2nd Cavalry, a detachment of artillery and some friendly Indians and white scouts. At Fort Peck he was joined by two companies of the 6th Infantry, and his entire command then numbered thirty-three officers, six hundred and forty-three enlisted men and one hundred and forty-three Indian and white scouts.

Miles' advance guard had one running fight with a force of Sioux estimated at three to four hundred, after which the Indians retreated north of the border. The troops then turned their attention to the Red River half-breeds who were alleged to have been trading with the

Sioux. These people lived in tents and moved their goods in Red River carts, primitive vehicles constructed of wood and rawhide. Captain Ovenshine and a portion of the command arrested one band on Porcupine Creek, capturing 143 carts and 193 horses. By the 8th of August, Miles had collected a total of 829 half-breeds and 655 carts which he turned back across the border. The Yellowstone country now returned to a state of comparative quiet until early the following spring.

In 1880, the Sioux began their depredations along the Yellowstone early in February. In a letter dated February 6th, L. A. Huffman, post photographer at Fort Keogh, wrote his father:

. . . . *The weather has been steadily moderating lately and things are unusually active about the post— On the 3rd the Gros Ventres and the Sioux had a big rumpus down the river a few miles— some ten dead and 12 wounded have been brought in  some reported to belong to S. Bulls band.*

*Yesterday morning three men came in from Powder River one wounded in the shoulder and one in the fore arm— they were attacked in a camp at a hay corrall and barely got off with their hair— they put the number of Sioux at 40— Sargt Glover and 25 men started to look them up this morning. . . .*

One of the men returned with the detachment and it was found that the party only numbered *six*. They found the body of one warrior and the *sign* indicated two had turned back. The remaining three were captured on Pumpkin Creek at the cost of one soldier killed and another wounded.

The editor of the newly established *Yellowstone Journal* devoted considerable space to accounts of Indian raids and the activities of troops from Fort Keogh. A story dated February 14th indicates that such news spread rapidly and—sometimes—was subject to wild exaggeration:

*The Indians the past week seem to have been exerting themselves to see how much they could annoy our settlers, and frequent raids have been made along the Tongue, and Yellowstone rivers and their numerous tributaries. One report reached here that not a head of stock was left on Bull creek, but upon investigation it was found that such was not the case, but still a number had been stolen all the same. Another rumor reached here and gained considerable credence, that Hubbell's teams had been taken in, and a few wildly excited groups were seen on our street corners, and in our saloons, talking of organizing a party and starting in pursuit of them. In a few hours however definite information was* received, and instead of the whole outfit being taken in, only one horse and a mule remunerated the Indians for their trouble, which information caused a great feeling of relief to pass over Mr. Hubbell. Another rumor was that the Crow Indians had broken out. . . .

On March 6th, several thefts were noted.

The Indians the past week have been enjoying themselves to their hearts content by running off stock along the Yellowstone, Tongue and Powder rivers. The first heard of them was their raid on a lot of stock in the Little Porcupine bottom, which they successfully got away with. Gen. Miles, however, concluding to teach them a lesson, immediately sent four companies after them the same day of receiving the dispatch, and on the next day sent three more. . . .

A week later—the *Yellowstone Journal* was printed each Saturday— the editor carried another long story which gave the details about the above-noted military operations. On the 5th of March, Lieutenant Miller with seventeen soldiers and Indian scouts had surprised a camp thirty miles west of the Rosebud. Although they killed three hostiles and eight ponies, and captured the baggage in camp, the remainder of the party got away with the "stock." This information had been promptly relayed to Lieutenant Baldwin who was on the north side of the Yellowstone with mounted infantry. He was fortunate enough to pick up the trail of the fugitives and, after running them for thirty miles, captured all the horses except those which the Indians were riding. Other troops were posted on the west branch of Sunday Creek— northwest of Miles City—to intercept the Indians if they came that way. The editor could not resist adding, "They . . . will probably, before this paper reaches all of its subscribers, have the Indians captured or killed."

There was more Indian news on the 27th of March:

This week a band of Sioux stole a large number of horses from the Crows within three miles of Fort Custer, and started in this direction. . . .

These hostiles, estimated at thirty or forty, had stolen about thirty ponies belonging to the Crow scouts at Fort Custer. After a forced march of some sixty miles, cavalry from the post succeeded in recapturing sixteen of the horses. Captain Huggins from Fort Keogh was more successful. He managed to find the trail and caught up with the Sioux on O'Fallon Creek where he attacked their camp and captured five warriors and all of the horses. The remainder of the party got into a "position of great natural strength, from which they escaped on foot in the darkness of that night."

During the next three months, a dozen accounts of Indian "deviltry"—stealing stock, fighting with the Crows, and burning stacks of buffalo hides—appeared in the *Yellowstone Journal*. Two of these attacks were unique in that they were made on stages. On the 30th of May:

> . . . the Bismarck stage came into town without our usual complement of mail. . . . From . . . [the driver and the agent of the line] we learned that the Indians had attacked three stations down the road and run off the stock from them. . . . Two men . . . were killed. . . . This is the first time the Indians have troubled this line, and it is sincerely hoped they will let it alone in the future.

This attack occurred just east of the divide between the Yellowstone and the Little Missouri: and the next one, noted on the 17th of July, occurred farther west:

> On Sunday last while coming on the stage on the route east of Pennel's station, Mr. L. Brunier, the grasshopper investigator, saw three objects a long distance off which by looking through his glass proved to be four Indians riding as if to cut off the stage. The driver, badly scared, thereupon whipped up his horses and ran them until all danger was passed. . . . On Monday, Henry Friese, a steady young German, started out from Pennel's station to drive his route to O'Fallon's creek, a distance of twenty-two miles. Up to date Friese, buckboard, team or mail had not been seen and it is the general impression that Poor Friese has met his death in the hands of the young bucks seen the day before. . . .

A partial sequel appeared in the next week's issue:

> . . . Cole . . . brought in the missing mail, which had been stolen by the Indians, and also the report that the body of the driver—"Dutchy"—had been found near with a bullet hole in the head. The sacks and harness were all cut to pieces. . . . It is thought that the registered packages were all taken. Troops from Fort Keogh have been sent out to punish the marauders.

Sioux scouts with these troops searched the area for a trail and then pronounced the task impossible. However, soldiers from a party protecting the surveyors staking out the line for the Northern Pacific Railroad also joined in the hunt. With them were three Cheyenne scouts and one of Bill Rowland's half-breed sons who was acting as an interpreter. One of the Cheyennes picked up the trail—

The following September, George O. Shields, an eastern sportsman and author, visited the camp of the railroad engineers. One bright moonlight night, while strolling about the camp, he stopped to talk with one of the "sentinels":

Among other questions, I ask him if there are any Indians in this part of the country now.

"No," said he, "there are none now. There was a band of five [sic four] Sioux through here a week ago. I was out on a scout with an officer and thirty other men, going over toward Powder river, and we struck their trail about fourty miles from here. The lieutenant detailed Sergeant Deavron [sic Devlin] and ten [sic eight] of us boys to follow the trail while he continued on his course. Two [sic three] Cheyenne scouts were sent with us to trail them. They laid down alongside of their ponies, their heads as near to the ground as they could get them, in order to be able to see the trail, and struck out at a lively trot. This was in the morning. All day long they followed that trail without difficulty, while for the greater portion of the time we could see nothing of it. Whenever we came to the top of a ridge the scouts would take the field glass with which they had been provided, and scan the country carefully as far as they could see. Late in the afternoon they spotted the Sioux crossing over a ridge about ten miles away. We could barely see them with the aid of the glass, and would not have guessed them to be Indians, but our scouts shouted, 'Sioux, Sioux, five Sioux!' We had ridden hard since morning, our horses were tired, and the sergeant ordered a halt here for rest and lunch, but our Indians wouldn't have it. They kept shouting, 'Sioux, Sioux, soldier heap damn lazy! Come on!' So the sergeant told them to go and we would follow them. Then they patted us on the backs and said, 'Soldier heap bully; come on.' At this they dropped the trail and made a bee line for the top of the hill where we had seen the Sioux. We rode this ten miles under spur, and took up the trail again on the hill, and followed it into a timbered ravine. The scouts now told us that we were close to them and that they had not yet seen us. We rode cautiously and carried our carbines at a 'ready.' Finally we sighted them at about five hundred yards, and before they knew they were followed at all we gave them a volley, killing one of them and wounding two others.

"They returned the fire and then skipped out. As our horses were badly worn out . . . we knew it was useless to follow them. When we fired the volley our scouts disappeared . . . . but in about half an hour they returned with three ponies that they had captured. . . . Then they went for the dead Indian's scalp, but the sergeant would not let them scalp him. After grazing our horses . . . we started back to the command. Pretty soon our scouts were missing again but that night they turned up and one of them had the dead Sioux's scalp. They also had about a dozen little scalps that they had cut off, after they got the main one, and these they gave to us boys."

The official report stated that this party killed two Indians and wounded one, and recaptured seven head of stock. Four of these horses carried packs and in them were bundles of letters and newspapers taken from Friese's stage.

Miles was not content to chase Sioux over the countryside—he wanted to get Sitting Bull's band to surrender. The three warriors captured by Sergeant Glover and the five brought in by Captain Huggins provided him with an opening wedge. He sent word to their people that they would be held until their relatives came in and surrendered and, in response to this ultimatum a delegation of eight warriors came in to see what surrender terms could be arranged. The major concern, however, was not the captives, but whether or not the surrender terms would be less objectionable than the empty stomachs which life in Canada sometimes entailed. These envoys were treated "civilly," and Miles did his best to impress them with the superiority of the white man. The telegraph was explained to them and they admitted that it was great medicine, but when half of the party was allowed to talk to the other half over the newly installed telephone

their hands shook visibly, their bodies trembled with emotion, and great drops of perspiration rolled down their bronzed faces. Then they carefully laid the instrument back upon the table and wished to go away immediately. They appeared to be as much struck with awe as if they had been in the presence of the Almighty. . . .

The "whispering spirit" made a very deep impression.

After this parley, various bands, each led by its own chief, began to straggle into Fort Keogh. The *Yellowstone Journal* turned from reporting raids to announcing the arrival of various bands, sometimes erring—perhaps naturally—in over-reporting the number which had surrendered:

(May 15, 1880)  A large band of Sioux Indians are camped on the other side of the Yellowstone river under Rain-in-the-Face trying to negotiate with the officials at Fort Keogh to come in and surrender. It is stated that they have been run off from the British provinces for killing two or three mounted police. . . .

(June 19, 1880) This week 81 lodges of Sitting Bull's band of Northern Sioux surrendered their arms and ponies to the commanding officer at Fort Keogh, and were placed on the reservation and rations issued to them. They are in a very destitute condition and were almost starved. The past winter over 5000 head of their horses died from exposure and starvation. In an interview with their chief, Yellow Twin, through Mr. William Rowland, we learned that a large band were now camped about 100 miles distant ready to surrender, should this party be well treated. The guns they have turned in were most all first-class Winchesters and Sharps rifles of the latest model. Their ponies will all be sold and the proceeds go to buying them farming implements. . . . The plan inaugurated by Gen. Miles of allowing Indians to cultivate ground and sell the products of the same for their own individual benefit, is productive of much satisfaction to the Indians, and has been a great factor in urging them to surrender.

(July 3, 1880) A large band of Indians under Rain-in-the-Face and Black Moon are within a few miles of Fort Keogh awaiting the arrival of Gen. Miles to surrender. They refuse to treat with any other officer as they are afraid of Miles and say they will only give up their arms and ponies to the "Big Chief."

(July 24, 1880) The hostile Indians are coming in, which will make times lively for everybody.

(September 11, 1880) On Wednesday 44 lodges or about 250 Northern Sioux from Sitting Bull's camp surrendered to Gen. Miles at Fort Keogh. This addition makes the total number of Sioux on the reservation close to 1500. [This was Broad Trail, sometimes called Big Road, and about 200 of his people.]

(October 22, 1880) . . . . A brother of Spotted Eagle arrived at Keogh during the week with a number of hostiles and surrendered to Gen. Miles, and reported that more of Sitting Bull's braves were coming in. . . .

(October 30, 1880) Spotted Eagle and Rain-in-the-Face, with about 600 Sioux Indians, were camped on Sunday creek last night. They will surrender to Gen. Miles, at Fort Keogh this evening. It will be remembered that Spotted Eagle was the Indian who was about to kill Gen. Terry when he had a quarrel with them a short time ago. Six hundred warriors will make quite a reduction of *Sitting Bull's band, and we now begin to think that he may be induced to surrender himself and braves.*

Miles wrote in his memoirs:

*In this way more than 2000 surrendered Indians were gathered at Fort Keogh. They remained peaceable, contented and industrious, fulfilling all the requirements made upon them, until, in 1881, when orders were received to move them down the Yellowstone and Missouri to the Indian agency on the lower Missouri. This was regarded by them as a serious disaster, as their crops were then well nigh half grown and in prosperous condition. They were contented and happy and anxious to stay. They went from one officer to another with tears in their eyes, begging, pleading and praying that they might be allowed to remain under the control of the military where they had been kindly and justly treated, and in a country agreeable to them.*

With plenty of unoccupied land in the surrounding country, Miles's plan had appeared feasible. A similar arrangement was working out very well with the Cheyennes who had a herd of beef cattle and raised corn and vegetables which they sold at the post and in Miles City. And shortly after their surrender, some of the Sioux had actually gone to work with a railroad grading crew—shoveling dirt for a dollar a day. The editor of the *Yellowstone Journal* was also struck with the injustice of the order and wrote a caustic editorial; however, the issue dated June 11, 1881, carried this information:

. . . . *Thursday the poor, friendless and homeless savages were ordered up and taken to the river bank and closely guarded by a cordon of soldiers, until the boats are ready to load up with them. The Indians are all sullen, and a look of moroseness is visible on all their faces at the outrageous manner in which faith has been broken with them. . . .*

It took five steamboats to carry the Indians. The *Eclipse,* with Captain Grant Marsh at the helm, was flagship of the fleet. Her cargo was 418 Oglalas; the *Josephine,* 323 Sans Arcs; the *Helena,* 528 Minniconjou; the *General Terry,* 181 Hunkpapa; and the *Sherman,* 191 Brules. For the captains, the affair was made to order for excitement —they staged a race to Standing Rock with their heavy-hearted passengers.

Although the bulk of Sitting Bull's followers surrendered in 1880, some endured the following winter and then straggled in to Fort Buford the following spring, a few coming to Fort Keogh. On the 19th of July, stout-hearted Sitting Bull bowed to the inevitable. The editor of the *Yellowstone Journal* estimated the news value of this story at one and three quarter lines: *Sitting Bull has come in to Fort Buford and surrendered.*

The days were gone when a raid by hostile Sioux might be expected at almost any time and any place. Stories about thefts still dotted the pages of the newspapers but these incidents were matters for civil officers—or the vigilantes. The soldiers had a stabilizing role to play for another decade and a half, but the days of Indian fighting were over in the Yellowstone valley.

Garrison life was also a part of the policing activities for often there were long periods between alarms. As some of the soldiers and many of the officers were married, some happenings involved the distaff side of the family—and the children. Life for the bulk of the enlisted men was often drab, and some sought freedom by deserting. In January 1880, the guard house at Fort Keogh held thirty would-be deserters; and the following June three deserters from Fort Custer almost starved to death on Clark Fork before being rescued by settlers.

Although Fort Custer was miles from the nearest settlement, Fort Keogh was only two miles from nearby Miles City—or Milestown as it was first called—and anyone with a pass and a little money in his pocket could, in the parlance of the day, "see the helephant." The place was a wide open frontier town with an abundance of saloons, dance halls, and brothels. Also the town supported one or more *variety houses*, as the saloon-vaudeville theatres were called. As the town population contained a good many bull whackers and hide hunters in the early days, trouble was usually expected during the "shank of the evening." Typical of many pay-day news items was this short note in the *Yellowstone Journal* of October 1, 1881:

*A row in which about 30 men, mostly soldiers, engaged in, occurred in Frank Reese's dance hall on Thursday night. Broken glass, chairs, tables, etc., were strewn promiscuously around, and had it not been for the prompt appearance of the officers, loss of life might have resulted.*

The cowboys, who followed the bull whackers and hunters, had a particularly strong dislike for soldiers and brawls in the *parlor houses* between these two groups were common. One old rancher recalled a fracas in Mag Burns' "44"—one of the fanciest houses in town—when a cowboy "gun-whipped" eight soldiers and laid them senseless on the floor.

Not all of the soldiers' amusements were of this nature. At Fort Keogh, the 5th Infantry had a fine library and a news item dated November 4, 1882, stated that the library received 58 domestic and foreign magazines, had 1,208 books on the shelves, and was visited by an average of 95 people daily. The son of one officer recalled, "The enlisted men had a social and dramatic club called "The Schury Club. They built a large log house and gave dramatic performances and dances in it." Hunting trips provided both recreation and a change in the daily menu. In October of 1879, Colonel Miles and a party of five officers, twelve soldiers and five Indians came back from a hunting trip along the Rosebud with ten six-mule wagons loaded with 60 large deer, 3 antelope, 1 mountain sheep, 5 elk, 17 buffalo, 70 prairie chickens, and 6 ducks. Horse racing was also a popular sport. Fort Keogh had a race track and, until Miles City also acquired an oval, races were run in Main Street.

The 5th Infantry had a fine band which gave concerts, played for dances and parades, and formed the source from which smaller groups like the Keogh Philharmonic Club were formed. This club gave occasional concerts in the variety houses in Miles City and—when a suitable place could be found—for the women and children of the town.

Dances were popular with the officers and their wives. The first "formal" affair at Keogh was held on board the *F. Y. Batchelor* in the summer of 1877 when General Sherman, General of the Army, and his staff came up the river on an inspection trip "and to see the wild and primitive country." The men wore their "campaign rigging of trousers reinforced with buckskin, their bespurred heels jingling and making occasional rents in the gowns of the ladies," and they danced until reveille. One very fancy affair—for which the ladies had sent East for expensive gowns—was interrupted at its height by a courier who arrived with the news that there was a band of Indians nearby.

There were other entertainments in season. During the late 1870's and early 1880's, the post and Miles City staged joint celebrations on the fourth of July. When winter came there was skating on the Tongue, and sleighing parties. Some of the officers owned their own sleighs— they cost $2.50 per hour with a $5.00 minimum at Miles City—and the son of one officer recalled, "The 1st sergeant of my father's company had a team of elk that he drove to a cutter." Horseback riding was popular with the ladies but it could have an element of uncertainty. There were occasional spills and more serious scrapes. On one occasion Lieutenant Baldwin's wife was chased by horse thieves, the girth on her side-saddle broke, and she was much embarrassed by having to complete the *race* riding "a-straddle."

Amateur theatricals were popular during the winter months. However, with part of the various casts coming from the Army, performances were not always certain. On November 20, 1879, the *Yellowstone Journal* noted:

> The officers and ladies of Fort Keogh are about resuming the dramatic entertainments which were so successfully sustained last winter until the command was suddenly ordered in to the field. . . .

These shows always played to packed houses and on one occasion the local press noted that there were "about forty invited guests from Miles City." One popular actor at Fort Keogh was Lieutenant J. M. T. Partello who was also a fine musician and one of the best riflemen in the United States.

Although but few records remain of the activities of the children, life was not dull for them. There was school to attend—in fact there were several schools. One of the better schools in the early 1880's was a semi-private affair held in the Sunday school room of the Episcopal Church in Miles City. The son of Captain Ovenshine recalled:

> A number of us children from Keogh used to go to a school in Miles City run by a Rev. Mr. Horsefall and his wife, driving there and back behind a four mule team. When the river was high we would cross on the ferry, or the bridge if it was there; in the fall when it was low we would ford and in the winter we would cross on the ice.

He also set down reminiscences which mirror life during the late 1870's and early 1880's:

> I used to see Two Moons, Rain-in-the-Face, Spotted Tail, Little Wolf and others of the well known chiefs often. Little Wolf at one time had his tepee pitched near the guard house for protection, and I went there several times and he strung a bow for me with sinews. His tepee was later removed to a small knoll along the road leading to the Yellowstone and several of us boys would take him sugar and other things in my small toy wagon. He made mocassins for my brother and myself. . . .

> The night before the Sioux were evacuated from Keogh to the Standing Rock Agency in 1881, they were camped along the Yellowstone and I and several boys spent the evening in and out of their tepees. We thought they were cooking their dogs. . . .

> My first two or three years at Keogh we could look out of our kitchen windows and see the hills across the Yellowstone covered with buffaloes.

In the fall of 1881, enroute to a camp at the mouth of the Powder River to guard supplies being landed from steamboats unable to pass the rapids on the Yellowstone, and to protect Northern Pacific graders, I saw the remains of hundreds of buffaloes with just their hides removed. . . .

A man who apparently had been scalped called on my father. He had no hair on top of his head, which was very red, showing the veins. He kept a bandana handkerchief on his head under his hat, and had the ends of all his fingers cut off. Who he was and how it happened I never knew.

In the days of the bull trains, hide hunters, famous Indians like Little Wolf, Rain-in-the-Face, and Spotted Eagle, and scouts like Yellowstone Kelly, Big Leggins Bruguier, and Liver-eating Johnson—the life of a boy at Fort Keogh was rich in many ways.

# 18

## Early Settlers

»»»»»»»««««««««« Yellowstone City was the first settlement in the Yellowstone Basin. This was a little mining camp tucked up against the towering Absaroka Mountains at the mouth of Emigrant Gulch and when the claims failed to yield a profitable return, it promptly dwindled to nothingness.

Two settlers who came to this "city" showed signs of remaining permanently. John J. Tomlinson set up a sawmill on Mill Creek about nine miles below and sawed lumber for the mackinaw boats which were built in this area. The other was Ben Strickland who, when he could not make a living from his claim, moved out into Paradise Valley and planted a field of wheat. This crop, grown in the summer of 1864, was the first of its kind in the valley. However, the first permanent settlers in the upper Yellowstone were the Boteler brothers—also spelled Bottler and Botteller—who settled near the mouth of Emigrant Gulch early in 1868. They established a "ranch" and, although pestered by thieving Indians, they prospered—their establishment becoming famous as a stopping place for parties going to the Yellowstone National Park.

The first permanent settlement was Benson's Landing at the Great Bend of the Yellowstone. Billy Lee built a crude ferry here to accommodate people traveling between Bozeman or Fort Ellis and the Crow Agency at the mouth of Mission Creek some fifteen miles further down stream. Then "Buckskin" Williams built a saloon and trading post at this point, and later Amos Benson and Dan Naileigh also erected a strong drink parlor. These were followed by another character named Horace Countryman who likewise established a saloon. These log huts were on the north side of the river as the south bank was on the Crow Reservation: and by 1873, the place was known as Benson's Landing. It was a resort of trappers and prospectors, and in 1877, became a stage stop. As might be expected, it was an unsavory sort of place and its *merchants* were regarded with disfavor by the Crow Agent.

On the north side of the Yellowstone, not far from the Crow Agency, were several hot springs which poured out an immense amount of hot water. These came to the attention of Dr. Andrew Jackson Hunter, a Missourian who came to Montana in 1864 to prospect. As Dr. Hunter was not successful in his search for gold, he took squatters rights, in February 1870, to the area containing the springs, and set about developing them as a health resort. In 1873, he built a house and, considering the times, some pretentious bath houses. Here he and his family lived until 1885 when he sold part of his holdings and retired to Bozeman.

During the greater part of the 1870's this was an exposed location in which to live as both the Piegans and the Sioux were prone to raid the nearby Crows. However, the Absaroka took a liking to the doctor and his family and looked out for them. On one occasion Chief Iron Bull demanded that they leave immediately and accompany the Crows on a buffalo hunt. Three days later they were told that they could go home —a band of Piegan raiders who had been in the area had now left! Hunter did a little farming and the Crows watched these operations with considerable interest. They were extremely fond of potatoes and on one occasion they carried away a green watermelon only to return later to ask how it should be eaten—cooking it, they said, only made it tougher.

As the Crow Reservation included all of that part of Montana lying south and east of the Yellowstone and west of the 107th Meridian, it acted as a barrier to further settlement in the upper part of the Yellowstone valley. And the prowling bands of renegade Sioux discouraged any would-be settlers who were prone to pay no attention to reservation boundaries. However, in 1870 a small party of prospectors found rich silver outcrops near the head of Clark Fork on the Crow Reservation; and before long the region was swarming with gold hunters. These ubiquitous trespassers entered this forbidden territory by going up the Yellowstone to the Park and then following the hunting trail used by the Nez Percé and the Bannocks in 1877 and 1878 to the *back door* of the forbidden area.

In 1877 a small smelter was erected on the head of Clark Fork but no bullion was taken out. These activities led to negotiations with the Crows and the Indians finally relinquished that part of their reservation lying west of Boulder Creek. This treaty was made in 1880 but the area was not officially opened until April 11, 1882. By this time prospectors had been into every nook and cranny, and a settlement called Cooke City existed on the head of Clark Fork. There was considerable activity in this area over the period of a decade or two but no one ever made a rich strike.

Aside from this treasure hunt, there was little activity in the valley of the Yellowstone until after 1876. Then a trickle of settlers started down the valley from the vicinity of Benson's Landing. This became larger with each succeeding year until, in 1882, a flood of farmers, merchants, and ranchers poured into the Yellowstone Basin from the east, south, and west. Even before 1876 a few venturesome souls edged down the valley. Three years after Hunter took up squatters rights, a man named Gage moved in six miles below the doctor and the Harrison brothers settled nearby. When the Crow agent moved the location of the Crow Agency, in 1875, to Rosebud Creek—a tributary of the Stillwater River —Horace Countryman and his partner, Hugo Hoppe, loaded up their whiskey kegs and other property and left Benson's Landing. They trailed down the river and set up shop on the north bank opposite the mouth of the Stillwater—as close to the new agency as the law would allow.

In the fall of 1876, other settlers moved eastward as far as the valley of the Rosebud. Some of these were not settlers in the strict sense of the word, but at least they were the advance guard of those who established permanent homes. Among these were Omar Hoskins and Thomas Mc-Girl. They established a store near where Major Baker had his fight with the Sioux in 1872 and the next year this became one of the stage stops on the newly established line betweeen Miles City and Bozeman. In 1877, the county assessor placed a valuation of $150 on their property and by 1880 this had increased to $8,300. Later, the two transferred their interests to raising cattle and McGirl became one of the wealthy ranchers in the valley.

Miles City, christened Milestown at its birth, was the first settlement of any size in the Yellowstone Basin. It came into being in the fall of 1876 when Colonel Miles, becoming irritated at having a bunch of *coffee-coolers* underfoot, ordered them to move to the other side of a stake which he had ordered set a couple of miles east of the cantonment. One of this group recalled later that before nightfall of the day they were ordered out of camp, they had a few tents up and two saloons and a gambling hall in operation. These *settlers* bore the colonel no ill will and, as soon as they had a few cabins erected, invited Miles and his staff to a banquet—consisting mostly of game and liquor.

In 1878, after Fort Keogh had been built two miles west of the Tongue, the Government relinquished all of that part of the ten-mile-square military reservation which lay on the east side of the river except for a small area for a ferry landing. The inhabitants of Old Town—as the original settlement was called—immediately stampeded to the vacated territory and put up a new town where Miles City now stands. The small area which was reserved became a sort of no-man's land—unruly soldiers retreated here to evade civil arrest in town, bullwhackers and other homeless people used it as a place to sleep off their jags, tramps camped there, and others found it a convenient place to dump trash. Eventually, it became Miles City's park but not before it acquired a reputation of sorts.

The story of Miles City is an inseparable part of the history of the Yellowstone frontier. Junction City and Coulson each had a small bit of fame and then dropped into obscurity. Glendive, Billings, and Livingston were *Johnny-come-latelys* which arrived with the railroad and promptly developed into more or less prosaic towns of the conventional pattern; and to the south on the eastern slope of the Big Horns, Big Horn and Sheridan grew up as supply points for ranchers and settlers. But not one had more than a smattering of the colorful past possessed by the city which developed from old Milestown.

When the *new* Milestown came into existence, one street was already laid out. A fragment of the trail between Fort Keogh and Bismarck became Main Street, and on either side of this road the business section of the town sprang up. Thus, along this street passed not only the business of the town but also the freighting trains, stages, and assorted travelers going to or from Bismarck, Bozeman, Fort Buford, Deadwood and various points in between. Main Street was definitely an artery of commerce and travel.

Miles City's importance and size was the result of several factors. The protection provided by the post was an invaluable asset, and the civilian employees of the Army provided a steady source of trade for the town. Before the day of the railroad, steamboats delivered great quantities of goods to the merchants and this made it a focal point for trade when settlers poured into this vast area. Even before this influx, the town was an important outfitting point for hide hunters—who spent a considerable sum of money each year with the merchants, saloon keepers, and others. And it was probably the most important market for buffalo hides in the Northwest.

In physical appearance, Miles City resembled the other frontier towns of its time. The first buildings were built of logs but as the merchants prospered frame buildings became common. In 1880, when it became obvious that the Northern Pacific Railroad would soon reach the town—after having been stalled at Bismarck since 1873—a building boom started which kept three sawmills busy for at least two years. Miles City was also the county seat of Custer County (originally called Big Horn County) which in those days embraced a section of southeastern Montana Territory that was almost as large as the state of Pennsylvania. In 1882, the county splurged by building a three story brick courthouse but the lustre of the new building was somewhat tarnished by a scandal involving the misuse of public funds during its construction. Previous to this time, court was held in a small log building with the crudest of furnishings, and the county jail was equally primitive. It too was of log construction with a stockade ten or twelve feet high, and was constantly crammed with criminals of the toughest sort. The only way these could be kept in custody was to mount an armed guard—assisted by the sheriff's pet bear—twenty-four hours a day. In 1880, this cost $900 a month—a sore spot with economy-minded grand juries.

The variety and amount of goods stocked by the large merchants reflected both the times and the geographical location. Before the day of the railroad, most of the goods came in once a year by steamboat as freighting by bull train from the end of the railroad 290 miles away involved high transportation costs. Thus if a merchant miscalculated his needs, he might find himself with depleted shelves before the next "June rise." Most stores offered a heterogeneous assortment of goods. In 1881, one such firm advertised:

> *Wholesale and Retail Dealers in* DRY GOODS AND GROCERIES! *crockery and glassware, hardware and tin-ware, boots and shoes, furnishing goods, Hats and caps, Carpets, wall paper, Wines, Liquors, and Cigars. Farming implements! Sole Agents for Mitchell Wagon! Dress'd Lumber of All Kinds. Furs, hides, Robes and peltries Bought and Sold.*

Each class of item noted represented a number of things. Thus the merchant who stocked ammunition—normally considered *hardware*—also carried powder, bar lead, primers, wax, and patching paper—the necessary components for reloading. It was not strange for a baker to sell tobacco, fruit in season, tea, coffee, eggs and butter, and even the barbers had their sidelines.

It took considerable capital to operate a mercantile establishment at this time. On November 5, 1881, the *Yellowstone Journal* carried this item:

> Judge D. S. Wade in an interview with the Helena Independent represents Miles City as a lively little town of 1,000 inhabitants. . . . There are several strong business houses in the place, notably those of Broadwater, Hubbell & Co., A. R. Nininger & Co., and Leighton and Jordan & Co., all engaged in general merchandise, the annual sales of each house, $300,000.

In 1877, A. R. Nininger had an assessed valuation of $12,510. By 1880 this had increased to $59,423, and at the same time the assets of Broadwater, Hubbell and Co. were listed at $100,725. It was not uncommon in 1879-1880 for these firms to advertise, e. g., that they had the "largest, best selected and most complete assortment of merchandise in the NORTHWEST amounting in value to OVER $150,000. . . ."

Stores were open from early in the morning until late at night and, until April 1880, seven days a week. On the 10th of this month a notice appeared in the paper that the merchants would close on Sunday, however, they reserved the right to "keep open a back or side door for the accommodation of our country customers." With a bit of nostalgia, one old lady recalled that Leighton and Jordan never had enough cats to keep the mice and rats down. One evening when a woman came in to purchase some rice, the clerk, on pulling the drawer open, discovered a mouse which he promptly killed. When the customer looked wryly at the desired article the clerk commented, "Maam, I can turn it over so there won't be any mouse on it." Merchants cheerfully made good any faulty merchandise and the customer's word was never doubted. All stores dealing in groceries kept a candy barrel for their patrons, and gave sweets regularly with orders of goods. And there was one hardware dealer who kept a barrel of whiskey and a tincup in the back of his store for his customers.

Not all of the food came from the grocery stores. Wagon loads of game were frequently peddled on the street and on January 17, 1880 the *Yellowstone Journal* noted that "Buffalo have knocked the butcher business almost in the head, it selling from two to three cents per pound." On October 15, 1881, it was noted that "John Hindeman of the Upper Yellowstone arrived in town Thursday with a boat load of speckled trout which he sold readily around town for 25 cents per pound." Potatoes, onions, and other vegetables from the Gallatin valley came down the river in mackinaw boats: and, while the Cheyennes lived in the vicinity of Fort Keogh, these Indians peddled melons during the late summer.

Before the railroad arrived, three stage and telegraph lines converged at Miles City, and in the spring—sometimes all summer—there were steamboat connections with the ports on the Missouri. It took ten days to two weeks to come up the river from the railhead at Bismarck, and this was the preferred means of transportation as it took five days *and* nights to cross the intervening prairie in a buckboard—an ordeal not recommended for women. Stages left two or three times a week going east and west, and, later, the companies inaugurated daily service. Gilmer, Salsbury & Co., who had a number of lines in southern Wyoming, took over the line from Miles City to Bozeman. However, the facilities consisted only of light, two-seated wagons called "jerkys"—the occasional passengers being entertained by the driver and, frequently, a bottle of "tarantular juice." It was 325 miles to Bozeman and the fare to this place, or to Bismarck, was $42.00. There was also regular service to Deadwood. Certainly Miles City was the hub of considerable travel and commerce, and much of it passed down "Main Street."

In 1879, a telephone was installed at Fort Keogh to connect the telegraph office and Colonel Miles' quarters. The townspeople were soon agitating for this modern convenience and in 1881 a "Central Office" was installed in a store owned by Bill Bullard and W. L. Lansing at 6th and Main. Originally there were twenty-five subscribers and there were connections with the post. This was the first telephone exchange in Montana. Although the town could boast of this convenience, decent hotel accommodations were difficult to find. One prominent citizen noted in 1880 that he "put up" with the sheriff and boarded at the jail as

*the people who frequented Miles City in those days usually came to town to stay up and see the sights. They did not feel the necessity for a bed or much to eat. They were just thirsty.*

However, in 1882, the Inter Ocean Hotel was built and this was soon acquired by "Major" Macqueen, a genial southerner who named it after himself. During the heyday of the open range, it is said no hostelry on the plains could compare with the Macqueen House. True, each room had to be heated by its own little stove in winter, the only bath was just off the barber shop, and the partitions were so thin that lady guests were sometimes both fascinated and embarrassed by the masculine conversations which they overheard—but it represented luxury on the frontier. Some measure of this is indicated by a menu for Christmas dinner in 1888. This listed some fifty-five items which ran the gamut from New York Counts through loin of beef with Yorkshire pudding to Charlotte Russe, Strawberry tarts and Edam cheese.

In the early days there were drug stores but no druggists. On April 24, 1880, the *Yellowstone Journal* carried this item:

*Hofflin and Gerrish have pretty nearly everything in their establishment. Among the rest of the calamities to be found is a large collection of patent medicines of every description. Yesterday a well-dressed gentlemanly appearing man stepped in and began surveying the display of patent nostrums. Carland, the boss clerk, stepping up, the stranger asked: "Have you a pharmaceutist here?"*

*This was a $25 word to Will, but not wishing to acknowledge himself "bushed" on a word, he adjusted his hat [the clerks wore derbies in those days] and with a wise expression of countenance cast his eagle eye over the collection for a second or two, and then turning to the questioner, said: "I sold the last damned one today."*

Between 1880 and 1882 there was a concerted effort on the part of the clergy to convert the heathen in this wide-open town. Reverend William Wesley Van Orsdel—beloved by all, and widely known as "Brother Van"—came on several occasions to preach the Methodist gospel, and others labored in their respective faiths. Soon there were three protestant churches, a catholic chapel, and members of the Jewish faith used a room over one of the stores. The editor did his bit by noting the services, and often began his inimitable page of local news with an exhortation—sometimes in verse—to attend church on Sunday. As he reported the shows at the Cosmopolitan Saloon with equal zeal, perhaps he was just being impartial. Thanks to this editorial attitude one choice bit of humor was recorded in the summer of 1880:

*A Sunday or two ago a certain Miles City woman, who sometimes takes a little of the ardent, took her little daughter to Sunday school. During the various exercises and while the children were singing, she thought that her daughter was not singing as loud as she could, so straightening herself up, she shouted, "Sing up Jenny! sing up! damn you, you can sing as loud as any of them." The scene which followed beggered description, and handkerchiefs were in requisition to prevent laughing.*

Street lighting came as a result of various merchants erecting street lights outside their places of business—with the saloons and dance halls pioneering movement. Water was a problem in several ways. In the spring when ice jammed an adjacent bend in the Tongue River, the town was flooded—the flood in March 1881 when row boats were used on Main Street was long remembered. The really serious problem came from the lack of a water system for fire fighting. Some merchants put down wells in front of their establishments and, fortunately, the town had a ready-made fire alarm system. As the saloons *never* closed, there were *watchmen* on duty twenty-four hours a day. All that was necessary to turn out the volunteer fire department, and the rest of the town for that matter, was for someone to walk into the street and empty his revolver in the air. Of course, if a couple of gents got into a very heated argument there was likely to be a false alarm.

In these early days, fire was a constant hazard. Hardly a month passed but that some admonition did not appear among the "Local Items" in the newspaper—haystacks within the area of the town were a menace, cigar butts dropped through the cracks in the wooden sidewalks could —and did—cause fires, and the editor applauded the town ordinance which outlawed tin stovepipes extending through the roof of a building. But, apparently, fires were inevitable. On June 7, 1885, one resident wrote in a letter to his father:

*Miles City needs only two more fires to entirely clean up every old landmark—the last two fires were hard blows even though they cost the Insurance Companys $100,000   there are now 13 two story brick buildings going up and the chances are good that during the summer at least six more will be built.*

However, fire was an efficient modernizer and in Miles City it brought fireproof construction along Main Street and, eventually, a modern water system. And what happened in this town happened in every town of any size in the Yellowstone valley—Glendive, Billings, and Livingston all had disastrous fires.

Among the enterprises of the town was the *Yellowstone Journal* which became one of the outstanding newspapers in Montana. It was founded in July 1879 by "Major" T. P. McElrath, then a correspondent for *The New York Times*. The next year W. D. Knight took it over and in July 1883 Sam Gordon entered the firm as editor and business manager, and it was the latter who guided it for many years afterward. During the early years, little of the town's doings seemed to have escaped Knight's eyes and ears for the page titled "Local News" is a colorful reflection of the gossip which eddied along Main Street. Here were chronicled weekly the details of the latest expedition dispatched from Fort Keogh, the topic of Reverend Horsefall's last sermon, the destination of dance hall girls who left for greener pastures, the "enterprising" skunk that took up residence near the sign painter's shop, and the latest land policy of the Northern Pacific Railroad. These were intermingled like bits of meat that had gone through a sausage grinder, and added to them, by way of seasoning, were bits of droll humor:

*Parties owning hogs are requested to keep them off the street as complaint has been made with regard to them.*

*A sensation resulted from the incarceration of one of our "soiled doves" in the county bastile on Thursday. Some philanthropist rustled and obtained bail.*

*There have been 30 births the past month, and more are under way we are told.*

*The knight of the razor who has been spending a day or two in jail for disturbing the peace, has been released.*

*Sheriff Tom Irvine has a tame frog whose nose he paints with molasses to entice the flies.*

However, Miles City is best remembered for things other than these substantial and eminently respectable enterprises. In 1883, a reporter wrote this description for *The New York Times:*

"*The town has a curious interest for the stranger. . . . It is more like a typical border town. . . . Cowboys with lariats hanging on their saddles are seen at every turn, riding on the stout little broncho ponies of the plains; rough-looking men are loafing on the street corners; occasionally a "big Indian" with a squaw or two following him, stalks across the scene, and on each side of the street are innumerable places of low resort, in which the combined attractions of rum and gambling are openly advertised. These places are so numerous, indeed, that they seem at first glance to constitute the chief industry of the town. At night they constitute a curious specticle. Nearly all are large rooms opening on the street. The doors are kept wide open when the weather will permit and inside may be seen a motley crowd of men and women. On one side of the room is a long bar from which beer and whiskey are dispensed and about which there is always a crowd. Scattered about the* room are three or four faro "lay-outs," with grim and intensely interested groups of players standing around them. Scattered among the group are several Chinamen. . . . At some of the tables women act as dealers of the game and apparently they are regarded with the utmost respect by the rough men who are tempting fortune and wasting their hard earned savings. Everything is conducted quietly and in the most orderly manner. To be sure, there is a revolver or two ostentatiously displayed at the side of a heap of money and chips on the table or sticking in a menacing way from a player's broad buckskin belt; but they are seldom used and seem to be carried more in a reckless bravado than for offensive or defensive purposes. In warm weather the gaming tables are removed to the edge of the plank sidewalks. . . .

The town also had saloons, dance halls, and "parlor houses"—which probably outnumbered the stores, restaurants, hotels, and blacksmith shops.

Saloons provided a necessary part of the social life of the community and there was no sharp dividing line between those with upright business principles and others where the management would not hesitate to roll a drunken sheepherder for his last dollar. In like manner there were parlor houses which were considered *respectable* while there were others like Annie Turner's down on "coon row" which got frequent mention because of the brawls which occurred there. As Sam Gordon once put it:

Society as then constituted demanded that all should meet on the level, consequently the specticle of the prominent citizen playing "a stack or two" against the "bank" or "settin' up the fizz" at one of the frequent soirées dansante of the demi-monde, excited absolutely no comment.

On March 13, 1880, the *Yellowstone Journal* announced:

We have 23 saloons in our town, and they all do a good business. We are to have one church soon.

On November 5, 1881, it carried this note:

Judge D. S. Wade . . . represents Miles City as a lively little town of 1,000 inhabitants, but "utterly demoralized and lawless. It is not safe to be upon the streets after night. It has forty-two saloons and there are on an average about a half dozen fights every night. Almost every morning drunken men can be seen lying loose about the city. . . ." The eminent and learned Judge hits our town pretty hard. . . .

Although the editor was a bit sensitive about the comments of the judge, the doubling of the saloon business in a period of eighteen months was caused by the proximity of the end of the railroad and the large floating population engaged in its construction. Every town and village from Glendive to Livingston had a similar experience with these brawling laborers. Also, the editor really had no grounds to take offense as but a few months before he announced that the consumption of beer in Miles City was 1,000 bottles a day, and that 1,300 gallons of whiskey were sold each month. And at this time, the Cottage Saloon, one of the largest and most popular, reported daily receipts of $200-300 per day—with drinks at "two bits" each.

Not all the drunks were railroad workers as this bit of newspaper humor indicates:

(September 10, 1881) Stranger, entering one of our crowded hotels late last night, and addressing the polite hotel clerk—"Are you full tonight?" Clerk—"I haven't been full for three months. I run with the temperance people now." Stranger said he owed one.

As a class, the hide hunters, bullwhackers, soldiers, cowboys and sheepherders were all hard drinking people and what money the saloon keepers did not get the gamblers and the girls did.

Sam Pepper, a professional gambler who ran a saloon which was the favorite hangout for many of the British remittance men, was also the son of a Methodist minister. The story is told that he once received word that his father was coming to Miles City and wanted to preach in the toughest saloon in town. Pepper finally approached the proprietor of the "I Excell" store and explained his difficulty. The storekeeper confessed that he had always wanted to run a saloon and the two traded places for a time. When Pepper's father arrived he preached in the Second National Saloon and when the "saloon keeper" passed the hat the "boys around town" made a generous contribution.

Liquor constituted only a part of a saloon's business. Years later, Sam Gordon wrote:

Every saloon had its games of stud, faro and roulette, with black-jack or chuck-a-luck and such like to tempt those who hadn't the nerve to go against the real thing. At times there would be a keno room started but these never lasted long; the rake-off was too heavy and the sports couldn't see what became of their money. "Stud" was the standby with faro and roulette patronized principally by the fleeting crowd who liked to keep on the move. . . . The men who played stud were stayers. They "sat in" early and they stayed late. . . .

Between the saloons at one end of the scale and the parlor houses at the other, there were several kinds of establishments. There were *saloons* which had girls who would dance and "rustle" drinks, there were *dance halls* where patrons could drink and gamble, and there were vaudeville or "variety" houses where drinks could be bought. The girls who worked in these places usually lived nearby, often in little one-room shacks conveniently located in the rear of the establishments.

The story of the parlor houses of the West has never been written and probably never will be. While a few fragmentary references to the business exist, research—outside the reminiscences of old-timers—is practically impossible. E.g., in the census listings of one Montana mining town—in which the occupation of each individual was recorded—not a single prostitute was listed as such EXCEPT a few Chinese and Negroes. This ancient profession does not need a halo painted around its head, nor need it be assumed that all the members of the profession were deserving of tar and feathers. Furthermore, it certainly was a definite part of life on the frontier.

Some of the madams were hard cases. One of these was a Negress named Annie Turner who hauled Eugene A. Allen into the District Court in 1878 on the charge that he was the father of her bastard child. The doings at Annie's place were chronicled in the *Yellowstone Journal* with considerable regularity. On July 15, 1882:

*Annie Turner's house in "Coon Row" is becoming a very hard hole. Not a night passes but that some of the inmates or visitors indulge in a wild carousel, always ending up in a fight. Wednesday night some of the festive coons became enraged at a white brother who was "taking in" the sights, and proceeded to jump him, which was accomplished with grand success. This enraged the colored landlady, who, deponent says, lives with the white brother mentioned, and she pulled her 44 and fired into the crowd of negroes, the ball piercing the ear of one of them. This ended the row. The officers should pull this low brothel.*

This source of news came to an end in the middle of the following December:

*About nine o'clock last night a fire broke out in Annie Turner's . . . by a lamp being upset by one of the children in the house.    At the time of the fire there were a number of girls in the house, preparing for the festivities of the evening, which usually consisted of a dance and wound up with a fight. The building being of logs, 25x60, with a string of shacks in the rear some forty feet more burned fiercely. . . . The loss including the furniture and clothing in the house will amount to close on to $2,500.*

It is doubtful if Annie had $2,500 worth of assets for the assessor's records for preceding years show approximately $100 worth of property.

Only the brief notes in the local newspaper chronicle those early happenings which are known today. There were fights in the dance hall run by William Reese, and later his brother Frank, and also in Kitty Hardiman's Saloon on Park Street. Brawls at Annie Turner's were an expected occurrence; and the press often noted the comings and goings of members of the profession in such notes as:

*Some of the shining lights of the demi-monde left this city for the progressive city of Billings yesterday. Some paid their bills before they left.*

And:

*Many new girls are arriving in town and even old-timers cannot keep track of them.*

According to one cowboy who wrote unabashedly about Miles City's sporting life, the cowboys demanded more attractive girls than those of the days of the hide hunters and, as they were free spenders, they got what they wanted.

During the twenty-five or thirty years that Miles City was an important shipping point for livestock, commercialized sex was a well-recognized business. A man who was a cashier at one of the banks at this time recalled that the largest certificate of deposit he ever made out was for $50,000—the depositor was Mag Burns, one of the best known madams in town. Some of the largest parlor houses were hardly more than the proverbial stone's throw from the main business district. However, there was a deep gulf between the sporting class and the "respectable" portion of the town as one twelve-year-old girl found out much to her surprise. During one of the big fires in the mid-1880's she went down town with her father to see the sights, and overheard comments about Connie Hoffman whose establishment was involved. "Who is Connie Hoffman?" she inquired of her father. Looking down sternly, he said, "Will you please shut your mouth. And don't open it again. Now go home."

The business was a paradox in some respects. Obviously, those engaged in it did not accept the Seventh Commandment but a number of them apparently had some admirable qualities. This was a woman-poor society and many men, because of their hard-drinking and reckless habits, were more or less ostracized by the relatively few "respectable" women. Naturally, many homeless men sought such female companionship as was available—and that they found in the dance halls and parlor houses.

Some of the girls floated from one town to another—Cheyenne, Deadwood, Miles City, Billings, and Helena. Others became residents of a sort but with some of the characteristics of migrant workers. Thus it was that a cowboy going to Oregon with a trail outfit met in Virginia City a girl known as Tiger Lily. She asked that he send a mutual friend "her best regards . . . and says she hopes to be back in Miles about beef shipping time." And an old cattleman, in commenting on the early shipping points in the days of the open range, recalled that, "The North Side shipped from Fallon [between Miles City and Glendive]. They always shipped the girls down for shipping time."

Among the fragmentary references are comments that many of the girls observed certain rules of etiquette. Although they might drink in private, most of them did not "belly up to the bar," and not all of them swore "like troopers." In a carefully considered comment, one well-to-do rancher referred to a girl on whom he had been "sweet" as a "*lady.*" When he met her years later she was the respected wife of a cattleman and the mother of a family. A few did marry and thus acquire respectability for, according to the code of the times, no one dared speak ill of them after they broke with the profession. Some came from prominent families. Two handsome girls in Miles City during the days of the open range were daughters of a wealthy merchant in Montana.

One old-timer in recalling these days noted that Fanny French and Mag Burns were probably the "most notorious" operators of "*hook shops.*" In the vernacular of the times, a prostitute was called a "hooker," a term believed to have originated during the Civil War because General Hooker is alleged to have allowed women in camp. These women became know as "Hookers" and thus a parlor house was also called a "hook shop." Fanny French was a "high yellow" and ran a negro house: she was also an excellent horsewoman and "rode a fine string." Frankie Blair—whose real name was Amy McGregor—was the madam in an imposing house which still stands on Main Street.

Of the half dozen or more madams who operated during the heyday of the open range, Mag Burns is best remembered. When she had her formal opening, she distributed *engraved* invitations. Her establishment became known as "The 44," the figures being painted on the glass above the front door. The story goes that, "A bunch got down there buying drinks and Mag said she would name the place for the one buying the most drinks. —— —— bought the most drinks and she put his brand over the door." This individual is alleged to have taken quite a fancy to Mag and spent some time "courting" her—but to no avail. "Bill Bullard was setting there *quietly* all the time." Bullard ran a brewery and a hotel and Maggie's money is said to have kept him in business. Finally, they retired together in the South.

E. C. Abbott—a cowboy widely known as Teddy Blue—has related one of his escapades which is said to have happened in the 44. He and some friends were trying to sing a popular ballad in Mag's parlor and she objected to the treatment they were giving her piano. One remark led to another and finally Abbott threatened to bring his horse into the parlor for reasons which need not be stated here. His friends egged him on until he did-just that. Maggie then locked the door and called the police. The only way out was through a large window which was not far above the ground, and the cowboy and his pony took it and headed for the ferry across the Yellowstone in considerable of a hurry. Whether the story is accurately told is not known, but on October 7, 1882, this item appeared in the *Yellowstone Journal*:

A half dozen cowboys got on a rampage and amused themselves by riding their bronchoes into "27," tearing up carpets, smashing furniture, etc. No arrests!

Two noted characters were Connie Hoffman and Cowboy Annie. Connie was a handsome brunette who was "kept" on several occasions by wealthy men, one of whom was an English remittance man. On one occasion, the latter took her to England with him when he returned on a visit. This was the courtesan about whom the previously-noted little girl asked her father. Cowboy Annie worked at the 44, and she had a dress on which was embroidered most of the brands of the outfits between the Platte and the Yellowstone. In the opinion of one old rancher, "Cowboy Annie seemed out of place in a sporting house—she didn't *belong*. She came out and met the roundup when it came near. *She always was a lady*." Perhaps she was a lady—except for her profession—for these women and their associates cannot be honestly judged except by the standards of their own times.

One kindhearted, amoral woman who spent considerable time in the Yellowstone valley was Calamity Jane. Much of what is in print about her is sentimental nonsense, and most, if not all, of the exciting adventures she related in her autobiography are impossibilities. Although there is no question that she worked at such masculine occupations as whacking bulls, there is no reliable evidence that she was ever a scout. However, there is no doubt that she was a chronic alcoholic, frequently an inmate of hook shops, and often disorderly—to the point of being obnoxious—when in her cups. But, as her heart was as big as the country in which she lived and as her vices were not of the vicious sort, many were charitably disposed toward her.

Just when Calamity came to the Yellowstone country, after working with Crook's supply train, is not clear. There is a photograph taken in Miles City on which the photographer wrote—probably years afterwards—"Taken in 1880." Although this date may not be correct, there is no reason to doubt the issue of the *Yellowstone Journal* dated February 14, 1882, which states, "Calamity Jane is in town." Or the issue of June 3rd which noted, " 'Calamity Jane' is now living on a ranch near Graveyard bottom."

Graveyard Creek, named by Jack Hawkins because of the many Indian burials in the cottonwoods along this valley, was about twenty miles west of Miles City.

During the following July and August, her visits to Miles City were noted by the editor of the *Yellowstone Journal*. On the 8th of July he wrote:

*Calamity Jane came to the metropolis last week from her Rosebud ranch, and "took in the town" in great shape. She is a queer freak of nature, and is as well known on the frontier as any living person. She looks as if she had seen hard usage of late.*

On September 2nd, it was noted that "Calamity Jane is at Billings"; and in December she was at Livingston. As the Northern Pacific Railroad was building track between Miles City and Livingston during this year, and as Calamity's whereabouts shifted westward at approximately the same speed as the end of the track, she was undoubtedly following the construction crews.

After the railroad passed Livingston, she returned and settled near Miles City where she again broke into the news on March 3, 1883:

*Kibble and Calamity Jane, charged with selling liquor to the Indians, got free owing to a technical error in the complaint.*

At one time she lived in a cabin on Canyon Creek near where Colonel Sturgis had his skirmish with the Nez Percé, and it is alleged—perhaps erroneously—that she was part of a horse stealing gang which hid their loot on a butte which is now called "Calamity Jane Horse Cache." In 1895 she was back in Miles City, living in a little shack behind the Grey Mule, a saloon on Park Street. After one of her sprees she was hauled—it took three men to put her in jail—before Judge Milburn who fined her, as she put it, "for being a celebrity." Around the turn of the century, she spent considerable time in the vicinity of Livingston selling her autobiography to tourists. In 1902, a judge in

Billings gave her 60 days in jail—partly for disturbing the peace and partly to remove her from temptation until she could recuperate her strength. But Calamity had burned the candle at both ends for too long and she died the following August in a village near Deadwood.

The election held in November 1882 was a memorable one in Miles City—and Custer County. Prior to this date there had not been any great amount of rivalry between the Republicans and Democrats, but this time the latter staged a determined fight. A few days after it was over photographer L. A. Huffman wrote to his father:

*Election day was a Daisy here—Many thousands changed hands on sheriff Joe Leighton had 4 $1000 bets and lost all—excitement ran high —Brass Bands and Banners—Gunpowder and gin were used extensively on both sides. . . .*

Voting was done at a faro table in the rear of Charlie Brown's saloon and the election board sat for five days—with frequent adjournments to indulge in other attractions close at hand. Many of the soldiers were clothed in civilian garments and "voted," and the total number of votes cast in Miles City was far in excess of the total population—even counting the women and children! One of the precincts which was tabulated in the total for the county was "Wooley's Ranch" which cast a unanimous 112 Democratic votes. This made it the third largest precinct in the county—and it has never been located on a map!

Another outstanding incident took place the following July. One Saturday morning a man named William Rigney and a companion, drunk and ugly from an all-night carouse, turned up at the residence of a respectable citizen while the family was at breakfast. When ordered out, they made obscene remarks about the wife and daughter—a thing which the frontier did not tolerate. Saloon keeper, Charlie Brown, who was passing by, walloped Rigney over the head with a "stout club" and stretched him senseless while the second tough took to his heels. Rigney was put in jail, only to be taken from the jailer about midnight by a group of citizens who hanged him from a nearby railroad bridge. The published account made the action appear to have been carried out by vigilantes but old timers say that Rigney was already dead when he was hanged, and the action was merely to cover the fact and prevent Brown from being tried for manslaughter.

This thug had been a hanger-on and part time employee at the Cosmopolitan Theatre, a variety house on the south side of Main Street at 6th Street. Early Sunday morning—a few hours after the *hanging*— this building was discovered to be on fire and the blaze swept the entire block before it stopped. This fire was obviously the work of an arsonist and many citizens believed Rigney's pals had started it as an act of retaliation. The town had long had a considerable number of tough characters, and the coming of the railroad in November 1881 had added to the assortment. After discussing the matter, the "vigilante committee" issued an ultimatum to the undesirable element to get out of town or take the consequences.

The leader of this faction was John Chinnick, one of the first settlers in the town. He was not a bad sort in some ways, and quite civic minded, but his saloon and cabin had always been the rendezvous of any shady characters who drifted up or down the Yellowstone—including Big Nose George Parrott whose story is told elsewhere. When he was informed on Monday morning that he had been banished from town, he first agreed to go but later showed signs of being unwilling to leave quietly. About noon he apparently had a scuffle in his cabin with his wife over a revolver and in the tussle he received a fatal wound in the abdomen. This caused his death a month later. With their leader in a critical condition, the rough element heeded the warning and left.

As settlers filtered into the gap between Bozeman and Miles City, two small trading centers sprang up which showed indications of developing into important towns. One of these was near the mouth of the Big Horn. The first signs of a permanent settlement in this area was the military depot known as Terry's Landing. This was located on the south bank of the Yellowstone about two miles above the mouth of the Big Horn. One day Captain C. E. Gilbreath, who had charge of this dump,

saw a boat come down the river and tie up on the opposite side near the ferry. As soon as a tent went up, I went over to see what was up. I found that a Jew named Batzinski [sic—one of the Basinski brothers] had put up a store tent. In it was everything imaginable, from fish hooks and calico to grain and provisions—there was even reading matter, in fact, about everything but pianos. Instead of one boat, he had three or four mackinaws with which he had brought his store from Bozeman or Helena. He had come down the river looking for a likely place to start a store.

This was the beginning—in 1877—of Junction City. Two and a half years later the editor of the *Yellowstone Journal* wrote:

. . . the folks at the mouth of the Big Horn ought to get a name for their town; it is now called Junction City, Peasefort, Big Bottom, Big Horn City, Terry's Landing, Sherman and Big Horn Junction.

Three years after Basinski put up his tent—he later moved to Miles City and became a prominent merchant—the Miles City editor reported the growth which had taken place:

Junction City is a thriving town. . . . Like all embryo western cities it has a number of saloons and maisons du pleasure, and one mercantile house—which is run by Paul McCormick, well known in this city. He keeps a large stock of dry goods, merchandise, whiskeys, etc, of all kinds, and is doing a rushing business. He is also express agent and postmaster and in taking care of his business has his time fully occupied. At the time of the JOURNALITE's visit the saloons were all booming and money was plenty. The saloon business was carried on by Burns Smith, who has a near and commodious place in the lower portion of town. he is doing a fine business and sells excellent "goods." Further along we come to Buckskin William's saloon and billiard hall [formerly at Benson's Landing] and find that his place is well patronized both the bar and the tables going all the time day and night. The Reed Brothers have a large eating house near and are feeding a number of borders all the time and as they set an excellent table are making money. Brown & Davis have the ferry and also a saloon and with a billiard table are doing well as games run all night in their house. There are a number of new houses going up and settlers are coming in rapidly.

In 1882, the Journal's reporter counted eight saloons—"all doing a good business at old time prices—drinks twenty-five cents"—2 large stores, a "bakery and confectionary," a hotel, a restaurant, and a livery, feed and sale stable. A year later there were fourteen saloons and three dance halls and an estimated 500 people in the place. The little town was booming.

The name Junction City was well chosen. It was at the head of navigation on the Yellowstone and merchandise was unloaded here to be freighted out to other points. A post named Fort Maginnis had been established at the edge of the Judith Mountains and a mining camp named Maiden was not far away. Freight and travelers for both of these places went north out of the town. Fort Custer was some thirty miles south up the Big Horn valley, and freighters also hauled goods as far south as Fort McKinney in Wyoming, and the nearby settlements of Buffalo and Big Horn. The story is told that on one occasion a box of silver currency was received by the postmaster to be forwarded to a bank in Buffalo. He persuaded a freighter to undertake the task and the box was labeled "bolts" and hidden under the other freight in the bottom of the wagon box—and delivered safely.

Although this was a tough little town, there was only one fatal shooting. On another occasion an irate German musician wielded a double-barreled shotgun on a would-be bad man who had tormented him, and plastered his back with birdshot. Considering the class of people who sometimes loafed here, perhaps it is strange that there was not more trouble.

Beginning in southern Utah, there was a *trail* which ran northward to Brown's Hole in northwestern Colorado, thence to some secluded areas in the southern part of the Big Horn Mountains, and then along the eastern slope of these mountains and northward to the Yellowstone. From Junction City, the *trail* continued north to the junction of the Musselshell and the Missouri, and from this point on to Canada. This was not a *trail* in the usual sense of the word but rather a general *route*. It had no name but it has been dubbed, quite appropriately, "The Outlaw Trail." Probably no one bunch of outlaws ever traveled its entire extent until the summer of 1901 when George Parker, alias "Butch" Cassidy, and his confederates rode southward along it from northern Montana.

When Junction City was a bustling little place, horse thieves rode the trail from above the Canadian line to the southern end of the Big Horn Mountains and the Black Hills. One hangout was a trading post operated by squaw man Billy Downs at the mouth of the Musselshell but there were no "bright lights" at this place. Junction City did have saloons and dance halls and the outlaws came to these attractions like moths to a light at night. As they contributed to the income of various establishments, the townspeople did not concern themselves with what their customers did outside of Junction City—after all this would have been a breach of frontier etiquette. Thus the town became a sort of *neutral ground*. In all probability the rustlers were not bad customers though they were a scourge to the countryside as indicated by dozens of items in the press of the valley during the early 1880's. But their days were numbered for in 1884 a vigilante organization, which was both efficient and thorough, shot or hung every rustler they could catch—which was most of them.

As with the other towns, fire took its toll. On April 5, 1883, three or four saloons and one of the stores burned. Men fought the flames by means of a bucket line which stretched between the river and the burning buildings. It is said that jugs of whiskey were passed along the line to stimulate the efforts of the workers, these passing more frequently as the fire was brought nearer control. In the end there were only five sober men left in town.

In spite of the promising start, the life of this town was destined to be short. Being bordered on the south by the Crow Reservation, there was only a limited area from which to draw trade and when the town of Billings was started in 1882 the end was in sight. Paul McCormick, the enterprising business man, transferred his activities to the new town and there was no one who could fill his place. The town slowly dwindled, and finally the restless Yellowstone cut away even the ground upon which it stood. Now, only the name remains.

At a spot about two miles below the city of Billings, another settlement sprang up. A man named Freth, Henry Kieser—a Crow squaw man and ex-trapper, and the McAdow brothers settled here in 1876. P. W. McAdow started a store and a hotel, and the latter also became a stage station the next year. Later, Ash and Boots built a brewery and McAdow set up a sawmill, the logs for which were rafted down the Yellowstone. Chicago Jane's Boudoir, a notorious hole, was located next door to the postoffice. Thus Coulson, like its neighbor down the river, showed promise of becoming an important town.

This settlement had no newspaper to chronicle its happenings but it had the earmarks of being a tough town. On the 14th of April, 1880, P. W. McAdow told a friend who was passing through on the stage that there were—already—sixteen graves in the boothill cemetery just above the town. One killing, on October 7, 1882, involved a thug named Lump and "Muggins" Taylor, a deputy. Taylor, the victim, had been a scout with Gibbon's men in 1876 and had carried the news of Custer's defeat to Bozeman and Fort Ellis. For a number of years, "Liver-eating" Johnson was an officer here. He was once asked how he kept order in a town which did not have a jail; and his reply was that he just "whooped" the unruly ones until they were glad to behave. As Johnson was an unusually powerful man, his fists were probably more feared than a jail would have been.

Johnson, one of the colorful characters in Montana, spent the latter part of his life in the Yellowstone Basin. He had been a trapper, then a scout with the troops at Fort Keogh, and later a police officer at various small towns. The peculiar nickname which attached itself permanently to him was acquired at a trading post at the mouth of the Musselshell. In June 1869, a Sioux war party jumped a band of trappers who had congregated at this point to celebrate the coming of the first steamboat of the season. The Indians got the worst of it and at the end of the fight Johnson is alleged to have cut out the liver of one warrior and eaten part of it. Unfortunately for this legend, Johnson claimed that he merely pretended to take a bite of the liver, a statement which is supported by another reliable witness of the incident.

Another little settlement grew up at the mouth of the Stillwater two miles below the combination store and saloon which Horace Countryman and Hugo Hoppe built in 1875. This was first named Eagle Nest. Shortly afterward it was called Sheep Dip—because some whiskey sold there had such a vile taste that a customer compared it to this liquid. For a number of years it was known as Stillwater—and was continually confused with Stillwater, Minnesota, and vice versa. Finally, the name was changed to Columbus. Shortly after 1880 three other settlements grew up to supply ranchers who settled east of the Big Horn Mountains. These were Buffalo, near Fort McKinney, Big Horn, and Sheridan, Wyoming. The latter was built on the campsite along Goose Creek used by Crook in 1876, and Buffalo became know later as the town in which a cowboy, alleged to have resembled Owen Wister's "Virginian," killed a rustler corresponding to "Trampas."

Financial difficulties arising from the panic of 1873 caused the Northern Pacific Railroad to let the railhead at Bismarck to lie dormant for almost five years. Then, in the spring of 1879, track construction was started again. When it built along the Yellowstone in 1881 and 1882, three towns mushroomed almost overnight. The first of these was at the mouth of Glendive Creek where Colonel Stanley had located a supply dump in 1873. A traveler reported early in August 1880 that

*there are altogether four families there now and that a larger number are expected from the east soon. . . . Grading will be commenced there soon. Mr. J. J. Graham [a Miles City merchant] has put in a stock of goods but has not as yet realized any flattering returns.*

When the track-laying crew reached the town on the 5th of July, 1881, work was already well under way on such facilities as the water tank, depots, and round house. Two lumber yards had been established, and there was a post office and a "palace of terpsichorean and theatrical art" which ran day and night. Approximately one hundred town lots had been sold during the preceding three weeks. In October, a special correspondent for the *Glasgow Herald* (Scotland) penned this description of the town:

*. . . I found the town to consist of about 100 habitations, and composed of about half and half of wood and canvas. The wooden buildings were of the roughest description . . . the line of houses constituting the only street . . . contained 46 houses and tents all told, 23 of these being liquor saloons, 3 dancing places of the lowest type, and the balance dwelling houses and stores, including the only hotel in the place, which is known as the "Grand Pacific." This hostelry is the most primitive one I have struck on my travels. . . .*

The next morning this reporter watched the loading of a steamboat. As it pulled up to the bank two laborers on board were settling an argument—one armed with a knife and the other with an axe.

*In talking to the captain of the boat I learned that all the scum, criminals, and roughs follow in the wake of the railroad construction. Certainly the class of laborers loading this boat were the most villainous lot of men I had ever seen together. I noticed one man take off his hat, and his head was literally seamed with scars and old wounds. These men do not carry pistols . . . but, even without, they are a lawless band of roughs.*

What this man observed about the appearance and the population of Glendive could have been seen in Billings the following summer, and again at Livingston about six months later.

There are two stories explaining the location of Billings. One is that a man named Alderson bought up a considerable acreage in the vicinity of Coulson, and that he and others held about two square miles of prospective townsite on which they hoped to realize a handsome profit when the railroad arrived. The high price demanded by these speculators irked the railroad officials so they established the town just outside these holdings. The more probable story is that certain railroad officials took steps which would line their own pockets with a handsome profit. In 1881—the railroad reached Billings on August 22, 1882— the Minnesota Land Improvement Company was organized with the major portion of the stockholders being officials of the railroad. This company bought up the desirable railroad land between Young's Point and Coulson, a total of 60,000 acres, and in April of 1882 were selling lots in the new town to eastern speculators. The people at Coulson were disagreeably surprised when surveyors began to lay out the town some two miles upstream. They, and others who expected to settle in the town, were even more disgruntled when they found the choice lots in the center of the town were in the hands of speculators who asked up to $250 for lots having a 25 foot frontage on the main street. There was considerable dissatisfaction—then and for a long time afterward—but the would-be settlers were over the proverbial barrel. Coulson hung on for a while and then finally gave up the struggle.

Billings, which was called "The Magic City," grew rapidly. Before long it contained 1,500 to 2,000 people, and a count made on October 22nd showed 155 business houses and 10 under construction, 99 residences and 13 under construction, 6 railroad buildings, 1 church and 1 under construction, and 25 tents. Miles City viewed the upstart with mingled envy and disbelief, and the editor of the *Yellowstone Journal* invariably referred to it—not without reason—as "Bilkings." The officials of the promotion company also hoped to sell the area of fine bench land which they owned to farmers. To promote this development, they obligated themselves to build 39 miles of irrigating ditch, which the people promptly named the "Big Ditch." Although this bit of construction proved to be both more difficult and more expensive than was anticipated, the company was obligated to complete it; and it constituted one bright spot among a host of unsatisfactory matters.

What happened at Billings and Coulson was repeated at Livingston. On July 16, 1882, a village began to grow near Great Bend around the warehouse and store of a track contractor. When the railroad reached this point on the 1st of December, Clark City was a going establishment with six general stores, two hotels, and forty-four other enterprises—of which *thirty* were saloons. However, the railroad officials decreed that Livingston should be located a short distance away—to the tune of a neat profit of $200,000. Again, the townspeople bought lots and moved. Some 2,000 people soon settled here, among them Calamity Jane who operated a hurdy gurdy.

With the establishment of Livingston, settlement in the Yellowstone Basin was practically complete except for a few small towns which sprouted later. After a year or two, and a few baptisms of fire, the three *Johnny-come-latelys* settled down to a prosaic existence with Billings maintaining its claim of being the "Magic City of the Plains." Miles City developed into an important livestock shipping point and, later, into a horse market. It was destined to remain a cowboy town for years and even today, under the veneer of modern trappings, there are things which recall the frontier days when this was the most important settlement in the Yellowstone Basin.

The route of the Northern Pacific was not definitely fixed for some time, and consideration was given to leaving the Yellowstone valley above Fort Keogh, crossing over to the valley of the Musselshell, and proceeding to Helena. In the end, the line built paralleled the river from Glendive to Livingston, being on the south bank except for a stretch of about 60 miles above Billings. The Crow Reservation posed a problem but in September 1881 a commission negotiated with the Absaroka and, for $25,000, secured a right of way. For a time after the road was completed, the Indians would climb into empty cars, bag and baggage, and ride from Billings to Livingston, and back on another train. This hitch hiking soon became a nuisance and the railroad officials were forced to put an end to these excursions.

After the surveyors established the line, construction crews went to work on the grade and these kept well ahead of the track-laying gangs.

Grading crews involved a large number of men. In the fall of 1880, the *Yellowstone Journal* reported that 1,500 men were to be scattered along the line between Miles City and Glendive to prepare grade for the track which was to be laid the following year: and on November 19, 1881, it was noted that 2,000 men and 1,600 mules were at work on the Yellowstone Division—which began at Glendive and ended at Billings. Track was laid at the rate of about a mile and a half a day. Supply cars were pushed up close to the end of the track and eighteen ties and two rails—sufficient to lay one length of track—were put on a dump car. A black horse named Old Nig pulled this up to where men had to carry the materials the rest of the way. Old Nig pulled this car all the way from Bismarck to Gold Creek where the junction was made with the line built eastward from the Pacific Coast.

Leap-frogging along—Glendive to Miles City to Billings to Livingston—came the headquarters of the Engineering Department with "Colonel" J. B. Clough in charge. This group was noted for the excellence of its mess, and one sportsman who ate at their table in the Little Missouri country was agreeably surprised to find

even ripe fruit, fresh oysters and new vegetables. . . . Cows are kept with each camp and fresh butter and milk greet the hungry traveler. . . . they spread before you game of a dozen different varieties all cooked to a turn . . . and in many instances the cuisine equals that of the Palmer House [in Chicago] or Grand Pacific.

In 1881, at Miles City, their Thanksgiving menu listed 3 kinds of soup, oysters prepared three different ways, 2 kinds of fish, 9 kinds of meat, 6 vegetables, 6 side dishes, 12 kinds of dessert, 3 kinds of fruit and "Coffee Tea Chocolate." And certainly there were cigars and various kinds of liquor.

Ties and bridge timbers were secured along the way. Some ties were chopped along the Powder but these became a total loss as there was not enough water to float them out. The upper Tongue supplied a large amount of such materials and these came down the river successfully. About the time the track reached Miles City, the *Yellowstone Journal* noted,

A contract has been let to Broadwater, Hubbell & Co. for 250,000 pine ties and 15,000 piles . . . besides a large quantity of bridge timbers and lumber. The branch road has been graded and the iron is now being laid to their saw mill and soon will convey the material to the front.

Presumably this material was sufficient to build a considerable distance toward supplies farther up the valley.

From time to time the *Yellowstone Journal* printed accounts of other incidents and difficulties which occurred. On the 9th of October, 1880, for example:

> The absence of game on the Little Porcupine caused the surveying party to make targets of Pete Jackson's hogs, resulting in a stump tail for one and the death of another, and a $10 accompaniment.

When the grade was still east of Miles City, one man shot another without any obvious cause. When he tried to escape by swimming the river, other men riddled him with bullets. Although the officers in Custer County followed the policy of letting the workers settle their own difficulties, they had to take action on May 28, 1882:

> Deputies Conley and King went up the railroad about fifteen miles on Sunday to arrest a man who, with the assistance of a six-shooter, had been running a railroad camp, much to the demoralization and terror of the peaceable inhabitants. It being . . . on Sunday, no work was being done, and the entire camp was roaring drunk and ripe for mischief. When Deputy Conley presented the warrant and reached forth to arrest the offender, the railroad camp gathered around and told the man he needn't go if he didn't want to; but when the brave deputies pulled their shooters and said they would shoot the first man who made a break at them, the courage of the railroaders ran out at their heels, and no attempt at a rescue was made. . . .

Thus the Northern Pacific Railroad pushed its way up the valley of the Yellowstone and, finally, into the Gallatin valley. The fight for a road east to the "States" had been won. With the railroad came some changes. Old-timers who had scorned all coins below a quarter found the nickles and pennies had come to stay; sightseers, and big game hunters in season, flooded the country; the Diamond R freighting outfit—one of the most famous in the West—folded and bull whackers had to find other sources of livelihood; and the tramps in Miles City no longer bedded down in the park but under the platform of the depot. One pioneer, in a moment of nostalgia, wrote:

> Then came the army of railroad builders. That—the railway—was the fatal coming. One looked about and said, "This is the last West." It was not so. There was no more West after that. It was a dream and a forgetting, a chapter forever closed.

# 19

## An Empire of Grass

»»»»»»»«««««««« There were fortunes to be made in the Yellowstone Basin. Every stockman on the high plains knew that. So did every man and woman in the United States and Europe who had a little money to invest and a desire to gamble on cattle and sheep. The grass was there—all that was needed was livestock to harvest it.

But there were three barriers to acquiring this wealth. Until the Sioux were immobilized and put on reservations, it was out of the question to think of trying to establish a ranch in this area. In their seasonal migrations the vast herds of buffalo engulfed any horses and cattle which were in their path, swept them along like a broad river carries floating leaves, and the owner usually never saw them again. And added to these was the difficulty of getting stock to market once it had been raised and fattened.

The solution to these three problems all came within the decade 1873-1883. The terminal of the Northern Pacific Railroad at Bismarck, D.T., was a promise that there would be transportation once the company could throw off the effects of the financial difficulties created by

the panic of 1873. Sitting Bull's defeat and Miles' vigorous campaigning along the Yellowstone in the years immediately after 1876
left no question about the final disposition of the Indian problem.
And as to the buffalo—by the mid-1870's the hide hunters on the
Southern Plains were looking for new hunting grounds and there was
only one place left to look. That was eastern Montana and adjacent
sections of Dakota and Wyoming Territories.

Miles City was located near the middle of this great hunting ground,
and the steamboats which plied the Yellowstone as far up as Junction
City provided transportation to the railroad terminals at Bismarck,
Sioux City, Omaha, and St. Louis. So it was natural that Miles City
became the most important outfitting and hide buying point on the
Northern Plains—as well as the most popular resort between hunting
seasons.

Although many buffalo were killed in the immediate valley of the
Yellowstone, some of the favorite hunting grounds lay just outside this
watershed. On the east, Beaver and Box Elder Creeks and, to the
north, the Musselshell River, Redwater Creek, Big Dry and Little Dry
were favorite hunting grounds: and it was in the country between the
Yellowstone and the Missouri that the last of the great herds were to be
found. However, the bulk of the hides from this vast area were sold to
hide buyers who either lived in Miles City or who traveled out from
this town.

In April and May, 1880, Granville Stuart, a pioneer rancher, made a
long reconnaissance trip hunting a desirable location for a ranch. He
came down the Yellowstone as far as Miles City, then went up the
Tongue a considerable distance, turned westward to the northern end
of the Big Horn Mountains, and then went north across the Yellowstone and the Musselshell Rivers to the edge of the South Judith
Mountains. From the time he left Miles City on the 24th of April until
he ended his trip on the 12th of May, his daily journal is studded with
comments like these—"Hundreds of buffalo in sight all the time"; "The
whole country is black with buffalo"; "Small bands of buffalo in sight
all the way down to Tongue River"; ". . . hundreds of buffalo in every
direction"; "Buffalo by the thousands in every direction. . . . Will
hardly run from us." Such were the conditions at the beginning of the
great slaughter. Three years later all that remained were a few—a very
few—wary survivors.

Of the scores engaged in hide hunting, Vic Smith was the most
famous. He was a marvelous shot, and a fearless man with a very likeable personality as well. Another well known hunter was F. R. "Doc"
Zahl who ran a road house at the mouth of Powder River during the

summer months. Among those who drifted up from the southern plains, bringing with them the hunting techniques which had been perfected there, were John Cook, Hyram "Hi" Bickerdyke—son of the famous Civil War nurse, "Mother" Bickerdyke, John Goff, and Jim White who had a reputation in the Southwest and—so he told a partner—a price of $5,000 on his head.

To some, hide hunting was a profession. Others, like photographer L. A. Huffman who made practically the only photographs of this business, hunted to bolster their meager incomes. And still others used this occupation to accumulate a grub stake. One of the latter was William Roach who left this record of his experiences:

Coming out from Minnesota in 1880 in company with my sister and Mr. Richard Tonner, who was my partner and hunting companion later on, I arrived in Glendive, Montana, in September of that year, Glendive was then the end of the Northern Pacific Railroad. From there we took the stage to Miles City. While passing through the Bad Lands the stage was held up by two masked bandits. . . . No one was hurt, but the hold up caused us several hours delay. . . .

Several months later Mr. Tonner, whom I called Dick, and I started on a hunting expedition, altho we were comparative strangers in Miles City we purchased $150.00 worth of provisions on tick, also we purchased Sharps rifles, 45-120 calibre on tick. In addition we secured four cheap horses and an old wagon and started on our buffalo hunt. Traveling north . . . we reached Crow Rock and camped a couple of weeks. . . .

We got a few buffalo here but game was not plentiful so we moved on to a place named Sunday Creek. Hunting was good. We started out early each morning and put in a long day, getting on an average of five or six a day. We skinned them, using what meat we wanted, and left the rest for the coyotes. Hides were worth about $3.50 each then.

We then moved to a place called Froze To Death Creek. There was lots of snow and it was very cold. After being there two weeks, we went out one morning to get some buffalo and knocked down nine. Thinking them all dead we went right into the center of the bunch to skin them, when three jumped up on one side and two on the other, having only been stunned, and all started charging. Dick . . . commenced shooting and killed all three on his side and then came to my rescue as my shots had not been as sure as his, and killed a huge buffalo within three feet of me.

Upon quitting here we went over toward the mouth of the Big Dry and put up a pole tepee with hides around it and camped as long as the hides were good up to the middle of March. When we got over to the Big Dry we had in the neighborhood of three hundred hides, not counting those stolen from us by the Indians. The Sioux would come and trade us hides for provisions. Finally Tonner caught on that they were stealing hides from us and that we were trading for our own hides. . . .

We had another little experience with Indians when one evening we went a little way into a thicket to hunt deer. When we separated . . . someone started firing at us. We laid down flat on the ground to avoid being hit, but I was shot in the calf of the leg. . . . We discovered that it was Indians doing the shooting and opened fire on them . . . . [and] what was left of them ran away. We later learned that they had stolen about a dozen horses from the whites. . . .

While still on the Big Dry I was lost one night. I heard a noise ahead of me and shot at it. It proved to be a big buffalo bull. I skinned him and wraped up in the hide to spend the night. During the night the hide froze and in the morning when I started to get up I discovered I was shut inside the frozen hide. I had left my gun on the outside but fortunately had my scabbord with me and was able to cut the hide sufficiently to permit me to climb out.

To sum up our hunting trip; between us we had six hundred buffalo hides and over one hundred smaller ones such as coyote, wolf, fox, etc. . . . . We frequently saw as many as seventy-five wolves in a single pack. We hauled these hides to Norris's Point on the bank of the Missouri River and sold them to the boats that came along.

\*     \*     \*

As this account indicates there were troubles of various kinds on the ranges. Occasionally a hunter would be found dead, apparently killed by a wounded buffalo. One white hunter resented the presence of Bill Stone on a bit of territory he had staked out for himself and started sniping at long range. Stone replied in kind and won the "argument." Horse thieves—red and white—left outfits afoot. And there were troubles with Sitting Bull's followers from across the border who destroyed hides and set fire to piles ricked up on the river banks. The story is told that on one occasion some Indians raided the camp of the Stone brothers and, while one was stealing a pony, another shot at Sam and broke his arm. At night, while Sam was gone to get his arm set, a warrior walked across the hide roof of the dugout in which the hunters were living and Bill shot up through the roof and hit the Indian in the neck.

Usually only the hides were taken. These sold for $1.25 to 3.50 each for the run-of-the-mill with fancy robes bringing $15 to 20.00 or more. Although it was wasteful to allow the meat to rot, there was practically no market for most of it. Dried tongues were a delicacy and were in demand; and when the Northern Pacific Railroad built up the Yellowstone valley, buffalo supplied cheap meat for the grading and track-laying crews. On one occasion at least, an effort was made to cure the meat in brine. About thirty miles north of Miles City along North Sunday Creek, a group of tub-shaped depressions could be seen for many years. With green hides for liners, these were used for pickling vats. Although this method of curing meat was used successfully on the Southern Plains, the results of this venture are no longer known. However, the locality was known as "Dry House" for many years.

No complete record was ever made of the hide hunting although a few hunters set down reminiscences during their sunset years. In 1886, only *three* years after the herds had ceased to exist, William T. Hornaday of the National Museum found it impossible to assemble anything resembling an accurate estimate of the number of hides which the Northern Herd had provided.

Perhaps the most extensive record of these days is that which can be patched together from the paragraphs which the editor of the *Yellowstone Journal* put in the columns headed "Local Items." These are some of the more interesting references to the business:

The buffalo herd is about twenty miles up the Yellowstone. (September 4, 1879)

Over 100 of our citizens are out hunting buffalo for their hides, which are worth on this market at present $1.50 each, one firm alone in this city have already on hand over 4000 hides, and many other houses have almost as many. (January 17, 1880)

Much difficulty is experienced by travelers and others in following the roads along the Yellowstone valley, as the trails are totally obscured in some places by the immense herds of buffalo. Several parties have got lost, and been obliged to camp out on this account. (January 17, 1880)

Jas. White, the boss buffalo hunter came to town Thursday to dispose of his hides, 2,000 of which he has secured this season. (January 17, 1880)

At Dillan's ranch, last week two Indians destroyed about 300 hides by burning them in the absence of the owner. This habit of burning hides seems to be quite a favorite pastime with the hostile Indian, but to prevent this pernicious practice we would suggest the hide owners to carefully insert a pound or two of giant powder in their piles of hides and if there are any Indians left to tell the tale of their diversions they won't be so anxious to burn hides afterward. (May 8, 1880)

From a careful estimate we find that about thirty-three thousand buffalo hides were shipped from this county this summer and spring. They were worth about $70,000 and the money went where it did the most good—to our hunters. (July 10, 1880)

Ed Martin says that in returning from Burn's ranch last week, he was obliged to turn from his course for about five miles to avoid an immense herd of buffalo near the ferry point. He could see them for twenty miles along his course. (August 14, 1880)

Geo. Dillon, hunting at the head of Cedar creek, shot 14 buffalo one day this week and when about to skin them was interrupted by a large party of what he supposes to be Poplar Creek Indians. He didn't stop to ask them however, but fled. (September 18, 1880)

Huffman, the rustling photographer, has at last succeeded in catching a full grown buffalo bull—on his camera—and has made some elegant pictures of him. During the performance the buff, made a charge at him, compelling him to throw aside his camera and other things and run for his life. Fortunately Mr. Geo. Meyer was near, and with a shot from his rifle checked the headlong charge of the infuriated animal. (July 16, 1881)

Buffalo seem to be quite numerous this season already, notwithstanding the tremendous slaughter last fall and winter. Hunters who have just come in from the range claim to have made very large killings. Just how many years it is going to take to annihilate the shaggy monster is beyond our knowledge, but it surely cannot be many years hence. (September 24, 1881)

Twelve hundred tons of hides were shipped from Montana this year by H. C. Tilhnghast & co., of Chicago. Three hundred tons were shipped from Benton, the same amount from the [railroad] terminus, and 600 tons from the Yellowstone. (October 15, 1881)

Judge D. S. Wade in an interview with the Helena Independent . . . . truthfully . . . [stated] that $500,000 was put in circulation in Miles City last year by the sale of buffalo hides alone. . . . (November 5, 1881)

Geo. W. Dillon, was in from his hunting camp on the Red Water, this week and reports the death of an unknown man on Elk Prairie Creek. The dead man was fortunately and singularly found by another hunter, who had heard a noise nearby and upon going over a hill discovered a wounded buffalo bull goring the dying man. He fired and brought down the infuriated animal with three shots. Upon approaching the prostrate man he found him to be dying, his intestines having been gored out and his head laid open. Who the dead man was our informant was at a loss to say, only knowing that he was hunting in that region. (November 5, 1881)

Buffalo hunters who have been spending the summer visiting relatives in the east are returning to Miles City and outfitting for the season's campaign. (September 2, 1882)

A gentleman just up from Tongue river, says that hunters are meeting with great success on the buffalo ranges, and that the season has opened most favorable. (September 23, 1882)

Hunters are numerous on the head of Big Porcupine and the bend of the Musselshell river. Buffalo are reported scarce in that country on account of so many Crow Indians out on the range. (October 7, 1882)

George Outhwait, a buffalo hunter on the Porcupine, not long ago had two head of his horses stolen from his camp by Indians. George . . . [trailed the Indians, located their camp and, after they went to sleep, crept in among the horse herd] and quickly lariated his horses. He singled out five more of the best horses in the herd and drove them out on the prairie and thence to his camp. . . . George . . . is now the happy possessor of five more head of horses than before the raid by the Indians. (December 16, 1882)

G. W. Baldwin, the hide buyer, shipped two carloads of buffalo hides to Chicago Thursday. That Baldwin can catch on where another would get left, is shown by his ceaseless shipping of hides, while other buyers complain of the dullness of the season. (March 3, 1883)

In spite of a few pathetically optimistic comments in the *Yellowstone Journal*, the hide business was slim during the winter of 1882-1883. Hunters outfitted and went out on the range the following fall, expecting the herds to drift back from Canada to their usual winter ranges. They never came—the great Northern Herd was gone. In the fall of 1886, William T. Hornaday managed to secure twenty-five specimens for the U. S. National Museum but he found the few which had survived as wild as deer and as wary as old wolves.

The summer of 1881 had seen Sitting Bull and the last of the hostile Sioux surrender: the winter snows of the same year found the railroad halfway up the Yellowstone valley: and another twelve months brought the almost complete annihilation of the buffalo. With the hostile Indians and buffalo gone, the prairies and valleys were empty. The iron horse had arrived. The stage was set for the *last* frontier—the era of the rancher on the open range.

Although the first trickle of settlers who came into the Yellowstone valley in the years immediately following 1876 were usually referred to as *ranchers*, their livestock could be counted by the dozen and not by hundreds or thousands. Many of them were actually farmers and the early issues of the *Yellowstone Journal* often noted yields of grain which were reported or the measurements of large vegetables. It took considerable capital to swing a ranching venture, and these pioneers did not have such assets.

The first trail herd to come into the Yellowstone Basin originated at Independence, Missouri, in the spring of 1833. It consisted of four cows and two bulls which were taken across the plains to a trapper rendezvous held in the valley of the Green River, then eastward to the valley of the Big Horn, and from thence down this valley to the mouth of the Yellowstone. One bull was bitten by a mad wolf and died. The remainder swam to the north bank of the Missouri with the trail driver, fur trade apprentice Charles Larpenteur, holding to "the bull's tail . . . and making use of my three loose limbs. . . ." Presumably they did not set hoof again in the Yellowstone valley.

These cattle were to form the nucleus of a little herd for the fur trading post of Sublette and Campbell. However, they were not the first cattle to arrive at the mouth of the Yellowstone for the *bourgeois* at Fort Union had brought in milk cows sometime during the preceding year—judging by what travelers wrote about the food served at the head table.

The 600 head of steers which Nelson Story drove up the Bozeman Trail in the fall of 1866 comprised the first trail herd of note to enter the

Yellowstone valley. These were destined to grace the butcher shops of the gold camps in the mountains and not to populate the ranges; but, until they were needed, some are said to have been kept on ranges along the upper Yellowstone. The McAdow brothers of Bozeman (who later founded Coulson) also used the upper Yellowstone for a range. In the fall of 1868, they drove their oxen over into the valley of Shields River to winter and left twelve herders to watch them. Early in the following March, Indians killed four of these men but no loss occurred to the cattle.

Some 1800 head of woolies formed the spearhead of the livestock population of these ranges. In 1875, an energetic rancher named John Burgess, assisted by his son, started a flock of sheep from Red Bluff, California for the mining camps of the Black Hills. After wintering in Prickly Pear Valley near Helena, the band was pushed eastward down the north side of the Yellowstone; and, in October, the soldiers of the Fifth Infantry who were engaged in building the Tongue River Cantonment were amazed to see the animals come pouring down the bluff to the edge of the river and cross on the ferry.

With the country full of hostile Sioux, Colonel Miles discouraged Burgess from attempting to go further. So the rancher built a brush wickyup near the present site of the Northern Pacific depot in Miles City and settled down to spend the winter. Some of the sheep were converted into mutton during the following months, and in the spring George M. Miles, a nephew of the colonel, and Captain Frank Baldwin bought the remaining 1,007 head for an even $2,000 in gold. This was not a particularly profitable venture at first but, by importing good rams, the owners finally got their venture on a profitable basis. During these early years, the clip from this flock was shipped to buyers in Boston.

In addition to the small *herds* of the early settlers, cattle were brought in to supply meat for the Army posts. At least one shipment of beef-on-the-hoof for the Tongue River Cantonment came up the Yellowstone on a steamboat in the fall of 1876. Alfred Meyers, who had trailed cattle into the valley of the Jefferson Fork of the Missouri in 1864, secured the beef contract at Fort Custer in 1877. He brought in yearlings and two-year-olds and secured a permit to run them on the Crow Reservation along Rotten Grass Creek, a tributary of the Big Horn. Here, at the mouth of the creek, he built a cabin for his cowboys, but spent much of his time at the post. The surplus was marketed as three- and four-year-olds by trailing to the Union Pacific Railroad at Cheyenne, W.T. In 1880-1881, Guthrie and Ming of Helena had the contract for Fort Buford and wintered a herd south of Fort Keogh on

Pumpkin Creek. These constituted the first shipment to be made from Miles City. In June 1881, a steamboat was brought close beside a high cut bank just east of the town. According to an old cowboy:

> Two long wings had been built of cottonwood poles which had been well fitted up to hold the cattle. Then with about twenty cowpunchers, and a lot of good luck, we rushed the cattle down the chute and on to the boat before they knew what was happening.

Although one historian has written,

> In 1879, a hundred thousand longhorns got by the Wyoming buyers and trailed north into Montana where they met the advancing herds of the cattlemen, moving out of the mountains,

there is no evidence in contemporary newspapers to support the statement. Furthermore, this would have represented 40 or 50 normal sized trail herds—too great a number not to have attracted considerable attention. However, on July 21, 1879, the Omaha *Journal of Commerce* stated, "From Montana and Oregon our estimate places the drive of 1879 at 100,000 . . . . ," which is a logical statement as it pertains to *exports* and not *imports*.

Stories in the newspapers in Cheyenne and Miles City indicate definitely that the first large scale ranching took place in the southern part of the Yellowstone Basin. On January 14, 1879, the Cheyenne *Sun* carried a long story pointing out the advantages of northern Wyoming. In this it stated:

> Thus we find [Wyoming] . . . today where Colorado was fifteen years ago. . . . Such opportunities for locating and acquiring first-class sheep, horse and cattle ranges have seldom been presented to the world. These opportunities cannot remain open much longer. Already the attention of rich livestock dealers in England and Australia has been drawn to the vast unclaimed meadows of Wyoming, and preparations are being made to introduce English colonies to the delightful valleys of the Sweetwater, Wind River, Powder, Stinking Water, Big Horn and Tongue Rivers. . . . It is only within the past two years, or since cattle ranges in Kansas and Colorado have become scarce and uninviting, that the attention of livestock dealers of the East have been attracted to Wyoming. . . . During the past years a great exodus northward has been going on among the cattle men. They have been steadily moving their immense herds northward, until now they have crossed the North Platte valley, and some of the more venturesome have reached the streams emptying into the Cheyenne river.

On the 9th of April, 1879, the *Sun* chronicled the start of the first ranching venture in the Yellowstone Basin:

*The Freuen [sic Frewen] Brothers yesterday loaded up a very complete and handsome looking outfit for their new cattle range near the head of Powder river. They send up provisions, arms, ammunition, tools, poultry, brands, plows, lumber, glass, sash and, in fact, everything necessary to establish a settlement. Mr. Richard Freuen will allow the wagon outfit to proceed north of Fort Fetterman when he will follow and join it between the Platte and Fort McKinney.*

Early the following spring another story recorded the progress made during the past year:

*. . . stockmen in and about North Platte last fall began to seek larger ranges for their cattle and turned their eyes toward northern Wyoming. The pioneers in that country were two Englishmen, Freuen Brothers, who secured a range located about twenty-five miles west of old Fort McKinney on Powder river. They placed 2,500 head upon it, and are so well pleased with the way the cattle are thriving there that they will still further increase their herd this season by purchase.*

*Their success has led a number of their fellow Britons to make semi-occasional trips into this country to propose to put their capital and to share in the enterprise. A stock company has been formed, which the Freuen brothers will manage independently of their own concern. There are a few other ranges running on Powder river below the fort, which were stocked last summer.*

*Last fall several of the heavy cattlemen of the North Platte region commenced prospecting for new ranges on Crazy Woman creek, Goose creek, and other streams. Stearns and Patterson have secured a range northwest of the Freuen; Barton and Dillon and Nichols, Beach & Co., ranges on the Powder river country. Dillon and Barton will put on 10,000 cattle, and the others somewhat lesser numbers. They are building their ranches and will stock them the coming summer.*

Moreton and Richard Frewen were members of an old, socially prominent family of southern England. Richard had something of the restless nature of an explorer while Moreton was more interested in business matters—an interest which had some of its roots in the simple matter of necessity. In the spring of 1878, Moreton met John Adair and his wife in New York: and the Adairs, who had backed Charles Goodnight in a ranching venture in the Palo Duro Canyon of west Texas, interested him in cattle.

After a hunting trip into the Yellowstone and Jackson Hole country the following fall, the brothers, an ex-prospector, and a Texas cowboy crossed the Big Horn Mountains in December and located a ranch site on the upper Powder River. It was here, near the junction of the Middle and North Forks some four miles east of the present town of Kaycee, that they built a large log ranch house, with features reminiscent of England, and founded the 76 outfit. In 1882, Moreton bought his brother out and organized the Powder River Cattle Company, Ltd. This had an English board of directors, £300,000 ($1,500,000) capital stock, and was managed by Moreton.

Although the northern part of the Yellowstone Basin was comparatively quiet during 1879, it was to explode with feverish activity the following year. On November 20, 1879, the *Yellowstone Journal* carried a long letter, copied from the Helena *Independent*, which gave an outline of the economics of this latest *gold rush*. This read, in part:

> . . . No one can spend a week in any part of Montana without hearing some of the most marvelous reports about the profits which have been realized during the last few years in the business of stock raising in this Territory. . . . It is only now and then that a band of cattle, sheep or horses yield a net income of from 40 to 60 or even 100 percent per annum: but I doubt if there is a single instance in which, taking a series of years together, the profits on stock raising have not been from 20 to 30 per cent on the original investment, and that, too, in cases where the animals have suffered severely from unusual cold weather and snow in the Winter or from disease.

*    *    *

> But it is not in those portions of the territory that have been longest settled that stock raising is most profitable. The valley of the Yellowstone River from near the National Park to its mouth is 650 miles long, and on the average ten to twelve miles wide. All of this land can be easily irrigated and placed under cultivation. Hundreds of families have settled there this year. On either side for almost the entire length of this valley are benches, foot hills and prairies, covered with bunch-grass and amply watered by small streams. Nor is this all. There flows into the Yellowstone from the south the Powder River and the Tongue River, Big Horn River, Clark's Fork and almost innumerable smaller streams, the valleys of each of which is from 30 to 100 miles in length, and nearly every one affords as good pasturage as to be found in the world. Nearly the whole of this country has been inaccessible until the last eighteen months or two years, and the tide of immigration has only just begun to flow in. A few bands of cattle have been driven into the valleys of all of the streams I have named, but it is safe to say that there is not one steer

there to-day where there is feed for a thousand. . . . it will be many years before it will be possible for the stock to begin to be crowded. . . . the grass . . . . is bunch grass that grows from one to two or three feet high. In most places the bunches stand close together and cure early in the summer. . . .

Very few of the stock men of Montana make any provision for feeding their cattle in the winter, and there is no herding in the summer. . . . Old cattle owners say that a herd that is fed occasionally when a heavy storm comes, will not winter as well as one that is not fed. . . .

The customary way of managing a band of cattle in Montana is simply to brand them and turn them out upon the range. Some stock-owners give no attention to their cattle until the next spring, when they round them up, and brand the calves, select those they intend to sell, and turn the remainder out again. . . . The more careful managers employ one man for every 1,500 or 2,000 head of cattle, whose duty it is to ride about the outskirts of the range, follow any trails leading away and drive the cattle back, and go among neighboring herds, if there are any, looking for stray animals and driving them home. At the spring roundup a few extra men have to be employed for several weeks. In starting a new herd cows, bulls and yearlings are bought. The older cattle of ordinary grade (they are all American—no long-horned Texans) cost from $15 to $25 a head and calves under one year running with the herd not being counted. Yearlings may be obtained from $5 to $7 each. The average cost of raising a steer, not counting interest on capital invested is from 60¢ to $1 a year so that a four-year-old steer raised from a calf and ready for market costs about $4. He is worth on the ranch, about $20, and if driven to Fort Benton or the railroad in Wyoming at least $25. A herd consisting of yearlings, cows and bulls will have no steers ready for the market in less than two or three years. Taking into account the loss of interest on capital invested before returns are received, all expences and ordinary losses, and the average profit of raising in Montana during the last few years has been at least 30 percent per annum. Some well-informed cattle men estimate it at 40 or 45 percent.

A large and increasing percentage of the cattle and sheep of Montana are owned by persons who do not manage them themselves, and some of whom do not reside in this Territory. Nearly all the leading bankers and merchants of Helena own interests in bands of stock, and lawyers, doctors, and Federal officers are following their example, and investing their own money or that of their friends in the East in cattle, sheep or horses. . . . . The return which capitalists obtain on their money . . . in a herd of cattle is never less than 15 per cent, in a flock of sheep 20 per cent and upward, and in a band of horses much greater than in either.

\*    \*    \*

The management of sheep is, of course, different from cattle. A band
of sheep containing 1,000 and upward, in good condition and free from
disease, may be bought here this season for $3 to $3.25 a head. They
must be herded Summer and Winter in separate bands of not more than
2,000 or 3,000 each, carralled every night and guarded against depredations of dogs and wild animals. Some hay must be provided with which
to feed them when there are deep snows, and sheds ought to be erected
to protect them from the most severe storms. . . . While a herd of
young cattle begin to yield an income only at the expiration of three
years, sheep yield a crop of wool the first Summer after they are driven
upon a range, and the increase of the band is much greater than that of
cattle, being from 75 to 100 per cent a year. The wool is of good quality
. . . and brings a good price on the ranch, the competition between the
buyers sent out here from the eastern cities being very great. Many thousand sheep have been driven into this Territory, this year from California, Oregon and Washington Territory, and every band that has arrived
has been gobbled up by men eager to increase their flocks or to start
new ones.

It is not my purpose to mislead any reader by reciting the cases in
which unusual profits have been realized in the business of stock raising,
but . . . Judge Davenport . . . four years ago last July purchased 1,000
ewes, which cost him in the neighborhood of $3,000. . . . The profits
of his investment of $3,000 for four years were . . . $14,500, or . . .
121⅔ percent a year. . . .

\*    \*    \*

. . . Of course the ranges are all Government land, to which no title
can be obtained, but the right of the first occupant to the land he uses
is universally recognized. . . .

Although the comments of this writer must be taken with some reservation, most of what he wrote was approximately correct at the *beginning* of the livestock boom. His enthusiasm for the business was typical
of that which brought scores of people to battle with the unmentioned
difficulties, and caused hundreds of others to invest their savings in this
*sure thing*.

During 1880, the *Yellowstone Journal* noted considerable activity in
the Montana portion of the Yellowstone Basin. Some stockmen added
to their holdings, others brought in cattle and sheep and started
ranches. Would-be ranchers arrived from the east and south. Among
these was C. C. Howes, a New Englander who had spent fourteen
years as a sea captain, and who, with George M. Miles and J. W.

Strevell, a hardware dealer, were to found the (later) well known Circle Bar outfit. Trailing to the railhead at Bismarck, which had started the year before with a total of about 2,000 cattle, increased in importance, and both herds of cattle and flocks of sheep were driven down the Yellowstone valley enroute to eastern markets. As there was a good ford across the Yellowstone about two miles above Fort Keogh, the south side of the valley became the common route followed by many of these trail herds.

The fate of one of these early ranches was long remembered—a grim example of what could happen. The Anglo-American Cattle Company, managed by B. B. Groom, formerly of Lexington, Kentucky, and financed by a Mr. Wilson of Kansas City, put a herd of Texas long-horns on the Tongue River late in the fall of 1880. Although the newspaper account stated that the herd totalled 5,000, old-timers—who are probably correct—recall that there were about 2,000 head. The wife of one early settler recalled:

[The cattle] Thin, tired from the long drive, unacclimated, [were] turned out on the Tongue River near Otter Creek, no shelter and later when the snow was deep—no feed. Cowboys in charge kept them "close herded" as a safeguard against theft by the Indians, instead of turning them out to rustle for themselves. The winter of 1880 and 1881 was not only a very cold one, but it was a long one, beginning early and the snow so deep on the level, even a snow-plow could not have laid bare the grass which was really abundant underneath. These cattle died like flies. As late as the fall of 1889 you could see the bones of hundreds piled up under an overhanging bank of the Tongue River, where the poor brutes had sought shelter. It was reported at the time only 120 survived.

On the 24th of the following September, the county sheriff sold the remaining assets of the company to satisfy the claims of the creditors.

The movement of cattle and sheep which began as a trickle in 1879 swelled into flood-sized proportions in 1881 and 1882. Scores of trail herds, usually 2,000-3,000 cattle each, were brought in and turned loose on what the journalists had called "almost-inexhaustable" ranges. Rancher-historian Granville Stuart estimated that by October 1883 "there were six hundred thousand range cattle . . . [on the plains of Montana] and these with the horses and sheep was as much stock as the ranges could safely carry." This flood was to continue for another three years, and then Mother Nature brought the situation back into balance with the grim winter of 1886-1887.

Perhaps the most desirable foundation stock for herds came from what is now Oregon and Washington. These animals were of good Shorthorn and Durham breeding which had been taken into the Northwest by emigrants for beef and milk purposes. This was hardy stock which had good feet and the ability to rustle for themselves. Also, the animals had good conformation, reasonably good dispositions—as range cattle went, and the cows produced enough milk to raise a good calf. As well bred bulls were imported during these beginning years, herds of good quality became common. Some stock was shipped in from the Mid-West. However, some of these cattle were of indifferent breeding and accustomed to shelter and feed in the winter. When turned loose on the open range, the results were sometimes tragic.

Although large numbers of Oregon cattle were trailed in, the largest single source of stock was the ranges of Texas, Colorado, and the Southwest where there was an over-abundance of cattle. These animals, especially those from Texas, were not particularly liked because of their Longhorn heritage. They did not have good lines and there were many off-colors which did not improve the appearance of any herd. But they could be had in quantity, and they had one valuable asset. An animal finished on the northern ranges would weigh 300 to 400 pounds or more than his or her counterpart grown to maturity on the home range. Even horses brought up from the South increased in size. This led to the practice of trailing up two-year-olds, "double-wintering" them, and sending them to market two years later as four-year-olds. During the later days of the open range, a number of Texas ranches, among them the great XIT, established branches and finished their cattle on the northern ranges.

Most of the cattle came in over two trails. The Texas, Northern, or Montana Trail came north by various routes to the head of Little Powder River. From this point the drivers went down the Powder to the vicinity of a stage stop named Powderville, then northwest across Mizpah Creek to Pumpkin Creek, thence down this stream and the Tongue River to the Fort Keogh Military Reservation. Here they swam the Yellowstone at a point about two miles above the post. Then they continued northward up Sunday Creek to ranges on the "North Side."

Cattle from the Northwest entered Montana from Idaho, crossing the Continental Divide by one of the passes just west of the Yellowstone National Park—usually Monida Pass. Then they followed down one of the forks of the Missouri, or their tributaries, and crossed the Bozeman Pass to the Great Bend of the Yellowstone from which point the trail boss took the best route directly to his destination.

The size of ranch holdings varied greatly. Five hundred to a thousand cattle was considered a small outfit; many had 10,000 to 20,000 or more. In 1885, the Powder River Cattle Company, which the Frewen brothers started with 2,500 head, was estimated to have owned about 58,000 head and counted a crop of 6,500 calves. In addition to the ranges on Powder River, this outfit also ran cattle on Hanging Woman Creek, a tributary of the Tongue just above the Montana-Wyoming line. However, accurate figures are hard to come by—as, for example, in the case of the N Bar outfit of E. S. "Zeke" Newman. The Niobrara Cattle Co., after being squeezed out on the Platte by homesteaders, located on the Powder River near the crossing of the Texas-Montana Trail in 1882. The next year Newman declared 7,000 head for tax purposes and the assessor—one-time sheriff Tom Irvine —made this skeptical notation beside the entry—"He has more cattle than this sure as hell." Other ranchers have been known to drive part of their cattle over the line into another state when the assessor came around.

It took considerable money to stock a large ranch, and this the average individual did not have. Old Montana brand books often listed capital investments of $100,000 to 500,000 and indicated that outfits represented a group of investors in the mid-west, east, or British Isles. Others, like the Home Land & Cattle Co. and the Mizpah Cattle Co., were owned by wealthy men. The former, the N-N which once had its headquarters on Sunday Creek north of Miles City was backed by the Neidringhaus brothers who manufactured enameled ware and stoves in St. Louis. The latter, the LO, was backed by the tobacco merchants, Liggett and Myers before the winter of 1886-1887. The cowboys never forgot that the owners expected the hands to use Star Brand chewing tobacco—*exclusively*, or that Mr. Liggett once lost a nickel between the ranch house and the corral and spent half a day hunting for it.

Men engaged in the active management were a varied lot. Some were experienced ranchers, like Zeke Newman, who had been crowded out by settlers elsewhere; others *spilled out* onto the plains from the mountain valleys of western Montana where they had been in the cattle business; and a few, like the Myers brothers, and Guthrie and Ming, had held meat contracts at the army posts. Some of the influx were from Texas and the Southwest and, like the XIT outfit, acted to supplement operations elsewhere. The earliest of these—the Hash-knife, the Milliron (which still operates in Texas), and the OX—located just outside the northeastern edge of the Yellowstone Basin but their cattle ranged the adjacent Powder River country. And still others came from various professions—even the classrooms of English universities.

Although they represented but a small fraction numerically, perhaps the group which contributed the most color were the English and Scotch. From an economic angle, they fell into two groups—the financially independent or self supporting, and the remittance men. Viewed from a social angle, some developed into solid citizens, some were shiftless floaters, and still others were bums. In this respect they were no different from any other group.

Even the lower strata made their contribution to the legends of the high plains. One of these—to all appearances only a liquor-wrecked horse wrangler—took an unsuspected interest in the outcome of an English university boat race which was being discussed within his hearing. From his lips slipped an exultant, "Thank God, we won." One present, who was unfamiliar with the code of the West, inquired why *he* should be so interested. The puncher, forgetting himself in the excitement of the moment, replied, "Why, man, once I stroked that crew."

Many of the English settled in the upper part of the valley of the Tongue. These made a lasting impression on their American neighbors who, in later years, never tired of reminiscing about them—as well as acknowledging their contribution in "their sportsmanship, their culture, and their horses."

Some, for one reason or another, were better remembered than others. There was J. H. Price who raised fine polo ponies on his Crown W ranch near Knowlton, Montana. Price always wore a monocle and never swore. He had been a professor at a college in Oxford, and his tongue could be as sharp as a razor as one lawyer found out who tried to belittle him while on the witness stand. E. S. Cameron, who ranched near Terry, Montana, became an authority on the birds of eastern Montana and even succeeded in raising sage hens in captivity —an extremely difficult operation. One old lady, with a typically feminine memory, recalled that Kirwan and Langley swept the dirt on the floor under the couch, and that when Mr. Kirwan inherited the family silver he wrote the other heirs that he would have much more use for a suit of clothes from Saville Row than the silver.

Captain and Mrs. E. Pennell Elmhirst, whose ranch was on Mizpah Creek, were a source of much interest to their neighbors even though they were regarded as "enjoyable people." The Elmhirsts employed a maid and a valet and, when they went to Miles City, packed along considerable baggage—sometimes even a collapsible bath tub! Fortunately, the Captain has preserved his impressions of the frontier in his book, *Fox-Hound, Forest, and Prairie,* and these are as amusing as the opinions of his neighbors. In relating his experiences in building a ranch house, he wrote:

[The Englishman] . . . has been accustomed to courtesy on the part of superiors, and to respect from inferiors, whether in the [military] service or out of it. . . . To these principles he has been educated, and any breech of them he has been taught to resent—especially, of course, when directed against his own status. Imagine him, then, brought on terms of closest intimacy, of the most unsparing familiarity, with men in his own employ in menial capacities—men whose only claim to intellect is based on their talent for chopping a log, whose accomplishments are confined to squirting tobacco juice across the floor, whose tastes soar no higher than New Orleans molasses at work and the most fiery of whiskey when at play; whose conversation, often inintelligible through its thickly interlarded and senseless oaths, is utterly pointless when purged of the same; whose personal cleanliness is limited to a dash of water (when not too cold) on hands and face once a day, and whose underclothing leaves not their bodies—day or night—till absolute necessity demands that the decayed garments be replaced by new. This is the company in which, at least until his house and premises be completed, he will have to spend day and night, probably in an old log shanty that is destitute of flooring, and consists of only a single room 12 by 14.

No doubt life on this frontier was something of a shock to many who began life as members of well-to-do English and Scottish families. However, it did offer to many an opportunity to attain financial independence which was denied them in their native land. The first son in each family was the favored one. The others, if any, were expected to make their own way in one of five professions—medicine, law, the ministry, the Army or Navy—as an officer of course, or foreign diplomatic service. Therefore, some of the energetic and resourceful—in whom there was a spark of the colonizing spirit which had characterized Great Britain in former years—looked to the High Plains for opportunity. Others were sent abroad by their relatives to get them out from under foot.

One of the latter was Sidney Paget who is still remembered as a "genuine all-around sport." The editor of the *Yellowstone Journal* recalled:

"Syd" Paget will stand out in the recollection of all the residents of that day as a type of genius. A thorough sportsman in everything that pertained to the open, he was always "game" for a horse race . . . as he had a few ponies that he thought pretty well of. . . . Whatever his allowance was, he was always ahead of it, but his credit was excellent, for when his debts became a matter of anxiety to his creditors, the money would be forthcoming from England to pay him out.

Although Paget was a hail-fellow-well-met with the crowd that used Sam Pepper's saloon for a hangout, he shocked others. One pioneer lady, remembering his association with the courtesan Connie Hoffman, wrote:

> There was a wealthy Englishman, among several such around Miles City at that time, whose brother later came into a title; and this man set her up in an establishment of her own with horses, carriage, everything, and was seen with her everywhere. . . . It was a most brazen performance and scandalized even Miles City.

Among these were several who attained recognition of a lasting sort. One was Malcolm Moncreiffe, the younger brother of Sir Robert Moncreiffe, baronet, of Perthshire, Scotland. After ranching near Gillette, Wyoming for thirteen years, he came to the upper Tongue in 1897 where he attracted attention as an outstanding polo player, a buyer and exporter of polo ponies, and a contractor of horses for the British army during the Boer War. Although he was an expert with horses, he owned and made money with cattle and then became a very successful breeder of Hampshire and Corriedale sheep, his flock of the latter being known as one of the finest in the world.

Perhaps the Englishman who carved the deepest niche in the memories of the old-timers was Oliver Henry Wallop, third son of the Fifth Earl of Portsmouth. "O.H.," as he was affectionately called, came to North Dakota to hunt in 1883 just after graduating from a college in Oxford. After roaming as far as the Pacific Northwest, he came back to Montana the next year and established a ranch on Otter Creek, a tributary of the Tongue. Here he began to raise horses. His father sent him some good stallions and his horses—the first purebred horses in the region—soon became known for their quality. In 1890, he acquired a ranch at the foot of the Big Horn Mountains near the head of Goose Creek and moved to Wyoming.

Although "O.H." demonstrated that he had ability as a rancher, it was not these qualities which endeared him to his neighbors and friends. He was the sort of man with whom it was easy to be friendly —generous, tolerant, witty, sometimes absent-minded, and—although he could and did dress impeccably on occasion—usually attired in clothes which even the rough frontier regarded as "disreputable." While sewing a button on his shirt, the wife of one rancher chided him for his careless appearance. He replied that at home he had to be so particular about his dress that it was a relief to go about as he pleased now that he was away from England.

He also had the *ability* to get into scrapes which others delighted in telling about. One old lady recalled that, when she was a girl, he was invited to Thanksgiving dinner at a rancher's house. He delayed washing his only suit of woolen underwear until there was not time for it to dry properly before putting it on. After a 28 mile ride in a "blizzard," he arrived hours late and so benumbed that he fell off his horse when he attempted to dismount. His hosts poured whiskey down him—a rather universal frontier remedy—and it took him three days to recover. "But," she concluded, "he got no turkey!"

During the Boer War (1899-1902), he and Malcolm Moncreiffe were the chief horse buyers for the British in the Northwest. In 1904 he became a naturalized citizen and five years later was elected to the first of two terms in the Wyoming State Legislature. In 1925, he succeeded to the family title and became the Eighth Earl of Portsmouth. Although this made his return to England almost imperative, he kept the Wyoming ranch, coming back each May and staying until October. After the death of his wife in 1938, he returned to Wyoming to stay until his death in 1943.

It is not easy to evaluate the contributions of men like Moncreiffe and Wallop. In private life they were successful ranchers. But they also had a sense of civic responsibility—in keeping with the tradition of their class in England—which made a substantial contribution to the development of the country. And last, but not least, they set an example in what might be called a gracious way of living.

As no one owned the range where their stock grazed, most ranchers did not build elaborate improvements. Thus the *home* ranch of an outfit, particularly if there was not a woman present, consisted of only the bare essentials—corral, a small barn, a bunkhouse for the cowboys, and another building which housed the kitchen, dining room, and provided quarters for the foreman. These were built of whatever native materials were available—logs, stone, adobe, or a combination of them.

Line camps occupied by cowboys who watched for drifting stock in the winter were little one-room cabins tucked away in some sheltered ravine, or dugouts built into the side of a hill or convenient cutbank. They had little to offer other than a place to eat and shelter from inclement weather. Often the only home-like touch might be that provided by a cat which one of the cowboys had lugged in to help keep the mice down and to provide a bit of companionship.

This was a man's world in many ways but some wives went out on the range in the very early 1880's. Most of these were women who had come west with their husbands, for if a rancher wished a wife it was almost necessary for him to travel to a more populated section to acquire one. A few married girls from the "parlor houses." Once a girl broke with the ancient profession, she was accepted and treated as a "lady," and some made good wives and raised respectable families. Still other wives were acquired through matrimonial agencies; and these were usually known as "heart and hand" women.

Isolated from their own sex to a large extent and subjected to many privations, life for these women was difficult and often dreary. The houses were usually rough affairs, there was little furniture and this of the crudest sort, and the walls might be covered with muslin or papered with old newspapers, the latter being used partly for insulation and partly to keep the bed bugs out of the cracks. And not infrequently water was scarce and often of abominable quality due to alkali salts.

Doctors were a problem—a double problem in fact. Not only were they usually miles away, but many had come West because they drank too heavily to hold a practice in the East. One of these recalled that he had a good practice because he never drank and could be depended upon. Women who were expecting often went to the nearest town— and at least one doctor was locked up as the time neared so that he would be sober. Accidents were another matter, and this danger was always present.

Providing children with schooling was difficult, and still is in places. One mother met the problem for a time by using Montgomery Ward catalogues as text books. On the upper Tongue, one rancher hired a teacher and "school" was held in one room of his house. And where there were enough children, a school was usually provided to which the youngsters came on horseback. One lady recalled that the school she attended ran erratically—sometimes three months in the fall and three months in the spring, sometimes it ran all year, and that during the first years the pupils were taught by subjects and not by grades.

For those who lived near the Cheyenne and Crow Reservations, there was the additional problem of Indians. One lady, whose parents moved into the valley of the Rosebud in 1882, recalled that once when her father had gone to Miles City for supplies a band of Indians came by and took what little food they had as well as the bedding and clothing which her mother had spread on the sagebrush to air.

Occasionally these contacts were amusing. One wife—then one of six women on the upper Tongue—lay down to take a nap. She awoke with the feeling that she was being watched to find the room lined with Cheyenne women who had come in silently while she was asleep. Another lady recalled that, "One big buck surprised my mother one day, looking in on her as she was taking a bath. In response to her consternation and yells, the old buck just grinned." However, there were times when there was, or seemed to be, considerable danger. One Indian scare resulted in a stampede from the vicinity of the Cheyenne Reservation in which settlers went as far as the settlements on the Yellowstone on the north, and to Sheridan and Buffalo, Wyoming on the south.

But life was not all hardship and toil. After the fall roundup was over, there was time for dances and parties and fifty or sixty miles was not an unusual distance to go to attend such a gathering. Often there was a trip to town to lay in supplies, an annual trip it is true but nevertheless an occasion of note. And in the spring when the Montana Stock Growers Association held their annual meeting in Miles City, there was a dinner and dance at the Macqueen House that was a gala affair.

Although the ranchers and their financial backers were a necessity in the business of ranching, it was their hired men—the cowboys—who created for it a permanent place in the minds of the public. So permanent has this interest become that much fiction is now regarded as fact. Even most of the old-timers have forgotten that many of the early boots were not as high heeled as fashion later dictated, that chaps were once nothing but leather pants without a seat and front, and the most popular shirt in the summer was a light colored cotton one.

One old rancher divided the cowboys he knew into two general groups. There were "Northern" punchers who had a tendency to be somewhat abusive, "loud voiced," and sometimes got into fist fights. The second group was made up of men from Texas and New Mexico who knew the handling of cattle from A to Z. These men had a code of their own, were soft-spoken, rarely carried a gun—though there was usually one in their bedroll, and enjoyed telling stories and tall yarns. If the rancher or his foreman yelled at one of these, he was likely to ride up and say, "I want my time. I'm no damned sheep dog." And now and then a paradox turned up among them. One such was a trail boss in the employ of one of the early outfits in the valley of the Tongue. This man would not trail on Sunday and, what was more, he said grace before each meal!

Few cowboys were thrifty and one of the things on which they spent their money, along with whiskey and women, was their outfit. For a man making $40.00 a month "and found," this cost considerable. In Miles City, during the latter part of the days of the open range, saddles cost from $40.00 to $60.00; hand-forged bits and spurs with silver inlays, $14.00 and $12.50 respectively; Angora goat skin chaps, $15.00; paulins (bed tarps), $7.00; and a bridle and reins from $7.00 to $14.00.

Tailor-made boots and Stetson hats were also expensive, and there were other necessities.

Although some cowboys' ideas of *mine* and *thine* were somewhat elastic when the government, Indians, or absentee owners were concerned, they were—as a class—scrupulously honest on a man to man basis. When a cowboy working on a roundup on the lower Powder River stole a $20.00 bill from a "kid" whose bedroll he had been sharing, he was promptly fired by the roundup boss. An old man working with the crew was much disappointed when the men did not hang him! The story is told that when a N Bar hand rode out of Miles City without paying Cowboy Annie for the week he had spent with her, the foreman discharged him. Then the other hands chipped in and settled his bill, said to have been $70.00, "because they wouldn't have a thing like that standing against the name of the outfit."

Even thieves subscribed to this code. Nate Champion, alleged leader of the rustlers on the upper Powder, once hired to a rancher to take care of his ranch during the latter's absence. When the rancher returned he noted that Champion was short of potatoes to cook. "Don't you know there are several wagon loads in the cellar?" the rancher asked. "Yes, I know," replied the rustler, *"but they weren't mine."*

Much of their amusement was self made, and humorous incidents were remembered and told over and over. In the lower part of the valley of Powder River there are old cowboys who still enjoy telling about the postal inspector who came to inspect a country postoffice which was in the home of a rancher. The postmaster was engaged in a game of poker and was in no mood to be interrupted by official duties. Finally the exasperated inspector said, "If you don't cooperate, I'll take the post office away from you." At this the postmaster arose, took the apple box which served as a letter box down off the wall, and threw it out the door. "There," he said, "take your postoffice and get out of here."

Sometimes the stories were fiction:

*Once up near my hangout there was a roundup and, because it was a big one, we brought out the best cook we could hire. Well, out on the range there wasn't any wood at all, yet the cook had to fix grub. He was a resourceful jasper. He lit a prairie fire and followed the flames with a frying pan. But it didn't work. When the first pan of bacon was done, he was eleven miles from the outfit.*

*Jim Shane told one about getting stuck in the mud at the edge of a pond. When a flock of ducks lit nearby, he threw his bed tarp over them and when they rose up and took off, they pulled him out of the mud.*

One of their chief avocations was "jobbing" someone. Some of these efforts were cleverly conceived and patiently prepared—in one case almost a year in advance. Others were the result of a situation of the moment. During one winter a traveler stopped overnight at the WL on Powder River. He lived on a ranch near Belle Fourche, South Dakota and had been to Havre, Montana to bring back some stolen horses. As it was storming the next day, he was urged to stay over. Then he took sick and died. The corpse, frozen hard as a rock, was suspended on wires from the rafters of the bunkhouse until the relatives could come for it.

The dead body made one of the men very nervous. He went to Miles City for a week but when he returned the corpse was still there. The others constructed a *ghost* from two crossed sticks and a bed sheet and hid it on the ground outside the cabin. A cord was attached which ran over the top of the wall, just under the eaves, and was hidden on the inside. That night when the uneasy man stepped outside to relieve his kidneys, the cord was pulled and the *ghost* pulled up into sight. Although the man would not admit noting anything unusual, he went back to Miles City—and stayed there. Later, he told one of the conspirators that he had seen a ghost and that it went up into the sky and out of sight.

Although the cowboy has always attracted the lion's share of attention, there were other hired men on the plains. Often they were drab and colorless but they were as steadfast and loyal as their flamboyant counterparts. These were the sheepherders—members of the lowest level of the social strata of the West.

Sheepherders, like the cowboys were a varied lot. The best were French and Spanish Basques, Scotsmen, and Mexicans, but there were also Americans, Englishmen and Scandinavians. Undoubtedly, there were among them many interesting individuals but most of these have gone unnoted. One newspaper man, after drinking with one herder in a little country saloon, discovered that the man was a graduate of Yale —but not *why* he was herding sheep.

Herding was a lonely life. The principal contact with the rest of the community was through the camp tender who came at regular intervals with supplies and checked to see that all was well. And the only recreation of many was a week or two in town once a year, during which time they spent most of what they had earned during the preceding year—usually $350-$400—gambling, drinking, and "playing the line." As there were many in the towns who were not above rolling a drunken sheepherder, his vacation might be limited to one short spree. One wealthy sheepman in Miles City had a back room off his office where it was not uncommon to see a herder on the floor, sometimes with his dog lying beside him, sleeping off a drunk in safety.

In the early range days, sheep wagons were unknown. The herders lived in tents or small cabins placed at strategic locations near watering places. When the feed became depleted in one location, the flock was moved to another spot. In later years, some owners insured possession of certain ranges by having their herders homestead these locations and then buying up the homesteads—a tactic which cattlemen also used.

Although the early ranchers in Wyoming were cattlemen, those who settled in the northern part of the Yellowstone Basin were a mixture of cattlemen, sheepmen, and horsemen. This was probably due to the fact that those who moved northward out of Colorado and Nebraska were predominantly cattlemen while those who had lived in the mountain valleys of Montana raised sheep and horses as well as cattle. Thus sheep were not common in the Wyoming portion of the Yellowstone Basin until the later days of the open range. Then they increased so rapidly, and to such an extent, that the southern part of the valley of the Big Horn became the scene of serious trouble between the sheepmen and the cattlemen.

In the Montana portion of the basin, sheep camps were quite widely scattered. There were, however, a few exceptions. Although Pumpkin Creek was "sheep country," the valley of Mizpah Creek to the east and that of Otter Creek to the west were not. Ranchers "closed" these areas to sheep and, although there was some trouble over the matter, made their edict stick. In like manner there was opposition to sheep in the valley of Stillwater River to the west of the Big Horn.

Much of the interest in horses, but by no means all of it, centered around the British operators who raised animals of good breeding. A few outfits trailed horses in from the southern ranges to supply the ranch market, while others specialized in draft breeds to supply markets in the Mid-West, East, and South. Some ranches ran both horses and cattle. A few, like the Diamond G, began as horse ranches, while others like the FUF, which became one of the largest, changed from cattle to horses after the hard winter of 1886-1887.

In due time Miles City developed into one of the largest horse markets in the West. In February 1890, the Custer County Horse Sales and Fair Association was organized. However, in the late 1890's, the market for horses was very poor. Then came the Boer War (1898-1902) and prices skyrocketed. A. B. Clarke organized the Montana Range Horse Co. in April 1901 and started a sale yard which attracted buyers from far and wide. But when the British buyers dropped out of the market, the market again declined and, for all practical purposes, horse raising ceased to be attractive.

Ranching was a business and, as such, had its problems. To meet some of these, the stockgrowers in Laramie County, Wyoming formed an organization which, eight years later, became the Wyoming Stock Growers Association. The first brand book (1882) listed nineteen outfits with ranges in the Yellowstone Basin and of these at least three had cattle north of the Wyoming-Montana line. When eastern Montana was occupied by ranchers, it was only natural that they too should organize. In October 1883, these stockmen (including some from the western edge of Dakato Territory) met at Miles City and organized the Eastern Montana Livestock Association. Recognizing the pioneer work of their sister organization in Wyoming, they adopted the by-laws of this group in their entirety. The next year a number of ranchers met in Helena and organized the Stockgrowers Association of Montana; and in April 1885 the Montana groups merged and became the Montana Stockgrowers Association. Both organizations played a very useful role in the livestock industry of their respective states. However, the Wyoming organization became, if anything, too powerful politically and finally brought down on their heads some—probably well merited—criticism for their high-handed participation in the affairs of the state.

Miles City was host to the annual meeting of the Montana Stockgrowers Association throughout the days of the open range. This three day meeting, held just before the start of the spring roundup, was an event of much importance in eastern Montana. Cattlemen and their wives, a considerable number of cowboys, and representatives of the various railroads and markets flooded the town.

In the very early days, the meeting began with a big parade composed of various dignitaries, the band and a detachment of soldiers from the post, and, of course, mounted cowboys. The Miles City Club held open house each day and set a table which became known far and wide for its *pièce de résistance* which was roast pig. Until it burned, the assembly was held in the roller skating rink, a large building which was used for various purposes. And on the evening of the last day a dinner and ball was held at the Macqueen House which was one of the social events of the year.

The meetings of the mid-1880's were unusually interesting. Ranchers in western Dakota were members and usually the Marquis de Mores and Theodore Roosevelt were present. The Marquis, a remarkable Frenchman who was the son-in-law of a wealthy New York banker, had about as many get-rich-quick schemes as a dog has fleas. One of these was to establish a string of packing plants in the West and ship dressed beef to the eastern markets. He built a plant at Medora, North Dakota—another was started at Miles City—and a string of icehouses along the Northern Pacific Railroad but the scheme folded in 1886. Nevertheless, the marquis was a forceful and dynamic figure and many listened thoughtfully to him. Roosevelt, although he was not much of a hand on a horse, was in his element at these meetings where he was certainly a "top hand" in assisting with the business of the Association.

Perhaps the most important piece of business performed at the meetings was the organization of the spring roundups. As cattle tended to stray from the range of their owner, it was necessary that they be thrown back on their proper range at regular intervals. It was also necessary that each outfit's calf crop be identified and properly branded. Both of these tasks were performed at this roundup. Such work had to be thorough and conducted efficiently and fairly. To this end the country was divided into districts, dates were set, and roundup foremen appointed. This action was published in the newspapers and became binding on all concerned. The description of one such district set up in 1885 read:

ROUNDUP NO. 2. Commence at the mouth of Logging creek on *Tongue River May 13th, 1885, work up Tongue river and its tributaries to mouth of Canyon, up Hanging Woman to Grinnell's Ranch, then join Wyoming roundup No. 17 at the boundary line, at the mouth of Squirrel creek, working with them on the west side of Tongue river to the mouth of Canyon; then commencing at Grinnell's Ranch working Hanging Woman creek and up the east side of Tongue river to boundary line, then to big bend of Rosebud and down the same to mouth of Muddy. Foreman, James Davis.*

In addition to setting up the roundups, there were problems related to marketing, and inspection at the markets to detect stolen stock. Members also had to decide on the number of bulls each rancher should have. Bounties for predators were still another problem as the wiping out of the buffalo herds had left many troublesome wolves behind to prey on the cattle.

An ever present problem was that of the rustler. Both associations employed range inspectors who were nothing but private detectives— often with civil authority as well. Billy Smith spent many years in the employ of the Montana association, respected by many but not by all. One Dakota officer refused to "work with" Smith because he regarded him as a killer who was prone to shoot before he asked questions. Steely-eyed Frank Canton, one-time sheriff of Johnson County, Wyoming, was another of these men. Canton still bears the reputation, in both Montana and Wyoming, as being an efficient officer—and a killer. In justice to the memory of such men it must be said that they had some tough, clever outlaws to handle.

Although ranchers occupied their rangers by a tacit recognition of their squatters' rights, there was nothing to stop others from elbowing in. By 1886 the ranges were filled to overflowing and then some. The summer of this year was extremely dry and hot, and the little creeks and waterholes dried up. To get water, the cattle moved closer to the larger streams and in doing so grazed closely what were normally winter ranges. Prairie fires took their toll. Then came fall with its ominous signs. Waterfowl and other migratory birds left early, animals grew a heavier coat of hair than usual, and, finally, the great white owls of the Arctic were seen. Old Indians pointed to these harbingers of winter and grunted, "Heap cold."

The cold and the snow came early—in November. The early part of December brought another storm with more cold and more snow, and in the middle of the month a blizzard hit which lasted three days. Then the weather cleared until the fore part of January when there was another cold wind and with it a foot and a half of snow. When the snow stopped falling, the temperature began to drop—first to twenty degrees below zero, then to thirty below, and finally to over forty below. This storm and frigid cold lasted for ten days. It was March before a chinook hit the plains and uncovered what grass there was to be had.

With the early fall snows covering the grass on the prairies, cattle congregated in the valleys and browsed on the shoots of willow and cottonwood, gnawed the bark from brush too large to eat, and even consumed the unpalatable sagebrush. Pieces of wood the diameter of a lead pencil were often seen in the manure. When the snow finally did melt and the "spring rise" was on, every stream carried a seemingly endless procession of carcasses bobbing along like large pieces of driftwood.

During the late winter, ranchers hoped blindly that the kill would not be as large as they feared it would be; and before the spring roundup there was a brief period of cautious optimism. But the roundup revealed the grim truth and the *wagons* that went as far south as the Platte hoping to find stock which had drifted before the storms returned empty handed. Southern trail herds thrown onto the ranges in the fall, and cattle which were in poor condition were gone almost to a critter. Of a herd of 2,000 which the Hashknife threw onto the range late in the fall, only *six* were found alive. Steers wintered better than the she stuff which had been suckling calves. Most of the immature cattle were gone. Some outfits were practically wiped out and one man who had been a small rancher recalled, "I had one cow left."

A few outfits escaped with moderate losses, and sometimes the kill was uneven. The son of "Captain" Joe Brown, who ran the Three Circle outfit on the Tongue, recalled that his father lost all of his pure-bred cattle but a thousand head of dry Texas cows which had just been trailed in "wintered, and wintered well," and that for many years this was considered a "miracle of the range." The captain's daughter remembered that they branded 700 calves from the 1,000 head the following spring. However, not many miles away, the Chariton Montana Cattle Company—the JO—branded 300 calves whereas the tally had been 1,900 the preceding spring. By and large, losses were estimated between 30 and 60 percent. John Clay, the astute Scotsman who was the economic historian of the range business, made this summary of the effects of the winter 1886-1887:

*From the inception of the open range business in the West and North-west, from say 1870 to 1888, it is doubtful if a single cent was made if you average up the business as a whole.*

In 1886, the cattle market began to show unmistakable effects of the results of over-expansion. As the crops of the Mid-west were hard hit by drouth the following year, those who were forced to liquidate the remnants of their herds realized a very poor sale; and Clay recalled that most eastern and British investors said, "Enough."

Some, however, held on with dogged determination and began to fight back. When the Montana Stockgrowers Association held their annual meeting, Joseph Scott was elected president. After being escorted to the chair, Scott addressed the meeting:

*"Gentlemen of the convention: It is with feelings of the greatest appreciation that I accept this honor. . . . I am proud that we have such an attendance; I think it is proof to us that we are not to bury this large industry, as some have stated, but we are here to revive it, and we are here to see that it does not die. It is true, the chilling winds of last winter have been felt on the range, and in many places you can smell the dead carcuses in the canyons; but the case is not as bad as it might have been. Had the winter continued twenty days longer, we would not have had the necessity of an Association. . . ."*

One of the men who laid the foundations for a fortune in these days of disaster was John Holt who purchased the interests of Liggett and Myers in the LO on Mizpah Creek. Another was Pierre Wilbaux who had chosen the western ranges in preference to a position in his father's textile mills in France. He immediately began to buy the holdings of the hard hit outfits, and southern trail herds, to restock his ranges along the northeastern edge of the Yellowstone Basin. One remnant which he purchased in the spring of 1889 was the "entire herd"—said to have been 10,000 cattle with 400 horses "thrown in"—of the Powder River Cattle Company for which Moreton Frewen had once had high hopes.

The old, careless days of the range were gone. No longer did a rancher dare turn a herd loose on the open range without provision for winter. As steers had demonstrated that they could withstand severe weather reasonably well, some operators began to bring in steers from the southern ranges to grow out and fatten. Others who maintained breeding herds, began to put up hay to supplement the winter range and trimmed their herds to a number which they could care for in event of an emergency. Nesters and small operators became more numerous, the government prosecuted large operators for illegal fencing, and the whole business of ranching underwent a slow but definite and permanent change.

Perhaps the largest outfit at the close of the days of the open range— about 1910—was the Spear Cattle Company. W. H. "Doc" Spear was vice president and manager, and associated with him was Willis Spear. The president of the company—the man who controlled its finances— was the president of the Stock Yards National Bank of Omaha, Nebraska, which, in turn, had considerable backing from the Armour and Cudahy families.

Leases on the Crow Reservation gave this outfit the grazing rights to about 1,250,000 acres, or a strip some 90 miles long and 20 miles wide. The company also controlled an area of considerable size on Clear and Crazy Women Creeks near their junction east of Sheridan, Wyoming. Collectively, their cattle wore twenty-five different brands. In 1911, the company branded 6,500 calves and went into the winter with 58,000 cattle on their ranges—of which they owned 32,000 head. The winter of 1912 was also a very severe winter and losses ran high in many areas: and this outfit lost an estimated 10,000 cattle and only branded 2,200 calves the following spring.

Along with the work connected with ranching, there was some play, and the English were responsible for bringing one unusual sport to the Yellowstone country. This was polo. The game originated in the Middle East, and came, by way of India, to England where the first game was played between the 10th Hussars and the 9th Lancers in 1869. In the early 1880's, Captain F. D. Grissell of the 9th Lancers settled on the

IXL ranch near Dayton, Wyoming; Captain Stockwell bought a ranch on Big Goose Creek in 1896, and it was not long before the two British officers recruited some cowboys and began to play in Sheridan, Wyoming. The next year Malcolm Moncreiffe, who was an experienced player, arrived and before long the Big Horn Polo Club was playing on an area which practically adjoined the front yard of Moncreiffe's ranch home on Little Goose Creek. In 1905, this club won from the team of the 10th U. S. Cavalry, then stationed at Fort Robinson, Nebraska, and went on the following year to make a creditable showing in other matches.

The winter of 1886-1887, hard as it was on the cattlemen, fostered the birth of a new industry in the West. In 1879, Howard Eaton came from Pittsburgh to establish the Custer Trail Ranch on the Little Missouri, a few miles south of where the town of Medora later sprang up. Howard Eaton, incidentally, had a banjo and the knack of improvising songs, and thus acquired for himself the reputation of being something of a troubadour. The following year, Alden Eaton, a brother, arrived to assist in the ranching venture, and the next year the third brother, Willis, arrived.

These brothers had a number of wealthy friends in the East and, as they were excellent hosts, their acquaintances came out each summer to hunt and to have a good time in the open. The winter of 1886-1887 left the brothers practically flat broke. When their friends arrived the next summer, they could no longer afford the luxury of a ranch house full of guests. "We're glad to see you," the brothers told them, "but we're broke and we can't keep you. However, if you want to chip in and pay for your keep, we'll be happy to have you stay." The guests were "happy" to pay for the privilege of eating the Eaton's grub and riding their horses which, being able to paw through the snow to grass, had not starved. The following year the Easterners arrived to do the same thing again—and dude ranching was started on its way to becoming a major industry in the West. The first paying "dude" actually preceded the hard winter. He was a man from Buffalo, N.Y., named Rumsey who contracted with Howard Eaton for a pack trip through the Yellowstone National Park in the summer of 1882.

Unfortunately for the Custer Trail Ranch, the campaign of the Northern Pacific Railroad to promote the settlement of the country brought a flood of honyockers into western North Dakota. The Eatons endured them for a short time and then, in 1904, sold out and moved to Wyoming where they settled at the foot of the Big Horn Mountains west of Sheridan. Here they established a new ranch where the son of one brother still wrangles both two and four legged critters. The two-legged species do not have to be branded, protected from rustlers, or fed hay when the snow gets too deep, and they have the habit of drifting back to the Arrowhead range year after year. Perhaps the Eaton brothers were fortunate that their cows did starve.

# 20

## Outside the Law

>>>>>>>>>«««««««« A cowboy, in reminiscing about some of the shadowy figures who rode the ranges, recalled:

One time we had a long dry spell an' the Mizpah was practically dry. But in one place there was a deep hole where there was a spring. Our wagon camped on a high bank that was right beside it. We were expecting a couple of reps from another outfit. A while after it got dark we heard a couple of men coming—spur and bridle chains jingling. They rode up to the waterhole and into the water to let their horses drink. One of us walked to the edge of the bank and hollered to the men and called them by name. But they never said a word. Just turned around and rode away.

The story of the criminals and officers of the open range days is, essentially, part of the story of the prairie and the mountains. Rustling, in one form or another, was the major occupation of many criminals and even the hold-up artists turned to it for additional income—or perhaps recreation.

Their activities, and those of the officers who pursued them, often extended beyond the limits of the Yellowstone Basin. Outlaws moving in a north-south direction usually followed the "Outlaw Trail." This came from Canada south to the mouth of the Musselshell River, to Junction City near the mouth of the Big Horn River, then along the eastern slope of the Big Horn Mountains and southwestward to Brown's Hole in the northwest corner of Colorado. The next stopping place was the Robbers Roost country in southeastern Utah and from thence the trail ran into northern Arizona. This was, however, not a *trail* but rather a general route; and probably only one gang ever rode it from northern Montana to Robbers Roost. Others used parts of it in their comings and goings.

Rustling was often a sort of shuttle operation. Teton Jackson and his gang, who used the Jackson Hole for a hangout, sometimes moved horses stolen in Idaho across the Yellowstone Basin and sold them in the Black Hills. Rustlers who stole in the Yellowstone Basin peddled their loot in Canada and then brought back stock stolen north of the border. And in the heart of the Yellowstone region, the Hole-in-the-Wall country, in the southern part of the Big Horn Mountains, was a famous retreat to which men could come knowing that they would be safe from unwanted attention.

The vigilantes who cleaned up the Montana goldfields in the 1860's hung every outlaw they could positively identify, and banished those they were uncertain about. This had a very wholesome effect on would-be criminals for some time, but when settlers began to come into the Yellowstone valley a new crop of outlaws assembled.

One of the first man hunts in the Yellowstone valley involved the notorious "Big Nose" George Parrott. In September 1878, he led a gang of outlaws in an attempt to derail a Union Pacific train in southern Wyoming. Although they were unsuccessful in this attempt to get a pay-car, the railroad officials put two detectives on their trail. The gang murdered these officers and were later identified by one of their own members who was captured and squealed.

As Wyoming was now too hot for them, the gang moved up to the Yellowstone valley and in January were hanging out in Miles City. About this time Morris Cahn, a hide buyer and merchant, left for the "States" to purchase a stock of merchandise. Although he took the precaution to travel with an army paymaster and his escort, he made no secret of the fact that he was carrying a considerable sum of money. Ten or twelve miles beyond the Powder River crossing, the trail to Bismarck dipped down into a small ravine for a short distance. Here Parrott and three companions relieved Cahn of $2,790—an expensive christening for what is now called Cahn's Coulee!

The gang then crossed to the opposite side of the Yellowstone, and the next night were back in Miles City spending money freely. Two months later, town marshall Hank Wormwood arrested the gang near Buffalo Rapids but they were released on the basis of perjured evidence. After the trial whenever Cahn would meet one of the gang on the street he would say, "Boys, don't kill me. I'll make you lots of money."

In July 1880, Parrott and one of his lieutenants, Bill Carey, were back in Miles City, staying at John Chinnick's cabin and peddling stolen horses. By this time circulars from the Union Pacific Railroad had reached the county sheriff and it was known that Parrott had a price of $2,000 on his head and Carey, $1,000. On the 17th of July the *Yellowstone Journal* reported the arrest of "two hard nuts," and three weeks later broke the fully story:

It will be remembered that the JOURNAL mentioned a short time ago, two noted blacklegs had been captured and incarcerated in the edifice known as the county jail. The reason why a more explicit account of the affair was not given, was owing to the request of the officers, Thos. Irvine and Jack Johnson, through whose instrumentality the villains were arrested. But now as they have been identified and are on their way to the territorial bastile, we will present the facts. For a long time the aforesaid officers held descriptions of "Big Nose George" alias George Parrott and his partner Bill Carey. The officers have kept a close look out and were at last rewarded by a sight of the villains who came in to town with a number of horses which they offered for sale. Knowing that they could not take the evildoers alive, the officers deputized Fred Schmalsle and Lem Wilson to make the arrest. The day before tackling George, Schmalsle and Wilson under the pretext of wanting horses, interviewed him and became acquainted. The next night at dark they proceeded to where George was stopping, leisurely sidled up to their victim who was setting in the doorway and in expressive words Fred told him to "throw up," placing a pistol to his left ear. George quickly obeyed accompanying the action with an exclamation of surprise. They then arrested Carey in a saloon who, when ordered up, made a motion for his pistol, but changed his mind as he saw the trigger of Fred's self cocker slowly rise. A day or two after the arrest, X Biedler [a U. S. marshall who was the most famous officer in Montana] arrived having trailed the prisoners to this place, but found them knabbed. On Saturday last, under escort of Detective Hines and Sheriff Rankins of Carbon county, Wyoming, heavily chained together, they were taken away to meet their doom, and can consider themselves in luck if they are not lynched before they reach their destination. . . . George has since [the Cahn holdup] been operating in the vicinity of Fort McKinney. . . .

Parrott actually was lynched later. He was tried in Rawlins, Wyoming, and sentenced to hang. While awaiting execution, he attempted a jail break which the jailer's wife foiled. When this became known a mob took him from his cell and hanged him, clumsily but effectively, from a telegraph pole.

The early settlers along the Yellowstone were plagued by thieves who sometimes posed as trappers and wood hawks [men who chopped wood for steamboats] anxious to earn an honest dollar. Although horses were usually the object of their attentions, they also stole cattle from the beef contractors near the army posts. In June 1880, after setting up a story about the mail contractor on the Miles City-Deadwood line who had already lost twelve horses since the first of the year, the editor of the *Yellowstone Journal* wrote a pointed editorial. In this he stated:

*The presence of horse thieves whether white or red is so apparent and their work so proven that it calls for some concerted action on the part of those most interested. Valuable animals are constantly disappearing and the losses incurred at this advanced portion of the season are irremediable. . . . And these predatory scoundrels are gathering fast. They have their organizations and . . . are desperate men. . . . They know they deserve to be strung up or shot down on short notice, and that when caught that method of disposing of them is usually resorted to. . . . While we are positively opposed to mob law except in the extremest cases, we are fully aware that something must be done for the protection of our property. . . .*

It was not until September of the following year that the editor was able to note that a "vigilance committee" had been formed. About the same time "Many Citizens" took Governor Potts to task in an open letter which this editor also published. Sheriff Irvine had trailed four thieves who had stolen 13 horses valued at about $1,000. Two had been apprehended in Dakota and two in Wyoming, but when Irvine asked for an official request for their extradition, the governor refused to grant it. And, as the letter writers pointedly put it—"the horse thieves have been turned loose and our citizens find that they have no redress for the property stolen." The orderly ways of the law were usually too slow and too uncertain to suit those who captured thieves.

Sometimes even the officers chafed under the legal restrictions. An old livestock inspector and officer who worked in western North Dakota recalled:

*A peace officer often had to break the law. In '92, I caught a man who had stolen a horse and saddle. It took me six weeks but I finally got him up northwest of Sheridan. Of course I didn't have a requisition for him but I started to take him back anyway. After we had gone a ways we met a couple of ranchers and the prisoner began to argue for his rights. They sized the situation up and finally one of them acted like he was in sympathy with my man. "Well," he said, "it looks like this officer don't have any business taking you back if you don't want to go. If you want to go back with us, we'll take you back. There's lots of good cottonwoods along this stream." The fellow got the point and decided right quick he would rather go with me.*

News items about stolen horses became commonplace in the Miles City and Billings papers—sometimes as many as a half dozen in a single issue. In June 1882, the publisher of the *Yellowstone Journal* editorialized again:

*There appears to be a horse stealing boom throughout the territory, and if it doesn't collapse the organization of the old-time necktye festivals will be in order.*

Horses were not the only things which interested some of these outlaws. On May 16, 1884, a story of the adventures of an army paymaster between Glendive and Fort Buford was telegraphed to the *Yellowstone Journal:*

*From an interview with Major Whipple the following details of the recent attempt of road agents to possess his treasure box was learned. Major Whipple's party consisted of himself, his clerk, Mr. Such, and escort of three men, including Sergeant Coonrad and two drivers in charge of an ambulance and wagon. The latter following the ambulance, carried the two soldiers, and the ambulance contained the paymaster, his clerk, Sergeant Coonrad and the driver, the two latter in the front seat. Contrary to usual custom this vehicle also carried the money chest. . . . While jogging along, without any thought of danger, the party were suddenly halted by seven masked and armed men at a point about . . . [20 ?] miles from Glendive, who at once opened fire on the cortege. . . . In this fire one of the mules was wounded and Sergeant Coonrad also received a wound, but he bravely responded to the fire, and kept it up* until, receiving a second wound he was disabled, meanwhile Major Whipple and Mr. Such had leaped from the ambulance, and about the same time the driver was hit, and lost control of the team, which at once started to run with the ambulance, which contained the money chest, and the wounded and dying sergeant. Major Whipple ran after it, and finally succeeded in overtaking it and gaining control of the team, but not before it had run some distance and reached a ranch [Halfway House near the present town of Savage. Here the sergeant died, and the outlaws, finding the strong box gone] . . . . destroyed the arms of the escort and rode off. . . . a courier was at once dispatched to Buford with the news of the attack and immediately Captain Bell's company of the Seventh cavalry was dispatched on the trail with three Indian scouts and guides. . . . The road agents are supposed to hail from Arizona, were well-armed and mounted. . . .

These scoundrels were never apprehended.

Such conditions could not be tolerated and when the Eastern Montana Livestock Association met in Miles City on March 21, 1884, the one problem which was foremost in the minds of most of the members was how to put a stop to rustling. Granville Stuart, a member of the Stockgrowers Association of Montana, was present and in the chair when the matter was discussed by the members on the floor. Stuart, who had been through the vigilante days in the gold fields, had—privately—urged that vigorous steps be taken; but when the question of raising a "small army of cowboys and raiding the country" was proposed from the floor, he argued against the idea. It was a hot session as the impulsive Marquis de Mores and two-fisted Theodore Roosevelt "openly accused me of 'backing water'." But Stuart carried his point, and it was decided to make no plans for an armed campaign.

Stuart knew all too well that effective action could not be initiated with a great fanfare. When he returned to the DHS, he and a few others gathered a committee of fourteen ranchers and cowboys, and one outsider, A. W. "Gus" Adams, a livestock inspector. About the same time, in the vicinity of Medora, North Dakota, "a small group of cowmen of that strong practical type who had already successfully pioneered the west" also organized, and "a well known stockman from Montana, with former vigilante experience, was called upon and played a prominent part."

Striking without warning, the Montana posse first cleaned out the gangs which had been using the badlands along the Missouri between the mouths of the Judith and the Musselshell as a base for their operations. Then:

. . . a small special train [consisting of one or two stock cars and a coach or two] on the Northern Pacific Railroad, carrying a "committee" of vigilantes and their horses, was taken eastward from a point near Billings, stopping at various places along the road where the "law enforcers" left the train to ride off and attend to the business at hand, returning to journey on to the next place and so on down the line, finally abandoning the train at Medora, Dakota. . . .

At Medora, Stuart joined the Dakota group and these men swept the little Missouri country and, probably, continued as far north as the Canadian line.

The shroud of secrecy which surrounds this campaign is almost as tight as the action was vigorous and effective. Some bits and pieces are know but no one involved in the cleanup has ever provided the public with a complete account. One old rancher, who probably knew whereof he wrote, put the story in a single sentence: "The total number of outlaws hung and shot in extreme eastern Montana and western Dakota was sixty-three."

Not all the comments about this cleanup were favorable. In an article for *The Century Magazine*, Theodore Roosevelt—who was not a participant—wrote, ". . . one committee of vigilantes in eastern Montana shot or hung nearly sixty—not, however, with the best judgement in all cases." Stuart, in defending the cleanup of the upper Missouri, wrote in his journal:

Several of the men who met their fate on the Missouri in July, 1884, belonged to wealthy and influential families and there arose a great hue and cry in certain localities over what was termed "the arrogance of the cattle kings." The cattlemen were accused of hiring "gunmen" to raid the country and drive small ranchers and sheepmen off the range. There was not a grain of truth in this talk.

On April 2nd of the following year, the Medora *Bad Lands Cowboy* admitted:

Whatever can be said against the methods adopted by the "stranglers" who came through here last fall, it cannot but be acknowledged that . . . . it seems as though a very thorough cleanup has been made.

The work of the Stranglers convinced any outlaws who escaped that eastern Montana was not a rustler's paradise. They moved elsewhere and left the field to the furtive operations of dishonest ranchers and cowboys. However, the rustlers in Wyoming were not bothered by any such fears. On September 7, 1885, the *Yellowstone Journal* carried this story:

Thursday there was a considerable excitement among cattle men, caused by the arrival of a letter from T. H. Brooks, foreman of Harris' horse ranch, thirty miles above Scott & Co.'s on Tongue river, announcing the fact that about the first of the month 200 head of horses had been stolen and run out of the country. A force of cowboys was organized and sent in pursuit of the thieves, but so far without satisfactory results. Some of the horses have been heard from at Sheridan, Wyo., where they were offered for sale. It is thought that the horses are being run south. . . .

The Big Horn Mountains and Jackson Hole in Wyoming, and the Black Hills of South Dakota were now to gain prominence as resorts for outlaws. And no place acquired more notoriety in the next decade and a half than the well-sheltered, spacious hideout in the southern part of the Big Horns that became known far and wide as the Hole-in-the-Wall country.

Beginning near the head of the Red Fork of Powder River, some fifteen miles west of the present town of Kaycee, a magnificent, westward-facing rampart of liver-red sandstone parallels the eastern edge of the Big Horns for approximately 35 miles. This towering reef of rock—known as the Red Wall—forms, for all practical purposes, an impassable barrier to all living things which cannot fly or scale sheer faces of rock. There are only four ways to get into the valley between the Red Wall and the backbone of the Big Horns—over the mountains from the west, up from the southern end, or by way of two entrances from the east. One of these, known as the Hole-in-the-Wall, is a gap about half or three quarters of a mile wide through which the Middle Fork of the Powder flows. The other means of access is called the Little-Hole-in-the-Wall. This is about twelve miles below the Hole-in-the-Wall and is a place where a watercourse runs to the top of the barrier. Here it is possible for horsemen to ride down the western face; and it was opposite this *entrance* that outlaws built their cabins and lived free from fear of pursuit.

After the campaign which Stuart directed, wholesale stealing in the Yellowstone Basin was pretty well limited, except for one effort on the Crow Reservation, to the work of gangs which lived in the Hole-in-the-Wall country. However, there were *little* rustlers, often single individuals, who kept right on "sleepering" calves and blotting brands. In Wyoming, these were divided into two classes—those who *ranched* and rustled on the side, and those who *rustled* and ranched on the side.

The branding of mavericks—often called *slicks* because they bore no mark of ownership—was sometimes the beginning point of stealing. It was not considered rustling to brand a slick although the Associations had rules which they applied to those gathered on the roundup. Some outfits, particularly those in the Wyoming portion of the Yellowstone Basin, adopted the policy of paying cowboys $2.00 to $5.00 for each maverick they found and branded. Soon some of the cowboys decided it was better to run on a brand of their own and possess a critter worth $10-30.00 than to get a few dollars for putting on the brand of the boss. Many a small rancher expanded his holdings in this manner; and old cowboys around Sheridan still joke about —— —— saying, "While we were getting our brand on one, he branded two." And a man who was the manager of several large outfits wrote frankly, "We were all guilty of it."

Next, the Wyoming cattlemen decided that, while it was all right to pay a cowboy for branding slicks for *them*, it was *wrong* for a cowboy to acquire cattle in the same manner. Cowboys owning a brand were black-listed by the cattlemen thus depriving them of employment. Naturally, this led to hard feelings and soon outright rustling of the big fellow's cattle was looked upon as a form of just retribution.

Of course some had no scruples about stealing—provided they did not get hung for it. On June 6, 1891, the *Yellowstone Journal* printed a letter from a prominent rancher which described in detail how the writer had watched a neighbor drive a bunch of cattle near the latter's home, and then run a cow and her calf around. When the horse knocked the calf down, the man took it up on the horse in front of him and was proceeding homeward, with the anxious cow following, when the interested observer approached. Finally, the thief put the calf down, whereupon it continued to follow his horse with the mother—plainly wearing the brand of another man—anxiously trying to reclaim her offspring. The writer noted in conclusion:

*This man is the owner of about 300 cattle, quite a band of horses, besides considerable other property, but takes no county paper, so will you please send me extra copies containing this article to give him. This kind of business is simply laughed at by many in this county, while the thief thinks he has done something smart. But when public sentiment will recognize the man who steals is a common thief, which he is, the community will be relieved of a very disagreeable element.*

Rustlers operated in many different ways. Stolen stock, particularly horses, might be driven to a distant point and sold with a fake bill of sale. Brands might be altered to conform with those which the rustlers

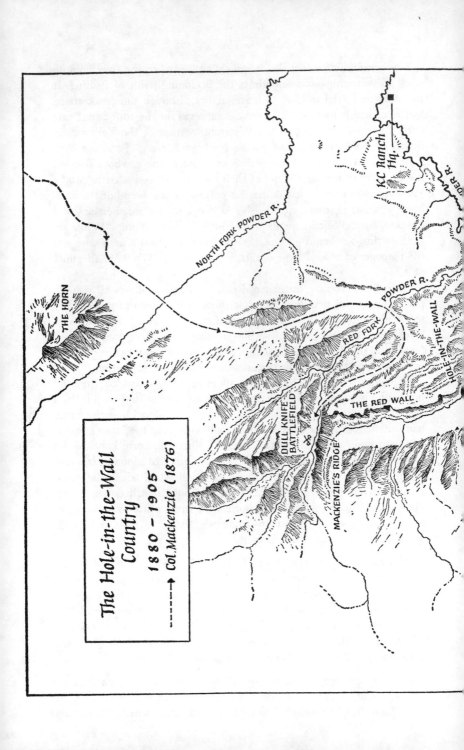

The Hole-in-the-Wall
Country

*1880 – 1905*

- - - → Col. Mackenzie (1876)

THE HORN

NORTH FORK POWDER R.

POWDER R.

RED FORK

THE RED WALL

HOLE-IN-THE-WALL

DULL KNIFE
BATTLEFIELD

MACKENZIE'S RIDGE

KC Ranch
Hq.

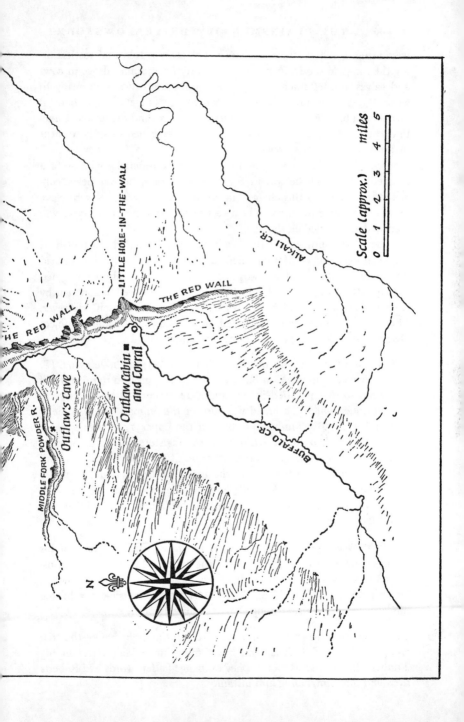

were using openly on their own stock. The story is told that rustlers using the range in the Hole-in-the-Wall country sometmies drove in cows
and calves and left them on the range until the calves were ready to
wean. Then they drove the cows back to the range of their rightful
owner, and branded the calves to suit themselves. And cattle were sometimes butchered and the meat—"slow elk," they called it—sold to meat
markets or construction crews.

Along the Yellowstone, Sim Roberts was considered to be quite a
character. Although he was in court several times, he was never convicted but once and this charge did not involve livestock. Nevertheless,
he was considered by many to be a very clever operator of the type who
"ranched and rustled on the side."

Roberts was born near Paris, Texas, and was riding with a trail herd
being brought out of Mexico when he was seventeen. By 1879 he had
drifted to Montana and was working for John T. Murphy who owned
the 79 outfit on the Musselshell. Later he was employed as foreman by
several large outfits, and finally began ranching for himself. However,
when he began to operate for himself, he immediately became an object
of suspicion. A judge who knew him personally recalled:

Sim had a brand, which was the dollar sign ($) on the left side. He
did not have a branding iron but used the end of an iron rod to run on
the brand so that it varied in size and shape according to the circumstances under which the brand was run on the animal. When Roberts
operated in the Big Timber country [on the upper Yellowstone] there
was a large cattle outfit near him with the registered brand of Seventy
Seven (77) on the left side, and another outfit with the pitchfork brand
on the left side. Both the 77 and the Pitchfork brand would fit under
the Dollarmark brand and a skilled operator, as was Sim Roberts, with
a running iron could turn a 77 and a pitchfork brand into a dollar sign
brand and do a good job of it.

Roberts was equally proficient with firearms. Although some of his
killings could be justified according to the code of the times, he was suspected in a few disappearances about which almost nothing was known.
One shooting involved Nate Young who was responsible for having
him arrested on a horse stealing charge. Young, the only witness,

did not arrive in town until about 10 o'clock the night before the trial
and put up his saddle horse and was coming down Main street in Big
Timber when he met Roberts. They exchanged a few words and Roberts
drew and shot him, killing him instantly.

Roberts was able to convince the jury that it was a case of self defense and was acquitted.

But this was not the end of the matter:

Shortly after this the decedent's brother, while walking along a road east of Big Timber, met Roberts driving a team with a hay rack. Young carried a rifle and as Roberts passed him, Roberts pulled his pistol and shot, the bullet passing through the front of Young's coat. Young opened up on Roberts with his rifle and Roberts jumped through the hay rack onto the doubletrees of the wagon and got away, with the horses at a dead run. Thereafter the rancher brother always carried a rifle and followed Roberts whenever he was out around the ranch or on the road. . . .

Not long after this situation developed, Roberts moved down into the Rosebud country where he spent most of the remainder of his life.

Roberts was more than just a man accused of being a clever thief. In his youth he was a top hand—a good rider, an expert roper, a fine trail boss, and had a thorough knowledge of how to handle horses and cattle. He was a likeable individual in many ways, could manage men, and left a creditable record as a foreman for several large outfits. Typical of those who knew him was a prominent rancher who, while admitting Roberts' shortcomings, insisted that he was a "wonderful cowman."

Many rustlers had similar qualities. Nate Champion, who worked in Johnson County, Wyoming, is said to have been another such man. However, to understand Champion and why he was killed, it is necessary to evaluate certain developments on the Wyoming ranges. Champion and Roberts, although similar, were parts of two entirely different situations.

In the Montana part of the Yellowstone Basin, small ranchers and farmers moved in and settled first, and these were followed by the large operators. Down in Wyoming, this movement was reversed with the small operators and nesters coming in and settling around Buffalo after the large cattle outfits had herds on much of the range. Also, the Wyoming Stock Growers Association was a dominant force in Wyoming politics while their sister organization in Montana never became as powerful politically. In fact at one time the wishes of the Wyoming association became almost the law of the state. And, as some of the large operators had a tendency to be arrogant, there were some who believed that the Wyoming Stock Growers Association had become "too big for its britches."

Some of the large outfits treated their smaller neighbors with con-

sideration but others which sprawled over the countryside impressed the
*little man* as being greedy and overbearing. The fact that some of these
were owned by absentee stockholders made this situation even worse,
and the blacklisting of cowboys who had cattle of their own added
more fuel to the fire. In the end, the two factions became solidly
aligned against each other; and rustling provided the fuse which
touched off this powder keg.

Losses sustained during the winter of 1886-1887 caused many cowboys to be thrown out of work. Some of these turned to rustling. Previous to this time, losses from rustling had been accepted as part of the
business howbeit disliked. Now all losses were severely felt and could
not be endured without danger of going broke. Also, homesteaders
crowded onto choice lands with water—water that sometimes was the
key to the use of the ranges between the streams. Tensions and hard
feelings increased until by 1890 the situation was as taut as a cord
stretched to the breaking point.

While conditions were getting worse on the ranges, the Wyoming
Stock Growers Association instituted a system of inspection at the large
markets which—although fundamentally sound—permitted them to
discriminate against and harass those whom they did not like. In 1891,
the Association, working through the Board of Livestock Commissioners, practically dictated who could and who could not sell cattle at
the large markets. The "rustler" element, in turn, organized an association of their own and in 1891 ran the roundups in northeastern
Wyoming. Also, it is said they drove some ranchers out of the country
and denied to others—under threat of death—the right to supervise
their property.

Buffalo, the county seat of Johnson County, was the focal point of
this trouble. The anti-cattleman or "rustler" element had elected a
sheriff and other county officials who ran the region to suit themselves:
and it is said that there were 180 charges of cattle stealing filed over a
four year period, and only *one* conviction resulted. There can be no
doubt but that considerable rustling went on in this area, and that
*honest* people were guilty of winking at this stealing. However, it is impossible to make a candid evaluation of this situation; and perhaps the
best that can be done is to liken it to that of the "pot calling the kettle
black."

"The Johnson County War" or "Cattlemen's Invasion" was preceded by several violent deaths. In at least two of these the finger of
suspicion was pointed at Frank Canton. Canton was a Texan who was
elected sheriff of Johnson County in 1882 and again in 1884. As a sher-

iff and range detective for the Wyoming Stock Growers Association, he was a tireless and efficient officer. But he was not particularly beloved by those among whom he lived—many regarded him as a cold-blooded killer. He had the steely eye, the reputation of being a fine marksman, and steady nerves when the chips were down, three things necessary for survival among the toughs of the West.

While he was sheriff, Canton stopped cattle stealing by the Shoshones by getting two braves sent to the penitentiary. His most notable arrest was that of "Teton" Jackson, a notorious outlaw leader who often trailed stolen stock across the Big Horn Mountains. Jackson was no pseudo bad man, he was the genuine article and it took a man of Canton's caliber to arrest him.

Perhaps the two hangings which occurred in 1889 along the Sweetwater, just south of the Yellowstone Basin, mark the beginning of the ruthless campaign which the cattlemen undertook. Jim Averill had a homestead near Independence Rock where he ran a combination store, bar, and post office. Nearby, Ella "Cattle Kate" Watson also had a homestead where she plied the most ancient of female professions. Jim managed to make himself disliked and Kate sometimes took her pay in mavericks or stock which her customers had rustled. The bodies of both were found dangling on ropes under a cottonwood.

Near Newcastle, Wyoming, in June 1891, Thomas Waggoner was taken from his home and hanged—for what and by whom was never known. Just before daylight, on the first of the following November, four men entered a little cabin on Powder River where Nathan "Nate" Champion and a man named Hall were sleeping, and shot at Champion. He grabbed his revolvers from under his pillow and drove off the would-be assassins, wounding one. About four weeks later, two men accused of rustling, Orley "Ranger" Jones and J. A. Tisdale, were *dry gulched* south of Buffalo.

No one was ever arrested in any of these incidents. In the Averill-Watson case, one witness *died* and the other *disappeared*. Canton was openly accused of the two bushwhackings. After the "Invasion," he returned to Buffalo—allegedly at his own wish—and stood trial but no evidence was brought against him.

Matters had now progressed to the point where the stage was set for desperate measures. In the spring of 1892, vigilante action was discussed at the meeting of the Wyoming Stock Growers Association. Although the Association took no steps, a small group took upon themselves the responsibility of taking action; and subsequent events indicate clearly that what these men did had the tacit approval of a great many of the members. Even the press was openly predicting a "war." On the 13th of February, the *Yellowstone Journal* copied a long, and surprisingly well written article from the *New York Sun:*

Men familiar with the situation between the cowmen and the rustlers in Wyoming have been saying for some time that there would be trouble on Powder river when the spring roundup was made, but the latest news from Buffalo, Wyo., as contained in a dispatch from Deadwood, indicates that there is a strong probability that the war will break out before the spring roundup comes on, if, indeed, it cannot be said to have already broken out.

Wherever cattlemen have organized outfits and located ranches cattle thieves have always followed, and there has been fighting. It is a singular fact that men who would assist at the lynching of a horse thief with cheerful good will would have no scruples at all about "rustling" cattle.

\* \* \*

The present trouble in Wyoming is the culmination of an ill-advised effort on the part of the Wyoming Live Stock Association to check the rustlers. It is a practical impossibility to devise any scheme by which cattle stealing could be wholly stopped, where the opportunities for profit from it are so large and where immunity from punishment is certain. The rustlers were few in number when the association was formed and their action was not concerted. They confined themselves almost wholly to the taking of mavericks. . . . But as the rustlers grew bolder and stronger they began not only to take mavericks but also to alter brands. In some cases instead of branding over the old brand they just put their brand on the cattle and forged a bill of sale. The rustlers were, for the most part, men who owned small ranches, or cowboys who had a few head of cattle on the range, or running with some other ranchers' stock.

The association made a regulation that no cow outfit in the association would give work to any cowboy who had been guilty of branding mavericks, or of assisting the rustlers, or of working with or for rustlers. A black list was kept of such cowboys. The result was that a good many cowboys found themselves unable to get work from the association outfits, and were compelled to become rustlers. Many of the other cowboys sympathized with their blacklisted friends. They argue that there is no certainty that they themselves will not be accused of assisting the rustlers and be blacklisted, in which case they would have to rustle themselves. The consequence is that in the present state of affairs it is almost impossible to find cowboys who would be of use to the cow outfits in case an open war with the rustlers breaks out, as now seems probable.

The numbers [sic rustlers] *have increased in numbers until there are now more than 125 of them. They are probably the best men physically in the cow country. A cowman well known in Wyoming . . . said to a reporter:*

*"There is not a man of the rustlers that cannot ride anything that ever wore horse hair. There is not a man among them who cannot rope, throw, tie and brand a steer single handed. They are the best riders, the best ropers, the best shots in the cattle business. They are the best cow punchers and cattle handlers in the state. They never knew what fear was, and now they are desperate. If they fight, somebody will get hurt."*

*The man who said that had been warned not to return to his ranch. His brother who is now in Buffalo, Wyo., has been warned not to attempt to visit the ranch. Recently John Durbin, one of the big ranchmen in Wyoming, while on a visit to Omaha, told the story of the situation to an Omaha reporter. Durbin has since been warned not to return to Wyoming, and the rustlers on Powder river openly threatened to shoot him at sight. . . . The rustlers are acting together and have been strong enough to elect one of their own men sheriff.*

*Several men have been killed, some on both sides. Tisdale, who was shot, and Jones, who was killed at the same time, were rustlers and not leaders. At the same time it was declared by the cowmen that the killing was due to a falling out among thieves. But it seems to have only made matters worse. It has been impossible to obtain a conviction in any case of rustling. When Henderson, a ranch manager, was killed, two men were convicted and got 20 years, although the crime was deliberate murder.*

\*     \*     \*

*The rustlers are very desperate. They have met their first serious check at the hands of the live stock commission. The commission places its inspectors at all the cattle markets, Omaha, Chicago, St. Louis, Kansas City and St. Paul. Every shipment of cattle is carefully inspected. If it comes from a rustler he must prove his title to every steer most conclusively or else the cattle are confiscated and sold and the money sent to the commission. . . . In this manner the rustlers have been deprived of a market for their cattle. In some cases their cattle have been seized even when they have shown bills of sale. This method, perhaps, could not be sustained in the courts, but so far no rustler has seen fit to make a fight for his property.*

*The rustlers have been forced to either butcher their cattle or to drive to Montana. The drive . . . does not insure a market . . . as all livestock commissions keep such a sharp watch on Wyoming cattle. The other scheme is not a satisfactory one, but they are compelled to adopt it. They have several butchers in Buffalo who do the killing for them, but even by this method they do not always get their meat marketed.*

*In the summer of 1891 the rustlers ran wagons openly on all three round-ups, and worked the roundup just as if they were a regular Association outfit. They also took all the mavericks, and no one was in a position to dispute with them. The spring roundup begins early in May, and the cowmen expect that it will be the signal for the war to begin.*

The preparations for the "Invasion" were rather elaborate. A "hat" was passed for expenses and $100,000 collected; and the secretary for the Association took care of some of the correspondence. Livestock detectives compiled a list of seventy suspects to be eliminated. One range detective, Tom Smith, went to Texas and enlisted twenty-five gunmen. Most of these came from around the town of Paris and were alleged to have been reliable ex-officers of the law. As some Southern families spawned both officers and outlaws, about all that can be said with certainty is that they were gunmen. Some horses and supplies were put on a special train at Denver, and additions were made to the party at Cheyenne.

This train was unloaded before daylight on the 7th of April just outside of Casper, Wyoming. Here the force consisted of 55 men, including the cooks, two newspaper correspondents, a doctor, and a young Englishman from Colorado along for the excitement. In addition to horses for the party, there were also three wagons loaded with supplies. The man who had command of this little army, at least most of the time, was "Major" Frank Wolcott, a dapper, nervy, little veteran of the Civil War.

After a miserable all-day march in mud and snow flurries, the little army laid over at Tisdale's ranch. Dawn of the following day found them with Winchesters ready, hidden around the Nolan KC ranch buildings along the Powder, just south of the present town of Kaycee. Here they expected to find Nate Champion and Nick Ray, another rustler.

Champion was perhaps the biggest thorn in the flesh of the cattlemen. He was a Texan who had come north with cattle, and for a time had been foreman at the EK ranch. He was a hard-working cowboy with ability as a leader, was "honest"—after the fashion of the times, a fine rider, fast with a gun, an "expert shot," and "dead game." But now he was known as the leader of the Red Sash Gang, the largest of the rustler groups.

Two trappers, over-night guests at the four-room, log ranch house, were the first to appear. These men were quietly captured. When Ray came out he was shot down near the door. Champion coolly dragged his wounded comrade inside and the battle was on. Late in the afternoon a wagon loaded with combustibles was pushed against the cabin and set afire. When all was a mass of flames, Champion ducked out of a back door and into the smoke, and then ran for a nearby ravine where waiting riflemen cut him down. In one of his pockets the cattlemen found a small notebook which contained a diary account of the day-long fight. Significantly, it contains no question as to the identity of his attackers, or why they were there. *He knew.*

Champion's account of his epic fight against fifty men is one of the classics of the West. He wrote:

*Me and Nick was getting breakfast when the attack took place. Two men here with us—Bill Jones and another man. The old man went after water and did not come back. Nick started out and I told him to look out, that I thought there was someone at the stable and would not let them come back. Nick is shot but not dead yet. He is awful sick. I must go and wait on him. It is now about two hours since the first shot. Nick is still alive. They are still shooting and are all around the house. Boys, there is bullets coming like hail. Them fellows is in such shape I can't get back at them. They are shooting from the stable and river and back of the house. Nick is dead. He died about 9 o'clock. I see a smoke down at the stable. I think they have fired it. I don't think they intend to let me get away this time.*

*It is now about noon. There is someone at the stable yet. They are throwing a rope out at the door and dragging it back. I guess it is to draw me out. Boys, I don't know what they have done with those two fellows that stayed here last night. Boys, I feel pretty lonesome right now. I wish there was someone here with me, so we could watch all sides at once. They may fool around until I get a good shot before they leave. There was a man in a buckboard and one on horseback just passed. They fired on them as they went by. I don't know if they killed them or not. I seen lots of men come out on horses on the other side of the river and take after them. I shot at the men in the stable just now; don't know if I got any or not. I must go and look out again. It don't look as if there was much show of my getting away. I see twelve or fifteen men. One looks like . . . [name scratched out]. I don't know whether it is or not. I hope they did not catch them fellows that run over the bridge toward Smith's. They are shooting at the house now. If I had a pair of glasses I believe I would know some of these men. They are coming back. I've got to look out.*

*Well, they have just got through shelling the house like hail. I hear* them splitting wood. I guess they are going to fire the house to-night. I think I will make a break when night comes, if alive. Shooting again. I think they will fire the house this time. It's not night yet. The house is all fired. Good-bye boys, if I never see you again.

NATHAN D. CHAMPION

The man whom Champion had noted passing the KC escaped. He confirmed what others had already suspected and riders rapidly aroused the entire countryside. When the "Regulaters" reached the TA ranch, fifteen miles south of Buffalo, a range detective warned them that they did not have enough men to occupy the county seat. So Wolcott prudently turned aside to the buildings of the TA and disposed his force to defend the place. Before long they were surrounded by 300 or more "rustlers." Both sides settled down to a sniping duel which lasted for two days with no casualties on either side. However, as the Invader's supply wagons had been captured, their situation soon became desperate.

Sheriff "Red" Angus, one of the "rustler" element, wired Governor Barber for the assistance of the state militia. This request was ignored as the cattlemen had already muzzled this organization. But when one of the besieged slipped through the lines at night and sent a telegram from nearby Fort McKinney, the governor immediately threw the weight of his office behind a request that the U. S. cavalry at Fort McKinney take the cattlemen into protective custody until the situation could be investigated. This involved having the two Wyoming senators get President Harrison out of bed and having him call the Secretary of War to issue the necessary order! By 4:00 A.M. the following morning the order had been received and three troops of cavalry were mounted and on their way.

The soldiers arrived as the cattlemen were about to make a "last ditch" attack, and Major Wolcott was most happy to surrender to Colonel Van Horn. All the force was taken to Fort McKinney, some three miles from Buffalo, and then were transferred to Fort D. A. Russell just outside of Cheyenne—the Johnson County officials clamoring loudly and futilely for their custody. It was not long before the prisoners were comfortably quartered in Cheyenne and soon the string-pulling resulted in a change of venue. Finally, late in January of the following year, the prosecuting attorney for Johnson County went to court and entered a *nolle prosequi,* and after a final bit of haggling the cattlemen were discharged. The gunmen had returned to Texas long before.

The invasion, a fiasco from the start, cost the cattlemen an estimated $105,000. Three years later, Johnson County had paid out $10,482.46

for legal expenses and owed an additional $17,295.92. Bitter feelings had been stirred up which lingered for decades—it is still impossible to make a candid appraisal of the trouble.

Trouble in Johnson County did not end with the removal of the Invaders, or the angry looting of some of the ranches. Late in April a notice, over the signatures of the sheriff and the county commissioners, appeared in the newspapers stating that "The authorities of Johnson County invite and desire" that owners of the various outfits send a representative to the roundups. The cattlemen countered by having an injunction issued to stop the illegal roundups. One such representative, the new foreman of the Hoe outfit and a U. S. Deputy Marshal, was ambushed and killed near Buffalo—by whom it was never known. There was a considerable stir about this and the outcome was that the President directed that a semblance of martial law be established in the trouble area.

However, the Invasion did create a feeling of uncertainty among some of the rustlers. Some Montana ranchers, living just north of Johnson County, observed a "steady stream" of riders passing through the country during the succeeding months. Who they were, why they were traveling, and where they were going—it was not polite to ask such questions. The supposition was that some were moving and others were trailing them. One rancher found two bodies hanging from a box elder tree at the forks of Pass Creek along the trail between Sheridan and Billings. They were never identified. One day the (Billings) *Post* informed its readers that two bodies had been found hanging within the town limits. Five or six rustlers who lived in a cabin in Dayton, Wyoming, a small town where the Bozeman Trail crossed the Tongue River, became obnoxious and occasionally shot up the place. When the residents posted a notice that this would not be tolerated, the outlaws took it as a dare and repeated the performance. So the settlers dug out their "buffalo guns" and killed one and wounded two others.

This exodus did not provide a cleanup for rustling was too deeply intrenched. Just three years before the war, three men were convicted in Casper, Wyoming for stealing horses in southeastern Montana and selling them in the vicinity of Casper. The leader was Phil Watson, then town marshall of Casper and deputy sheriff for part of Carbon County. One of the big dealers in stolen stock in central Wyoming is alleged to have become a prominent banker, and some officers of the law were suspected of providing tips about impending searches. And five years after the Invasion, Buffalo's reputation as a "rustler town" was the subject of pointed editorial comments in other newspapers of the state. Even after the cattlemen and officers had demonstrated that they dared to comb the Hole-in-the-Wall country for stolen stock, the infamous Wild Bunch often holed up there after a foray, and the outlaws hid out by working as cowboys for nearby ranches.

There was no better spot in all the West for rustlers than the Hole-in-the-Wall country. Secure behind the towering Red Wall, they leisurely worked over brands and held their loot until a market could be arranged. In the summer of 1897, three large outfits—the CY (one of the largest in Wyoming), the Ogallala Company, and the Pugsleys—decided to work the Hole. To make certain that there was no mistake about their intentions, the foreman of the CY wrote an open letter to the *Casper Tribune*. This read, in part:

· CASPER, WYOMING, July 19, 1897

EDITOR, Casper Tribune.

*I have seen all sorts of reports bearing upon John R. Smith and Nolan gang stopping the roundup from working the Hole-in-the-Wall country. They will have a hard time of it. Neither the CY boys, the Keystone or the Pugsley outfits are hunting a fight. We are all working men and only want such cattle as belong to our employers. . . . I am going to work that country and have asked the sheriffs of Natrona and Johnson counties to work with us and see that everybody is treated right. . . . And if those men want to fight us, when we know we are right, I say fight.*

R. M. DEVINE

The thieves then wrote an ultimatum which also appeared in print:

*Bob Devine you think you have played hell   you have just begun you will get your dose   there is men enough up here to kill you.   we are going to get you or lose 12 more men   you must stay out of this country if you want to live   we are not going to take any chances any more but will get you any way we can   we want one hair a piece out of that damned old chin of yours   you have give us the worst of it all the way through and you must stay out or die.   dont stick that damned old grey head of yours in this country again if you dont want it shot off we are the twelve men appointed a purpose to get you if you dont stay out of here*

REVENGE GANGE

Accompanied by a U. S. deputy marshall and a Montana livestock inspector, the foremen and their cowboys proceeded with the announced roundup. While hunting cattle near the Hole-in-the-Wall ranch house, Devine and his men met Bob and Al Smith and Bob Taylor. On being asked if they had seen any CY cattle, Bob Smith pulled his six-shooter. When the dust and smoke settled, Devine and his son were wounded, Bob Smith lay on the ground dying, Bob Taylor had both hands in the air, and Al Smith was out of sight. Taylor was arrested and later released—it was no use trying to convict a rustler in Johnson County.

The success of Devine's roundup launched a second soon afterward. With this one rode the sheriff of Johnson County—an honest man who had succeeded the "rustler" supported Red Angus, the sheriff of Natrona County (just to the south), and an officer from South Dakota who was looking for outlaws. This drive brought out about 550 head of stolen stock; and it inspired a number of barbed comments against Johnson County and the town of Buffalo in particular. The *Douglas News* stated:

*The attitude of a number of Johnson county people in upholding the Hole-in-the-Wall thieves is not likely to increase the number of advocates favoring a state appropriation of money to pay for the Invasion trial expenses. . . . If the Hole-in-the-Wall gang had been in any other county of the state the whole outfit would have been in the penitentiary years ago for the full limit of the law.*

The editor of the Basin City *Herald* cut even deeper. In commenting on the chase of a gang of robbers—who also hid out behind the Red Wall—he wrote:

*Should O'Day's companions in the Belle Fourche [bank] robbery be arrested or killed by the posses in pursuit, it will go far toward breaking up the gang which has defied the authorities for so long with such a strange immunity. But the death or capture of these men will not be a full satisfaction of justice. The moneyed scoundrels who aid and abet them, who take their stolen stock, who make their stealing possible and profitable, are far more guilty than O'Day and the rest of the gang.*

It may be noted in passing that O'Day got out of this scrape but six years later was captured in the Big Horn Mountains with twenty stolen horses. This time—after two hung juries—he was convicted.

Although the rustlers were the major concern of the cattlemen, sheriffs and U. S. marshalls for miles around were particularly interested in a gang of outlaws which was first known as the Hole-in-the-Wall Gang and later became part of the notorious Wild Bunch. Obviously, most of what is *known* about them has been pieced together from bits and pieces and the holes filled in by deduction.

Apparently the group was first called the Red Sash Gang. Allegedly led by Nate Champion, the chief activity was rustling. Prominent in this group was "Flat Nose George" Curry, son of a Nebraska rancher. Curry has sometimes been confused with "Big Nose George" Parrott who was captured in Miles City and lynched in Rawlins. Parrott was undoubtedly familiar with the country behind the Red Wall, but probably was not a member of the gang. For a time the Logan brothers— Harvey, later called "Kid Curry," Lonny, and Johnny—and their cousin Bob Lee rode with this group. The Logan brothers, also known as the Curry or Currie brothers were quarter blood Cherokees and tough nuts, especially Harvey "Kid Curry" Logan.

Sometime before the Invasion, the Logan brothers went to Montana and settled north of the Missouri near a little town named Landusky. Here they assumed the name of "Currie." To this area, in 1892, came others of their kind. On December 27, 1894, Harvey got into a fight with Powell "Pete" Landusky and killed him. As Landusky had friends who were certain to take offense, the three brothers left at once for the Hole-in-the-Wall.

During this Montana sojourn, Champion had been killed and George Curry had taken over the leadership of the gang which still continued to use the Nolan KC ranch as a headquarters. These outlaws enlarged the scope of their operations and terrorized the surrounding countryside. On April 13, 1897, they murdered a deputy sheriff of Johnson County who, in a moment of overconfidence, tried to arrest the gang. A week after this murder, Butch Cassidy's gang—the notorious Wild Bunch—pulled off an $8,800 robbery in Utah which apparently fired the imagination of Curry and his men.

On June 26, 1897, six men rode into Belle Fourche, South Dakota and took approximately $4,000 from the Butte County Bank. All rode safely away except Tom O'Day whose horse bolted and left his rider to become the occupant of the local jail. Dakota officers took up the trail in earnest and chased the outlaws over parts of northern Wyoming, North and South Dakota and almost to the Canadian line in Montana. Finally the thieves doubled back and vanished into a rugged part of the valley of the Big Horn.

This relentless pursuit, added to the two forays of the cattlemen, convinced the outlaws that they should move. Apparently there was an exodus from the Hole-in-the-Wall country to northwestern Colorado where the Wild Bunch of George LeRoy Parker, alias "Butch" Cassidy, were using Brown's Hole as a rendezvous. The Wyoming outlaws now dropped stock rustling, except perhaps as an avocation, and joined Cassidy in hunting large stakes.

Cassidy was not a stranger to the Hole-in-the-Wall Gang as he had hidden out behind the Red Wall as early as 1894. He was an unusual outlaw leader of the legendary Robin Hood type—extremely likeable, used liquor in moderation, was never quarrelsome, and had none of the attributes of a gunman. Strange to say, he never killed a man during his holdups.

A couple of years after this merger, a Union Pacific train was held up about 70 miles south of Casper, Wyoming and a large sum of unsigned bank notes—reported to have been $60,000—taken from the express car. A few days later, three suspicious characters, probably George Curry and Harvey and Lonny Logan, were seen a few miles north of Casper. A posse of eleven men started after them and were ambushed near Salt Creek where a sheriff was fatally wounded. The outlaws, having reached familiar territory and friends, now vanished into the Hole-in-the-Wall country. The resulting search was futile but it did result in the press making the name "Hole-in-the-Wall" well known throughout the United States.

The Wild Bunch now began to thin out. Next year "Flat Nose George" Curry was shot while rustling cattle in Utah. In the summer of 1901, Butch Cassidy, Harvey Logan, Harry Longabaugh—the "Sundance Kid," and a new member, Camilla Hanks, rode the Outlaw Trail to northern Montana for one last job. On the 3rd of July they robbed a Great Northern train near Warner and headed back down the trail with $40,000 in new bank notes which—alas—lacked the signatures of the bank officials. Later, Harvey Logan tried to pass some of the loot in Knoxville, Tennessee and was arrested. Before the officers could get him safely into the penitentiary, he escaped and turned up in the Hole-in-the-Wall country where he joined up with an old crony. Then the two stole some horses and the sheriff came to investigate. The outlaws escaped but not before Logan was wounded. Shortly afterward a doctor in Thermopolis, on the western slope of the Big Horns was forced to make two trips at night to attend a seriously wounded man. Nothing more was heard about the patient and the doctor assumed that he died. In 1903 a rustler was shot in Colorado whom a railroad detective identified—positively—as Harvey Logan.

Now only two were left of the long-riders who knew the trails from Robbers Roost in Utah to the country behind the Red Wall, and on up into Montana. They were Cassidy and the Sundance Kid. These two, who were similar in many respects, now went to South America together. Between holdups, they worked like honest men but finally, after a robbery, soldiers cornered them and the *Yanqui* bandits shot it out rather than surrender.

Tall, handsome Harry Longabaugh was an experienced outlaw before he wandered into the Hole-in-the-Wall and joined Curry's gang.

However, on one occasion, he met his match in "Eph" Davis, a frontiersman, and Billy Smith, the Montana stock inspector. They caught him in June 1887 at the N Bar ranch on the Powder, and delivered him safely to the jail in Miles City after a series of depredations which began near the Canadian line and extended to the Newman ranch. Even then he picked the lock on some fancy handcuffs with a horseshoe nail one night and would have escaped except that Davis was playing "possum" while pretending to be asleep. The Montana officers turned him over to a Wyoming sheriff, from whom he had recently escaped, and the Kid continued to be an outlaw for another twenty-two years.

Another noted figure to come to the Hole-in-the-Wall country was Tom Horn. Horn had been a packer and scout in Arizona during the troubles with the Apaches, and he had handled pack mules for General Shafter in the Spanish-American War. He was employed by the Pinkerton Detective Agency for a time, and then by the Swan Land and Cattle Company in southern Wyoming. Cowboys on the Wyoming range at the turn of the century knew him as a range detective but details about his employers are shadowy. It is said that he was hired to kill rustlers: and he was seen in the Hole-in-the-Wall country but no killings there have been ascribed to him. He was hung in Cheyenne in 1903 for the alleged murder of the son of a sheepman—a silent, controversial figure whose guilt was never proven to the satisfaction of many.

Sheepmen, as well as the rustlers, were a source of concern to some ranchers. Part of the dislike of cattlemen for sheep was based on fact and part on imagination. In time it was demonstrated that sheep and cattle could live together on the range, but sheep often nibbled grass to its very roots and a range which had been overgrazed by "woolybacks" was often ruined for years. Be that as it may, some cattlemen did not like sheep and refused to tolerate them on the range where their cattle ran. And there was trouble.

For the most part, the cattlemen and sheepmen got along reasonably well in that part of the Yellowstone Basin north of the Wyoming-Montana state line. Sheep were trailed in in quantity almost as early as cattle, and these flocks were settled on the range with but a small amount of friction. Of course cowboys did not like sheep and they regarded a sheepherder as an inferior sub-species of the *homo sapiens* and this caused friction which sometimes came close to gunplay.

There were two areas in Montana which certain cattlemen "closed" to sheep. These were the Otter Creek area—a tributary of the Tongue, and the Mizpah Creek watershed—which emptied into the lower Powder. A man who herded woolies in the early days recalled:

The only acts of aggression that occurred was the work of over enthusiastic range foremans, and would be Montgomery Ward [sic—imitation] cow hands. As a sample of their work I will offer a few occurrences of 1885.

Some cow hands came into a sheep camp, no one was at home and they opened fire on a Dutch oven, next they tried to run a bull over a sheep herder. The bull would not do it so they quirted the herder over the head; next, three of them rode into a sheep camp before sunrise expecting the herder to be in bed. He was not. When they came down over the brink of the draw in which he was camped he had heard the commotion and had shoved his Colt's Navy cap and ball six-shooter down between his suspender straps and was standing before his tent ready for eventualities. Mr. Sabers, the roundup boss for the Niobrara Cattle Company, fell off his horse before the horse stopped spouting invective about sheep and whosoever. Then motion and language ceased. He had appraised the situation. . . . Then the herder spoke, "Mr., the owner of these sheep lives over yonder hill. I have nothing to do with them except to see that nothing happens to them." And Ed decided he, the owner, was the man he wanted to see.

*　　　*　　　*

A few days after this a bunch of cow punchers rode into one of W. E. Harris' camps at night and emptied their six shooters into the band of sheep and killed 25 and crippled many more. These were the only acts that occurred in 1885 in a vast range country. In 1886, the drouth year, W. E. Harris, who was ranging 7000 sheep on Pumpkin Creek, decided to move over into Otter Creek country where there was more feed at that time, but not enough to winter the stock that already belonged there. He was met on the divide by a delegation of stockmen who took his sheep back to Pumpkin Creek.

A cowboy who rode for the LO recalled that on another occasion W. E. Harris—usually called "Charlie" Harris—edged over into the Mizpah country. Riders wrecked the herder's camp and shot through a case of tomatoes so as to puncture every can. The sheep were pulled back to Pumpkin Creek.

Tempers flared in the valley of the Stillwater where sheep were also not welcome. In the fall of 1896, the body of Gottleib Heide was found riddled with buckshot, and 400 sheep were killed. It was believed cattlemen were responsible for the killing.

There were several squabbles in the Otter Creek country. On one occasion a sheepman named Philbrick who ranged on the Rosebud tried to edge into the Liscomb Creek valley. Cattlemen eased horses into the flock in the daytime and tried to drift the sheep out of the country. When this did not work, the ranchers sent one of their number to talk with the herder. The *talk* developed into a heated argument during which the herder called the rancher a liar whereupon the latter "gun-whipped" the herder with his Winchester. When the matter got into court the wrong person was charged with the whipping and the judge threw the case out.

Although there were sheep along the lower Powder in the early days, additional flocks were viewed with disfavor. In 1901 when Hank Greenway, of Greenway and Harris, moved to the Powder he received a "whitecap" message which read: IF YOU TAKE SHEEP TO POWDER RIVER BRING YOUR COFFIN ALONG. YOU WILL NEED IT.

One of the most serious incidents in this part of the Yellowstone Basin, although it did not involve a killing, occurred on January 2, 1901. R. R. Selway of Sheridan, Wyoming—an early sheepman on the head of Pumpkin Creek—tried to edge a flock which John Daut was handling on shares over into the "closed" range of the Otter Creek country. One morning at daybreak, eleven men with masks made from gunny sacks rode into the sheep camp, then on the head of Toomey Creek, just as the herder was coming out of his wagon. While one man held Daut at the point of a pistol, the others entered the corral and clubbed over 2,000 sheep. According to one old-timer, "Only twelve got away."

The herder, "bugg-eyed" with fright, came in to the Three Circle ranch on the Tongue and the news was phoned to the sheriff at Miles City. He came out and picked up the ash clubs which were used but did not make any arrests. Selway offered a $2,000 reward for information but to no avail, in fact the local people joked about the matter. It was pretty well known who did the job but whenever any discussion gets around to the subject of names, knowledgeable old-timers shut up like clams.

Sometime later a bank in Miles City received $15,000 in an anonymous letter with the request that the money be deposited to Selway's credit. But Selway refused to accept the money. Although no one was ever arrested, action was brought in Wyoming charging John B. Kendrick, a prominent rancher who lived in Sheridan and owned the OW on the Tongue, with being the person who was responsible. As the overt act was committed in another state, the Wyoming courts refused to consider the case. However, the clubbing was a blessing to the half-starved Cheyennes who lived nearby. They trailed up the creek to the site of the killing for days to get mutton.

Although the sheepmen and cattlemen in Montana got along without much serious trouble, relations in Wyoming were often violent. In fact, in the early 1900's, brutal incidents became so common that some killings are said to have never been noted by the press. The Big Horn valley was ablaze with feuds.

In 1893, Joe Gans, a well known Montana sheepman was arrested for trailing across Wyoming. This became the subject of correspondence between the two governors. Late in the summer of the next year about 500 sheep belonging to George Crosby were rushed over a cliff into a deep gorge. This was alleged to have been done by Montana cattlemen in retaliation for grazing a flock just south of the Pryor Mountains in Montana. A "Stockmen's Protective Association," formed by the cattlemen of the upper Shoshone valley in 1901, set arbitrary deadlines on the range and for two years threatened sheepmen with violence if they crossed them. And in the Wind River, Owl Creek, and Big Horn Basin areas, bands of masked riders destroyed camps, killed flocks, and terrorized sheepmen.

While herding sheep on Kirby Creek about twenty miles from Thermopolis, Lincoln Morrison—referred to by some as a "boy"—was shot through the abdomen in May 1904. A reward of $2,500 was offered for the arrest and conviction of the gunman—or $1,000 for his dead body. The boy finally recovered but the guilty party was never apprehended. Fifteen months later, ten masked men rode into a camp belonging to Louis A. Gantz which was located on Shell Creek some forty miles from Basin. They clubbed and shot about 4,000 sheep, and killed a team of horses. The camp wagons and about $700 worth of supplies were destroyed—the raiders even tied the sheep dogs to the wagon wheels where they burned to death. The complaint was that the sheep, some 7,000 in number, were destroying the range they were trailed across. One newspaper editor wrote later, ". . . nothing was ever done to bring the men to justice who committed the act, although it was well known who perpetrated the henious deed."

The most publicized case of violence occurred on the night of April 3, 1909 on No Wood Creek south of Tensleep. However, it was not, in the opinion of one editor, an isolated incident:

*The . . . case was similar to many cases that had previously occurred and a number that have since been committed, except that the perpetrators of the crimes were not even brought into court.*

Joseph Allemand—a sheepman of good reputation, Joseph Emge—an unpopular ex-cattleman, and Jules Lazair—a French herder, together with two additional helpers, were trailing flocks to high ranges in the Big Horns. They had been warned not to cross the cattle country but the approved route was so long that they took the risk. After having crossed the forbidden territory, they camped on the range of a sheep-man.

That night the two extra herders were taken a few hundred yards away from their wagon and held under guard. The remainder of the attacking party then surrounded the other sheep wagon and riddled it with bullets. After they had gathered sagebrush with which to fire the wagons, Allemand—apparently wounded—came out of the wagon and was ordered to hold up his hands. When he did so, another shot him saying, "This is a hell of a time of night to come out here with your hands up." The raiders then burned all the wagons, and killed the sheep dogs and about twenty-five sheep. The dead were left where they fell, Emge and Lazair being burned almost beyond recognition.

This crime was so revolting that there was considerable clamor for the arrest and conviction of the murderers. A reward, which finally to-talled $5,500, was offered. Seven men were arrested—George H. Sabin —a prominent and wealthy cattleman, Milton A. Alexander—another prominent citizen, Herbert L. Brink—allegedly an unsavory character, Ed Eaton—a cowboy who was an ex-cattleman and ex-saloon keeper, Thomas Dixon, Charles Faris, and Albert F. Keys—also known as Bill Kise.

Faris and Keys turned state's evidence claiming that they had done no shooting and had gone along having been promised that no one would be killed. Feeling ran so high that they had to be taken to Sheridan for safety. In fact, when the trial was held in Basin two companies of the National Guard were stationed in town to insure that the ends of justice were served.

Brink was quickly convicted and sentenced to hang. The other four then confessed and were sentenced accordingly: Sabin and Alexander received 20 to 26 years for second degree murder, and Eaton and Dixon, three to five years for arson. Eaton died in prison and Dixon served his term. Alexander was paroled in five years and pardoned three years later. Sabin was soon made a trusty and served four years, "escaping" while working in friendly territory. Brink's sentence was reduced to life imprisonment and, later, commuted to 25 to 26 years. Eight years after he was committed, he was paroled. This parole he promptly violated, and was apprehended five years later. With law enforcement records like this, it is not strange some pioneers preferred to use a piece of rope or a gun.

Trouble continued in the Big Horn Basin until the newly organized U. S. Rangers—predecessors of the U. S. Forest Rangers—and government management of public grazing lands brought order out of chaos.

Some cattlemen learned to tolerate sheepmen, others took to running sheep themselves. But rustling never stopped.

In the spring of 1901, Montana newspapers carried stories about the capture of two sets of thieves. Up in the northeastern part of the Yellowstone valley and adjacent part of North Dakota, Jim McPeake and others had been suspected of stealing in North Dakota and selling the stolen stock on the upper Yellowstone in Carbon County, Montana. One evening when McPeake rode in to a little ranch in western North Dakota a posse of eight men, led by inspector Billy Smith, was waiting. Jim wheeled his horse and made a run for it but the officers dropped both him and the horse as he topped a little hill. Not long afterward the livestock inspector at Glendive notified Smith that he had recovered 61 horses that had been stolen on the lower Yellowstone.

While McPeake was rustling a few head of stock at a time, other thieves—alleged to have been two rustlers and a certain public official—planned a larger take. On the Crow Reservation, the Absaroka had a sizable herd of cattle wearing the brand I D. According to the (Billings) *Post* (which was probably correct), the brands on 752 head were altered to **⊄⊅** , which some old-timers called the *squashed pumpkin* and others, the *two-pole pumpkin*. The animals with the blotted brands were driven from their normal range into the northern part of the Big Horn Mountains, around the head of Black Canyon, and into a snug hideout on the Wyoming-Montana line. This area, now called the Garvin Basin, is sealed off on the west by the upper reaches of the canyon of the Big Horn River, and is walled in by rimrock on the other sides. There were but two ways in or out. One was the mountain trail and this was easily obstructed by a barricade of logs: the other was through a narrow gap in the rock in the extreme southwest corner and this was closed by stretching a log chain across the opening.

Not wishing to venture into such formidable territory to try to arrest individuals who were regarded as tough characters, officials waited until one of them, Robert Lee, came out of the mountains. When taken into custody, this man produced a bill of sale and swore that the cattle were his—but the government inspectors thought otherwise. Lee was bound over under a $4,000 bond at Billings, and a far-flung search instituted for his "confederates." Eventually, Lee was convicted and did time, but his helper, thought to have been a man named Sam Garvin, was never caught. After his release, Lee once confided to a friend that the man who masterminded this attempted rustling was ——— (a prominent official), a statement which old-timers do not doubt.

These men were followed by others. One Montana rustler, who is still remembered as having been very clever, on one occasion loaded an entire stock train at night with stolen cattle—and "got away with it." But there finally came a day when forged bills of sale and other subterfuges did not prevail. He was convicted and his lawyer's fees broke him.

# 21

## Twilight of a Way of Life

### THE CHILDREN OF THE LARGE-BEAKED BIRD

>>>>>>>>><<<<<<<<< "On the seventh day of May, in the year of our Lord one thousand eight hundred and sixty-eight," eleven Crow chiefs, led by Che-ra-pee-ish-ka-ta (Pretty Bull) and Chat-sta-he (Wolf Bow), signed their "X"s to a treaty "made and concluded at Fort Laramie in the Territory of Dakota." This marked for the Absaroka the beginning of a vast change in their way of life. Perhaps it was not good —but it was so. Unfortunately, it was inevitable.

The blueprint of the changes which Pretty Bull, Wolf Bow, and their people faced was set down in this eight-page document.

In Article III:

The United States agrees, at its own expense, to construct on the south side of the Yellowstone, near Otter creek, a warehouse or store-room for the use of the agent in storing goods belonging to the Indians, to cost not exceeding twenty-five hundred dollars; an agency building for the residence of the agent, to cost not exceeding three thousand dollars; and five other buildings, for a carpenter, a farmer, blacksmith, miller, and engineer, each to cost not exceeding two thousand dollars; also a schoolhouse or mission building, so soon as a sufficient number of children can be induced by the agent to attend school, which shall not cost exceeding twenty-five hundred dollars.

The United States agrees further to cause to be erected on said reservation, near the other buildings herein authorized, a good steam circular saw-mill, with a grist-mill and shingle machine attached, the same to cost not exceeding eight thousand dollars.

Article V specified:

The United States agrees that the agent for said Indians shall in the future make his home at the agency building; that he shall reside among them and keep an office open at all times for the purpose of prompt and diligent inquiry into such matters of complaint, by and against the Indians, as may be presented for investigation under the provisions of their treaty stipulations, as also for the faithful discharge of other duties enjoined on him by law. . . .

Other sections stipulated that the government would provide a physician, teachers, carpenter, miller, engineer, farmer, and blacksmiths; furnish certain articles of clothing annually for each person; and give them "one pound of meat and one pound of flour per day" for four years for each Indian over four years of age. To make certain that the goods issued were of the proper quality, "the President shall, annually, detail an officer of the army to be present and attest the delivery of all goods and the manner of their delivery."

In the summer of 1869, an agency was established a few miles below the Great Bend of the Yellowstone. The buildings were located on a high bench on the south side of the river near the mouth of Mission Creek; and, although the place was named Fort Parker—for E. S. Parker, then Commissioner of Indian Affairs in Washington—it was often referred to as the "Mission" agency. On the 27th of November it was near enough complete so that Alfred J. Sully, Superintendent of Indians in Montana Territory, notified the Commissioner of Indian Affairs to pay the contractor $5,000 for the work which had been completed. Sully added:

I required the contractor to enclose the buildings with a stockade 10 feet high with a gate and build a stable inside the fort capable of holding the animals, this work is also finished. I also required him to erect two block houses, two stories high and a corral inside the work of the stockade 8 feet high. This work is also in a fair way of being finished by two weeks. The buildings are all constructed of solid logs squared and set into a frame work with shingled roofs. The workmen are now painting the buildings with lime and building stone chimneys.

E. M. Camp, a captain in the army, was appointed agent on the 25th of October but a shift in government policy threw him out of office shortly after he assumed his duties. F. D. Pease, who was married to a Crow woman, was then selected and became, in accord with the custom of the times, "Major" Pease. The physical facilities lasted but slightly longer than the first agent for they burned the following spring. The second agency—referred to as the "New Agency"—was similar to the first one except that adobe brick were used in its construction. This material was not only fireproof but it did not shrink and let in the weather as had the cottonwood logs used in building the previous one.

By June 1871, Pease had built two miles of irrigating ditch and three miles of fence, and had 100 acres under cultivation. The prospects for a crop looked "splendid," but the Crows were not interested in farming—although they were fond of pumpkins and potatoes.

Except when the Piegans or Sioux raided, life at this agency was a carefree sort of existence. Work details sent out some distance from the headquarters usually loafed and accomplished little or nothing. Perhaps the only person with any worries was the agent, and his troubles were few. Many of the white employees formed alliances with Crow women and led a half-civilized sort of existence. This careless sort of life did not meet with the approval of official visitors. After a visit in March 1873, the Superintendent of Indians in Montana wrote the Commissioner of Indian Affairs that he had found white men living with Indian women and others residing in the camps. He ordered those with red consorts to get married within thirty days or get out. The loafers were given twenty-four hours to get off the reservation—"Of this the Indians bitterly complain." One man who had two squaws finally told one to leave "because of the governmental disfavour I might incur."

Life went on pretty much as it always had for the Crows, except in two respects. Now, they had someone to whom they could complain about the encroachment of the whites, and they received an annual issue of various items. A couple of licensed traders at the agency supplied an assortment of articles, and the squaw men acted as middlemen in most of the trading transactions. Flour was accepted to get the sacks, bacon was tried out for the grease, and sometimes the beef which was issued was fed to the dogs. With plenty of buffalo and wild fruit and berries in season, there was no absolute dependence on the issues of staple foods. Tribal life remained practically unchanged—except for those children who could be *corralled* in what was called a school.

The Absaroka had divided into two groups years before when the Sioux drove them out of the valleys of the Powder and the Tongue. The "Mountain" Crows ranged south of the Yellowstone for the most part and came regularly to the agency. In January 1874, these numbered 233 lodges or 2,200-2,400 people. The "River" Crows, who spent considerable time with the Gros Ventre near the Missouri, totalled 110 lodges with 1,000-1,200 men, women, and children. They were the more dissipated of the two groups and sometimes hung around Camp Cooke in the Musselshell country where the men—apparently—traded the ·favors of their squaws for whiskey. At this time the Mountain Crows still looked with disfavor on the use of liquor and sometimes punished those who transgressed with a heavy hand. For a number of years various officials tried to get the River Crows to stay on the reservation and, although this was eventually accomplished, it took a long time.

The agency had hardly been built when the settlers in the Gallatin valley began to agitate for the removal of the Indians. This grasping, miserly attitude toward Indians was, of course, nothing new on the frontier. In 1871, a party of Indians raided the Gallatin country and, although the marauders were quite definitely identified as Sioux, this incident provided an excuse for periodic clamoring. A year later, the Montana press was reporting rumors that the Crows were preparing to raid the settlements. This provoked two caustic retorts in the (Bozeman) *Avant Courier*. On the 28th of April, the paper printed a long letter written by the Crow agent in which it was stated emphatically that

*there is not the slightest foundation for these rumors, and they must have been put in circulation by some evil disposed person or persons, for the sake of creating excitement among the citizens. . . . Such conduct is to say the least villianous and its consequence liable to lead to very serious results. . . .*

About a month later, a long editorial pointedly called attention to the disagreeable possibilities which might be expected if the citizens of the valley continued to support a bill which had been introduced in Congress calling for the removal of the Crows. The editor pointed out:

*We believe this bill has been introduced . . . and fostered by designing persons for other ends than the public good. It is a well known fact . . . that the Crow Indians . . . have been an aid to the military posts . . . as, by their well-known animosity to the various bands of* the Sioux nation they assist in keeping that warlike tribe away from our settlements. . . .

Then he went on to point out that "at least half" of the produce of the Gallatin valley was sold to the army posts and the agency, and if this market were to vanish a drastic drop in prices could be expected:

We are convinced that the people are acting against their own best interests in thus persistently agitating the removal question, both in the matter of protection and profit. . . .

In 1873, the government seriously contemplated moving the Crows to the Judith Basin which lay between the Missouri and the Musselshell. Lieutenant C. C. Doane and Major Pease, assisted by Mitch Buoyer and Horace Countryman, made a survey of the area, and the matter progressed smoothly with the Indians. However, when the news of this possible change leaked out, settlers promptly squatted along the road which connected Helena and Carroll, a *low-water* port on the Missouri, and screamed that *their* rights were about to be violated.

The government commission, which surveyed both the situation on the reservation and the possibilities, reported:

We found that the principal region already occupied by the miners was along Emigrants Gulch, extending thirty or forty miles eastwardly into the mountains from the Western border of the reserve, and upon Clarks fork . . . and that the prospectors were gradually extending their operations and could not long be prevented from overrunning the entire mountain region bounded by Clarks fork and the Yellowstone river. . . .

They also eyed enviously the fine lands further east and ventured the hypocritical opinion that with a railroad pending, together with one or more roads from the south, demands for their use will "make the removal of the Crow Indians a necessity." And they recommended that the Absaroka be moved while there were still suitable lands available.

This controversy involved the reservation guaranteed the Crows by the treaty of 1868. It embraced about 8,000,000 acres, and consisted of that part of Montana lying north of the present Wyoming-Montana state line which was bounded on the west and north by the channel of the Yellowstone River, and on the east by the 107th Meridian. The treaty of 1851, which was never ratified, assigned to the Crows almost the entire Yellowstone Basin—over 338,500,000 acres.

All this study came to naught. The squatters blocked the move to the Judith Basin, and the government left the prospectors with their claims.

Finally, on June 12, 1880, the Absaroka agreed to cede the area the miners wanted and, on July 10, 1882, the territory lying west of Boulder Creek and adjacent to the northeastern part of the Yellowstone National Park, was officially opened to settlement. The consideration was $600,000 payable in installments over a period of twenty years. However, before this happened the agency had been moved to the valley of the Stillwater River.

As early as March 1873, James Wright, Superintendent of Indian Affairs in Montana complained to the Commissioner of Indian Affairs that the location at the mouth of Mission Creek was not satisfactory. Timber and logs had to be hauled at least twelve miles; there was not enough land for farming; it was a "very uncomfortable location because of wind"; and there were no sheltered places nearby for the Indians to camp. Also, Wright was concerned about the whiskey problem. He urged Pease to try to get the River Crows to come in and live near the agency, and the following October he addressed a letter to the officials in Washington about a problem spot:

*I have the honor to address you on a subject vital to the interests of this Agency. There is just across the river from this reservation a whiskey Shop kept by one Benson professionally under a permit granted by the United States, and licensed in the county of Gallatin, Montana Territory.*

*Men pass by this shop and obtain whiskey, get drunk, come here on business and annoy us very much.*

*This establishment amounts to a serious nuisance. If his U S license could be revoked the establishment could be broken up. Can the Revenue Dept be induced to revoke the license. . . .*

The little settlement of Benson's Landing was a hard hole. Amos Benson and Dan Naileigh had a saloon, Buckskin Williams had another, and Horace Countryman operated a third. The place was "the rendezvous of all the thieves and bummers in the country" who gambled, peddled whiskey (on one occasion in "Pain killer" bottles), bought goods issued to the Indians, and—probably—stole ponies. As the squaw men and some of the employees acted as intermediaries in this illicit traffic, the situation was almost impossible to control.

Wright wrote repeatedly to the Commissioner of Indian Affairs about this thorny problem and, when Dexter E. Clapp took over the agency later in December of 1874, this new agent took up the battle in earnest. Clapp had been a general officer in the Union Army and his letters indicate that he was a man of considerable ability and a vigorous administrator. Whether or not he was guilty of accepting bribes from contractors—a common failing of agents—can no longer be determined. However, it is obvious that he tried to do much of benefit to his wards while he held this position.

On December 22, 1874, Clapp wrote the Commissioner of Indian Affairs—then the Reverend E. P. Smith who acquired an unsavory reputation during the next year or so—that he had had a reconnaissance made and believed that the valley of the Stillwater, near the mouth of Rosebud Creek, would be a suitable location for an agency. He argued that the location was twenty miles from the north boundary of the reservation and thus illicit trading could be controlled better, that there was every opportunity for farming, and that this place was out of line of the "terrible Cañon winds" and probably free from rheumatic diseases. On the 12th of the following April, the change was approved and Clapp estimated that $15,000 would be sufficient to effect the change and build a new set of buildings. The agent lost no time in getting the project under way, and late in June was able to report that substantial progress had been made with the improvements at the new location.

This change raised a furor. The commanding officer at Fort Ellis looked with understandable disfavor on a move which would take the agency 73 miles nearer the renegade Sioux. The citizens of Bozeman voiced their objections to Governor Potts in no uncertain manner. Some of these were fabricated, some imagined, a few real, and all of them selfish. Potts protested to the Secretary of the Interior—the agency would be no further from the Yellowstone, it was a poor place to winter horses, it was on a trail used by the Sioux and therefore liable to continual attack, the Crows did not want to move, and the estimated $15,000 would not start to construct the agency buildings.

The objection that the Sioux would cause trouble was well founded, as noted in chapter XIV, and, on the 5th of July, Clapp wrote to the Commissioner of Indian Affairs asking that the Secretary of Interior bring pressure to bear on the Secretary of War for a detail of soldiers— "the guard can be obtained only by an order from Washington as General Gibbon has refused to furnish any for the New Agency." But the Army was adamant in their stand and the agent had to get along as best he could.

In his annual report dated September 10th, Clapp devoted considerable space to bitter criticism of the military policy:

*The efforts of the Military Authorities to protect the settlements, and the U S property during the summer have simply been a worthy subject of ridicule. Various parties have been sent out in different directions, but as far as I can learn without seeing a hostile Indian . . . and at the same time, I could scarcely send a man to my lime, or timber parties, nor could a man travel the public road from the Yellowstone Crossing [at Benson's Landing] to Fort Ellis without falling into deadly ambush.*

\*       \*       \*

*These facts interpreted in the light of remarks made to me in person by the Commanding Officer of the district force me to the belief that the exposure of this agency . . . has been unnecessary and intentional and caused by his avowed displeasure at the removal of the Agency.*

No doubt there were two sides to this question. Although there was probably some truth in Clapp's accusations, neither was Fort Ellis flush with troopers. In the late summer when an escort of 50 cavalry was requested to protect the train moving the families to the new location, the Commanding Officer reported to General Gibbon, and the latter to the Department Headquarters, that he had a total of 10 officers and 149 enlisted men. Of the latter *only* 19 noncoms and 34 privates were listed "for duty."

By the fore part of September, the building crew had made remarkable progress. In addition to getting a saw mill and two "adobe mills" into operation and an irrigation ditch dug, eight buildings and a corral had been completed and seven more structures were in varying stages of completion. With justifiable pride, Clapp wrote the Commissioner that if the Sioux had not caused him a loss of $4,500 to 6,000 he would probably have stayed within his original estimate.

In less than a month after the agent made the first move, the whiskey peddlers at Benson's Landing began to stir. There were rumors of three "expeditions" being organized but in the end only Countryman and Hoppe moved. They came down the Yellowstone to a short distance above the mouth of the Stillwater—as close to the agency as they could get. Clapp now asked that the reservation boundary be extended north of the river; and on October 20th an executive order added that part of the "North Side" lying west of the 107th Meridian. As this would have put the head of navigation on the reservation, the agent recommended that the eastern end of this extension be moved west to a point eight miles upstream from the mouth of Prior Creek which "will leave the north bank of the river at the head of navigation unencumbered" for the "contemplated establishment of a route for freight and passengers . . . by way of the Yellowstone." Apparently the objections raised by the settlers in western Montana carried considerable weight for the extension was cancelled completely on March 8, 1876. This left Countryman free to peddle whiskey to those who were willing to ride the intervening fifteen or twenty miles. This maneuvering explains why Clapp was so vitriolic in his letter (quoted in Chapter XIV) pertaining to the "relief" of Fort Pease which

deposited across the river from the Agency, and on the Reservation, two barrels of Whiskey.

Soon after the order revoking the extension of the Agency was received, and thereafter for two weeks, that whiskey made this Agency almost a pandemoneum of drunkenness and brawling.

Life at the New Agency during its first year was far from dull. The Sioux kept everyone in suspense through the summer of 1875. When fall came, there were still some essential buildings which were not completed, no hay had been put up, and the country was grazed short for considerable distance about the post. Some of the annuity goods—freighted from Corrine, Utah, via Virginia City and Bozeman—arrived in poor condition. The Mountain Crows came in earlier than usual—"in excellent spirits, but very hungry. We have no sugar or coffee on hand. . . ." The wolfers at Fort Pease were trespassing on the reservation and, apparently, received some rough treatment at the hands of Crows who found them—which resulted in complaints to Washington. The River Crows came in for the first time: and in March 1876, Clapp estimated that he had one third of the goods on hand which would be needed for the annual issue in April. March brought the "relief" of Fort Pease, and a few weeks later officers came to recruit Crow scouts for the summer campaigns.

While Crook and Terry were experiencing troubles with the Sioux, Clapp had his at the agency. Early in August, he wrote the Commissioner that the warriors of the Mountain Crows had gone "en masse" to assist in the campaigns and he had nothing but beef to feed the families left in his care. He had asked for an army inspector to witness the issue of the annuities and had been told none could be spared; and he urged that he be allowed to use some funds from the appropriations of the previous year to purchase much needed supplies otherwise "the beef on hand will be exhausted and there will be nothing whatever to feed the Crows."

Clapp was replaced not long after this and it must have been with feelings of relief that he embarked in a boat on the Yellowstone "for the states." Lewis H. Carpenter, who inherited his problems, soon began to send a steady stream of letters to Washington—there was no hay, grain, or pasture for the horses, the arrival of the annuity goods was uncertain which will "be particularly unfortunate for me," the saw mill burned, the Indians were dissatisfied—and one ended with this plaintive plea, "I write you this so you can give me some instructions in regard to matters."

The agency remained on Rosebud Creek until May 26, 1883, when it was moved to its present location, Crow Agency, on the Little Big Horn River. The ceding of the area west of Boulder Creek in 1880-1882 and the sale of the right-of-way to the railroad in 1881, were followed by a third release on March 3, 1891. This time the Crows retained only those lands lying (generally) in the valleys of Prior Creek, Little Big Horn River, and the Big Horn River, a total of about 3,000,000 acres. For this last block of territory the government paid $946,000.

There is no more malodorous chapter in the history of the frontier than that of the dealings involving supplies for Indian Agencies. Even honest men were harassed and subjected to libelous statements, and in the end the Indian was the loser. The investigation which took place at the Crow Agency in the winter of 1875-1876 provides a documented *example* of how slippery these dealings could become. The principals in this one were: Dexter E. Clapp—the agent, Ed Ball—Captain in the 2nd Cavalry and "Inspector of Indian Supplies," and two Montana contractors—L. M. Black and Nelson Story.

Ball signed a formal statement that he had been asked to inspect 57 barrels of "mess pork" of which only seven were packed in "pork barrels," the remainder being in "whiskey barrels." He opened three of the whiskey barrels and found that they contained an average of 231 pounds of pork. This was a mixture of satisfactory meat together with heads, backbones and trimmings. Story had proposed that he pass this at 450 pounds per barrel—for $1,000. When he inspected Story's flour he was told there were 2,000 sacks in the warehouse but he could find but 1,197, and this was double-sacked. (Double-sacking was an old dodge. The inspector had to stamp each sack which he counted and, when he turned his back, the outside covering was stripped off and the sack could be stamped and counted again.) Although inspection of cattle was not his concern, Ball added that Dr. Hunter had told him that during the preceding September Story had sent 40 head of agency cattle with an ox-train to the Missouri River, and that a reliable citizen in Bozeman had told him that this man had Indian Department cattle in two of his herds and had put his brand on others. He also stated that he believed that some of Story's offers could only have been carried through with the cooperation of the agent—of which Story seemed to be quite certain.

Agent Clapp signed an affidavit that on two occasions Black had asked him to cooperate in "making money illegitimately out of the

Agency," had assured him that he (Black) was instrumental in having Ball appointed inspector and that the two were good friends, and that he was out to "make . . . a great deal of trouble" for Story. He also swore that in September 1875, Black delivered 561 sacks of flour to the agency warehouse and that Ball had asked him to certify that they weighed 100 pounds each instead of 98 pounds; also that "A large portion of this flour [was] not equal to the sample furnished from Washington. . . ." He stated further that after Ball made his report of attempted fraud, he was notified that he had been transferred to the Fort Peck Agency on the Missouri: that Black had boasted to General Sweitzer (a former Inspector at Fort Ellis then living in Washington) that he was responsible for Clapp being transferred: and that Sweitzer had promptly gone to his friends in the Cabinet and informed them that if the order was not revoked it was likely to cause a scandal.

The grand jury which investigated these claims did not return any indictments, nor was the government inspector who went over the matter able to make any charges. Nevertheless, Story had trouble collecting his "accounts." A year after Ball made his charges, Story presented a sworn affidavit in rebuttal to the various allegations.

Story claimed that he had not offered Ball a bribe to pass the pork, and that he was innocent of the condition of the meat. He had had the pork repacked to conform with the contract, after which Ball refused to pass it although Clapp accepted the consignment when he presented affidavits from three responsible parties that it was satisfactory. As to Ball, he stated that he drank and gambled to excess; and he presented a testimonial statement signed by prominent citizens to the effect that they did not believe Ball and that they regarded Story as "incapable of dishonesty, indirection, and attempt at bribery charged by Captain Ball. . . ." In regard to a lot of 467 cattle, he had not seen them as they were delivered by a sub-contractor. Although the lot did contain yearlings—the contract called for mature cattle—there were no calves: the yearlings were accepted on the basis of their own weight. (It was the practice to determine the weight of a herd by taking a couple of average individuals and weighing their carcasses.) As to the flour which was double-sacked, this was done to insure safe delivery as the rough road made it necessary to unload and load several times during the trip to the agency. No false vouchers were ever presented.

And he charged that although Judge Blake had insinuated that he was "a conniver at Indian frauds," he could not refer to any "positive" evidence of fraud. The judge's own record, he stated, was not above suspicion as it was a notorious fact that in the summer or fall of 1875, Judge Blake actually issued a license to trade with the Crow Indians to one Horace Countryman.

(Clapp had refused to honor this license and, when asked by the Commissioner of Indian Affairs to justify his action, wrote a scathing letter about Countryman's character in which he even quoted Governor Potts to support his appraisal.) As might be expected, Story supported Clapp:

The agent has at all times, and in the most positive manner, denied all complicity with me in any wrongful act or intention, and of knowledge of any intended fraud. This denial and the high character which the agent has heretofore sustained, are facts which, surely, I am entitled to have considered, and considered favorably. . . .

These sworn statements are best understood when considered along with other background data. L. M. Black and Nelson Story were bitter rivals. Captain Ball was, allegedly, appointed as an inspector as a result of Black's influence, and was a friend of the contractor. Judge Blake, who presided at the grand jury investigation, was also a friend of Black's and most of the grand jury appointed by him came from Virginia City where the judge resided. When this jury failed to return any indictments, the judge rebuked its members and insinuated that they had not done their duty. These insinuations touched off an investigation by a government inspector who, as has been noted, did not make any charges either.

Information concerning Clapp is scanty. Two months after he was replaced, his successor wrote the Commissioner as follows:

. . . I find that anyone who wanted to cut hay on the Reservation has done so, and such persons desire to sell it to me. . . . I also find that the hay which is at this Agency, and which is claimed by Mr. Millan is hay that was cut August last and I find that he was on the Pay roles as an Employee in August and the same for September.

Although this is not proof of wrongdoing, it does illustrate the trend of these times.

As to Story, it is doubtful if his reputation was as spotless as his character testimonial would make it appear. He was rather notorious for running stock on the Crow Reservation and George W. Frost, who followed Carpenter a year after Clapp left, had occasion to complain to the Commissioner about Story's trespassing. In a letter dated October 31, 1877, he stated that Story had admitted to him that he had

3,000 cattle and 1,000 horses on the reservation—and that he had told a mutual acquaintance that there were 4,700 cattle.

> . . . *I am of the opinion that he must have between five and six thousand [cattle] now here. . . . In my judgement there must be at least 1500 [horses] at the present time, and many who have seen them (I have not) say there are 2000. . . .*

Ten months later, Frost had been removed for crooked dealing and, soon after, his successor was writing about the frauds of *his* predecessors!

The truth was hard to come by for, according to the run-of-the-mill morals of the times, it was not a sin to swindle or steal from either the Indians or the Government. A former employee on the reservation recalled that, "The new agent came here poor but left a rich man a year and a half later when General Clapp took charge." And *many* years later, stories were told—if not boastingly at least unblushingly—in the Gallatin valley of rocks being packed in barrels of pork, of loads of hay being counted more than once, of flour which was *double-sacked*, of the largest beeves in a herd being killed to determine the amount for which the government was obligated, and other similar methods of fraud. What went on was no secret to the general public—but proving it in court was an entirely different matter.

Perhaps the most brazen attempt to swindle the Crows began in 1884 when John T. Blake and J. C. Wilson, acting as trustees for a "syndicate of cattlemen," attempted to lease the greater part of the reservation for ten years at *one cent* per acre. The Billings *Post* broke the story with the following statement:

> *Ugly rumors have got around about this transaction and one of them associates the name of Secretary Teller's brother with the syndicate. Who are behind Blake and Wilson no one seems to know. . . . The charge that the syndicate consisted of Colorado men who were getting this lease in return for helping Teller to an election as United States senator he pronounces false.*

Secretary Teller, as head of the Department of Interior, was in a poor position to deny connection with a plot involving his brother. Later stories named "one United States senator, one member of the house of representatives, the Clerk of the United States Court at Topeka, a gentleman formerly mayor of Topeka, and a certain United States official" as the interested parties.

Some editors in Montana and Wyoming got quite stirred up about the matter. One wrote, perhaps more truthfully than he intended:

*We profess but scanty sympathy for these . . . thieving rascals . . . but that their lands should be taken from them on the shallow pretext of a lease . . . will result in constant and endless complication. Even if the Crows were disposed to barter this immense territory for a nominal price . . . the people of Wyoming and Montana . . . [are] bitterly opposed to this wholesale gobbling of the public domain.*

This might be interpreted to mean that if any "gobbling" was to be done, the "people of Wyoming and Montana" wanted to do their part.

Members of the Billings Board of Trade took it upon themselves—with the approval of the Commissioner of Indian Affairs and the chairman of the Senate Committee on Indian Affairs—to conduct an investigation. On February 5, 1885, the Billings *Post* devoted almost the entire front page to a detailed story of their findings. Of the twenty-six chiefs who represented 3,123 persons, fourteen were consulted, and in addition 108 adult Crows who were found in the vicinity of the agency were also interviewed. All of these except one chief, "a sort of agency pet" who would take no positive stand, were emphatic in demanding a cancellation of the lease. Agent H. J. Armstrong, although professing indifference in the matter, "by his actions belied his words."

This study publicized the method which had been used to secure the lease. A letter was received from the Commissioner of Indian Affairs stating that there would be no allowance for beef rations between April 1st and July 1st, 1885. As the lease money could be used to buy beef to keep them from starving, this letter was used as a "lever" by the agency officials and as a threat by Blake to make the Crows "touch the paper." As soon as the signatures had been secured, the Commissioner of Indian Affairs informed the agent that an allowance had been granted to cover the three months in question! The group concluded that:

*Agent Armstrong and [Clerk] Barstow in asking the Indians to make the lease were, in all probability, acting in good faith, with the view of using the rent . . . to bridge over the shortage of rations. Giving Agent Armstrong the benefit of this charitable view he was guilty of gross stupidity in not insisting on his wards receiving some adequate consideration for leasing their land. Had he chosen to call for bids he could readily have obtained $90,000 or $100,000 instead of the ridiculously inadequate price of $30,000 provided for in the lease.*

For all practical purposes, this ended the manipulations of the mysterious Colorado Syndicate. On December 6, 1885, "General" Henry E. Williamson replaced Armstrong. Williamson, another ex-Confederate officer, was to smell gunpowder before he ended his stay at Crow Agency.

Although some old-timers state that the Indians never stole from them, newspapers occasionally reported friction. Some trouble was to be expected, particularly from unruly young men who were light-fingered and reckless with guns. However, these troubles were not all one-sided. Stockmen driving cattle between Wyoming and Montana sometimes found it convenient to follow the old Bozeman Trail and thus trespass on the reservation. In 1878, Frost set the charges for trailing cattle across the reservation at $1.00 a head—charges it was easier to assess than to collect. In August of this year, when the agent attempted to collect from one cattleman the latter claimed the Indians had threatened him. He refused to pay toll but finally posted a bond and then— apparently ignored the matter. When he tried to drive another herd through, Frost turned the matter over to the Commanding Officer at Fort Custer who sent troops to enforce the regulation.

There was one bit of friction which resulted in some tense moments. Chees-chi-bah-aish, also known as Wraps-Up-His-Tail, aspired to become a leader among his people and, in proper Indian fashion, he went to the Big Horn Mountains where he fasted. In the vision which he had, he saw the son of the Morning Star make a sweeping motion with a sword and trees fell before him. This the warrior interpreted to mean that soldiers would fall before him if he made a similar motion with a sword, and he believed that bullets from their rifles would not harm him. He gathered about him a handful of followers and attempted to share with them the *power* of his vision. They all dressed in a sort of uniform made of red flannel, carried swords, and rode horses of the same color.

Early in October 1887, some twenty young men under the leadership of Wraps-Up-His-Tail—now known also as Sword Bearer—returned from a successful raid on the Piegan herds with about 60 horses. Williamson, who took a dim view of this ancient sport, sent his police to arrest the group for horse stealing, but the band met the agent's orders with scorn, indignation, and disrespect.

Williamson is remembered as a Southerner who disliked Northern soldiers, and as a man whom the Crows had sized up as a weak character who could be bluffed. Chees-chi-bah-aish seized the opportunity to display, not only his disdain for the agent's authority, but also the *power* of his medicine. He and his followers promptly rode into the Agency and shot the place up. Fortunately, no one was injured. With the agent cowed, the chief clerk assumed the responsibility of calling for help from nearby Fort Custer. A detachment of cavalry was sent to quiet the place down but, when the matter was reported to Department Headquarters, General Terry ordered the troops to confine their activities to guard duty until the causes for the trouble could be investigated.

When the troops assumed a defensive attitude, Sword Bearer went ahead with his preparations. A week or two later, he and a small party visited the adjacent Cheyenne reservation and tried to get some of the young men there to join his band, but his proposition got a cool reception. In the meantime, a few troops were called in from Forts McKinney and Maginnis. There was a small flurry at Fort Keogh when some troops took the train to Junction—and then returned. Wraps-Up-His-Tail had now reached a point from which there could be no face-saving retreat.

On November 5th, the officer in charge of the troops forced a showdown. The soldiers were camped on a commanding elevation near the agency and the troublemakers had their camp not far away: it was either surrender or fight. Strong in the belief that his medicine was strong, Sword Bearer made a bravery ride in front of the troopers and waved his sword. But the white men did not fall, and when they fired he was wounded in the heel and his horse was also hit. When this happened the little party disintegrated. Their leader fled to the hills east of the Little Big Horn and his father raced after him, pleading with his son to come back and act like a warrior. Seizing the bridle reins, he turned the horse around and led him back. When they reached the Little Big Horn, at a point a couple of miles north of the agency, Wraps-Up-His-Tail dismounted and lay down at the edge of the stream to drink. While thus engaged an Indian policeman named Fire-bear came up. Remarking that, "This is for getting all these people into trouble," he shot him in the back of the head. As might be expected, white accounts credited a soldier with firing the fatal shot but this is not true. The Crows disapproved of Fire-bear's act and, although he had been a warrior of considerable stature, he was no longer respected.

Thus ended the Crow rebellion. The rebel band fell apart and seven of the warriors were arrested. These were sent to Fort Snelling, Minnesota and tried, eventually serving time at the prison at Carlisle.

The big change in the life of the Crows came with the passing of the buffalo which was the foundation of their previous way of life. Tepees now had to be made of canvas, travois gave way to wagons, and other things of the white man—like matches—came into common use. But for buffalo meat there was no substitute—it was "hard meat" and it made "good muscles." The substitution of beef—"soft meat"— was accepted with reluctance; and in some cases it even caused families to break up. To a people who had been hunters as far back as their legends went, the prospect of becoming farmers was a grim one. For the young men the prospects were even grimmer. A man's standing was based on his exploits in war and his prowess as a horse thief. With opportunities of this kind gone—for the most part—ambitions were frustrated. Among the Cheyennes this feeling of hopelessness was one of the fundamental causes for a grim tragedy in 1890.

Some things remained unchanged. Old tribal clans continued to exist —and still do, and lineage is traced through the female side of the family. Marriage was taken more casually than with other peoples: it was a mark of distinction for a man not to become so attached to his wife that he was reluctant to give her up. Children sired by the same father, but having different mothers, belonged to the same *teasing clan*—they were privileged to say anything they pleased to their half-brothers and sisters and custom demanded that they be accepted without any show of temper. And their beliefs in omens, taboos, and *powers* associated with various "medicines" remained virtually unchanged. This is not strange for even white men who have had a long association with them will not attempt to explain some of the strange happenings associated with an Indian's *medicine* or their medicine men.

Typical of the various incidents pertaining to *medicine*, is the experience of Fox-Just-Coming-Over-Hill who was a prominent and respected warrior. This Crow was hit in the shoulder by a bullet in the Battle of the Rosebud; and after his return to the Crow village the wound festered and he wasted away during the hot summer days. The family called in the prominent medicine men, but the man steadily became worse. Finally his uncle, whose name was His-Medicine-Is-Wolf, was called in to "doctor" him. He instructed the village cryer that on a certain day all the dogs in camp should be tied up, and that the family should prop the sick man up in bed, uncover the wound, and place a "crackling" of dried marrow gut just inside the door of the lodge. At daybreak all the dogs in the camp barked. Then a coyote pushed the door-flap aside and stuck its head in. As the others in the tepee watched, the coyote quickly ate the crackling, walked clockwise around the tepee to the bed of the patient, nuzzled the wound a few times, and then went hurriedly out the way it had come in. The warrior began to improve at once and the uncle—who thought his nephew's chances of living a long life were very poor—renamed him Old Coyote, that he might live a long time like a crafty old coyote.

Visiting and story telling have long been favorite recreations among the Crows. And, as the wild free days slipped farther into the past, those who had known them well enjoyed recalling the time when there was plenty of fat buffalo and Sioux and Piegan horses could be had for the stealing. Old Coyote was a noted story teller and his two grandsons were often allowed to listen while their grandfather and his friends told and retold favorite stories and legends. The boys particularly enjoyed the stories about the Crow hero, Plays-With-His-Face.

The medicine of this Indian had come from a bear who had surprised him along the Little Big Horn as he was allowing his horse to drink from the river. The bear wrestled with him and finally lifted him from the ground. Then he said, "Look, son." And Plays-With-His-Face saw the panorama of the four seasons—coming of life (spring), height of life (summer), waning of life (fall), and the serenity of winter. Then the bear said, "This is what you will live to see. Reach into my mouth, son." When the young man did so he felt only the gums of the jaws— the teeth were gone. "This," said the bear, "is the way your mouth will be before you die." So thereafter Plays-With-His-Face was never afraid and when his companions would remonstrate about his being too reckless, he would reply, *"Death is my teasing brother"* (who would not harm him).

There were many stories about this Crow—how, in the winter, he plunged through one hole in the ice and came out another, how he stabbed a bear which he teased out of a hole, how he deliberately fell off his horse and rolled in a patch of cactus, how he took off his shirt and fell on a big rattlesnake, how he rode a *mad bull* (buffalo), and how the Sioux cornered him on a point of rimrock and he made a parachute of his robe and escaped. But the story the grandsons liked best was of one of the feats he performed in a fight with the Sioux.

A small boy and his sister had been attacked by a Sioux warrior, and the boy gave his horse to his sister so she could escape. The girl wanted her brother's death revenged but did not know how to accomplish the task. Finally, she appealed to Plays-With-His-Face. He set out with a small party of carefully selected warriors and scouted the various Sioux camps until he found the one containing the Sioux who had killed the boy. Then he set a trap with his friends. He waited until the warrior left the camp circle to defecate and, when he was in an embarrassing position, Plays-With-His-Face approached and said, "How, Kola. I am Plays-With-His Face come to kill you." The Sioux immediately sprinted for the camp and the Crow allowed him to reach the center of the circle of lodges before he killed him and counted coup. The aroused Sioux then chased the warrior out of camp and into the trap which had been set. Here his friends rose up and delivered a deadly fire. The Crows counted many coups and the hero rode away singing his war song.

With all the depressing influences of reservation life, it is not strange that the old men liked to recall the days when buffalo meat was their staff of life. Nor is it strange that the boyhood heroes of the youngsters were men like Plays-With-His-Face whose *teasing brother* was death.

## THE CUT ARMS PEOPLE

Unlike the Crows, the Northern Cheyennes had no home of their own as the reservation days approached. During the treaty making at Fort Laramie in 1868, this small group agreed to accept space on the reservation of their southern relatives or on those of the Sioux. The surrender in 1877 split them between Fort Keogh and the Red Cloud Agency, and the group which surrendered in Nebraska were split again as a result of the move to Indian Territory. In 1878, Little Chief became dissatisfied with the life at Fort Keogh and was moved to the reservation of the Southern Cheyennes. A few years later, still dissatisfied, he was back with the Sioux on the Pine Ridge Reservation. The result was that these people were scattered in Montana, South Dakota, and Indian Territory.

After the surrender of the Sioux in Canada, the soldiers at Fort Keogh had but little need for scouts, and when Colonel Miles was transferred to the Department of the Columbia in November 1880, the ties which held the Cheyennes to the post were loosened. A few families at a time, they drifted away and settled on Lame Deer and Muddy Creeks (tributaries of the Rosebud) and along the Tongue River between the mouths of Otter and Hanging Woman Creeks. Perhaps Little Wolf started this movement when he took up residence here in the early part of his self-imposed exile. In the early 1880's, the Cheyennes were well established in these two areas, living in tepees and little cabins, and subsisting, for the most part, on game and what they raised in small gardens.

As the buffalo disappeared an occasional *cow* was killed and this practice led to complaints by the ranchers. In March 1883, a special agent was sent to investigate the conditions. On the basis of his findings, the Commissioner of Indian Affairs recommended that a special agent be appointed to take charge of the Cheyennes temporarily and to distribute such supplies as they were entitled to receive. He also stated that the commanding officer at Fort Keogh had indicated that these Indians were deserving of assistance and should be allowed to remain where they were. This led, eventually, to an Executive Order dated November 26, 1884, which set aside a tract of land—east of the Crow reservation and south of the "40 mile limit" of the Northern Pacific Railroad grant—for the use of the Northern Cheyennes—"parties captured by the military in 1877 and 'hostiles' from the Pine Ridge Agency who have been permitted to settle in the vicinity of the Tongue and Rosebud Rivers."

This was the *legal* beginning of the reservation for the Northern Cheyennes. Its *moral* foundation undoubtedly dated back to 1877 for Two Moon, White Bull, Black Wolf, and others argued a few years later that General Miles had told them that they could "stay here permanently," a fact which Miles tacitly admitted in 1889. However, it took more than the Executive Order to make the reservation a permanent reality. It took years to get the boundaries fixed, to separate the white settlers with legitimate homestead claims from those who came after the deadline set by the order, and to establish lines so that timber thieves and encroaching flocks and herds could be turned away or arrested.

As if these were not troubles enough, many of the people in southeastern Montana were bitterly opposed to the establishment of this reservation. Members of Congress were petitioned to return the land to the public domain and the newspapers—the *Yellowstone Journal* in particular—often carried editorials and articles the theme of which was, "The Indian Must Go." Some of the reasons advanced were devious, to say the least. This clamor kept the white settlers stirred up, and the Cheyennes also for the general context of some of these articles filtered down to them. This added appreciably to the difficult problems of the various agents who were caught in the cross-fire from both sides.

This attitude simmered along until the summer and fall of 1890 when two murders, caused—indirectly—by starvation rations, brought matters to a white heat. An Indian commission, of which General Miles was an important member, made a study of the situation and after several months consideration recommended that the reservation remain where it was. To this recommendation, the commission tied a stinging rebuke aimed at those whites who trespassed on the reservation and those who persistently stirred up ill feelings. Other recommendations put an end to the shuttling back and forth of visitors between the reservations in Montana and South Dakota which had been a continual source of trouble. In the winter of 1890-1891, just after the conclusion of the Ghost Dance trouble in Dakota, Little Chief and his people were brought up to Fort Keogh and, on October 5, 1891, placed with their relatives. Three years later a census showed 1,227 Indians on the reservation. Of these 241 were men over 18, 384 were women over 18, and 311 were children of school age (6 to 16).

Army officers stationed at Fort Keogh were the first to act in the capacity of "agent" to the Cheyennes. Then, in the fall of 1883, "Colonel" W. S. Dyer arrived from Washington and took over the business of dispensing rations once a month. As these issues were made at Miles City, the Indians spent most of their time shuttling back and forth between their camps and the town. The next spring Dyer established an "agency" and a warehouse on Muddy Creek—a few miles west of the present agency—and went back to Washington—having turned the business of being agent back to a captain at Fort Keogh.

The first regularly appointed agent, Major N. J. Walton—an ex-Confederate officer from Arkansas—arrived late the following November with two subordinates. They made a hasty trip to the reservation and soon were back in Miles City. The editor of the *Yellowstone Journal* reported:

After having looked the ground over carefully, he decided that in the present state of affairs he could neither do justice to himself or the Indians and on his return to the railroad at once telegraphed his resignation. . . .

Walton wanted no part of what he saw.

His successor, Captain R. L. Upshaw—another ex-Confederate officer, this time from Texas—arrived at Miles City late in January 1886. Upshaw refused to be discouraged by remarks made by the editor of the *Journal*. He found a place for his wife in the home of W. W. Alderson, a rancher on Tongue River, and assumed his duties on the 1st of February. As his father had been the first Choctaw agent in Indian Territory some forty years before, the new agent was not unfamiliar with his tasks, formidable as they were.

During the four and a half years Upshaw served as agent, he was frequently criticized, sometimes bitterly, by some of the nearby ranchers, by whites who had settled within the reservation boundaries, and —of course—by the anti-Indian *Yellowstone Journal*. However, old letter files are mute evidence that he fought stubbornly and persistently for the good of his charges. He was a well educated man and apparently a far sighted one for he established a small but efficient police force, tried—with limited opportunity—to get the men to work, promoted an agency school and gave hearty support to a Catholic Mission school, watched for white encroachment, repeatedly recommended cattle raising as a means of livelihood, and worked to consolidate and enlarge the reservation.

Although Upshaw labored diligently, he never developed a real affection for the Cheyennes. In his first annual report he described them as

*. . . dirty, ignorant, obstinate and hard to control, but generally the men are honest and the women virtuous, two characteristics which seem to me to be a good foundation for superstructure, but they are a long way from being civilized. . . .*

In other annual reports these comments are repeated. On one occasion he added, "They . . . will pay their debts better than any people I ever saw. . . ." He also reported very little drunkenness, and the agency physician invariably reported that he had observed no cases of venereal disease.

Apparently, Upshaw's services came to an end as the result of two developments. He was caught in an explosive situation which grew out of a continual food shortage; and he had a severe—almost violent—fallout with his charges. The Indians asked him to discharge the interpreter, a half-breed named Jules Seminole whom they distrusted. The agent refused. Then, while killing beef on issue day, Jules shot and killed—"accidentally on purpose" as one old-timer put it—a Cheyenne man named Deafy. Indian tempers flared and Upshaw was practically forced to ask the Commissioner of Indian Affairs to replace him as soon as possible.

Beginning reservation life in close contact with white settlers, who were generally intolerant of Indians at the best, it was inevitable that friction should result. With the Indians short of food and cattle running unattended on the ranges, trouble was doubly inevitable. However, the first, and probably the second, incidents were the result of overt acts by the whites.

The first incident occurred in March 1884. Two cattlemen, Zook and Alderson, had built a cabin on Lame Deer Creek about where the present agency building is located, and were running a small herd of cattle in the vicinity. Mrs. Alderson had gone to Miles City for the birth of her first child and two cowboys had been left in charge. Black Wolf, a chief who had brought his band up from Pine Ridge, came begging for a meal. The cowboys fed the Indian and not long afterward Hal Taliafero (Mrs. Alderson's cousin) made a wager with his companion that he could shoot the Indian's hat off without touching his head. According to the deposition the Indian made three years later, the shooting occurred in the house but legend in the Alderson family says that he was sunning himself on a pile of poles in the yard when the bullet struck dangerously low and plowed a furrow in his scalp. The cowboys fled in search of help and the chief finally regained consciousness and staggered about three miles back to his camp. And,

as soon as my relations saw me they were very much excited, and went
right up and burned the house. . . .

When the cowboys returned, the Indians shot at them and then set
fire to the house. A posse from Miles City arrested thirteen of the band
without serious trouble and they were tried a few weeks later. Black
Wolf was acquitted. Four others were convicted and sentenced to five
years in the penitentiary, and charges against the others were dropped.
One man died in prison and the others were pardoned a year later. The
real culprit took Alderson's top horse and headed south. Officers trailed
him as far as the Wyoming line and then gave up the chase.

Zook and Alderson now moved over to the valley of the Tongue and
settled at the mouth of Hanging Woman, still in close proximity with
the Cheyennes. Here another cowboy, A. J. Morris—better known as
Packsaddle Jack, is alleged to have driven cattle to water over the garden
of an Indian named Iron Shirt. The two got into a quarrel and Packsaddle Jack shot and broke the Indian's arm. Alderson set Iron Shirt's arm
and, fortunately, had no difficulty in placating him with a gift of meat,
sugar and coffee. The cowboy gave himself up and was acquitted—receiving the advice that he had best hunt another range.

On June 30th, five months after beginning his duties, Upshaw began
to urge that the rations be increased. On this occasion, after protesting
a cut in the new beef contract, he stated:

*The supplies heretofore issued have barely sufficed, with an occasional
dog, to keep them from a starvation point. No depredations on cattle
have been reported by cattlemen and only one Sheep (that not certainly) killed by Indians. White men on short rations with children crying for food—even though civilized would be sorely tempted by the
sight of fat cattle, and even men under military discipline and control,
under such circumstances have been known to commit depredations.
What can we expect from people emerging from barbarism?*

On the 16th of July, he again protested to the Commissioner of Indian
Affairs that rations were too small. And on the 23rd of October, he
pointed out that the summer had been so dry that the Indian's crops
had not added to their food supply, "The 25 per cent added to the ration does not bring it up to a half ration, but to 5/12 of a ration."

In his annual report dated October 26, 1887, Upshaw noted that

*it is almost impossible to keep the Indians in the limits [of the reserva-
tion] while rations is so small and the temptation to seek game outside
is so great.*

On November 17, 1888—after having complained about the matter in the preceding August and September—he again hammered away at the distant office in Washington with a prophetic statement:

*I have to repeat my request that the steps be taken to supply these Indians with a further supply of beef and flour—the quantities on hand will only admit of a daily ration of 7/10 of a pound of beef and 36/100 of a pound of flour—which I deem to be inadequate to their healthy subsistence during the extreme cold winters of this country. The want of such proper subsistence during a hard winter, will possibly, lead to depredations on the stock of the neighboring stockmen and consequently to still greater evils—I am happy to state that I have had no complaints of depredations of this character for a long time and wish to use every possible means to prevent them. . . .*

With these proud people being given but starvation rations, it is remarkable that Upshaw was able to report to Fort Keogh, during the Wraps-Up-His-Tail uprising, "The Crows left here on Saturday. They received very little sympathy from the Cheyennes."

In 1889, Upshaw was still fighting doggedly for adequate rations but time was now running out. He made no mention of depredations but undoubtedly cattle disappeared—completely—in the secluded valleys of the Lame Deer Hills and along the breaks of the Tongue. The daughter of an early settler on the Rosebud recalled that her mother always worried when her father went to the hills to gather cattle, and that she never told the children when he was gone.

"It was fatal," she said, "to find Indians butchering beef. Men were afraid to ride over the crest of a hill for fear of stumbling on to a butchering party."

Even the Cheyennes made no secret of what they would try to do if discovered stealing meat. It was impossible that such a situation could continue month after month without a serious incident.

Violence came early in May 1890. On the 13th of June, Upshaw reported to the Commissioner of Indian Affairs:

*On May 6th Mr. Robert Ferguson living about 35 miles from here at a point supposed to be on the Crow reservation near the eastern line, went to look for horses and did not return. About the 17th of May search was made for him and on the 24th his horse was found shot through at a point 20 miles from here in the Little Wolf Mountains on the Crow reservation. On the 28th the body of Mr. Ferguson was found buried near where his horse was found and the fresh carcass of a beef* being found at no great distance from the same place, suspicions pointed to Indians who were supposed to have been discovered in the act of killing cattle as the murderers. On the 31st "Little Eyes" was arrested here as a participant in the murder. Since then three other Cheyennes have been arrested at Fort Keogh (being enlisted scouts and enlisted since the murder) and are being surrendered to the authorities.—All of whom are in jail at Miles City—There has been intense excitement among the neighboring people and among the Indians—tho no collisions have taken place and every precaution is being taken to prevent any and every endeavor to allay excitement—The White people are fearful of an outbreak and the Indians of an attack. . . .

Troops made patrols, settlers organized home guard units, and even the Indians built a few breastworks for defense. When Black Medicine, Little Eyes and White Buffalo came to trial, witnesses with incriminating evidence failed to appear and the Indians were released a few weeks later.

When this tension was at its highest pitch, a lieutenant stationed at Lame Deer with a detachment of cavalry wrote a long, blistering letter to the editor of the *Yellowstone Journal*. In this he pointed out that

. . . this question should be looked squarely in the face and the blame of such outrage placed unflinchingly and plainly where it belongs. . . . It is sufficient to know that the location [of this reservation] was approved by the interior department, and that when it placed the Indians here that department was vested with the obligation to feed and care for them. . . . Instead of feeding them the department has kept them on half rations. . . . It has for eleven years kept many of them separated from their husbands, wives and children, who are confined in their turn on a reservation 300 miles away. . . . it is astonishing that their instincts . . . should have been restrained so long and that cattle and human life should not have suffered years ago. . . . Indian morality could hardly go on forever deaf to the cravings of an empty stomach. . . . That the Cheyennes had eked out their rations for a year or more by . . . killing [cattle] is indisputable. For four years their daily food supply has been: Beef (including bone) ¾ lb; flour 4/10 lbs.; coffee 3/10 oz.; sugar 5/10 oz.; salt 3/10 oz. This is issued to them every two weeks, the Indians are sometimes compelled to come 30 miles to draw it. This petty ration is their all. . . . Compare the above ration with that of the U. S. soldier, with less capacity for food than the Indian. He gets of meat, twice as much; flour, five times; coffee, three times; sugar, seven times; and vegetables and other stuff ad libitum! . . . these Indians generally eat their

*scanty rations within the first week of issue. . . . These Indians are*
*still suffering for food. . . .*

Colonel Curtis, aide de camp of Governor Toole, met with the Indians and surveyed the situation—emphasizing that the governor did not want them carrying guns around and worrying the settlers. The Cheyennes had no quarrel with this point, but said that they were hungry. American Horse, a minor chief, summed it up by saying that rations for seven days would only last three days, and that if they had not been very tough Indians they would have been dead now.

This airing of the situation cleared the atmosphere: and the Commissioner of Indian Affairs sent J. A. Cooper to replace Upshaw. However, any feeling that Ferguson's death might mark a turning point for the better was rudely shattered two months later.

H. Gaffney had a homestead along Lame Deer Creek about three miles south of the Agency. This man had a nephew named Hugh Boyle, a young man of about eighteen or nineteen who had come out from the East for his health. On the evening of September 7th it looked like it might rain and, as Gaffney's daughter Anne prepared to mount her horse to go in search of the cows, her cousin volunteered to go instead. He rode away up the valley, following the road which led over the divide to Tongue River. The next morning the horse was found not far from the cabin, riderless, and with spur marks on the cantle indicating that his rider had been thrown.

Late that afternoon, Wolf Tooth, who lived along Tongue River, came down this trail in a wagon, together with his squaw and a grandson. Rations were to be issued in six days. A fine drizzle was falling and it was almost dark when, not far above the forks of Lame Deer Creek, Wolf Tooth's team suddenly shied violently at something beside the trail. Today, this grandson is a highly respected historian of his tribe and his account of what happened beside the trail—and subsequently—is the most complete and by far the most enlightening. These are John Stands In Timber's recollections of what occurred between the evening of September 7th and the "fifth day"—Friday, September 13th.

American Horse's band was camped at the forks of Lame Deer Creek when Head Chief, an unruly young buck about twenty-five years old, and Heart Mule, a young lad of about thirteen, came to visit their friend Sitting Man. When his wife set before them a dish of coffee and bread, she said, "This is all we have been eating for a long time." To this, Head Chief replied, "That's all right. When I finish eating I will go out and get you fresh meat. Get me a fresh horse." Heart Mule insisted on going along, and about three miles above the forks of the creek they found a cow which Head Chief shot and butchered. Packing the meat back of their saddles, they started to return.

When about halfway back,

*they saw someone coming. The boy said, "That's a white man." Head Chief said, "Don't be afraid of white man. There are two of us." They met on Tongue River Trail—Indians facing one way, white boy facing the other. Head Chief did not understand English—Heart Mule understood some. Head Chief said, "What is our friend talking about?" Heart Mule said, "Our friend is mad at us. He call us dogs that we kill his cow." Then the boy said, "Look out!" White boy started to strike with bull whip. Head Chief's horse dodge sideways and back. Head Chief started to pull his Springfield carbine out from under meat. When white boy saw hidden rifle, he wheel his horse and start to run back down trail.*

Head Chief threw off meat and took after him with Heart Mule right behind. [After a chase of six or seven hundred yards and when within fifty or seventy-five yards] Head Chief shot on run and hit boy in back and he fell off. Head Chief make circle and reload. Shot top of his head off with second shot. Then he picked up the brains in boy's cap and hid it under some grass and rosebushes near creek. Then they picked up body and packed it on Head Chief's horse. Rode double on boy's horse and led pack horse. Headed for Tongue River.

As it soon became very dark, they got lost in the pine-covered hills and made a circle. Then, discovering where they were, the two hid the body under a ledge high on the side of a ravine and picked up the meat and went on into camp. Here Head Chief told American Horse that he had killed young Boyle:

*Told him, "I don't want women and children held responsible. Go down to Agency and tell them, 'I killed the boy.' Next Friday I will go to the Agency and make play with the soldiers."*

Head Chief had no intentions of surrendering and being hung—that was no way for a *Cheyenne* to die. On the "fifth day," in the presence of all the Indians assembled to draw their rations, he would attack the soldiers and die in battle.

Head Chief now returned to the camp of his relatives along the Tongue at the mouth of Otter Creek. His father was a man who held stubbornly to the old ways and refused to recognize that times were no longer the same as when he was a boy. When his son had tried to do things in a mature way, he had never been satisfied and had always nagged and belittled, making Head Chief feel that he was still only a boy.

When Head Chief got back to his father's camp, his mother gave him dinner. Then Head Chief said, "Mother, tell father to come in. Tell all to come in. I have something to tell." After they had come in, Head Chief said, "My father, you have been talking to me like there was still a war. There is no war—no enemies. But you always tell me I am not man enough when I try to do things that are hard. Now I think I am man enough. I have killed a man at Lame Deer, and this has been reported to the agent and the Army. I am going to have a play with the soldiers on the fifth day in the afternoon. I will be killed among the soldiers. I will be man enough to die that way. When this is done don't cry. Be a man, father—dance in a victory dance. I will return to get ready."

The warrior then returned to Lame Deer, riding in boldly through the cavalry camp with his war clothes on and singing the battle song of the Elk Society. American Horse's camp had been moved to Alderson's Gulch near the agency buildings. Here Head Chief visited during the evening, spending part of the time in the lodge of John Crazy Mule, John Timber's uncle.

. . . then went to talk with his girl friend, American Horse's daughter, for the last time. Talked outside tepee for a long time. His friends laid down all around—watching. Then he climbed Squaw Hill.

Rugged breaks, tipped with red scoria rocks and covered with patches of pine, edge both sides of the valley of Lame Deer Creek. On the east side, immediately in front of the agency building, a high, flat-topped butte juts out from the line of hills and dominates the valley. It was to the top of this commanding elevation that Head Chief and his friends now climbed, with Heart Mule doggedly following along. Here, on a point overlooking the agency, the party spent the remainder of the night and the next forenoon, telling stories and, at last, making medicine for a successful charge. Then, about mid-day, Head Chief sent his friends to warn the Indians to leave the immediate vicinity of the butte.

First, the young men rode down the west face of the hill to a low spur just above the infantry who had been stationed in front of the agency. Here they made a bravery ride during which Heart Mule's pony was hit. Then they scrambled back up the steep face of the butte to the top where more shots were exchanged and the pony expired. When Head Chief saw the cavalry approaching from the camp to the south, he rode down off the eastern end of the butte, dashed across the little valley of Alderson Gulch and up the hill on the opposite side. As he topped this, he was directly in front of the line of troops. Charging straight at them, he shot once and then threw his rifle away. When he got close, the watching Indians saw a cloud of smoke blossom all along the line. Then the warrior emerged in the rear, rode about one hundred yards and fell off his horse. Two or three soldiers ran up to the prostrate form, there were two more puffs of gunsmoke—and all was quiet.

In the meantime, Heart Mule slipped down the south side of Squaw Butte and hid behind one of the cutbanks in Alderson's Gulch. Two Moon and American Horse now asked that the boy's life be spared, and this was granted:

*No soldier wanted to kill boy. When they shot they make target beyond. Then bugle sounded—all still. Boy came out and start to talk to Bill Rowland. One shot sounded and boy fell dead. They say that Indian policeman shot boy.*

Whatever shortcomings Head Chief and Heart Mule may have had in life, the manner of their dying has enshrined their memory in the minds of the Cheyennes. Those who know how to read Indian *sign*, can follow this tragedy, step by step, from the place where the fatal encounter took place to the spot where Head Chief made the final payment for his folly.

Before the death of Ferguson, a worry began to develop which was to last for at least a couple of years. In late March or early April, an Indian visited the Cheyennes and told them about the new Messiah who had foretold that the white men would soon pass away and the buffalo would return. This—the Ghost Dance Religion—was to reach its highest point the following winter and end, for all practical purposes, with the tragedy which has been called the *Battle* of Wounded Knee where about 300 Sioux were shot down.

On the 19th of June, Upshaw wrote to the Commissioner of Indian Affairs:

*The prophet is here—"Porcupine" who really belongs at Pine Ridge Agency and was here on a visit, according to his own account went to "Wind River" Agency, Wyoming—thence to the "Fort Hall" Agency thence as is supposed from his description of the country and the people to "Walker River," Nevada, where he says he saw a man who was the "Christ," who had been crucified, and had returned to this earth and who delivered him a message for his people—the message comprised the commonly received Christian virtues—And he claims that the Christ appears to him in dreams and gives other messages—This in my opinion constitutes his danger if there is any in him—*

Although the Ghost Dance Religion did not make a strong appeal to the Cheyennes, Porcupine continued to preach this new religion for a couple of years. In his monthly report for August 1892, the agent—now John Tully—noted:

*Some little excitement and alarm among the settlers was caused during the month by "Porcupine" and his "Ghost Dancers" who it appears have resurrected the "Messiah craze" and have been carrying on their foolish dancing and starving to some extent: however this has been allayed and no trouble is now expected.*

Although the killing of Ferguson and Boyle are the best remembered events of these early years, there were other affairs which got into court. One young Cheyenne broke into the post office at Ashland and was apprehended by the agent. When a deputy sheriff was taking him to Miles City, a "war party" of four took him away from the officer. Indian police then brought the "war party" into town and, as they could not be tried for about four months, Captain Ewers at Fort Keogh and "Major" Macqueen put up their bond—which raised a few eyebrows. But when word was sent to them to come in for trial, they arrived— promptly—and without police escort.

One experiment which was viewed with skepticism was that of enlisting Indians in the Army. In 1888, Lieutenant E. W. Casey of the 22nd Infantry secured permission to try to make soldiers out of some of the Cheyennes and Troops L and M of the 8th Cavalry came into existence. There were times when Big Red Nose, as the Indians called Casey, and Lieutenant Getty had their hands full trying to keep their men out of mischief, but the experiment was not a failure. Frederic Remington, who saw them in the fall of 1890 wrote that "they fill the eye of a military man until nothing is lacking." And when he accompanied them in the campaign against the Sioux Ghost Dancers, he found them good soldiers.

In the late winter of 1884-1885, Father Joseph Eyler and four Ursuline nuns arrived in Miles City to start a mission on the reservation. The nuns left Miles City on the 29th of March with a military escort consisting of four wagons, an ambulance and a small detachment of soldiers. A week later a construction crew of eleven men and "six teams" followed them. Buildings were erected at the mouth of Otter Creek at a cost of about $7,000 and the place named St. Benedict Joseph Labre Mission. The government gave the Mission a contract for a day school and most of the annual reports of the agents mention the work, invariably with kind words for the efforts of the staff.

For several years after 1890, there were no open clashes between the settlers and the Indians but the situation was far from being quiet. Three agents within the four years following Upshaw's departure did not help the situation. In the winter of 1891-1892, when two bucks refused to be arrested for killing cattle and threatened to kill the agent and the captain of the Indian police, it became necessary to station a company of soldiers permanently at the agency. The old problem created by homesteaders within the reservation was still present, and the boundaries of the reservation had never been surveyed and marked. As a result, one agent reported:

*I am of the opinion that cattle and sheep men are herding thousands of their stock on the reservation, that there are two sawmills located on and cutting timber from the reservation; but . . . it is impossible for me to substantiate the fact. . . .*

Some trespassers paid no attention to notices to move their stock. And the settlers were plagued by the killing of stock, firing of hay stacks, young bucks who were "saucy" and insolent, and Indians who roamed outside of the reservation without passes.

George W. H. Stouch, Captain 3rd Infantry, who took over in May 1894, was not the sort who could be bullied by either the Indians or the whites; and he was firmly in the *saddle* when trouble flared again three years later. On the 27th of April, 1897, Fred Barringer, whose father was running sheep about three miles north of the reservation and the same distance west of Tongue River, took John Hoover, a herder, out to one of the flocks and left him. Hoover, who had recently come from Missouri, was a very short man, inclined to be "hump-backed," and about twenty-four years of age. Six days later some of Hoover's sheep came to the ranch and a search was immediately instituted for the herder. For the next two days a party combed the range.

*Then . . . [we] gave up the search, for in the opinion of all, if he had been hurt and was lying on the ground, we would have found him or his dog; but if killed by the Indians (which is the opinion of everyone here) it was useless to search farther.*

On the 23rd of May, two men accidentally found Hoover's body. It lay in a very small depression not far from his camp and the remains of the dog lay beside the corpse. Both had been shot and there was no doubt in anyone's mind but that Indians had done the deed. This news spread like a prairie fire before a high wind, and wild tales and rumors of Indian uprisings followed in its wake. As the tension mounted, women on the upper Tongue picked up a few cherished belongings and headed for Sheridan. On the 31st of May, the *Yellowstone Journal* reported that thirteen wagon loads of settlers had come in to Miles City from the valley of the Powder and, "As we go to press the arrival of eight wagon loads of Tongue river settlers is noted." In the valley of the Rosebud, people went to Rosebud. One lady recalled:

*People came by all afternoon going to Rosebud, and they would stop and tell my folks they had better go. Night came and the wagons still went by, but mother wanted to stick it out because of her garden and the cows. Finally about nine o'clock a man stopped and said there were no whites left. Then my folks got scared and loaded a wagon. Father stayed to turn the cows out and an old soldier who lived with us drove the wagon. The man who stopped to warn us, got in the wagon and sat on my feet. They went to sleep and I was too scared to ask him to get off. A neighbor down the road waved us down with a lantern and we stopped there. Mother was so worried that she walked the floor all night. We did not go home for two weeks.*

Stouch now requested that his forces be augmented to four troops of cavalry and a company of infantry, and set about finding the murderers. White Bull's followers, who were in the vicinity of the crime, were ordered in to the agency where Stouch told the chief that he suspected someone in his band and ordered him to take some of his old men and try to find the killers. The civil authorities now proceeded to complicate the situation. Sheriff Gibb arrived with 25 armed men and, after the agent explained how he was trying to solve the case, "They blustered and made all manner of demands." However, the agent finally got rid of all of them but four deputies.

It was not long before White Bull came in with the information that a young man named David Stanley—or Whirlwind—had confessed, but that he would not surrender. He would fight at three o'clock that afternoon. When the time came the warrior and his squaw were on the Squaw Butte, the former "in his war dress and paint, and . . . heavily armed; . . . all ready for the fight." The officer with the cavalry, who returned a half hour later, was willing to accept the challenge, but Whirlwind sent word he wanted to fight the deputies. Billy Smith, who was in charge, wished to tackle the job—provided Stouch would keep the Indians off his back. With the hills near the agency covered with armed Indians awaiting the show, it was hard to predict what would happen; and the agent flatly refused to permit anything but an orderly arrest.

The deputies now became more of a problem than Whirlwind and Stouch was forced to give Smith written orders to get off the reservation "at once." Finally, after several days maneuvering, Whirlwind was induced to surrender his arms and go to jail. As soon as this happened the sheriff and his deputies returned to demand the prisoner—and with a warrant for Stouch's arrest charging him with resisting officers trying to make an arrest! The agent politely but bluntly refused to be arrested —and gave the sheriff a letter which stated, "I consider the presence of yourself or deputies here on this reservation handicaps me in the performance of my plain duties under the revised statutes of the U. S. . . . ." Gibb left but ordered the deputies to remain. In three days of questioning Stouch failed to make any progress with the prisoner so he sent him, with a troop of cavalry as escort, to the railroad station at Rosebud, and wired Sheriff Gibb to pick up his prisoner. The comic opera was over.

Whirlwind, who had previously stated that he alone was to blame, made a confession in July implicating Spotted Hawk, Little Whirlwind, and a fifteen-year-old boy named Shoulder Blade. According to the testimony which he gave on the witness stand during the trial, these four Indians went riding in the hills above Barringer's ranch on either the 2nd or 3rd of May:

> . . . we found a two year old beef and killed it. While we were skinning the beef someone called to us and we looked up and saw a white man standing on the hill above us. He talked in English to Spotted Hawk and Spotted Hawk talked in English to him. Spotted Hawk said that the white man told him that we would all get into trouble for killing the beef. The white man went back to his sheep. After we had gone a little way we said, now the white man has been close to us and saw us skinning this beef and he knows us and will tell and make us lots of trouble, so we concluded to follow and watch him. After a while we all rode close to him and charged upon him, firing as we charged. The white man fell but tried to get up again. Spotted Hawk then rode right up to him and fired, shooting him in the breast. The dog was running around the man crying and making a noise, and Little Whirlwind shot the dog and placed it alongside the dead man. After this we rode slowly off, Spotted Hawk going to his tepee and Little Whirlwind to his and I went to Calf's. When I got to Calf's tepee Shoulder Blade was there, he having started home just after we killed the beef.

Shoulder Blade was dismissed. Whirlwind's testimony was questioned as he had a bad record when a soldier at Fort Keogh, and Spotted Hawk tried to prove an alibi. The jury believed Whirlwind and found all three guilty, but the counsel for Spotted Hawk appealed his conviction and, eventually, succeeded in getting the case against this individual dropped.

This was the last murder by the Cheyennes. The settlers, having found out they could not get the Indians moved, settled down and learned to live with a situation which they did not like. Small depredations continued for years but this—probably—was not a one way business for on at least one occasion the agent had to ask a prominent rancher—the brand is still used on the Tongue—how it happened that a calf bearing his brand was found following an "I D" cow.

Some of the problems which plagued the early agents were finally solved. Sometimes progress was made under a good agent but too often it was undone by his successor. Then, too, there were handicaps inherent in the Indians which were formidable. As one intelligent old Cheyenne summed it up briefly and succinctly: "Indian looks at today and tomorrow—not far ahead."

# 22

## Sunset

>>>>>>>>>><<<<<<<<< At least a shadow of the frontier lasted for a little over a decade after the turn of the century. Many ranchers were still grazing their stock—at least to some extent—on public lands, and the ways of the early days had not been completely forgotten. But the farmer was soon to blot out many of these remnants.

Strangely enough, the man with a plow was not a stranger on this frontier, even in the beginning. *Ranchers* who farmed were not uncommon along the Yellowstone from Paradise Valley, south of the Great Bend, to its mouth. In the days immediately after the Sioux War, they were also among the first settlers on the lower Rosebud and the Tongue —raising small grain, hay, and vegetables. In the early issues of the *Yellowstone Journal*, items may be found about the production of wheat and oats, and the importation of threshing machines. Also noted were a squash that weighed 64 pounds, an onion that topped 1½ pounds, carrots and parsnips that were over two feet long, and stalks of corn almost twelve feet high.

An interest in irrigation developed early. In 1876 a man named Gage, who settled six miles below Hunter's Hot Springs, dug one of the first irrigating ditches in the Yellowstone valley, and in 1882 was selling alfalfa hay to the government. Early in August 1882, the Tongue River Irrigating and Ditch Company was organized in Miles City with capital stock placed at $100,000. This project had its ups and downs but water was finally turned into its main ditch in October 1889. Another project, conceived as part of the speculation scheme of the Minnesota and Montana Land Development Company, was probably planned in 1881. Because of the tight spot in which these speculators placed themselves, perhaps inadvertently, they were obliged to complete their "Big Ditch" more promptly than the Miles City company.

Farming developed steadily all through the 1880's and 1890's. As the Northern Pacific Railroad grant included all odd-numbered sections in a strip extending out 40 miles on either side of the right-of-way, this company was very much interested in encouraging the immigration of the tillers of the soil. In the 1880's the price of these lands was about $2.50 per acre; and in 1882 the Railroad published an elaborate guide book describing the country, climate, crops, ranching, and public improvements as well as outlining the procedure to follow in securing land under the homestead law, tree culture claims, and pre-emption claims.

The developments during these *frontier* days was on a reasonably sound basis. Then, during the years just after 1900, a period of intense promotion began which lured a flood of homesteaders with the promise of 160 acres of land in return for maintaining a residence for five years and plowing a few furrows. Some of these people were unmarried men and women with their belongings in a single trunk, others were families traveling in a box car with their household goods in one end and their livestock in the other. Most of them can be compared only to moths attracted to a candle—which was soon to singe their wings.

These people, nicknamed *honyockers*, scattered out over the prairies. Some squatted in dugouts and others in dwellings built of sod, rock, or logs. The usual habitation was a single-roomed frame shack 12 x 14 feet with a door and not more than two windows. Sometimes the outside was covered with tar paper to keep out the biting winter winds. Many were miles from water, fuel, and a store. Once located, these people set about breaking the sod and planting crops to meet the government requirements.

As many immigrants settled near springs and along the streams, their fences tended to keep any stock on the range away from water. Naturally, they were regarded with disfavor by the stockmen. And when they began to set their dogs on livestock which pushed through their flimsy fences, they slipped farther down the scale to the status of "pests." Sometimes ranchers hired men to ride the range and shoot mean dogs. A homesteader came up to one of these men one day and said, "Mr. H——, what does this word *honyocker* mean?" "Oh, that's a name they give some people," the rider replied. "Well," persisted the other, "just *who are* these honyockers?" The reply was, "They are undesirable citizens like you."

When these settlers took up large areas of the best range lands and blocked off access to necessary watering places, those ranchers whose operations were based on free grass were forced to sell their stock. Then they sold their chuck wagons and the day of the open range was over. The last shadow of the frontier was gone.

Five years was a long time to try to exist on a quarter section in this dry country. The searing heat of summer, grasshoppers, drouth—these all took their toll, and the rosy picture of financial independence painted by the promoters changed to one of grim reality. In the end most of the *honyockers* were forced to leave their claims. Tumble weeds took over the abandoned fields which were once a part of an empire of grass. And sprinkled over the prairies were vacant shacks—like tombstones in a vast graveyard of blasted hopes.

# Some Interesting Books

>>>>>>>>>>>«««««««« Charlie Russell once remarked, "There ain't no such thing as bad whiskey. Some kinds are just better than others." He might also have added that it was sometimes difficult for a thirsty cowboy to acquire a drink. In these respects, whiskey might be likened to books about the West.

This list has been prepared to guide the general reader who wishes to delve further into the story of the Yellowstone frontier. It does not constitute a bibliography—such a listing would fill a good many pages. Those who are interested in knowing the source material used should read the text carefully where they will find, in most cases, either a definite reference to the original or helpful clues. In making this selection, the writer is well aware of the fact much of this material will be available only in a *good* library. Furthermore, many references do not cover a field adequately, and some may not be completely reliable—for various reasons. Again, a critical reading of the text will often reveal an evaluation of the item in question.

Perhaps the most valuable single source of secondary reading are the ten volumes of the *Collections of the Historical Society of Montana,* particularly Volumes I, II, and X. Here will be found many journals, diaries, and articles which contain fascinating accounts of various events. The rare *Chronicles of the Yellowstone* by E. S. Topping is also very good—if a few errors are accepted.

*The Journal of François Antoine Larocque,* Publication No. 10 of the Canadian Archives or somewhat abridged in Vols. XIV and XV of *The Frontier,* is extremely interesting—particularly when read in conjunction with parts of the *Original Journals of the Lewis and Clark Expedition* edited by Reuben Gold Thwaites. Those who enjoy riddles will find a translation of the journal of Chevalier de la Verendryé in Vol. VII of the *South Dakota Historical Collections.* Burton Harris' *John Colter* is a well-prepared study of this outstanding frontiersman.

Those who are interested in the days of the fur trade should start with *The History of the American Fur Trade of the Far West* by Hiram M. Chittenden and *Jedediah Smith and the Opening of the West* by Dale Morgan. Among the several journals of the trappers and traders, *Journal of a Trapper* by Osborne Russell and *Forty Years a Fur Trader on the Upper Missouri* by Charles Larpenteur are two of the best. Three excellent publications of the Bureau of American Ethnology are *Of the Crow Nation* by Edwin Denig (Bulletin 151) and his "Indian Tribes of the Upper Missouri" in the 46th Annual Report, and the *Journal of Rudolph Friederich Kurz* edited by J. N. B. Hewitt (Bulletin 115). Maximilian's *Travels in the Interior of North America* is available in *Early Western Travels* edited by Reuben Gold Thwaites, and De Smet's letters will be found in *Life, Letters and Travels of Father Pierre-Jean De Smet* edited by Hiram M. Chittenden and Alfred Talbot Richardson.

Although formal government reports are sometimes difficult reading, no reader need shy away from *Report on the Exploration of the Yellowstone River* by General W. F. Raynolds. Only the first few pages will be found tedious.

*Soldiers of the Overland* by Fred B. Rogers covers Connor's "futile campaign" and other material will be found in C. G. Coutant's *History of Wyoming.* An interesting account of Sawyer's road exploring expedition is contained in *Pioneering in the Northwest* by Constant Marks and Albert Holman.

Part of the story of the Montana Road may be found in *AB-SA-RA-KA Land of Massacre* by Col. Henry B. Carrington (4th edition) and *An Army Boy of the Sixties* by Alson Ostrander. A number of first hand narratives are contained in *The Bozeman Trail* by Grace Hebard and E. A. Brininstool.

Strange as it may seem, in view of the scores of books which have been published, really good items on the Sioux War of 1876 are not plentiful. Two of the best dealing with Crook's campaigns are *On the Border With Crook* by John G. Bourke and *Warpath and Bivouac* by John Finerty. Among the dozens dealing with Custer, *Custer's Luck* by Edgar Stuart and *The Custer Myth* compiled by W. A. Graham are outstanding. One of the best Indian accounts is *A Warrior Who Fought Custer* by Thomas Marquis. John Vaughn's *With Crook at the Rosebud* is an excellent account of a single battle.

The days which followed the Indian and the buffalo are covered by a number of noteworthy books. Outstanding among these is *Forty Years on the Frontier* by Granville Stuart. Among the books dealing with the range days are *The Cowboy* by Philip Ashton Rollins, *Wyoming Cattle Trails* by John Rollinson, and *We Pointed Them North* by E. C. Abbott and Helena Huntington Smith. Smith also collaborated with Nannie Alderson to produce another fine book, *A Bride Goes West*. Noteworthy for their illustrations, if nothing else, are *The Frontier Years* and *Before Barbed Wire* by the author and W. R. Felton which contain the fine frontier photographs of L. A. Huffman of Miles City, Montana.

Of the several books dealing with "outlaws," *The History of Natrona County, Wyoming* by Alfred Mokler is close to bed-rock, and *The Outlaw Trail* by Charles Kelly contains considerable material not available elsewhere. Those interested in the Johnson County War should read *both* A. S. Mercer's *The Banditti of the Plains* and Robert David's *Malcolm Campbell, Sheriff* for both sides of this struggle.

There are other books which, although not specifically related to the Yellowstone Basin, are part and parcel of the literature of the Northwest and helpful in a general appreciation of its people and ways. No one should miss Charlie Russell's incomparable *Trails Plowed Under*, trail boss Andy Adams' *Log of a Cowboy* and *The Outlet*, John Neihardt's poetry in *The Song of the Indian Wars* (and others), or any of Frank Bird Linderman's books. Nor should Theodore Roosevelt's *Ranch Life and Hunting Trail* be overlooked.

Pictures also add to an understanding of this area. Examples of Russell's work are included in his *Trails Plowed Under* and in *The Charles M. Russell Book* by Harold McCracken. The above-noted Huffman photographs are an invaluable record of the period 1878-1910. William Henry Jackson's splendid photographs of "The Wonderland" in 1871 are contained in *Picture Maker of the Old West* by Clarence Jackson. Charles Bodmer's work is reproduced in the *Atlas* which accompanies Maximilian's *Travels*; Alfred Jacob Miller's watercolor sketches of the fur trade days form the basis for *The West of Alfred Jacob Miller* edited by Marvin Ross. Two folios, *Drawings* and *Frontier Sketches*, contain some of the work of Frederic Remington and the work of Charles Schreyvogel is reproduced in *My Bunkie and Others*. *Artists and Illustrators of the Old West* by Robert Taft contains a sampling of the work of a number of artists; and Foster Harris' *The Look of the Old West* gathers together a wide assortment of odds and ends.

# Acknowledgments

»»»»»»»»«««««««««« It is a pleasure to acknowledge the assistance of others in an undertaking of this sort. However, in this case, the bulk of the thanks rightfully belongs to those men and women who set down in journals, diaries, letters and articles a record of their experiences and observations on this frontier. From such records have come the bits and pieces which were indispensable to this task. Unfortunately, except for a very few, these people have crossed the Big Divide.

Much material was made available by the Historical Society of Montana, Helena, Montana; and librarian Virginia Walton went out of her way to be of assistance. Merrill J. Mattes and Ray H. Mattison, Region 2 Office National Park Service, Omaha, Nebraska, provided files and made suggestions which saved considerable time and expense. The U.S. Military Academy, West Point, New York, graciously permitted the use of parts of the journals of Captain John G. Bourke to whom all students of the West are deeply indebted. Thanks are due the Missouri

Historical Society, St. Louis, Missouri, and John C. Ewers of the U.S. National Museum, Washington, D.C., for permission to quote from Edwin Denig's *Of the Crow Nation*, Bureau of American Ethnology, Anthropological Paper No. 33, Bulletin 151, and also to John W. Vaughn, Windsor, Colorado, for the use of material from his *With Crook at the Rosebud*.

L. G. Lippert, Crow Agency, Montana, and Carl Pearson, Lame Deer, Montana, made available valuable files in their respective agency offices. John Stands In Timber, Lame Deer, Montana, spent considerable time with the author going over points of interest. Among the Crow Indians, Barney and Henry Old Coyote, and Joe Medicine Crow, Crow Agency, Montana, were very helpful.

Others who supplied information or helped in various ways were: Floyd and Irving Alderson, Birney, Montana; William C. Almquist, Miles City, Montana; Army War College, Carlisle Barracks, Pennsylvania; Ben Bird, Medora, North Dakota; Chester Brooks, Medora, North Dakota; Dr. Merrill G. Burlingame, Montana State College, Bozeman, Montana; Dick, Bob and Luke Conway, Miles City, Montana; William B. Clarke, Miles City, Montana; Edwin and Virginia Crocker, Storm Lake, Iowa; Will and Patty Eaton, Wolf, Wyoming; W. R. Felton and W. R. Felton, Jr., Sioux City, Iowa; Dwight Ferguson, Kirby, Montana; E. T. Flaherty, Sioux City, Iowa; F. Hoyte Freeman, Bellevue, Nebraska; Robert and Genie Fulmer, Forsyth, Montana; Harry Fulmer, Big Horn, Wyoming; Rodger T. Grange, Jr., Fort Robinson, Nebraska; Mr. and Mrs. Sam Hotchkiss, Miles City, Montana; Ed Holt, Miles City, Montana; George Hoyt, Cherokee, Iowa; Amelia Huffman, Lame Deer, Montana; Ashton Jones, Broadus, Montana; Harvey M. Jopling, Bellevue, Nebraska; Michael Kennedy, Helena, Montana; Hans and "Missy" Kleiber, Dayton, Wyoming; Elmer Kobold, Kirby, Montana; Fred C. Kreig, Billings, Montana; Dr. John D. Lutton, Sioux City, Iowa; Anne McDonnell, Helena, Montana; Ralph Miracle, Helena, Montana; Miles City Public Library, Miles City, Montana; National Archives, Washington, D.C.; Shy Osterhout, Medora, North Dakota; Col. E. G. Ovenshine, Washington, D.C.; Mrs. Rodolphe Petter, Lame Deer, Montana; Anna Polk, Miles City, Montana; Bertha M. Richard, Bentley, Alberta; Don Rickey, Hardin, Montana; Harry Roberts, Medora, North Dakota; Robert J. Scanlon, Miles City, Montana; Harry and Mildred Schlosser, Miles City, Montana; Ruth and Vern Scott, Miles City, Montana; Erwin D. Sias, Sioux City, Iowa; Lola Lewis Smead, Denver, Colorado; Colville Terrett, Billings, Montana; Julian Terrett, Miles City, Montana; R. Price Terrett, Paso Robles, California; K. Ross Toole, New York, New York; Mat Tschirgi,

Wyola, Montana; Oliver and "Towlie" Wallop, Big Horn, Wyoming; Paul Wellman, Los Angeles, California; Dudley White, Columbus, Montana; Lewis Woodcock, Miles City, Montana; and Natalie Brown Woodward, Birney, Montana.

Last, but not least, thanks are due to Helen Dull, Bellevue, Nebraska, who searched the small errors while putting the manuscript in final form, and to the writer's wife, Alice, who permitted him to bury himself in this task for months at a time.

MARK H. BROWN

ALTA, IOWA

# Index

"Dry House," 366
Dude ranching, 393-94
Dull Knife, Chief, 297, 299, 301, 304, 307, 320
Durbin, John, 411
Dusold, Captain, 235
Dyer, W. S., 447

Eastern Montana Livestock Association, 388, 400
Eaton, Alden, 393-94
Eaton, Ed, 424
Eaton, Howard, 393-94
Eaton, Willis, 393-94
Eclipse, steamboat, 330
Edgar, Henry, 130, 133, 134
Edmonton, Alberta, 63
Egan, Captain Teddy, 245, 246
Eighteenth Infantry, 250
Eighth Cavalry, 456
Ellis, Fort, 172, 191, 192, 193, 196, 197, 212, 219, 223, 231, 232, 238, 241, 250, 251, 300, 319, 433, 434
Elmhirst, Captain E. Pennell, 379-80
Emge, Joseph, 423-24
Emigrant Gulch, 134, 135, 178, 335, 431
Estes, Ben, 149
Evans, Governor, 141
Everts, Truman C., 191, 192
Ewers, Captain, 456
Explorations 110-24
Eyler, Father Joseph, 456

Fairweather, Bill, 130, 133, 134
Famished Elk, 13, 321
Faris, Charles, 424
Farming, 462-63
Far West, steamboat, 254, 255, 256, 278
Feather-on-the-head, scout, 297
Ferris, Warren, 188
Fetterman, Captain William J., 160, 161, 162
Fetterman, Fort, 240, 242, 249, 257, 268, 294, 295
Fifth Cavalry, 260, 269
Fifth Infantry, 149, 272, 279, 310, 317, 331, 370
Finerty, John, 257, 261, 268-69, 286, 287, 321
Fink, Mike, 65-66
Firebear, 442
Firehole River, 119, 191
First Dakota Volunteer Cavalry, 149
Fisher, Isaac, 161, 162
Fisher, S. G., 312-14
Fitzpatrick, Thomas, 16, 55, 72-74, 95, 96, 97, 126, 127
Flathead Indians, 26, 51, 59, 98, 99, 100
Floyd, Fort, 75
Folsom, David E., 190
Folsom-Cook party, 190, 192
Forest Rangers, U.S., 424
Forsyth, Major George A. "Sandy," 203
Forsyth, Colonel James W., 220
Four Horns, Chief, 186
Fourth Cavalry, 280, 294
Fox-Just-Coming-Over-Hill, 267-68, 443-44

French, Fanny, 349
Frewen, Moreton, 372-73, 378, 392
Frewen, Richard, 372-73, 378
Friese, Henry, 326
Frost, George W., 438-39, 441
Frost, Mr., 204, 209
Fur trade, 58-85

Gaffney, H., 452
Gall, Chief, 202, 229, 279, 292
Gallatin River, 121, 129, 133
Gans, Joe, 423
Gantz, Louis A., 423
Gardnier, Baptiste "Little Bat," 243
Gardnier River, 193
Garrett, Frank, 134
Garvin, Sam, 425
Gass, Sergeant, 24
General Appropriations Act (1851), 126
General Terry, steamboat, 330
Geological Survey, U. S., 193
Ghost Dance Religion, 455-56
Ghost Dance War, 307, 446
Gibb, Sheriff, 458-60
Gibbon, General, 182, 250-54, 256, 270, 273, 277, 283, 310, 433, 434
Gibbon River, 191
Gibson, George, 32, 33
Gilbreath, Captain C. E., 353
Gillette, Warren C., 191
Gillette, Wyoming, 149, 381
Gilmer, Salsbury & Company, 341
Girard, Major, 317
Glass, Hugh, 55, 66-67
Glendive Creek, 196, 205, 209, 289, 338, 343, 346, 357-58
Glover, Sergeant, 321, 328
Goff, John, 364
Gold, prospecting for, 129-35, 170, 227, 337
Good Heart, Chief, 261
Gordon, Sam, 343, 345, 346
Gordon, William, 62-63, 76
Gore, Sir George, 106-09, 123
Gorman, Jack, 200
Graham, J. J., 357
Grant, Colonel F. D., 220
Grant, Orvil, 254
Grant, General U. S., 148-49, 194, 249, 254-55
Graveyard Creek, 351
Great Porcupine Creek, 36, 209, 216, 252
Green River, 68, 73, 95
Greens, O. D., 219
Greenway, Hank, 422
Greenwood, Caleb, 55
Grissell, Captain F. D., 392
Groom, B. B., 376
Gros Ventre Indians, 26, 41, 42, 324, 430
Grouard, Frank, 243, 245, 248, 257, 260, 261, 265, 267, 268, 283, 295, 305
Grounds, Benjamin Franklin, 217
Grummond, Lieutenant, 162

Hall, Fort, 73, 193, 319
Hall, Hugh, 32, 34, 35
Hamilton, James Archdale, see Palmer, Archibald